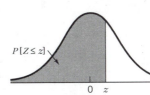

Standard Normal Probabilities (Continued)

$P[Z \leq z]$

z	.00	.01	.02	.03	.04	.05	.06	.07	.08	.09
.0	.5000	.5040	.5080	.5120	.5160	.5199	.5239	.5279	.5319	.5359
.1	.5398	.5438	.5478	.5517	.5557	.5596	.5636	.5675	.5714	.5753
.2	.5793	.5832	.5871	.5910	.5948	.5987	.6026	.6064	.6103	.6141
.3	.6179	.6217	.6255	.6293	.6331	.6368	.6406	.6443	.6480	.6517
.4	.6554	.6591	.6628	.6664	.6700	.6736	.6772	.6808	.6844	.6879
.5	.6915	.6950	.6985	.7019	.7054	.7088	.7123	.7157	.7190	.7224
.6	.7257	.7291	.7324	.7357	.7389	.7422	.7454	.7486	.7517	.7549
.7	.7580	.7611	.7642	.7673	.7703	.7734	.7764	.7794	.7823	.7852
.8	.7881	.7910	.7939	.7967	.7995	.8023	.8051	.8078	.8106	.8133
.9	.8159	.8186	.8212	.8238	.8264	.8289	.8315	.8340	.8365	.8389
1.0	.8413	.8438	.8461	.8485	.8508	.8531	.8554	.8577	.8599	.8621
1.1	.8643	.8665	.8686	.8708	.8729	.8749	.8770	.8790	.8810	.8830
1.2	.8849	.8869	.8888	.8907	.8925	.8944	.8962	.8980	.8997	.9015
1.3	.9032	.9049	.9066	.9082	.9099	.9115	.9131	.9147	.9162	.9177
1.4	.9192	.9207	.9222	.9236	.9251	.9265	.9279	.9292	.9306	.9319
1.5	.9332	.9345	.9357	.9370	.9382	.9394	.9406	.9418	.9429	.9441
1.6	.9452	.9463	.9474	.9484	.9495	.9505	.9515	.9525	.9535	.9545
1.7	.9554	.9564	.9573	.9582	.9591	.9599	.9608	.9616	.9625	.9633
1.8	.9641	.9649	.9656	.9664	.9671	.9678	.9686	.9693	.9699	.9706
1.9	.9713	.9719	.9726	.9732	.9738	.9744	.9750	.9756	.9761	.9767
2.0	.9772	.9778	.9783	.9788	.9793	.9798	.9803	.9808	.9812	.9817
2.1	.9821	.9826	.9830	.9834	.9838	.9842	.9846	.9850	.9854	.9857
2.2	.9861	.9864	.9868	.9871	.9875	.9878	.9881	.9884	.9887	.9890
2.3	.9893	.9896	.9898	.9901	.9904	.9906	.9909	.9911	.9913	.9916
2.4	.9918	.9920	.9922	.9925	.9927	.9929	.9931	.9932	.9934	.9936
2.5	.9938	.9940	.9941	.9943	.9945	.9946	.9948	.9949	.9951	.9952
2.6	.9953	.9955	.9956	.9957	.9959	.9960	.9961	.9962	.9963	.9964
2.7	.9965	.9966	.9967	.9968	.9969	.9970	.9971	.9972	.9973	.9974
2.8	.9974	.9975	.9976	.9977	.9977	.9978	.9979	.9979	.9980	.9981
2.9	.9981	.9982	.9982	.9983	.9984	.9984	.9985	.9985	.9986	.9986
3.0	.9987	.9987	.9987	.9988	.9988	.9989	.9989	.9989	.9990	.9990
3.1	.9990	.9991	.9991	.9991	.9992	.9992	.9992	.9992	.9993	.9993
3.2	.9993	.9993	.9994	.9994	.9994	.9994	.9994	.9995	.9995	.9995
3.3	.9995	.9995	.9995	.9996	.9996	.9996	.9996	.9996	.9996	.9997
3.4	.9997	.9997	.9997	.9997	.9997	.9997	.9997	.9997	.9997	.9998
3.5	.9998	.9998	.9998	.9998	.9998	.9998	.9998	.9998	.9998	.9998

BUSINESS STATISTICS

BUSINESS STATISTICS

Decision Making with Data

RICHARD A. JOHNSON
Department of Statistics, University of Wisconsin

DEAN W. WICHERN
College of Business Administration, Texas A & M University

JOHN WILEY & SONS, INC.

New York • Chichester • Brisbane • Toronto • Singapore • Weinheim

ACQUISITIONS EDITOR	Brad Wiley II
DEVELOPMENTAL EDITOR	Madalyn Stone
MARKETING MANAGER	Jay Kirsch
DESIGNER	Laura Nicholls
MANUFACTURING MANAGER	Mark Cirillo
PHOTO RESEARCHER	Elaine Paoloni
PHOTO EDITOR	Mary Ann Price
ILLUSTRATION	Jaime Perea
COVER ART	Marjory Dressler
COVER PHOTOS	(*top*) Jon Riley/Tony Stone Images
	(*center*) Greg Pease/Tony Stone Images
	(*bottom*) Charles Thatcher/Tony Stone Images
CHAPTER OPENER PHOTO	Greg Pease/Tony Stone Images, New York, Inc.
PRODUCTION SERVICE	Susan L. Reiland

This book was set in Garamond Light by Publication Services and printed and bound by R. R. Donnelley and Sons/Willard. The cover was printed by Phoenix Color.

Recognizing the importance of preserving what has been written, it is a policy of John Wiley & Sons, Inc. to have books of enduring value published in the United States printed on acid-free paper, and we exert our best efforts to that end.

The paper in this book was manufactured by a mill whose forest management programs include sustained yield harvesting of its timberlands. Sustained yield harvesting principles ensure that the number of trees cut each year does not exceed the amount of new growth.

Library of Congress Cataloging-in-Publication Data

Johnson, Richard Arnold.
    Business statistics : decision making with data / Richard A.
Johnson, Dean W. Wichern.—1st ed.
      p. cm.
    Includes index.
    ISBN 0-471-59213-7 (cloth : alk. paper)
    1. Industrial management—Statistical methods.   2. Statistical
decision. I. Wichern, Dean W. II. Title.
HD30.215.J64   1997   96-30259
658.4′033—dc20   CIP

Printed in the United States of America

10 9 8 7 6 5 4 3 2 1

PREFACE

The body of methodology concerned with the art and science of gathering, analyzing, and using data to identify and resolve problems and make decisions is known as statistics. We introduce and develop statistical methods in business contexts. The applications presented come from the traditional functional areas of business: accounting, finance, marketing, management, production, and so forth, but we try to stress problems that span several of these areas.

Our goal in writing this book is to make the study of statistics interesting and relevant for operating successfully in a competitive business environment. Managers, at all levels, make many decisions every day. Some decisions are routine and require little thought. Many, however, are more complex and depend on numbers to suggest and justify subsequent courses of action. We believe that good data contain information and, when carefully interpreted, increase knowledge. We believe that the use of statistical methods, when coupled with sound organizational practice, can be a key to good management and effective leadership in business settings.

Basing decisions on data can be viewed as a piece of an effective management strategy that incorporates a scientific approach to learning, a commitment to quality, and an emphasis on process improvement. Although our focus may appear to be rather narrow at times, the reader should not forget these broader issues. We indicate how the material in this book "fits into the larger organizational picture," and attempt to emphasize the "why" rather than the "how." We do this primarily through our Statistics in Context sections at the end of Chapters 1–13, and with our discussion of the managerial issues associated with process improvement and the use of statistics in Chapter 13.

Fortunately, the development of good statistical computer programs has improved the use of statistical procedures. Comprehensive statistical software is now readily available for personal computers as well as mainframes. In this book we use the Minitab statistical package because of its ease of use and widespread availability. However, the output displayed in the text is generic enough to be used with virtually any statistical software package selected by the instructor. In addition, the data sets on the Data Disk can be conveniently accessed by any common statistical software.

This book has several pedagogical strengths.

DISTINGUISHING FEATURES

- We stress statistical thinking applied to business problems. The clear exposition of statistical concepts and tools is immediately followed by illustrative examples using, in most cases, real data from the various functional areas of business.

- Throughout the book we cast statistical methods as useful tools for generating, summarizing, and analyzing numerical information with the goal of helping managers make decisions that will improve processes and products, and add economic value to the organization.

- We have deliberately focused our discussion of inference to means and proportions with an emphasis on large sample results. However, the small sample, normal theory based inferences are also given, and consequently we include discussions of assessing normality and transformations to near normality.

- There is an abundance of exercises. These exercises range from simple drill to analyses of large data sets requiring the use of computer software. Manipulating the data sets is relatively easy using the Data Disk included with the text. Some exercises are designated as team or class projects. Several review exercises relate to each Statistics in Context section. Exercises requiring the use of a computer are marked with a computer disk icon.

- The Statistics in Context sections at the ends of Chapter 1–13 are mini-cases that illustrate the use, in real business situations, of the material in the chapters. A Statistics in Context mini-case can typically be discussed after studying only the first few sections of the chapter.

ORGANIZATION

- The book is organized into six general areas: (1) data description and summary (Chapters 1–3), (2) data collection (Chapter 4), (3) foundations for inference (Chapters 5–7), (4) inferences about means and proportions (Chapters 8–10), (5) linear models (Chapters 11 and 12), and (6) statistics and management (Chapter 13). There is more than enough material for a one-quarter or one-semester course. Although we generally proceed in a linear fashion, an instructor can pick and choose material from various parts of the book in a nonlinear fashion to suit his or her needs.

- Chapter 4: Collecting Data has an extensive section on questionnaire design. For those interested in sample surveys, this material could be covered toward the end of the course, perhaps in conjunction with a student project assignment.

- The summary material in Chapter 13: Management and Statistics can be studied anytime after completing Chapters 1–3, although most students will get more out of it if they have had a little inference and some exposure to simple regression models.

- Confidence intervals and tests of hypotheses are both discussed for a given population parameter (see Chapters 8–10). We do not put estimation in one chapter and testing of hypotheses in another. In fact, we discuss the relation between confidence intervals and two-sided tests for means. We emphasize the interpretation of P-values in the context of tests of hypotheses.

- We have indicated sections and subsections that are optional in a first course; however, the level of these sections is no different from the level of the remaining sections. For those with a greater interest in time series analysis and forecasting, for example, some of our optional sections and exercises may be appropriate.

COURSE SEQUENCING

A possible one-quarter or one-semester course sequence follows. You should regard this sequence as a guide. It probably does not fit anyone's course exactly, including our own.

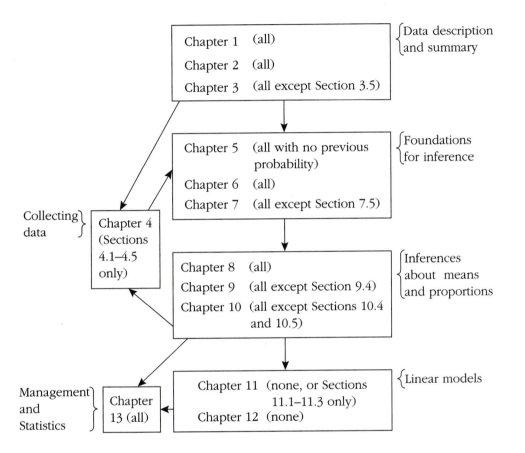

A course emphasizing linear models and forecasting would use more of Chapters 11 and 12. One-way analysis of variance (Section 9.4) might be covered instead of straight-line regression (Section 3.4 and Chapter 11). Finally, a two-quarter or two-semester course might use the entire book.

SUPPLEMENTS

This book comes with the following ancillary materials:

- An Instructor's Manual containing solutions to all the exercises
- A Data Disk containing files for the data sets used in the examples and exercises
- A Test Bank containing potential examination questions. The Test Bank is available in both hard copy and electronic, IBM-PC and Mac version, formats.

ACKNOWLEDGMENTS

We would like to thank Robert L. Armacost (University of Central Florida), Hamparsum Bozdogan (University of Tennessee), Y. C. Chang (University of Notre Dame), Dale F. Duhan (Texas Tech University), Michael Evans (University of Toronto), Donald C. Freeburg (Fitchburg State University), Ron Gulezian (Drexel University), William G. Koellner (Montclair State University), Johannes Ledolter (University of Iowa), David O'Donnell (University of Southern California), Toni Somers (Wayne State University), Ralph St. John (Bowling Green State University), Richard Stockbridge (University of Kentucky), Faye Teer (James Madison University), Cindy van Es (Cornell University), and Peter H. Westfall (Texas Tech University) for their helpful reviews of preliminary versions of this book. We would especially like to thank Robert Aubry, Gil Churchill, Jon Cryer, Mark Finster, Jed Frees, Joseph Haefner, Jim Hickman, Paul Kharouf, José Ramirez, and the Canadian flower importer for their contributions to the Statistics in Context sections. Any errors that remain are, of course, our responsibility and we would appreciate having them brought to our attention. Our e-mail addresses are: rich@stat.wisc.edu and d-wichern@tamu.edu.

To the students, we hope, at the end of this book, you will become a critical consumer of statistical information presented by others. More important, we hope that you will be able to generate and assemble numerical information in a way that will lead to better decisions and, hence, to improved processes and products.

Richard A. Johnson
Dean W. Wichern

CONTENTS

CHAPTER 4: COLLECTING DATA   164

CHAPTER 5: PROBABILITY   212

CHAPTER 6: RANDOM VARIABLES AND PROBABILITY DISTRIBUTIONS   272

CHAPTER 7: CONTINUOUS RANDOM VARIABLES AND SAMPLING DISTRIBUTIONS   326

CHAPTER 8: FROM SAMPLES TO POPULATIONS: INFERENCES ABOUT MEANS   379

CHAPTER 9: COMPARING MEANS   441

After reading this chapter, you should be able to:

- Define statistics.
- Discuss and use the scientific method.
- Discuss quality and understand how a scientific approach, supplemented with data, can lead to better decisions, and improved products and processes.
- Understand variation and know how to construct a measure of the variation in a set of numbers.
- Construct bar charts, pie charts, Pareto diagrams, cause-and-effect diagrams, fishbone charts, and flowcharts.
- Calculate the sample mean, the sample variance, and sample standard deviation.
- Distinguish between a sample and a population.

CHAPTER ONE

Introduction

1.1 BUSINESS DECISIONS AND DATA

Today, changes occur rapidly. To take advantage of these changes, decisions with long-term implications must often be made quickly. Information is vital. Managers, for example, must be conscious of customer needs and must determine how to react to changing economic, political, and social situations inside and outside their businesses to maintain a competitive advantage and remain profitable.

The question is whether our decisions, based on the information we receive, are making things better, having no effect, or making things worse. We will argue that decisions based on numerical information or data, if the data are collected and processed correctly, typically make things better.

Consider the following situations where decisions seem to naturally depend on data.

A survey of customers indicates that a bank should improve the quality of its customer service. What should the bank do? The first step might be to concentrate on the teller–customer interaction. To improve service, the bank might use data on the lengths of time for teller transactions, the number of customers waiting in line, the teller error rates, the costs of handling exceptional requests, the amount of teller turnover, and so forth. These data could then be used to examine the entire *process* of providing customers with exceptional service.

Capital for company projects can be raised by selling bonds or issuing additional shares of stock. The choice of one or the other (or some combination of the two) depends, to some extent, on the likely behavior of interest rates, inflation, tax policy, and other economic variables. These variables are described by sets of numbers or data. Interest rates may be given by a set of short-term (90-day Treasury bill, 6-month certificate-of-deposit) and long-term (10-year Treasury note, 30-year Treasury bond) rates. Tax policy may be characterized by a set of tax brackets.

A drug company has developed a drug for combating the HIV virus that, according to the company, is more effective than current drugs and has fewer side effects. Before the company can produce and market the drug, however, it must receive government approval. Approval from the U.S. Food and Drug Administration requires that the company successfully complete a set of *clinical trials*. That is, the proposed drug must be tested, under carefully controlled conditions, on groups of human subjects. Data on the effectiveness and side effects must be collected, analyzed, and reported as part of the company's case. As part of its review, the government agency must decide whether the company's claims are sound. Were the data collected properly? Were the data interpreted correctly?

Sound decisions involve the collection of pertinent data and the application of appropriate techniques for extracting the information contained in the data.

1.2   STATISTICS AND THE SCIENTIFIC METHOD

If we knew exactly what was going to happen, when it was going to happen, and to whom it was going to happen, we could prepare for it. Knowing everything makes decision making easy but life less interesting. If a power company in the northeast knew how cold it was going to be next winter, it would be simple to plan for the amount of heating fuel to have available. On the other hand, operating with complete uncertainty is frustrating and often costly. Fortunately, there is a middle ground. Often we can collect or generate numerical information that, although not eliminating uncertainty entirely, will allow us to learn enough about the underlying situation to perform effectively.

As we mentioned in the Preface, **statistics** is the body of methodology concerned with the art and science of gathering, analyzing, and using data to identify and solve problems, and to make decisions. Statistical methods should be regarded as valuable tools. They do not replace critical thinking and common sense. However, if used correctly, statistical methods enable us to generate and assemble numerical information in a way that will help us pick out the signals in the fog, make better decisions, and create more rapid improvements in processes and products.

Let's return to the power company and heating fuel example. Numbers indicating the actual use of heating fuel for the past several winters are available from company records. These numbers will not tell us exactly what will be required this winter because **variation** in the weather from year to year and changes in the customer base introduce conditions not represented in the previous years' data. However, the power company has found that the uncertainties associated with determining the amount of heating fuel to have on hand during a particular winter can be greatly reduced by examining the actual heating fuel used for the past few years.

Some would say, particularly from a business perspective, that statistics is the study of variation. The Director of Statistical Methods for Nashua Corporation maintains that the central problem of management, in all its forms, including planning, research and development, procurement, manufacturing, sales, personnel, accounting, and law, is the failure to completely understand variation. What are its causes? What does it mean? The director is referring to the differences in numbers of the same type and the failure to understand the information contained in these differences.

Variation can often be summarized in simple graphs. Pictures are often easier to interpret than tables or lists of numbers. Spreadsheet programs can be used to construct familiar displays like **bar charts** and **pie charts.** For the former, amounts are indicated by the heights of bars. For the latter, amounts are indicated by the areas of pie slices.

EXAMPLE 1.1   Construction of a Bar Chart

Questions about the largest companies in the United States or the world can often be addressed by consulting the annual lists in *Fortune* magazine. In a recent issue, *Fortune* listed the world's 500 largest diversified service companies. The numbers of companies on the list by country follow.

Country	Number of Companies
United States	135
Japan	128
Germany	45
Britain	42
France	33
Canada	18
Spain	16
Italy	15
Switzerland	15
Other	53
Total	500

Construct a bar chart. How do the United States and Japan compare with the rest of the world?

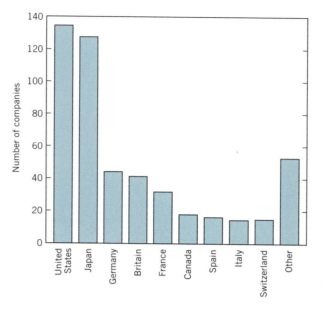

Figure 1.1 Bar Chart of Largest Diversified Service Companies by Country

Solution and Discussion. The name of each country is located along a horizontal axis in the order given in the table. Vertical bars of equal widths whose heights represent the number of companies for each of the countries are constructed. The result is shown in Figure 1.1. We easily determine that the United States and Japan have about the same number of companies on the list because the heights of their bars are about the same. The United States has slightly more of the companies on the list than Japan, and each of these countries has many more firms on the list than any other country. Together the two countries account for $\frac{135+128}{500} = .53$ or just over half of the world's largest 500 diversified service companies.

EXAMPLE 1.2   Comparing a Bar Chart and a Pie Chart

Companies continually monitor their markets to maintain market share. The *New York Times* recently reported the market shares, by type of beverage, in the carbonated soft-drink market. The results follow.

Type of Beverage	Market Share (%)
Caffeinated cola	48.0
Caffeine-free cola	10.4
Lemon-lime	9.8
Dr Pepper	3.9
Other	27.9

Graphically illustrate the market shares with a bar chart and a pie chart.

Solution and Discussion. To construct a pie chart, you must first calculate the angle of the slice. The angle of the slice is equal to the proportion of market share times 360°. With this choice, the *area* of any slice corresponds to the proportion. For example, the angle for caffeinated cola is $(.480)(360) = 172.8°$.

Most statistical software and spreadsheet packages require only the names of the categories and the counts or proportions (or percentages) to construct bar charts and pie charts. The market share bar chart is shown in Figure 1.2(a) and the pie chart in Figure 1.2(b). Both charts show the degree to which cola, both caffeinated and caffeine-free, dominates the carbonated soft-drink market.

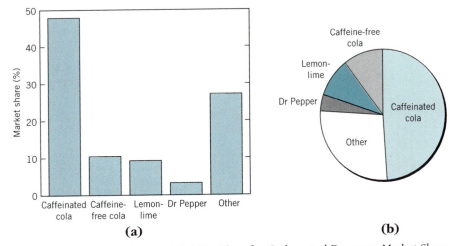

Figure 1.2   (a) Bar Chart and (b) Pie Chart for Carbonated Beverage Market Share

Psychologists have suggested that most people are able to compare bar heights better than they are able to compare pie slices. Pie slices are even harder to compare visually when the pie is tipped or given a thick edge as is often done in magazines and newspapers.

As we learn more, we typically get better results. Learning is a repetitive process, improved by applying a logical procedure for reasoning from available evidence. This is known as the **scientific method.**

Briefly stated, the scientific method is represented by the following sequence of steps:

- Observation
- Hypothesis
- Deduction
- Verification

In any practical application of the scientific method, these steps usually run together, must often be repeated, and are supplemented with trial and error, guesswork, and luck. However, the systematic approach to discovery represented by the scientific method remains an efficient and accepted means to new knowledge.

Observation is simply recognition of a particular phenomenon or outcome. Recognition may be triggered by an event, a need for action, an unusual set of numbers, or some other occurrence that draws our attention to an outcome. Observation leads to a hypothesis or conjecture that attempts to explain what was observed. If the hypothesis is true (the conjecture is correct), certain logical conclusions (predictions) follow by the process of deduction. These logical conclusions can be verified or checked. If there is agreement between what is suggested by the hypothesis and what is observed at the verification stage, the hypothesis can be taken as a working explanation of what has occurred, and new knowledge results. If there is disagreement, the original hypothesis must be abandoned altogether or modified, in which case there is another round of deduction and verification until a satisfactory match between explanation and experience occurs.

The scientific method requires that hypotheses (conjectures) be verified. This verification is ordinarily accomplished by running experiments and collecting data. An experiment may be as simple as sending out a questionnaire, or as complex as carefully varying the levels of several variables under controlled laboratory conditions to assess their effect on the outcome of interest. Ordinarily, an analysis of the data leads to a confirmation or revision of the hypothesis and, potentially, a repeat of the whole procedure.

EXAMPLE 1.3   Using the Scientific Method to Select a Commercial for a New Product

The marketing department of a large cereal manufacturer wanted to launch a new product that was related to their top-selling, donut-shaped cereal. Past experience with other new products has shown that a successful commercial was needed to get people to try the new product (*observation*). Two commercials were made. One featured a group of young women singing and the other featured a housewife. It was thought that they would not be equally effective (*hypothesis*), although it was not known which would be better. If one commercial is more effective than the other, a higher proportion of its viewers should remember the key message about the new product (*deduction*).

New cable technology was used to show one commercial to half of the cable audience in a viewing area and the other commercial to the other half. Several hours after the broadcast, telephone interviews were conducted with people randomly selected from each half of the audience. The response of interest was the number of viewers in each group who remembered a key idea from the commercial. In this instance, the second commercial featuring the housewife proved better (*verification*). The verification step is crucial before continuing with larger-scale operations.

The following example illustrates another application of the scientific method.

EXAMPLE 1.4   Using the Scientific Method to Discover Losses in Cheese Production

The production of cheese is big business in the United States. The National Cheese Institute represents a broad collection of member companies (Kraft, Land O Lakes, and others) that consider common problems and issues. At one time within this membership, there was significant interest in the procurement, trade, settlement, and accounting for bulk cheese as an ingredient in processed cheese forms.

Courtesy Dean Wichern

Figure 1.3   Sampling Cheese Through the Top of a 500-Pound Barrel

Several companies had consistently experienced unaccountable losses of cheese solids during the production of processed cheese (*observation*). One possibility was that the unaccounted-for solids were not there in the first place (*hypothesis*); that is, the procuring companies were receiving less solid cheese from their suppliers than they were anticipating (and paying for). This would imply that the moisture content within the 500-pound barrels of cheese received by the procuring companies was higher than expected (*deduction*). With the support of the National Cheese Institute, a proposal for data collection (an experimental design) and analysis was developed. The overall objective was to see whether the generally accepted sampling procedure for determining the moisture content of 500-pound barrels of cheese was faulty and, if so, to determine a better procedure. Measurements were collected and it was indeed discovered that the sampling method used (see Figure 1.3) led to estimates of moisture content that were too low (and amounts of cheese solids that were too high).

The experimental evidence suggested that the initial hypothesis was true (*verification*): The companies were paying for cheese solids they were not receiving. A new sampling procedure was developed to accurately measure the moisture content of barrel cheese. The new procedure was approved by the U.S. Department of Agriculture and is now the industry standard.

1.3   THE SCIENTIFIC METHOD IN A MANAGERIAL CONTEXT—IMPROVING QUALITY

A **process** is a collection of activities organized to achieve some goal. A process generally involves transforming inputs to a desired output. Getting dressed in the morning is a process. Routing a purchasing voucher for signatures is a process. Manufacturing paper is a process. A process may be composed of smaller processes (associated with subgoals). A collection of related processes and the environment that goes along with it is a **system.** For example, the network of interacting units associated with getting new cars from the factory to the consumers may be regarded as the distribution system. It may help to think of processes as local and systems as more encompassing and global in nature.

The business organization is a system comprising (1) inputs provided by suppliers, (2) steps and processes by which work is done, and (3) customers who receive the outputs. Customers provide feedback that can be used for the design and redesign of products and services. This view of the organization was developed and promoted by Dr. W. Edwards Deming (see Figure 1.4), the principal architect of the quality revolutions in Japan and the United States.

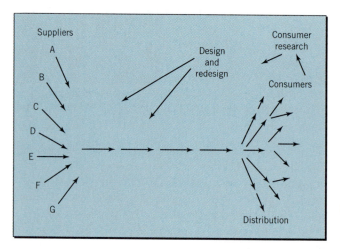

Figure 1.4 The Organization as a System with Consumer Feedback

The diagram in Figure 1.4 reminds us that work flows between functions and departments, and that customers are the reason a business organization exists.

By the 1950s, Dr. Joseph M. Juran, another force behind the quality revolution in the United States, had found that only about 20% of the production-level problems were worker-controllable. By worker-controllable, Dr. Juran meant that workers had the means for knowing what they should be doing, had the means for knowing what they were actually doing, and had the means for closing the loop between what they were doing and what they should be doing.

The majority of the problems—roughly 80%, according to Dr. Juran's studies—were beyond the control of the individual worker. In other words, if employees did their jobs as well as they could every time, only about a fifth of the problems would disappear. The majority of the problems come from the processes, the methods, the policies, the materials, the equipment, the training—things only management can change. Dr. Deming has suggested that as many as 96% of the problems can be removed by management, with about 4% the responsibility of individual employees.

Thus, large gains are possible if managerial decisions lead to improvements in the way work is done and in the tools for doing it. Managerial decisions, in turn, are most effective when based on a systematic approach to gathering and interpreting numerical information.

Dr. Deming has argued that improving the quality of what we do and how we do it eventually leads to decreased costs and increased productivity. This leads to lower

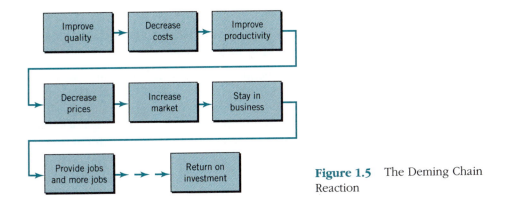

Figure 1.5   The Deming Chain Reaction

prices. With better quality and lower prices, we can expand our market share, stay in business, and provide jobs and more jobs. Another step to the chain reaction initiated by an improvement in quality has been suggested by Dr. Brian L. Joiner—namely, a better return to investors. The Deming chain reaction is pictured in Figure 1.5.

Ultimately, customers outside the company define quality. To customers, quality typically means more than just the characteristics of the product or service they initially receive. It is defined by *all* their interactions with the company. **Quality** products and services are those that meet and exceed customer expectations; that is, they *delight* the customer.

We buy a particular brand of television, for example, because we believe the quality is better than that of a comparatively priced set produced by another manufacturer. What does this mean? It means the perceived performance of the television (picture sharpness, sound, ease of operation, repair record) more than measures up to our standards—it exceeds our expectations. Moreover, we know the company stands behind its product and, if necessary, will resolve problems with the television in an expeditious and courteous manner.

Of course, a company may have internal customers and may itself be a customer of external suppliers. The same principles apply. The customer defines quality. Quality is achieved if the product or service meets and exceeds customer expectations.

Notice that quality is a moving target. Our notion of quality changes as our expectations change. In addition, quality may be assessed differently by different customers. For example, what is the quality of a college textbook? To the student, quality may involve the clarity of the exposition, the format for the transmission of information (text, pictures, tables), the relevance of the exercises, the book's entertainment value, and so forth. To the author, quality may be determined by the exposition, the content, the layout, the ancillary materials, and sales. To the publisher, quality is sales. Finally, to the printer, quality involves the style of the type, the materials used, minimal typographical errors, and legibility. Quality could be high (exceed expectations) for the author and printer, and low for the student and publisher.

Deming and his disciples have argued, as part of their program for quality improvement, that there is no substitute for knowledge. They have advocated the use of a scientific approach to solving problems that necessarily depends heavily on knowledge gained as a result of collecting and analyzing data.

EXAMPLE 1.5   Using the Scientific Method and Data to Improve the Quality of a Service

The manager of computing services at a large state university was concerned because the number of complaints about the quality of service at a particular "help desk" had increased, and she was responsible for general help-desk policy and staffing. Of course, the manager had to operate within a budget that had remained essentially the same for the past several years while the demand for service at the help desk had increased dramatically. What could the manager do to eliminate the complaints and increase the quality of service?

Solution and Discussion.   The first step was to learn more about the problem. From several visits to the help-desk area, the manager *observed* that some students waited to have their questions answered; some questions could not be answered by the student "consultants" on duty; some consultants were busier than others; some students became irritated because consultants refused to answer questions dealing directly with course assignments; and, finally, there were some periods during the day when the help desk was understaffed. In addition, although the computing center to which the help desk was attached was used primarily by business students, some of the traffic came from nonbusiness majors.

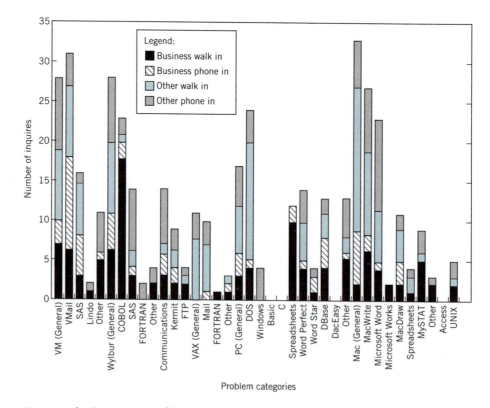

Figure 1.6   Frequencies of Initial Problem Categories, May 4–8

From these observations, the manager *hypothesized* that many of the questions were similar and were probably associated with certain software packages or operating systems; that is, the observations suggested a hypothesis or conjecture to be tested. Consequently, she *deduced* that many of the problems could probably be solved with handouts and, particularly, a better training program for the student consultants.

To test her hypothesis, the manager asked each consultant to maintain a daily log for a period of four consecutive weeks. Thirty-seven categories of questions were identified, including questions about the programming language COBOL, the software package Microsoft Word© , and the text editor Wylbur. Also included was the catchall category "other." The consultants simply recorded the number of times they encountered a problem in one of the categories. These frequencies were further organized according to major (business or nonbusiness) and whether the inquiry was a walk-in or phone-in question. Finally, the consultants kept track of the number of problems solved in a particular category and the number of problems referred.

Figure 1.6 contains a *segmented* bar chart of the total frequencies obtained from the consultants' daily logs for the first full week in May. The lengths of the segments in each vertical bar represent frequencies associated with the different ways complaints were received as indicated in the legend.

Although Figure 1.6 gives a good first-step summary, there are too many problem categories. Choosing more general problem categories helps to readily identify problems that can be corrected. Figure 1.7 is a segmented bar chart of the same frequencies after the initial problem categories were consolidated into seven general subject-matter categories. As the legend indicates, the segments in each bar refer to the number of problems solved or referred.

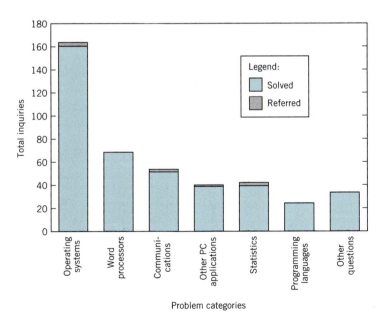

Problem categories	Solved	Referred
Operating systems	160	4
Word processors	70	0
Communications	52	2
Other PC applications	39	1
Statistics	39	2
Programming languages	24	1
Other questions	34	0

Figure 1.7   Frequencies of General Problem Categories, May 4–8

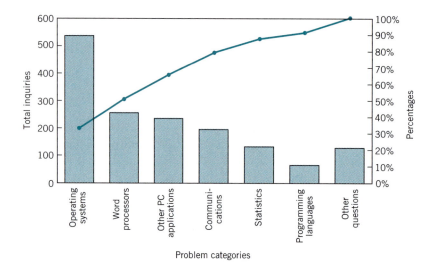

Figure 1.8   Total Frequencies for Four Weeks, April 13 to May 8

The data collection was extended to four weeks and the resulting four-week totals for the seven general problem categories are shown in Figure 1.8. The right-hand vertical scale in Figure 1.8 shows the cumulative percentage of problems in the various categories. From Figure 1.8, we see that 34% of the questions related to the operating system. Moreover, an appreciable percentage of the inquiries were about software packages, for example, word processing. The data appeared to *verify* the manager's hypothesis; that is, many of the problems were related and most of them were concerned with operating systems or a few kinds of software packages.

The bar chart in Figure 1.8 is called a **Pareto chart.** A Pareto chart is a special form of a vertical bar chart that helps you to determine which problems to solve and in what order. Constructing a Pareto chart from either a log or other forms of data collection helps direct attention and effort to the truly important problems. You will generally gain more by working on the tallest bar than from tackling the smaller bars. For example, in Example 1.5, operating systems questions occurred with the greatest frequency (see Figure 1.8). This single category, if eliminated, would reduce the help-desk traffic considerably. A Pareto chart is a useful tool for identifying frequently occurring categories of problems.

We have argued that the scientific method is an efficient way to acquire new knowledge. In this section, we have shown how the scientific method can be used in a general way to solve problems of quality. The scientific method invariably requires us to collect and analyze data (the subject matter of statistics), and it is this aspect of the method on which we will focus our attention in the remainder of this book. With a little practice, applying the scientific method becomes routine, and there is no need to go over the steps repeatedly. Keep in mind that the overriding objective is to learn something important about a process and to use this knowledge to make better decisions.

EXERCISES

1.1   Refer to Example 1.1 and the number of companies by country on *Fortune* magazine's list of the 500 largest diversified service companies. Calculate the proportion of companies on *Fortune*'s list for each of the countries: United States, Japan, Germany, Britain, France, Canada, Spain, Italy, and Switzerland.

1.2   Refer to Table 1.1, which gives the world's 25 largest diversified service companies. Construct a bar chart showing the sales according to country. Compare your chart with the bar chart for the top 500 companies in Figure 1.1. Do the United States and Japan still have about equal numbers of firms on the list? Comment on any major differences between the two bar charts.

TABLE 1.1   World's 25 Largest Diversified Service Companies

Company (Major industry)	Country	Sales ($ billions)
Itochu (trading)	Japan	156.3
Sumitomo (trading)	Japan	145.4
Mitsubishi (trading)	Japan	142.7
Marubeni (trading)	Japan	138.9
Mitsui (trading)	Japan	137.6
Nissho Iwai (trading)	Japan	86.2
American Telephone & Telegraph (telecomm.)	U.S.	65.1
Tomen (trading)	Japan	61.8
Nippon Telegraph & Telephone (telecomm.)	Japan	52.2
Nichimen (trading)	Japan	51.7
Kanematsu (trading)	Japan	47.7
Veba (trading)	Germany	39.6
Cie Generale des Eaux (construction)	France	27.1
RWE Group (energy)	Germany	26.6
Shimizu (eng., constr.)	Japan	19.1
Taisei (construction)	Japan	19.0
Kajima (eng., constr.)	Japan	17.6
BCE (telecomm.)	Canada	17.2
Toyota Tsusho (trading)	Japan	16.4
Hyundai (trading)	South Korea	14.5
Enron (natural gas)	U.S.	14.1
Takenaka (eng., constr.)	Japan	14.1
Time Warner (entertainment)	U.S.	13.1
Kawasho (trading)	Japan	13.0
Fleming (wholesale)	U.S.	12.9

1.3   Refer to Table 1.2 (page 14), which lists the world's 25 largest banks in 1992. Construct a bar chart showing the number of banks on this list from each country. What proportion of the banks on the list are from Japan?

TABLE 1.2 World's 25 Largest Commercial Banks

Company	Country	Assets ($ billions)
Dai-ichi Kangyo Bank	Japan	493.4
Fiji Bank	Japan	493.4
Sumitomo Bank	Japan	490.9
Sanwa Bank	Japan	485.0
Sakura Bank	Japan	470.8
Mitsubishi Bank	Japan	460.8
Norinchukin Bank	Japan	379.1
Industrial Bank of Japan	Japan	370.0
Crédit Lyonnais	France	350.7
Deutsche Bank	Germany	306.6
Crédit Agricole	France	298.1
Mitsubishi Trust & Banking	Japan	293.3
Tokai Bank	Japan	292.0
Long-term Credit Bank of Japan	Japan	290.4
Banque Nationale de Paris	France	283.7
Sumitomo Trust & Banking	Japan	280.7
Bank of China	China	279.4
Mitsui Trust & Banking	Japan	265.3
HSBC Holdings	Britain	257.9
Société Générale	France	256.9
Bank of Tokyo	Japan	254.8
ABN AMRO Holding	Netherlands	253.1
Asahi	Japan	251.9
Daiwa	Japan	224.2
Barclays Bank	Britain	222.7

1.4 Referring to Table 1.2, calculate the proportion of assets held by banks from each of Japan, France, and the United States.

1.5 Referring to Table 1.2, construct a horizontal scale from 200 to 500 billion dollars, and mark a dot above the scale at each asset listed. Are there any large gaps in the pattern? If so, how many banks would you place in a group of the very largest banks? Which country dominates this group?

1.6 Table 1.3 gives the total population and area of some of the world's largest cities. Make a bar chart for total population, arranged from largest to smallest.

TABLE 1.3 Total Population, Area, and Density of Some of the World's Largest Cities

City	Population (millions)	Area (square miles)	Density (thousands/square mile)
Bombay	12.101	95	127.5
Chicago	6.529	762	8.6
Hong Kong	5.693	23	247.5
London	9.115	874	10.4
Los Angeles	10.130	1110	9.1
Mexico City	20.899	522	40.0
New York	14.625	1274	11.5
Tokyo-Yokohama	27.245	1089	25.0

1.7   Refer to Exercise 1.6 and Table 1.3. What proportion of persons in these cities live in the United States?

1.8   Refer to Exercise 1.6 and Table 1.3. The total population divided by the area gives the population density in the last column. Construct a bar chart for population density arranged from largest to smallest. Compare your answer with that given in Exercise 1.6, and comment on any major differences.

1.9   List examples of academic processes that, from your perspective, need improvement. Suggestions include the registration process, method of instruction, and grading process. Using the scientific method, list specific steps that might reasonably be used to improve the processes you have identified.

1.10 List examples of financial transactions that, from your perspective, need improvement. Suggestions include student loans, check cashing, and parking ticket payments. Using the scientific method, list specific steps that might reasonably be used to improve the processes you have identified.

1.11 Consider the following list of personal items: winter coat, swimsuit, sunglasses, and tennis shoes. Define quality for each of these items. As part of your definition, list the factors that you think determine quality. Order the factors from most important to least important.

1.12 Consider the following list of services: airline service, public transportation (bus, subway), drive-through banking, hotel service, and maintenance (apartment, dorm) service. Define quality for each of these services. As part of your definition, list the factors that you think determine quality. Order the factors from most important to least important. Identify any common factors of general service quality.

1.13 Refer to Exercise 1.11. Given the factors that determine the quality of sunglasses, how should quality be measured? That is, what are the numbers (data) that could and should be collected to assess quality? [*Hint:* If the quality of sunglasses is determined by weight, amount of light allowed to pass through the lens, design, and so forth, some of these variables are easily measured. Others, for example, design, may have to be assigned a number on a scale ranging from, say, "terrible" to "outstanding."]

1.14 Refer to Exercise 1.12. Given the factors that determine the quality of airline service, how should quality be measured? What are the numbers (data) that could and should be collected to assess quality? [*Hint:* To assess service quality, we may have to keep certain records for a period (month, year) of time. For airline service, potentially important variables such as percentage of on-time departures and arrivals, amount of luggage lost, time spent at check-in, and so forth should be examined over time.]

1.4 VARIATION

The energy planning section of a large midwest power company is responsible for providing estimates of the amount of gas needed for heating. The amount of gas shipped on a daily basis can be determined from company records. A day in the middle of the week may be representative of weekday usage. For five Wednesdays in the previous January, the amount of gas sent out was

$$5.0 \qquad 3.8 \qquad 3.4 \qquad 4.6 \qquad 4.7$$

in heating units called megatherms. These values are not identical nor should they be. Each day's shipment of gas is influenced by daily weather conditions, including temperature, wind velocity, and the amount of cloud cover, as well as other uncontrollable variables.

The five numbers for Wednesday gas sendouts vary; that is, they are different. This state of disagreement is called **variation.** As we said, a central problem of management is the failure to understand variation. This general topic is explored in Chapter 13. For now, we present a numerical measure of variation known as the variance, and a closely related measure known as the standard deviation.

Consider the gas shipments. To create a useful measure of variation, we need a quantity that will be 0 when there is no variation (no differences, or all the numbers the same) and large when there is a lot of variation (big differences). This suggests measuring the variation relative to an internal reference point, rather than, say, the origin.

Let x_1 denote the first number, x_2 denote the second number, and so on to x_n for the nth and last number. In the present example, the size of our sample of Wednesdays is $n = 5$, and $x_1 = 5.0$, $x_2 = 3.8$, $x_3 = 3.4$, $x_4 = 4.6$, and $x_5 = 4.7$.

Our internal reference point will be the arithmetic average of the n numbers. This point is called the **sample mean** and is denoted by $\bar{x}$:

Sample mean: $\displaystyle \bar{x} = \frac{1}{n}\sum_{i=1}^{n} x_i = \frac{1}{n}(x_1 + x_2 + \cdots + x_n)$

The sample mean is the arithmetic average of a set of numbers.*

For the sendout of gas,

$$\bar{x} = \frac{1}{5}(5.0 + 3.8 + 3.4 + 4.6 + 4.7) = \frac{21.5}{5} = 4.3$$

Note that the sample mean, 4.3, falls within the set of numbers, but, in this case, is not one of the original numbers. The sample mean is located in the set such that the sum of the differences of the numbers from the mean is zero. In this sense, the sample mean represents the center of gravity (balancing point) of the numbers—the group of negative differences cancel out the group of positive differences.

Thus, subtracting $\bar{x} = 4.3$ from each of the gas sendout numbers, we get the differences

---

*A reader wishing to review the summation notation $\sum_{i=1}^{n} x_i$ can consult Appendix A.

$$5.0 - 4.3 = .7$$
$$3.8 - 4.3 = -.5$$
$$3.4 - 4.3 = -.9$$
$$4.6 - 4.3 = .3$$
$$4.7 - 4.3 = .4$$

These differences sum to zero. More generally (see Exercise 1.21), for any data set,

$$\sum_{i=1}^{n} (x_i - \overline{x}) = \sum (\text{differences}) = 0$$

The difference of a given number from the mean is sometimes called a **deviation from the mean.**

It should be clear from the expression for $\overline{x}$ that if all the numbers are the same, the mean will equal this common number, and, in this case, all the deviations from the mean will be zero. If the numbers vary, the deviations from the mean are not all zero. The larger the differences among the numbers, the larger (in absolute value) the deviations.

To measure variation, we need a single number that is zero if the numbers are the same (no variation) and increases as the differences increase. The sum of the deviations from the mean is not useful because it is always zero. To eliminate the influence of the signs of the deviations, we might consider the sum or mean of the absolute deviations. Another possibility is to construct a summary measure based on the squared deviations, since these quantities are always nonnegative. This leads to the definition of the **sample variance,** denoted by s^2:

Sample variance: $s^2 = \dfrac{1}{n-1} \sum_{i=1}^{n} (x_i - \overline{x})^2 = \dfrac{1}{n-1} \sum (\text{deviations})^2$

Here $x_1, x_2, \ldots, x_n$ are n numbers.

Because we are (essentially) averaging *squared* deviations to get the sample variance, the unit of measurement for the variance is the square of the unit of measurement for the original numbers. For example, s^2 will be in (megatherms)^2 units in the case of the gas shipments. A related measure of spread in the same units as the original numbers is the **sample standard deviation,** denoted by s.

Sample standard deviation: $s = +\sqrt{s^2} = \sqrt{\dfrac{1}{n-1} \sum_{i=1}^{n} (x_i - \overline{x})^2}$

The sample variance is almost the arithmetic average of the squared deviations.* Note that the sample variance and the sample standard deviation are, indeed, measures of spread. They are both zero when the deviations are all zero (the numbers are all the same), and they both increase as the deviations increase (the differences in the numbers get larger). Since the standard deviation is in the same units as the original numbers, it is often easier to interpret.

EXAMPLE 1.6   Calculation of the Sample Mean and Sample Standard Deviation

Calculate the sample mean and the sample standard deviation for the gas shipment data reproduced in the first column in the following table.

Solution and Discussion.   It is convenient to arrange the calculations in the form of a table, as follows:

x_i	$(x_i - \bar{x})$	$(x_i - \bar{x})^2$
5.0	.7	.49
3.8	−.5	.25
3.4	−.9	.81
4.6	.3	.09
4.7	.4	.16
Total 21.5	0	1.80

$$\bar{x} = \frac{21.5}{5} = 4.3 \qquad s^2 = \frac{180}{5-1} = .45$$

$$s = \sqrt{.45} = .67$$

The sample mean sendout is 4.3 megatherms and the sample standard deviation is .67 megatherm.

Together, the sample mean and sample standard deviation provide useful summaries of a data set. The mean indicates a central or typical value, and the standard deviation is a measure of spread about this central value.

EXAMPLE 1.7   Relating the Concentration of Data to *s*

The accompanying table contains five determinations of the moisture content of a plug of cheese from the study described in Example 1.4. The plug was ground, and the weights (in grams) of five portions of the ground plug were recorded before and

---

*There is a technical reason for using $n - 1$ in the definition of the sample variance rather than n. This reason is explored in Chapter 2.

after drying the portions in a vacuum oven. The moisture numbers are the weight losses expressed as percentages of the initial weights.

Replication	1	2	3	4	5
Moisture (%)	33.8	34.0	34.1	33.9	34.2

The following table contains the information required to calculate the sample mean and the sample standard deviation.

	x_i	$(x_i - \overline{x})$	$(x_i - \overline{x})^2$
	33.8	$-.2$	.04
	34.0	.0	.00
	34.1	.1	.01
	33.9	$-.1$	.01
	34.2	.2	.04
Total	170.0	0	.10

$$\overline{x} = \frac{170}{5} = 34 \qquad s^2 = \frac{.10}{5-1} = .025$$

$$s = \sqrt{.025} = .16$$

The sample mean, 34.0, falls in the bulk of the observations and is an indication of magnitude or location. (Here, the sample mean is equal to one of the original numbers. However, as we observed in Example 1.6, this is not always the case.) The sample standard deviation, .16, is a measure of spread.

Determine the percentage of observations in the mean centered interval $\overline{x} - 2s$ to $\overline{x} + 2s$.

Solution and Discussion.   The interval $\overline{x} - 2s$ to $\overline{x} + 2s$, or $34.0 - .32$ to $34.0 + .32$, contains all five, or 100%, of the data points. We will learn that a typical percentage is 95%.

Data need to be stable over time for the mean $\overline{x}$ and standard deviation s to provide reasonable summaries.

EXAMPLE 1.8   Checking Stability for a Large Data Set

Many of the numbers of interest in business become available over time. Examples include annual sales, quarterly earnings, and monthly inventory levels. Observations recorded in chronological order are called *longitudinal* or *time series* data. Table 1.4 (page 20) contains the monthly inventory levels (expressed in thousands of dollars) of diesel engines at Hatz Diesel of America, Inc.* The data cover the period from December 1987 through June 1992 and are organized chronologically by rows in the table.

---

*Data courtesy of A. G. Crownover.

TABLE 1.4   Engine Inventory Levels

772	701	681	620	618	543	551
848	1114	1079	1143	1040	1018	923
862	881	903	948	952	915	1096
965	1067	1049	948	863	1072	1440
1638	1669	1640	1699	1714	1571	1583
1481	1418	1255	1166	1037	914	993
1008	1094	1454	1334	1184	1180	1033
994	847	719	778	866	804	

Plot these data versus time to check stability. Comment on any pattern.

Solution and Discussion.   The inventory numbers are displayed as a time series plot in Figure 1.9. We see that the monthly inventory of engines reached its peak in mid-1990 and that there was quite a bit of up-and-down movement (variability) over the $4\frac{1}{2}$-year period represented by the data. In fact, the large upward swing at about time 30 coincided with a change in the way inventory was evaluated. Once the new system was understood, inventory could be reduced and savings realized.

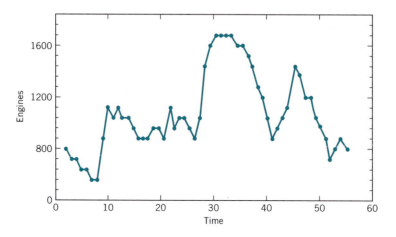

Figure 1.9   Time Series Plot of Inventory Levels

A computer program calculates a mean monthly inventory of $\bar{x} = 1067$ and a standard deviation of $s = 307.3$. However the mean 1067 is not a good summary because of the large upward swing. Neither is s a good summary.

Variability is not necessarily bad, and there is a lot to be learned from analyzing it. In fact, if all the daily gas sendouts had been exactly the same, we might suspect the data had been manipulated. Sendouts should be higher on colder days and lower on warmer days.

When numbers of the same kind vary within predictable ranges, we say the process that produced the numbers is in a state of **statistical control**—the sources of variation are stable or constant. We should not be unhappy with such variation. If we want to uniformly reduce the variation, we must change the process, as we discuss in Chapter 13.

EXERCISES

1.15 Given the five observations

$$-3 \quad 1 \quad 0 \quad 3 \quad 4,$$

calculate the sample
a. Mean
b. Variance
c. Standard deviation

1.16 Given the four observations

$$7 \quad 3 \quad 4 \quad 10$$

calculate the sample
a. Mean
b. Variance
c. Standard deviation

1.17 The power company records, referred to on page 16, also included the following actual values for gas sendouts for the four Saturdays in January:

$$3.5 \quad 2.9 \quad 3.4 \quad 4.3$$

Calculate the sample
a. Mean
b. Variance
c. Standard deviation

1.18 Refer to Exercise 1.17 and the results in Example 1.6 of the text. Compare the gas sendouts on Saturday with those of Wednesday. Some differences are due to different weather conditions but, according to planners, the fact that offices and industrial plants close on Saturday has a major impact. Does this explanation coincide with the direction of the difference suggested by these small data sets?

1.19 At the beginning of a recent year, the five nuclear generating plants in U.S. Region VII (Iowa, Kansas, Missouri, Nebraska) had net summer generating capabilities (in megawatts) of 530, 1135, 1125, 778, and 476. Determine the mean net summer capacity for the five plants (*Supplement to the Annual Energy Outlook 1992,* DOE/EIA-0554(92), Feb. 1992, Table 52).

1.20 At the beginning of a recent year, the United States had 111 nuclear generating units with a total net summer capability (in megawatts) of 99,624. How many generating plants in Exercise 1.19 had net summer capability above the U.S.

mean (*Supplement to the Annual Energy Outlook 1992,* DOE/EIA-0554(92), Feb. 1992, Table 52)?

1.21 Let $x_1, x_2, \ldots, x_n$ be n numbers.

a. Using the definition of $\bar{x}$ and some algebra, show that, for any set of numbers, $\sum_{i=1}^{n}(x_i - \bar{x}) = 0$.

b. Using the definition of $\bar{x}$ and some algebra, show that $\bar{x} = x_i$ for each i if all the numbers are exactly the same.

1.22 The moisture determinations in Example 1.7 were made at a cheese processing plant in Decatur, Georgia. Similar moisture determinations, using the same cheese, were made at a cheese processing plant in Clinton, Missouri. The latter numbers are given here:

Replication	1	2	3	4	5
Moisture (%)	34.1	34.0	33.8	33.8	33.9

a. Determine the sample mean, $\bar{x}$.

b. Calculate the differences of the observations from the sample mean, and show that their sum is zero.

c. Determine the sample variance, s^2, and the sample standard deviation, s.

d. Compare the sample mean, $\bar{x}$, and sample standard deviation, s, calculated in parts **a** and **c** with the corresponding quantities determined from the moisture numbers in Example 1.7. Are the Decatur, Georgia, and Clinton, Missouri, plants getting equally reliable determinations of moisture content? Discuss.

1.23 Gate receipts (in millions of dollars) for a recent season are given here for the $n = 26$ major league baseball teams (Ozanian, M., and Taub, S. "Big Leagues, Bad Business." *Financial World,* July 7, 1992, pp. 34–51).

19.4	26.6	22.9	44.5	24.5	19.0
27.5	19.9	22.8	19.0	16.9	15.2
25.7	19.0	15.5	17.1	15.6	10.6
16.2	15.6	15.4	18.2	15.5	14.2
9.5	10.7				

a. Compute the mean, $\bar{x}$, and standard deviation, s.

b. Using the results in part **a,** determine the proportion of observations that fall in the intervals $\bar{x} \pm s$ and $\bar{x} \pm 2s$, respectively.

1.5 SAMPLE AND POPULATION

We have argued that to acquire new knowledge, relevant data must be collected. Some amount of variability is unavoidable even though observations are made under the same or very similar conditions. It is also true that access to a complete set of data is either physically impossible or, from a practical standpoint, not feasible. No matter how many field or laboratory experiments have been performed, more can always be done. In public opinion or consumer expenditure surveys, a complete body of information would emerge only if data were gathered from every individual in the nation—undoubtedly a monumental if not an impossible task. To collect an exhaustive set of data related to the damage sustained by all cars of a particular model under collision at a specified speed, every car of that model coming off the production lines would have to be subjected to a collision! Thus, the limitations of time, resources, and facilities, and sometimes the destructive nature of the testing, mean that we must work with incomplete information—the data that are actually collected in the course of a study.

A distinction exists between the data set that is actually acquired through the process of observation and the vast collection of all potential observations that can be conceived in a given context. The statistical name for the former is a sample; for the latter, it is a population or statistical population.

Each measurement in the data set that constitutes the sample originates from a distinct source. This source may be a firm, a household, an employee, a patient, an invoice, or some other entity depending on the object of a study. The source of each measurement is called a **sampling unit** or simply a **unit.** The entire collection of units is called the **population of units.**

The data arise from measuring the value, for each unit, of a characteristic or variable of interest. Several characteristics may be of interest for a given population of units (see Table 1.5).

TABLE 1.5   Examples of Populations, Units, and Variables

Population	Unit	Variable or Characteristic
All firms in Dallas, Texas	Firm	Annual revenue Number of employees Annual amount spent on employee health care
All students currently enrolled in school	Student	Grade point ratio Number of term credit hours Hours of work per week

All households in
    Madison, Wisconsin
	Household	Household income
		Number of cars
		Quarterly amount spent on
		    entertainment

> **Population of units:** The complete collection of units about which information is sought
>
> **Unit:** A single entity, usually a person or an object, of the population of units

We are now in a position to formally define a population.

> The collection of *values* of a variable, obtained for every unit in the population of units, is the **statistical population,** or just the **population.**

Henceforth, we will refer to the population of units only when there is a need to differentiate it formally from the entire collection of values.

The population represents the target of an investigation. We learn about the population by taking a sample from the population—that is, by taking a subset of the population of units and recording the values of the variable of interest for the units in the subset. A **sample** or **sample data set** then consists of the measurements recorded for those units that are actually observed.

Sample: The set of measurements that are actually collected in the course of an investigation

---

EXAMPLE 1.9   Identifying the Population of Units, the Variable of Interest, and the Sample

A host of a radio talk show announced that she wants to know the favorite seafood restaurant among city residents. Listeners were then asked to call in and name their favorite seafood restaurant. Identify the population of units, the variable of interest, and the sample. Comment on how to get a sample that is more representative of the city's population.

Solution and Discussion.   The population of units is the entire collection of individuals who live in the city at the time of the announcement; the variable of interest is seafood restaurant preference. Because it would be nearly impossible to question all the residents of the city, we must necessarily settle for taking a sample.

Having listeners make a local call is certainly a low-cost method of getting a sample. The sample would then consist of the seafood restaurants named by each person who calls the radio station. Note that here the "values" of the variable are categories—the names of seafood restaurants.

Unfortunately, with this selection procedure, the sample is unlikely to be representative of the responses from all city residents. Those who listen to the radio show are already a special subgroup with similar listening tastes. Furthermore, those listeners who take the time and effort to call are usually those who feel strongest about their opinions. The resulting responses could well be much stronger in favor of a particular restaurant than is the case among the total population of city residents, or even those who listen to the station.

If the purpose of asking the question is really to determine the favorite seafood restaurant, we have to proceed differently. One commonly employed procedure is a phone survey where the phone numbers are chosen at random. For instance, we can write the numbers, 0, 1, 2, 3, 4, 5, 6, 7, 8, and 9 on separate pieces of paper and place them in a hat. Slips are then drawn one at a time with replacement. (Computers can mimic this selection quickly and easily.) Four draws will produce a random telephone number within a three-digit exchange. Telephone numbers chosen in this manner will certainly produce a much more representative sample than the self-selected sample of persons who call the station.

Self-selected samples consisting of responses to call-in or write-in requests will, in general, not be representative of the population. They arise primarily from subjects who feel strongly about the issue in question. To their credit, many TV news and entertainment programs now state that their call-in polls are nonscientific and merely reflect the opinions of those persons who responded.

Data collected with a clear-cut purpose are very different from **anecdotal data.** Many of us have heard people say they made money in the commodities market, but we have not heard much about their losses. People tend to tell good things about themselves. In a similar vein, some drivers' lives are saved when they are thrown free of car wrecks because they were not wearing seat belts. Although such stories are told and retold, you must remember that there is really no opportunity to hear from those who would have lived if they had worn their seat belts. Anecdotal information is usually repeated because it has some striking feature that may not be representative of the mass of cases in the population. Consequently, it is not apt to provide reliable answers to questions.

EXERCISES

1.24 A consumer magazine article asks,

HOW SAFE IS THE AIR IN AIRPLANES?

and then says that its study of air quality is based on measurements taken on 158 different flights of U.S.-based airlines. Identify the units, the population of units, the statistical population, and the sample.

1.25 A magazine that features the latest electronics and computer software for homes enclosed a short questionnaire on a postcard. Readers were asked to answer questions concerning their use and ownership of various software and hardware products, and to send the card to the publisher. A summary of the results appeared in a later issue of the magazine. The data were used to make statements such as "40% of readers have purchased program X." Identify a statistical population and sample, and comment on the representativeness of the sample. Are readers who have not purchased any new products mentioned in the questionnaire as likely to respond as those who have purchased?

1.26 Each year a local weekly newspaper gives out "Best of the City" awards in categories such as restaurant, deli, bakery, and so on. Readers are asked to write their favorites on a form enclosed in this free weekly paper and then send it to the publisher. The establishment receiving the most votes is declared the winner in its category. Identify the statistical population and sample, and comment on the representativeness of the sample.

1.27 Which of the following are anecdotal and which are based on a sample?

a. Erik says the checkout is faster at the grocery store on Tuesday than any other night of the week.

b. Out of 58 cars clocked on a busy road, 22 were exceeding the speed limit.

c. During a tornado, a man wrapped himself in a mattress in his bedroom. He was sucked out of the house along with his mattress, but he was unhurt.

1.28 Which of the following are anecdotal and which are based on a sample?

    a. Joan says that adding a few drops of almond flavoring makes her cookies taste better.

    b. Out of 102 customers at a quick-stop market, 31 made their purchases with a credit card.

    c. Out of 80 persons who purchased catsup at the supermarket one night, 71 purchased the same brand as their previous purchase.

1.6 STATISTICS IN CONTEXT

Throughout the chapters in this book, we will illustrate the use of statistical methods in real business contexts. These minicases will allow us to reinforce ideas and concepts introduced previously in the text. Here is a typical situation in a large firm where a process was statistically scrutinized to see how the process could be improved.

A department within a computer manufacturing company had a problem with distributing the mail.* Although mail was delivered to the department's mail stop twice a day (three times on Monday) by a company mailroom employee, the mail did not get to departmental mailboxes in a timely fashion. Often, the mail was handled by a departmental staff member only when he or she happened to be in the area. In addition, the staff seemed to spend an inordinate amount of time processing mail that, for one reason or another, did not belong to the department.

After forming a team of staff members to investigate the problem (the K-Team as it was called), a plan of action was devised that called, in part, for data on current operations. The first data collected were arrival times for departmental mail. The company mailroom had scheduled deliveries at 11 A.M. and 3 P.M. each day (and, additionally, at 8:30 A.M. on Monday), but data collected over a two-week period showed that the mail arrived at the department as much as 30 minutes late and never at the scheduled times. The arrival time frequencies, rounded to the nearest 15 minutes, for the 11 A.M. and 3 P.M. periods are indicated by vertical columns of dots in Figure 1.10.

Based on these data, we can reasonably assume that the mail will always reach the department no later than 11:45 A.M. and 3:45 P.M. The team decided to schedule mail pick-up at these times and then distribute it.

A **flowchart** for the department mail distribution process was created and is displayed in Figure 1.11. A flowchart is a series of boxes connected by arrows that shows the sequence of activity for the process. The diamond boxes in the chart indicate points where a decision must be made. If the condition in a diamond box is not met, an extra step, indicated by a dotted line in the chart, is added to the sequence. Thus, the dotted lines correspond to opportunities for improvement.

One major concern, suggested by the flowchart and reinforced by data collected over another two-week period, was the amount of time spent processing mail that did not belong to the department. Misaddressed mail had to be either tossed or readdressed and set out for pick-up by mail room personnel. Unwanted mail simply sent back to

---

*Project description and data courtesy of José Ramirez, Digital Corporation.

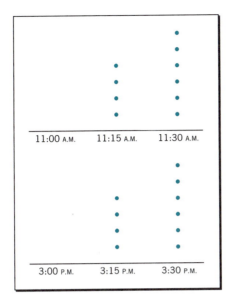

Figure 1.10 Mail Arrival Times

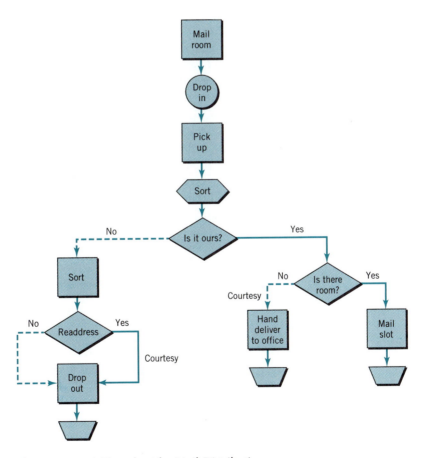

Figure 1.11 A Flowchart for Mail Distribution

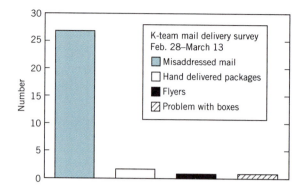

Figure 1.12 A Pareto Chart for Extra Work with Mail Distribution

the mail room would, in most cases, come back to the department. Figure 1.12 is a Pareto chart showing the two-week frequencies of the types of extra work involved with distributing the mail. Misaddressed mail is by far the most frequent source of difficulty. How can this problem be eliminated?

After a little brainstorming, the K-Team created a **cause-and-effect diagram** or **fishbone chart.** This diagram is shown in Figure 1.13.

The center line in the figure represents the problem or effect (misaddressed mail), and the larger diagonal lines are possible causes of the problem. The smaller lines attached to the diagonal lines represent subcases of the causes. The result has the appearance of the skeleton of a fish and, hence, the name, fishbone chart. The cause-and-effect diagram or fishbone chart identifies the causes that must be considered to eliminate the problem (time spent dealing with the wrong mail) and improve the process. Following the diagram in Figure 1.13, the K-Team took steps to reduce the amount of misaddressed mail. Change-of-address forms were located near the departmental mailboxes, and people were encouraged to update their addresses when they moved.

This quality improvement project was a success. The K-Team believed they had made a significant contribution. The mail is now available at specific times, with the secretarial staff sharing the distribution responsibility. The time it takes to handle the mail has been reduced substantially.

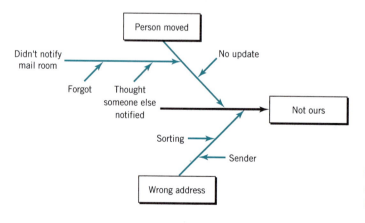

Figure 1.13 Cause-and-Effect Diagram for Receiving Wrong Mail

The collection of relevant data and summary by a graph allowed employees to set a pick-up time that could be consistently met. The other problem of taking too much time to distribute the mail was also addressed by collecting appropriate data and summarizing them in a Pareto chart. This highlighted specific difficulties, which were then remedied. A paradigm of this kind can be used to improve any process.

1.7   CHAPTER SUMMARY

In this chapter, we have learned:

- **Statistics** is the body of methodology concerned with the art and science of gathering, analyzing, and using data to identify and resolve problems and to make decisions.

- A **process** is a collection of activities organized to achieve some goal.

- A **system** is a collection of processes.

- **Quality** products and services are those that meet and exceed customer expectations. Quality is defined by the customer.

- Improved processes and products result from a focus on quality, a scientific approach to problem solving, and teamwork.

- Ultimately, management is responsible for improving processes.

- Problem solving can be enhanced by applying a systematic approach known as the scientific method.

- The **scientific method** is represented by four steps: Observation, Hypothesis, Deduction, and Verification.

- Data, in conjunction with the scientific method, are necessary to improve business decisions.

- Data can be summarized with simple graphical displays like **bar charts, pie charts,** and **Pareto charts.**

- Understanding variation (or differences) is a crucial part of resolving problems.

- The arithmetic average of a set of numbers is called the **sample mean.** The position of the sample mean in a set of numbers is such that the sum of the differences of all numbers from the mean is zero.

- The variation in a set of numbers is measured by the **sample variance** or **sample standard deviation.** The sample standard deviation is the positive square root of the variance and is expressed in the same units as the original numbers.

- A **population** is the complete set of measurements, or record of a qualitative trait, corresponding to the collection of all units about which information is desired.

- A **unit** is the single entity on which the variable of interest or characteristic is measured.

- A **sample** from the population is the set of measurements that are actually collected.

- Additional simple graphical tools for improving processes include **flowcharts** and **cause-and-effect diagrams** or **fishbone charts.**

1.8   IMPORTANT CONCEPTS AND TOOLS

CONCEPTS

Anecdotal data, 25
Deviation from the mean, 17
Population, 23
Population of units, 23
Process, 7
Quality, 9
Sample, 24
Sample mean, 16

Sample standard deviation, 17
Sample variance, 17
Scientific method, 5
Statistical control, 21
Statistics, 2
System, 8
Unit, 23
Variation, 16

TOOLS

Bar chart, 3
Cause-and-effect diagram, 28
Fishbone chart, 28
Flowchart, 26
Pareto chart, 12
Pie chart, 3

1.9   KEY FORMULAS

$$\overline{x} = \frac{1}{n} \sum_{i=1}^{n} x_i$$

$$s^2 = \frac{1}{n-1} \sum_{i=1}^{n} (x_i - \overline{x})^2$$

$$s = +\sqrt{s^2}$$

REVIEW EXERCISES

1.29   Table 1.6 gives the total exports and population size for the leading export nations in 1992. Construct a bar chart for total exports arranged from largest to smallest.

TABLE 1.6   Total Exports and Population Size

Country	Exports (billions U.S.$)	Population (millions)
Brazil	31	148.0
Canada	124	26.8
China	70	1151.5
France	216	56.6
Germany	391	79.5
Japan	314	124.0
United Kingdom	185	55.4
United States	422	252.7

1.30   Refer to Exercise 1.29 and Table 1.6. Calculate the sample mean and sample variance of the total exports for these countries.

1.31 Refer to Exercise 1.29 and Table 1.6. Divide each country's total exports by population size to obtain the exports per capita.

    a.   Construct a bar chart for exports per capita arranged from largest to smallest.

    b.   What major differences do you see between the bar chart of total exports and the bar chart of exports per capita?

1.32 U.S. energy consumption (in units of quadrillion BTUs) by fuel type is given here for a recent year (*Supplement to the Annual Energy Outlook 1992,* DOE/EIA-0554(92), Feb. 1992, Table 1).

Fuel Type	Consumption
Petroleum products	33.8
Natural gas	19.4
Coal	19.1
Nuclear power	6.2
Other	6.6

    a.   Determine the *percentage* of total energy consumption by fuel type, and construct a bar chart showing the percent consumption. [*Hint:* Mark the fuel types at equal intervals along the horizontal axis, and construct vertical bars centered at the fuel types whose heights are the appropriate percentages. Should the widths of the bars be equal? Should the bars touch one another? Discuss.]

    b.   Suppose we record U.S. energy consumption by fuel type for several years. If we want to track changes in, say, the dependence on natural gas (relative to the other fuels) as an energy source, should we use the original consumption numbers or the consumption percentages? Explain.

1.33 List examples of processes associated with daily living that, from your perspective, need improvement. Suggestions include room cleanup, local transportation system, and grocery shopping. Using the scientific method, list specific steps that might reasonably be used to improve the processes you have identified.

1.34 Consider the following list of foods: pizza, frozen yogurt, orange juice, potato chips, and chocolate chip cookies. Define quality for each of these foods. As part of your definition, list the factors that you think determine quality. Order the factors from most important to least important.

1.35 Refer to Exercise 1.34. Given the factors that determine the quality of a pizza, how should quality be measured? What are the numbers (data) that could and should be collected to assess quality? [*Hint:* Measurable factors influencing the quality of pizza may include amount of toppings, temperature, thickness of crust, and so forth.]

1.36 Given the five observations

$$12 \quad 6 \quad 8 \quad 0 \quad 14$$

calculate the sample

    a.   Mean

    b.   Variance

    c.   Standard deviation

1.37   The research and development (R&D) expenditures as a percentage of sales for the world's twelve largest automakers are given here for a recent year. (*Financial World,* Apr. 14, 1992, pp. 58–59).

R & D (as % of sales)	4.4	3.6	4.4	3.7	9.6	3.9
	3.6	3.5	3.0	4.5	3.9	2.2

   a.   Order the observations from smallest to largest, and plot the numbers as dots on a horizontal axis.

   b.   Calculate the sample mean, $\bar{x}$, and the sample standard deviation, s.

   c.   Mark the location of the sample mean on the diagram in part **a.** Notice that one expenditure, 9.6, seems to be substantially larger than the others. This is the R&D expenditure for Daimler-Benz, the maker of Mercedes-Benz automobiles. Remove this "outlier" from the set, and recalculate the sample mean and sample standard deviation.

   d.   Compare the sample means and sample standard deviations from parts **b** and **c.** Comment on the effect of a single atypical observation on the calculation of $\bar{x}$ and s.

1.38   A consumer magazine article asks readers to respond to the question, "How do you like to spend your free time?" From the responses of 100 persons, the article concluded that 74% consider shopping at least a hobby. Identify the statistical population and the sample, and comment on the representativeness of the sample.

1.39   Review the mail delivery case discussed in Section 1.6. As part of their investigation for ways to improve the mail service, the departmental staff recorded the amount of time needed to put the mail into slots and to hand carry oversize packages to departmental offices. These times (in minutes) for most of a two-week period are given here. (The mail processing times for some of the delivery periods were not recorded over the two-week interval.)

   10   5   5   10   5   5   10   5   3   5   5   10   2   2

   a.   Plot these data using dots over the different numbers to indicate frequencies (see Section 1.6).

   b.   Calculate $\bar{x}$ and s. Mark the location of the sample mean on the plot in part **a.** Does it appear as if the dot diagram "balances" at the sample mean? Should it?

1.40   Refer to the mail distribution times in Exercise 1.39.

   a.   Suppose 3 minutes is added to each of the mail distribution times. What effect does this have on the sample mean? Calculate $\bar{x}$ with 3 added to each of the numbers in Exercise 1.39. Compare this sample mean with the sample mean in part **b** of Exercise 1.39.

   b.   Given the result in part **a,** can you make a general statement about the effect on the sample mean of adding an arbitrary constant, c, to each number in a data set?

1.41 Refer to the mail distribution times in Exercise 1.39.

a. Suppose each mail distribution time is multiplied by 3. What effect does this have on the sample variance and sample standard deviation? Do you expect both to increase? Calculate s when each observation in Exercise 1.39 is multiplied by 3. Compare this sample standard deviation with the sample standard deviation in Exercise 1.39 part **b.** [*Hint:* Compare the ratio of the standard deviations to 3.]

b. Given the result in part **a,** can you make a general statement about the effect on the sample standard deviation of multiplying each number in a data set by an arbitrary positive constant c? Must the constant be positive?

c. Suppose an arbitrary constant, c, is added to each number in a data set. Do you think the sample standard deviation will change? Discuss.

1.42 Refer to Exercises 1.40 and 1.41. Recalling that $\bar{x}$ is a measure of location and s is a measure of spread, investigate the effects on these quantities of multiplying each number in a data set by a positive constant and then adding a constant to each of the modified numbers. (This operation is called a linear transformation.) Use the data set consisting of the following $n = 5$ numbers:

$$2 \quad 3 \quad 6 \quad 9 \quad 5$$

a. Calculate $\bar{x}$ for these numbers. Multiply each number by 2 and add 10. Recalculate $\bar{x}$. Plot the two sets of data, with dots, and mark the sample means. Compare the two means. Does the additive constant, 10, or the multiplicative constant, 2, affect the sample mean? Do you think different values for the constants would change your conclusion about the sample mean? Discuss.

b. Calculate s for these numbers. Multiply each number by 2 and add 10. Recalculate s. Compare the two sample standard deviations. Which of the constants, 2 and 10, affect the sample standard deviation? Do you think different values for the constants would change your conclusion about the effects of additive and multiplicative constants on the sample standard deviation? Discuss.

CHAPTER TWO

Describing Patterns in Data

2.1 INTRODUCTION

In Chapter 1, we stated that numerical information (data) is often required for gaining new knowledge, effectively improving business processes, and, in general, making better decisions. We also suggested that some amount of variability in the data is unavoidable even though measurements are made under identical or very nearly identical conditions. This chapter is concerned with methods for describing and summarizing data to highlight any important features or patterns they may contain. The goal is to make the information in data obvious. Because there are several types of data, a particular procedure for displaying and summarizing one kind of data may not be appropriate for another. However, there are general categories of methods that work, to a greater or lesser extent, for everything. These categories include tables, plots, and numerical summaries. The practice of examining data with a collection of relatively simple tables, plots, and numbers is called **exploratory data analysis.**

2.2   ENUMERATIVE VERSUS ANALYTIC STUDIES

We said in Chapter 1 that the population often represents the target of the numerical inquiry, although the population may be difficult to define or simply unavailable for study. In general, however, we learn about the population by sampling from it.

To illustrate situations where defining the appropriate population is difficult and generalizations *beyond* the sample observations must be carefully interpreted, we must distinguish between enumerative and analytic studies.*

In an **enumerative study,** interest centers on the identifiable, unchanging, generally finite collection of units from which the sample was selected. For example, we may be interested in the 1996 per capita cost of health care for all U.S. companies with at least 100 employees. To get some idea of what the average 1996 per capita cost might be, a sample of these firms is selected and health care costs determined. The per capita costs for the units (firms) in the sample are the sample observations. The per capita costs for the entire collection of units (firms) are the population observations. The population numbers include the sample numbers and, if time and resources allow, a complete enumeration of the population is possible.

A list, or similar mechanism, for identifying the entire set of relevant sampling units is called a frame.

> **Frame:**   A list of the entire set of relevant sampling units

In the example on health care cost, a frame is a list of all U.S. firms with at least 100 employees as of December 31, 1996. Enumerative investigations are typically concerned with making generalizations (inferences) from the sample data to the complete collection of units in the frame. Along these lines, enumerative studies have two distinguishing characteristics. First, the frame (entire collection of units) does not change. This ordinarily means that enumerative studies pertain to an environment existing at a particular point in time. Second, a 100% sample of the frame provides the complete answer to the question posed.

An internal audit conducted to determine the extent to which long-distance telephone calls are business related is an enumerative study. The frame is a list of all long-distance calls made by the several hundred employees of a particular firm for the previous month. A sample of employees is selected, and their long-distance calls are audited. The results will be used to determine the amount the employer paid for nonbusiness-related calls. Perhaps the audit will suggest an investigation of all the items in the frame.

---

*A distinction emphasized by Dr. Deming and others.

Product acceptance sampling is another good example of an enumerative study. A shipment of parts from a supplier is accepted or rejected depending on the number of defective parts in a sample of parts from the shipment. The frame is the aggregate collection of parts in the shipment, say, a truckload, and interest centers on the number of defective parts in the truckload.

An **analytic study** is a study that is not enumerative. Analytic studies generally take place over time and are concerned with processes or cause-and-effect systems. The most effective analytic studies involve a plan for collecting the data. The objective is to improve future practices or products. Analytic studies often involve comparisons. Will this material or that material lead to more durable products? Will this method of training or that method of training lead to more productive employees? Will this type of service or that type of service lead to a higher retention of customers?

In analytic studies, we are interested in drawing conclusions about a process or product that often does not exist at the beginning of the study. We are no longer dealing with a collection of identifiable units and, consequently, there is no relevant frame (population) from which to sample. Instead, we are typically dealing with observations derived from a current process or product, and we must *predict* what will happen at some future time if, for example, certain actions are taken.

Consider a public opinion poll of registered voters held *before* an election. If interest centers on the proportion of people voting for, say, the Republican candidate on election day, the pre-election-day poll is an analytic study. Even a 100% sample of the registered voters will not allow us to predict the outcome of the election with certainty. Between the time of the poll and election day, some voters will change their minds, additional eligible people may register, some voters will not vote for one reason or another, and these "stay-at-homes" may well differ in their voting preferences from those who do vote. We want to draw conclusions about a future process (election-day voting) from information on a current process (pre-election voting indications) that might be quite different. However, an *exit poll* to determine the proportion of voters who have voted for a particular candidate is an enumerative study, since a 100% sample provides perfect information (provided all voters tell the truth).

New products are frequently test-marketed before full-scale production occurs. Consumer responses to a prototype product are used to fine-tune the product before full production or, perhaps, to abandon it altogether. Full evaluation of all test-marketed products still may not tell us about the process of interest—the process associated with producing the final product. Studies involving prototypes or trial products are analytic.

The vast majority of numerical studies in business are analytic and we have to be careful about making statements or taking actions based on observations from current processes. If a process is stable and unchanging (in a state of "statistical control") and remains so, current data may be used to reach conclusions about future performance of the process. However, the validity of extrapolating from current conditions should always be thoroughly examined. Enumerative studies, too, must be conducted with care. The validity of inferences from enumerative studies depends, in part, on how well the frame represents the target population.

The issues raised either explicitly or implicitly in this section—collecting appropriate data, summarizing numerical information, monitoring processes, generalizing beyond the data or time period, reaching valid conclusions, and so forth—will be considered as we progress through this book. After-the-fact analysis cannot compensate for a poorly planned investigation and, as we shall see, the planning process is different for analytic than for enumerative studies.

2.3   VARIABLES AND DATA

We have used the term *data* to mean numbers or measurements obtained from sampling units. In the previous chapter, sampling units included Wednesdays in January, engines, and time intervals. More formally, **data** are numbers that represent particular characteristics of sampling units. The characteristics themselves are called **variables.** Income is a variable and, if you are a sampling unit, your particular income is a measurement or data. Gender is a variable and, if you are a sampling unit, your gender is data.

The previous examples indicate that variables are of two types:

Quantitative variable: A variable that is naturally numerical, such as income
Qualitative variable: A variable whose values are categories, such as gender

The values of a quantitative variable fall on some scale of measurement. Qualitative variables are somewhat different. The variables "gender," "employment status," and "Moody's bond rating" are not naturally numerical. The "values" for these variables are categories such as male/female, employed/unemployed, and Aaa, Aa, . . . , C, respectively. We can make variables like these numerical by assigning numbers to the categories, and sometimes it is convenient to do so.

Nominal data: The numbers assigned to distinguish the separate categories of a qualitative variable

The number 1 assigned to "male" and the number 2 assigned to "female" are nominal data. Sometimes, however, it is useful to retain the original verbal descriptions of the categories.

If the outcomes for qualitative variables are ordered, that is, if there is an implied hierarchy of categories, an increasing (or decreasing) set of numbers can be assigned to represent the ordered categories.

Ordinal data: An increasing (or decreasing) set of numbers assigned to the ordered categories of a qualitative variable

For example, Moody's has nine categories of bond ratings ranging from C (extremely poor in investment quality) to Aaa (a "gilt-edge" security). We might code these categories using the integers 1 through 9 with category C assigned the number 1 and category Aaa assigned the number 9. The increasing order of the integers matches the increasing order—from worst (extremely risky) to best (virtually no risk)—of the bond categories. A group of 10 bonds might yield the data 4, 9, 9, 5, 6, 8, 2, 7, 7, 6, where the numbers correspond to the Moody's ratings.

The magnitudes of the numbers we have assigned have meaning: 7 is a better (less risky) bond than 6 because 7 is larger than 6. But arithmetic operations performed on these numbers have no meaning, since there is no well-defined origin and no natural unit of measurement. For example, we can compute the difference $9 - 8 = 1$, but we cannot say that this is the difference between Aaa bonds and Aa bonds. We could just as well have assigned the number 20 to Aaa bonds, 15 to Aa bonds, and so forth. In this case, the implied difference between the two highest-rated bond groups is 5. The differences (or sums or products or ratios) could be anything we want them to be, because there is no natural (unique) choice for an increasing set of numbers to represent the bond categories.

For a qualitative variable with two unordered categories, it is often helpful to assign the number 0 to one category and the number 1 to the other. With employment status, we might make the assignment

$$\text{employed} = 1$$
$$\text{unemployed} = 0$$

and, if several people were involved, the data would consist of a sequence of 0's and 1's, where a single digit corresponds to a specific person.

> **Binary coding:** Assigning 0 and 1 to the only two unordered categories of a qualitative variable

Using binary coding, a group of five people, three of them employed, could yield the data 0, 1, 1, 0, 1. For binary coding, summing the data gives the count in the category designated by 1. There are $0 + 1 + 1 + 0 + 1 = 3$ people employed in our group of five. Dividing the sum by the total number of items gives the *proportion* of items in the 1 category. For our five people, a proportion $\frac{3}{5} = .60$ are employed. Because of the interpretation of these specific arithmetic operations, binary, or 0–1, coding is useful.

Closer scrutiny of quantitative variables reveals two distinct types. American shoe sizes, such as $7, 7\frac{1}{2}, 8, \ldots$, proceed in steps of $\frac{1}{2}$. Stock prices are expressed in steps of $\frac{1}{8}$'s of a dollar. Counts such as number of directors or vote tallies are, of course, integers.

> **Discrete variable:** A quantitative variable whose values are distinct numbers with gaps between them

Shoe size, stock price, number of directors, and vote tally are examples of discrete variables.

On the other hand, there are quantitative variables whose values can, in principle, take any value in an interval.

> **Continuous variable:**   A quantitative variable whose value can be any value in an interval

To a reasonable approximation, net income, time to equipment failure, total sales, and weight are examples of continuous variables. In these cases, the measurement scale does not have any gaps. Ideally, any value along a continuum is possible.

A truly continuous scale of measurement is an idealization. In practice, continuous measurements are always rounded either for the sake of simplicity or because the measuring device has a limited accuracy. However, even though weight may be recorded to the nearest pound or time to failure to the nearest minute, their actual values occur on a continuous scale so the data are referred to as continuous. Variables that are inherently discrete are treated as such, provided they take relatively few distinct values. When the values for a discrete variable span a wide range, however, they may be treated as continuous. The number of shares (volume) of stock traded per day is a discrete variable, but daily volume data may, for practical purposes, be viewed as continuous.

The point to keep in mind is that, regardless of whether the variables (characteristics of interest) are naturally numerical, ultimately we will be dealing with numbers.

EXERCISES

2.1   Classify the following as enumerative or analytic studies. Justify your choice.
   a.   A telephone company wishes to estimate the proportion of all telephones in a city that are working at a given time.
   b.   An airport executive wants to know the number of on-time arrivals at a municipal airport yesterday.
   c.   A construction company executive wants to estimate the amount of supervisory time for each worker-day of time allocated to its jobs.
   d.   During the summer, a university administration wants to estimate the number of admitted freshmen who will attend school in the fall.

2.2   Classify the following as enumerative or analytic studies. Justify your choice.
   a.   A rating service wishes to estimate the number of households in the United States watching a particular Monday night television program.
   b.   A company wants to determine the number of defective golf balls in a recently produced batch.
   c.   A consumer products company wants to know whether increasing advertising expenditures will lead to increased sales of an item.
   d.   A mail order firm wants to estimate the time it takes to ship the goods once an order is received.

2.3 Refer to Exercise 2.1. For each of the studies, define the variable (characteristic) of interest. Indicate whether the variable is quantitative or qualitative. If the variable is quantitative, indicate whether it is discrete or continuous.

2.4 Refer to Exercise 2.2. For each of the studies, define the variable (characteristic) of interest. Indicate whether the variable is quantitative or qualitative. If the variable is quantitative, indicate whether it is discrete or continuous.

2.5 Consider the collection of students in the class.
   a. Describe two enumerative studies for which the students in the class may be regarded as a sample from a larger population.
   b. Describe two enumerative studies for which the students in the class may be regarded as the population. Suggest a frame for this population.

2.6 A sample of $n = 15$ people were asked whether they favored or opposed a new system of high-speed rail transportation. The responses were coded as follows: favored = 1, opposed = 0. The data are

$$1\ 0\ 0\ 0\ 1\ 1\ 1\ 1\ 0\ 0\ 1\ 0\ 0\ 0\ 0$$

   a. Sum these numbers and interpret the result.
   b. Calculate the sample mean, $\bar{x}$, and interpret this quantity for 0–1, or binary coded, data.

2.7 A sample of ten recent graduates in accounting were asked about job satisfaction. The responses were coded as follows: satisfied = 1, not satisfied = 0. The data are

$$1\ 0\ 1\ 1\ 0\ 0\ 1\ 1\ 1\ 1$$

   a. Sum these numbers and interpret the result.
   b. Calculate the sample mean, $\bar{x}$, and interpret this quantity for 0–1, or binary coded, data.

2.4 GRAPHICAL DISPLAYS OF DATA DISTRIBUTIONS

Recall the sendouts of gas on Wednesdays in January discussed in Example 1.6 or the monthly inventory levels of diesel engines introduced in Example 1.8. These examples illustrate that repeated measurements of a given variable are different. The measurements vary. When the data set is very small, the differences are readily apparent. We can immediately see, for example, whether all the numbers are close together or whether one number is considerably smaller than all the rest. With moderate to large data sets, however, the pattern of variability is generally not evident. Until the data are organized in some meaningful fashion, it is often not clear what the data are telling us. Organizing the data graphically is a necessary first step to understanding the information contained in them. Graphical displays can provide an immediate interpretation not visible in the raw numbers.

The pattern of variability in a data set is called its **frequency distribution.** This distribution indicates the possible values, or categories, for the variable and the number of times each value or category occurs. Frequency distributions are best characterized by graphs or plots. The best display in a particular case depends on the nature and size of the data set.

DOT DIAGRAM

We have already seen an example of a **dot diagram** in Figure 1.10. This figure showed the frequencies of the mail arrival times for a department in a computer manufacturing company. For relatively small data sets that contain either discrete or (rounded) continuous measurements, a dot diagram provides a useful display of the variability. To create a dot diagram, draw a line with a scale covering the range of values of the measurements, and then plot the individual measurements above the line as prominent dots.

EXAMPLE 2.1   Constructing a Dot Diagram

The monthly inventory levels for diesel engines (in thousands of dollars) were given in Table 1.4 (see Example 1.8). Construct a dot diagram for these data.

Solution and Discussion.   The dot diagram, constructed with the help of a computer program, is given in Figure 2.1. The dot diagram indicates that most of the monthly inventories cluster around the 1000 ($1,000,000) level, with a few levels above 1500 and none below 500. The dot diagram shows the pattern of the variation in these data—a pattern that is not obvious from examining the rows of numbers in Table 1.4.

Figure 2.1   Dot Diagram for Inventory Levels

The dot diagram is the simplest way to display data. However, for moderate to large data sets, it is sometimes difficult to determine the actual numerical values from the scale beneath the dots. The dots blend together, or nearly identical data get rounded and plotted as the same numbers. Other graphical displays can be constructed that picture the frequency distribution and convey information about the magnitudes of the numbers themselves.

STEM-AND-LEAF DIAGRAM

A view of a frequency distribution that features the actual numerical values in the display is provided by a **stem-and-leaf diagram.** Stem-and-leaf diagrams work best for small- to moderate-size data sets where the measurements are all positive two- or three-digit numbers.

A stem-and-leaf diagram is created from data arranged in ascending order of magnitude (smallest to largest). The diagram uses the information in the leading digits of the numbers. For two-digit numbers, the first digits are the stems and the second digits are the leaves, and the arrangement of the leaves on the stems provides a pictorial representation of the distribution.

EXAMPLE 2.2 Constructing a Stem-and-Leaf Diagram for a Small Data Set

Consider the R&D expenditures for the twelve largest automakers given in Exercise 1.37. Create a stem-and-leaf diagram for these data.

Solution and Discussion. The R&D expenditures as a percentage of sales are reproduced here:

4.4	3.6	4.4	3.7	9.6	3.9	3.6	3.5	3.0	4.5	3.9	2.2

We represent 2.2, for example, as 2|2, where the first digit is the stem and the second digit is the leaf. The numbers 3.0 and 3.5 become 3|05, where 0 and 5 are the leaves attached to the same stem, 3. Continuing in this way we obtain the stem-and-leaf diagram in Figure 2.2.

```
2 | 2
3 | 0566799
4 | 445
5 |
6 |
7 |
8 |
9 | 6
```

Figure 2.2 Stem-and-Leaf Diagram for R&D Expenditures

In summary, the integers 2, 3, ..., 9 in the first column are the stems. (The column of stem digits is often called the stem for convenience.) The integers in the horizontal lines coming from the stems are the leaves. Each leaf digit corresponds to a number. Since the leaf digits, for this data set, are in tenths, we say the leaf unit is .10. The first line in the stem-and-leaf diagram, 2|2, indicates a value of 2.2 for the smallest number in the data set.

The second line, 3|0566799, indicates that there are seven numbers with the stem, or first digit, 3, and with the leaf unit .10; the seven numbers are 3.0, 3.5, 3.6, 3.6, 3.7, 3.9, and 3.9. There are no numbers in the data set with the stems (first digits) 5 through 8, because there are no leaves attached to these stems. The final and largest R&D expenditure is 9.6.

It is clear that most of the data are associated with the stem (category) 3. That is, the majority of the automakers in this group spend between 3% and 4% of sales on research and development. The expenditure 9.6 (Daimler-Benz) is large relative to the rest of the data. Observations that are far removed from the bulk of the data are called "outliers" and are ordinarily subjected to additional scrutiny to determine why they are different.

When the stem-and-leaf diagram in Figure 2.2 is turned on its side with the stem as a horizontal axis, we get a view of the pattern of variation.

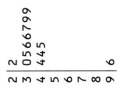

In this case, the distribution is characterized by a mound of values (leaves) on the left that tail off to the one relatively large value at the right. The display is informative because, in addition to giving us a picture of the variation, every R&D number can be reconstructed exactly from the stem and corresponding leaf integers.

Stem-and-leaf diagrams are extremely versatile displays. A stem-and-leaf display involving a larger data set of three-digit numbers is given in Example 2.3. Other examples and variants of the stem-and-leaf diagram are considered in the exercises. Of particular interest is the use of back-to-back stem-and-leaf diagrams to compare two distributions. The distributions of the ratio (current assets)/(current liabilities) for bankrupt and nonbankrupt firms are examined in Exercise 2.12 using back-to-back stem-and-leaf diagrams with a common stem.

EXAMPLE 2.3   A Computer-Generated Stem-and-Leaf Diagram for a Large Data Set

In Table 2.1, the national 800-meter-dash records for women are listed for 55 countries.* The times are recorded in minutes. Construct a stem-and-leaf diagram for these data.

TABLE 2.1   National 800-Meter-Dash Records for Women

2.15	2.01	2.05	2.24	2.02	2.00	2.00	1.89
2.30	2.19	2.00	2.05	2.10	1.93	2.19	2.11
2.28	2.12	2.03	1.99	2.18	2.09	1.96	2.07
2.07	1.99	2.22	2.02	2.00	2.24	2.08	1.97
1.92	1.89	2.04	2.10	1.96	2.15	1.98	2.09
1.98	2.10	2.02	2.03	2.03	2.05	2.15	2.33
2.21	2.27	2.16	2.10	2.20	1.95	1.95	

Solution and Discussion.   The stem-and-leaf diagram is shown in Figure 2.3. This diagram was produced by Minitab. There are several things to notice about the display in Figure 2.3. Since we are dealing with three-digit numbers, the stem consists of two-digit numbers with, as usual, single-digit leaves. Second, some of the stem numbers, for example, 20, are repeated. Third, the leaf unit is .01, so when an individual value is reconstructed from the diagram, the decimal point falls between the two stem digits; that is, the first line in the figure, 18|99, corresponds to the values 1.89, 1.89.

---

*SOURCE: IAAF-ATFS Track and Field Statistics Handbook for the 1984 Los Angeles Olympics.

```
 2     18 | 99
 4     19 | 23
13     19 | 556678899
25     20 | 000012223334
(8)    20 | 55577899
22     21 | 000012
16     21 | 5556899
 9     22 | 01244
 4     22 | 78
 2     23 | 03
```

Figure 2.3   Stem-and-Leaf Diagram for 800-Meter Data

Finally, the first column of cumulative frequencies, which the software adds to the traditional stem-and-leaf picture, counts the cumulative number of values in the stem categories. The frequencies are added from each end of the distribution until the "middle" category, indicated here with a parenthetical frequency of 8, is reached. So, for example, there are 25 values less than or equal to 2.04, and 9 values greater than or equal to 2.20.

With a fairly large data set, the number of leaves attached to a stem may be large, and, because the stem categories are always defined by one- or two-digit integers, the stem-and-leaf diagram may not be particularly informative. When this occurs, a given stem category may be repeated, with the leaf digits 0 through 4 associated with the first occurrence of the category, and the leaf digits 5 through 9 associated with the second occurrence. This was the case with stem categories 19, 20, 21, and 22 above. Ordinarily, a stem category is not repeated more than once.

Turning the stem-and-leaf diagram on its side, we see that the pattern of variation in the 800-meter times tends to fan out to the right.

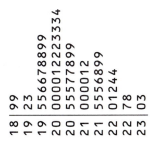

The smallest value is 1.89 and the largest value is 2.33, a range of .44 minute. However, most of the times cluster around 1.95 to 2.12, a fairly narrow range of .17 minute; that is, the bulk of the distribution is closer to the minimum, 1.89, than it is to the maximum, 2.33. Distributions that have this property are said to have a long right-hand tail or to be skewed to the right. As you might expect, nations with highly developed track and field programs, like the United States, the former Soviet Union, and the former German Democratic Republic, have the fastest times, and these times are nearly the same. Countries with less developed programs have times that are slower and more varied.

Since stem-and-leaf diagrams use, at most, only the first few digits of the numbers they represent, some information may be lost when constructing these diagrams from numbers with more than three digits. In these cases, the remaining digits are simply ignored or truncated. For moderate to large data sets, a better graphical representation of variability is provided by histograms.

HISTOGRAMS

As we have mentioned, constructing a dot diagram for a large data set can be tedious, and overcrowding of the dots can destroy the clarity of the diagram. Stem-and-leaf diagrams display actual numerical values, but they too can be awkward and difficult to interpret for large data sets. In such cases, it is often convenient to group the observations according to intervals and, for each interval, to record the frequency or

$$\text{Relative frequency} = \frac{\text{Frequency}}{\text{Total number of values}}$$

of values falling in the interval.

Ordinarily, the intervals are equal, consecutive, and cover the range of the data. However, the intervals may be unequal and even open-ended. In this sense, the data categories are more flexible than those of a stem-and-leaf plot. The frequency distribution is given by listing the intervals and their associated frequencies or relative frequencies. In this format, the intervals of the frequency distribution are called **class intervals** and their endpoints are called **class boundaries** or **class limits.** *We shall adopt the convention of putting observations that fall exactly on the right-hand boundary (larger class limit) into the next interval.* In this way, the numbers represented by a class interval include the left-hand endpoint but not the right-hand endpoint. If the data are discrete, the class intervals may be centered on the individual values with widths extending halfway to the observations on each side.

A display of a frequency distribution using a series of vertical bars with heights proportional to the frequencies or relative frequencies is called a **histogram.**

The number and positions of the class intervals of a frequency distribution are somewhat arbitrary. The number of classes usually ranges from 5 to 15, depending on the size of the data set. With too few intervals, much of the information concerning the distribution of the observations within individual intervals is lost, since only frequencies are recorded. With too many intervals and particularly with small data sets, the frequencies from one cell to the next can jump up and down in a chaotic manner, and no clear pattern is evident. It is best to begin with a relatively large number of intervals, combining intervals until a smooth pattern emerges. In other words, constructing a frequency distribution (and the histogram) requires some judgment.

EXAMPLE 2.4   Constructing a Histogram for the 800-Meter Data

Let's return to the 800-meter data. A frequency distribution for these data is shown in Table 2.2, using the endpoint convention. For this example, there are 10 class intervals of equal width, .05 minute. Draw the histogram for this frequency distribution.

TABLE 2.2   Frequency Distributions for 800-Meter Data

Class Interval	Frequency	Relative Frequency
[1.875–1.925)	3	$\frac{3}{55}$ = .055
[1.925–1.975)	6	$\frac{6}{55}$ = .109
[1.975–2.025)	12	$\frac{12}{55}$ = .218
[2.025–2.075)	9	$\frac{9}{55}$ = .164
[2.075–2.125)	9	$\frac{9}{55}$ = .164
[2.125–2.175)	4	$\frac{4}{55}$ = .073
[2.175–2.225)	6	$\frac{6}{55}$ = .109
[2.225–2.275)	3	$\frac{3}{55}$ = .055
[2.275–2.325)	2	$\frac{2}{55}$ = .036
[2.325–2.375)	1	$\frac{1}{55}$ = .018
Total	55	1.001[a]

[a]This entry is 1.000 within rounding error.

Solution and Discussion.   Making use of two vertical axes, we can display both the frequency distribution and the relative frequency distribution in the same figure as a single histogram. The histogram for the 800-meter data is pictured in Figure 2.4. The heights of the bars in the figure are the frequencies or relative frequencies (see the axes at the left and right of the figure), and the widths of the bars are the class interval widths.

The bulk of the distribution, represented by the highest bars, is to the left. Since the distribution falls off to the right from its left-hand peak, it is skewed to the right—a description of the variation that is consistent with the stem-and-leaf diagram in Figure 2.3. The histogram, in this case, gives a clearer picture of the distribution of women's 800-meter records than the stem-and-leaf diagram. This usually happens for large data sets. On the other hand, the individual values cannot be determined from the frequency distribution (or the histogram).

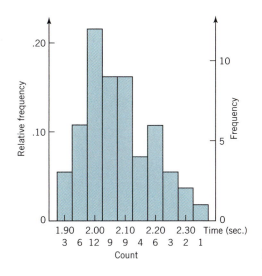

Figure 2.4   Histogram for 800-Meter Data

Again we see that most of the national 800-meter times are within about .2 minute (12 seconds) of one another, and these are the countries with the fastest times. There is more separation among the relatively few countries with 800-meter times that are slower.

Histograms are versatile data displays. With a little experimentation, they can provide clear representations of variability. A quick glance at a histogram will give the location and general shape of the data pattern. The pattern can be described as **symmetric** or **skewed** (single long tail). A pattern is symmetric if the pattern of variability on one side of a vertical line through the center is a mirror image of the pattern on the other side. A pattern is skewed if much of the distribution is concentrated near one end of the range of possible values—that is, if one tail extends farther from the center than the other. Patterns of data that were skewed to the right were exhibited in Examples 2.2 and 2.3. In these examples, the bulk of the data was on the left and, consequently, the right-hand tails (higher values) were much longer than the left-hand tails (lower values). Distributions with (relatively) long left-hand tails are said to be skewed to the left.

The number of peaks in a histogram is also of interest because two distinct peaks, even if one is lower than the other, may indicate two groups of numbers that are different from one another in some fundamental way. For example, the histogram in Figure 2.4 has two peaks, although one is considerably smaller than the other. The second peak occurs at an 800-meter time of about 2.2 minutes. The first peak at about 2 minutes is associated with national record 800-meter times for large developed countries. Countries with national record times near the second peak are small and less developed.

A relatively simple display like a histogram can provide a considerable amount of useful information, as the next example illustrates.

EXAMPLE 2.5   Using a Histogram to Convey Important Stock Market Information

Dealers who are market makers on the NASDAQ exchange give bid and asked prices on securities. The quotes are given in dollars and eighths of dollars. With competition among several hundred dealers, we expect each of the fractions of dollars, $\frac{0}{8}, \frac{1}{8}, \frac{2}{8}, \ldots, \frac{7}{8}$, to occur about equally often.

Two investigators* collected all bid and asked prices for 100 of the most actively traded stocks on the NASDAQ for 1991. The distribution of inside bid and asked quotes is summarized by the histogram shown in Figure 2.5. The percentage along the vertical axis is an average of the frequencies at the bid and asked prices, computed using all inside quotes for all 100 stocks throughout 1991. Interpret this histogram.

---

*Christie, W. B., and Schultz, P. H., "Why do NASDAQ market makers avoid odd-eighth quotes?" *Journal of Finance*, XLIX, No. 5, 1994, pp. 1813–1840.

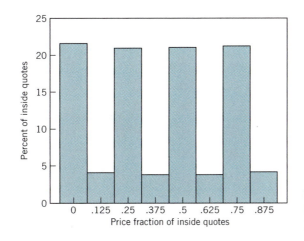

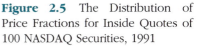

Figure 2.5 The Distribution of Price Fractions for Inside Quotes of 100 NASDAQ Securities, 1991

Solution and Discussion. We expected a flat or uniform pattern, suggesting that all eighths are "equally likely." Instead, the histogram is a comb pattern. There are very few odd price quotes—many fewer than would be expected if prices were set in a competitive manner. If dealers agreed to avoid odd-eighth quotes, then the bid–asked spread would always be at least $\frac{2}{8}$ dollar or 25 cents. Maintaining a bid–asked spread of this nature imposes a real cost on investors.

A histogram showing price fractions for 100 similar securities traded on the NYSE/AMEX exchanges is essentially flat, with all eighths represented equally. The presentation in the national press of the data shown in Figure 2.5, which suggests but does not prove collusion among NASDAQ dealers, led to almost immediate changes in the nature of bid–asked quotes for heavily traded issues. Here the message from the data is clearly and forcefully given by the histogram.

Like stem-and-leaf diagrams, histograms with a common set of equal class intervals can be used to compare two distributions. The best way to do this is to plot the histograms back-to-back along a common scale. We explore this possibility in Example 2.6.

EXAMPLE 2.6 Using Histograms to Compare Two Data Distributions

Paper is manufactured in continuous sheets several feet wide. Because of the orientation of fibers within the paper, it has a different strength when measured in the direction produced by the machine (machine direction) than when measured across, or at right angles to, the machine direction. The latter direction is called the cross direction. Several plies of paper are used to produce cardboard and, as part of the cardboard manufacturing process, the strengths of samples of the various plies of paper are measured. The histograms in Figure 2.6 show the patterns of the measurements for strength in the machine direction and strength in the cross direction for 41 pieces of paper.*

---

*Source: Data courtesy of SONOCO Products, Inc. The complete data set is contained in Table 6, Appendix C.

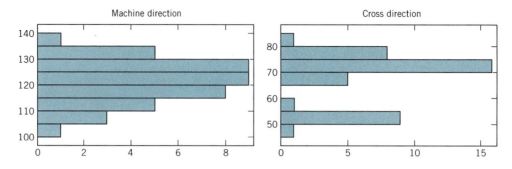

Figure 2.6   Histograms of Strengths in the Machine Direction and Cross Direction

There are two clear peaks in the histogram of cross direction strengths—one at about 52 and the other at about 72. Eleven of the pieces of paper were relatively old. The remaining 30 pieces of paper were new at the time the measurements were made. Construct back-to-back histograms of strength in the machine direction for the old and new paper.

Solution and Discussion.   Figure 2.7 displays the histograms of the machine direction strengths for the old paper and new paper in a back-to-back format with a common set of class intervals. It is clear from this figure that, in general, the new paper is stronger in the machine direction than the old paper.

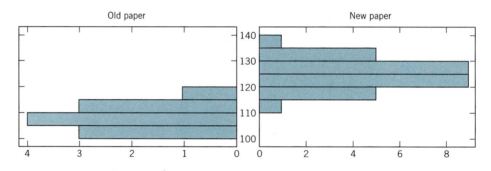

Figure 2.7   Back-to-back Histograms of Machine Direction Strengths

The differences in strengths in the machine direction for the old and new paper are "hidden" in the histogram in Figure 2.6. However, two peaks in machine direction strengths are evident if the histogram is constructed with narrower class intervals (see Exercise 2.14).

Once the reason for the distinct peaks in the histogram of cross direction strengths (age of paper) was identified, the strengths in the machine direction were examined for the same characteristic. In this example, the two groups of machine direction strengths were then compared using back-to-back histograms.

When the relative frequency in a class interval is represented by the area, rather than by the height of a bar, the histogram is called a **density histogram.** The bar has the same width as the class interval and a height adjusted to make its area (height × width) equal to the relative frequency. The adjusted height is called the density. Densities are determined from the relative frequency distribution using the definition

$$\text{Density} = \frac{\text{Relative frequency}}{\text{Interval width}}$$

and, consequently,

$$\text{Relative frequency} = \text{Class interval width} \times \text{Density} = \text{Area}$$

In fact, this is how we scaled the two histograms in Figure 2.7 because the sample sizes, 11 and 30, were unequal.

We see that *density measures the concentration of observations per unit of interval width*. Consequently, for two class intervals of equal widths and the same relative frequencies, the densities will necessarily be the same. For two class intervals of different widths, the same relative frequencies lead to different densities because the two intervals will have different proportions of observations per amount of interval width.

Comparing relative frequency distributions spread out over a set of unequal class intervals is difficult, because relative frequency calculations are influenced by class interval widths. How do we compare two identical relative frequencies when they are associated with two class intervals of considerably different widths? The scaling caused by using areas to represent relative frequencies allows an unambiguous comparison because the sum of the areas of the bars of any density histogram is always 1.00 by construction. The next example illustrates this point.

EXAMPLE 2.7   Constructing a Density Histogram

An article in the November 25, 1992, *Wall Street Journal* discussed the differences in earnings for male and female doctors. The article pointed out that, although one-third of the residents and 40% of the medical students in America were female, female doctors in private practice earned considerably less than their male counterparts. This income disparity occurred even in specialties in which women were heavily concentrated.

To indicate the magnitude of the differences, two relative frequency histograms (one for males, one for females) of income were displayed. The relative frequency distributions, based on a survey of 17,000 group-practice doctors, are shown in Table 2.3 (page 52) along with the density distributions created by dividing the relative frequencies by the corresponding class interval widths.*

Looking at the relative frequency distributions, we see, for example, that the largest relative frequency for male doctors occurs for the 1991 income category $150,000 to $200,000, whereas the largest relative frequency for female doctors is associated with the categories $0 to $60,000 and $80,000 to $100,000. Generally speaking, female

---

*The relative frequency distributions in Table 2.3 differ slightly from the ones in the *Wall Street Journal*. However, the minor changes that we made do not change the results appreciably.

TABLE 2.3   Distributions of 1991 Income for Male and Female Doctors

Income ($1,000's)	Male		Female	
	Relative frequency	Density	Relative frequency	Density
[0, 60)	.0737	.0012	.1919	.0032
[60, 80)	.0842	.0042	.1414	.0071
[80, 100)	.1053	.0053	.1919	.0096
[100, 125)	.1579	.0063	.1616	.0065
[125, 150)	.1263	.0051	.0909	.0036
[150, 200)	.1684	.0034	.1111	.0022
[200, 250)	.1263	.0025	.0606	.0012
[250, 300)	.0947	.0019	.0404	.0008
[300, 400)	.0632	.0006	.0101	.0001
Total	1.0000		1.0000	

doctors appear to make less than male doctors, since the largest relative frequencies for women are associated with the lower income categories, and the largest relative frequencies for men are associated with the middle income categories. But direct comparisons using relative frequencies are difficult in this case because the interval widths are different. Instead, compare the distributions of income with back-to-back density histograms.

Solution and Discussion.   The density distributions in Table 2.3 are plotted as back-to-back density histograms in Figure 2.8. The picture is clear. Salaries of female doctors are fairly tightly concentrated (dense) in the $60,000 to $125,000 range, with less concentration in the upper income categories. Salaries of male doctors, on the other hand, are concentrated (dense) in the $80,000 to $150,000 range, with appreciable concentration (relative to females) in the upper income categories. This survey indicates that female doctors make less than male doctors, and the nature of

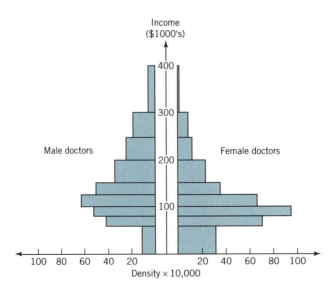

Figure 2.8 Density Histograms of 1991 Incomes for Male and Female Doctors

the discrepancy is evident. Incomes of females are more tightly concentrated (less variable) than those of males, and this concentration occurs at the lower end (relative to male incomes) of the income scale.

The graphical displays described in this section are extremely useful ways of looking at data. Modern computer software makes them easy to implement. Carefully constructed pictures provide an immediate impression of the general features of a data set and often suggest avenues for further study. Plots, charts, and graphs are key elements of exploratory data analysis.

EXERCISES

2.8 The R&D expenditure numbers discussed in Example 2.2 are given here:

| 4.4 | 3.6 | 4.4 | 3.7 | 9.6 | 3.9 | 3.6 | 3.5 | 3.0 | 4.5 | 3.9 | 2.2 |

   a. Construct a dot diagram.

   b. Is the dot diagram consistent with the stem-and-leaf diagram in Figure 2.2? Discuss.

2.9 What, if anything, is wrong with the following choices of intervals for constructing a frequency distribution for data that run from 0 to 99?

   a. [0, 25), [25, 50), and [55, 100)

   b. [0, 20), [20, 40), [40, 80), and [75, 100)

2.10 (*Minitab or similar program recommended*) In the first phase of a study of the cost of transporting milk from farms to dairy plants, a survey was taken of firms engaged in milk transportation. One of the variables measured was fuel cost. The fuel costs on a per-mile basis for 36 gasoline trucks and 23 diesel trucks are given here (data courtesy of M. Keaton).

FuelCost.dat

Gasoline		Diesel	
16.44	7.19	8.50	7.42
9.92	4.24	10.28	10.16
11.20	14.25	12.79	9.60
13.50	13.32	6.47	11.35
29.11	12.68	9.15	9.70
7.51	9.90	9.77	11.61
10.25	11.11	9.09	8.53
12.17	10.24	8.29	15.90
10.18	8.88	11.94	9.54
12.34	8.51	10.43	10.87
26.16	12.95	7.13	11.88
16.93	14.70	12.03	
10.32	8.98		
9.70	12.72		
9.49	8.22		
13.70	8.21		
15.86	9.18		
12.49	17.32		

a. Construct a dot diagram of the fuel costs for gasoline trucks. Construct a separate dot diagram of the fuel costs for diesel trucks using the same scale as that for gasoline trucks. Comment on the differences (if any) between the two types of trucks.

b. Construct separate stem-and-leaf displays for the fuel costs of gasoline and diesel trucks. Use the same scale. Let the leaf unit be tenths. Truncate (rather than round) the hundredths digit.

c. Repeat part **b** with a leaf unit of hundredths.

d. Using part **b** or part **c**, construct a back-to-back stem-and-leaf diagram of fuel costs for gasoline and diesel trucks. Are the differences (if any) consistent with those of the dot diagrams in part **a?**

2.11 Refer to the data in Exercise 2.10.

a. Construct a frequency distribution (see as an example Table 2.2) for the fuel costs of gasoline trucks. Use 10 class intervals of equal length 3. Set the midpoint of the first class interval equal to 3 and the midpoint of the last class interval equal to 30. Your table should include both frequencies and relative frequencies.

b. Repeat part **a** using the fuel costs of diesel trucks. Use the same class intervals.

c. Using the results in parts **a** and **b,** construct back-to-back relative frequency histograms of fuel costs for gasoline and diesel trucks. Are there any differences between gasoline and diesel trucks with respect to fuel costs?

d. Would the configuration of the histograms in part **c** change if densities rather than relative frequencies were used to construct the back-to-back histograms? Discuss.

Bankrupt.dat

2.12 (*Minitab or similar program recommended*) Annual financial data were collected for firms approximately 2 years before bankruptcy and for financially sound firms at about the same time. The accompanying table gives data on the variable (Current assets)/(Current liabilities) = CA/CL for 21 bankrupt and 25 nonbankrupt firms (Moody's Industrial Manuals).

Bankrupt		Nonbankrupt	
1.09	1.51	2.49	2.01
1.01	1.45	3.27	2.25
1.56	.71	4.24	4.45
1.50	1.37	2.52	2.05
1.37	1.42	2.35	1.80
.33	1.31	2.17	2.50
2.15	1.19	.46	2.61
1.88	1.99	2.23	2.31
1.51	1.68	1.84	2.33
1.26	1.14	3.01	1.24
1.27		4.29	1.99
		2.92	2.45
		5.06	

a. Construct a dot diagram on the interval [0, 6] using all the observations of CA/CL. Comment on its general appearance.

b. Construct separate dot diagrams of CA/CL for bankrupt and nonbankrupt firms. Use the interval [0, 6] in both cases. Compare the results. Based on the evidence here, do you think this variable may be useful in distinguishing bankrupt from nonbankrupt firms?

c. Construct a back-to-back stem-and-leaf diagram of CA/CL for bankrupt and nonbankrupt firms. Let the leaf unit be .10. Truncate the hundredths digit. Is the result consistent with the separate dot diagrams in part **b?**

2.13 Refer to the data in Exercise 2.12.

a. Construct a frequency distribution (for example, see Table 2.2) of CA/CL for bankrupt firms. Use four class intervals of equal length .5. Let the first class midpoint be .5 and the last class midpoint be 2. Your table should include both frequencies and relative frequencies.

b. Repeat part **a** using the data for nonbankrupt firms. (Use 10 class intervals of length .5. Let the first class midpoint be .5 and the last class midpoint be 5.)

c. Using the results in parts **a** and **b,** construct back-to-back relative frequency histograms of CA/CL for bankrupt and nonbankrupt firms. Interpret the results.

d. Would the configurations of the histograms in part **c** change if densities rather than relative frequencies were used to construct the back-to-back histograms? Discuss.

2.14 (*Minitab or similar program recommended*) Consider the observations on "strength in the machine direction" discussed in Example 2.6 and given in Table 6, Appendix C.

PaprStrg.dat

a. Using all the data on strength in the machine direction, construct a frequency histogram using class intervals all of equal length 3. Set the midpoint of the first class interval at 104 and the midpoint of the last class interval at 134. Compare the result with the histogram of strengths in the machine direction given in Figure 2.6.

b. Repeat part **a** using class intervals all of equal length 2. Using the results in Figure 2.6 and part **a,** comment on the effect of changing the class interval length on the appearance of the histogram. Are the observations for the old and new paper distinguishable?

2.15 The following frequency distribution shows the magnitudes of raises by percentage for 4145 quality professionals surveyed by *Quality Progress* magazine (Bemowski, K., "1992 Quality Progress Salary Survey." *Quality Progress,* Sept. 1992, p. 28).

Size of Raise	Frequency
[−.1, .1)	602
[.1, 3.1)	715
[3.1, 5.1)	1405
[5.1, 7.1)	805
[7.1, 10.1)	386
[10.1, 15.1)	178
[15.1, 20.1)	54

a. Complete the table by adding a relative frequency column and a density column.

b. Using the results in part **a,** plot the density histogram for sizes of raise. Comment on the general appearance of the density histogram.

2.16 The following table gives the class midpoint weights (in grams) and class frequencies for 100 newly minted U.S. pennies.

Class Midpoint Weight	Frequency
2.99	1
3.01	4
3.03	4
3.05	4
3.07	7
3.09	17
3.11	24
3.13	17
3.15	13
3.17	6
3.19	2
3.21	1

Source: Adapted from Table 1 in Vardeman, S., "What About Other Intervals?" *The American Statistician,* Vol. 46, No. 3, Aug. 1992, p. 195.

a. Create a frequency distribution for these data by specifying the class limits (assume all intervals are of the same length) and adding a relative frequency column.

b. Plot the relative frequency histogram of penny weights, and comment on its appearance. Would the configuration of the histogram change if densities rather than relative frequencies were used in its construction? Discuss.

2.17 The accompanying table gives the frequency distributions of household incomes for white and nonwhite families in the United States as of 1987. We report only household incomes up to $50,000.

Income ($1000's)	White Households Frequency (1000's)	White Households Relative Frequency	Nonwhite Households Frequency (1000's)	Nonwhite Households Relative Frequency
[0, 5)	3926	.0639	2235	.1561
[5, 10)	7930	.1290	2679	.1871
[10, 15)	7852	.1277	2119	.1480
[15, 25)	14683	.2388	3351	.2341
[25, 35)	12956	.2107	2066	.1443
[35, 50)	14133	.2299	1867	.1304

Source: *Statistical Abstract of the United States 1990,* U.S. Dept. of Commerce, Bureau of the Census, Washington, D.C., pp. 444–445.

a. Plot the relative frequency histograms for white household incomes and nonwhite household incomes. Compare the two histograms. Can you make any statements about the distribution of white household incomes relative to the nonwhite household incomes? Discuss.

b. Add a column of densities to each of the income distributions. Plot the density histograms for white household incomes and nonwhite household incomes. Compare the two density histograms. (You may want to plot back-to-back density histograms.) Do your conclusions about the distribution of white household incomes relative to the distribution of nonwhite household incomes change from part **a?** Explain.

c. Refer to your results in parts **a** and **b.** When comparing distributions over class intervals of unequal lengths, is it better to use relative frequency histograms or density histograms? Discuss.

2.5 NUMERICAL SUMMARIES OF DATA DISTRIBUTIONS

MEASURES OF LOCATION

As we have seen, data sets can be visually compared using density histograms. More succinct summaries are provided by single numbers that represent particular features of data sets. For example, we may be interested in the center of a data set, or the smallest value, or the typical distance from the center, and so forth. These single-number summaries may be of interest in their own right, or they may be used in conjunction with density histograms to allow more objective comparisons.

Why are single-number summaries important? They provide immediate impressions of order of magnitude, and they allow simple comparisons. A current U.S. unemployment rate of 6.4% provides us with an immediate indication of the overall jobless situation—particularly when this number is compared with last month's figure of 6.7%. We know that some areas of the country will have unemployment rates higher than 6.4% and some areas will have lower rates, but it is difficult to convey to the general public the nature of unemployment by publishing the entire collection of unemployment rates for, say, all the U.S. standard metropolitan areas. We need a *summary* measure of unemployment.

At one of the Ford Motor Company plants, it takes a total of 20.4 hours to build a new car. Do you believe that *every* vehicle takes exactly 20.4 hours to build? Of course not. Sometimes it takes more than 20.4 hours, sometimes it takes less. The number 20.4 is a "typical" figure. It is a useful way to summarize one aspect of productivity. It can be compared with the 19.5 hours it takes to build a vehicle at one of the Toyota plants in the United States.

Initially, we will concentrate on the following numerical measures of magnitude or location:

- Mean
- Median
- Percentiles

Later, we will consider numerical summaries of other features of data sets.

To clarify the ideas and to present effectively the associated calculations, it is convenient to use the symbols $x_1, x_2, \ldots, x_n$ to represent the n measurements in the data set. We introduced this notation in Chapter 1. Now the x_i's may be measurements of quantitative variables or numbers assigned to observed categories of qualitative variables. The subscripted x notation allows a general discussion since we are not then anchored to a specific set of numbers.

The two most commonly used measures of center are the mean and the median. The sample mean was introduced in Chapter 1. Recall that the sample mean is the sum of the sample measurements divided by the sample size and is denoted by $\bar{x}$.

For n measurements

Sample mean: $$\bar{x} = \frac{1}{n} \sum_{i=1}^{n} x_i$$

To understand how the sample mean indicates the center or middle, we present the following example.

EXAMPLE 2.8   Interpreting the Sample Mean

Two measures of productivity for the 10 most productive vehicle assembly operations in North America, according to a 1994 Harbour Report, are listed in Table 2.4.

TABLE 2.4   Productivity in Auto Manufacturing

Plant	Number of Workers per Vehicle	Total Number of Hours to Build a Vehicle
Nissan truck (Smyrna, Tenn.)	2.20	17.6
Nissan car (Smyrna, Tenn.)	2.32	18.6
Toyota car (Georgetown, Ky.)	2.44	19.5
Ford car (Kansas City, Mo.)	2.48	19.8
Ford car (Atlanta, Ga.)	2.49	19.9
Nummi truck (Fremont, Calif.)	2.52	20.2
Ford car (Chicago, Ill.)	2.55	20.4
Ford truck (Norfolk, Va.)	2.70	21.6
Ford truck (Louisville, Ky.)	2.71	21.7
Chrysler car (Belvidere, Ill.)	2.72	21.8

SOURCE: *San Diego Union-Tribune,* June 24, 1994.

Construct a dot diagram for the total hours needed to build a vehicle, and indicate the sample mean on the diagram.

Solution and Discussion.   The dot diagram, with the value of the sample mean, 20.11, indicated by a fulcrum, is shown in Figure 2.9.

If we imagine the horizontal axis of the dot diagram as a weightless bar and the dots representing the data as balls of equal size and weight, the mean is the point at which the bar balances. The sample mean is affected by extreme observations.

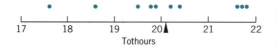

Figure 2.9   Total Number of Hours to Build a Vehicle and the Location of the Sample Mean

Imagine, for example, that the smallest total hours figure, 17.6, is decreased (moved to the left in the figure) while the other numbers remain the same. To maintain balance, the mean (fulcrum) must decrease (move to the left). If we change 17.6 to 13.3, for example, the sample mean becomes 19.68. Is the sample mean a good measure of center? It is, provided you interpret the center as the balancing point.

For large samples, the sample mean is ordinarily not appreciably affected by a few extreme measurements. Summary measures that are not affected by extreme values are said to be **resistant** or **robust.** One way to make the sample mean robust is not to include extreme values in its calculation. Suppose we order the observations from smallest to largest and then ignore, say, 5% of the measurements at each end. If we calculate the sample mean from the remaining observations, the result is called the 5% **trimmed mean.** Ignoring 10% of the observations at each end gives the 10% trimmed mean and so forth.

A trimmed mean is the balancing point or center of gravity of the measurements from which it is calculated. In this sense, its interpretation is the same as that of the sample mean. Computer programs will usually compute a trimmed mean along with the sample mean. Five percent is a typical amount of trimming.

To obtain an even more robust summary statistic, arrange the data from smallest to largest. The sample median is the value that divides the data set in half; that is, 50% of the measurements are less than the median, and 50% are larger than the median.

Sample median: The value that divides the ordered data in half

---

If the number of measurements is odd, the median is the middle measurement. If the number of measurements is even, the median is defined to be the average of the two middle measurements, or the value halfway between them.

To calculate the sample median:

1. Arrange the n observations in numerical order, from smallest to largest.
2. If the number of observations is odd, the sample median, M, is the middle observation, determined by counting $(n + 1)/2$ observations up from the smallest value in the ordered set.
3. If the number of observations is even, the sample median, M, is the average of the two middle observations in the ordered set.

Notice that the calculation of the median is not influenced by the values of the measurements at the ends of the ordered data set. Consequently, the sample median is a robust measure of location. Moreover, the median corresponds to our intuitive notion of middle: the value that divides the ordered observations exactly in half.

The sample mean and sample median determined from the same data set will, in general, be different. This should not be surprising since they correspond to different notions of center. They measure the overall location of a data set in different ways.

The sample mean is the most popular measure of location but, in cases where the mean and median are considerably different, both should be reported. A collection of incomes, for example,

$$\$40,000 \quad \$50,000 \quad \$58,000 \quad \$60,000 \quad \$136,000$$

is best summarized by the sample median, $M = \$58,000$, since it will not be influenced by exceptionally large incomes. Large incomes tend to inflate the sample mean, in this case $\bar{x} = \$68,800$, and make it less useful as a measure of typical income.

EXAMPLE 2.9   Calculating the Sample Median for an Even Number of Observations

The total number of hours needed to build a vehicle are arranged from smallest to largest in Table 2.4 of Example 2.8. Calculate the sample median.

Solution and Discussion.   There are $n = 10$ observations, so the sample median is the average of the two middle values, 19.9 and 20.2; that is, $M = 20.05$. The median is in position $(n+1)/2 = \frac{11}{2} = 5.5$ or halfway between the 5th and 6th largest observations.

EXAMPLE 2.10   Calculating the Sample Median for an Odd Number of Observations

A University Association Group Life Insurance Plan paid 31 death claims during a recent policy year. The claim amounts are given from smallest to largest in Table 2.5. Calculate the median.

TABLE 2.5   Death Claim Amounts for Group Life Insurance Plan

1750	2800	3500	4025	4025	4375	4375	4375
5775	5775	6125	6125	6125	6475	6825	6825
6825	7350	7350	7350	7350	8050	9450	13125
13125	26250	26250	54600	64750	89600	95550	

Solution and Discussion.   Since $n = 31$ is odd, the median is the middle observation given, in this case, by counting $\frac{n+1}{2} = 16$ observations from the smallest number. Thus, $M = 6,825$.

The median indicates a central value. However, if the *total* payments for claims is important, the total is (Number of claims) $\times$ (Mean claim) $= 31 \times \bar{x}$, whereas $31 \times M$ is not related to total payments.

Percentiles are numbers that divide the data into percentages. The sample median is the 50th percentile, because the sample median divides an ordered data set in half.

Sample 100pth percentile: The value in an ordered data set such that at least $100p$% of the data set is at or less than this value and at least $100(1 - p)$% of the data set is at or above this value

---

Setting $p = .25$, $p = .5$, and $p = .75$ generates the 25th, 50th, and 75th percentiles, respectively. These numbers, taken as a group, divide the data set into quarters and, not surprisingly, are known as the **sample quartiles.**

We adopt the convention of taking an observed value for the sample percentile except when two adjacent values satisfy the definition, in which case, their average is taken as the percentile. This procedure is consistent with the way we calculate the sample median.

To calculate the sample 100pth percentile,

1. Arrange the n observations in numerical order, from smallest to largest.
2. Determine the product (Sample size)(Proportion) $= np$.
3. If np is not an integer, round it up to the next integer and find the observation in this position. This value is the percentile. If np is an integer, say, k, calculate the average of the kth and $(k + 1)$st ordered values. This average is the percentile.

Some statistical software packages use slight variations of our definition of percentiles. For large samples, they all tend to give essentially the same numbers.

The sample percentiles used most frequently are the median, and the first and third quartiles. The sample quartiles are summarized here in terms of the percentiles they represent. From these representations, you can see that the first and third quartiles are themselves medians. The first quartile, Q_1, is the median of the observations less than the sample median, and the third quartile, Q_3, is the median of the observations greater than the sample median.

Sample Quartiles

First quartile	Q_1 = 25th percentile
Second quartile (or median)	Q_2 = 50th percentile
Third quartile	Q_3 = 75th percentile

To illustrate the calculation of sample quartiles, we turn once more to the productivity data listed in Table 2.4 (see Example 2.8).

EXAMPLE 2.11   Calculating Sample Quartiles

From Table 2.4, the $n = 10$ total number of hours needed to build a vehicle are, in order,

| 17.6 | 18.6 | 19.5 | 19.8 | 19.9 | 20.2 | 20.4 | 21.6 | 21.7 | 21.8 |

The sample median (or 50th percentile or second quartile) was calculated in Example 2.9. Recall that $M = 20.05$. Calculate the first and third quartiles.

Solution and Discussion.   To calculate the first quartile, set $p = .25$. Then $np = 10(.25) = 2.5$. Since 2.5 is not an integer, round it to the next integer, 3, and take the observation in the 3rd position as the required quartile. Thus, $Q_1 = 19.5$. Three of the 10 observations (at least 25%) are at or below 19.5, and 8 observations (at least 75%) are at or above 19.5, confirming that it is the first quartile.

Similarly, to get the third quartile, set $p = .75$ so that $np = 10(.75) = 7.5$. Round 7.5 to the next integer, 8, and take the observation in the 8th position as the required quartile. Consequently, $Q_3 = 21.6$. Eight of the 10 observations (at least 75%) are at or below 21.6, and 3 observations (at least 25%) are at or above it.

The three quartiles, $Q_1 = 19.6$, $Q_2 = M = 20.05$, and $Q_3 = 21.6$, divide the data set into quarters.

If, in Example 2.11, the last number in the data set were 25.3 instead of 21.8, the quartiles would not change. Similarly, if the two smallest values were, for example, 16.9 and 18.8 instead of 17.6 and 18.6, respectively, the quartiles would not change. Percentiles in general, and quartiles in particular, are not heavily influenced by the particular values of the observations. Extreme values have no influence on percentiles located toward the center of the distribution. This is what we mean when we say that *percentiles are robust measures of location.*

We have discussed measures of location in terms of the original set of observations. If the data are displayed as dot diagrams, stem-and-leaf diagrams, or density histograms, measures of location can be indicated on the diagrams. We have already seen, for example, with the 800-meter data in Figure 2.3, that the statistical software identifies the median class in its version of the stem-and-leaf diagram and prints the cumulative frequencies from each end of the data distribution. This allows easy identification of the sample quartiles.

The sample mean always retains its interpretation as the balancing point. Therefore, its location on the variable axis of a dot diagram and, to a good approximation, a density histogram, is the point at which a fulcrum would just balance the configuration of points or pattern of vertical bars.

Because the sample mean is not a robust measure of location, it will typically be larger than the median for a histogram with a long right-hand tail, and less than the median for a histogram with a long left-hand tail. The two measures of location will almost coincide for nearly symmetric histograms, because the balancing point and the value dividing the distribution in half are the same (see Exercise 2.22).

MEASURES OF VARIATION

We talked about measuring variability in Chapter 1, where we introduced the sample variance and sample standard deviation. Here, we will not only review these measures, we will also introduce the sample range and sample interquartile range as additional measures of variability.

The sample variance, s^2, and sample standard deviation, s, can be useful single-number summaries of variability. This is particularly true for relatively large, mound-shaped data sets.

Sample variance: $$s^2 = \frac{1}{n-1}\sum_{i=1}^{n}(x_i - \overline{x})^2$$

Sample standard deviation: $$s = +\sqrt{s^2}$$

The sample variance is essentially an average squared distance from the mean; consequently, its value can be heavily influenced by observations far from the middle. Since the standard deviation is closely connected to the variance, its value can also be heavily influenced by observations far from the middle. The sample variance and sample standard deviation are not robust measures of variability.

The number $n-1$ in the definition of the sample variance (or sample standard deviation) is called the **degrees of freedom** because it represents the number of deviations from the mean that are "free to vary." Let's see what this means.

In Chapter 1, we showed that the sum of the deviations $x_i - \overline{x}$ is always 0. Consequently, the final deviation can be determined once we know any $n-1$ of the other deviations. For example, given the $n = 4$ numbers

$$x_1 = 2 \quad x_2 = 3 \quad x_3 = 4 \quad x_4 = -1$$

you may verify that $\overline{x} = 2$, and the first three deviations from the mean are $2 - 2 = 0$, $3 - 2 = 1$, and $4 - 2 = 2$. Since the sum of all deviations must be zero, the last deviation must be $-(0 + 1 + 2) = -3$. Only $3 = n - 1$ of the deviations are free to vary.

The sample range is simply the difference between the largest and smallest observations. It is the length of the interval that just contains all the data.

Sample range: Largest observation − Smallest observation

The range is very easy to calculate and interpret. However, by definition, the range is extremely sensitive to the existence of even a single very large or very small value in the data set. It is also not a robust measure of variability.

The sample interquartile range is a measure of variability based on the first and third quartiles.

Sample interquartile range:	IR $= Q_3 - Q_1 =$ Third quartile $-$ First quartile

The interquartile range is the length of the interval just containing the middle 50% of the observations. This interval is not centered on the median unless the data distribution is symmetric. Because the interquartile range depends only on the first and third quartile numbers, its value is not affected by a few extreme measurements at each end of the distribution. The sample interquartile range is a robust measure of spread. It is often used to measure spread when the median is used to measure middle.

The center and the extent of spread in a data set are key pattern features. For (nearly) symmetric and mound-shaped data distributions, the mean and standard deviation are worthwhile measures of location and spread. Their usefulness is enhanced by the **empirical rule.**

The empirical rule provides intervals that contain certain proportions of the data when we know only the values of $\bar{x}$ and s. This rule works best with large data sets (for example, more than 30 numbers) that tend to have a mound of values around the mean and fewer values far from the mean in each direction. It gives the approximate proportion of values within 1, 2, and 3 standard deviations of the mean.

Empirical Rule

Approximately   68% of the data lie within $\bar{x} \pm s$

95% of the data lie within $\bar{x} \pm 2s$

99.7% of the data lie within $\bar{x} \pm 3s$

With only the two values $\bar{x}$ and s, the empirical rule allows us to create an expanding set of intervals that contain increasing proportions of the data set.

When data distributions are skewed to the right or to the left, no single measure of spread is entirely satisfactory because the nature of the variability on one side of the center is different from that on the other side. If a single measure of spread is required, it may be best to use a number that is robust to extreme values.

EXAMPLE 2.12   Summarizing Variation with the Empirical Rule, the Range, and the Interquartile Range

Table 2.6 gives the cost per kilowatt (KW) capacity in place for a particular year for $n = 22$ U.S. public utility companies. Obtain the range, the interquartile range, and the intervals $\bar{x} \pm s$ and $\bar{x} \pm 2s$. Compare the proportions of the observations in the latter intervals with the proportions suggested by the empirical rule.

TABLE 2.6   Cost per KW Capacity in Place for U.S. Public Utilities

151	104	96	168	168	174	136	178
175	202	148	164	197	192	111	150
199	245	113	204	252	173		

Solution and Discussion.   The Minitab printout follows:

	N	MEAN	MEDIAN	TRMEAN	STDEV
CostprKW	22	168.18	170.50	167.60	41.19

	MIN	MAX	Q1	Q3
CostprKW	96.00	252.00	145.00	197.50

From the printout, Min = 96, Max = 252, Q_1 = 145, Q_2 = M = 170.5, and Q_3 = 197.5. We can easily calculate

$$\text{Range} = \text{Max} - \text{Min} = 252 - 96 = 156$$

and

$$\text{IR} = Q_3 - Q_1 = 197.5 - 145 = 52.5$$

All of the observations are within 156 units of one another. The middle 50% of the costs per KW capacity in place are contained in an interval of length 52.5.

The empirical rule suggests that about 68% of the costs should fall in the interval

$$\bar{x} \pm s = 168.18 \pm 41.19 \quad \text{or} \quad (126.99,\ 209.37)$$

Similarly, about 95% of the observations should fall in the interval

$$\bar{x} \pm 2s = 168.18 \pm 82.38 \quad \text{or} \quad (85.80,\ 250.56)$$

In fact, $(\frac{16}{22})100\% = 73\%$ of the costs are included in the first interval, and $(\frac{21}{22})100\% = 95\%$ of the costs are contained in the second interval. For this relatively small data set, the empirical rule gives a fairly accurate picture of the distribution of cost per KW capacity in place.

BOXPLOTS

Together with the smallest and largest observations, the quartiles Q_1, Q_2, Q_3 provide a fairly comprehensive five-number summary of a distribution of measurements. Let Min and Max represent the smallest and largest observations in the data set, respectively. The **five-number summary**

$$\text{Min} \quad Q_1 \quad Q_2 = M \quad Q_3 \quad \text{Max}$$

is represented pictorially as a **boxplot.**

Figure 2.10 is a horizontal boxplot of the cost per KW capacity in place data from Example 2.12.

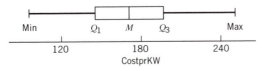

Figure 2.10   Boxplot of Costs per KW Capacity in Place for 22 U.S. Public Utilities

There are five vertical lines in the boxplot: the lines forming the ends of the box (rectangle), the line within the box, and the small vertical lines at the ends of the horizontal lines (whiskers) that extend in opposite directions from the box. These vertical lines correspond to the five summary numbers. Reading from the scale beneath the figure, we see that the vertical line within the box identifies the median. The ends of the box correspond to the 1st and 3rd quartiles, and the lines at the ends of the whiskers denote the minimum (Min) and maximum (Max) values. The length of the box is the interquartile range, and the distance between the Min and Max is the overall range. The median line is nearly in the middle of the box and the whiskers are nearly of the same length, so this data distribution is very nearly symmetric.

Boxplots are not as informative as stem-and-leaf plots or density histograms because they do not show the patterns of the data within the quartile boundaries. They are, however, useful for assessing symmetry (or asymmetry) and for comparing distributions. Figure 2.11 shows side-by-side boxplots of average Graduate Record Examination (GRE) verbal scores for students admitted to graduate study in departments classified according to the general categories displayed. The departmental averages are based on data for students who took the GRE over a five-year period.*

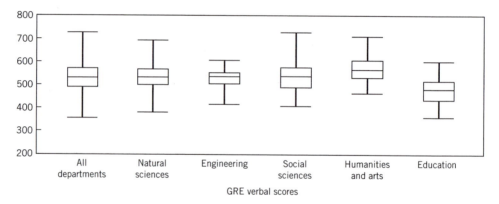

Figure 2.11   Boxplots of Departmental Means for GRE Verbal Scores

The center, spread, and range of the distributions of average scores are immediately apparent. We see, for example, that the average GRE verbal scores for Engineering departments are tightly concentrated about a median average score of about 540. The highest median of average verbal score occurs for students admitted to departments in the Humanities and Arts. The interquartile range is about the same for all the categories with the exception of Engineering, where it is smaller. Finally, although there are some differences in overall spread as measured by the range, the median scores do not vary a great deal. Boxplots for departmental averages of GRE quantitative scores are considered in Exercise 2.29.

MODIFIED BOXPLOTS

The whiskers in boxplots ordinarily extend to the smallest and largest observations. However, if some of the observations are significantly smaller or larger than the

*Source: Schneider, L. M., and Briel, J. B. *Validity of the GRE: 1988–89 Summary Report*. Princeton, N.J.: Educational Testing Service, Sept. 1990.

rest—potential outliers—they are not evident using this procedure. Boxplots can be modified to reveal potential outliers by extending the whiskers to the smallest and largest observations only if these points are sufficiently close to the rest of the data. If they are not, those observations far removed from the majority of cases are plotted as individual points. A common measure of closeness is $1.5 \times$ IR.

A **modified boxplot** is constructed by extending the whiskers to the smallest and largest observations *only* if these values are within $1.5 \times$ IR of the first and third quartiles, respectively. Otherwise, the whiskers are extended to the most extreme values still contained in these limits and the remaining observations are plotted individually. Modified boxplots work best for a moderate number of observations. If the number of observations is too large, an inordinate number of outliers may be identified.

EXAMPLE 2.13 Constructing a Modified Boxplot

The actual costs (ActualCo) in millions of dollars of 26 construction projects at a large industrial facility are given in Table 2.7. Construct a modified boxplot for these data.

TABLE 2.7 Actual Construction Costs

.918	7.214	14.577	30.028	38.173	15.320
14.837	51.284	34.100	2.003	20.099	4.324
10.523	13.371	1.553	4.069	27.973	7.642
3.692	29.522	15.317	5.292	.707	1.246
1.143	21.571				

SOURCE: Schmoyer, R. L. "Asymptotically Valid Prediction Intervals for Linear Models." *Technometrics,* Vol. 34, Nov. 1992, pp. 399–408.

Solution and Discussion.   The modified boxplot is shown in Figure 2.12 and indicates one potential outlier. For the construction costs, you may verify that Min = .707, $Q_1 = 3.692$, $M = 11.947$, $Q_3 = 21.571$, and Max = 51.284. Consequently, IR = $Q_3 - Q_1 = 21.571 - 3.692 = 17.879$ and $1.5 \times$ IR $= 1.5(17.879) = 26.819$. The smallest observation in the data set, Min = .707, is well within 26.819 of $Q_1 = 3.692$; therefore, the left-hand whisker extends to this smallest value. The number $Q_3 + (1.5)$IR $= 21.571 + 26.819 = 48.390$ is greater than all the construction costs except Max = 51.284. Thus the right-hand whisker extends to the largest number in the data set less than or equal to 48.390 (here 38.173) and the remaining case, 51.284, is plotted individually.

The distribution of construction costs is skewed to the right and the extreme value, 51.284, will have a significant influence on the calculation of, for example, the sample mean. In this example, there is nothing wrong with the number 51.284, but it is highlighted as a project whose construction cost is considerably higher than that of the other projects.

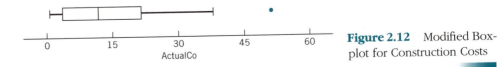

Figure 2.12   Modified Boxplot for Construction Costs

The data displays and summary numbers we have considered to this point are helpful in organizing large sets of numbers, and they are particularly appropriate for measurements of quantitative variables.

EXERCISES

2.18 Given the four observations

$$3 \quad 1 \quad 0 \quad 4$$

calculate the sample variance, sample standard deviation, range, and interquartile range.

2.19 Calculate the sample mean, variance, and standard deviation for each of the following data sets:

a. 6, 9, 7, 9, 14

b. 23, 29, 22, 26

c. −1.1, .8, − .2, 1.6, 2.9

2.20 Annual salaries (in thousands of dollars) for ten of the top-ranking officers in a large corporation are given here:

175   150   210   650   425   230   190   260   300   250

Calculate the sample mean and sample median. Comment on the appropriateness of these numbers as summary measures of top executive salaries.

2.21 Refer to Exercise 2.20. Obtain the sample quartiles of top executive salaries.

2.22 Sketch three density histograms: a symmetric histogram, one with a long right-hand tail, and one with a long left-hand tail. Keeping in mind that the mean is the center of gravity, or balancing point, of the data distribution and that the median divides the data in half, indicate the relative positions of the sample mean and the sample median on each of your density histograms.

2.23 Vendors doing business with a particular state were sampled to determine the economic impact of state business on their gross sales. A sample of 15 firms that provide services to the state had the following percentages of total annual sales as a result of sales to the state:

27.0   12.0   14.9   1.2   .1   1.0   .1   5.3
7.6   5.0   1.0   1.0   3.2   3.0   7.0

a. Find the sample median, first quartile, and third quartile.

b. Find the range and interquartile range.

c. Find the sample 90th percentile.

2.24 The mean and median salaries of machinists employed by two competing companies, A and B, are as follows:

	Company	
	A	**B**
Mean salary	$27,000	$23,500
Median salary	$22,000	$25,000

Assume that the salaries are set in accordance with job competence and that the overall quality of workers is about the same in the two companies.

a. Which company offers a better prospect to a machinist having superior ability? Explain.

b. Where can a medium-quality machinist expect to earn more? Explain.

2.25 Consider the data on workers per vehicle for the 10 most productive vehicle assembly plants listed in Table 2.4 (see Example 2.8).

a. Plot these data as a dot diagram. Calculate the sample mean, $\bar{x}$, and indicate the mean on the dot diagram.

b. Calculate the 5% trimmed mean. [*Hint:* Round 10(.05) up to the next integer when determining the number of observations to delete from the ordered data.]

c. Calculate the sample median, M, and indicate the median on the dot diagram in part **a.** Compare the mean and median. What does the discrepancy (if any) tell you about the symmetry of this data set?

2.26 Consider the R&D expenditures (as a percentage of sales) given in Example 2.2.

a. Calculate the 5% trimmed mean. [*Hint:* Round 12(.05) up to the next integer when determining the number of observations to delete from the ordered data.]

b. Compare the 5% trimmed mean with the sample mean (see Exercise 1.37 of Chapter 1).

c. Calculate the sample median.

d. Discuss the relative effects of outliers on the 5% trimmed mean, the sample mean, and the median for this particular example.

2.27 (*Minitab or similar program recommended*) Consider the death claim amounts given in Example 2.10.

DeathClm.dat

a. Calculate the sample mean, $\bar{x}$, and the 5% trimmed mean. [*Hint:* See Example 2.10 for the ordered claims. Round 31(.05) up to the next integer when determining the number of observations to delete from the ordered set.]

b. Calculate the first and third quartiles, Q_1 and Q_3, and determine the interquartile range, IR.

c. Using the data and the median from Example 2.10 and the results in part **b,** display the boxplot (or modified boxplot) for the death claim amounts.

2.28 The sample variance may be written

$$s^2 = \frac{1}{n-1}\left[\sum_{i=1}^{n} x_i^2 - \frac{1}{n}\left(\sum_{i=1}^{n} x_i\right)^2\right]$$

This formula is known as the *computing formula* for the sample variance. It leads to faster calculations because it uses the basic quantities, $\sum x_i^2$ and $\sum x_i$, directly and does not require the intermediate quantities $(x_i - \bar{x})$. You are given the four observations

1,000,000   1,000,001   1,000,000   1,000,000

Calculate the sample variance using the definitional formula,

$$s^2 = \frac{\sum_{i=1}^{n}(x_i - \overline{x})^2}{n - 1}$$

Calculate the sample variance using the computing formula *assuming your hand-held calculator can keep only 8 digits in any number.* Compare the results. Consider the statement, "Although the computing formula leads, in general, to faster calculations, it may lead to inaccurate results because of round-off error for a set of uniformly large numbers." Do you agree?

2.29 Side-by-side boxplots of GRE Quantitative scores for students admitted to graduate study in departments classified as Natural Sciences, Engineering, and so forth are shown here. The boxplots are based on GRE scores accumulated over a five-year period.

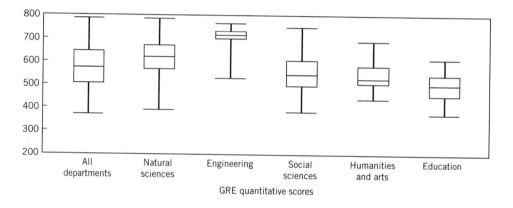

a. Using the vertical scale in the diagram, interpret the boxplot for Education.

b. Which departments tend to have the highest Quantitative scores? Which departments have the most highly concentrated Quantitative scores about the median score as measured by the interquartile range? Which departments have the largest range of Quantitative scores?

c. Looking at the boxplot for all departments, would you say the distribution of Quantitative scores is symmetric or skewed? Justify your choice. The scores of which departments are the most heavily skewed? Are these scores skewed to the right or left?

2.30 Select the appropriate phrase to make the sentence correct.

a. The mean of a data set with the outliers eliminated will be {smaller than; larger than; smaller or larger than; equal to} the average of the data set with the outliers included.

b. The standard deviation of a data set with the outliers eliminated will be {smaller than; larger than; smaller or larger than; equal to} the standard deviation of the data set with the outliers included.

c. The median of a data set with the outliers eliminated will be {smaller than; larger than; smaller or larger than; equal to} the median of the data set with the outliers included.

AgePres.dat

2.31 (*Minitab or similar program recommended*) The following table shows the age at inauguration of each U.S. president.

Name	Age at Inauguration	Name	Age at Inauguration	Name	Age at Inauguration
1. Washington	57	15. Buchanan	65	29. Harding	55
2. J. Adams	61	16. Lincoln	52	30. Coolidge	51
3. Jefferson	57	17. A. Johnson	56	31. Hoover	54
4. Madison	57	18. Grant	46	32. F. D. Roosevelt	51
5. Monroe	58	19. Hayes	54	33. Truman	60
6. J. Q. Adams	57	20. Garfield	49	34. Eisenhower	62
7. Jackson	61	21. Arthur	50	35. Kennedy	43
8. Van Buren	54	22. Cleveland	47	36. L. Johnson	55
9. W. H. Harrison	68	23. B. Harrison	55	37. Nixon	56
10. Tyler	51	24. Cleveland	55	38. Ford	61
11. Polk	49	25. McKinley	54	39. Carter	52
12. Taylor	64	26. T. Roosevelt	42	40. Reagan	69
13. Fillmore	50	27. Taft	51	41. Bush	64
14. Pierce	48	28. Wilson	56	42. Clinton	46

a. Make a stem-and-leaf diagram of the age at inauguration. Let the leaf unit = 1.

b. Find the median, M, and the first and third quartiles, Q_1 and Q_3.

2.32 (*Minitab or similar program recommended*) The article "The Best Cities for Knowledge Workers" (*Fortune,* Nov. 15, 1993) states that one measure of the brainpower that employers need is the number of workers 25 years old and older who hold a postbaccalaureate (graduate) degree. Consider the following table.

CitGrad.dat

City	% Graduate Degree	City	% Graduate Degree	City	% Graduate Degree
Raleigh/Durham	11.6	Dayton	6.9	Norfolk	6.5
New York	10.5	Denver	9.4	Oakland	10.8
Boston	11.2	Detroit	6.4	Oklahoma City	7.3
Seattle	8.8	Ft. Lauderdale	6.4	Orlando	6.1
Austin	10.3	Fort Worth	6.2	Phoenix	6.9
Chicago	8.7	Grand Rapids	5.6	Pittsburgh	6.8
Houston	7.9	Greensboro	5.1	Portland	7.6
San Jose	12.0	Hartford	10.3	Richmond	7.7
Philadelphia	8.3	Honolulu	7.9	Rochester	8.7
Minneapolis	7.7	Indianapolis	7.4	Sacramento	6.9
Albany	10.2	Jacksonville	5.6	St. Louis	3.8
Atlanta	8.1	Kansas City	7.5	Salt Lake City	7.0
Baltimore	9.2	Las Vegas	4.7	San Antonio	6.8
Birmingham	6.6	Los Angeles	7.8	San Diego	8.8
Buffalo	7.5	Louisville	6.7	San Francisco	12.8
Charlotte	5.2	Memphis	6.4	Scranton	5.1
Cincinnati	7.1	Miami	7.6	Tampa	5.6
Cleveland	6.5	Milwaukee	6.5	Tulsa	6.0
Columbus	8.0	Nashville	7.1	Washington, D.C.	15.8
Dallas	8.2	New Orleans	6.9	West Palm Beach	7.6

a. Construct a stem-and-leaf diagram of "% graduate degree."

b. Which cities have an unusually large percentage of workers holding graduate degrees?

CitGrad.dat

2.33   (*Minitab or similar program recommended*) Refer to Exercise 2.32. Consider the first ten cities in the first column of the list. Construct back-to-back stem-and-leaf diagrams of these ten cities and the remaining cities. Does there appear to be a difference between the two groups of cities with respect to the percentage of workers with graduate degrees?

2.6   THE NORMAL DENSITY FUNCTION

Density histograms provide good visual representations of data distributions. But the appearance of a density histogram can change as the number and width of the class intervals change. The outline of a density histogram, by construction, is not very smooth. Moreover, density histograms are somewhat awkward to use. If we want to find the proportion (relative frequency) of the data set falling in some fixed interval, we must sum the areas of the vertical bars over the chosen interval. If one or both of the endpoints of our fixed interval fall within class intervals, as in the diagram shown here, then it is necessary to interpolate to find the required proportion.

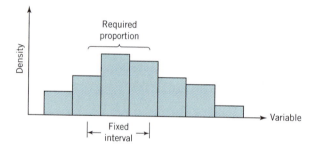

When density histograms are symmetric about a single peak and look like the outline of a bell, they can often be closely approximated by a smooth curve known as the **normal density function.** (You may already be familiar with the bell-shaped normal density curve because it often serves as a model for the distribution of examination scores.) Areas under a normal density curve can then approximate density histogram relative frequencies.

The advantage of using a single mathematical function, like the normal density function, to represent a distribution of data is that it is always available in a compact form. Histograms of data from a variety of sources may display very similar features. If so, they may all be represented by the same mathematical function. This function can be used to make statements about the size of future measurements and to develop procedures that allow us to generalize from a sample to a population.

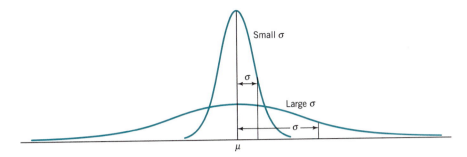

Figure 2.13 Two Normal Density Functions with Different Standard Deviations

The normal density function is usually associated with Pierre Laplace and Carl Gauss, who, working somewhat independently in the 18th and 19th centuries, figured prominently in its development. Gauss, motivated by errors in astronomical measurements, derived the function mathematically as a distribution of errors. He called his error distribution the "normal law of errors." Subsequent scientists and data collectors in a wide variety of fields found that their histograms exhibited the common feature of first gradually rising in height to a maximum and then decreasing in a symmetric manner. Although there are other functions exhibiting this property, the normal density seemed to "fit" the data in so many real-life situations that many of its proponents believed that if data did not conform to the normal curve, the data collection process must be suspect. In this context, Gauss's function became known as the **normal distribution** and the name held.

There are many normal distributions, but all normal curves have the same overall shape. A particular normal distribution is determined once its mean μ (mu) and standard deviation σ (sigma) are specified. The mean is the balancing point of the normal curve; because a normal distribution is symmetric, it is also the median. Changing the value of the mean changes the location of the normal curve on the horizontal axis. The standard deviation measures spread. As the standard deviation decreases, the normal curve becomes more tightly concentrated about its center (mean). Two normal density functions with the same mean but different standard deviations are shown in Figure 2.13.

The two points along the horizontal axis at which the normal curve changes from curving more steeply downward to curving less steeply downward (beginning to flatten out) are located a distance σ on each side of the mean μ. Consequently, it is possible to guess the values of μ and σ from a graph of the normal density function.

The normal density function with mean μ and standard deviation σ will be denoted by $N(\mu, \sigma)$. So if we want to refer to a normal distribution with $\mu = -4$ and $\sigma = 3$, we write $N(-4, 3)$. Furthermore, we shall use uppercase letters, such as X, to represent the variable whose measurements have a theoretical distribution like the normal distribution, and we shall use lowercase letters, for example, x, to represent a particular measurement.

With a little mathematics, it is possible to show that the total area under any normal curve is 1. In addition, we have the following rule:

The Normal Distribution 68–95–99.7 Rule

For any normal density function,

- 68% of the area under the curve is contained within 1 standard deviation of the mean.

- 95% of the area under the curve is contained within 2 standard deviations of the mean.

- 99.7% of the area under the curve is contained within 3 standard deviations of the mean.

The **68–95–99.7 rule** allows us to think about the nature of normal distributions without having to make repeated mathematical calculations. Note the similarity between this rule and the empirical rule. Recall that the empirical rule talks about the proportion of a data set that falls within 1, 2, and 3 sample standard deviations of the sample mean. Specifically, the empirical rule states that

- At least 68% of the data fall within s of $\overline{x}$.

- At least 95% of the data fall within $2s$ of $\overline{x}$.

- At least 99.7% of the data fall within $3s$ of $\overline{x}$.

In fact, the empirical rule comes from assuming that a data frequency distribution can be approximately represented by a normal distribution with a mean μ equal to the sample mean $\overline{x}$ and a standard deviation σ equal to the sample standard deviation s. For small data sets, it is difficult to determine whether a normal distribution approximation is warranted because there is little information in few observations. With large data sets, we can get a better picture of the shape of their distributions. If a normal density curve provides an adequate model for the data distribution, the empirical rule will provide an accurate summary of the variation.

Figure 2.14 illustrates the 68–95–99.7 rule for a normal distribution with $\mu = 0$ and the measurements expressed in units of σ; so, for example, -2 in the figure stands for

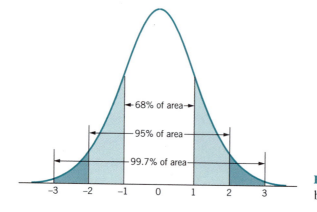

Figure 2.14 The Normal Distribution 68–95–99.7 Rule

-2σ and so forth. In particular, for $\sigma = 1$, the plot in the figure is the $N(0, 1)$ density function.

Normal distributions serve as good data models for scores on psychological tests or subject-matter examinations taken by a broad spectrum of individuals. Measurements from homogeneous biological populations that yield data on, say, bone lengths or corn production, tend to be normally distributed. Data from stable processes collected over time, such as stock rates of return, are often well represented by a normal distribution. Finally, repeated careful measurements of the same quantity, like the moisture content in portions of ground cheese from Chapter 1, are nearly normally distributed.

THE STANDARD NORMAL DISTRIBUTION

If two variables x and y are related by the expression

$$y = a + bx$$

then y is said to be a **linear transformation** of x. The name linear transformation comes from the fact that a plot of $y = a + bx$ is a straight line.

Let X be a variable whose values, theoretically, are normally distributed with mean μ and standard deviation σ, and let $Y = a + bX$ be a linear transformation of X. Then the values of Y will have mean $a + b\mu$ and standard deviation $|b|\sigma$. In addition, Y will have a normal distribution.

A Linear Transformation of a Normal Variable

If X is distributed as $N(\mu, \sigma)$, then $Y = a + bX$ is distributed as $N(a + b\mu, |b|\sigma)$.

One linear combination is particularly convenient for normal data. Define the variable

$$Z = \left(\frac{-\mu}{\sigma}\right) + \left(\frac{1}{\sigma}\right)X = \frac{X - \mu}{\sigma}$$

This variable is called a **standardized variable.** By construction, a standardized variable always has mean 0 and standard deviation 1. Consequently, from our previous result, if X has a $N(\mu, \sigma)$ distribution, Z has a $N(0, 1)$ distribution.* A normal distribution with mean 0 and standard deviation 1 is called the **standard normal distribution.**

---

*In this section, we focus our attention on a normal variable and patterns of data that are well approximated by the bell-shaped normal curve. We will encounter other data models in this book, and we will often find it convenient to work with standardized variables in those contexts.

We can turn the expression $Z = (X - \mu)/\sigma$ around and write the variable X in terms of the standardized variable Z. With a little algebra, we have

$$X = \mu + Z\sigma$$

If μ and σ are the mean and standard deviation of the normal distribution, then this equation implies that any value of the normal variable X can be written as the mean plus a multiple Z of the standard deviation.

In practice, data are often standardized with the sample mean, $\bar{x}$, playing the role of μ and the sample standard deviation, s, playing the role of σ. If there are n observations, then

$$z_i = \frac{x_i - \bar{x}}{s} \qquad i = 1, 2, \ldots, n$$

are the **standardized observations,** and these values have sample mean 0 and sample standard deviation 1 (see Exercise 2.46). If the original data are approximately normally distributed, the standardized observations are approximately normally distributed.

AREAS UNDER A NORMAL CURVE

Areas under the standard normal curve have been tabulated. Table 3 in Appendix B is a table of the area under the standard normal curve to the *left* of a particular value of z. Thus, the table gives the area under the $N(0, 1)$ curve over the interval $(-\infty, z]$. Figure 2.15 demonstrates how to read and interpret the standard normal table for $z = 1.26$.

Since the total area under any normal curve is 1, the area under the standard normal curve to the *right* of $z = 1.26$ is $1 - .8962 = .1038$. Moreover, as we have indicated in Figure 2.14, about .68 (actually, .6827) of the area under the curve is between -1 and 1, and about .95 (actually, .9545) of the area is between -2 and 2. Of course, since the mean is also the median, .5 of the area under the $N(0, 1)$ curve is to the left of 0 and .5 of the area is to the right. Using Table 3, the symmetry of the normal density function, and simple arithmetic operations, we can determine any area under the standard normal curve.

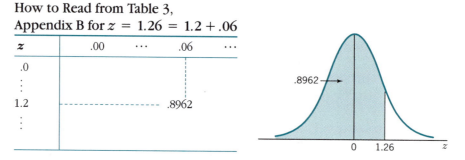

How to Read from Table 3,
Appendix B for $z = 1.26 = 1.2 + .06$

z	.00	$\cdots$	.06	$\cdots$
.0				
:				
1.2			.8962	
:				

Figure 2.15   Area Under the $N(0, 1)$ Curve to the Left of $z = 1.26$

EXAMPLE 2.14 Using the Normal Table

Find the area under the standard normal curve for the following cases:

1. Area to the left of $z = -.53$

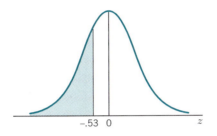

Solution and Discussion. This area can be read directly from Table 3. The table entry corresponding to $z = -.53$ is .2981. Because of the symmetry of the standard normal curve, .2981 is also the area to the *right* of $z = .53$.

2. Area to the right of $z = 1.45$

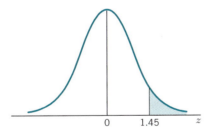

Solution and Discussion. The desired area is $1 - (\text{Area to the left of } z = 1.45)$ $= 1 - .9265 = .0735$ since .9265 is the table entry corresponding to $z = 1.45$. Equivalently, the area to the right of $z = 1.45$ is equal, from symmetry, to the area to the *left* of $z = -1.45$. The latter area can be read directly from Table 3 and is, as expected, .0735.

3. Area between $z = 0$ and $z = 2.01$

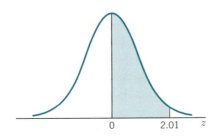

Solution and Discussion.   The area between $z = 0$ and $z = 2.01$ is given by the area to the left of $z = 2.01$ minus the area to the left of $z = 0$. We know the area to the left of 0 is .5 (verify with the table). Table 3 indicates that the area to the left of 2.01 is .9778 and, consequently, the area between 0 and 2.01 is .9778 − .5000 = .4778.

4.   Area between $z = -1.195$ and $z = .830$

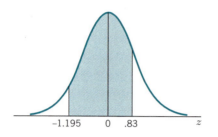

Solution and Discussion.   Again, the area between $z = -1.195$ and $z = .830$ is the area to the left of .830 minus the area to the left of −1.195. From Table 3, the area to the left of .830 is .7967. To determine the area to the left of −1.195, we must interpolate since the z values in the table are given to only two decimal places. Interpolating* between the table entries for −1.200 and −1.190, we find the area to the left of −1.195 to be .1161. The required area is then .7967 − .1161 = .6806.

Hint: When evaluating areas under a normal curve, it is a good idea to sketch the curve and then darken the required area. This will often immediately indicate the arithmetic required (if any) to determine the area from Table 3 entries.

Notice that virtually all the area under the standard normal curve is contained between −3.5 and 3.5. Areas to the left of −3.5 and to the right of 3.5 are extremely small. Table 3 gives .0002 for each area. Consequently, for z values more extreme than these, we typically ignore the areas to the left of the negative extreme values and to the right of the positive extreme values.

A table of standard normal curve areas and the relationship $z = (x - \mu)/\sigma$ can be used to find the area under any normal density curve. To illustrate, suppose a normal density function with mean 10 and standard deviation 2 is a good representation of a particular density histogram, and we are interested in the proportion of the data between, say, 6 and 11. This proportion is approximated by the area under the $N(10, 2)$ curve over the interval $[6, 11]$. The values of a normal variable can be converted to the values of a standard normal variable. In this case, $\mu = 10$ and $\sigma = 2$, so a value of $x = 6$ corresponds to a value of $z = \frac{6-10}{2} = -2$. Similarly, a value of $x = 11$ converts to a standard normal value of $z = \frac{11-10}{2} = .5$.

The area under the $N(10, 2)$ function over the interval $[6, 11]$ is exactly the same as the area under the standard normal curve, $N(0, 1)$, over the interval $[-2, .5]$. The latter

---

*Since −1.195 is halfway between −1.200 and −1.190, the table entry corresponding to −1.195 is halfway between the table entries for −1.200 and −1.190, respectively.

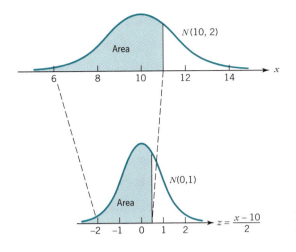

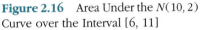

Figure 2.16   Area Under the $N(10, 2)$ Curve over the Interval [6, 11]

area can be determined with the help of the standard normal table. This situation is illustrated in Figure 2.16.

In general, we have the following. Suppose we are interested in the area under the $N(\mu, \sigma)$ distribution curve between two numbers c and d with $c < d$. Then

Area under $N(\mu, \sigma)$ over the interval $[c, d]$

$$= \text{Area under } N(0, 1) \text{ over the interval } \left[\frac{c - \mu}{\sigma}, \frac{d - \mu}{\sigma} \right]$$

Since single points have zero width, the area under a normal curve over the interval $[c, d]$ is the same as the area over the interval (c, d)—the interval without the endpoints. That is, the area under the curve does not change if we include or exclude one or both of the endpoints of the target interval.

EXAMPLE 2.15   Determining Areas Under Normal Curves

1. Suppose X is approximately distributed as $N(100, 5)$. Determine the area under this normal density between 97 and 110.

Solution and Discussion.   When $c = 97$ and $d = 110$, the area under the curve between $x = 97$ and $x = 110$ is the same as the area under the standard normal density between

$$z = \frac{97 - 100}{5} = -.60 \quad \text{and} \quad z = \frac{110 - 100}{5} = 2.00$$

Using Table 3, the latter area is the area to the left of $z = 2.00$ minus the area to the left of $z = -.60$, or $.9772 - .2743 = .7029$.

2. Suppose X is approximately distributed as $N(-12, 3)$. Determine the area to the right of -8.5.

Solution and Discussion. Since the total area under any normal curve is 1, the area to the right of $x = -8.5$ is equal to

$$1 - (\text{Area to the left of } x = -8.5)$$

Converting $x = -8.5$ to $z = \dfrac{-8.5 - (-12)}{3} = 1.167$, we calculate the required area:

$$1 - (\text{Area to the left of } z = 1.167) = 1 - .8784 = .1216$$

where .8784 is obtained by interpolating between the entries corresponding to $z = 1.16$ and $z = 1.17$ in Table 3.

3. Suppose X is approximately distributed as $N(44, 6)$, and we know that a proportion .90 of the area under this curve is to the left of a value x. That is, x is the 90th percentile of the $N(44, 6)$ distribution. Determine x.

Solution and Discussion. We are given

$$(\text{Area to the left of } x) = .90$$

This implies that

$$\left(\text{Area to the left of } z = \frac{x - 44}{6}\right) = .90$$

From Table 3, we can determine the value of z that has .90 (or approximately .90) of the area under the standard normal density to the left of it. Using the table, we find

$$(\text{Area to the left of } z = 1.28) = .8997$$

which is nearly .90. Setting

$$\frac{x - 44}{6} = 1.28$$

and solving for x, we get $x = 44 + (1.28)6 = 51.68$. Consequently, $x = 51.68$ is the 90th percentile of the $N(44, 6)$ distribution.

On occasion, we might want to judge whether the observed value of a normal variable is, in some sense, unexpected. If area is determined from a $N(\mu, \sigma)$ curve, an unexpected or unusual value x is one that is too far from the mean μ. Equivalently, the absolute value of $z = (x - \mu)/\sigma$ is too large. A value for the standardized variable less than -2 or greater than 2 could be considered large because each of the tail areas is .0228 and the combined area $2(.0228) = .0456$ is small. We will continue to elaborate on this idea of "unusual" or "unexpected" as we develop the central statistical procedures.

John Chase

An Outlier?

Not all data patterns can be reasonably approximated by a normal curve. Therefore, if a normal distribution is tentatively assumed to be a plausible data model in a particular case, this assumption must be checked once the sample observations are in hand. We consider this in Chapter 7, where we discuss the normal distribution in greater detail.

EXERCISES

2.34 Find the area under the standard normal curve to the left of
  a. $z = 1.16$
  b. $z = .24$
  c. $z = -.57$
  d. $z = -2.1$

2.35 Find the area under the standard normal curve to the left of
  a. $z = .77$
  b. $z = 1.68$
  c. $z = -.21$
  d. $z = -1.39$

2.36 Find the area under the standard normal curve to the right of
  a. $z = .84$
  b. $z = 2.25$

    c. $z = -.1$

    d. $z = -1.595$ (interpolate)

2.37 Find the area under the standard normal curve to the right of

    a. $z = .21$

    b. $z = 2.03$

    c. $z = -.67$

    d. $z = -1.115$ (interpolate)

2.38 Find the area under the standard normal curve over the interval

    a. $z = 0$ to $z = .37$

    b. $z = -.42$ to $z = 1.06$

    c. $z = -1.62$ to $z = .09$

    d. $z = .25$ to $z = 1.966$ (interpolate)

2.39 Find the area under the standard normal curve over the interval

    a. $z = -2.07$ to $z = .04$

    b. $z = -1.12$ to $z = -.35$

    c. $z = -.77$ to $z = 0$

    d. $z = .69$ to $z = 1.893$ (interpolate)

2.40 Identify the z values in the following diagrams of the standard normal distributions (interpolate as needed).

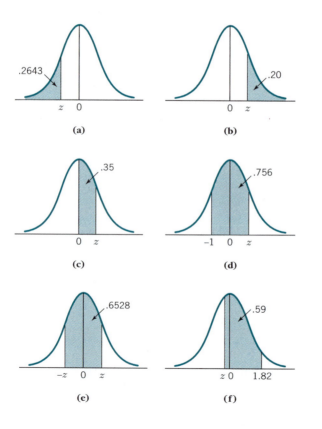

2.41   Identify the z values in the following diagrams of the standard normal distributions (interpolate as needed).

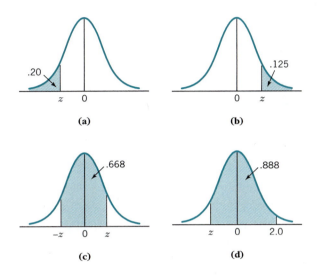

(a)   (b)

(c)   (d)

2.42   Determine the quartiles of the standard normal distribution.

2.43   Find the following:

  a.   The area under the standard normal curve to the left of $z = .35$

  b.   The 35th percentile of the standard normal distribution

  c.   The area under the standard normal curve to the left of $z = .60$

  d.   The 60th percentile of the standard normal distribution

2.44   Find the following:

  a.   The area under the standard normal curve to the left of $z = .15$

  b.   The 15th percentile of the standard normal distribution

  c.   The area under the standard normal curve to the left of $z = .99$

  d.   The 99th percentile of the standard normal distribution

2.45   If the variable X has the $N(50, 20)$ distribution, determine the distributions (including the means and standard deviations) of the following linear combinations.

  a. $Y = 10 + 3X$

  b. $Y = -50 + .2X$

  c. $Y = (X - 25)/2$

  d. $Y = -4X$

2.46   Show that standardized observations have sample mean 0 and sample standard deviation 1. [*Hint:*   Since s is a constant, $\sum_{i=1}^{n} z_i = \sum_{i=1}^{n}(x_i - \overline{x})/s = 0$ (see Exercise 1.21 of Chapter 1). Also, $\sum_{i=1}^{n} z_i^2 = \sum_{i=1}^{n}(x_i - \overline{x})^2/s^2$.]

2.47   If X is normally distributed with $\mu = 40$ and $\sigma = 3$, find the following:

  a.   The area under the normal curve to the left of $x = 43$

  b.   The area under the normal curve to the left of $x = 45$

    c.   The area under the normal curve to the left of $x = 38$

    d.   The area under the normal curve to the right of $x = 40$

    e.   The area under the normal curve to the right of $x = 36$

    f.   The area under the normal curve over the interval $x = 37$ to $x = 41$

2.48   If X is normally distributed with $\mu = 15$ and $\sigma = 6$, find the following:

    a.   The area under the normal curve to the left of $x = 16.5$

    b.   The area under the normal curve to the left of $x = 7$

    c.   The area under the normal curve to the right of $x = 22$

    d.   The area under the normal curve to the right of $x = 11$

    e.   The area under the normal curve over the interval $x = 17$ to $x = 27$

    f.   The area under the normal curve over the interval $x = -1$ to $x = 19$

2.49   For the $N(200, 4)$ distribution, find the value c such that

    a.   The area under the normal curve to the left of c is .8461.

    b.   The area under the normal curve to the right of c is .5897.

    c.   The area under the normal curve to the left of c is .0116.

    d.   The area under the normal curve to the right of c is .2297.

2.50   For the $N(-10, 2)$ distribution, find the value c such that

    a.   The area under the normal curve to the left of c is .7995.

    b.   The area under the normal curve to the right of c is .9429.

    c.   The area under the normal curve over the interval $-c$ to c is .6826.

    d.   The area under the normal curve over the interval $-c$ to c is .9544.

2.51   Scores on a certain nationwide college entrance examination follow a normal distribution with a mean of 21 and a standard deviation of 3. Find the proportion of scores (students)

    a.   Over 25

    b.   Under 20

    c.   Between 19 and 27

2.52   Refer to Exercise 2.51.

    a.   If a school admits only students who score over 24, what proportion of the test takers would be eligible for admission?

    b.   What limit would you set that makes 50% of the test takers eligible for admission? (Round to the nearest integer.)

    c.   What would be the cutoff score if only the top 20% of the test takers are to be eligible? (Round to the nearest integer.)

2.7 MORE GRAPHS AND CHARTS

We cannot overemphasize the importance of graphing your data. If a feature you expect to see is not present in the plots, statistical analyses will, generally, be of little use. Some would argue that well-constructed graphs and charts convey virtually all

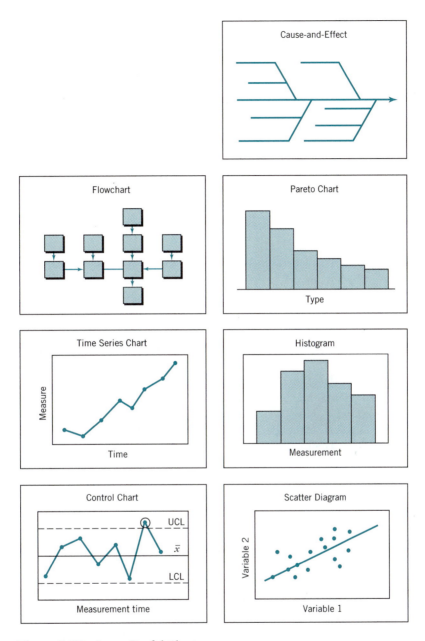

Figure 2.17 Seven Useful Charts

the information contained in the data. Figure 2.17 contains seven charts found to be particularly helpful in business and economics.* We have already introduced most of these charts. The remaining charts will be introduced shortly.

Creative graphics can highlight features in the data and even provide new insights. A classic example is the display by Charles Minard showing the ill-fated attempt of

*These charts are adapted from similar displays appearing in Walton, M. *The Deming Management Method*. New York: Perigee Books, 1986.

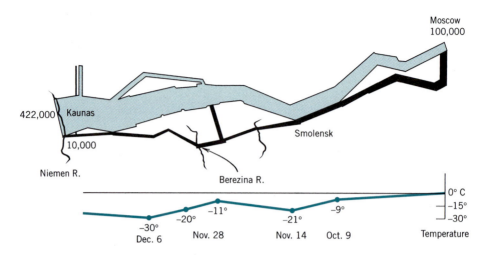

Figure 2.18   The Demise of Napoleon's Army in Russia, 1812–1813 (based on display by Charles Minard)

Napoleon's Grand Army to capture Russia. A simplified version of the original graphic appears in Figure 2.18.*

The 422,000 troops that entered Russia near Kaunas are shown as a wide (shaded) river flowing toward Moscow, and the retreating army as a small (black) stream. The width of the band indicates the size of the army at each location on the map. Napoleon had to provide 422,000 soldiers in Poland to field 100,000 troops in Moscow.

Even the simplified version (Fig. 2.18) of the original graphic dramatically conveys the losses that left the army with 10,000 returning members. The temperature scale at the bottom of the graph, pertaining to the retreat from Moscow, helps to explain the loss of life, including the incident where thousands died trying to cross the Berezina River in subzero temperatures.

Another informative graph is presented in Figure 2.19. In this graph, countries of the world are scaled to approximate size according to 1992 stock market capitalization. We see that most of the world's money resides in the United States, Japan, and, to a lesser extent, the United Kingdom.

Although we do not intend to pursue graphics, the impact of these examples should motivate you to think creatively when displaying data.

2.8   STATISTICS IN CONTEXT

The quality control department of a midwest manufacturer of microwave ovens is required by the U.S. government to monitor the amount of radiation emitted when the doors of the ovens are closed. Observations of the radiation passing through the closed doors of $n = 42$ ovens were obtained and are given in Table 2.8.†

---

*A copy of Minard's original map and additional discussion are contained in Tufte, E. R. *The Visual Display of Quantitative Information*. Cheshire, Conn.: Graphics Press, 1983.
†Data courtesy of J. D. Cryer.

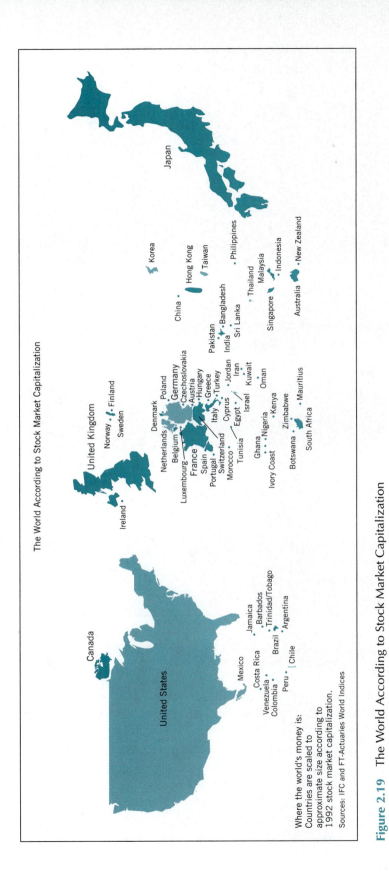

The World According to Stock Market Capitalization

Where the world's money is:
Countries are scaled to
approximate size according to
1992 stock market capitalization.

Sources: IFC and FT-Actuaries World Indices

Figure 2.19   The World According to Stock Market Capitalization

TABLE 2.8   Radiation Through Closed Doors of
Microwave Ovens (mw/cm²)

.15	.09	.18	.10	.05	.12	.18
.05	.08	.10	.07	.02	.01	.10
.10	.10	.02	.10	.01	.40	.10
.05	.03	.05	.15	.10	.15	.09
.08	.18	.10	.20	.11	.30	.02
.20	.20	.30	.30	.40	.30	.05

To determine the chance of exceeding a prespecified tolerance level, a pattern of variation for the amounts of radiation was required. Can we regard the observations here as being normally distributed?

Panel 2.1 shows the stem-and-leaf diagram and the boxplot of the radiation data in Table 2.8. We call the radiation variable RADiaTioN Door Closed in the Minitab plots. It is clear from these plots that the radiation data are skewed to the right, with several ovens having relatively large values of .30 and .40.

```
RADTNDC
                                      Stem-and-leaf of RADTNDC   N  = 42
                                      Leaf Unit = 0.010

    N     MEAN    MEDIAN     STDEV
   42   0.1283    0.1000    0.1003           6    0 112223
                                            17    0 55555788899
  MIN     MAX        Q1        Q3          (11)   1 00000000012
0.0100  0.4000    0.0500    0.1800          14    1 55588
                                             9    2 000
                                             6    2
                                             6    3 0000
                                             2    3
                                             2    4 00
```

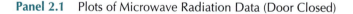

```
     |------|-----------+----------|------------------|               *
   |-------|-----------|----------|------------------|----------| RADTNDC
  0.00     0.10       0.20       0.30               0.40
```

Panel 2.1   Plots of Microwave Radiation Data (Door Closed)

To bring the large radiation measurements more in line with the remaining observations, we consider a reexpression or transformation of the data. The objective here is to create a set of data that can reasonably be described by a normal distribution.

One transformation that brings large (positive) values relatively closer to the remaining values is the square root transformation. (For example, the numbers $\sqrt{9} = 3$ and $\sqrt{100} = 10$ are closer together than the original numbers 9 and 100.) If we apply the square root transformation twice, that is, take the fourth root, $\sqrt[4]{x}$, of each observation, we get the results shown in Panel 2.2. We label the reexpressed data Fourth ROOT Door Closed in the plots.

It is evident from the stem-and-leaf diagram and boxplot in Panel 2.2 that the transformed observations are reasonably symmetric and, we would argue, nearly normal.

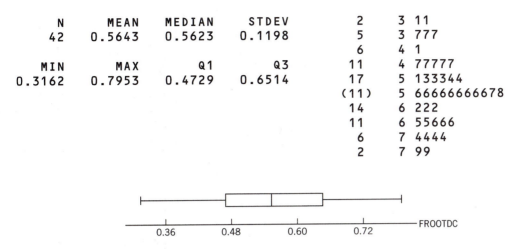

```
                                            Stem-and-leaf of FROOTDC   N  = 42
              FROOTDC                       Leaf Unit = 0.010

      N      MEAN    MEDIAN    STDEV            2     3 11
     42    0.5643    0.5623   0.1198            5     3 777
                                               6     4 1
     MIN     MAX       Q1        Q3           11     4 77777
   0.3162  0.7953    0.4729    0.6514         17     5 133344
                                            (11)    5 66666666678
                                             14     6 222
                                             11     6 55666
                                              6     7 4444
                                              2     7 99
```

Panel 2.2   Plots of the Transformed Microwave Radiation Data (Door Closed)

The radiation data are measurements of a particular characteristic associated with the manufacture of microwave ovens. The extent to which these measurements depict the behavior of radiation readings for yet-to-be-manufactured ovens depends on the stability of the manufacturing process. As we explain in Chapter 13, if the process is "in-control"—that is, if the causes of variation in the radiation measurements remain the same (*constant* or *common causes*)—then we would expect the current observations to tell us something about future values. If something unusual occurs, or the manufacturing process changes in some fundamental way, for example, there is a new supplier of raw materials or parts, or a new method of assembly, then the current radiation measurements may have little to say about future emissions through closed doors. The validity of any generalizations beyond the data in hand depends very much on the crucial assumption that the future is much like the past.

We are generally concerned with the radiation emitted through the closed doors of all ovens that have been or *will be* produced. Consequently, a study of the radiation measurements to see whether the microwave ovens meet government standards is an analytic study. A 100% sample of all the ovens currently available will not provide perfect information about the performance of future ovens.

Suppose the data in Table 2.8 are recorded in the order in which the ovens were manufactured. That is, the first observation in the first row is the radiation measurement for the oldest oven, the first oven of the group produced. The second observation in the first row is the radiation measurement for the second oldest oven, and so forth. Thus, as we read across the rows in the table, we encounter more recent observations. A time-ordered plot of the transformed radiation measurements is given in Figure 2.20 (page 90).

There are three horizontal lines in the figure. The middle line is at the value of the mean of the observations. The upper line is at 3 standard deviations above the mean. This line is called the **upper control limit (UCL).** The lower line is located at 3 standard deviations below the mean. This line is called the **lower control limit (LCL).** Because

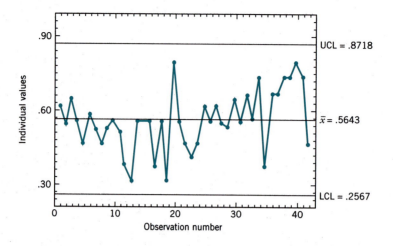

Figure 2.20   A Time-Ordered Plot of the Transformed Radiation Measurements

of their location with respect to the mean, the UCL and LCL are sometimes called the three-sigma (3σ) limits.*

A chart like the one in Figure 2.20 is called a **control chart.** A control chart is simply a time-ordered or time series plot with upper and lower control limits drawn on each side of the mean of the observations. Control charts are used to display variability and to discover how much variability in the observations is due to random or common cause variation, and how much is due to unique events or *special causes.* We discuss control charts in Chapter 13. At this point, we use the control chart simply to display the time-ordered radiation measurements relative to their mean and 3 standard deviation limits. Let's interpret what we see.

We see that all the transformed radiation measurements are within 3 standard deviations of the mean. However, there is some tendency for the radiation values for the older ovens to be below the mean and the values for the more recently manufactured ovens to be above the mean. This could indicate some change in the manufacturing process leading to higher levels of emitted radiation. The evidence is inconclusive and additional monitoring may be required, but the slight upward drift in the data illustrates the importance of looking at observations in the time order in which they were produced.

If the process is stable (in control), we would expect the observations in the control chart to vary about the centerline (mean), within the 3σ limits, with no specific pattern of variation. A few observations outside the 3σ limits or a long sequence of observations above (or below) the mean suggest that the process is not stable. That is, the causes of variability in the numbers are not constant or common over time. A change has occurred. As we discuss in Chapter 13, once a change is detected, we search for the reason for the change.

Sometimes subgroup means rather than the individual observations are plotted in control charts. This often produces a clearer picture of the measured characteristic. Let's look at the measurements in Figure 2.20. Suppose we collect the observations into subgroups of size 3. The rationale might be that the first three observations are a

---

*The standard deviation used in the construction of the control limits is an estimate of σ based on the range and produces a slightly different number than the sample standard deviation s.

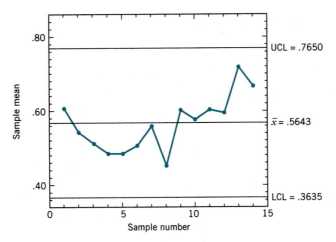

Figure 2.21   An *X*-bar Chart for the Transformed Radiation Data

sample from a batch of microwave ovens produced at about the same time. The second three observations are a sample from a later batch of ovens, and so forth. The subgroup means are plotted in the control chart in Figure 2.21. Since the points plotted are means, the chart is called an **X-bar chart.** The 3σ limits (UCL and LCL) are determined using the standard deviation of the subgroup means. This standard deviation is less than the standard deviation of the original observations. Since we have 42 observations, there are $\frac{42}{3} = 14$ sample (subgroup) means plotted in the chart.

Notice the upward drift in the mean radiation numbers over time. This pattern is consistent with the pattern for the individual observations in Figure 2.20. The drift in the means is clearer than the drift in the original observations, suggesting that there may be a problem with the more recently manufactured ovens.

2.9   CHAPTER SUMMARY

In this chapter, we have learned:

- The general practice of summarizing data with a collection of relatively simple tables, plots, and numbers is called **exploratory data analysis.**

- An **enumerative study** is a study about an identifiable, unchanging, generally finite population done at a particular point in time. The list of sampling units for an enumerative study is called a **frame.** An enumerative study is like a snapshot.

- An **analytic study** is a study that is not enumerative. Analytic studies generally take place over time, like a moving picture. The objective is to use current information to predict what will happen in the future. Analytic studies often involve comparisons.

- The characteristic of interest in either an enumerative or analytic study is called a **variable.** Variables are of two types: **quantitative** and **qualitative.** Qualitative variables are non-numerical. The "values" for qualitative variables are categories. Numbers are often assigned to the categories to distinguish them. If the categories have no particular order, such as male/female, the numbers assigned to the categories are called **nominal data.** If the categories are ordered, such as the bond ratings, Aaa, Aa, . . . , the ordered numbers assigned to the categories are called **ordinal data.** Quantitative variables are naturally numerical and may be **discrete** or **continuous.** Discrete variables are those variables whose values are numbers with gaps between them, such as the number of votes received by candidates in an election. Continuous variables are those variables that can, in principle, take any value in an interval. Sometimes discrete variables are treated as continuous variables.

- The pattern of variability in a set of data is called its **frequency distribution.** A frequency distribution indicates the values, or categories, for the variable and the number of times each value, or category, occurs.

- Frequency distributions are best characterized by graphs or plots. Possible plots for displaying a frequency distribution include: a **dot diagram,** a **stem-and-leaf diagram,** a **histogram** or **density histogram,** and a **boxplot.**

- Summary numbers indicating location include the **mean,** $\bar{x}$, the **median,** M, and **percentiles.** The location of the mean is such that the sum of the deviations of the observations from the mean is zero. The median divides the ordered data in half. **Quartiles,** Q_1, Q_2, Q_3, are percentiles that divide the ordered data into quarters. Consequently, the second quartile, Q_2, is also the median, M.

- Summary measures that are not appreciably affected by a few extreme observations are said to be **robust** or **resistant.** The median, for example, is a robust measure of location.

- Summary numbers measuring variation include the following: the **variance,** s^2, the **standard deviation,** $s = +\sqrt{s^2}$, the **range,** Range $=$ Max $-$ Min; and the **interquartile range,** IR $= Q_3 - Q_1$. The interquartile range is a robust measure of variation.

- **Boxplots** are pictorial representations of the **five-number summary,** Min, Q_1, $Q_2 = M$, Q_3, and Max.

- Variables x and y that are connected by the expression $y = a + bx$ are said to be connected by a **linear transformation.** We say that y is a linear transformation of x.

- When density histograms are symmetric about a single peak and look like the outline of a bell, they can often be approximated by a smooth curve known as the **normal density function.** The normal density function with mean μ and standard deviation σ is denoted by $N(\mu, \sigma)$. The mean locates the middle of the normal density function along the x-axis, and the standard deviation controls the spread or concentration of the normal curve about the mean. As the standard deviation decreases, the normal curve becomes more tightly concentrated about its mean. The normal density function is also called the **normal distribution.**

- The **empirical rule** allows us to summarize the locations of increasing proportions of a set of numbers using only the sample mean and sample standard deviation. The empirical rule tells us that about 68% of the data lie in the interval $\bar{x} \pm s$; about 95% of the data lie in the interval $\bar{x} \pm 2s$; and about 99.7% of the data lie in the interval $\bar{x} \pm 3s$. The empirical rule works best for large, mound-shaped data sets.

- The **68–95–99.7 Rule** summarizes the area under the normal curve in terms of standard deviation intervals centered at the mean. For any normal density function,

  1. 68% of the area under the curve is contained within 1 standard deviation of the mean.
  2. 95% of the area under the curve is contained within 2 standard deviations of the mean.
  3. 99.7% of the area under the curve is contained within 3 standard deviations of the mean.

- The 68–95–99.7 rule and the empirical rule are related. In fact, the empirical rule comes from assuming that a data frequency distribution can be approximately represented by a normal density function with a mean μ equal to the sample mean $\bar{x}$ and a standard deviation σ equal to the sample standard deviation s.

- The **standard normal distribution** is a normal distribution with mean 0 and standard deviation 1.

- If X is distributed as $N(\mu, \sigma)$, then $Y = a + bX$ is distributed as $N(a + b\mu, |b|\sigma)$.

- The variable

$$Z = \frac{X - \mu}{\sigma}$$

is called a **standardized variable.** A standardized variable Z is a linear transformation of the variable X of the form $Z = a + bX$ with $a = -\mu/\sigma$ and $b = 1/\sigma$.
- Using a table of standard normal curve areas and the symmetry of the normal density function, we can determine areas under any normal curve.

2.10   IMPORTANT CONCEPTS AND TOOLS

CONCEPTS

Analytic study, 37
Binary coding, 39
Class boundary, 46
Class interval, 46
Class limit, 46
Continuous variable, 40
Data, 38
Degrees of freedom, 63
Discrete variable, 39
Enumerative study, 36
Exploratory data analysis, 36
Five-number summary, 65
Frame, 36
Frequency distribution, 41
Interquartile range, 64
Linear transformation, 75
Lower control limit, 89
Nominal data, 38
Normal density function, 72
Normal distribution, 73

Ordinal data, 38
Percentiles, 61
Qualitative variable, 38
Quantitative variable, 38
Range, 63
Resistant summary measure, 59
Robust summary measure, 59
Sample mean, 58
Sample median, 59
Sample quartiles, 61
Sample variance, 63
Skewed data pattern, 48
Standard normal distribution, 75
Standardized observations, 76
Standardized variable, 75
Symmetric data pattern, 48
Trimmed mean, 59
Upper control limit, 89
Variable, 38
X-bar chart, 91

TOOLS

Boxplot, 65
Control chart, 90
Density histogram, 50
Dot diagram, 42
Empirical rule, 64
Histogram, 46
Modified boxplot, 67
68–95–99.7 rule, 74
Stem-and-leaf diagram, 42

2.11   KEY FORMULAS

$$IR = Q_3 - Q_1$$

$$\text{Range} = \text{Max} - \text{Min}$$

Sample mean: $\bar{x} = \dfrac{1}{n} \sum_{i=1}^{n} x_i$

Sample variance: $s^2 = \dfrac{1}{n-1} \sum_{i=1}^{n} (x_i - \bar{x})^2$

Computing formula for s^2: $s^2 = \dfrac{1}{n-1} \left[\sum_{i=1}^{n} x_i^2 - \dfrac{1}{n} \left(\sum_{i=1}^{n} x_i \right)^2 \right]$

Standardized variable: $Z = \dfrac{X - \mu}{\sigma}$

REVIEW EXERCISES

2.53 Classify the following as enumerative or analytic studies. Justify your choice.

  a. A postal employee wants to estimate the number of two-day letters, sent from the postal station, that arrive at their destination within 48 hours.

  b. A manager wants to know the number of employees in her division who were absent at least one-half day during the previous month.

2.54 Refer to Exercise 2.53. For each of the studies, define the variable (characteristic) of interest. If the variable is quantitative, indicate whether it is a discrete or continuous variable.

2.55 The following table gives the frequency distribution for the length of time (in minutes) of taxi rides originating at the local airport.

Time (min.)	Frequency
$[0, 10)$	8
$[10, 20)$	17
$[20, 30)$	14
$[30, 40)$	10
$[40, 60)$	11

  a. Complete this table by adding a relative frequency column and a density column.

  b. Using the results in part **a,** plot the density for time of ride. Comment on the general appearance of the density histogram.

2.56 Consider the statement, "The $238,544 figure for net worth is the mean, a figure halfway between the highest and lowest amounts," that appeared in an article in the February 19, 1996, issue of *USA Today.* What is wrong with this statement?

2.57 Given the four observations

$$6 \quad 2 \quad 4 \quad 0$$

obtain the following:

  a. The sample mean and median

  b. s^2 using the definitional formula, $\sum_{i=1}^{n}(x_i - \overline{x})^2/(n - 1)$

  c. s^2 using the computing formula (see Exercise 2.28)

2.58 The numbers of years of service for ten upper-level managers are

$$3 \quad 12 \quad 7 \quad 21 \quad 15 \quad 8 \quad 18 \quad 25 \quad 16 \quad 9$$

Calculate the following:

  a. The sample mean

  b. The sample quartiles

  c. The range

  d. The sample interquartile range

2.59 (*Minitab or similar program recommended*) Collect a set of data that interests you. Try to collect 40 or more observations. The data set might be the starting salaries of undergraduate marketing, accounting, finance, or management majors; the difference or spread in football scores for professional games; daily living expenses; selling prices of comparable homes; and so forth.

a. Is your data set symmetric? Discuss with reference to a stem-and-leaf diagram, a boxplot, and a frequency histogram.

b. Compute the sample mean and median. Which number is a better measure of location for your data set? Why?

c. Compute the sample standard deviation, the range, and the sample interquartile range. Recalculate these quantities after discarding the two largest observations in your data set. Do these measures of variation change appreciably? Should they? Discuss.

d. Demonstrate the accuracy (or inaccuracy) of the empirical rule for your data set.

2.60 (*Minitab or similar program recommended*) Refer to the microwave radiation data in Table 2.8. Transform these observations by taking their fourth roots. Let

MicroRad.dat

x represent a transformed observation. Construct 21 sample means based on samples of size 2 by taking every pair of observations along the rows in the table. For example, the first sample mean is

$$\overline{x} = \frac{\sqrt[4]{.15} + \sqrt[4]{.09}}{2} = .59$$

The second sample mean is

$$\overline{x} = \frac{\sqrt[4]{.18} + \sqrt[4]{.10}}{2} = .61$$

and so forth.

a. Determine the mean, $\overline{x}$, and the standard deviation, s, for the 21 sample means.

b. Taking the 21 sample means in the order in which they were computed, plot the means on an X-bar chart with a centerline equal to $\overline{x}$, the mean of the means, and 3σ limits given by UCL = $\overline{x} + 3s$ and LCL = $\overline{x} - 3s$.

c. Interpret the X-bar chart in part **b**. Are the radiation measurements stable over time? Discuss with reference to the discussion in Section 2.8.

2.61 (*Minitab or similar program recommended*) The radiation emitted through the *open* doors of the $n = 42$ microwave ovens discussed in Section 2.8 was also

MicroRad.dat

measured. The open-door radiation measurements (mw/cm²) are given here (data courtesy of J. D. Cryer).

.30	.09	.30	.10	.10	.12	.09
.10	.09	.10	.07	.05	.01	.45
.12	.20	.04	.10	.01	.60	.12
.10	.05	.05	.15	.30	.15	.09
.09	.28	.10	.10	.10	.30	.12
.25	.20	.40	.33	.32	.12	.12

a. Are open-door radiation measurements normal? The evidence for your answer should include the summary numbers and displays like the ones in Panel 2.1.

b. Let *x* denote the radiation emitted through the open door of an oven. Transform the observations by taking their fourth root, $\sqrt[4]{x}$. Are the transformed radiation measurements normal? Discuss with reference to summary numbers and plots like the ones in Panel 2.2.

2.62 Using the fourth roots of the data in Exercise 2.61, construct an *X*-bar chart similar to the one in Figure 2.21. That is, using the transformed open-door radiation measurements, form samples of size 3 along the rows in the table in Exercise 2.61. Compute the 14 sample means and the mean of these means, $\bar{x}$. Compute the standard deviation, *s*, of the 14 sample means. Use $\bar{x}$ and *s* to determine the centerline and 3σ limits in your *X*-bar chart.

2.63 Refer to Exercise 2.62.

a. Is the *X*-bar chart in Exercise 2.62 similar in appearance to the one in Figure 2.21? In other words, do the open-door radiation measurements drift over time, with the older measurements below the centerline and the more recent measurements above? Would you expect the two charts to be similar? What if the open-door and closed-door observation pairs are not from the same ovens? That is, what if the first open-door measurement in Exercise 2.61 is not from the oven that produced the first closed-door measurement in Table 2.8 and so forth?

b. In general, would you expect the radiation measurements through the open doors of the ovens to be larger or smaller than the corresponding measurements through closed doors? Are the *X*-bar charts in Exercise 2.62 and Figure 2.21 consistent with your answer? For which set of measurements does the variation appear to be larger?

CitiesBA.dat

2.64 (*Minitab or similar program recommended*) Refer to Exercise 2.32. The article "The Best Cities for Knowledge Workers" (*Fortune*, Nov. 15, 1993), also gives the percentage of workers 25 years and older that hold a baccalaureate (BA) or higher degree for various cities.

City	% BA or Higher	City	% BA or Higher	City	% BA or Higher
Raleigh/Durham	31.7	Dayton	19.1	Norfolk	19.8
New York	25.4	Denver	29.1	Oakland	29.9
Boston	28.8	Detroit	17.7	Oklahoma City	21.6
Seattle	29.5	Ft. Lauderdale	18.8	Orlando	20.4
Austin	30.7	Fort Worth	22.4	Phoenix	21.4
Chicago	24.5	Grand Rapids	17.8	Pittsburgh	18.7
Houston	25.0	Greensboro	17.5	Portland	23.3
San Jose	32.6	Hartford	26.0	Richmond	23.8
Philadelphia	22.6	Honolulu	24.6	Rochester	22.9
Minneapolis	26.9	Indianapolis	20.2	Sacramento	22.7
Albany	23.6	Jacksonville	18.6	St. Louis	17.7
Atlanta	26.1	Kansas City	23.2	Salt Lake City	22.9
Baltimore	23.1	Las Vegas	13.3	San Antonio	19.3
Birmingham	19.7	Los Angeles	22.3	San Diego	25.3
Buffalo	18.8	Louisville	17.2	San Francisco	34.9
Charlotte	19.6	Memphis	18.7	Scranton	13.6
Cincinnati	19.9	Miami	18.8	Tampa	17.3
Cleveland	18.5	Milwaukee	21.3	Tulsa	20.3
Columbus	23.3	Nashville	21.4	Washington, D.C.	37.0
Dallas	26.9	New Orleans	19.3	West Palm Beach	22.1

a. Construct a stem-and-leaf diagram of the percentages with a double stem.

b. Which cities have an unusually high or unusually low percentage of workers holding college degrees?

 2.65 (*Minitab or similar program recommended*) Refer to Exercise 2.64. Consider the first ten cities in the first column of the list. Make back-to-back stem-and-leaf diagrams of these ten cities and the remaining cities on the list. Does there appear to be any difference between the two groups of cities with respect to the percentage of workers with college degrees?

CitiesBA.dat

 2.66 (*Minitab or similar program recommended*) Refer to Exercise 2.64.

CitiesBA.dat

a. Obtain the mean and standard deviation of the percentages on the list.

b. Compare the number of observations in the interval $\bar{x} - 2s$ to $\bar{x} + 2s$ with the number predicted by the empirical rule.

 2.67 (*Minitab or similar program recommended*) Refer to Exercise 2.64.

CitiesBA.dat

a. Obtain the minimum and maximum percentages and the quartiles.

b. Obtain the interquartile range.

c. Construct a boxplot, and identify the quartiles and interquartile range from the boxplot.

2.68 (*Minitab or similar program recommended*) Collect the closing Friday price of your favorite stock for the last year.

a. Plot the $n = 52$ stock prices over time. Is there any apparent pattern?

b. Calculate and plot the $n = 51$ weekly returns by subtracting the previous Friday's price from the current Friday's price and dividing the difference by the previous price. Is there any pattern in the stock returns over time?

c. Are your stock rates of return normal? Discuss with reference to summary numbers and plots like the ones in Panel 2.1.

 2.69 (*Minitab or similar program recommended*) Consider the "operating income" numbers listed in Table 7, Appendix C, for $n = 102$ professional sports franchises.

SportFrn.dat

a. Are these data normal? Discuss with reference to summary numbers and plots like the ones in Panel 2.1.

b. Construct side-by-side boxplots of operating income for the four types of sport franchises: baseball, football, basketball, and hockey. Comment on the results. Can you identify any outliers?

c. For each sport franchise, does operating income appear to be normally distributed? Discuss with reference to summary numbers and plots like the ones in Panel 2.1.

2.70 (*Minitab or similar program recommended*) Consider the "guaranteed accumulation after 10 years" (GurAcc10) numbers listed in Table 5, Appendix C, for the universal life policies of $n = 182$ insurance companies. Are these data normal? Discuss with reference to summary numbers and plots like the ones in Panel 2.1.

LifeIns.dat

CHAPTER OBJECTIVES

After reading this chapter, you should be able to:

- Construct and interpret scatterplots of bivariate observations.
- Calculate and interpret the sample correlation coefficient.
- Calculate and interpret the sample autocorrelation coefficients.
- Fit a line to a scatterplot using the method of least squares.
- Plot and analyze residuals.
- Model exponential growth.
- Arrange frequencies associated with two categorical variables in two-way tables.
- Arrange time series data in two-way tables to show trend and seasonality.

CHAPTER THREE

Organizing Data: Association and Relationships

3.1 INTRODUCTION

Investigations involving data rarely focus on a single variable. In business settings, we are often interested, for example, in a set of financial ratios or several economic indicators or a collection of measures of productivity. From a managerial perspective, we use data on several variables to describe past performance, to make informed conjectures about the future, to evaluate current performance, to study cause-and-effect relations, and to investigate unusual occurrences that occasionally turn out to be useful surprises. In our effort to discover and extract information from multivariable data, we will introduce and illustrate some new graphical and numerical tools. These new tools, in addition to the ones introduced in Chapter 2, will allow us to effectively communicate numerical information.

In this chapter, we concentrate on three types of displays:

1. Two-dimensional scatterplots of pairs of observations on two continuous variables
2. Two-way tables of counts (frequencies) associated with two categorical variables
3. Time sequence or time series plots of continuous variables

After tables and graphs, we discuss numerical summaries. Our attention will be focused on the relations between two variables. In some circumstances, such as studying the longitudinal pattern of change of a particular characteristic, time implicitly becomes the second variable. Relations among more than two variables are considered in Chapter 12.

Observations on two variables recorded for individual sampling units are called bivariate data.

Bivariate data: Measurements on two variables for each sampling unit

---

Both characteristics observed may be qualitative traits (categorical variables), in which case the data are ordinarily counts or frequencies. Both characteristics may be quantitative variables, in which case the data are pairs of (usually) continuous measurements. Or one characteristic may be qualitative and the other quantitative.

Although we introduce a variety of displays and numerical summaries in the sections that follow, we concentrate on those that measure linear association or describe straight-line relations between two variables. Procedures that focus on straight-line relations between two variables are among the most useful statistical tools and are part of a collection of methods collectively labeled regression and correlation.

A study of data on two (or more) variables is often accompanied by a discussion of whether there is a **cause-and-effect relation** between the variables. For example, business people like to think that increased advertising expenditures (potential cause) lead to increased sales (potential effect). Data on sales and advertising expenditures, which are closely linked, tend to support this assertion, but is the situation more complex? Are there other variables that affect both sales and advertising? In fact, do sales respond to advertising expenditures or is the reverse true? That is, are advertising expenditures determined by previous sales? Answers to these questions provide a framework for making decisions about the magnitudes, durations, and mix of advertising expenditure levels. We will encounter other situations where it is natural to think in terms of a cause-and-effect relation as we work through the examples in this chapter.

In studying the relation between two variables, we distinguish between the response variable and the **predictor** or **explanatory variable.**

Response variable: The variable that measures the outcome of a study

Predictor variable: The variable that attempts to explain the response variable

---

In some cases, several predictor or explanatory variables may be used to explain a response variable.

In the previous advertising–sales example, sales is ordinarily the response variable and advertising expenditures is the predictor variable. On the other hand, if the study is one that attempts to link current advertising expenditures with previous sales, then advertising expenditures is the response variable and previous sales is the predictor variable.

As you may recall from our discussion of enumerative and analytic studies, there is a difference between investigations that are focused on a particular time period and those that are focused on a sequence of time periods—not unlike the distinction between a snapshot and a moving picture. Enumerative studies are more like snapshots, and analytic studies are more like moving pictures. To review, data gathered on different sampling units at a particular point in time are called **cross-sectional data.** Data accumulated over a sequence of (usually) equally spaced time periods are called **longitudinal** or **time series data.**

The most effective cross-sectional studies of cause-and-effect between two (or more) variables depend on direct management intervention and planned experimentation to improve process performance. Studies based on planned experimentation often allow us to readily sort out the relations among variables. In many situations, however, experimentation is not feasible and we must be content with recording "happenstance data"—that is, data that are passively observed. In these latter cases, determining cause-and-effect relationships is more difficult.

Similarly, most longitudinal data (such as quarterly earnings, monthly sales, or annual personnel turnover) result, at least in part, from general economic factors beyond the control of any individual company. In this sense, time series data arising in the course of business are not ordinarily the result of planned experimentation and are passively observed.

Observations collected over time on a single variable are often related. For example, market share this period is related to market share next period. Consequently, we devote some discussion to understanding data on a single variable in a longitudinal context. Many of the methods for detecting and measuring the association between two variables can be used, with minor modification, to detect and measure the association within a single time-ordered variable.

Our focus in this chapter is on association and two-variable relationships. We begin with two variables in a cross-sectional context.

3.2 SCATTERPLOTS

Consider two variables, each measured on a numerical scale. For reference, we label one variable X and the other variable Y. Ordinarily, Y is the response variable and X is the explanatory variable. Two numerical observations (x, y) are recorded for each sampling unit; x is a value for the variable X, and y is a value for the variable Y. The observations are *paired* in the sense that an (x, y) pair arises from the same sampling unit. An x observation from one pair and an x or y from another pair are unrelated. For n sampling units, we can write the bivariate observations as $(x_1, y_1), (x_2, y_2), \ldots, (x_n, y_n)$.

If we disregard the y measurements, the x measurements alone constitute the data set for one variable. The methods of Chapter 2, including plots depicting the pattern of variation and numerical summary measures, can be used to describe these measurements. Similarly, the y measurements can be studied while ignoring the x measurements. However, the purpose of collecting bivariate observations is to answer such questions as:

Are the variables related?

If so, is it a cause-and-effect relation?

What is the nature of the relationship indicated by the data?

Can we quantify the strength of the relation?

Can we predict one variable from the other?

Studying the x measurements by themselves or the y measurements by themselves would not help us answer these questions.

As we stated in Chapter 2, an important first step in examining data is to plot them. With bivariate data, we create a plot by regarding the horizontal axis as the explanatory variable X and the vertical axis as the response variable Y in a two-dimensional coordinate system. The pairs of observations (x, y) are then plotted as points on the graph.

Scatterplot: A graph of the bivariate observations (x, y)

The scatterplot provides a visual impression of the relation between the X and Y variables. If the points cluster along a line, a linear relation is indicated. Points that band around a curve indicate a curvilinear relation. If the points form a patternless cluster, no relation among the variables is indicated.

EXAMPLE 3.1   Constructing and Interpreting a Scatterplot

Total revenue (millions of dollars) and operating income (millions of dollars) for the $n = 21$ teams in the National Hockey League (NHL) for the 1990–1991 season can be determined from the data given in Table 7, Appendix C. Suppose we believe that total revenue determines or explains, to a large extent, operating income. Plot these pairs of observations as a scatterplot.

Solution and Discussion.   The scatterplot of total revenue and operating income for the NHL teams is shown in Figure 3.1. Since we have identified total revenue as the explanatory variable, the X variable, and operating income as the response or Y variable, values of total revenue are plotted along the horizontal axis, and the corresponding values of operating income are plotted along the vertical axis.

The points in the scatterplot tend to increase in a linear fashion, although the points do not lie exactly along a straight line. Not unexpectedly, low values of total revenue tend to be paired with low values of operating income, and high values of total revenue occur with high values of operating income. When this happens, we say there is a positive association or positive relation between the two variables. As an

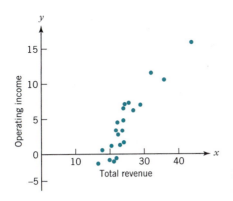

Figure 3.1 Scatterplot of Operating Income and Total Revenue

aside, we see that some of the operating income numbers are negative, suggesting that operating expenses exceeded income during this season for some of the teams.

Two variables are *positively associated* when below-the-mean values of one variable tend to occur with below-the-mean values of the other variable and, likewise, above-the-mean values tend to occur together. Two variables are *negatively associated* when above-the-mean values of one variable tend to accompany below-the-mean values of the other variable and vice versa.

In addition to providing a graphical description of the association between two variables, scatterplots often reveal information that is not evident from looking at the numbers themselves. The next two examples illustrate this point.

EXAMPLE 3.2   Scatterplot Illustrating a Linear Relation with Increasing Variation

We encountered the actual costs (millions of dollars) for $n = 26$ construction projects in Example 2.13. These costs along with the corresponding estimated costs, as determined by engineering calculations, are given in Table 3.1. Plot the bivariate construction cost data as a scatterplot.

TABLE 3.1   Construction Costs

Estimated Cost	Actual Cost	Estimated Cost	Actual Cost
.575	.918	8.947	13.371
6.127	7.214	3.157	1.553
11.215	14.577	3.540	4.069
28.195	30.028	37.400	27.973
30.100	38.173	7.650	7.642
21.091	15.320	13.700	3.692
8.659	14.837	29.003	29.522
40.630	51.284	14.639	15.317
37.800	34.100	5.292	5.292
1.803	2.003	.960	.707
18.048	20.099	1.240	1.246
8.102	4.324	1.419	1.143
10.730	10.523	38.936	21.571

Solution and Discussion. Let the explanatory variable, X, be estimated cost and the response variable, Y, be actual cost. The (x, y) values are graphed as a scatterplot in Figure 3.2, with the horizontal axis representing estimated cost and the vertical axis representing actual cost. For example, the first point to be plotted is $(x_1, y_1) = (.575, .918)$. Again, the southwest to northeast pattern of the points indicates a positive association between estimated cost and actual cost; that is, (relatively) high estimated costs tend to occur with (relatively) high actual costs, and (relatively) low estimated costs with (relatively) low actual costs.

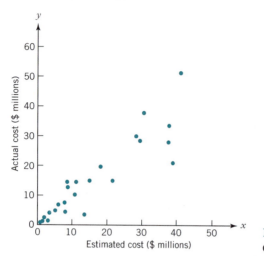

Figure 3.2 Scatterplot of Construction Costs

If the engineers could explain (predict) construction costs with no error, the estimated cost would equal the actual cost for each project and all the points would lie along the 45° line through the origin. Notice that the points in the scatterplot "fan out" as the values increase. The points corresponding to small projects are more tightly banded about the 45° line than the points corresponding to big (expensive) projects. The deviation (difference) of actual cost from estimated cost appears to increase with the size of the project. The engineers typically come close to determining the costs of smaller projects. They are less successful with the larger ones.

EXAMPLE 3.3   **Scatterplot with Two Distinct Sets of Points**

The strengths measured in the cross and in the machine directions for $n = 41$ pieces of paper used to construct mailing tubes are given in Table 6, Appendix C. Plot these data as a scatterplot.

Solution and Discussion.   In this case, the choice of an explanatory variable and a response variable is arbitrary. The scatterplot of the paper strengths is shown in Figure 3.3, with the horizontal axis representing strength in the cross direction X and the vertical axis representing strength in the machine direction Y.

This scatterplot is interesting. First, there are two distinct clusters of points. The 11 points in the lower left portion of the diagram are the strength measurements for units of "old" paper. The 30 points in the upper right portion of the diagram are the strength measurements for units of "new" paper. Second, all the points taken together exhibit positive association. In general, (relatively) small cross-direction strength occurs with

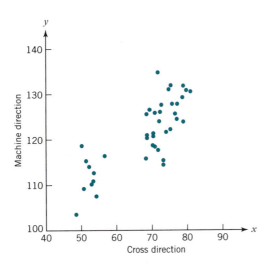

Figure 3.3   Scatterplot of Paper Strengths

(relatively) small machine-direction strength, and large cross-direction strength occurs with large machine-direction strength.

At issue is whether the relatively strong positive association indicated by all the points is maintained within each of the clusters. If not, how do we interpret the apparent positive relation between cross-direction strength and machine-direction strength? We will explore the nature of the association within each of the two clusters and continue our discussion of the scatterplot in Figure 3.3 in Example 3.5.

These examples have all indicated a positive relation between two variables. Of course, two variables may be negatively related—one increases while the other decreases—or they may not be related at all. We now turn to a numerical measure of the strength and direction of the association between two variables.

3.3   THE CORRELATION COEFFICIENT—A MEASURE OF LINEAR RELATION

The scatterplot gives a visual impression of the relation between the x and y values in a bivariate data set. In many cases, the points appear to cluster around a straight line. A numerical measure of the closeness of the scatter to a straight line is provided by the sample correlation coefficient.

The **sample correlation coefficient,** denoted by r, is a measure of the strength of the linear relation between the X and Y variables. The manner in which the correlation coefficient assesses the strength of the linear relation is summarized as follows:

1.   The value of r is always between -1 and $+1$.

2.   The magnitude of r indicates the strength of the linear relation, and its sign indicates the direction. In particular,

$r > 0$ if the pattern of (x, y) values is a band that runs from lower left to upper right

$r < 0$ if the pattern of (x, y) values is a band that runs from upper left to lower right

$r = +1$ if all (x, y) values lie exactly on a straight line with a positive slope (perfect positive linear relation)

$r = -1$ if all (x, y) values lie exactly on a straight line with a negative slope (perfect negative linear relation)

3. A value of r close to -1 or $+1$ represents a strong linear relation.

4. A value of r close to 0 means that the linear relation is very weak.

It is a good idea to interpret r in conjunction with a scatterplot of the bivariate data. If there is no visible relation, that is, if the y values do not change in any direction as the x values change, then r will be close to 0. Also, a value of r near 0 can occur if the scatterplot points band around a curve that is far from linear. These situations, and others, are illustrated in Figure 3.4. *Keep in mind that the correlation coefficient is a measure of a linear or straight-line relation.* A value of r close to 0 indicates the absence of a linear relation, but it does not necessarily indicate the absence of a relation of any kind.

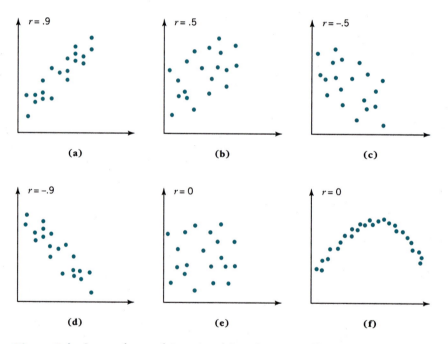

Figure 3.4   Scatterplots and Associated Correlation Coefficients

Figure 3.4 illustrates the correspondence between scatter diagram patterns and the value of r. Notice that (e) and (f) correspond to situations where $r = 0$. The zero correlation in (e) is due to an absence of any relation between X and Y. The zero correlation in (f) is due to a relation that is quite strong but far from linear.

CALCULATION OF r

The correlation coefficient can be expressed in several ways. We give one version here; other versions are given in Exercises 3.8 and 3.9.

In words,

$$\text{Sample correlation} = \frac{\text{Sample covariance}}{(\text{Sample std. dev. of } x)(\text{Sample std. dev. of } y)}$$

The **sample covariance**

$$s_{xy} = \frac{1}{n-1} \sum_{i=1}^{n} (x_i - \overline{x})(y_i - \overline{y})$$

is also a measure of linear association, but its value is unrestricted. This makes the sample covariance difficult to interpret. Dividing the covariance by the product (standard deviation of x) × (standard deviation of y) creates a coefficient that lies between -1 and 1.* The sample correlation coefficient is just the sample covariance of the pairs of standardized observations $(x_i - \overline{x})/(\text{std. dev. of } x)$ and $(y_i - \overline{y})/(\text{std. dev. of } y)$. Because the standardized observations are free of the measurement scale, so is the correlation coefficient.

Substituting the algebraic formulas for the covariance and the standard deviations of x and y, and performing a little manipulation, we get

---

Sample correlation coefficient: $r = \dfrac{S_{xy}}{\sqrt{S_{xx}}\sqrt{S_{yy}}}$

---

where, with n pairs of observations $(x_1, y_1), \ldots, (x_n, y_n)$,

$$S_{xy} = \sum_{i=1}^{n} (x_i - \overline{x})(y_i - \overline{y})$$

$$S_{xx} = \sum_{i=1}^{n} (x_i - \overline{x})^2$$

$$S_{yy} = \sum_{i=1}^{n} (y_i - \overline{y})^2$$

The quantities S_{xx} and S_{yy} are, respectively, the sums of squared deviations of the x observations and the y observations from their sample means. S_{xy} is the sum of the cross-products of the x deviations with the y deviations.

S_{xx} and S_{yy} are always positive. S_{xy} or, equivalently, the sample covariance, determines the sign of r. When x values below their mean tend to be paired with y values above their mean or vice versa, S_{xy}, and hence r, will be negative. When x values below their mean tend to be paired with y values below their mean, and when x values above their mean tend to be paired with y values above their mean, S_{xy}, and hence r, will be positive.

---

*The proof of this assertion is beyond the scope of this book.

When n is small or moderate, the value of r can be influenced significantly by one or two extreme bivariate observations (see Exercise 3.13). Because of this phenomenon, we say that the correlation coefficient r is not a resistant measure of linear association.

EXAMPLE 3.4   Calculation and Interpretation of r

A commodities trader contacted a midwest supplier of field corn seed to learn about demand. The supplier provided the average price per bushel (in dollars) and the number of bushels sold (in thousands) for an eight-year period. The data follow:

Price (x) per bushel	Sales (y) per year
1.25	125
1.75	105
2.25	65
2.00	85
2.50	75
2.25	80
2.70	50
2.50	55

Determine the sample correlation coefficient, r, and interpret this quantity.

Solution and Discussion.   The following table displays the numbers required for the calculation of r.

	x	y	$x - \bar{x}$	$y - \bar{y}$	$(x - \bar{x})^2$	$(y - \bar{y})^2$	$(x - \bar{x})(y - \bar{y})$
	1.25	125	$-.90$	45	.8100	2025	-40.50
	1.75	105	$-.40$	25	.1600	625	-10.00
	2.25	65	.10	-15	.0100	225	-1.50
	2.00	85	$-.15$	5	.0225	25	$-.75$
	2.50	75	.35	-5	.1225	25	-1.75
	2.25	80	.10	0	.0100	0	0
	2.70	50	.55	-30	.3025	900	-16.50
	2.50	55	.35	-25	.1225	625	-8.75
Total	17.20	640	0	0	1.560	4450	-79.75
	$\bar{x} = 2.15$	$\bar{y} = 80$			S_{xx}	S_{yy}	S_{xy}

Consequently,

$$r = \frac{S_{xy}}{\sqrt{S_{xx}}\sqrt{S_{yy}}} = \frac{-79.75}{\sqrt{1.56}\sqrt{4450}} = -.957$$

The value of r is close to -1. This means that the linear association is very strong and, in particular, the (x, y) values lie nearly along a line with a negative slope. For this data set, as the price per bushel increases, the sales tend to decrease in a linear fashion.

The correlation coefficient r measures the strength of the linear relation for two quantitative variables. Moreover, it was natural, in Example 3.4, to label sales as the response variable (Y) and price as the explanatory variable (X) since a change in price is expected to produce a change in sales. The correlation coefficient, however, does not distinguish between response and explanatory variables.

When calculating r, the choice of the X variable and, hence, the Y variable is arbitrary. The correlation coefficient measures linear association and has nothing directly to say about cause-and-effect.

EXAMPLE 3.5   Calculating r for Sets of Observations

Figure 3.3 on page 105 is a scatterplot of strength in the cross direction and strength in the machine direction for $n = 41$ pieces of paper. Recall that 11 of the paper pieces were older than the others. Calculate r using all the data, the data for the old paper, and the data for the new paper, respectively. Interpret the three correlation coefficients.

Solution and Discussion.   The data in Table 6, Appendix C, and a computer program were used to produce the following results.

Data	r
All paper ($n = 41$)	.81
Old paper ($n = 11$)	.29
New paper ($n = 30$)	.50

The two clusters of points that are located on a southwest to northeast diagonal in Figure 3.3 are responsible for the large positive value $r = .81$. When the clusters are examined individually, the correlation coefficient declines dramatically. The strength measurements for the new paper still exhibit a fairly large positive linear association. However, the smaller correlation coefficient for old paper strengths suggests that this positive linear relation weakens as the paper ages and its strength deteriorates. That is, for old paper, there is not much evidence that the two strength measurements are linearly related.

The clusters of points in Figure 3.3 represent samples from two different populations: old paper strengths and new paper strengths. As we have seen, the nature of the linear relation is different for the two types of paper. Consequently, it is inappropriate and misleading to calculate a correlation coefficient for the entire set of bivariate observations. Faced with distinct clusters like the ones in Figure 3.3, it is best to try to determine the underlying reason for the separation. If the two (or more) sets of points are fundamentally different in some way, linear association should be examined within individual clusters.

AUTOCORRELATION (OPTIONAL)

By their very nature, longitudinal data typically have characteristics that are not present in cross-sectional data. For example, observations of a variable that are close together in time tend to be related. We expect today's stock price to be similar to yesterday's price, but it may be substantially different from the price a year ago. The tendency for successive observations to be related is called autocorrelation. Many, but not all, time-ordered sequences are autocorrelated, and this property can often be used to develop meaningful forecasts of future observations. We discuss forecasting methods in Chapters 11 and 12.

> **Autocorrelation** measures association *within* a particular chronological sequence of observations.

Autocorrelation is often manifested in patterns that appear in plots of time series. Regardless of the general economy, we expect the sales of fireworks to be relatively large each July in the United States and France because of Independence Day activities. A plot of monthly U.S. fireworks sales would exhibit July sales peaks whose values are somewhat larger than those of the surrounding months. *Searching for patterns is an integral part of analyzing time series data*. A pattern that indicates a steady increase or a steady decrease over time is called a **trend.** A wavelike pattern that may repeat itself several times over a period of years is called a **cycle.** A pattern, like firework sales, that repeats itself over a shorter period, for example, annually, is called a **seasonal component** (see Chapter 12).

Figure 3.5 contains a time sequence or time series plot of the number of workers employed in what the state of Wisconsin calls Food and Kindred Products. The data are monthly employment figures (in thousands) for a period of several years (see Table 8, Appendix C). It is clear from this plot that food products employment is remarkably periodic and stable, although there is a slight upward drift at the end of the series. In Wisconsin, work in the food industry is very seasonal, reaching a yearly

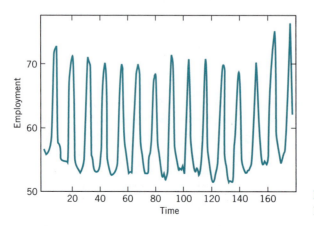

Figure 3.5 Employment in Food and Kindred Products

peak with the summer harvest and canning activities. We say this series exhibits a *seasonal component,* that is, a pattern connected with the seasons that repeats itself, in this case, year after year.

If someone told you, for example, the July employment number for people who produce food products, you would also have a pretty good idea of what the August value is going to be. It would be close to the July figure. Similarly, if you knew the January number, you would be able to make a reasonable guess at the February number. It should be close to the January value. Moreover, all the July numbers tend to be similar and so forth. The food products employment series is *autocorrelated.*

Autocorrelation occurs when time sequence observations a fixed number of time periods apart are linearly related. Let y_t denote an observation in a time sequence. We use the subscript t to denote time; for example, y_1 indicates the first or earliest observation. The pair (y_{t-1}, y_t) indicates the observation at time $t-1$ and the next observation at time t. The pair (y_{t-12}, y_t) indicates the observation at time $t-12$ and the observation 12 periods later at time t. In this way, we can create pairs of observations from a single time series and examine a linear association in the same way that we would if we had pairs of observations on two variables, X and Y.

Figure 3.6 contains a scatterplot of the (y_{t-1}, y_t) pairs for the employment series. For example, from Table 8, Appendix C, we see that $(y_1, y_2) = (56.3, 55.7)$, $(y_2, y_3) = (55.7, 55.8)$, and so forth. In the scatterplot, the y_{t-1} values are plotted along the horizontal or x-axis and the y_t values are plotted along the vertical or y-axis.

The scatterplot in Figure 3.6 has a positive orientation. The correlation coefficient for the pairs of observations 1 month apart is $r_1 = .77$. The subscript on the correlation coefficient indicates the *lag* or number of time periods separating the observations in each pair. It is called the lag 1 **sample autocorrelation coefficient.**

In the same manner, we might examine the linear association between observations separated by 12 time periods. The correlation coefficient constructed from the pairs (y_{t-12}, y_t) is denoted by r_{12} and is called the lag 12 sample autocorrelation coefficient. In general, the lag k sample autocorrelation coefficient is denoted by r_k. Sample autocorrelation coefficients are ordinarily calculated for all lags $0 < k \leq \frac{n}{4}$. For our purposes, we shall rarely calculate autocorrelation coefficients beyond the first few lags unless there is a seasonal pattern in the time series. Sample autocorrelations can be computed using the following formula.

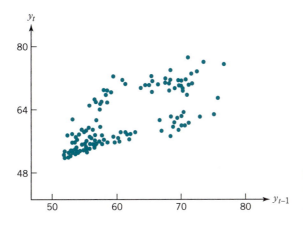

Figure 3.6 Scatterplot of Pairs of Consecutive Employment Observations

> **Sample autocorrelation coefficient:** $r_k = \dfrac{\sum_{i=1}^{n-k}(y_i - \bar{y})(y_{i+k} - \bar{y})}{\sum_{i=1}^{n}(y_i - \bar{y})^2}$

The sample autocorrelations help in the development of models that allow us to forecast future values of the time series.

EXAMPLE 3.6   Determining a Sample Autocorrelation

Using the employment data, plot the pairs of observations (y_{t-12}, y_t) as a scatterplot. Calculate the sample autocorrelation r_{12}.

Solution and Discussion.   To construct the scatterplot we need to create the pairs of observations (y_{t-12}, y_t). Using Table 8, Appendix C, we have, for example, $(y_1, y_{13}) = (56.3, 55.3), (y_2, y_{14}) = (55.7, 54.9), (y_3, y_{15}) = (55.8, 54.9)$, and so forth. The scatterplot with $x = y_{t-12}$ and $y = y_t$ is shown in Figure 3.7.

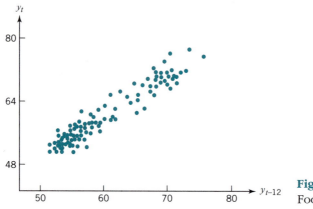

Figure 3.7   Scatterplot of (y_{t-12}, y_t), Food and Kindred Products Data

The lag 12 sample autocorrelation coefficient is $r_{12} = .88$. As we suspected from a plot of the employment series, observations 12 months apart are highly positively correlated. If employment this January is relatively small, employment next January will be relatively small. July numbers tend to be large and so forth.

As we have pointed out, correlation patterns are useful for designing models that describe linkages between variables or between, in the case of autocorrelation, observations of a single variable at different time points. These models can then be used for various purposes. Often they are used with current data to predict future observations. We discuss some of these models in later chapters of this book.

CORRELATION AND CAUSATION

Large correlations calculated from happenstance data—that is, data that are routinely recorded and not the result of planned experimentation—do not necessarily signify a causal relation between two variables.

We are all aware of "strange" or "nonsense" correlations. The large positive correlation between teachers' salaries and liquor sales, the large negative correlation between divorce rates and death rates, and so forth. The correlations are real, but the interpretations of the correlations are nonsense. Do teachers routinely spend their salary increases on liquor? Can we conclude that divorce necessarily lengthens one's life?

Observed correlations, like the ones just described, are often the result of another variable, sometimes called a lurking variable. A **lurking variable**[*] is a variable that was not included in the initial study but does affect both the measured variables. Economic growth over a period of several years might lead to both higher teacher salaries and larger liquor sales, resulting in the positive linear relation between teacher salaries and liquor sales.

Age may be the lurking variable in the second example of nonsense correlation. In the United States, older couples tend to have lower divorce rates and higher death rates. Younger couples tend to have higher divorce rates and lower death rates. A mixture of observations for old couples and young couples could easily result in the strong negative correlation observed between divorce rates and death rates.

According to Mosteller and Tukey,[†] to establish cause, we must establish *consistency, responsiveness,* and *mechanism.* For our purposes, a variable, X, is a *cause* of a variable, Y, if a change in X is always accompanied by a change in Y (responsiveness), and the manner in which these changes take place (mechanism) remains the same for a variety of contexts (consistency). Notice that a change in X precedes a change in Y.

As the next example illustrates, care must be exercised in attributing cause-and-effect relationships to variables that appear to be associated over time.

EXAMPLE 3.7 Correlation Due to Lurking Variables

A scatterplot of the total federal debt versus the number of golfers in the United States is shown in Figure 3.8(a). This diagram shows a strong correlation, with r greater than

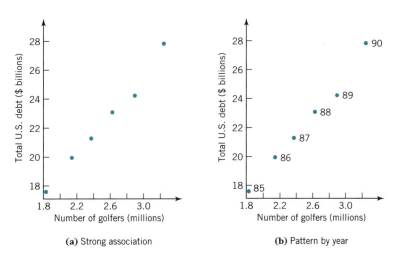

(a) Strong association

(b) Pattern by year

Figure 3.8 A Scatterplot of U.S. Debt and Number of Golfers

---

[*]The term *lurking variable* is attributed to Dr. G. E. P. Box.
[†]Mosteller, F., and Tukey, J. W. *Data Analysis and Regression.* Reading, Mass.: Addison-Wesley, 1977.

.99. Would cutting the number of golfers by taxing them or making the sport illegal reduce the federal debt? Comment.

Solution and Discussion. We observe a strong association, but common sense suggests that there is no cause-and-effect relation between the federal debt and the number of golfers. In Figure 3.8(b) we have repeated the scatter diagram but have labeled each point according to the year. For example, 86 stands for 1986 and so on. The years march up the points from the lower left to the upper right of the diagram. Many things change over the course of a year, and the year is just a stand-in, or proxy, for all of them.

Adding the year notation to the points makes it clear that other variables are leading to the observed association. Such a graph can help discredit claims of causal relations. However, if the years had been scrambled along the curve represented by the points, then a causal relation might be indicated.

Ideally, to establish cause, we must examine the behavior of X and Y in an environment that excludes the influences of all other factors (isolation). In the real world, this ideal is unobtainable, and the closest we can come is to attempt to control or mitigate the effects of extraneous variables. This is best accomplished through carefully planned experiments. Unfortunately, opportunities to carry out designed experiments in business are rare, and we must often be content with data that are passively observed, not actively generated. This condition makes establishing a cause-and-effect relationship difficult.

EXERCISES

3.1 Would you expect a positive, negative, or nearly zero correlation between the following pairs of variables? Discuss.

a. The number of import cars sold in the United States and the number of business school graduates for the years 1970, 1975, 1980, 1985, 1990, and 1995

b. The number of luxury car sales and the number of certified public accountants for cities of differing sizes in a given year

c. The number of sales persons and the total dollar amount of real estate sold during a year for real estate firms of various sizes in a large metropolitan area

d. The number of felonies and the number of persons in upper management positions for cities of differing sizes in a given year

3.2 Refer to Exercise 3.1. Either specify the nature of the causal relation or suggest a lurking variable responsible for the likely nonzero correlation in parts **a–d.**

3.3 Data consisting of five pairs of observations are displayed in the first two columns in the following table.

x	y	$x - \bar{x}$	$y - \bar{y}$	$(x - \bar{x})^2$	$(y - \bar{y})^2$	$(x - \bar{x})(y - \bar{y})$
0	7					
1	4					
6	1					
3	3					
5	0					

a.   Construct a scatter diagram.

b.   Guess the sign and value of the correlation coefficient.

c.   Complete the table and calculate the correlation coefficient.

3.4   Consider the following data set:

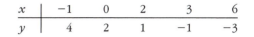

x	−1	0	2	3	6
y	4	2	1	−1	−3

a.   Construct a scatterplot.

b.   Guess the sign and value of the correlation coefficient.

c.   Calculate the correlation coefficient.

3.5   Plot the scatter diagram for the following data, and calculate the correlation coefficient.

x	−2	4	1	7	0
y	−1	3	0	5	3

3.6   A selection of four receipts from a university bookstore provided, among other things, the number of books sold and the total dollar amount for each sale. The data are given in the table.

x (number of books)	4	5	4	3
y (dollar sales)	142	152	148	158

a.   Plot the data as a scatterplot, and calculate the correlation coefficient.

b.   Let $\tilde{y} = y/100$, so that dollar sales is expressed in hundreds of dollars. Notice that $\tilde{y}$ is a linear transformation of y. Calculate the correlation coefficient between x and $\tilde{y}$. [The first $(x, \tilde{y})$ pair is $(4, 1.42)$ and so forth.] Is the result surprising?

3.7   A morning newspaper lists the following used car prices for a particular model Japanese car with age x in years and asking price y in thousands of dollars.

x (age)	2	2	11	8	6	5	2	11	4	5	3	3
y (price)	10	5.8	1.8	2.2	2.8	3.5	9.4	1.1	4.5	7	8.5	13

a.   Plot these data as a scatterplot, and guess the value of the correlation coefficient.

b.   Calculate the means, $\bar{x}$, $\bar{y}$, the standard deviations, s_x, s_y, and the correlation coefficient, r.

3.8   Refer to Exercise 3.7. Construct the standardized observations, $\tilde{x}_i = (x_i - \bar{x})/s_x$ and $\tilde{y}_i = (y_i - \bar{y})/s_y$. Verify that the sample correlation coefficient can be written

$$r = \frac{1}{n-1} \sum_{i=1}^{n} \tilde{x}_i \tilde{y}_i = \frac{1}{n-1} \sum_{i=1}^{n} \left(\frac{x_i - \bar{x}}{s_x} \right) \left(\frac{y_i - \bar{y}}{s_y} \right)$$

where n is the number of observations and s_x and s_y are the sample standard deviations of the x's and y's, respectively.

3.9   It is often convenient to use the alternative "computing formulas" for S_{xx}, S_{yy}, and S_{xy} when determining r:

$$S_{xx} = \sum_{i=1}^{n} x^2 - \frac{(\sum_{i=1}^{n} x)^2}{n}$$

$$S_{yy} = \sum_{i=1}^{n} y^2 - \frac{(\sum_{i=1}^{n} y)^2}{n}$$

$$S_{xy} = \sum_{i=1}^{n} xy - \frac{(\sum_{i=1}^{n} x)(\sum_{i=1}^{n} y)}{n}$$

Calculate r using the data in Example 3.4 and the computing formulas for S_{xx}, S_{yy}, and S_{xy}. Compare the result with the value for r in Example 3.4.

3.10   Let $\tilde{x} = a + bx$ and $\tilde{y} = c + dy$ be linear transformations of x and y, respectively. Show that linear transformations of x and y do not change the value of the correlation coefficient provided the constants b and d have the same sign. (Refer to Exercise 3.6 for a numerical example.) What happens to the value of r if b and d have opposite signs?

3.11   The *London Economist* reported that there is an inverse relation between a nation's number of central bankers per capita and its Gross Domestic Product (GDP) growth rate. What does this imply about the sign of the correlation coefficient between number of central bankers and GDP growth rate? Do you believe the key to prosperity may lie in controlling (decreasing) the supply of central bankers? Suggest some lurking variables that may be responsible for the inverse relation between number of bankers and economic growth. What would you have to do to establish a cause-and-effect relation between the number of central bankers and the GDP growth rate?

3.12   The following scatterplot shows the population of Oldenberg, Germany, at the end of each year and the number of storks observed in that year. The data cover the period 1930–1936 (*Ornithologische Monatsberichte*, Vol. 44, No. 2, Jahrgang, 1936, Berlin, and Vol. 48, No. 1, Jahrgang, 1940, Berlin; and *Statistiches Jahrbuch Deutscher Gemeinden*, 27–33, Jahrgang, 1932–1938, Gustav Fischer, Jena).

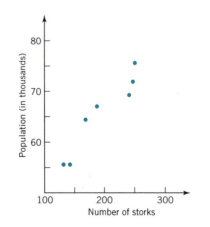

Do storks bring babies? Suggest some lurking variables that may be responsible for the positive association between the number of storks and the population of Oldenberg during this period.

3.13 The following table lists the number of employees, x, and the profits per employee, y, for $n = 16$ publishing firms (*Forbes,* April 30, 1990).

x (1000's employees)	9.4	6.3	10.7	7.4	17.1	21.2	36.8	28.5
y (1000's dollars)	33.5	31.4	25.0	23.1	14.2	11.7	10.8	10.5

x (1000's employees)	10.7	9.9	26.1	70.5*	14.8	21.3	14.6	26.8
y (1000's dollars)	9.8	9.1	8.5	8.3*	4.8	3.2	2.7	−9.5

*These observations correspond to Dun & Bradstreet.

a. Plot these data as a scatter diagram, and locate the Dun & Bradstreet data point. Calculate the correlation coefficient.

b. Remove the Dun & Bradstreet data, and calculate the correlation coefficient with the remaining $n = 15$ observations. Compare this value of r with the value of r computed in part **a.**

c. Add the data points $(60, 30)$ and $(80, 40)$ to the scatter diagram in part **a.** Calculate the correlation coefficient using the original data and the two new bivariate observations. Compare the result with the results in parts **a** and **b.** Comment on the effect of a few outlying observations on the calculation of r.

3.14 The average team salary (as determined by the owners) and the final won/lost percentage for American League East baseball teams as they were aligned in 1990 are given here.

Team	x (avg. sal. in $1000's)	y (won/lost %)
Boston Red Sox	766	54.3
Toronto Blue Jays	678	53.0
Detroit Tigers	671	48.8
Cleveland Indians	502	47.5
Baltimore Orioles	277	47.2
Milwaukee Brewers	495	45.7
New York Yankees	721	41.4

a. Plot these data as a scatter diagram, and identify the New York Yankees data point. Calculate the correlation coefficient. Discuss the association between player salary and won/loss record.

b. Repeat part **a** after removing the New York Yankees from the data. Comment on the effect of this one data point on the calculation of r.

c. Can a championship team be bought? Discuss with reference to the information in parts **a** and **b.** What must be done to establish a cause-and-effect relation (if any) between player salaries and won/loss percentage?

3.15 Match the following values of r with the correct diagrams at the top of page 118:

(a) $r = -.7$ (b) $r = .9$ (c) $r = .5$ (d) $r = 0$

[*Hint:* (d) goes with diagram (2).]

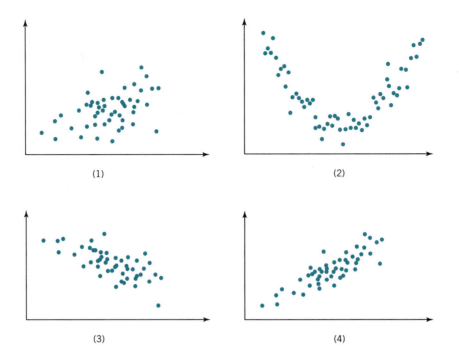

3.16 Construct scatterplots of the four data sets, and describe the four relationships implied by the diagrams. As usual, plot x on the horizontal axis and y on the vertical axis.

Data Set 1		Data Set 2		Data Set 3		Data Set 4	
x	y	x	y	x	y	x	y
10	8.04	10	9.14	10	7.46	8	6.58
8	6.95	8	8.14	8	6.77	8	5.76
13	7.58	13	8.74	13	12.74	8	7.71
9	8.81	9	8.77	9	7.11	8	8.84
11	8.33	11	9.26	11	7.81	8	8.47
14	9.96	14	8.10	14	8.84	8	7.04
6	7.24	6	6.13	6	6.08	8	5.25
4	4.26	4	3.10	4	5.39	19	12.50
12	10.84	12	9.13	12	8.15	8	5.56
7	4.82	7	7.26	7	6.42	8	7.91
5	5.68	5	4.74	5	5.73	8	6.89

SOURCE: Anscombe, F. "Graphs in statistical analysis." *The American Statistician*, Vol. 27, Feb. 1973, pp. 17–21.

3.17 The following table contains undergraduate grade point averages (GPA) and total Graduate Management Admission Test (GMAT) scores for a selection of students admitted to a graduate program in Business.

x (GPA)	3.46	3.29	3.03	3.19	3.78	3.40	3.58	3.33	3.76	3.80
y (GMAT)	690	530	630	660	590	550	560	565	650	520

x (GPA)	3.37	3.60	3.26	3.38	3.50	3.47	2.96	3.59	3.35	3.44
y (GMAT)	560	610	660	605	570	550	600	590	520	690

a. Plot these data as a scatter diagram, and calculate the correlation coefficient.

b. We might expect a reasonably strong positive association between the grade point average and the GMAT score for students admitted to a graduate program. Do you think this association is present in the grade point averages and test scores for students who applied but were not admitted to the graduate program? Discuss.

c. Of course, the real issue is whether the undergraduate grade point average and GMAT score are predictors of success in the graduate business program. Identify variables that could be plotted against GPA or GMAT scores that may begin to address this issue.

3.18 (*Optional*) (*Minitab or similar program recommended*) The following table contains the S&P 500 Index monthly rates of return (expressed as percentages) for the years 1988–1991. The data are listed chronologically in columns. Notice the first rate of return is for February 1988.

S&P500RR

	1988	1989	1990	1991
Jan.		6.87	−7.13	4.07
Feb.	4.10	−2.94	.85	6.51
Mar.	−3.39	2.06	2.40	2.20
Apr.	.94	4.89	−2.73	.03
May	.32	3.45	8.80	3.79
June	4.23	−.80	−.89	−4.91
July	−.54	8.47	−.52	4.39
Aug.	−3.94	1.54	−9.91	1.95
Sept.	3.90	−.66	−5.25	−1.93
Oct.	2.56	−2.55	−.67	1.18
Nov.	−1.91	1.64	5.82	−4.49
Dec.	1.46	2.12	2.45	10.58

a. Let y_t denote the rate of return at time t. Construct the observation pairs (y_{t-1}, y_t). For example, the first pair is $(y_1, y_2) = (4.10, -3.39)$, the second pair is $(y_2, y_3) = (-3.39, .94)$, and so forth. Plot these observation pairs as a scatter diagram with y_{t-1} plotted along the x-axis and y_t plotted along the y-axis.

b. Calculate the lag 1 autocorrelation coefficient using the formula for the sample correlation coefficient r with $x = y_{t-1}$ and $y = y_t$. Interpret the result.

3.19 (*Optional*) (*Minitab or similar program recommended*) The autocorrelation function (ACF) for lags 1 through 12 for the food products data in Figure 3.5 is given at the top of page 120. The employment data are in a column labeled C1.

WiscEmpl.dat

a. Compare the values for r_1 and r_{12} with those in the text. (See Example 3.6 and the discussion preceding it.)

b. Using statistical software, compute r as in Exercise 3.18b, then compute r_1. Compare the values of r and r_1. The difference in numerical values is due to the slightly different formulas used to calculate the correlation coefficient and the lag 1 autocorrelation coefficient.

```
ACF of C1

            -1.0 -0.8 -0.6 -0.4 -0.2   0.0   0.2   0.4   0.6   0.8   1.0
            +----+----+----+----+----+----+----+----+----+----+----+
   1    0.773                                 XXXXXXXXXXXXXXXXXXXXX
   2    0.325                                 XXXXXXXXX
   3   -0.115                           XXXX
   4   -0.384                  XXXXXXXXXXX
   5   -0.522              XXXXXXXXXXXXXX
   6   -0.564              XXXXXXXXXXXXXXX
   7   -0.518               XXXXXXXXXXXXXX
   8   -0.378                 XXXXXXXXXX
   9   -0.116                          XXXX
  10    0.288                                XXXXXXX
  11    0.691                                XXXXXXXXXXXXXXXXXX
  12    0.882                                XXXXXXXXXXXXXXXXXXXXXXX
```

MicroRad.dat

3.20 (*Minitab or similar program recommended*) The following table contains pairs of radiation measurements for $n = 42$ microwave ovens. The first measurement was obtained with the door open. The second measurement was obtained with the door closed. (See Section 2.8 and Exercise 2.61.) Suppose the microwave ovens were produced in lots of six. The mean radiation emitted through open and closed doors for ovens in a particular lot can be determined by averaging the measurements in a row in the table.

x (door open)	.30	.09	.30	.10	.10	.12
y (door closed)	.15	.09	.18	.10	.05	.12

x (door open)	.09	.10	.09	.10	.07	.05
y (door closed)	.08	.05	.08	.10	.07	.02

x (door open)	.01	.45	.12	.20	.04	.10
y (door closed)	.01	.10	.10	.10	.02	.10

x (door open)	.01	.60	.12	.10	.05	.05
y (door closed)	.01	.40	.10	.05	.03	.05

x (door open)	.15	.30	.15	.09	.09	.28
y (door closed)	.15	.10	.15	.09	.08	.18

x (door open)	.10	.10	.10	.30	.12	.25
y (door closed)	.10	.20	.11	.30	.02	.20

x (door open)	.20	.40	.33	.32	.12	.12
y (door closed)	.20	.30	.30	.40	.30	.05

a. Determine the mean radiation (to two decimal places) through open doors, $\bar{x}_1$, for the six microwave ovens in the first lot. Similarly, determine the mean radiation (to two decimal places) through closed doors, $\bar{y}_1$, for ovens in the first lot. Repeat this procedure for the six remaining lots of ovens.

b. Plot the original microwave radiation measurements as a scatter diagram. Plot the open-door data along the horizontal axis and the closed-door data along the vertical axis.

c. Plot the $n = 7$ pairs of mean radiation measurements calculated in part **a** on the scatter diagram in part **b.** Guess the magnitudes of the correlation coefficients for the original data and the mean data.

d. Calculate the correlation between open-door and closed-door radiation for the original data and for the mean data. Compare the results.

e. Discuss the statement: Correlations calculated from means or aggregates can be misleading when applied to individual cases.

3.4   FITTING STRAIGHT LINES

The correlation coefficient measures the strength of the linear association between two variables but tells us little about its nature. If two variables appear to be linearly related, it is often helpful to write down a mathematical equation (model) that describes the relationship between the variables. Such an equation allows us to predict the value of the response variable Y from a known value of the explanatory variable X. For example, given the scatterplot of construction costs in Figure 3.2, a project administrator might want to predict the actual cost of a new project using an engineer's estimate. A state of Wisconsin official may be interested in predicting next July's employment in the food industry from the employment figure for this July. A personnel supervisor may wish to predict the score of a trainee on a skill test given the length of a training program.

You can see that models help us answer *if–then* questions. *If* certain conditions apply or, equivalently, if our predictor variable has this value, *then* certain consequences follow or, equivalently, the response variable is expected to have this value. Good models allow us to examine the consequences of our actions over a range of conditions. Simple models are often gross approximations of reality, yet they can be useful. The simplest interesting model is a function whose graph is a straight line. We consider elements of this model next.

GRAPHING A STRAIGHT LINE

A straight line has the equation

$$y = a + bx$$

where y is the value of the response variable and x is the value of the explanatory variable. In a two-dimensional coordinate system, y is plotted on the vertical axis and x is plotted on the horizontal axis. The constant a is the *intercept,* the height at which the line crosses the vertical axis, and the constant b is the *slope,* the amount by which y changes if x increases by 1 unit. Figure 3.9 (page 122) illustrates these concepts.

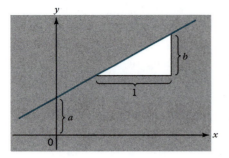

Figure 3.9   The Line $y = a + bx$

The line with equation $y = -3 + 6x$ has an intercept of -3 and a slope of 6. A graph of this line crosses the y-axis 3 units below the origin and slants upward with an inclination determined by the slope. In this case, as the x-coordinate of a point on the line increases by 1 unit, the y-coordinate increases by 6 units. This line has a much steeper inclination than, say, the $45°$ line, since the latter has a slope of 1.

The points in the scatterplots of the previous section cluster along straight lines; but it is clear we cannot pass a *straight* line through *all* the points in any of the scatter diagrams. A straight line can, however, be "fit" to the points in a scatterplot using the **method of least squares** (see Chapter 11). The fitted line is referred to as the **least squares line** and passes through the scatter such that, at the observed x values, the sum of the squares of the vertical distances of the points from the line is as small as possible.

In many cases, we could visually draw a line through the points of a scatterplot. However, different people could draw different lines. The least squares line is an objective result. Everyone using the method of least squares to determine a line through the same scatter of points will get the same line.

The least squares line is also called the *estimated regression line*. The term *regression* is attributed to Sir Francis Galton (1822–1911), who, in his studies of heredity, noticed, for example, that children of tall parents tended to be taller than average but not as tall as their parents. This "regression toward mediocrity" was interesting to Galton, and the methods he used to describe the relationship between the size of parents and the size of their progeny form a small part of what today we call regression methods—those statistical methods associated with analyzing the relationship between a response variable and explanatory variable(s).*

The data on the sales and price of field corn seed, introduced in Example 3.4, are plotted in Figure 3.10. Recall that price is an average price over the year in dollars per bushel and sales is annual sales in thousands of bushels. The data cover an eight-year period. The least squares line is also plotted.

Let x be price per bushel and y be annual sales so that (x, y) represents the coordinates of a data point in the scatterplot. The least squares line seems to characterize the scatter pretty well in the sense that the line passes through the points in a manner that is consistent with the general downward trend. Notice that some of the data points are close to the least squares line, but none of the data points fall

---

*For more about the history of regression, see Stigler, S. M. *The History of Statistics*. Cambridge, Mass.: Harvard University Press, 1986.

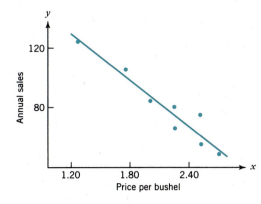

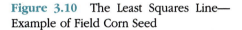

Figure 3.10 The Least Squares Line—Example of Field Corn Seed

exactly on the line. In addition, recall there are two values of price, $x = 2.25$ and $x = 2.50$, where each has two values of sales associated with it. For example, the average price was $2.25 in two different years. During one of these years, 65 thousand bushels of corn were sold; during the other year, 80 thousand bushels of corn were sold. Thus, in this case, price appears to be closely related to sales, but it does not determine sales exactly.

We distinguish between a data point with coordinates (x, y) and the corresponding point on the least squares line. For the given x, we denote the y coordinate of the point on the least squares line by $\hat{y}$. The "hat" represents a fitted or predicted value of y at x.

The least squares line in Figure 3.10 has the equation

$$\hat{y} = 189.91 - 51.12x$$

so that, for example, for the point on the least squares line at $x = 2.25$, the "fitted y" is

$$\hat{y} = 189.91 - 51.12(2.25) = 74.89$$

This value can be compared with the actual y values at $x = 2.25$ of 65 and 80. The differences between the actual y values and the corresponding fitted y values, the $\hat{y}$'s, are called the **residuals.** The residuals are the vertical distances (positive or negative) of the data points from the least squares line.

We have the identity

$$\text{Observation} = \text{Fit} + \text{Residual}$$

or, in symbols,

$$y = \hat{y} + (y - \hat{y})$$

In this context, the fit represents the overall pattern of the data, and the residuals represent the deviations from this pattern. The split into fit plus residual applies to patterns other than straight lines, and we will make use of it repeatedly throughout this book.

It is important to remember that fitted straight lines or, more generally, fitted functions, may be good representations of local behavior; that is, they may be useful over the range of the data in hand but may not be useful globally. We might be hard pressed to argue that a price of $x = 0$ (free seed corn) would yield sales of 190 thousand bushels (the y-intercept in the least squares line equation) unless this was the largest amount that could be obtained by the supplier in a year. Until we have established a cause-and-effect relation, we must treat models determined from the data as tentative specifications, subject to possible modifications as more information arises.

CALCULATION OF SLOPE AND INTERCEPT

How did we determine the least squares line in Figure 3.10? Where did the values for the slope (-51.12) and intercept (189.91) come from? Starting with the criterion of finding a line that minimizes the sum of squares of the vertical distances of the data points from the line,

$$\sum (\text{Vertical distance } y_i \text{ to line at } x_i)^2 = \sum (y_i - a - bx_i)^2$$

we use a little mathematics to yield formulas for the slope and intercept that depend only on the observations $(x_1, y_1), (x_2, y_2), \ldots, (x_n, y_n)$. These formulas are

$$
\begin{aligned}
\textbf{Slope:} \quad & b = \frac{S_{xy}}{S_{xx}} = \frac{\sum_{i=1}^{n}(x_i - \overline{x})(y_i - \overline{y})}{\sum_{i=1}^{n}(x_i - \overline{x})^2} \\
\textbf{Intercept:} \quad & a = \overline{y} - b\overline{x}
\end{aligned}
$$

Once the slope is calculated, the intercept is easily determined. The least squares line is constructed to yield the smallest sum of squared residuals.

Comparing the formula for the correlation coefficient, r, with the formula for the least squares slope coefficient, b, we have

$$b = \left(\frac{\sqrt{S_{yy}}}{\sqrt{S_{xx}}} \right) r$$

so that b is proportional to r and has the same sign. Along the least squares line, a change of 1 standard deviation in x gives a change of r standard deviations in y.

Statistical software does regression calculations quickly and reliably. In practice, we merely enter the data, manipulate them, and issue commands that ask for the required calculations, graphs, and output. We display some of the computational formulas simply to illustrate how we might proceed with small data sets and no computer. In addition, the formulas allow us to indicate the relationship between the slope coefficient and the correlation coefficient. In more complex situations, we will rely on the computer to do the arithmetic.

EXAMPLE 3.8   Calculating the Slope and Intercept of Least Squares Line

Verify the equation for the least squares line for the field corn seed data. Also, determine the sum of squares of the vertical distances of the data points from the least squares line.

Solution and Discussion.   From Example 3.4, we have

$$\bar{x} = 2.15 \quad \bar{y} = 80 \quad S_{xx} = 1.56 \quad S_{yy} = 4450 \quad S_{xy} = -79.75$$

In addition, to three decimal places, $r = -.957$. Consequently,

$$b = \frac{S_{xy}}{S_{xx}} = \frac{-79.75}{1.56} = -51.12$$

and

$$a = \bar{y} - b\bar{x} = 80 - (-51.12)2.15 = 189.91$$

Since we already calculated the correlation coefficient r, the slope of the least squares line can also be determined as

$$b = \left(\frac{\sqrt{S_{yy}}}{\sqrt{S_{xx}}}\right) r = \left(\frac{\sqrt{4450}}{\sqrt{1.56}}\right)(-.957) = -51.12$$

The equation of the least squares line is thus $\hat{y} = a + bx = 189.91 - 51.12x$.

To determine the sum of squares of the vertical distances of the data points from the least squares line, we must first determine the residuals, $y - \hat{y}$. The details are set out in the following table.

x	y	$\hat{y} = 189.91 - 51.12x$	$y - \hat{y}$	$(y - \hat{y})^2$
1.25	125	126.01	−1.01	1.02
1.75	105	100.45	4.55	20.70
2.25	65	74.89	−9.89	97.81
2.00	85	87.67	−2.67	7.13
2.50	75	62.11	12.89	166.15
2.25	80	74.89	5.11	26.11
2.70	50	51.89	−1.89	3.57
2.50	55	62.11	−7.11	50.55
Total			0	373.04

The sum of squares of the vertical distances or, equivalently, the residual sum of squares is 373.04. No other straight line will yield a smaller sum of squared deviations.

PREDICTING A NEW OBSERVATION

The least squares line can be used to predict or forecast a new observation. Suppose, in the example on field corn seed, the average price in a year is $3 per bushel. What is the best guess of annual sales? Assuming $3 per bushel is close enough to the current observations to justify extrapolating the least squares line, the predicted sales is

$$\hat{y} = 189.91 - 51.12(3) = 36.55$$

thousand bushels. This operation is illustrated geometrically in Figure 3.11. We see that a predicted y is simply obtained by evaluating the least squares equation at a specified value of x.

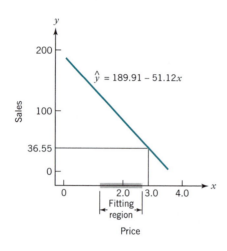

Figure 3.11 The Predicted Value at $x = 3$

The predictions we are discussing in this section are guesses of y at *new* values of x. These are conceptually different from the fitted values that are the predictions of y made at the *observed* values of x. The prediction issue arises because in business we often want to know what will happen if we try something different. That is, we want to know the likely response (sales, productivity, deposits) if we set a potential explanatory variable (amount of rebate, length of training, interest rate) at a value not previously considered.

EXAMPLE 3.9 Predicting Operating Income

A scatterplot of operating income, y, and total revenue, x, for 21 National Hockey League (NHL) teams is shown in Figure 3.1 and, again, in Figure 3.12. Fit the least squares line to these data, and predict operating income if a team expects total revenue for the current season to be 39 million dollars.

Solution and Discussion. Statistical software and the appropriate NHL data from Table 7, Appendix C, yield the least squares line with equation

$$\hat{y} = -13.13 + .70x$$

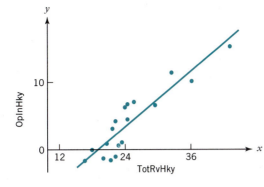

Figure 3.12 The Least Squares Line, NHL Example

This line is shown superimposed on the scatterplot in Figure 3.12. The predicted operating income, if total revenue is 39 million dollars, is

$$\hat{y} = -13.13 + .70(39) = 14.2$$

million dollars.

Notice that the intercept of the least squares line is -13.13. This suggests a loss of 13.13 million dollars of operating income when total revenue is zero. Although this figure could represent start-up commitments for a new franchise, the scenario of no revenue and an associated expenditure of operating income is unlikely. Once again, the least squares line is probably best viewed as describing the general nature of the relationship between operating income and total revenue *over the fitting region* or, equivalently, over the range of total revenue figures actually observed. Extrapolating the least squares line beyond this range may not provide accurate predictions.

EXAMPLE 3.10 Predicting Future Employment (Optional)

The state of Wisconsin food products employment data were discussed in Example 3.6. Figure 3.7 contains a scatterplot of (y_{t-12}, y_t). Let y represent the current month's employment, y_t, and let y_{t-12}, employment 12 months earlier, play the role of x. Fit the least squares line to the data (y_{t-12}, y_t) and forecast employment a year from now if this month's employment, a figure just determined, is 66.7. Can the least squares equation be used to forecast next month's employment?

Solution and Discussion. The equation of the least squares line is

$$\hat{y} = 1.21 + .98x \quad \text{or} \quad \hat{y}_t = 1.21 + .98y_{t-12}$$

To use the least squares equation to forecast a year (12 months) ahead, we set the explanatory variable equal to the current month's value (with time index t) and do the arithmetic. The value of the response variable (with time index $t + 12$) is the forecast. Consequently, if current employment is $x = y_t = 66.7$, employment a year from now is projected to be

$$\hat{y} = \hat{y}_{t+12} = 1.21 + .98(66.7) = 66.6$$

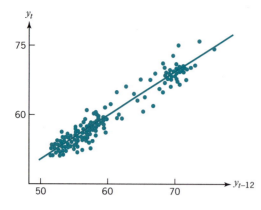

Figure 3.13 The Least Squares Line, Employment Example

thousand people. Employment for the same month a year ahead is nearly equal to the current monthly employment. This is not surprising, given the very regular periodic nature of this employment series, as shown in Figure 3.5.

The least squares line is shown on the (y_{t-12}, y_t) scatterplot in Figure 3.13. The least squares equation can be used to forecast next month's employment, y_{t+1}, since it relates employment figures 12 months apart. To predict next month's employment, we need y_{t-11}, the employment eleven months ago.

It may seem strange that our model allows for association only between employment figures 12 months apart. We might expect that this month's employment is related to last month's employment; consequently, our model should include a y_{t-1} term as well as a y_{t-12} term. This is indeed the case, but we will delay further discussion until Chapter 12 when we discuss forecasting with simple time series models.

We have assumed that the fitted line adequately describes the general nature of the relationship between the explanatory and response variables. Successful prediction does not require a causal relationship between the explanatory variable x and the response variable y. Both variables could be responding to the effects of the same unmeasured lurking variables. As long as the general (x, y) pattern continues to be well represented by a straight line, it may be possible to predict y from x even though x has no direct influence on y.

If the fitted line does not adequately describe the general nature of the relationship between x and y, then any deficiency should show up in the residuals. The residuals are the deviations from the fit; consequently, they allow us to assess how well the fit captures the pattern in the data.

EXAMINATION OF RESIDUALS

If the fit captures all the information in the data about the relationship between the explanatory variable and the response variable, then the residuals

$$y_1 - \hat{y}_1, y_2 - \hat{y}_2, \ldots, y_n - \hat{y}_n$$

should be "informationless." That is, the residuals should not contain any systematic patterns or be associated with variables either in or out of the current model. They should appear to be completely random and not related to anything. If the residuals do exhibit systematic patterns or are related to other variables, then the original model is faulty and can be improved.*

Residuals can be examined using many of the numerical summary measures and plots we have introduced previously. Ordinarily, however, we focus on one or two summary measures and a few scatterplots.

Although some residuals are positive and some negative, a property of the least squares procedure ensures that *the sum of the residuals is always zero.*[†] The residuals from the least squares lines developed in this section sum to zero. This was demonstrated numerically with the field corn seed data in the table in Example 3.8. Thus the residuals will always have a sample mean of zero.

Because the mean of the residuals is zero, their standard deviation is the square root of their sum of the squares divided by the appropriate degrees of freedom. When the residuals are deviations from a least squares line, the number of degrees of freedom is $n - 2$, two less than the number of data pairs.[‡] Denoting the standard deviation of the residuals by s, we have

Standard deviation of residuals: $\quad s = \sqrt{\dfrac{1}{n-2} \sum_{i=1}^{n} (y_i - \hat{y}_i)^2}$

The standard deviation indicates the typical size of the residuals. It can be used in conjunction with a dotplot or histogram to summarize the distribution of the residuals and to look for outliers—that is, exceptionally large deviations from the fitted straight line.

Residuals are also examined by constructing special plots called **residual plots.** Specifically, we

1. Plot the residuals against the fitted values.
2. Plot the residuals against the explanatory variable.
3. Plot the residuals against any variable suspected to affect the response.
4. Plot the residuals against time if the data are chronological.

Ideally, the points in all of these plots should appear as a horizontal band centered at zero on the vertical axis. Any deviation from a horizontal band indicates a need for adjusting the original model—in our case, a straight line—to accommodate the displayed pattern. The nature of residual plots is best illustrated with several examples.

---

*This issue is discussed in more detail in Chapter 11.

†This statement is generally true. There are cases where the residuals do not sum exactly to zero. For example, fitting a least squares line that is constrained to go through the origin (no intercept term) will produce residuals that do not sum to zero (see Exercise 3.31).

‡One degree of freedom is lost because the residuals sum to zero. Only $n - 1$ of the residuals are free to vary. This is analogous to the degrees-of-freedom argument associated with the calculation of the sample standard deviation discussed in Chapters 1 and 2. A second degree of freedom is lost because, for a least squares fit, the sum of the products of the fitted values and residuals, case by case, is zero. In general, the number of degrees of freedom associated with the residual sum of squares varies with the number of terms in the model being fit to the data. Different models fit to the same data set yield different degrees of freedom.

EXAMPLE 3.11 Plot of the Residuals Against the Explanatory Variable

The least squares line relating operating income and total revenue for 21 NHL franchises was given in Example 3.9. Plot the residuals versus the explanatory variable, total revenue, for this example.

Solution and Discussion. The residual plot is shown in Figure 3.14. A horizontal line through zero (the mean of the residuals) is drawn on the plot to serve as a baseline. The residuals should not be related to the values of total revenue and should appear to vary in a haphazard fashion about the baseline. The plot also contains two additional horizontal lines. The lines are drawn equidistant above and below zero and are spaced so they just contain all the residuals. The residuals should be spread evenly throughout the horizontal space created by the upper and lower lines. That is, the spread of the residuals at small values of x should be the same as the spread at large values of x. There should be no relationship between the size or sign of the residuals and the values of x. In this case, the residuals are fairly evenly distributed in a horizontal band. With only 21 residuals, a pattern would have to be clearly evident before we would think about modifying the original straight-line fit.

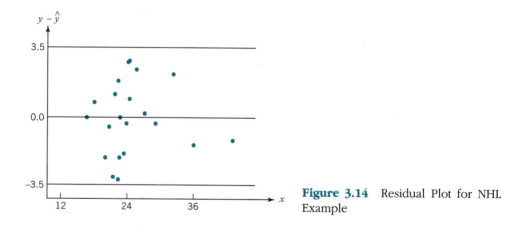

Figure 3.14 Residual Plot for NHL Example

EXAMPLE 3.12 Plot of Residuals Against the Fitted Values

Consider the "Anscombe" data sets introduced in Exercise 3.16. As we shall see in Exercise 3.37, the least squares line fit to each of the four data sets is exactly the same. For this example, we fit the least squares line to data set 2 and label the bivariate observations (x_2, y_2). The equation of the least squares line is

$$\hat{y}_2 = 3.0 + .5x_2$$

The scatterplot and the superimposed least squares line are shown in Figure 3.15. Plot the residuals versus the fitted values, $\hat{y}_2$, and interpret the result. Suggest how the original model should be modified to improve the fit.

Solution and Discussion. It is clear from the scatterplot that the least squares line does not capture the nature of the relationship between x_2 and y_2. The relationship

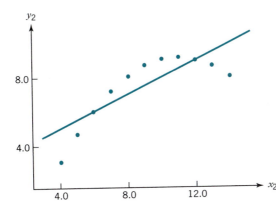

Figure 3.15 Scatterplot and Least Squares Line, Anscombe Data Set 2

is curvilinear not linear. The data points are below the line for small values of x_2 or $\hat{y}_2$, above the line for moderate values of x_2 or $\hat{y}_2$, and below the line for large values of x_2 or $\hat{y}_2$. Consequently, a plot of the residuals against either x_2 or $\hat{y}_2$ will have a curvilinear pattern: negative residuals followed by positive residuals followed by negative residuals. This pattern is clearly visible in the plot of the residuals versus the fitted values in Figure 3.16.

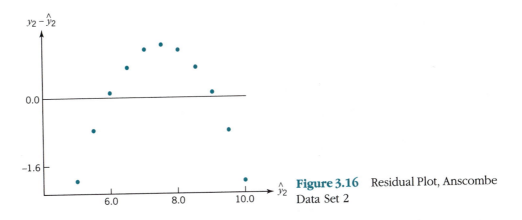

Figure 3.16 Residual Plot, Anscombe Data Set 2

The original model can be improved by adding a term to account for the curvature in the data. This can be accomplished by adding a second-order term in x_2 to the equation relating y_2 and x_2. The fitted function would then have the general form

$$\hat{y}_2 = a + bx_2 + c(x_2)^2$$

Procedures for fitting functions more general than straight lines to data are considered in Chapter 12.

EXAMPLE 3.13 Residual Plots for Time Series Data (Optional)

Examine the residuals from the model fit to the employment data. Can the original model be improved?

Solution and Discussion. Figure 3.17 is a plot of the employment residuals over time. The residuals vary about zero with no obvious pattern, although there are sequences where all the residuals are negative or all the residuals are positive. Figure 3.18 is a plot of the residuals versus the explanatory variable, y_{t-12}. Horizontal lines are drawn equidistant from the baseline. It appears that the residuals vary in a haphazard fashion within a horizontal band. There does not seem to be any association of the residuals with the explanatory variable. A plot of the residuals against the fitted values, $\hat{y}_t$, looks the same.

However, the dependence among successive residuals is not evident from these plots. As we show in Chapter 12, the dependence among the residuals can be used to improve the model.

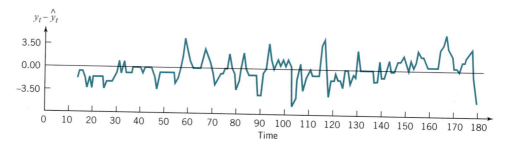
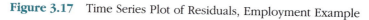

Figure 3.17   Time Series Plot of Residuals, Employment Example

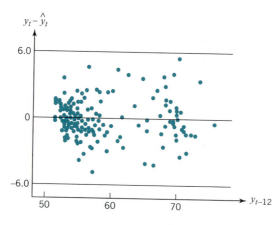

Figure 3.18   Residual Plot with Explanatory Variable, Employment Example

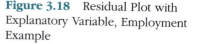

Analyzing residuals is an important part of the modeling effort. Failure to examine residuals often leads to mathematical descriptions of relationships that are, at best, inadequate and, at worst, completely misleading.

UNUSUAL AND INFLUENTIAL OBSERVATIONS

We have described outliers as unusual observations or observations far from the rest of the data. In a regression setting, outliers are individual observations that are far from the fitted straight line and, consequently, produce large residuals. They are cases that seem to be outside the general pattern.

Influential observations are those data points that significantly affect the location of the least squares line in the sense that, if they were removed, the location of the least squares line would change considerably. Sometimes influential observations are outliers and sometimes they are not. Often influential observations are points separated in the x direction from the remaining data.

Outliers and influential observations should be investigated to see why they are outside the pattern. Was there an error made in the collection of the data? If so, the errors should be corrected or the erroneous data points simply deleted.

Do the unusual cases correspond to situations that are somewhat different from that of the other observations? If so, the unusual cases may lead to new insights, and may or may not be retained in the analysis of the data.

EXAMPLE 3.14   **Effect of an Influential Observation**

Figure 3.19 is a scatterplot of Anscombe data set 3 from Exercise 3.16. The least squares line with equation

$$\hat{y}_3 = 3.0 + .5x_3$$

is superimposed on the scatterplot. Detect the influential observation and demonstrate its effect on the fit.

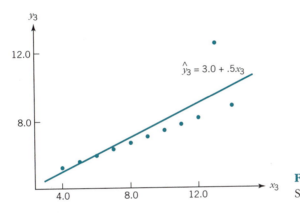

Figure 3.19 Scatterplot and Least Squares Line, Anscombe Data Set 3

Solution and Discussion.   It is clear from the scatterplot that the point with coordinates $(x_3, y_3) = (13, 12.74)$ is quite different from the other observations. Although 13 is consistent with the other values for the explanatory variable, 12.74 is much larger than the remaining responses. The residual plot in Figure 3.20 indicates systematic

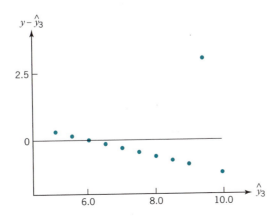

Figure 3.20 Plot of Residuals Versus Fitted Values, Anscombe Data Set 3

deviations from the fitted line; one particularly large residual is evident. This large residual identifies $(13, 12.74)$ as an outlier.

The outlier in Figure 3.19 seems to be lifting the least squares line toward it. To check on the influence of this observation, the point $(13, 12.74)$ was deleted from the data set and a least squares line fit to the remaining data. The result is shown in Figure 3.21. The line in Figure 3.21 has the equation

$$\hat{y}_3 = 4.0 + .345x_3$$

and within the resolution of the computer graph, passes through all the data points. Comparing the equations from the fits of Figures 3.19 and 3.21, we see that the single outlier has a considerable effect on the location of the least squares line. We conclude that this observation is also influential.

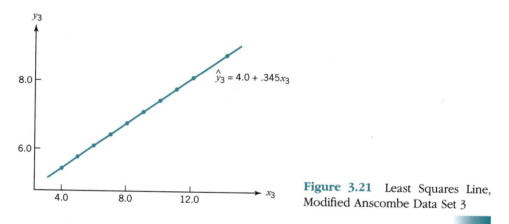

Figure 3.21 Least Squares Line, Modified Anscombe Data Set 3

The next example illustrates the effects of more than one outlier.

EXAMPLE 3.15   Effect of Several Outliers

The data in the following table are the number of pairs of telephone wires (x) and the time in hours (y) needed to splice these wires. There are $n = 40$ cases.

x	y	x	y	x	y
50	.27	500	3.35	1300	5.02
50	.72	600	5.00	1350	5.97
52	.58	700	1.98	1624	4.08
100	3.92	802	3.42	1800	5.10
150	1.48	900	7.57	1800	5.93
200	1.15	916	2.52	1800	6.27
200	1.98	1000	5.13	1800	9.37
200	2.62	1200	2.48	1808	5.58
300	1.15	1200	2.70	1814	3.10
300	4.33	1200	6.05	1827	3.62
400	3.58	1200	6.38	1950	6.10
400	6.30	1204	3.02	2116	5.92
406	1.47	1204	3.25		
450	2.02	1300	4.73		

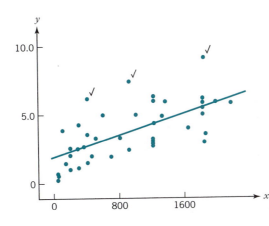

Figure 3.22 Scatterplot and Least Squares Line, Telephone Data

A scatterplot of these data along with the least squares line is shown in Figure 3.22. The time required to splice pairs of wires should be proportional to the number of pairs with an additional additive constant to account for some fixed setup time. This argument, plus the pattern in the scatterplot, led to the consideration of a linear relationship between x and y.

The equation of the least squares line is

$$\hat{y} = 1.89 + .0021x$$

Three cases, $(400, 6.30)$, $(900, 7.57)$, $(1800, 9.37)$, have been identified with check marks in the scatterplot. These are potential outliers since they are relatively far from the least squares line. Verify that these points are outliers, and examine their influence.

Solution and Discussion. A plot of $y - \hat{y}$ versus x is given in Figure 3.23. Figure 3.24 (page 136) contains a histogram of the residuals. It is clear from the two graphs that the points we have identified are outliers. These points have large residuals.

The scatterplot of the data with the three outliers removed is shown, along with the corresponding least squares line, in Figure 3.25. The least squares line for the modified data set has the equation

$$\hat{y} = 1.65 + .0020x$$

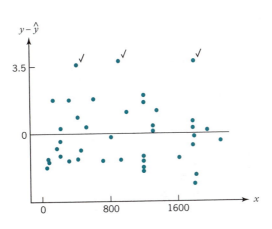

Figure 3.23 Residual Plot, Telephone Data

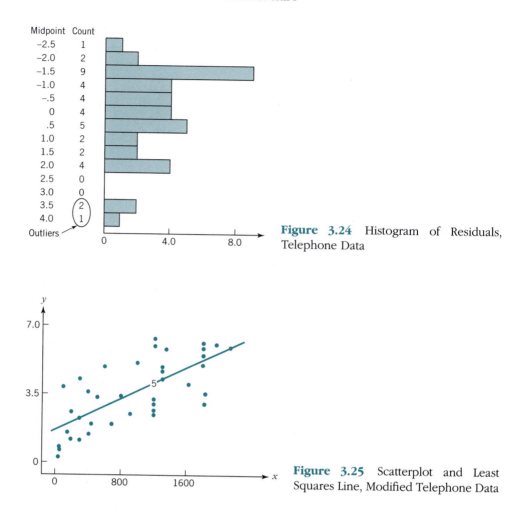

Figure 3.24 Histogram of Residuals, Telephone Data

Figure 3.25 Scatterplot and Least Squares Line, Modified Telephone Data

The slope coefficients for the two least squares lines are nearly the same. The intercepts, however, are different. Removing the outliers causes the least squares line to be relocated parallel to the old line but closer to the x-axis.

We have removed the outliers to demonstrate their numerical effect on the least squares line. Collectively, they are influential observations. These three cases should be examined in the context of the subject matter to see why they are different from the remaining observations.

We have concentrated on linear relationships—relationships that can be represented by a straight line. Sometimes it is possible to convert nonlinear relationships to linear ones by transforming one or both of the variables X and Y. If this can be done, it often simplifies the analysis.

LINEAR AND EXPONENTIAL GROWTH

If a response measured over time increases by the same *percentage* each time period, it is said to exhibit **exponential growth.** If a response increases by the same *amount* each time period, it is said to exhibit **linear growth.**

Consider the data listed here. These data chart the growth in the number of electronic mail (e-mail) users for a large university over a five-year period. The first row of data contains the number of e-mail users for each of the five years, rounded to the nearest thousand. The second row contains the natural logarithm of the number of e-mail users for each of the five years. For example, in 1986, there were 4000 e-mail users on the campus and $\ln(4000) = 8.29$.

Year	1986	1987	1988	1989	1990
Users	4000	7000	12000	20000	35000
Logarithm of users	8.29	8.85	9.39	9.90	10.46

Although the percentage increase in e-mail users is not exactly the same from year to year, it is not far from the average annual growth rate of 72%. The increase in the number of e-mail users from year to year, however, is quite different. The increases in magnitude range from a low of 3000 over the 1986–1987 period to a high of 15000 for the 1989–1990 period.

When we reexpress or transform the numbers of e-mail users by taking their natural logarithms (logarithms to any base will do), we convert exponential growth to linear growth. The magnitude of the increase in the logarithm of the number of e-mail users from one year to the next is roughly the same. Figure 3.26 shows plots of the number of e-mail users and the logarithm of the number of users for the five-year period.

The curvature representing exponential growth in Figure 3.26(a) has been straightened out in Figure 3.26(b) by the logarithmic transformation. This is true in general. That is, a response variable exhibiting exponential growth can be converted to a variable exhibiting linear growth by taking its logarithm. This implies that the logarithms of data that appear to grow exponentially will resemble a straight line when plotted against time. A least squares line can be fit to the logarithms with time as the explanatory variable. The least squares slope coefficient can be manipulated algebraically to determine the growth rate. The growth rate (in percent) is

$$\text{Growth rate} = 100[\text{antilog}(\text{Slope coefficient}) - 1]\%$$

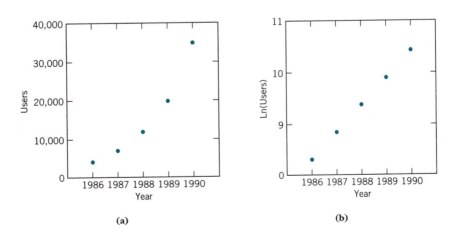

(a)   **(b)**

Figure 3.26 (a) Number of E-Mail Users and (b) Logarithm of Number of E-Mail Users

EXAMPLE 3.16   Estimating a Growth Rate and Forecasting a Future Value

On the Double, a chain of campus copy centers, began operations with a single store in 1983. The number of copy centers in operation, y_t, is recorded for 14 consecutive years. The data are given in the following table, where, for convenience, we set the time index $t = 1$ for 1983, $t = 2$ for 1984, and so on. We have also recorded the natural logarithm of the number of copy centers, $\ln y_t$.

Year	t	y_t	$\ln y_t$
1983	1	1	0
1984	2	2	.69
1985	3	2	.69
1986	4	6	1.79
1987	5	10	2.30
1988	6	16	2.77
1989	7	25	3.22
1990	8	41	3.71
1991	9	60	4.09
1992	10	97	4.57
1993	11	150	5.01
1994	12	211	5.35
1995	13	382	5.95
1996	14	537	6.29

Determine the annual growth rate for On the Double, and predict the number of copy centers in operation in 1997.

Solution and Discussion.   Figure 3.27 shows time series plots of the number of copy centers before and after the logarithmic transformation.

The plot of the logarithms resembles a straight line, and the least squares line fit to these data has the equation

$$\widehat{\ln y_t} = -.308 + .483t$$

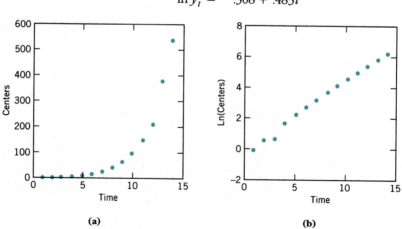

(a)   **(b)**

Figure 3.27   (a) Number of Copy Centers and (b) Logarithm of Number of Copy Centers

where t is the time index. The annual growth rate is estimated to be

$$100(e^{.483} - 1)\% = 100(1.621 - 1)\% = 62.1\%$$

where e is the base of the natural logarithms.

To predict the number of copy centers for 1997, we set $t = .15$ and compute

$$\widehat{\ln y}_{15} = -.308 + .483(15) = 6.94$$

Consequently,

$$\hat{y}_{15} = e^{6.94} = 1033$$

is a prediction of the number of copy centers operating in 1997.

Example 3.16 illustrates the potential danger of extrapolating exponential growth beyond the fitting region. The estimated number of On the Double copy centers in 1997 may or may not be a realistic figure. A phenomenon exhibiting exponential growth increases very rapidly for some period of time. However, exponential growth may not be sustainable. A saturation level is often reached and the growth slows or even declines.

Situations leading to exponential growth occur frequently in business. Funds earning compound interest grow exponentially. Sales of a (successful) new product often grow exponentially during the early period of the product's life cycle. Targeted expenditures sometimes exhibit exponential growth. The bar graph in Figure 3.28 shows federal spending on AIDS in the United States for the period 1982–1993. Spending on AIDS grew exponentially over this period.

As we have seen, *adding* a fixed amount in each time period leads to linear growth. Exponential growth occurs when a quantity is *multiplied* by a fixed number, $1 +$ (Growth rate), each time period. A variable growing exponentially can be converted to a variable growing linearly by taking its logarithm. Analysis of data in the linear framework can then be used to make statements about the original variable with the help of antilogarithms.

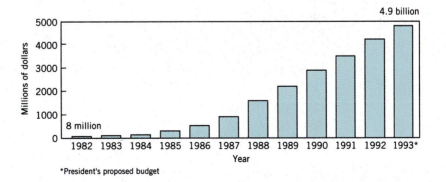

Figure 3.28 Federal Spending on AIDS. Source: U.S. Department of Health and Human Services, The Public Health Service. Strategic Plan to Combat HIV and AIDS in the United States. November 1992.

EXERCISES

3.21   Plot the lines represented by the following equations. For each line, identify the slope and intercept.

    a. $y = 3 + 7x$

    b. $y = -4 + 2x$

    c. $y = 7 - x$

3.22   Plot the lines represented by the following equations. For each line, identify the slope and intercept.

    a. $y = -1 - 8x$

    b. $y = 4x$

    c. $y = -10x$

3.23   The following data consist of five pairs of observations:

x	y	$x - \bar{x}$	$y - \bar{y}$	$(x - \bar{x})^2$	$(x - \bar{x})(y - \bar{y})$
1	0				
2	2				
3	3				
4	7				
5	8				

    a.   Construct a scatter diagram.

    b.   Guess the sign of the slope of the least squares line.

    c.   Complete the table and determine the equation of the least squares line. Graph this line on the scatterplot.

    d.   Predict a new value of y at $x = 4$.

3.24   The following data consist of five pairs of observations:

x	y	$x - \bar{x}$	$y - \bar{y}$	$(x - \bar{x})^2$	$(x - \bar{x})(y - \bar{y})$
-2	1				
-1	6				
0	3				
1	12				
2	13				

    a.   Construct a scatter diagram.

    b.   Guess the sign of the slope of the least squares line.

    c.   Complete the table and determine the equation of the least squares line. Graph this line on the scatterplot.

    d.   Predict a new value of y at $x = 1$.

3.25   Refer to Exercise 3.23.

    a.   Obtain the five residuals.

    b.   Determine the standard deviation of the residuals.

3.26   Refer to Exercise 3.24.

    a.   Obtain the five residuals.

    b.   Determine the standard deviation of the residuals.

3.27 The data on number of books sold (x) and total dollar sales (y) described in Exercise 3.6 are reproduced here.

x (number of books)	4	5	4	3
y (dollar sales)	142	152	148	158

a. Calculate the slope and intercept coefficients of the least squares line relating total dollar sales to the number of books sold.

b. Calculate the slope coefficient, b, using the correlation coefficient, r, calculated in Exercise 3.6. Verify that this method of calculating the least squares slope coefficient gives the same result as that in part **a.**

3.28 The following data are research and development expenditures, x, and earnings, y, for $n = 14$ companies.

x (R&D)	8.5	12.0	6.5	4.5	2.0	.5	1.5
y (earnings)	83	147	69	41	26	35	40

x (R&D)	14.0	9.0	7.5	.5	2.5	3.0	6.0
y (earnings)	125	97	53	12	34	48	64

a. Construct the scatter diagram for these data.

b. Determine the equation of the least squares line, and plot the least squares line on the scatter diagram in part **a.**

c. Plot the residuals, $y - \hat{y}$, against R&D, x. Does it appear that the least squares line provides an adequate description of these data?

d. Predict the earnings for a company with research and development expenditures of 5.5.

3.29 Consider the construction cost data in Example 3.2.

a. Determine the equation of the least squares line relating actual cost, y, to estimated cost, x.

b. Plot the residuals, $y - \hat{y}$, against the estimated costs, x. Comment on the appearance of the plot. Would you agree that estimated costs are better predictors of actual costs (closer to target) for smaller projects than for larger projects?

ConsCost.dat

3.30 (*Minitab or similar program recommended*) Refer to the construction cost data in Example 3.2.

a. Construct the bivariate observations ($\ln x, \ln y$) where x is estimated cost and y is actual cost. Plot these observations as a scatter diagram.

b. Fit a least squares line to the bivariate observations in part **a.**

c. Plot the residuals from the fit in part **b** against the logarithm of the estimated costs, $\ln x$. Compare this residual plot with the residual plot in Exercise 3.29**b.** Are the deviations of $\widehat{\ln y}$ from $\ln y$ roughly the same throughout the fitting region?

d. Using the least squares equation in part **b,** predict the actual cost of a construction project if the estimated cost is 19.5 million dollars.

ConsCost.dat

3.31 (*Minitab or similar program recommended*) Refer to the construction cost data in Example 3.2.

a. As we argued in Example 3.2, we might expect the relationship between actual costs and estimated costs to be represented by the 45° line through the origin—that is, a line with the equation $y = x$. The general expression for the slope coefficient of a least squares line *through the origin* is

$$b = \frac{\sum xy}{\sum x^2}$$

Fit a least squares line through the origin (no intercept) to the construction cost data, where y is actual cost and x is estimated cost.

b. Compare the least squares line through the origin with the least squares line in Exercise 3.29**a.** Which provides a better representation of the construction cost data? Support your argument with appropriate plots.

c. Determine the residuals from the fit in part **a** and show that their sum is not zero. In general, the residuals from a fitted function without an intercept term do not sum to zero.

3.32 Consider the used car data in Exercise 3.7.

a. Determine the equation of the least squares line, where y = price and x = age.

b. Using the value of the correlation coefficient from Exercise 3.7**b** and the value for the slope coefficient in part **a,** show that $b = (\sqrt{S_{yy}}/\sqrt{S_{xx}})r$.

c. Show that the residuals sum to zero.

d. Predict the selling price of a used, 7-year-old Japanese car.

3.33 The Capital Asset Pricing Model (CAPM) is used in finance to relate the expected return on an individual security (or portfolio of securities) to its systematic risk. The model has the rather simple form

$$y = a + bx$$

where y = expected return, a = risk-free rate, b = (Expected market return) − (Risk-free rate) or the "market risk premium," and x is the systematic risk, sometimes called the "beta coefficient." Regulatory agencies often use CAPM to determine the required rate of return for a public utility. Suppose the CAPM for a given utility is $y = .045 + .084x$.

a. Express the risk-free rate as a percentage. Can you identify a security yielding a risk-free rate?

b. Graph the utility's CAPM. Let the y-axis be the expected rate of return and the x-axis be the systematic risk. Predict the required rate of return if the systematic risk is currently .70.

MarketAs.dat

3.34 (*Minitab or similar program recommended*) The following data were collected as part of a study of real estate property valuation. The numbers are observations on x = assessed value (in thousands of dollars) on city assessor's books and y = market value (selling price in thousands of dollars) for n = 30 parcels that sold in a particular calendar year in a certain neighborhood.

Parcel	Assessed	Market	Parcel	Assessed	Market
1	68.2	87.4	16	74.0	88.4
2	74.6	88.0	17	72.8	93.6
3	64.6	87.2	18	80.4	92.8
4	80.2	94.0	19	74.2	90.6
5	76.0	94.2	20	80.0	91.6
6	78.0	93.6	21	81.6	92.8
7	76.0	88.4	22	75.6	89.0
8	77.0	92.2	23	79.4	91.8
9	75.2	90.4	24	82.2	98.4
10	72.4	90.4	25	67.0	89.8
11	80.0	93.6	26	72.0	97.2
12	76.4	91.4	27	73.6	95.2
13	70.2	89.6	28	71.4	88.8
14	75.8	91.8	29	81.0	97.4
15	79.2	94.8	30	80.6	95.4

a. Plot the market value against the assessed value as a scatter diagram. Determine the least squares line relating market value to assessed value.

b. The city assessor claims to assess properties at 60% of market value. Is the assessor achieving his goal? Explain.

c. Examine the residuals. Can you identify any observations that may have a significant influence on the location of the least squares line? Justify your choice(s).

SportFrn.dat

3.35 (*Minitab or similar program recommended*) Player cost (millions of dollars) and operating expense (millions of dollars) for the $n = 26$ Major League Baseball (MLB) teams for the 1990–1991 season can be determined from the data given in Table 7, Appendix C.

a. Plot these pairs of observations as a scatter diagram with $x =$ player cost and $y =$ operating expense. Determine the least squares line relating operating expense to player cost, and graph it on the scatter diagram.

b. Using the least squares line in part **a,** predict operating expense if a baseball team has a player cost of 15 million dollars. Do you think player cost represents the bulk of the operating expense for MLB teams? Explain.

c. Determine the residual standard deviation, s, and plot the residuals versus the fitted values. Construct horizontal lines s and $2s$ from zero in both directions on the residual plot. Does the residual plot have the appearance of a horizontal band? Why is this important?

d. Using the value of s in part **c,** determine the fraction of residuals within 1 and 2 standard deviations of zero. Do the results agree with the empirical rule?

e. Construct a boxplot of the residuals.

GPAGMAT.dat

3.36 (*Minitab or similar program recommended*) Exercise 3.17 contains data on undergraduate grade point average (GPA) and Graduate Management Admission Test (GMAT) score for $n = 20$ students admitted to a graduate business program.

a. Determine the least squares line relating GMAT score to undergraduate GPA. Based on these data, is undergraduate GPA a good predictor of GMAT score? Discuss.

b. Using the least squares line, predict the GMAT score of an undergraduate with a GPA of 3.5.

c. Using the correlation coefficient calculated in Exercise 3.17 and the information in part **a**, verify that $b = (\sqrt{S_{yy}}/\sqrt{S_{xx}})r$.

3.37 (*Minitab or similar program recommended*) Consider the Anscombe data sets listed in Exercise 3.16.

Anscombe.dat

a. Determine the least squares line relating y to x for each of these data sets, and verify that the lines are all the same.

b. Sketch the least squares line on the scatterplot of each of the data sets (see Examples 3.12 and 3.14). Which data set seems to be best represented by the least squares line? Why?

c. Plot the residuals, $y - \hat{y}$, against x for each data set. Examine the residual plots. Which data set is best represented by the least squares line? Is your choice the same as the one in part **b**? Should it be? Explain.

d. Using the information in parts **b** and **c**, identify the influential observation in data set 4. Justify your choice.

3.38 (*Minitab or similar program recommended*) The data listed here are the dollars spent per student in each state (and the District of Columbia) and the state's ranking according to 1992 Scholastic Aptitude Test (SAT) math scores.

StSATExp.dat

State	Avg. Exp.	SAT Rank	State	Avg. Exp.	SAT Rank
New Jersey	9159	39	Kansas	5009	6
New York	8500	42	Hawaii	5008	44
District of Columbia	8210	49	Georgia	4860	50
Connecticut	7914	35	Iowa	4839	1
Alaska	7877	31	California	4826	34
Rhode Island	6989	43	Colorado	4809	23
Pennsylvania	6534	45	North Carolina	4802	48
Massachusetts	6351	33	Nevada	4564	29
Maryland	6184	32	New Mexico	4446	15
Delaware	6016	37	Missouri	4415	13
Wisconsin	5946	7	Kentucky	4390	18
Maine	5894	41	Nebraska	4381	8
Vermont	5740	36	South Carolina	4327	51
Ohio	5639	24	Texas	4238	46
New Hampshire	5504	28	Arizona	4231	25
Virginia	5360	38	Louisiana	4012	16
Oregon	5291	26	Oklahoma	3742	11
Minnesota	5260	3	South Dakota	3730	5
Michigan	5257	20	Tennessee	3707	9
Wyoming	5255	21	North Dakota	3685	2
Montana	5184	19	Alabama	3648	14
Florida	5154	40	Arkansas	3334	17
Illinois	5062	10	Mississippi	3322	12
Indiana	5051	47	Idaho	3200	22
West Virginia	5046	27	Utah	2993	4
Washington	5045	30			

SOURCE: *Wall Street Journal*, June 22, 1993.

a. Plot the data as a scatter diagram with x = average expenditure and y = SAT rank. What does this plot suggest about the relationship between student expenditures and performance on the math section of the SAT?

b. Fit a least squares line to these data, and predict SAT rank if average expenditure is $7000.

c. Do you believe the prediction in part **b?** Notice that the per student expenditures for Iowa and South Carolina are not very different ($4839 and $4327), yet they rank first and last in SAT math scores, respectively. Is the positive association between average expenditure and SAT rank misleading? Can you suggest a lurking variable that may be partially responsible for the nature of the scatter plot in part **a?** [*Hint:* The percentage of high school seniors taking the SAT in the various states is quite different. The percentage is relatively small in Iowa.]

S&P500RR.dat

3.39 (*Optional*) (*Minitab or similar program recommended*) Exercise 3.18 contains data on the monthly rates of return on the S&P 500 Index for the 1988–1991 period.

a. Let y_t be the rate of return at time t, and let y_{t-1} be the rate of return at time $t - 1$. With y_{t-1} playing the role of x, determine the least squares line relating the rate of return at time t to the rate of return at time $t - 1$.

b. Plot the residuals versus time, and compute the lag 1 residual autocorrelation coefficient. Is there any obvious pattern in the residuals that appears over time? Explain.

c. Using the least squares relation in part **a,** forecast the monthly S&P returns for January 1991, March 1991, June 1991, and September 1991. Compare your forecasts with the actual rates of return for these months.

d. One model for stock returns would use this month's return as the forecast of next month's return. Use this model to forecast the monthly returns for January 1991, March 1991, June 1991, and September 1991. Compare the forecasts with the actual rates of return for these months. Given these results and the results in part **c,** which model appears to produce the best forecasts?

3.40 The following data are the numbers of connections to an AppleTalk computer network for a ten-year period.

Year	1	2	3	4	5	6	7	8	9	10
Connections	20	24	30	32	44	76	90	148	187	220

a. Compute the natural logarithms of the connections. Construct scatterplots of the connections versus year and the natural logarithms of connections versus year. Comment on the general appearance of the two scatterplots.

b. Let y = natural logarithm of connections and x = year. Determine the least squares line relating y to x, and graph it on the appropriate scatterplot in part **a.**

c. Using the least squares slope coefficient from part **b,** calculate the annual growth rate for the number of AppleTalk connections.

d. Predict the number of AppleTalk connections for year 11. Do you think the forecast of the number of connections for, say, year 20 would be a realistic number? Discuss.

3.5   TWO-WAY TABLES

When the outcomes for two variables are categories, for example, when we are measuring traits or characteristics of experimental units, the resulting data can be summarized in the form of a two-way frequency table. The categories of one trait are marked along the left margin, those for the second trait are marked along the top of the table, and the frequency counts are recorded in the cells. Data in this summary form are sometimes called **cross-classified** or **cross-tabulated data.** The table itself is sometimes referred to as a **contingency table.** In particular, if we let r denote the number of row (left margin) categories and c denote the number of column (top margin) categories, the resulting table is often called an $r \times c$ contingency table.

Ordinarily, frequencies associated with the categories of two *qualitative* variables are cross-classified. However, contingency tables can be constructed for a qualitative variable and a quantitative (measured) variable or two quantitative variables. If a quantitative variable is used, its values must be divided up into several nonoverlapping intervals that serve as categories. The construction of these intervals is analogous to the choices of the number of classes and class widths when constructing histograms. Constructing tables with quantitative variables requires some experimentation and judgment in determining the appropriate categories.

EXAMPLE 3.17   Calculating Relative Frequencies in a Contingency Table

A sample of 500 persons is questioned regarding political affiliation and attitude toward a proposed national health care plan. The responses are cross-classified according to the political affiliation and opinion categories displayed in the following 2×3 contingency table.

Affiliation	Attitude Favor	Attitude Indifferent	Oppose	Total
Democrat	138	83	64	285
Republican	64	67	84	215
Total	202	150	148	500

We have a single sample, and each sampled individual (sampling unit) yields two types of outcomes: political affiliation and attitude. Frequencies associated with the pairs of outcome categories are given in the table. For example, individuals who are Democrats and favor the national health plan are counted in the upper left-hand cell of the table. There are 83 Democrats who are indifferent toward the plan, and so forth. In addition, the totals for each row and column, called the *marginal totals*, are displayed along with the *grand total.*

Are the qualitative variables political affiliation and attitude related? If they are, then political affiliation would convey some information about a person's attitude toward the national health care plan and vice versa. For example, we might conclude that Democrats tend to favor the plan whereas Republicans tend to oppose it.

To gain further understanding of how the responses are distributed, calculate the relative frequencies of the cells and the relative frequencies for the margins. Convert these relative frequencies to percentages.

Solution and Discussion. To calculate the cell relative frequencies, we divide each cell frequency by the sample size 500. The cell relative frequencies (for instance, $\frac{64}{500} = .128$) are given in the body of the following table.

The marginal relative frequencies obtained by dividing the marginal totals by 500 are also displayed. Notice that the cell relative frequencies sum to 1, as do each of the sets of marginal relative frequencies.

Percentages are obtained by multiplying the relative frequencies by 100. These numbers are given in parentheses beneath the relative frequencies. In the body of the table, we see that the two largest relative frequencies (percentages) occur in the Democrat–Favor and Republican–Oppose cells.

Relative Frequencies (%)

Affiliation	Favor	Attitude Indifferent	Oppose	Total
Democrat	.276 (27.6%)	.166 (16.6%)	.128 (12.8%)	.570 (57%)
Republican	.128 (12.8%)	.134 (13.4%)	.168 (16.8%)	.430 (43%)
Total	.404 (40.4%)	.300 (30%)	.296 (29.6%)	1.000 (100%)

The relative frequencies in the table in Example 3.17 seem to indicate an association between political affiliation and attitude. However, before we can be more definitive, we need to know what we would expect to see in a sample of 500 if, in fact, there is no association between political affiliation and attitude. After all, in a sample, it is possible by chance to get a distribution of frequencies that suggests some association. What is needed is a way to compare expected frequencies with observed frequencies. We return to this issue in Chapter 10.

There is some art to displaying data in the form of a contingency table. When categorical data are collected, variables with many categories may be used. However, when reporting and analyzing categorical data, we may want to combine some categories. This is usually a good strategy if there is no significant distortion of information because it provides a clearer picture and simplifies the analysis.

SIMPSON'S PARADOX

Two characteristics may appear to be strongly related because of the common influence of a third factor that is not included in the study. For example, an association between family income and the number of automobiles owned may be heavily influenced by family size. Lurking variables can change or even reverse a relationship between two categorical variables. This phenomenon is known as **Simpson's Paradox.**

Consider the following table of data on graduate admissions at a major university.*

Gender	Status		Total
	Admit	Deny	
Female	220	180	400
Male	375	225	600

We see that ($\frac{375}{600}$) or 62.5% of the male applicants were admitted to these graduate programs, but only ($\frac{220}{400}$) or 55% of the female applicants were admitted. Is there a bias against admitting female applicants?

The results summarized in the previous table are for two graduate programs: business and veterinary medicine. The admissions numbers for the individual professional schools are summarized in a three-way table with professional school (business and veterinary medicine) representing the third variable.

	Business			Veterinary Medicine	
	Admit	Deny		Admit	Deny
Female	160	40	Female	60	140
Male	350	150	Male	25	75

The counts in the table show that proportionally more women were admitted to business than men. The business school admitted ($\frac{160}{200}$) or 80% of the female applicants and ($\frac{350}{500}$) or 70% of the male applicants. Similarly, proportionally more women were admitted to veterinary medicine than men. The school of veterinary medicine admitted ($\frac{60}{200}$) or 35% of the female applicants and ($\frac{25}{100}$) or 25% of the male applicants. The individual schools admit a larger proportion of female applicants than male applicants, but the overall admission rates show a larger proportion of males were admitted to the combined graduate programs. How can this be? The answer can be seen by expressing the overall rates as weighted averages.

A **weighted average,** denoted by $\bar{x}_w$, is given by

$$\bar{x}_w = \sum_{i=1}^{n} w_i x_i \quad \text{where} \quad \sum_{i=1}^{n} w_i = 1$$

The coefficients w_i, multiplying the observations x_i, are called the *weights,* hence the name weighted average. If $w_i = 1/n, i = 1, 2, \ldots, n$, the weighted average is the sample mean. The sample mean can be viewed as a weighted average with equal weights $\frac{1}{n}$.

Now consider the female admission rates. The overall admission rate (.55) can be written as the weighted average of the female admission rates (.80 and .30) for the two professional schools. The weights (multiplicative coefficients) are the proportions of

---

*The data are hypothetical but the situation is real. A more complex, but similar, example is discussed in Bickel, P.J., and O'Connell, J.W. "Is there a sex bias in graduation admissions?" *Science,* Vol. 187, 1975, pp. 398–404.

the total number of females applying to each of the two schools. In this case, half (.50) of the 400 females applied to the business school and half (.50) of the 400 females applied to veterinary medicine, so we can write

$$\textbf{Female rate:} \quad \frac{220}{400} = \frac{200}{400}\frac{160}{200} + \frac{200}{400}\frac{60}{200}$$

or

$$.55 = .50(.80) + .50(.30)$$

Because of the equal weighting of .50, the overall rate is midway between the individual rates of .80 and .30.

Similarly, we can express the overall admission rate for males as the weighted average

$$\textbf{Male rate:} \quad \frac{375}{600} = \frac{500}{600}\frac{350}{500} + \frac{100}{600}\frac{25}{100}$$

or

$$.625 = .83(.70) + .17(.25)$$

Many more males applied to the business school than to the school of veterinary medicine. In fact, five times as many males applied to the business school than to the school of veterinary medicine. When the overall admission rate for males (.625) is written as a weighted average of the male admission rates for the two professional schools (.70 and .25), the weights (multiplicative coefficients) are .83 and .17. These numbers represent the proportions of the total number of males applying to the business school and school of veterinary medicine, respectively. Consequently, the male admission rate for the business school gets more weight in the weighted average, and the overall male admission rate is closer to the business school rate.

The apparent contradiction in admission rates is an example of Simpson's Paradox. As we pointed out, Simpson's Paradox can result when a third (lurking) variable is responsible for a change or reversal in the relationship between two categorical variables. In our case, the third variable is professional school. The real situation was not apparent until we constructed a three-way table to allow for the effects of this third variable. The very different numbers of applicants and the different proportions of female and male applicants for the two schools are hidden when the data are combined in a two-way table, and a misleading conclusion results.

TIME SERIES DATA

Two-way tables of time series data complement plots and provide numerical evidence of interperiod differences. The row and column categories are ordinarily time periods. These categories are determined by the frequency of the data and the periods of suspected patterns.

For example, a table on daily volume on the New York Stock Exchange might have the rows representing the trading days of the week and the columns representing the weeks of the year. The idea is to see whether there is a weekly pattern in volume. Does volume tend to be highest on Mondays? Is daily volume fairly uniform throughout the week? Answers to questions like these can be provided, in part, by the numbers in the two-way table.

A two-way table of time series data is essentially a listing of the data in the form of an array rather than a single column or row of numbers. The margins of the table usually contain averages, which can be examined to detect patterns.

EXAMPLE 3.18   Organizing Time Series Data in a Two-Way Table

A list of the monthly peak power demand for the Wisconsin branch of Northern States Power Company is given in the data disk and labeled NPowPeak.dat. The data cover a nine-year period beginning in January and ending with November of the last year. The data represent the maximum amount of power, measured in megawatts, generated during one month by the Wisconsin utility. Arrange the data in a two-way table with months forming the rows and years determining the columns. Compute the average monthly peak demand and the average yearly peak demand, and place these numbers in the margins of the table. Examine the margin averages for patterns.

Solution and Discussion.   Table 3.2 is a two-way table of the data. The averages are indicated in the margins of the table. The yearly averages, in the last row of the table, suggest that peak demand is trending upward; that is, the general level is increasing throughout the time period covered by these data. A given year's average peak demand is always greater than the previous year's.

The monthly averages, in the last column of the table, suggest a seasonal pattern with winter (November–February) and summer (July–August) highs, and dips in the spring and fall. This pattern is consistent with winter heating and summer cooling requirements in the upper midwest. Notice that the winter high is greater than the

TABLE 3.2   Northern States Power (Wisconsin) Peak Demand

Month	Year									Average
	1970	1971	1972	1973	1974	1975	1976	1977	1978	
January	385	406	420	432	446	468	496	572	574	466.6
February	375	411	418	412	440	467	498	543	564	458.7
March	372	388	397	396	426	433	477	554	544	443.0
April	365	387	368	390	428	411	423	464	486	413.6
May	360	361	415	390	409	440	405	462	527	418.8
June	370	386	381	418	393	473	490	527	546	442.7
July	376	367	420	434	471	496	489	562	539	461.6
August	383	382	429	451	438	495	504	492	597	463.4
September	382	387	389	395	431	403	476	504	586	439.2
October	365	360	390	412	417	406	476	487	483	421.8
November	391	377	424	410	421	440	518	530	593	456.0
December	406	412	438	433	442	495	528	560	—	464.3
Average	377.5	385.3	407.4	414.4	430.2	452.3	481.7	521.4	549.0	

summer high. In a typical year, winter heating generates more demand for electricity than summer cooling.

In summary, the marginal averages reveal an annual seasonal pattern superimposed on a general growth trend.

Two-way tables of time series data are most useful when used in conjunction with plots of the time series and tables or graphs of autocorrelation coefficients. If common patterns are suggested by all three sources of information, then one can be fairly confident the patterns are stable. These patterns can then be projected to develop forecasts of future values.

EXERCISES

3.41 At one time there was not enough space in Texas state prisons to hold inmates. Many state prisoners were sent to county jails until space in state prisons became available. The sheriff of Travis County requested a study of the number of inmates discharged to the county by the state and the number of inmates sent to the state by the county for 1991. In 1991, the state discharged 2303 inmates to Travis County and received 693 inmates from Travis County. Of the 2303 inmates sent to Travis County, 735 were incarcerated for burglary, 632 for drug related offenses, 411 for larcency, and 525 for other offenses. Of the 693 inmates sent to the state, 203 were incarcerated for burglary, 131 for drug related offenses, 61 for larcency, and 298 for other offenses.

    a. Construct a two-way frequency table with status of state prisoners (discharged, received) representing the rows and type of crime (burglary, drugs, larceny, other) representing the columns. Be sure to include the marginal totals.

    b. Calculate the relative frequencies separately for each row in the table.

    c. Comment on any apparent differences in type of criminal between those prisoners discharged to Travis County by the state and those received from Travis County by the state.

3.42 Refer to Exercise 3.41. Of the 2303 prisoners discharged to Travis County by the state of Texas, 833 were 17–26 years old, 998 were 27–36 years old, 362 were 37–46 years old, and 110 were 47 years old or older. Of the 693 prisoners received from Travis County by the state, 271 were 17–26 years old, 235 were 27–36 years old, 141 were 37–46 years old, and 46 were 47 years old or older.

    a. Construct a two-way frequency table with status of state prisoner representing the rows and age representing the columns. Record the marginal totals.

    b. Calculate the relative frequencies separately for each row.

    c. Comment on any apparent differences in the age profiles of prisoners discharged by the state to Travis County and those received from Travis County by the state.

3.43 A stock brokerage company conducted a survey of a random sample of 400 of its customers. One question on the survey asked respondents whether they had been experiencing problems with any aspect of the service within the past three months. In addition, on the basis of respondents' stock transactions, the company was able to group the respondents into "low-volume" and "high-volume" categories. Frequencies are recorded in the following two-way table.

	Volume		
Problem	Low	High	Total
No		120	300
Yes		40	100
Total			400

a. Fill in the remaining cells and marginal totals in the table.

b. Convert the frequencies to relative frequencies.

c. Given these data, are customers who experience problems likely to do less business than those not experiencing problems? Explain.

3.44 A random sample of 500 households was surveyed, and data on three variables, household income, household size, and number of cars owned, were collected. The data are summarized in the following three-way frequency table.

		Number of cars	
Income	Household size	2 or fewer	More than 2
Less than $30,000	4 or fewer	125	100
	More than 4	15	60
$30,000 or more	4 or fewer	100	50
	More than 4	10	40

a. Make a two-way table of income by number of cars owned for the combined household sizes by summing entries in the three-way table. Include the marginal totals.

b. Discuss the nature of the apparent association between household income and number of cars owned. Is the result counterintuitive?

c. Make a two-way table of household size by number of cars owned by summing entries in the three-way table. Include the marginal totals.

d. Discuss the nature of the apparent association between household size and number of cars owned.

3.45 You are interested in comparing two hospitals that serve your community, Hospital I and Hospital II. The data on the survival of patients after surgery follow. All patients undergoing surgery in a recent time period are included. "Survived" means that a patient lived at least 6 weeks following surgery.

Status	Hospital I	Hospital II	Total
Died	88	21	109
Survived	2112	679	2791
Total	2200	700	2900

Calculate the percentage of surgery patients each of the two hospitals lost. If you were scheduled for surgery, which of the two hospitals would you choose?

3.46 Refer to Exercise 3.45. Not all surgery cases are equally serious. You discover data broken down by the condition of the patients before surgery. Here are the data for patients classified as being in either "good" or "poor" condition.

Status	Good condition			Status	Poor condition	
	Hospital I	Hospital II			Hospital I	Hospital II
Died	14	15		Died	74	6
Survived	686	585		Survived	1426	94
Total	700	600		Total	1500	100

a. Calculate the percentage of patients in good condition who died after surgery at each of the two hospitals. Make the same calculations for patients in poor condition.

b. Given the results in part **a,** which hospital would you choose if you needed surgery? Is this decision consistent with the one in Exercise 3.45? Explain any discrepancy. (This is an example of Simpson's Paradox.)

c. Write the overall attrition rate for Hospital I as a weighted average of the attrition rates for patients in good condition and patients in poor condition at this hospital. Do the same thing for Hospital II. Interpret the weights (coefficients) in the weighted averages.

3.47 A random sample of 400 supermarkets was taken to determine the effects of promotional expenditures and price on recent sales of a certain brand of detergent. As a first step in the analysis, the sample medians were determined for each of the two variables. The data were organized in the form of a two-way frequency table, as follows:

Promotional expenditure	Sales		Total
	Below median	Above median	
Below median	100	100	200
Above median	100	100	200
Total	200	200	400

a. Does there appear to be any association between promotional expenditure and sales? Rearrange the cell frequencies so there is a positive association between promotional expenditure and sales. Rearrange the cell frequencies so there is a negative association. Can the marginal totals change for either rearrangement? Explain.

b. You are told that of the 200 supermarkets with promotional expenditures *above* the median, 40 have prices above the median price and sales above the median sales. In addition, 70 have prices below the median price and sales above the median sales. Create a two-way frequency table of price by sales for this group of supermarkets. Comment on the nature of the association.

c. Of the 200 supermarkets with promotional expenditures *below* the median, 35 have prices above the median price and sales above the median sales. Also, 55 have prices below the median price and above the median sales. Construct a two-way frequency table of price by sales for this group of supermarkets. Comment on the nature of the association.

d. Using the information in parts **b** and **c,** discuss association between price and sales at the different levels of promotional expenditure. Given this evidence, what would you do as a supermarket manager to increase sales of this brand of detergent?

3.48 Consider the Wisconsin food products employment data displayed in Figure 3.5 and listed in Table 8, Appendix C. Cross-tabulate the data, with months representing the rows and years representing the columns. Record the row and column averages in the margins of the table. Examine the row averages for a seasonal effect. Examine the column averages for a yearly effect. Are your conclusions consistent with the time series plot in Figure 3.5? Explain.

3.49 The monthly inventories of diesel engines (in thousands of dollars) at Hatz Diesel of America, Inc. are given in Example 1.8 on page 19. The data cover the period December 1987 through June 1992. Beginning with the January 1988 value (701), construct a months by years two-way table of inventory numbers. Put the row and column averages in the margins of the table. Examine the monthly averages for an annual seasonal pattern. Is there any evidence for a trend in inventory levels over the years covered by these data?

3.50 The aging of commercial aircraft can make them more vulnerable to "skincracking" rivets. In 1987, a major manufacturer collected the following data on its three most popular aircraft models in active use to determine the magnitude of the problem.

	Age		
Model	≤ 20 Years	> 20 Years	Total
B07	90	123	
B27	1214	435	
B37	1042	9	

Compare the aging of the three types of planes by calculating the relative frequencies.

3.6 STATISTICS IN CONTEXT

As is typical for public utilities, Wisconsin Gas Company is required to appear before regulatory agencies to argue for rate structures and investments that will allow the company an appropriate rate of return. One way to determine the required rate of return is to use the Capital Asset Pricing Model (CAPM). The CAPM is an equation that represents the equilibrium relationship between a security's (or portfolio's) expected return and its systematic risk. The model has the straight-line form

$$y = a + bx$$

where y = expected return, a = risk-free rate, b = (expected market return) − (risk-free rate) or the "market risk premium," and x is the "systematic risk," sometimes called the "beta coefficient."

It can be shown that the beta coefficient or systematic risk is related to the correlation between the security return and the market return. This correlation is responsible for the name "systematic risk" since the correlation measures the extent to which the security moves with the market.

To determine the required or expected rate of return, we need values for (i) the risk-free rate, a, (ii) the market risk premium, b, and (iii) the systematic risk or beta coefficient, x.

(i) The risk-free rate is generally taken to be the current rate of return on an investment with little chance of default, such as a 3-month U.S. Treasury bill. Sometimes other U.S. Treasury offerings, such as the 30-year bond, are used. At the time of the Wisconsin Gas hearings, the 3-month rate was 4.55% and the 30-year rate was 7.95%.

(ii) The market risk premium is often determined by independent companies and is based on the return of stocks, bonds, bills, and inflation relative to a risk-free rate. Ibbotson Associates of Chicago, Illinois, is one firm that calculates market risk premiums. For example, Atlanta Gas and Light had a market risk premium of 8.4% using the 3-month bill and 7.3% with the 30-year bond.

(iii) The beta coefficient is generally estimated by determining the slope parameter in a straight-line fit of a firm's stock rates of return (or the rates of return on a portfolio of stocks of similar firms) against the rates of return on a proxy for the market of all financial assets. The proxy often used is the S&P 500 Index. Beta coefficients for particular firms are available from independent investment information services, such as Value Line. For example, the beta coefficient for Atlanta Gas and Light was quoted as .70.

In its 1993 rate hearings before the Wisconsin Public Service Commission, Wisconsin Gas argued for an increase in natural gas rates. The company calculated required rates of return using CAPM for a reference set of seven other natural gas suppliers. Here is some of the CAPM information presented by Wisconsin Gas Company for the reference set of gas companies, including Atlanta Gas and Light.

	3-Month T-Bill			30-Year T-Bond	
	Risk-free rate	Market risk premium	Beta	Risk-free rate	Market risk premium
Atlanta Gas and Light	4.55%	8.4%	.70	7.95%	7.3%
Bay State Gas	4.55%	8.4%	.75	7.95%	7.3%
Brooklyn Union Gas	4.55%	8.4%	.55	7.95%	7.3%
Indiana Energy	4.55%	8.4%	.70	7.95%	7.3%
Northwest Natural Gas	4.55%	8.4%	.70	7.95%	7.3%
Piedmont Natural Gas	4.55%	8.4%	.70	7.95%	7.3%
Washington Gas and Light	4.55%	8.4%	.60	7.95%	7.3%

Let's first calculate the required rate of return based on the 3-month Treasury bill. For Atlanta Gas and Light, the risk-free rate of return is given by the (average) yield on a 3-month Treasury bill or 4.55%. The available market risk premium, assuming the T-bill yield is the risk-free rate, is 8.4%. The published beta coefficient for Atlanta Gas and Light is .70. Converting the percentage rates of return to decimals and using CAPM, we calculate the required rate of return as

$$.0455 + .084(.70) = .104$$

or 10.4%.

A similar calculation, assuming the (average) 30-year Treasury bond yield is the risk-free rate of return, gives a required rate of return of

$$.0795 + .073(.70) = .131$$

or 13.1%.

The required rates of return for each choice of the risk-free rate for all the companies in the reference set are given in the following table.

	Required Rate of Return		
	T-bill	T-bond	Average
Atlanta Gas and Light	10.4%	13.1%	11.7%
Bay State Gas	10.9%	13.4%	12.1%
Brooklyn Union Gas	9.2%	12.0%	10.6%
Indiana Energy	10.4%	13.1%	11.7%
Northwest Natural Gas	10.4%	13.1%	11.7%
Piedmont Natural Gas	10.4%	13.1%	11.7%
Washington Gas and Light	9.6%	12.3%	11.0%

The mean of the seven average required rates of return for the reference companies is 11.5%, and this "expected return" was proposed as the required rate of return for Wisconsin Gas Company. Of course, the staff of the Wisconsin Public Service Commission had an opportunity to challenge this number. Given that CAPM is the appropriate tool to determine the required rate of return, what questions would you ask if you were a member of the Wisconsin Public Service Commission staff? You might ask whether it is appropriate to average the 3-month and 30-year rates. You might ask how the companies on the reference list were selected. Ideally, these and other hard questions are asked, and solid answers required, in the give and take leading to new gas rates.

3.7 CHAPTER SUMMARY

In this chapter, we have learned:

- How to construct and interpret **scatterplots** of bivariate data
- How to calculate and interpret the **sample correlation coefficient** r. We found

$$r = \frac{\text{Sample covariance}}{(\text{Sample std. dev. of } x)(\text{Sample std. dev. of } y)} = \frac{S_{xy}}{\sqrt{S_{xx}}\sqrt{S_{yy}}}$$

1. The value of r is always between -1 and $+1$.

2. The magnitude of r indicates the strength of the linear relation, and its sign indicates the direction. In particular,

$r > 0$	if the pattern of (x, y) values is a band that runs from lower left to upper right
$r < 0$	if the pattern of (x, y) values is a band that runs from upper left to lower right
$r = +1$	if all (x, y) values lie exactly on a straight line with a positive slope (perfect positive linear relation)
$r = -1$	if all (x, y) values lie exactly on a straight line with a negative slope (perfect negative linear relation)

3. A value of r close to -1 or $+1$ represents a strong linear relation.

4. A value of r close to 0 means that the linear relation is very weak.

- **Autocorrelation** measures association within a particular chronological sequence of observations. The sample autocorrelation coefficient r_k at lag k is given by

$$r_k = \frac{\sum_{i=1}^{n-k}(y_i - \overline{y})(y_{i+k} - \overline{y})}{\sum_{i=1}^{n}(y_i - \overline{y})^2}$$

- A **lurking variable** is a variable that was not included in the initial study that affects the measured variables.

- Correlation does not establish a **cause-and-effect relation.** To establish cause, we must establish consistency, responsiveness, and mechanism.

- A straight line is determined by its **slope** and **intercept.**

- The **least squares line** or estimated regression line minimizes the sum of squares of the vertical distances of the points from the line.

- The **least squares slope coefficient** b and **intercept coefficient** a are given by

$$b = \frac{S_{xy}}{S_{xx}} = \frac{\sum_{i=1}^{n}(x_i - \overline{x})(y_i - \overline{y})}{\sum_{i=1}^{n}(x_i - \overline{x})^2}$$
$$a = \overline{y} - b\overline{x}$$

- $b = (\sqrt{S_{yy}}/\sqrt{S_{xx}})r$, so along the least squares line, a change of 1 standard deviation in x gives a change of r standard deviations in y.

- The **standard deviation of the residuals** s is

$$s = \sqrt{\frac{1}{n-2}\sum_{i=1}^{n}(y_i - \hat{y}_i)^2}$$

- Residuals should be plotted to examine the fit of the least squares line. Useful **residual plots** are:

1. A plot of the residuals against the fitted values
2. A plot of the residuals against the explanatory variable
3. A plot of the residuals against any variable suspected to affect the response
4. A plot of the residuals over time if the data are chronological

- **Influential observations** are those data points that significantly affect the location of the least squares line. **Outliers** are observations far removed from the rest of the data. Outliers may or may not be influential.

- A response exhibits **exponential growth** if it increases by the same percentage each time period.

- A response exhibits **linear growth** if it increases by the same amount each time period.

- We can convert exponential growth to linear growth by taking the logarithms of the response. The slope coefficient of the least squares line relating the logarithms of the response to time can be used to estimate the growth rate. In particular,

$$\text{Growth rate} = 100[\text{antilog}(\text{Slope coefficient}) - 1]\%$$

- The frequencies associated with two categorical variables can be summarized in a **contingency table.**

- An association between two categorical variables that is changed or even reversed because of a variable not included in the study is known as **Simpson's Paradox.**

- A **weighted average** $\bar{x}_w$ is given by

$$\bar{x}_w = \sum_{i=1}^{n} w_i x_i \quad \text{where} \quad \sum_{i=1}^{n} w_i = 1$$

- Patterns in time series data, like **trend** and **seasonality,** can often be recognized by organizing the data in a two-way table with larger time periods (e.g., years) as the columns and smaller time periods (e.g., months) as the rows.

3.8   IMPORTANT CONCEPTS AND TOOLS

CONCEPTS

TOOLS

3.9   KEY FORMULAS

Sample covariance: $s_{xy} = \dfrac{1}{n-1}\sum_{i=1}^{n}(x_i - \bar{x})(y_i - \bar{y})$

Sample correlation coefficient: $r = \dfrac{S_{xy}}{\sqrt{S_{xx}}\sqrt{S_{yy}}}$

where

$$S_{xy} = \sum_{i=1}^{n}(x_i - \bar{x})(y_i - \bar{y})$$

$$S_{xx} = \sum_{i=1}^{n}(x_i - \bar{x})^2 \qquad S_{yy} = \sum_{i=1}^{n}(y_i - \bar{y})^2$$

Computing formulas: $S_{xx} = \sum_{i=1}^{n}x_i^2 - \dfrac{\left(\sum\limits_{i=1}^{n}x_i\right)^2}{n} \qquad S_{yy} = \sum_{i=1}^{n}y_i^2 - \dfrac{\left(\sum\limits_{i=1}^{n}y_i\right)^2}{n}$

$$S_{xy} = \sum_{i=1}^{n}x_i y_i - \dfrac{\left(\sum\limits_{i=1}^{n}x_i\right)\left(\sum\limits_{i=1}^{n}y_i\right)}{n}$$

Least squares slope coefficient: $b = \dfrac{S_{xy}}{S_{xx}} = \dfrac{\sum\limits_{i=1}^{n}(x_i - \bar{x})(y_i - \bar{y})}{\sum\limits_{i=1}^{n}(x_i - \bar{x})^2}$

Least squares intercept coefficient: $a = \bar{y} - b\bar{x}$

Relation between b and r: $b = \left(\dfrac{\sqrt{S_{yy}}}{\sqrt{S_{xx}}}\right)r$

Standard deviation of residuals: $s = \sqrt{\dfrac{1}{n-2}\sum_{i=1}^{n}(y_i - \hat{y}_i)^2}$

Weighted average: $\bar{x}_w = \sum_{i=1}^{n}w_i x_i$ where $\sum_{i=1}^{n}w_i = 1$

REVIEW EXERCISES

3.51 The following table gives the federal deficit (billions of dollars) and the number of golfers (millions) in the United States.

Year	Deficit (billion $)	Golfers (million)
1985	17.5	1.81
1986	19.9	2.12
1987	21.2	2.35
1988	23.0	2.60
1989	24.2	2.87
1990	27.8	3.21

SOURCE: *Statistical Abstract of the United States 1992.*

a. Determine the correlation between number of golfers (in millions) and the federal deficit (in billions of dollars).

b. Suppose we take as data the total number of golfers and the federal deficit in dollars. The data for 1985 are 1,810,000 and 17,500,000,000. What is the correlation between the number of golfers (total number) and the federal deficit (total dollars)? Answer without doing any further calculation.

c. If deficit is replaced by surplus so that a deficit of 17.5 becomes −17.5 and so on, what is the correlation between the number of golfers and the surplus? Answer without doing any further calculations.

3.52 Given the following data with five pairs of observations:

x	y	$x - \bar{x}$	$y - \bar{y}$	$(x - \bar{x})^2$	$(x - \bar{x})(y - \bar{y})$
0	11				
2	14				
6	2				
3	7				
4	1				

a. Construct a scatterplot.

b. Guess the sign of the correlation coefficient and the slope of the least squares line.

c. Complete the table and determine the equation of the least squares line. Graph this line on the scatterplot.

d. Predict a new value of y at $x = 5$.

3.53 Refer to Exercise 3.52. Determine the correlation coefficient r.

3.54 Refer to Exercise 3.52.

a. Obtain the five residuals.

b. Calculate the standard deviation of the residuals.

3.55 Given the following data with five pairs of observations:

x	y	$x - \bar{x}$	$y - \bar{y}$	$(x - \bar{x})^2$	$(x - \bar{x})(y - \bar{y})$
0	5				
1	4				
2	4				
3	10				
4	12				

a. Construct a scatter diagram.

b. Guess the sign of the correlation coefficient and the slope of the least squares line.

c. Complete the table and determine the equation of the least squares line. Graph this line on the scatterplot.

d. Predict a new value of y at $x = 1.5$.

3.56 Refer to Exercise 3.55. Determine the correlation coefficient r.

3.57 Refer to Exercise 3.55.

a. Obtain the five residuals.

b. Calculate the standard deviation of the residuals.

3.58 Refer to Exercise 1.2 and Table 1.1 on page 13. Among the world's 25 largest diversified service companies, 20 are from either the United States or Japan.

These firms can be further categorized as having sales of less than 50 billion dollars, or 50 billion dollars or more.

	Sales (billions of dollars)		
	Under 50 billion	50 billion or more	Total
Japan	7	9	
U.S.	3	1	
Total			

    a.   Determine the marginal totals.

    b.   Determine the relative frequencies for each entry in the table. Comment on the pattern.

3.59   Refer to Exercise 3.58. Add an additional row representing "Other countries" to the table, and repeat the two parts to that exercise.

3.60   Refer to Exercise 1.3 and Table 1.2 on page 14. Among the world's largest commercial banks, 8 are from Europe and 17 from Asia. These banks can further be categorized as having assets of less than 300 billion dollars and 300 billion dollars or more.

	Assets (billions of dollars)		
	Under 300 billion	300 billion or more	Total
Asia	9	8	
Europe	6	2	
Total			

    a.   Determine the marginal totals.

    b.   Determine the relative frequencies for each entry in the table. Comment on the pattern.

CitiesBA.dat

3.61   (*Minitab or similar program recommended*) Refer to Exercise 2.64 on page 96. The top ten cities on the list are ranked in order according to their number of knowledge workers, with Raleigh/Durham ranked first, New York ranked second, and Minneapolis ranked tenth.

    a.   Make a scatterplot with the percentage of workers holding a baccalaureate or higher degree on the *y*-axis and the rank of the city on the *x*-axis.

    b.   Determine the correlation coefficient between rank and percentage of workers holding baccalaureate degrees or higher.

3.62   It seems to be a fact that a larger proportion of drivers with fuzzy dice hanging from the rearview mirror exceed posted speed limits than those without fuzzy dice. Would removing the fuzzy dice from cars improve compliance with the speed limit? Comment and suggest a possible lurking variable responsible for the association.

3.63   Volvo, Lincoln Town Car, and Cadillac Fleetwood appeared on the list of the safest cars. The Corvette, Camaro, Charger Shelby, and Ford Mustang are on the unsafest list based on the number of fatalities per 10,000 units. Comment and suggest a possible lurking variable responsible for the association.

3.64 The following chart showing the annual increase in the number of Outback Steakhouses appeared in the October 10, 1993, issue of the *Houston Chronicle*.

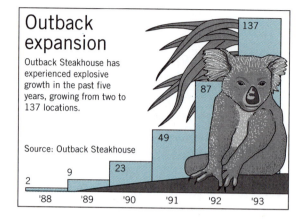

Outback expansion

Outback Steakhouse has experienced explosive growth in the past five years, growing from two to 137 locations.

Source: Outback Steakhouse

137
87
49
23
9
2

'88   '89   '90   '91   '92   '93

a. Does there appear to be linear or exponential growth in the number of steakhouses? Explain.

b. Use a least squares line to estimate the annual growth rate for Outback Steakhouse.

c. Predict the number of Outback Steakhouses in 1994.

3.65 The Minitab commands for determining the equation of the least squares line relating operating income, y, to total revenue, x, for the NHL data (see Figure 3.1 on page 103) are given here. Operating income is in a column named 'OpInHky' and total revenue is in a column named 'TotRvHky'. We also show the command for computing the correlation coefficient, r, between operating income and total revenue.

```
MTB > Correlation 'OpInHky' 'TotRvHky'.

Correlation of OpInHky and TotRvHky = 0.915

MTB > Regress 'OpInHky' 1 'TotRvHky'.

The regression equation is

OpInHky = - 13.1 + 0.701 TotRvHky

Predictor          Coef
Constant        -13.130
TotRvHky         0.70106
```

a. Compare the output with the results in Example 3.9.

b. Given $S_{xx} = 718.99$ and $S_{yy} = 422.41$, verify the relationship

$$b = \left(\frac{\sqrt{S_{yy}}}{\sqrt{S_{xx}}} \right) r$$

3.66 (*Minitab or similar program recommended*) Refer to Example 3.15. Verify the equation of the least squares line given in this example. Note that the $n = 40$ pairs of observations are listed in Example 3.15.

TeleWire.dat

3.67 (*Optional*) (*Minitab or similar program recommended*) Refer to the NSP (Wisconsin) peak power demand data in Example 3.18.

NPowPeak.dat

a. Compute the autocorrelation coefficients for the first 12 lags. Does there appear to be a strong annual seasonal pattern? Discuss.

b. Let y_t be the current demand and let y_{t-12} be the demand 12 months previously. Determine the least squares line relating y_t to y_{t-12}.

c. Plot the residuals from the fit in part **b.** Calculate the residual autocorrelation coefficients for the first 12 lags. Does there appear to be some association among the residuals? Do you think the initial model relating y_t to y_{t-12} can be improved? Discuss.

d. Using the least squares line from part **b,** predict next May's peak demand if the peak demand for this May is 500 megawatts.

3.68 Given the nine pairs of (x, y) values

x	1	1	1	2	3	3	4	5	5
y	9	7	8	10	15	12	19	24	21

a. Plot the scatter diagram.

b. Calculate $\bar{x}$, $\bar{y}$, S_{xx}, S_{yy}, and S_{xy}.

c. Determine the equation of the least squares line, and draw the line on the scatter diagram.

d. Find the predicted y corresponding to $x = 3$.

3.69 A least squares fit of a straight line produces the following residuals:

$\hat{y}$	11.3	14.8	18.4	22.0	25.5	27.0	31.2	32.7	34.1
Residuals	−.4	.2	−5.4	2.0	.5	5.0	−9.2	6.3	12.9

$\hat{y}$	36.2	39.8	43.4	45.5	46.2	46.9	46.9
Residuals	−4.2	−14.8	7.6	−1.5	16.8	1.1	−16.9

Plot these residuals against the fitted values. Does the fitted straight line appear to adequately represent the data? Explain.

After reading this chapter, you should be able to:

- Distinguish primary data from secondary data.
- List the steps involved in data collection.
- Discuss the issues associated with surveying a sample from a target population.
- Use a random number table.
- Distinguish probability samples from nonprobability samples.
- Discuss sampling designs.
- Construct good questionnaires.
- Distinguish nominal, ordinal, interval, and ratio scales of measurement.
- Discuss and implement experimental designs for comparing two treatments.

CHAPTER FOUR

Collecting Data

4.1 INTRODUCTION

Data are best collected with a purpose. Consequently, before we can effectively collect data, we should ask these questions:

What do we want to know?

Why do we want to know it?

Data collected in a thoughtful and systematic manner are a valuable aid to decision making. On the other hand, data collected without much thought and care may be useless and, in fact, may lead to inappropriate decisions. Data contain information, and the quality of the information is only as good as the quality of the data. Sophisticated methods of display, summary, and analysis cannot compensate for poor data.

There are many ways to collect data. The data collection process must balance the quality of the answers to the questions being addressed and the constraints of time, money, and the availability of sampling units. In this chapter, we discuss key issues connected with gathering data, and we highlight some important data collection procedures.*

4.2 ELEMENTS OF DATA COLLECTION

Collecting data from a complex environment can be time-consuming and expensive. Consequently, it is necessary to have a plan and a systematic collection method that gains maximum information at minimum cost. Every effort should be made to comply with sound data collection principles so that the information received is as accurate and relevant as possible.

There are two types of data: primary data and secondary data. **Secondary data** are collected by someone else and are available in published sources. Quarterly profits published in the *Wall Street Journal* are secondary data. As another example, the U.S. Department of Commerce's *Survey of Current Business* contains data collected by the government on a large number of indicators of the business environment, including gross national product, national income, personal income and expenditures, income and employment by industry, and government receipts and expenditures. Other secondary data sources of potential use to people in business are listed in Section 4.7. Knowledge of the steps in data collection discussed in this section will allow the investigator to assess the usefulness of data collected by others.

For our purposes, **primary data** will refer to data collected directly by the investigator or by the organization employing the investigator. Primary data are collected by a variety of methods: simple observation, checksheets, personal interviews, mail questionnaires, electronic data capture, experiments simulated on a computer, and controlled laboratory or field experiments.

Controlled experimentation is a method of data collection in which the environment is deliberately manipulated to determine the effects of change. For example, two individuals may be deliberately paired according to their age, gender, educational background, and so forth, and each shown the same 30-second television commercial but with the sponsor's information arranged in two different formats. At some later point, the viewers' abilities to recall certain product facts can be compared to judge the relative effectiveness of the two formats.

Designs are arrangements for collecting primary data that address such issues as: How much data should we collect? How should the experimental units be selected? If comparisons between groups of experimental units are involved, how should the groups be formed? Which variables should be examined, and how should they be

---

*The literature associated with collecting data is vast, and the interested reader could consult these books for further study: Box, G. E. P., Hunter, J. S., and Hunter, W. G. *Statistics for Experimenters*. New York: Wiley, 1978; Cochran, W. G., *Sampling Techniques,* 3rd. ed. New York: Wiley, 1977; Deming, W. E. *Sample Design in Business Research*. New York: Wiley, 1960; Scheaffer, R. L., Mendenhall, W., and Ott, L. *Elementary Survey Sampling,* 4th. ed. Boston: PWS-Kent, 1990; and Sudman S., and Bradburn, N. M. *Asking Questions. A Practical Guide to Questionnaire Design*. San Francisco: Jossey-Bass, 1982.

measured? Data collected without the aid of a design are often incomplete and difficult to interpret because important variables are not controlled and their effects are hopelessly intertwined or **confounded.**

STEPS IN DATA COLLECTION

Certain steps help to ensure data quality. Collecting data properly, particularly data collected as part of a survey, is often an intricate process. Data collection requires careful reflection on the complexities involved in a population structure, the practical feasibility of sampling methods, the coordination and supervision of field work, and finally the processing, analyses, and reporting of the data. We briefly introduce these issues by examining the principal steps involved in the collection of primary data. Our treatment is intended to be illustrative rather than exhaustive.

1. **Determine the purpose of the study.**

   The need for a clear statement of the *purpose* of the study cannot be overemphasized. Without establishing the goal of the investigation, including what we hope to learn from the data, a meaningful choice among alternative data collection plans will be impossible. By initially defining the purpose of the study as specifically as possible, we are unlikely to overlook vital information.

2. **Determine the data to be collected.**

   Guided by the statement of purpose, we should determine the *nature of the data* that are to be collected. Care should be taken to include all the essential data and, at the same time, to avoid collecting data that are irrelevant to the purpose of the study. In sampling human populations, the primary vehicle for gathering data is the questionnaire. A well-designed questionnaire is crucial to the success of a survey. In laboratory settings where the objective is to uncover the effects of controllable variables on a particular response variable, a well-designed experiment can provide an abundance of information, and save time and money.

3. **Determine the plan for collecting the data.**

   Available resources and the purpose of the investigation will generally dictate the particular method for collecting the data. Determining the appropriate *sampling design* and choosing the *sample size(s)* are two key issues that must be resolved. The choice of the sampling design is based on such factors as the structure of the population, the type of information sought, and the administrative facilities and personnel available to carry out the plan. In conjunction with choosing the appropriate data collection method, we determine the required sample size by specifying the degree of precision desired in the sample summary measure. Since there are always costs associated with collecting data, the sampling procedure and the associated sample size must be consistent with the budget allocated for the study.

4. **Train personnel.**

   Training is frequently required for the people responsible for actually recording the observations and organizing them in files. Training may take several forms and may be ongoing if the data collection takes place over an extended period of time. Everyone should understand the importance of the data so that data collection is taken seriously. Why are the data being collected? What difference does it make to the organization? What happens if the data contain errors?

5. **Analyze and report the data.**

Once the data collection plan is established and the data are collected, the full force of graphic and numerical techniques can be used to interpret the results. Ingenuity in creating plots and careful data analysis can suggest interesting relationships and conclusions that may be considered in additional studies.

Data may be reported as lists of numbers, as summary measures, in graphical form, in tables, or as an equation, or they may simply be described verbally. In general, data should be reported so the information is readily apparent to those who will use it to make decisions. If the appropriate presentation method is unclear, ask the user. Alternatively, imagine yourself as the decision maker. Which methods work for you?

EXAMPLE 4.1   Illustrating the Steps in Data Collection

An evaluation of each manager in an organization is about to begin. As part of this exercise, information is to be solicited from subordinates about the performance of their managers. Describe the possible steps in a data collection process.

Solution and Discussion.

1. *State the purpose of the study.* The objective is to solicit information from subordinates about the performance of their managers. This project is important because changes in organizational structure, salary adjustments, and advancement opportunities will depend, in part, on the outcomes. Data will be collected with a questionnaire distributed to all subordinates. Responses will be confidential.

2. *Determine the data to be collected.* Performance variables might include the following: ability to communicate goals and objectives; accessibility; leadership ability; ability to delegate; commitment to quality; management of resources; interpersonal skills; availability of feedback; and overall effectiveness. Questions related to these variables will be included on the questionnaire. The response to each performance variable question will be indicated on a 5-point scale.

$$1 \quad\quad 2 \quad\quad 3 \quad\quad 4 \quad\quad 5$$
Almost never   Almost always

A sample question follows.

My supervisor:

5. Gives me honest feedback that helps me improve my performance.

1 2 3 4 5
◯ ◯ ◯ ◯ ◯

In addition, the top of the questionnaire will provide a space for the manager's badge number and group acronym. The respondent will also indicate the length of time with the current supervisor by checking one of the three response categories: less than 1 year, 1–2 years, or more than 2 years.

3. *Describe the plan for collecting the data.* The data will be collected from all subordinates of the managers of eight groups in the organization. A two-person team in the personnel department has been designated to construct and distribute

the questionnaire. The questionnaire will be limited to a single page. The team will follow-up with nonrespondents, and tabulate and summarize the data.

4. *Train personnel.* Each of the team members has completed a short training course on questionnaire construction and ways of dealing with people who do not respond. The division head has instructed each of the team members on the importance of this project. A draft version of the questionnaire will be tested with a small group of people in the personnel department to be sure the questions are clearly stated and provide the information required.

5. *Analyze and report the data.* After the questionnaires are produced and distributed, the team will allow a week for the questionnaires to be returned. The team will follow-up with nonrespondents to get 100% participation.

   As the questionnaires are returned, they will be checked for the manager's badge number and group acronym. Response categories will be scanned to be sure questions have been answered. Data will be entered into a file in a spreadsheet program as the completed questionnaires are received. One member of the personnel team is responsible for data entry. Another member of the team will check a printout of the file for errors.

   The data will be summarized for each manager by tabulating the number of responses in each of the five response categories for each question. The mean response for each question will be computed. The data summary for one manager will be checked by hand to be sure the spreadsheet is producing the correct numbers.

   Reports for each division head, including a sample questionnaire and the data summaries, will be prepared and forwarded. Each report will also indicate where the raw data are stored and how they can be accessed. The members of the team will be identified as the authors of the reports.

EXERCISES

4.1 The primary data for one organization may be the secondary data for another organization. Do you agree with this statement? Explain.

4.2 Identify the following as primary or secondary data.

   a. Financial information (sales, profits, dividends, market value) listed annually for each firm in the Business Week 1000

   b. Customer perceptions of a new bank marketing strategy

   c. The annual salaries (including bonuses and exercised stock options) of the 20 highest paid U.S. CEOs last year

   d. The quarterly unemployment rate for Brazos County, Texas

   e. The number of U.S. households watching prime-time programming on each of the television networks, ABC, CBS, NBC, and Fox, on Monday evenings during March

   f. The performance (travel time, accuracy, cost, overall effectiveness) of a trucking firm subject to different plans for assigning drivers to routes, different pricing mechanisms, and different training opportunities

4.3   A social club has noticed a decline in the number of its members. Describe a data collection process designed to provide the club with reasons for its declining membership. Be sure to include an explicit statement of purpose.

4.4   Highway welcome centers are used in many states as part of their tourism marketing plan. Describe a data collection process that can be used to evaluate the influence of the welcoming centers on traveler behavior. Issues may include required information about destinations, and state policies about littering, speeding, and so forth. Include an explicit statement of purpose for this study.

4.5   List several factors, in addition to cost, that will influence the choice of a method for collecting data.

4.6   Collecting data in a haphazard manner is likely to result in confounding, which is the intermingling of effects of several variables. It is difficult, if not impossible, to sort out cause-and-effect relations in these circumstances. Suppose, for example, that one ethnic group of students has lower scores, on average, than another group on graduate school entrance exams, such as the Graduate Management Admission Test (GMAT). Does this necessarily imply that the first group of students does not have the ability to score as well as the second group on these tests? Suggest some factors (variables) that might be responsible for the lower scores but whose effects cannot be determined from the scores themselves.

4.7   Refer to Exercise 4.6. If you could wave a magic wand to create the necessary conditions, can you think of a way to generate test score data that would allow you to determine the effects of the factors you identified?

4.3   SAMPLING DESIGNS WITH AN EMPHASIS ON SAMPLE SURVEYS

Much of the data studied by market researchers, human resource administrators, and others in the organization are obtained by means of a survey. Surveys are used to identify consumers' perceptions of a new product, to examine employee attitudes toward proposed organizational changes, and to determine the effectiveness of new internal controls. More generally, surveys are used to forecast crop harvests, to identify prevailing social and economic conditions, such as employment, health care, and inflation, and to gauge public reaction to such events as a new minimum wage, the actions of world leaders, or a major change in foreign trade policy.

We will assume in this section that we are dealing with a finite but perhaps very large population of size N and that there are certain population characteristics that are of interest. A **census** or complete evaluation of all members of the population can conceivably provide all the desired information. However, circumstances often prevent such an extensive evaluation. Cost considerations (the year 2000 U.S. Decennial Census will cost about 50 million dollars), the lack of qualified personnel and, if required, highly specialized equipment can severely limit the size of a proposed survey. For these reasons and when fairly accurate information must be obtained quickly, it is wise to forego a census and to survey a *representative sample* from the population in question.

The process of surveying a representative sample is referred to as **survey sampling** or conducting a **sample survey.** When the sampling is properly planned and executed, samples numbering several hundred can provide accurate information about populations numbering in the hundreds of thousands.

If the sample is selected by a chance mechanism so that there is no favoritism by the sampler nor self-selection by the respondents, the sample is called a **probability sample.** Probability samples are representative in the sense that they can be used to make objective inferences about the characteristics of the population. This is not true for other, nonprobability, sampling plans. We discuss a common probability sampling design known as simple random sampling later in this section.

Surveys must be carefully managed to produce high-quality results. Sample surveys, particularly of human populations, are generally part of enumerative studies done during relatively short time intervals that provide cross-sectional snapshots of the populations during these periods. Many variables are measured on each experimental unit, frequently by completing a questionnaire, and large data bases are often generated.

EXAMPLE 4.2   Well-known Surveys

Give three examples of well-known sample surveys.

Solution and Discussion.

1. The U.S. Bureau of Labor Statistics (Dept. of Labor) surveys 370,000 employers to determine the number of people who worked for them at any time during the month. The data are collected with a mail questionnaire, and the same establishments are surveyed every month. About 90% respond. Farmers, people who are self-employed, and domestic help are excluded from the survey. The Bureau of Labor Statistics sample survey results are used to determine the total U.S. work force.

2. J. D. Power and Associates annually survey automobile owners. In one J. D. Power survey, about 45,000 people who bought new cars or light trucks during the year are questioned about their satisfaction with the way dealers treated them. Among other things, the survey measures how well salespeople explain a vehicle's features, how well the vehicle is "prepped," and how customers are treated when they pick up their new cars or trucks. The results are used to construct a dealer satisfaction index. Different brands of vehicles are ranked according to their index scores. The J. D. Power rankings are widely publicized in the United States.

3. A third example of a well-known sample survey is the Gallup poll of public opinion. Samples of about 1500 people are periodically surveyed to determine, for example, performance ratings for the president.

SELECTING THE SURVEY SAMPLE

Once the decision has been made to obtain information by means of a sample, we are immediately faced with two tasks: carefully defining the population we wish to study and selecting the characteristic or characteristics to be recorded. The latter often follows directly from the objectives of the study.

> **Target population:**   The population about which we wish to make statements on the basis of the sample

Although specifying a population may seem to be a straightforward procedure, some cases can present difficulties in even the simplest survey. To conduct a survey of the employment status of college students, we would have to decide whether to include non–degree-seeking students and degree-seeking students carrying fewer than the specified minimum number of hours during the semester.

Sampling a finite population requires a *frame,* a list of sampling units, from which the sample can be drawn. The frame should contain all the units in the target population. Can you imagine, however, the difficulties of constructing a frame for the homeless people living in a city?

In practice, frames frequently differ from the target population in various ways. They may be inadequate (units of particular types are excluded), out of date (units no longer in the target population), incomplete (units missing for no obvious reason), inaccurate (units not qualified to be in the frame or wrong information), and duplicative (units listed more than once). Nevertheless, it is usually possible to develop a reasonably good frame by expending some care and thought about the structure of the target population. Ultimately, generalizations from the sample to the population are generalizations defined by the frame.

> **Characteristic:**   The basic unit of information of interest obtained from the sampling units

The characteristic can be a person's opinion about the quality of a particular brand of automobile or the dollar amount spent on groceries. In most surveys, several characteristics are studied simultaneously.

To be able to use statistical methods correctly to draw inferences about a population from a sample, it is essential that randomness enter the selection process in an explicit manner. Before the selection is made from the frame, the method of selection should specify the *chance* that any particular unit or group of units will be included in the sample. *The introduction of chance distinguishes probability samples from nonprobability samples.*

Examples of nonprobability samples are samples chosen because they are convenient or because they correspond to the sampler's idea of what a "representative sample" should be: a questionnaire inserted in a magazine mailed to all subscribers or a group of people interviewed at a shopping mall. Each application of a nonprobability sampling method must be treated as a census and evaluated individually. No reliable assessments of the uncertainty associated with the sample results are available. Nonprobability selection methods should be avoided whenever possible.

We are now ready to examine the technical aspects of drawing a probability sample. We will discuss the *simple random sample* sampling design. This design can be implemented using a chance mechanism known as a **table of random digits.**

Table 4.1 contains a list of random digits. These digits were generated by a mechanism that can be conceptualized as follows. Suppose that 10 identical balls

TABLE 4.1 Table of Random Digits

Row									
1	0695	7741	8254	4297	0000	5277	6563	9265	1023	5925
2	0437	5434	8503	3928	6979	9393	8936	9088	5744	4790
3	6242	2998	0205	5469	3365	7950	7256	3716	8385	0253
4	7090	4074	1257	7175	3310	0712	4748	4226	0604	3804
5	0683	6999	4828	7888	0087	9288	7855	2678	3315	6718
6	7013	4300	3768	2572	6473	2411	6285	0069	5422	6175
7	8808	2786	5369	9571	3412	2465	6419	3990	0294	0896
8	9876	3602	5812	0124	1997	6445	3176	2682	1259	1728
9	1873	1065	8976	1295	9434	3178	0602	0732	6616	7972
10	2581	3075	4622	2974	7069	5605	0420	2949	4387	7679
11	3785	6401	0540	5077	7132	4135	4646	3834	6753	1593
12	8626	4017	1544	4202	8986	1432	2810	2418	8052	2710
13	6253	0726	9483	6753	4732	2284	0421	3010	7885	8436
14	0113	4546	2212	9829	2351	1370	2707	3329	6574	7002
15	4646	6474	9983	8738	1603	8671	0489	9588	3309	5860
16	7873	7343	4432	2866	7973	3765	2888	5154	2250	4339
17	3756	9204	2590	6577	2409	8234	8656	2336	7948	7478
18	2673	7115	5526	0747	3952	6804	3671	7486	3024	9858
19	0187	7045	2711	0349	7734	4396	0988	4887	7682	8990
20	7976	3862	8323	5997	6904	4977	1056	6638	6398	4552
21	5605	1819	8926	9557	2905	0802	7749	0845	1710	4125
22	2225	5556	2545	7480	8804	4161	0084	0787	2561	5113
23	2549	4166	1609	7570	4223	0032	4236	0169	4673	8034
24	6113	1312	5777	7058	2413	3932	5144	5998	7183	5210
25	2028	2537	9819	9215	9327	6640	5986	7935	2750	2981
26	7818	3655	5771	4026	5757	3171	6435	2990	1860	1796
27	9629	3383	1931	2631	5903	9372	1307	4061	5443	8663
28	6657	5967	3277	7141	3628	2588	9320	1972	7683	7544
29	4344	7388	2978	3945	0471	4882	1619	0093	2282	7024
30	3145	8720	2131	1614	1575	5239	0766	0404	4873	7986
31	1848	4094	9168	0903	6451	2823	7566	6644	1157	8889
32	0915	5578	0822	5887	5354	3632	4617	6016	8989	9482
33	1430	4755	7551	9019	8233	9625	6361	2589	2496	7268
34	3473	7966	7249	0555	6307	9524	4888	4939	1641	1573
35	3312	0773	6296	1348	5483	5824	3353	4587	1019	9677
36	6255	4204	5890	9273	0634	9992	3834	2283	1202	4849
37	0562	2546	8559	0480	9379	9282	8257	3054	4272	9311
38	1957	6783	4105	8976	8035	0883	8971	0017	6476	2895
39	7333	1083	0398	8841	0017	4135	4043	8157	4672	2424
40	4601	8908	1781	4287	2681	6223	0814	4477	3798	4437

numbered $0, 1, \ldots, 9$, respectively, are placed in a barrel. After the balls are mixed, one is drawn blindly, and the digit on it is recorded. The ball is returned to the barrel and the operation is repeated. The numbers in Table 4.1 were actually generated by a computer that closely simulates this procedure.

The chance mechanism underlying the random number table ensures that all single digits have the same chance of occurrence, that all pairs of digits $00, 01, \ldots, 99$ have the same chance of occurrence, and so on. Moreover, each digit and consequently any collection of digits, is unrelated to any other digit in the table. This latter condition makes the digits random.

EXAMPLE 4.3   Using a Table of Random Digits

Suppose we have 40 boxes of low-fat frozen dinners. Use Table 4.1 to select a sample of size $n = 5$ dinners to study their fat content.

Solution and Discussion.   The first step is to number the boxes from 1 to 40 or to stack them in some order so that they can be identified. In Table 4.1, the digits must be chosen two at a time because the population size $N = 40$ is a two-digit number. We begin by arbitrarily selecting a row and a column in the table. Suppose we select row 8 and column 25. We read the pairs of digits in columns 25 and 26, and proceed downward to get

$$31 \quad 06 \quad 04 \quad 46 \quad 28 \quad 04 \quad 27$$

We ignore the number 46 because it is greater than 40. We also ignore any number when it appears a second time, as 4 does here. We continue reading pairs of digits until five different numbers in the appropriate range are selected. Here boxes of frozen dinners numbered

$$31 \quad 6 \quad 4 \quad 28 \quad 27$$

are tested for fat content.

For large-scale samplings or frequent applications, it is more convenient to use a well-tested random number generator on a computer.

SIMPLE RANDOM SAMPLING

There are two main types of random sampling:

> **Random sampling with replacement:**   The sampling units are replaced after each draw.
>
> **Random sampling without replacement:**   The sampling units are *not* replaced after each draw.

The mechanism of drawing balls from a barrel used to illustrate the construction of a random digit table is an example of sampling with replacement. Each ball is selected, its digit recorded, and the ball is returned to the barrel before the next ball is drawn. This procedure yields a sequence of random draws in which it is possible to select the same sampling unit more than once.

If a ball is selected from the barrel, its digit recorded, and the ball is *not* returned to the barrel before the next ball is selected, the result is sampling without replacement. Sampling without replacement yields a collection of different units. The same sampling unit cannot appear more than once in a sample chosen without replacement.

When sampling without replacement, the number of units remaining in the population is reduced by one with each single draw. However, in spite of the feature of a changing population size, all samples of a given sample size, n, can be shown to have the same ultimate chance of being selected.

In survey sampling, sampling without replacement is known as *simple random sampling*. The sample of frozen dinners in Example 4.3, selected using a table of random digits and rejecting a duplicate number, is an example of a simple random sample of size 5.

Simple random sample: A sample selected in such a way that every possible set of n units has the same chance to be in the sample actually selected

---

A simple random sample may be selected by assigning a different number to each of the N population items in a frame and then, using a table of random digits, drawing numbers until n different sampling units are chosen.

EXAMPLE 4.4   Selecting a Simple Random Sample

An audit of a Fee Account is required to verify that expenditures were not made to supplement the salary of a county official. It is decided to sample the checks written from this account in fiscal year 1996 to ensure that, for each check selected, the expenditure can be traced to a Request-for-Nonappropriated-Funds form and to a vendor invoice or other appropriate support documentation. Sixty checks are to be selected for testing. Select a simple random sample of size 60 from the checks written on this Fee Account in fiscal year 1996.

Solution and Discussion.   An inspection of the check register for fiscal year 1996 reveals that 172 checks were written on the Fee Account. The first check number was 1116 and the last check written on the account during this year had number 1287. A computer program designed to produce nearly random numbers was used to generate 60 different numbers from 1116 to 1287. (The seed number at the top of the following display simply starts the random number generator.) The results, shown in ascending order, are given on page 176. Checks with these numbers were chosen for testing.

RANDOM NUMBERS   VERSION 2.00

COMPANY: Fee Account Check Sample

Random number generator seed used was: 94967258
To generate next continuous series use: 1504064036

Selected 60 numbers from the following sequence(s):
    Sequence 1: From 1116 to 1287

Group 1 (Primary sample of 60)

Ascending order

Number	Number	Number	Number	Number
1116 ⊠	1167 ⊠	1190 ⊠	1216 ⊠	1252 ⊠
1131 ⋎	1168 ⊠	1191 ⊠	1219 ⊠	1255 ⊠
1133 ⊠	1170 ⋎	1193 ⊠	1220 ⊠	1258 ⊠
1136 ⊠	1172 ⊠	1194 ⊠	1223 ⊠	1259 ⊠
1137 ⊠	1175 ⊠	1199 ⊠	1229 ⊠	1263 ⊠
1141 ⊠	1176 ⊠	1200 ⋎	1233 ⊠	1264 ⊠
1143 ⋎	1177 ⊠	1207 ⊠	1234 ⊠	1267 ⊠
1147 ⊠	1178 ⊠	1208 ⊠	1238 ⊠	1269 ⊠
1160 ⊠	1184 ⊠	1209 ⊠	1240 ⋎	1276 ⊠
1161 ⊠	1185 ⊠	1211 ⊠	1244 ⊠	1281 ⊠
1165 ⊠	1187 ⊠	1213 ⊠	1245 ⊠	1283 ⊠
1166 ⊠	1188 ⊠	1215 ⊠	1251 ⊠	1285 ⊠

⊠   Check valid and selected for testing

⋎   Void check

In this case, five of the checks in the sample were checks that were voided. Testing could proceed with a sample of size 55 rather than 60. Alternatively, replacements for the voided checks could be selected, at random, from the remaining checks in the population.

Suppose the characteristic of interest measured on each of the sampling units is denoted by X. Measurements of the characteristic on the n units in the random sample can be denoted by $x_1, x_2, \ldots, x_n$, where the subscripts indicate the different units. Often, a primary purpose of sampling is to learn about a population mean or a population total. Inferences about these population quantities are naturally based on the sample mean, $\bar{x} = \frac{1}{n}\sum_{i=1}^{n} x_i$, or the sample total, $\sum_{i=1}^{n} x_i$.

In some cases, an inherent characteristic or attribute is of interest. Examples include people who are retired and voters favoring a school bond issue. A natural estimate of the proportion of units in the population that have the attribute is provided by the proportion in the simple random sample with the attribute.

With the measurement variable, X, coded 0–1 to indicate the absence or presence of the attribute, the sample values, $x_1, x_2, \ldots, x_n$ will be a sequence of 0's and 1's. The sample sum counts the number in the sample with the attribute so that the sample proportion, $\hat{p}$, is given by

$$\textbf{Sample proportion:} \quad \hat{p} = \frac{\sum_{i=1}^{n} x_i}{n}$$

which is of the same form as the sample mean. Keep in mind, however, the x_i's in the definition of the proportion all have the values 0 or 1.

Inferences about population proportions, based on simple random samples, are considered in more detail in Chapter 10.

OTHER PROBABILITY SAMPLING METHODS

The principal objective of a sampling design is to make efficient use of the budget allocated to a study by obtaining as precise an estimate of a population quantity as possible. Simple random sampling is the most basic sampling technique that not only ensures a representative sample but also yields an estimate of a population quantity and a statement of precision. Many ramifications have evolved from the concept of simple random sampling that permit more precise estimates to be attained for different types of populations. One of the most practically useful designs, called **stratified sampling,** first divides the population into homogeneous segments and then draws separate simple random samples from these individual subpopulations.

At first, it may seem surprising that the technique of simple random sampling can be improved. To clarify this point, consider a city in which the northern districts are predominantly high-income areas and the southern districts are predominantly low-income areas. To estimate the average cost of housing for the entire city, it is intuitively apparent that relatively small simple random samples taken separately from the northern and southern districts are likely to provide more accurate information than a single sample taken from the whole city. Why? The essence of stratification is that it capitalizes on the known homogeneity of the subpopulations, so that only relatively small samples are required to estimate the characteristic for each group. These individual estimates can then be easily combined to produce an estimate for the whole population. In addition to savings in sample size, a valuable by-product of the stratified sampling scheme is that estimates obtained from different subpopulations can be subsequently used to make comparisons.

Randomization and stratification constitute the core concepts of survey sampling. However, other sampling designs have been developed either to exploit specific population structures or for administrative convenience. One of these designs, **systematic sampling,** selects every kth unit in the frame for the sample, beginning with a unit chosen at random from the first k units. The purpose of this type of sampling technique is usually to spread the sampled units evenly over the frame. Since the sample size, n, is specified in advance and the population size, N, is fixed, $k = N/n$. Once the starting point is selected, the remaining units in the sample are determined, so there are only k possible samples.

In many situations, a substantial cost saving can be achieved by conducting a survey with randomly chosen groups or *clusters* of the sampling units rather than taking a simple random sample from the population. To obtain information about children as consumers, suppose that a sample is to be selected from the population of all seventh-grade students in a particular state. We can view each school in the state as a cluster of the basic sampling units, the seventh-grade students. In **cluster sampling,** first we choose a simple random sample of clusters (schools) and then interview *all* of the units (seventh graders) in those clusters (schools).

Most of the sample survey results, such as the Gallup poll, the Consumer Price Index, and the Unemployment Rate, that regularly appear in print and other mass media not only employ stratification and sampling without replacement but also use strata within strata or even a combination of stratification and cluster sampling.*

NONSAMPLING ERRORS AND BIAS IN SURVEYS

Errors that result as a consequence of collecting a sample rather than examining the entire population are called *sampling errors.* For probability samples, the magnitudes of sampling errors can generally be quantified, and it is usually possible to reduce sampling errors by increasing the sample sizes.

Errors that are not sampling errors are called *nonsampling errors.* These errors occur, for example, because of a substantial difference between the sampled population and the target population, or because of an inadequate measuring instrument, such as a poorly worded questionnaire, or because the selected units cannot be measured for some reason.

Nonsampling errors introduce *bias* or systematic errors in the way in which the sample represents the population.

Bias: The consistent departure, in a particular direction, of the sample estimator from the target population quantity

Source of bias: Any cause of the consistent departure of the sample estimator from the target population quantity

---

Of course, choosing the wrong formula to construct an estimator from the sample data can be a source of bias, but this can often be corrected and is far from the most important source of bias.

A frame that does not include all of the target population is an important source of bias. This *undercoverage* can produce a sampled population substantially different from the target population. One of the most dramatic and frequently cited situations in which this problem surfaced was the failure of the *Literary Digest*'s poll to predict a winner in the national presidential election of 1936 between the candidates F. D. Roosevelt and A. Landon. Although a large-scale survey was conducted, the pollsters drew their sample from a list consisting of telephone and car owners. In 1936, such amenities were much more common among upper-income groups, and the sample failed to adequately represent low-income groups. Because support for the Republican candidate happened to be strongest in upper-income classes, the poll

---

*We have barely scratched the surface of the sampling design methodology. The books by Deming; Scheaffer, Mendenhall, and Ott; and Cochran, referenced in the footnote on page 166, are excellent places to learn more about advanced sampling techniques.

wrongly predicted a defeat for Roosevelt. Moreover, the sampling was nonprobabilistic; no error limits could be placed on the estimated percentage of votes, even for the population actually sampled.

A faulty measuring device that produces observations different from what were intended can be a major source of bias. Casually constructed survey questionnaires are notorious for poorly worded questions that are likely to produce incorrect or misleading responses. How would you interpret a "no" response to the question: "Do you feel firms today are concerned about their employees and customers?" The bias arising from an inaccurate measuring instrument is called *response bias*.

Finally, another primary source of bias emerges when a large number of the sampling units selected for the sample cannot be measured for the characteristic of interest. In surveys of human populations, this can occur when people refuse to be interviewed or refuse to fill out a mail questionnaire. Nonrespondents typically differ from respondents regarding the characteristic being surveyed, making the population actually sampled quite different from the target population. This *nonresponse bias* can sometimes be reduced with a follow-up study of the nonrespondents. Substituting units that are conveniently available for nonrespondents can introduce additional bias. An interviewer who finds no one at home at a designated residence may decide to interview the neighbors, who may have an entirely different lifestyle from the intended subjects.

Every effort should be made to reduce nonsampling errors. When they exist, however, it is virtually impossible to precisely determine their effects. This suggests that we should read and interpret survey results with extreme caution. Good design is part, but only part, of a trustworthy survey.

SAMPLING IN ENUMERATIVE AND ANALYTIC STUDIES

The discussion of probability sampling plans to this point has assumed that the investigator is involved with an enumerative study in which the frame does not differ in any important respects from the target population. However, sampling designs are pervasive in statistical studies. It is possible, and desirable, to sample processes as part of an analytic study of process characteristics. For example, a process producing thin film may be sampled systematically every hour to generate measurements of thickness, strength, and so forth. These measurements may be plotted on control charts to monitor the consistency of the film.

The flow diagram in Figure 4.1 (page 180) illustrates the role of sampling in enumerative and analytic studies.* The enumerative study side of the diagram and comments (1)–(5) below the diagram summarize much of our discussion in this section.

As indicated in the flow diagram, sampling in an analytic study has a different orientation from that of an enumerative study. By definition, an analytic study evolves over time. We are observing a *current* process but are interested in making decisions about or taking actions on a *future* process. Thus, there is generally no fixed finite population—and no frame—to sample. Sampling in analytic studies is usually done to monitor manufacturing processes or to provide representative units for testing purposes.

---

*Source: Hahn, G. J., and Meeker, W. Q., "Assumptions for statistical inference," *The American Statistician*, Vol. 47, No. 1, Feb. 1993, pp. 1–11.

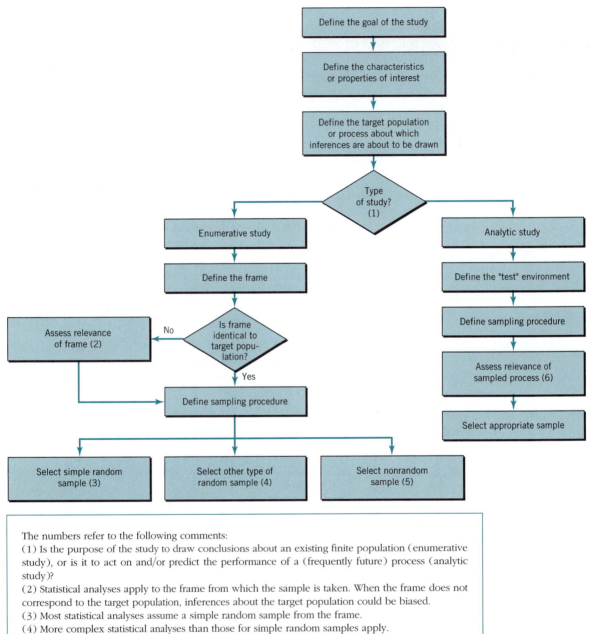

The numbers refer to the following comments:
(1) Is the purpose of the study to draw conclusions about an existing finite population (enumerative study), or is it to act on and/or predict the performance of a (frequently future) process (analytic study)?
(2) Statistical analyses apply to the frame from which the sample is taken. When the frame does not correspond to the target population, inferences about the target population could be biased.
(3) Most statistical analyses assume a simple random sample from the frame.
(4) More complex statistical analyses than those for simple random samples apply.
(5) Statistical analyses do not apply.
(6) Statistical analyses apply to the sampled process, and not necessarily to the process of interest.

Figure 4.1   Role of Sampling in Enumerative and Analytic Studies

Sampling does not provide direct information on what would happen if the present environment were different or deliberately changed—a necessary ingredient for process improvement. Collecting observations under specially selected operating conditions, as we discuss in Section 4.5, is better suited for this purpose, and is a primary means of collecting information in analytic studies.

EXERCISES

4.8   Classify the following as a probability or nonprobability sample.

  a.   A television news show asks viewers for their position on a particular issue. Viewers are asked to call one phone number if they support the issue and another phone number if they are opposed. A number of viewers respond.

  b.   A collection of invoices is organized sequentially according to invoice number in a file. An invoice is selected at random from the first 10 invoices and then every 12th invoice is chosen until the end of the file is reached. These invoices form the sample.

  c.   A frame is created by listing the 10-digit serial numbers of all automobile engines of a particular type built within a certain period of time. A computer program is used to generate five 10-digit random numbers from the range of numbers covered by the frame. The engines corresponding to the five numbers generated are chosen for the sample.

4.9   Classify the following as a probability or nonprobability sample.

  a.   Fragile ceramic plates are packed in large boxes. The sample consists of the top plates in the first 20 boxes.

  b.   Large rolls of material are used in the manufacture of Scotch tape. Several pieces of material of the same size are cut from the end of the roll to create a sample of material.

  c.   Phone operators at a mail order house handle calls of varying lengths during the course of their shifts. A sample of call lengths is selected by measuring the length of the current call every 30 minutes.

4.10   Refer to Exercise 4.8. For each situation identified as a probability sample, determine the type of probability sample described. Identify, in general terms, the types of nonprobability samples.

4.11   Refer to Exercise 4.9. For each situation identified as a probability sample, determine the type of probability sample described. Identify, in general terms, the types of nonprobability samples.

4.12   Find four examples of recent surveys in newspapers, magazines, or other published sources. For each example,

  a.   Indicate the organization conducting the survey.

  b.   Identify the survey as a census, a nonprobability survey, or a probability survey.

  c.   Discuss the objectives of the survey, and indicate how the survey information was summarized. Were the limits of sampling variation indicated? If so, what do you think these mean?

  d.   Identify the target population and discuss potential sources of error in the survey results. Can the survey findings be reliably generalized to the target population? Why or why not?

4.13   Some would argue that politicians allow public opinion surveys to set their agendas rather than exhibiting leadership to chart appropriate courses of action. Some have suggested that polls "harden" opinions that people have not really formed yet because of the need to avoid embarrassment by responding in a seemingly knowledgeable way. What implications do these two assertions have for using the results of opinion polls in political situations? Should opinion polls be banned in the best interests of the country? Discuss.

4.14 Discuss the appropriate choices of the sampling units and the frame in each of the following surveys:

a. The Director of Human Resources at a large manufacturing plant is interested in determining the effectiveness of the Targeted Selection Program (TSP) currently in use at the plant. The objective is to assess the strengths and weaknesses of the TSP to improve the plant's employee selection process.

b. A software company sells a popular computer program that is stored on a single $3\frac{1}{2}$-inch diskette. The company wants to be sure disks are being produced with no or very few defects.

c. A student at a large university, as part of a class project, wants to determine the proportion of students who work part-time.

d. The marketing division of a pharmaceutical company wishes to ascertain the percentage of hospitals in the country that use its brand of disinfecting solution to sterilize surgical equipment.

4.15 For each survey in Exercise 4.14, discuss:

a. The construction of the frame and any difficulties that might be encountered in the process

b. The selection of a probability sample and a suitable method for conducting the sampling: direct measurement or personal observation, mail questionnaire, telephone call, or other relevant methods

c. The advantages and possible disadvantages of using your suggested sampling method in part **b**

4.16 Discuss the appropriate choices of the sampling units and the frame in each of the following surveys:

a. A local community newspaper that carries few stories and lots of advertising is circulated without charge. Many copies of the paper are deposited at a large number of drop sites in the community. The publisher wants to verify circulation figures to sell advertising space at profitable rates.

b. A large number of people working for a county in central Texas have access to the county's computer system. The county wishes to determine the proportion of people with computer access who are no longer county employees.

c. The U.S. Bureau of Labor Statistics wishes to determine the number of unemployed workers in a given month.

d. An elected judge wishes to determine how her constituency feels about a proposed piece of antiobscenity legislation.

4.17 For each survey in Exercise 4.16, discuss:

a. The construction of the frame and any difficulties that might be encountered in the process

b. The selection of a probability sample and a suitable method for conducting the sampling: direct measurement or personal observation, mail questionnaire, telephone call, or other relevant method

    c. The advantages and possible disadvantages of using your suggested sampling method in part **b**

4.18 Identify the major sources of bias in each of the following situations:

    a. A survey is conducted to study the extent of the use of convenience foods (such as frozen dinners) by households in a community. A random sample of households is selected, and the data are collected by telephone interviews made during working hours (8 A.M. to 5 P.M.). The nonrespondents are ignored.

    b. A radio station conducts a poll to determine the best restaurants in a community by asking its listeners to call the station and state their opinions.

    c. An agriculture organization wishes to survey a sample of ranches in Texas. Darts will be thrown at a state map. The two ranches closest to the location of each dart will be surveyed.

    d. An organization is interested in monthly household expenditures for groceries. Representatives of the organization conduct exit surveys of every third shopper, at several major supermarkets, weekday afternoons to collect the expenditure data.

4.19 A resort area has 32 motels, which are collectively taken as a population. The characteristic to be studied is the charge per day for double-occupancy rooms. The population values are the following rates per day in dollars:

65	60	75	61	62	62	64	65
70	68	64	60	60	65	60	59
65	63	60	64	68	64	64	62
68	66	63	65	62	67	65	63

    a. Using a random number table, draw a simple random sample of size 10 from this population. Record the daily double-occupancy rates.

    b. Use the results in part **a** to calculate the sample mean.

4.20 CapExpFa.dat (*Minitab or similar program recommended*) Suppose that 588 farms located in a particular area constitute a population and that their last year's capital expenditure on farm machinery and equipment is the characteristic to be studied. The record for the whole population is provided in Table 4.2 (page 184), divided into three data sets based on farm size (courtesy of Harlan Hughes).

    a. From the whole population of 588 farms, draw a simple random sample of size 60 using a table of random digits. Record the expenditures on farm machinery and equipment.

    b. Use the results in part **a** to calculate the sample mean.

4.21 CapExpFa.dat (*Minitab or similar program recommended*) Refer to Table 4.2. The farms in the table are already *stratified* according to size.

    a. Using a table of random digits, select a simple random sample of 10 farms from each stratum (small, medium, and large). Calculate the sample mean for each stratum. Denote the sample means by $\bar{x}_1$, $\bar{x}_2$, and $\bar{x}_3$, respectively.

    b. Calculate an overall sample mean $\bar{x}$ by constructing a weighted average of the sample means for each stratum. The weights will depend on the number of farms in each stratum. Let N denote the total number of farms.

TABLE 4.2   Capital Expenditures on Machinery and Equipment (in thousands of dollars)

Small Farms

17	38	9	7	11	14	17	10	31	24	22	21	9	41	19
9	13	26	36	18	8	11	23	19	16	14	14	17	20	20
9	18	6	19	52	14	5	27	14	14	28	17	9	11	12
25	19	28	15	18	24	23	27	24	20	21	27	21	34	26
21	9	29	22	10	18	45	24	16	95	40	42	11	17	17
13	14	23	17	27	18	34	18	16	17	20	23	18	42	22
18	23	16	26	11	37	23	32	24	16	24	34	37	31	29
15	41	38	21	34	23	24	27	34	5	34	29	22	26	30
26	27	39	30	31	28	39	28	34	28	24	44	22	23	40
16	5	19	36	36	17	21	43	21	19	14	14	31	27	39
30	41	28	19	32	18	19	33	27	28	26	23	32	36	21
24	32	19	18	31	25	26	21	18	36	29	47	26	31	26
32	27	43	45	45	25	17	30	27	28	16	44	20	15	31
21	42	27	32	33	21	35	44	24	26	38	57	54	24	37
21	33	19	20	32										

Medium Farms

37	30	41	17	38	29	32	21	39	41	28	33	35	24	36
28	20	23	27	34	33	36	25	28	39	36	22	25	54	53
36	14	22	32	21	35	35	39	32	40	24	48	41	30	42
20	38	23	17	38	16	23	28	32	18	60	28	47	61	25
22	25	48	53	35	25	23	44	18	56	42	55	39	24	38
42	27	30	34	43	29	35	43	62	25	15	66	34	25	11
45	28	40	32	38	33	48	46	54	45	35	31	30	42	22
23	46	14	42	33	31	75	50	44	33	41	32	45	44	51
39	35	22	44	35	24	29	23	32	30	35	50	28	21	21
12	30	28	60	35	49	33	22	58	25	23	39	40	44	41
14	37	32	22	27	23	37	59	50	46	40	47	41	38	48
40	32	31	22	24	25	33	54	36	52	39	61	46	36	16
37	38	51	25	35	49	9	46	35	53	43	59	41	52	51
47	72	46	29	25	42	42	43	46	43	29	58	47	85	52
48	23	39	40	43	52	36	35	27	56	47	39	51	48	48
23	24	39	30	59	35	39	32	51	18	27	38	36	41	11
42	42	65	27	34	72	49	39	44	57	64	51	53	55	63
39	31	48												

Large Farms

53	63	44	66	40	42	48	44	27	56	37	39	37	40	66
49	39	54	30	68	36	42	28	29	41	57	30	39	28	80
79	61	81	53	57	54	29	94	77	52	61	49	52	67	36
35	57	63	32	48	57	50	62	51	52	59	55	22	18	84
57	86	50	54	96	45	28	59	64	42	41	77	76	83	36
42	39	72	84	34	55	51	66	96	63	88	87	63	91	117
107	48	56	71	54	64	45	61	59	68	50	74	100	144	80
64	101	105	77	85	60	63	66	36	95					

Here $N = 588$. Let N_1, N_2, and N_3 be the number of farms in the small, medium, and large stratum, respectively. Here $N_1 = 215$, $N_2 = 258$, and $N_3 = 115$. The overall sample mean is given by the formula

$$\overline{x} = \frac{N_1}{N}\overline{x}_1 + \frac{N_2}{N}\overline{x}_2 + \frac{N_3}{N}\overline{x}_3$$

c. Using a computer, determine the mean capital expenditure for all 588 farms in the population. Compare the sample means computed in Exercise 4.20**b** and part **b** of this exercise with the population mean. (The sample means are computed for samples of sizes 60 and 30, respectively.)

4.22 Errors present in the accounts receivable are of vital concern to auditors. An auditor who works for a shipping company wishes to estimate the proportion of instances in which customers receive faulty bills. During a given period of time, suppose that the customer clearances of 2325 accounts receivable are filed at the auditor's office. A simple random sample of 500 of these accounts is taken, and 48 of them are found to involve faulty billing.

a. Calculate the sample proportion of accounts receivable that involved faulty billing.

b. Do you think this examination of the accounts receivable is an enumerative or an analytic study? Defend your position.

4.4 DESIGNING QUESTIONNAIRES

The tool most frequently used to collect data from sample surveys is the **questionnaire.** Questionnaires are generally inexpensive to produce and relatively easy to administer. (You are probably most familiar with mail questionnaires or questionnaires that are used by interviewers over the telephone.) It is important to remember, however, that questions and response categories must be carefully constructed to encourage respondent participation and to produce data that are trustworthy and address the intended issues. In this section, we briefly discuss some of the issues associated with producing effective questionnaires.

MEASUREMENT SCALES

Consideration of the kinds of information collected in surveys indicates that the characteristics or variables of interest are of different types. This has implications for the wording of questions, the choice of response categories, and the nature of the analysis once the data are collected.

We have previously distinguished between two broad categories of variables: *quantitative* variables and *qualitative* variables. Quantitative variables can be either *discrete* or *continuous*. Qualitative variables, when numerically coded, are always discrete. With these broad distinctions in mind, we distinguish four levels of measurement or types of scale.

The values of variables on a **nominal scale** are denoted by arbitrary labels or symbols. We introduced the nominal scale previously in our discussion of binary or 0–1 coding. Employment status is a qualitative variable measured on a nominal scale.

Its "values" are unemployed or employed. These labels may be conveniently assigned the numbers 0 and 1, respectively; however, any numerical assignment with two distinct numbers is possible.

The **ordinal scale** is similar to the nominal scale but each name or symbol can be associated with the extent to which some underlying property is possessed. In the bond rating discussion, riskiness is the variable or underlying property. The symbol Aaa is associated with little risk, whereas the symbol C is associated with considerable risk. That is, the order of the names or symbols is meaningful. Any set of distinct numbers of increasing magnitudes can be used to represent the outcomes on an ordinal scale. Notice, however, that for numbers used in an ordinal scale, their difference is not meaningful. We could say that an Aaa bond is a 9 and a C bond is a 0, but to say the difference between an Aaa bond and a C bond is 9 minus 0 is nonsense. All the methods suitable for summarizing and analyzing nominal data can be used on ordinal data.

The **interval scale** can be thought of as an ordinal scale where outcomes are labeled with numbers rather than category names and where the numerical difference between two numbers is a measure of the amount of difference in the underlying characteristic. The position of zero on this scale is arbitrary. Temperature is a common example of a variable measured on an interval scale. There are several standard temperature scales, but temperature can be measured accurately, and a difference between two temperatures on the same scale is a meaningful measure. All the methods suitable for summarizing and analyzing nominal and ordinal data can be used on interval data.

The **ratio scale** is similar to the interval scale but the position of zero is unique and indicates the absence of the characteristic. Most variables of a quantitative type are measured on a ratio scale. Income, consecutive years employed, and earnings per share are all examples of variables measured on a ratio scale. All statistical methods may be used with data on a ratio scale.

The four types of measurement scales form a hierarchy with an ascending order of complexity. The nominal scale is least complex, and the ratio scale is most complex (and most informative). A ratio or interval scale can be changed to an ordinal scale by grouping values into categories, for example, high, medium, and low. An ordinal scale can be changed to a nominal scale by using labels or symbols and dropping any indication of order. However, the reverse is not true; that is, a nominal scale cannot be changed to an ordinal scale unless we have more information than is contained in the nominal or ordinal scale categories alone.

QUESTIONNAIRE DESIGN

Designing questionnaires may appear to be simple. Once you have a clear notion of the information desired, it should be easy to construct appropriate questions and arrange them in the form of an instrument. However, experience suggests there are no rules that guarantee a flawless questionnaire. Practice helps, but even questionnaires produced by skilled researchers are often flawed. Questionnaires should be pretested on subjects who are similar to the intended respondents. Remember, the questionnaire must:

1. Communicate to the respondent what the investigator is asking for, and

2. Communicate to the investigator what the respondent has to say.

The accuracy of the data depends on the lack of misinformation in these two channels of communication.

Once the objective of the investigation is determined and the appropriate types of variables are identified, the data requirements must be translated into a set of rough questions. Questionnaire design may require several iterations. Certain critical checks of the rough draft have to be made. Does each question have the most appropriate *form?* Is each question *relevant* and *properly worded?* Is the *sequencing* of the questions appropriate? Do the *layout* and *appearance* of the questionnaire allow for easy data collection?

Each of these checks will invariably suggest changes in the rough draft. The checks are interrelated so that, for example, a change in the sequencing of questions may require changes in the form and wording of some of the questions. Several repetitions through the sequence of checks may be required before a questionnaire is ready for *pretesting.* Changes resulting from pretesting may require another loop through the checks, and so on, until a final draft of the questionnaire is ready.

Our discussion pertains to designing questionnaires for face-to-face, telephone, or mail surveys. Depending on the method of administration, there may be unique requirements concerning certain questionnaire features that we will not address. For example, the cover letter is an important component of mail surveys. Good discussions of additional issues associated with questionnaire design are available in marketing research texts and books dealing specifically with questionnaire construction.*

QUESTION FORMAT

Question format is essentially determined by the nature of the allowable responses. A question with *fixed response categories* that is *worded in the same way for every respondent* is called a **completely structured question.** The response categories are mutually exclusive (do not overlap) and exhaustive (cover all possibilities). At the other extreme, an *open-ended* question without fixed response categories that *may be worded differently for different respondents* is called a **completely nonstructured question.**

Questionnaires consisting mostly of structured questions are known as **structured questionnaires,** and those consisting mostly of nonstructured questions are known as **nonstructured questionnaires.** In general, the more focused and concise the research objective, the more structured the questionnaire. Nonstructured questionnaires are more likely to be used in relatively small-scale exploratory research projects where the objective is to identify issues for further study.

EXAMPLE 4.5   **Constructing a Question**

A discount long-distance telephone service wants to survey households in a particular area to assess potential demand. Construct a structured question dealing with the number of long-distance telephone calls made by people in a particular household per week.

---

*See, for example, Churchill, G. A., Jr., *Marketing Research: Methodological Foundations,* 5th ed. Hinsdale, Ill.: Dryden Press, 1991; Parasuraman, A., *Marking Research,* 2nd ed. Reading, Mass.: Addison-Wesley, 1991; and Dillman, D. A., *Mail and Telephone Surveys: The Total Design Method.* New York: Wiley, 1978.

Solution and Discussion. The following question is one solution.

Approximately how many long-distance telephone calls do you and other members of your household make per week?

_____ 0 to 1 call
_____ 2 to 3 calls
_____ 4 to 5 calls
_____ 6 to 7 calls
_____ More than 7 calls

The question is direct, asking for specific information from the respondent, and the response categories are fixed. To answer the question, the respondent must check one of the blanks. The fixed response categories are mutually exclusive and exhaustive to provide unambiguous and comprehensive data.

The variable being examined in this case, number of long-distance calls, is a discrete quantitative variable measured on a ratio scale. Because of the structure of the categories, however, the measurement is only accurate to within a range of phone calls. We can easily convert the question to a nonstructured question by simply leaving the response open-ended, as follows:

Approximately how many long-distance telephone calls do you and other members of your household make per week? _____
(Please specify)

For this question an open-ended response may be preferable. On the other hand, it may be easier for respondents to specify a range of phone calls rather than a single value.

Apart from the response category issue, is this question a good one? Is the meaning of "approximately" clear? How about "members of your household"?

Many business-related surveys attempt to measure attitudes in addition to personal or demographic characteristics, such as education level, age, and income, and behavioral variables such as frequency of visits to a store and the extent to which a catalog is used. An attitude can be defined as an underlying mental state that often results in a predisposition to respond in a particular way to certain stimuli. For example, an attitude of general support for education might manifest itself in the following statements: Education is important. I will vote for the current school bond issue.

Attitudes can only be inferred and cannot be directly observed or measured. Nevertheless, considerable insight can often be obtained by asking relatively direct questions in the form of rating scales on which respondents check off positions that best reflect their feelings.

A person's attitude toward a particular supermarket may be represented by the expressed extent of agreement to the following 5-point scale items:

	Strongly Disagree	Disagree	Neither Agree Nor Disagree	Agree	Strongly Agree
1. Prices in the store are reasonable.	_____	_____	_____	_____	_____
2. The store has a wide variety of products.	_____	_____	_____	_____	_____
3. The store's operating hours are inconvenient.	_____	_____	_____	_____	_____

The responses may be analyzed for each question separately, or the respondent's overall attitude may be measured by summing* the numerical ratings on the statements making up the scale.

The general principles underlying attitude measurement are also useful in measuring other internal variables, such as beliefs, opinions, preferences, and motives.

Rating scales used in most surveys have between 5 and 9 categories. The categories usually have labels with *anchor labels* that define the two extremes. The labeled categories are typically regarded as equally far apart so that consecutive integers attached to the categories for the purpose of analysis are regarded as a set of *interval scale* measurements. Consequently, on a 5-point scale, the difference between "agree" and "neither agree nor disagree," $(4 - 3)$, is regarded as equal to the difference between "disagree" and "strongly disagree," $(2 - 1)$.

To summarize, question format is determined by the variable being measured, the type of information required (the analyses to be done), and the ability of the respondents to make mental judgments. The same variable can be recorded on different measurement scales, and these scales may be defined by fixed response categories or may result from an open-ended question. One question form may elicit more accurate responses than another.

Consider a person's use of a new rapid transit system. This variable can be measured on a nominal scale at one extreme (Have you used the rapid transit system at any time during the last month? Yes, No) or on a ratio scale at the other extreme (How many times have you used the rapid transit system in the past month? Please specify: _____; or, perhaps, Check one: _____ 0 to 3, _____ 4 to 7, and so forth). The nominal-scale question is easy to answer. The accuracy of the response to the ratio-scale question will depend on the respondent's ability to remember the number of times the rapid transit system was used in the last month.

EXAMPLE 4.6   Format and Measurement Scales

Specify the format and type of measurement scale for the following questions:

1.   What is your current annual salary before taxes? _____

---

*Before summing, numbers must be assigned to the scale categories in such a way that a high (or low) numerical rating on each statement always represents the *same* attitude direction.

2.   How likely are you to buy a new automobile within the next year?

Will Definitely Not Buy	**Extremely Unlikely**	**Unlikely**	**Likely**	**Extremely Likely**	**Will Definitely Buy**
_____	_____	_____	_____	_____	_____

3.   If you had additional money to invest, which of the following would be most attractive to you?

_____ Stock mutual fund

_____ Bond mutual fund

_____ Balanced mutual fund

_____ Money market account

_____ Other account _____
                                        (Please specify)

Solution and Discussion.   Question 1 is a nonstructured question with a response (dollars) measured on a ratio scale. This is one of those questions that, depending on the respondent's perception of how the information will be used, may not generate an accurate response. Some people tend to inflate their salaries, whereas others tend to understate them.

Numerical summaries like the mean, standard deviation, and percentiles may be calculated from the responses to this question. Computing and interpreting ratios makes sense. We can say that a respondent with an annual salary of $80,000 makes twice as much as a respondent with an annual salary of $40,000.

Question 2 is a structured question with ordered response categories. Attaching an increasing sequence of numbers, for example, 1 to 6, to the categories produces an ordinal scale. In addition, it is possible to argue that the differences in response categories are about equal. In this case, the numbers 1 to 6 represent an interval scale, and the differences between them are meaningful.

Assuming an interval scale, we can calculate the mean, standard deviation, percentiles, and other descriptive numerical measures. These measures must be interpreted within the context of the particular numbers assigned to the categories. Computing and interpreting ratios does not make sense because there is no uniquely defined starting point or origin for the category numbers. We could just as easily have created interval-scale measurements by assigning the numbers -2, -1, 0, 1, 2, and 3 to the six categories.

The response categories in Question 3 have distinct verbal descriptors with no natural relative positions or order. Attaching a set of distinct numbers to the categories results in a nominal scale. Although one of the response categories allows an open-ended response, we regard the question as structured because it has fixed response categories.

With nominal-scale data we can count the number (frequency) of responses in each category. These counts may be converted to relative frequencies or percentages. No other numerical operations are permitted because they have no meaning.

We turn now to a second issue in questionnaire design, that of question wording.

QUESTION WORDING

The key to writing good questions is to imagine yourself as the respondent. Even then, some of the questions may have to be modified as a result of pretesting.

Each question must be examined to be sure it has the ability to generate data consistent with the purpose of the study. Questions that do not clearly contribute to the research objective should be deleted with the possible exception of open-ended questions designed to kindle the respondent's interest or to put the respondent at ease.

Thoughts to keep in mind while writing a question include: Can the respondent answer this question? Will the respondent answer this question? Does this question address more than one issue? Does the question lead the respondent in one direction or another? Does the question imply the same frame of reference to all respondents?

The wording of a question and its influence on responses is situation-specific and complex. Words that are too difficult for use with one population may be perfectly acceptable for another. A question that makes little sense by itself may be quite clear as part of a sequence of questions. We will examine several examples to demonstrate some of the problems that can occur as a result of question wording and discuss ways to minimize the difficulties.

Consider the following question from a mail questionnaire concerned with professors' perceptions about students majoring in finance.

In your opinion, how many students in your finance courses are potentially successful financial managers?

Ten percent _____

Twenty percent _____

Thirty percent _____

_____ percent _____

Although this question deals with professors' perceptions of their students and is therefore relevant to the study, most respondents could not provide a meaningful answer. The number requested is likely to be beyond the realm of experience of most respondents. In addition, the response categories are confusing. The specified percentage categories have gaps. The open-ended category allows for any number but is the requested number to be interpreted as something above thirty percent? How about:

How much has your family spent on toothpaste in the last six months? $_____

Again, the respondent has little chance to answer this question accurately. How many respondents would be able to remember the amount they spent on toothpaste during the previous six months?

Questions that raise several separate issues with only one set of responses are very difficult to interpret. These questions are called **double-barreled questions.**

How is a "no" response to the following double-barreled question to be interpreted?

Do you feel firms today are concerned about their employees and their customers?

_____ Yes _____ No _____ No opinion

A "no" response can be interpreted three different ways:

- The respondent feels firms are concerned about neither employees nor customers.
- The respondent feels firms are concerned about employees but not customers.
- The respondent feels firms are not concerned about employees but they are concerned about customers.

Only the respondent knows which of these interpretations is accurate. The way to remedy this question is to break it up into two questions with the same set of response categories: one question dealing with employees and the second question dealing with customers.

A **leading question** is one that may steer respondents toward a particular response regardless of their true position. Leading questions can be very subtle, and the risk of asking them is particularly great when the focus of the study is on people's attitudes, beliefs, or opinions.

Don't you think offshore drilling for oil is environmentally unsound?

_____ Yes   _____ No   _____ No opinion

This question implies that offshore drilling is environmentally unsound, and some respondents, including those who really have no opinion, will be tempted to answer "yes." Those respondents who yield to the temptation generate inaccurate data. The question can be made more neutral as follows:

What category best describes your feeling about the environmental impact of offshore drilling for oil?

_____ Offshore drilling is environmentally sound.
_____ Offshore drilling is environmentally unsound.
_____ No opinion

One-sided questions are questions that are oriented toward one side of an issue. A variation of one-sidedness can occur in multiple-category questions when the alternatives presented are loaded toward one side. Consider:

How important is price to you in buying a new television?

_____ More important than any other factor
_____ Extremely important
_____ Important
_____ Somewhat important
_____ Unimportant

The alternatives listed are _unbalanced_. Four of the five categories suggest price is an important criterion. The question can be improved by rewriting the question with _balanced_ alternatives.

How important is price to you in buying a new television?

_____ Very important

_____ Relatively important

_____ Neither important nor unimportant

_____ Relatively unimportant

_____ Very unimportant

The balanced alternatives offer a wider choice to respondents who do not consider price to be an important factor.

EXAMPLE 4.7   A Question with Ambiguous Response Categories

The responses to some questions can be greatly influenced by what respondents assume in answering them. That is, the questions do not provide the same frame of reference to all respondents. Consider the question:

How often do you eat breakfast?

_____ Frequently

_____ Occasionally

_____ Rarely

_____ Never

Discuss the problem with this question. Fix the problem by rewriting the question.

Solution and Discussion.   The problem with this question is that different respondents may attach different meanings to the first three response categories. One way to provide the same frame of reference for all respondents is to rewrite the question as:

On the average, how many days per week do you eat breakfast?

_____ Every day

_____ 5 or 6 days

_____ 3 or 4 days

_____ 1 or 2 days

_____ Less than 1 day per week

_____ Never eat breakfast

Questions must be written so that they will be interpreted the same way by all respondents.

Question wording is perhaps the most crucial determinant of data accuracy in surveys. Particular attention must be paid to identifying and correcting double-barreled, leading, and one-sided questions, as well as questions with ambiguous response categories.

QUESTION SEQUENCING

Although there are no generally accepted guidelines for question wording, there are certain principles that govern the sequencing of questions.

In general, questions should follow a logical sequence subject to the following broad guidelines:

- Place questions about respondents' personal or demographic characteristics (age, education level, income, and so forth) at the end of the questionnaire. These questions provide *classification data* useful for constructing a profile of the respondent sample. However, asking these questions at the beginning may irritate some respondents and affect their willingness to complete the rest of the survey.

- Place sensitive questions likely to embarrass respondents near the end of the questionnaire. This placement is especially important if the questionnaire is to be administered through face-to-face or telephone interviews. Again, asking sensitive questions early may affect the respondent's willingness to continue.

- Questions related to the same topic should appear together.

- Questions within a topic should go from general to specific; that is, follow a funnel sequence.

- Avoid skip patterns such as, "If the answer to Question 6 is no, proceed to Question 11."

Certain situations may require a change in one or more of these principles, but, in most cases, they provide a good template for question sequencing.

QUESTIONNAIRE LAYOUT

The appearance and layout of a questionnaire can influence the degree of respondent cooperation as well as the quality of the data collected. That is, questionnaire appearance and layout, if ignored, can lead to confusion, low response rates, and coding errors. Appearance and layout are especially crucial in mail surveys because the questionnaire has to sell itself.

In general, a questionnaire must appear attractive, neat, and uncluttered. It must also be convenient to handle, easy to read, and simple to fill out.

EXERCISES

4.23 One firm, evaluating the results of a survey of users and nonusers of its products, declared:

> On the average, users are only half as old as nonusers.
>
> The image that users have of our company is twice as positive as that of nonusers.

Can the company legitimately make these statements? Discuss.

4.24 Two different samples of 200 people each responded to the following question. The number of responses in each category is indicated in the table.

How likely are you to buy an automobile within the next six months? (Please check the most appropriate category.)

Response Category		Number of Respondents (First Sample)	Number of Respondents (Second Sample)
Will definitely not buy	_____	10	120
Extremely unlikely	_____	10	40
Unlikely	_____	70	10
Likely	_____	60	10
Extremely likely	_____	20	10
Will definitely buy	_____	30	10
		200	200

a. Assign numbers 1 to 6 to the six response categories beginning with "will definitely not buy" and compute the mean response for the first sample. Does the mean response make sense here? Discuss.

b. Repeat part **a** for the second sample.

c. Compare the mean responses in parts **a** and **b.** Can we conclude, for example, that respondents in the first sample are twice as likely to buy a new car as respondents in the second sample? Discuss.

4.25 Suppose you want to determine the extent to which students in your class are paying for their educational expenses with their own earnings. Assuming you want to ask just one question, write it as:

a. A nonstructured question

b. A structured question with two response categories

c. A structured question with multiple response categories

4.26 Refer to Exercise 4.25. For each question form, determine the measurement scale and, consequently, the type of data obtained.

4.27 Construct an example of your own to illustrate

a. A double-barreled question

b. A leading question

c. A one-sided question

4.28 Refer to Exercise 4.27. For each example, suggest a revised question or questions that will correct the problem.

4.29 Identify a problem with the wording in the following questions. Rewrite each question, including response categories if necessary, to minimize the problem.

a. Would you agree or disagree that deregulation in the airline industry has benefited consumers?

b. Are you favorable, indifferent, or unfavorable toward a proposed 5% increase in the city tax rate?

c. Do you think the quality of products on the market today is as high as it was 10 years ago?

4.30 Construct response categories consistent with the indicated measurement scale for the following questions.

    a. *Ratio scale.* How many years of formal education have you completed?

    b. *Nominal scale.* Which of the following media influences your purchasing decision the most?

    c. *Interval scale.* Which of the following best describes your supervisor's accessibility?

    d. *Ordinal scale.* How long do you spend studying on a typical school day?

4.31 (*Team or class project*) Construct a short (10 or so questions) questionnaire designed to elicit student opinions and recommendations about a particular campus topic. Topics might include quality of on-campus health care, participation in elections for student officers, need for (expanded) student tutoring or help sessions, and quality of registration process.

4.5   DESIGN OF EXPERIMENTS

Advances are made when new products or procedures are developed and then shown to be better than the old products or procedures. How do we decide whether something is better? One way is to make changes, collect data, and then compare the new with the old. Statistical ideas play an integral role in the comparison of products or procedures. The plan for collecting the data when we actually do something to people, animals, or objects is called the **experimental design.** The choice of an appropriate experimental design is crucial to making valid comparisons.

In this section, the term **experiment** is used in the usual scientific sense. It refers to an operation carried out under controlled conditions to discover or confirm the effect of one set of variables on another variable. Consistent terminology will allow us to discuss various types of experimental studies.

The objects that are subjected to the experimental conditions are called the **experimental units** or, if the objects are people, the **experimental subjects.** The particular experimental condition applied to the units is called a **treatment.** A treatment may be as simple as a price reduction, an increase in temperature, or a new drug. Alternatively, a treatment may be complex and consist of some combination of the values of several variables. The characteristic that is observed and measured as a result of applying a treatment to an experimental unit is called the **response.** For a price change, the response may be sales. For a temperature change, the response may be yield. For a new drug, the response may be concentration in the bloodstream after 30 minutes.

We have said that experiments are conducted to determine the response of one variable to deliberate changes in other variables with the goal of revealing or confirming a cause-and-effect relation. The manipulated, or explanatory, variables are called **factors.** In experiments that study the joint effects of several factors, each treatment consists of a combination of specific values, called **levels,** one for each factor.

EXAMPLE 4.8   A Simple Experiment

The manager of a supermarket is running out of linear shelf space. Describe a simple experiment to answer the question: Will decreasing the shelf space allocated to Brand X detergent by 25% significantly lower sales?

Solution and Discussion. Dodging the issue of what "significantly lower" means, we can answer the question by comparing sales over a period of time for each of two amounts of linear shelf space: the current amount and a 25% reduction in the current amount. The amounts could be measured in square feet. In this case, the explanatory variable or factor is "shelf space" with two levels: "current amount" and "25% reduction." Because there is only a single factor, each factor level is a treatment. The experimental units are "boxes of detergent," and the response is "sales." (Each unit either sells or does not sell over the study period.) A comparison between total sales for current shelf space with that for a 25% reduction in shelf space will provide an indication of the effect of shelf space on sales.

EXAMPLE 4.9 Identifying Factors in a Health Care Experiment

Managers for a health care provider became aware that doctors and nurses were taking too long, on average, to return calls to patients giving them information requested earlier in the day. Calls are received at two different locations within the facility. To determine a reference for improvements in the current return call procedure, data on the time to return calls will be collected for each of the two locations. Describe the data collection plan with experimental design terminology, and suggest some variables that may be responsible for the delays.

Solution and Discussion. The experimental units or subjects are the individual medical personnel returning phone calls. The response is "length of time to return phone call." Several factors or explanatory variables that may contribute to the apparent delays are listed here. In some cases, the levels of these factors are clear. In other cases, the levels have to be carefully articulated.

Potential explanatory variables include:

- Location receiving call
- Method of documenting information requested
- Type of call
- Day of week
- Staffing level
- Person responding to initial call

There are other variables that could be identified as contributing to delays in responding to patients' requests for information.

Once the levels of each of the factors have been established, a treatment consists of a combination of levels, one level from each factor.

EXAMPLE 4.10 Identifying all the Components of an Experiment to Compare Battery Performance

A manufacturer of batteries is interested in comparing the performance of its AA-size alkaline battery with the performance of a comparable battery of its major competitor. Tests are performed every second and fourth quarter. To simulate different operating conditions, fresh batteries are discharged through different resistances (representing different applications such as toy, camera, and so forth) to different voltage endpoints (points at which the batteries no longer work for the application being simulated). The length of service life (measured in minutes) is recorded for each combination of resistance and voltage endpoint.

Suppose there are 3 different resistances (measured in ohms) and 3 different voltage endpoints. Identify the experimental units, the response, the explanatory variables or factors, their levels, and, finally, the treatments for the experiments carried out by the battery manufacturer.

Solution and Discussion. The experimental units are the individual AA batteries selected for the tests. The response is "service life." There are two factors: "resistance" and "voltage endpoint." As indicated, resistance has 3 levels or different values of ohms at which the tests are made. Similarly, endpoint voltage has 3 different voltage levels. A treatment consists of a combination of resistance and endpoint voltage. (Each battery is discharged under a specific resistance to a specific voltage endpoint.) Consequently, there are $3 \times 3 = 9$ treatments.

An experimental design specifies the manner in which the units or subjects are selected and assigned to treatments. We can control the environment of the experimental units to study the effects of the chosen treatments on the response with little interference from extraneous factors. This feature of experimental data distinguishes them from data that are collected passively as part of observational studies. In observational studies, there is no direct control of the environment and, consequently, no way to untangle the effects of possible factors from other unobserved variables.

Complete control of the environment is an ideal that is rarely achieved in practice. However, employing a few principles of good experimental design, an experimenter can make a valid comparison of treatments.

The first principle of good experimental practice is **randomization.** Randomization refers to an impartial assignment of experimental units to treatments accomplished by using a chance mechanism. Randomization can ensure that influences other than the treatments being studied operate equally on all groups of units. Thus, certain outcomes are not favored. This is not the case if the assignment is based on expert judgment.

Randomization introduces chance into the study, but it does so in a regular way that can be described by the laws of probability. We are able to infer that observed differences in the response variable must be due to the effects of the treatments. That is, the treatments *cause* the observed differences in the response.

EXAMPLE 4.11   Illustrating Randomization

A company wants to select one e-mail computer program to be used throughout the firm. The company has narrowed its consideration to one of two different programs. To get employee input into the decision, 50 users are selected to try one of the two programs for a week and rate it on a 5-point scale with respect to ease of use. Twenty-five of the 50 employees will rate e-mail Program A, and the remaining 25 employees will rate e-mail Program B. The ratings will be compared to see which of the two programs receives the highest ratings. Assign the employees (experimental subjects) to e-mail programs (treatments).

Solution and Discussion.   In spite of her best intentions, a manager may bias the results by assigning employees to programs. For example, in her attempts to balance the number of males and females using each of the two programs and the number of clerical and nonclerical staff using each of the two programs, she may, unknowingly, assign those with substantial computer experience to Program A and those without much experience to Program B. The way to ensure that all variables *not explicitly controlled by the experimenter* operate equally on the response (rating) is to randomly assign employees to e-mail programs.

Suppose we number the employees from 1 to 50. Using a table of random digits we can select 25 two-digit numbers from 1 to 50 (see Table 4.1 and Example 4.3). Employees corresponding to these numbers are assigned to Program A and the remaining 25 employees to Program B.

There will be some differences in the measured characteristic even if the treatments have no effect. This happens because it is impossible to hold *all* outside variables constant, that is, to completely eliminate the effects of extraneous factors.

How much of the observed differences in the response are due to chance (extraneous factors), and how much are due to treatments? Although we can answer this question by randomly assigning units to treatments and running the experiment once, repeating the experiment several times can reduce the amount of chance variation in the response and make the treatment effects more apparent. Repeating the experiment is referred to as **replication.** Replication is another important principle of good experimental practice.

COMPARING TWO TREATMENTS

Often we are interested in comparing just two treatments, training versus no training, drug versus no drug, one form of advertising versus another form, new procedure versus old procedure, and so forth. The two basic designs for comparing two treatments are:

Independent samples (complete randomization)

Matched pair sample (randomization in matched pairs)

The case of **independent samples** arises when the experimental units are randomly divided into two groups: One group is assigned Treatment 1, and the other group is assigned Treatment 2. The response measurements for the two treatments are then unrelated because they arise from separate and unrelated groups of units. Consequently, each set of response measurements can be considered a sample from a population of possible measurements, and we can speak in terms of a comparison between two population distributions.

With the **matched pair design,** the experimental subjects are chosen in pairs so that the members in each pair are alike, whereas those in different pairs may be substantially different. One member is randomly selected from each pair to receive Treatment 1, and the other member of the pair receives Treatment 2.

When a single treatment is being studied with human subjects, it is best to compare the treatment with no treatment. This eliminates the *placebo effect* that is likely to occur when a single treatment is examined in isolation.

A placebo is a benign treatment, such as colored water or a sugar pill. Many subjects respond positively to any treatment, even a fake treatment. A response to a placebo, the placebo effect, can be quite strong. Consequently, if a treatment is administered and a response is observed, it is not clear whether the treatment caused the response or we simply observed a placebo effect.

We can control for the placebo effect by creating a second group of experimental subjects. The first group of subjects receives the treatment, and the second group of subjects receives the placebo or no treatment. The group of subjects receiving no treatment is called the **control group.** When the responses from the two groups of subjects are compared, the placebo effect and other environmental variables operate on both sets of responses. Therefore, any significant differences between the two groups of responses must be due to the treatment.

Creating a control group, particularly in single-treatment experiments, is an important principle of good experimental design.

EXAMPLE 4.12   Independent Samples and Matched Pair Designs

A key aspect of organizational buying is negotiation. A manager is interested in comparing two types of bargaining strategies: competitive bargaining and coordinative bargaining. A *competitive* strategy is characterized by inflexible behavior aimed at forcing concessions, whereas a *coordinative* strategy involves a problem-solving approach to negotiations with a high degree of trust and cooperation. Eight organizational buyers are recruited to participate in a negotiation experiment. Four buyers will use the competitive strategy, and four buyers will use the coordinative strategy. The response is amount of savings (in dollars) achieved by each negotiator.

The experimental subjects consist of four men and four women. Two women have 3 years of experience, and the other two women have 1 year of experience each. Two men have 2 years of experience, and the other two men have 1 year of experience each. Describe a design of independent samples where the eight buyers are split into groups of four. Describe a matched pair design with two buyers per pair, controlling for gender.

Solution and Discussion.   The eight buyers are shown on the left in Figure 4.2(a), labeled with their years of experience. To implement an independent samples design, we divide the group at random using a table of random numbers. Number the buyers and, from the table, select four digits from 1 to 8. Suppose the numbers are 3, 8, 7, and 1. These buyers will use the competitive strategy, and the remaining four buyers will use the coordinative strategy. The savings realized using the competitive strategy will have no relation to the savings realized using the coordinative strategy because the selection of buyers in the two samples is left completely to chance.

To implement a matched pair design, we first select the buyers in pairs. The two buyers in each pair should be alike with respect to their gender. This preexisting condition is the same for each member of the pair so it affects the response equally. The condition may be different from one pair to another. After the buyers are paired, one buyer is randomly selected from each pair for the competitive strategy, the other buyer in the pair is assigned the coordinative strategy. The random selection in a pair can be accomplished by tossing a fair coin. See Figure 4.2(b).

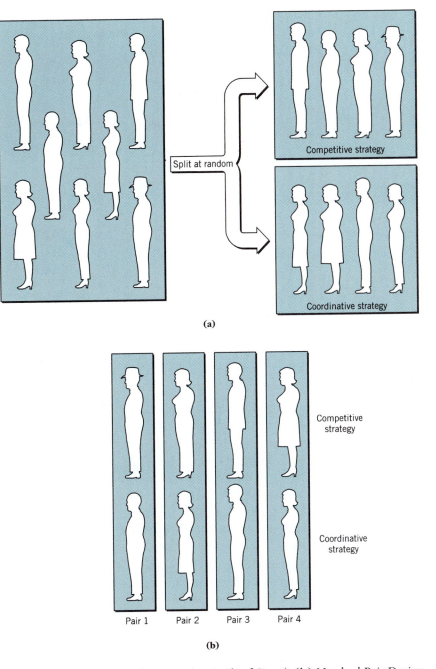

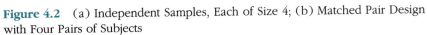

Figure 4.2 (a) Independent Samples, Each of Size 4; (b) Matched Pair Design with Four Pairs of Subjects

In contrast to the situation in Figure 4.2(a), we would expect the responses of each pair to be related because they are influenced by the same preexisting conditions of the subjects.

We will learn how to analyze data from the independent samples and the matched pair designs in Chapter 9.

In summary, a carefully designed experiment is crucial to a successful comparative study. The design determines the structure of the data. In turn, the design provides the key to selecting an appropriate analysis.

EXERCISES

4.32 Six students in a marketing course have volunteered to serve as subjects in a matched pair experiment.

Name	Age	Gender
Tom	18	M
Sue	20	F
Erik	18	M
Grace	20	F
Chris	18	F
Andy	18	M

a. List all possible sets of pairings if subjects are paired by age.

b. If subjects are paired by gender, how many pairs are available for the experiment?

4.33 Al, Bob, Carol, Dennis, and Ellen are available as subjects. Make a list of all possible ways to split them into two groups, with the first group having two subjects and the second group three subjects.

4.34 Identify the following as either matched pair or independent samples. Also, identify the experimental units, treatments, and response in each case.

a. Twenty previous donors to a charitable organization are solicited for donations again this year. Another 20 previous donors are mailed an attractive brochure describing the organization's activities and soliciting larger contributions. The donation amounts actually received will be recorded.

b. Ten newly married couples will be interviewed. Both the husband and the wife will respond to the question, "How many children would you like to have?"

c. A businesswoman issues a large number of checks, some of which are not cashed. To find out why checks were not cashed, the uncashed checks were divided into two groups: those written for less than $500, and those written for $500 or more. Forty checks are selected from the first group, and sixty checks are selected from the second group.

4.35 For each of the following experimental studies, identify the experimental units, the explanatory variable(s) or factors, and the response variable.

a. A fruit grower wishes to evaluate a new spray that is claimed to reduce the loss due to damage by insects. To test the claim, the grower treats 12 of the trees in his orchard with the new spray and the remaining 15 trees with the standard spray. The fruit yield (in pounds) from each tree is recorded.

b. A university system now requires each system component to provide training for all personnel "involved in voucher preparation and approval." To investigate the effectiveness of the planned training session, one campus in the system selects 50 people at random to take the training. Another 50 people do not take the training and are identified as a control group. Vouchers prepared by all these individuals are monitored for 6 months, and the number of errors on each voucher is tabulated.

c. Two work designs are being considered for possible adoption in an assembly plant. A time study is conducted with 10 workers using Design 1, and 12 workers using Design 2. The time (in minutes) to assemble a standard piece of equipment is measured for each worker.

4.36 Carefully explain why each of the following studies is *not* an experiment.

a. Some years ago, the record industry noticed that the Duran Duran (a British rock group) album *Rio* was being sold out at half the record stores in Dallas and was gathering dust in the other half. A check of the local television listings showed that the parts of the city that were wired for cable and carrying the MTV cable channel were the very same areas where the album was flourishing. An MTV executive infers that "Duran Duran owes its life to MTV."

b. Checking the records of her sales staff for the past year, the sales manager of an industrial marketing firm noticed that those people who averaged 6 sales calls per customer had, as a group, significantly higher sales than the group of people who averaged 4 sales calls per customer. The sales manager wants to require all sales people to average 6 sales calls per customer.

c. A manufacturer of television reception products observes the bill-paying behavior of three independent distributors of its products. When payment on a bill is received, the manufacturer records the number of days since the bill was issued. Time series plots of the "days until payment" for each distributor show that two of the distributors have relatively consistent payment patterns with payments averaging about 30 days. However, the "days until payment" for the third distributor have roughly doubled from about 25 to 50 days over the last half of the observation period. This seemed to occur at about the time the manufacturer changed the payment terms from 1%–10 days, net 30 days to 1%–10 days, net 35 days. The manufacturer is considering reverting to the old payment terms.

4.37 Refer to Exercise 4.36. Although the studies in Exercise 4.36 are not experiments, they have explanatory and response variables. Name these variables in each case.

4.38 Refer to Exercise 4.36. For each of the studies, identify potential lurking variables that may be responsible, at least in part, for the implied conclusion. (When the effects of the lurking variables cannot be separated from those of the explanatory variables, we say the effects are *confounded* or that the *variables are confounded*.)

4.39 Briefly describe the design of a matched pair experiment to determine whether consumers prefer the taste of Pepsi or Coke in a blind test in which neither product is identified. Can you think of any advantage(s) the matched pair experiment might have over an independent samples experiment in this situation?

4.40   Briefly describe the design of an experiment for determining the effectiveness of two potential television commercials, Commercial A and Commercial B, for a brand of automobile tires. Assume the response will be a numerical score of "brand image."

4.41   Think of a question of interest to you that might be answered with the aid of an experiment. Carefully describe an appropriate experimental design.

4.6   STATISTICS IN CONTEXT

American Trust is one of several commercial lending institutions located in the Tennessee community of Northwest Hills. The bank maintains two branch offices in the northern and southern districts of town. Its main office is located in downtown Northwest Hills.

During the recent past, changes in the banking industry in Northwest Hills have paralleled those taking place nationally. The environment has become increasingly complex and competitive. Deregulation, technological innovation, changing interest rates, and competition from insurance companies and multiservice investment firms have all made it difficult for banks to attract and keep customers. As a result, lending institutions are focusing increased attention on meeting customer needs and developing strategies to increase their client base. American Trust is no exception.

A 1992 study of commercial banking in Northwest Hills showed American Trust to have an above-average proportion of older households, long-time residents of the community, and middle-income persons as customers. The bank appeared to be less successful in attracting younger households, college graduates, and new residents of Northwest Hills. In addition, the study found noncustomers of American Trust to have a weak image of the bank, even though customers had a very positive image. Bank officials sensed that these 1992 results were typical of the current situation as well. However, because the officials were in the process of developing a comprehensive marketing plan, they wanted more up-to-date and detailed information to help formulate an appropriate marketing strategy. Consequently, bank officials contracted with the McGuire Research Agency to study current bank customers. The objectives of the study given to the McGuire Agency were (1) to determine demographic profiles of current bank customers; (2) to determine customer awareness, use, and overall perception of present bank services; and (3) to identify new bank services desired by customers.

After several sessions designed to increase the research team's familiarity with American Trust's current clientele and service offerings, a questionnaire was developed to collect the information required by the objectives of the study. Because the information required was general yet personal in nature, a mail survey was selected for data collection purposes. To encourage a high response rate, a cover letter describing the research objectives and the importance of responding was written by the bank president and mailed with each questionnaire, along with a stamped, self-addressed envelope. Furthermore, those who returned completed questionnaires became eligible to participate in a drawing to win one of five $50 bills.

The questionnaire itself was also designed to encourage high response. The instructions made it clear that the information would remain confidential, and the more sensitive questions were asked last. In addition, the questionnaire was extensively pretested using bank customers of various ages and backgrounds.

The relevant population for the study was defined as all noncommercial customers of American Trust who lived in Northwest Hills and who were not employees of the bank. The total number of customers meeting these requirements was 8200.

The researchers thought that 500 survey responses were required to adequately perform the analysis. Anticipating a 30% to 35% response rate, the researchers needed to mail 1500 to 1600 surveys. Given the list of 8200 population elements and the estimated sample size of 1600, the researchers decided to send a questionnaire to one of every five names on the list. The first name was determined by selecting a random number between 1 and 5 from a table of random digits. It was the fourth name on the list. Questionnaires were sent to the fourth, ninth, fourteenth, ..., names on the list. In all, 1621 questionnaires were mailed, and 673 were returned for a response rate of approximately 42%.

Responses to questions other than the demographic questions were typically recorded on a 5-point scale. Tables 4.3–4.5 contain summaries of the data according to the research objectives. Table 4.6 (page 207) is a cross-tabulation of the responses to the overall rating of American Trust services by age of customer.

From the demographic data, we see that the typical survey respondent is married (49%), either 22–40 years old (44%) or 51 and over (36%), high school educated or better, having an annual income of less than $25,000 (52%), and having lived in the area for more than 10 years (66%).

TABLE 4.3   Demographic Characteristics of American Trust Customers

Characteristic/Category[a]

Marital status					
Married	330	(49%)	Widowed	67	(10%)
Single	204	(30)	Divorced/Separated	48	(7)
Age					
Under 18	1	(0)	41–50	64	(10)
18–21	31	(5)	51–64	113	(17)
22–30	160	(24)	Over 65	126	(19)
31–40	133	(20)			
Education					
Grade school	19	(3)	Attend college	119	(18)
Some high school	15	(2)	College graduate	128	(19)
High school graduate	119	(18)	Post graduate study	154	(23)
Vocational/technical	77	(12)			
Total household income					
$0–$9,999	111	(17)	$25,000–$29,999	54	(8)
$10,000–$14,999	88	(13)	$30,000–$39,999	92	(14)
$15,000–$19,999	73	(11)	$40,000–$49,999	58	(9)
$20,000–$24,999	73	(11)	$50,000 or more	67	(10)
Number of years living in Northwest Hills					
Less than 1 year	29	(4)	6–10 years	53	(8)
1–3 years	59	(9)	More than 10 years	444	(66)
4–5 years	48	(7)			

[a]The percentages in a category may not add to 100% because some of the questions were not answered by all of the respondents.

TABLE 4.4 Use and Awareness of Services at American Trust

General Bank Services at American Trust

Service	Using service		Aware of service		Number answering question
Checking					
Regular	525	(80%)	651	(99%)	654
NOW account	110	(18)	528	(86)	613
Savings					
Regular	346	(54)	636	(100)	637
Certificate of deposit	149	(24)	561	(91)	619
Partnership savings	89	(15)	411	(68)	602
IRA	59	(10)	553	(92)	598
U.S. savings bond	46	(8)	504	(84)	602
Repurchase agreement	16	(3)	253	(43)	590
Loans					
Personal	132	(22)	560	(92)	608
Auto	96	(16)	547	(90)	605
Mortgage/home improvement	49	(8)	517	(86)	603

Special Bank Services at American Trust

Service	Using service		Aware of service		Number answering question
TYME card	276	(44%)	608	(96%)	631
Traveler's cheques	272	(43)	584	(93)	628
U.S. Treasury bills and notes	250	(37)	662	(99)	669
VISA/MASTERCARD	247	(39)	573	(90)	635
Direct deposit	202	(32)	530	(84)	629
Safe deposit	164	(25)	597	(93)	644
Telephone transfer	99	(16)	352	(56)	627
24-hour depository	87	(14)	546	(87)	629
Overdraft protection	81	(13)	354	(57)	618

TABLE 4.5 Response to Potential New Services at American Trust

Service	Would use service	
Discount brokerage	85	(13%)
Insurance	71	(11)
Tax preparation	138	(21)
Financial counseling	229	(34)
Travel service	193	(29)
In-home banking	106	(16)

TABLE 4.6 Overall Rating of Services by Age of Customer

Age group		Overall service rating					No reply
		Excellent 1	Good 2	Acceptable 3	Poor 4	Unacceptable 5	9
Under 18	Number	0	0	1	0	0	0
	Row percent[a]	(0)	(0)	(100)	(0)	(0)	(0)
	Column percent[a]	(0)	(0)	(1)	(0)	(0)	(0)
18–21	Number	7	16	7	0	0	1
	Row percent	(23)	(52)	(23)	(0)	(0)	(3)
	Column percent	(2)	(7)	(10)	(0)	(0)	(20)
22–30	Number	62	67	30	1	0	0
	Row percent	(39)	(42)	(19)	(1)	(0)	(0)
	Column percent	(18)	(28)	(42)	(20)	(0)	(0)
31–40	Number	46	68	14	2	10	2
	Row percent	(35)	(51)	(11)	(2)	(1)	(2)
	Column percent	(14)	(28)	(19)	(40)	(33)	(40)
41–50	Number	31	25	7	0	1	0
	Row percent	(48)	(39)	(11)	(0)	(2)	(0)
	Column percent	(9)	(10)	(10)	(0)	(33)	(0)
51–64	Number	71	33	7	1	0	1
	Row percent	(63)	(29)	(6)	(1)	(0)	(1)
	Column percent	(21)	(14)	(10)	(20)	(0)	(100)
65 Plus	Number	101	19	4	0	1	1
	Row percent	(81)	(15)	(3)	(0)	(1)	(1)
	Column percent	(30)	(8)	(6)	(0)	(33)	(20)
No reply	Number	24	15	2	1	0	1
	Row percent	(56)	(35)	(5)	(2)	(0)	(2)
	Column percent	(7)	(6)	(3)	(20)	(0)	(20)
Total	Number	342	243	72	5	3	6
	Row percent	(51)	(36)	(11)	(1)	(0)	(1)
	Column percent	(100%)	(100%)	(100%)	(100%)	(100%)	(100%)

[a]The row and column percentages may not add to 100 because of rounding.

The bank does not appear to be attracting young (less than 22 years old) and middle-age (41–50 years old) customers. Relatively few customers have incomes in the $25,000–$29,999 and $40,000–$49,000 ranges, and the bank did not have very many customers who were newcomers to the community.

Compared to the 1992 study, American Trust still has a large proportion of older households and long-time residents of the community as customers. However, the bank does appear to be more successful in attracting younger customers.

Table 4.4 shows that customers are highly aware of most general bank services, but the overall awareness level was lower for special services. No special service was used by over 44% of the respondents. Notice that awareness and use of special bank services appear to be related. The three most frequently used special services are TYME card, traveler's cheques, and VISA/MASTERCARD. These services also have among the highest awareness levels.

The data in Table 4.5 indicate that the bank might benefit from instituting financial counseling and travel service.

Is the overall rating of American Trust services related to age? The cross-tabulated data in Table 4.6 show that older customers tend to have the most favorable image of the bank's services compared to other age groups. The fact that older groups are most satisfied with bank services, whereas younger groups tend to be least satisfied, could have important implications for the long-run viability of the bank.

4.7   GUIDES TO SECONDARY DATA SOURCES

In this section, we simply list some sources or guides to sources of secondary data likely to be useful to those in business. We have made no attempt to include all the possibilities in this area.

Survey of Current Business (U.S. Department of Commerce, Bureau of Economic Analysis: Government Printing Office). This monthly publication provides a comprehensive statistical summary of the national income and product accounts of the United States. There are some 2600 different data series reported, covering such topics as general business indicators, commodity prices, construction and real estate activity, income and employment by industry, transportation and communications activity, and personal consumption expenditures by type.

Statistics of Income (U.S. Internal Revenue Service: Government Printing Office). Published annually, this publication is prepared from federal income tax returns of corporations and individuals. There are different publications for each type of tax report: one for corporations, one for sole proprietorships and partnerships, and one for individuals.

Statistical Abstract of the United States (U.S. Department of Commerce, Bureau of the Census: Government Printing Office). Published annually since 1878, this publication is designed to serve as a convenient volume of data references and as a guide to other data sources. It contains summary statistics on the social, political, and economic organizations of the United States.

Business Information Sources (revised ed., Daniells, L. M., Berkeley: University of California Press, 1985). A guide to the basic sources of business information organized by subject area.

Encyclopedia of Business Information Sources (7th ed., Detroit: Gale Research, 1988). A guide to the information available on various subjects, including basic data sources, periodicals, directories, handbooks, and on-line databases.

Where to Find Business Information: A Worldwide Guide for Everyone Who Needs the Answers to Business Questions (2nd ed., Brownstone, D. M., and Carruth, G., New York: John Wiley & Sons, 1982). This publication lists over 5000 books, periodicals, and databases of current interest and contains subject, title, and publisher indexes.

4.8 CHAPTER SUMMARY

In this chapter, we have learned:

- The general steps involved in data collection with particular reference to explicitly stating the study objectives and then devising a data collection plan consistent with these objectives

- The distinction between **primary data** and **secondary data.** Several methods for collecting primary data were discussed, including **sample surveys** and **designed experiments.** Sources for secondary data were listed in Section 4.7.

- How to select a simple random sample using a table of random digits. **Simple random sampling** is the most common probability sampling design used in sample surveys. Other probability sampling designs include **stratified sampling, systematic sampling,** and **cluster sampling.**

- The role of sampling in enumerative and analytic studies

- The elements of good questionnaire construction. Consideration of the kinds of information collected by questionnaires led to a discussion of the **nominal, ordinal, interval,** and **ratio scales** of measurement.

- That good questionnaire construction depends on **question format, question wording, question sequencing,** and **questionnaire layout**

- That a highly efficient and productive form of data collection involves making comparisons under controlled conditions. The plan for determining the controlled conditions and the nature of the comparisons is called the **experimental design.**

- How to assign experimental units to treatments so that the response of interest could be measured. Principles associated with good experimental design include **randomization** and **replication.**

- How to implement two designs for comparing two treatments: **independent samples** and a **matched pair sample.** When comparing two treatments, one treatment is often a **placebo** or no treatment. The group receiving the placebo is called the **control group.**

4.9 IMPORTANT CONCEPTS AND TOOLS

CONCEPTS

Bias, 178
Census, 170
Characteristic, 172
Cluster sampling, 178
Completely nonstructured question, 187
Completely structured question, 187
Confounded, 167
Design, 166
Double-barreled question, 191
Experiment, 196
Experimental subjects, 196
Experimental units, 196
Factors, 196

Interval scale, 186
Leading question, 192
Levels, 196
Nominal scale, 185
Nonstructured questionnaire, 187
One-sided question, 192
Ordinal scale, 186
Primary data, 166
Probability sample, 171
Random sampling with replacement, 174
Random sampling without replacement, 174
Randomization, 198

Ratio scale, 186
Replication, 199
Response, 196
Sample survey, 170
Secondary data, 166
Simple random sample, 175
Source of bias, 176
Stratified sampling, 177
Structured questionnaire, 187
Survey sampling, 170
Systematic sampling, 177
Target population, 172
Treatment, 196

TOOLS

Control group, 200
Experimental design, 196
Independent samples, 199

Matched pair sample, 199
Questionnaire, 185

Simple random sample, 175
Table of random digits, 173

4.10   KEY FORMULAS

With the measurement variable X coded 0–1 to indicate the absence or presence of the attribute,

Sample proportion: $\hat{p} = \dfrac{\sum_{i=1}^{n} x_i}{n}$

where x_i is the ith observation in the sample of size n.

REVIEW EXERCISES

4.42   Refer to Section 4.6 and Table 4.3. Do you agree with the assertion that American Trust customers tend to be older, long-time neighborhood residents, educated, and have relatively low incomes? Support your answer by computing the proportions of survey respondents that

a.   Are over 40

b.   Have some post–high school education

c.   Have lived in the area more than 5 years

d.   Have an annual income of less than $30,000

4.43   Refer to Section 4.6 and Table 4.6. Do you agree with the statement that older customers tend to have a more favorable image of American Trust's services than customers in the remaining age groups? Support your answer by consolidating the frequencies in the age categories 51–64 and 65 plus in Table 4.6 into a single 50 plus category, and then computing the percentages of respondents that rate the overall service as good or excellent for each age category.

4.44   A city analyst wished to compare the "degree of support" for a new rapid transit system among the following three groups of people: university employees, downtown businesspeople, and state government personnel. Assuming that a "rapid transit support index" can be constructed from responses to a questionnaire, describe a survey design that could be used to make the comparisons.

4.45   Give an example of a variable that could be measured on a

a.   Nominal scale

b.   Ordinal scale

c.   Interval scale

d.   Ratio scale

4.46   A manufacturer of prefabricated homes is concerned with declining sales. To get a better perspective on their customers so they can target their marketing efforts, management decides to conduct a sample survey. Among other things, management would like to have answers to the following questions. What is the demographic profile of our typical customer? What initially attracts these customers to one of our homes? A questionnaire is to be developed to address these issues.

a. Consider the first question. Construct structured questions with multiple response categories to determine the annual income and educational level of a typical customer.

b. Consider the second question. List five potential features or items that might attract customers to prefabricated homes. For each feature, construct a question designed to indicate its importance for attracting customers.

c. Refer to part **b.** Identify each of your questions as structured or non-structured, and indicate the measurement scale defined by your response categories.

4.47 Describe a simple experiment to address the marketing vice president's question, "Can we improve the profitability of our fashion clothing line by increasing its price by 10%?"

4.48 We want to evaluate a new method of teaching calculus to business students. There is a standardized test that adequately measures proficiency in calculus. The new method is to be compared with the traditional lecture method. Describe an experimental design that could be used to compare the two methods of instruction, assuming 30 students in a typical calculus class and 60 students available for the experiment.

4.49 Two brands of tires, Brand A and Brand B, are to be tested for durability. Durability is measured as the tread depth remaining after 10,000 miles of normal driving. Twenty tires of each brand are available for the tests. Describe an experimental design that can be used to compare the durability of Brand A with that of Brand B, assuming one tire of each brand will be installed on the rear axle of 20 cars.

4.50 Two appraisers are to be compared to see whether they assign the same assessed values to homes in a certain city. Describe an experimental design that can be used to compare the appraisers, assuming time and resources permit assessments of 50 homes.

4.51 Describe an experiment in a business setting that would lead to

a. Independent samples

b. A matched pair sample

After reading this chapter, you should be able to:

- Identify the sample space associated with an experiment, and determine whether it is discrete or continuous.

- Define events as collections of elementary outcomes of the sample space.

- Discuss probability as a numerical measure of uncertainty, and understand how probability can be assessed using the equally likely principle and long-run relative frequency.

- Describe the complement of an event, the union of two events, and the intersection of two events.

- Distinguish incompatible or mutually exclusive events from independent events.

- Discuss conditional probability.

- Calculate probabilities using the Law of the Complement, the Addition Law, and the Multiplication Law.

- Use Bayes' Theorem to revise the probability of an event given the occurrence of a related event.

- Use the Rule of Combinations to simplify some probability calculations.

- Define a random sample from a finite population.

CHAPTER FIVE

Probability

5.1 INTRODUCTION

The business environment is fraught with uncertainty. To reduce that uncertainty, data can be collected and summarized using methods suggested in the previous chapters. However, even in situations where data are available, the data typically represent only a portion, or *sample*, of the information that can be accumulated. In a decision-making context, we must be able to generalize beyond the available data to a target *population* in the case of enumerative studies, or to a collection of future outcomes in the case of analytic studies.* In statistics, the process of using data to make statements about the target population or collection of future outcomes is called **inference.**

What is our current market share? Which stocks will increase in price over the next year? Will this new design concept result in a high-volume product? Are our current accounting controls appropriate? Can we reduce the number of defects produced by this manufacturing process? Data can help to answer these questions, and sound decisions can then be made. Yet, for example, as we determine a product's current market share from a survey of selected metropolitan areas or predict the future price of stocks based on historical prices, some uncertainty is still associated with our inferences. We simply do not, or cannot, have all the information required for unambiguous conclusions. That is, the decisions may be sound but not always correct.

Sound decisions can be made when the uncertainty can be quantified. Probability is a way to quantify uncertainty and provides the key for understanding the reasoning that leads to appropriate generalizations from sample evidence. This chapter is devoted to a discussion of probability.

A NUMERICAL MEASURE OF UNCERTAINTY

In everyday conversations, we all use expressions of the kind:

"It is unlikely that interest rates will be higher next year."

"I have an even chance of getting an internship this summer."

"Most likely our basketball team will win this Saturday."

The phrases "unlikely," "even chance," "most likely," and so on are used qualitatively to indicate the chance that an event will occur. In general terms, the probability of an event is a numerical value that gauges how likely it is that an event will occur. We assign probability values on a scale from 0 to 1. A value close to 0 indicates the event is extremely unlikely, a value close to 1 indicates the event is very likely, with intermediate values interpreted accordingly. A value of 0 is assigned to an event that never occurs; the value of 1 is assigned to an event that always occurs.

A full appreciation for the concept of a numerical measure of uncertainty and its role in inference can be gained only after the concept has been explored in some detail. We can, however, preview the role of probability in one kind of statistical reasoning.

A corporation claims that its new luxury automobile, Car C, will give a more comfortable ride than its main competitor's best seller, Car L. To gather experimental evidence to support this claim, 15 current owners of Car L are selected for study. One by one they are blindfolded and given a test ride, over the same stretch of road, in each of the cars. If 12 of 15 owners say that Car C has the most comfortable ride, does this demonstrate that Car C gives a more comfortable ride?

Let us scrutinize the claim from a statistical point of view. If the two cars really give equally comfortable rides, there would still be a 50–50 chance that

---

*The collection of future outcomes can frequently be conceptualized as a population.

any particular person would say Car C is more comfortable. Observing 12 preferences for Car C out of 15 amounts to obtaining 12 heads in 15 tosses of a fair coin. We will see later that the probability of at least 12 heads in 15 tosses of a fair coin is .018, indicating that the event is not likely to happen. Thus, tentatively assuming the model (or hypothesis) that both cars are equally comfortable, 12 or more preferences for Car C is very unlikely. Rather than agree that an unlikely event has occurred, we reject the equally comfortable model and conclude that the experimental evidence strongly supports the corporation's claim.

This kind of reasoning, called *testing a statistical hypothesis,* will be discussed in Chapter 8. For now, we are concerned with introducing the ideas that lead to assigned values for probabilities.

5.2   PROBABILITY OF AN EVENT

The probability of an event is viewed as a numerical measure of the chance that the event will occur.

As we have suggested, we assign probability to an event using a scale of 0 to 1. A small value near 0 indicates the event is extremely unlikely, and a value close to 1 indicates the event is very likely. We have used the terms *event* and *experiment* assuming you have some notion of their meaning. In Chapter 4, we pointed out that our use of the term *experiment* is not limited to studies conducted in a laboratory setting. Rather, *experiment* is used in a broad sense to include any operation of data collection or observation where the outcomes are subject to variation. Consequently, rolling a die, drawing a card from a shuffled deck, sampling a number of customers for an opinion survey, and, in a more traditional sense, recording the temperature and pressure that produce the best backing for Scotch tape are examples of experiments.

> **Experiment:** The process of observing a phenomenon that has variation in its outcomes

Before attempting to assign probabilities, it is essential to consider all the possible outcomes of the experiment. We introduce the following terms which are explained in subsequent examples.

> **Sample space:** The collection of all possible distinct outcomes of the experiment
>
> **Elementary outcome** or **Simple event** or
> **Element of the sample space:** Each outcome of an experiment
>
> **Event:** The collection of elementary outcomes possessing a designated feature

The elementary outcomes, which together comprise the sample space, constitute the specification of the potential results of an experiment. For instance, in rolling an ordinary die, the elementary outcomes are the numbers 1, 2, 3, 4, 5, and 6, which together make up the sample space. At the specified announcement time, a company could declare a dividend on its stock, announce that there will be no dividend, or postpone the announcement. The collection of the three elementary outcomes, dividend, no dividend, and postponement, is the sample space. The outcome of a football game is a win, a loss, or a tie for the home team. Win, loss, and tie constitute the sample space.

Each time an experiment is performed, one and only one elementary outcome can occur. A sample space can be specified either by listing all the elementary outcomes, using convenient symbols to identify them, or by making a descriptive statement that characterizes the entire collection. For general discussion, we denote

the sample space by S,

the elementary outcomes by $e_1, e_2, e_3, \ldots$,

events by A, B, and so forth.

In specific applications, the elementary outcomes may be given other labels that provide a more vivid context identification.

An event A occurs when any one of the elementary outcomes in A occurs.

EXAMPLE 5.1   The Sample Space for Two Tosses of a Coin

Toss a coin twice and record the outcome head (H) or tail (T) for each toss. Let A denote the event of getting exactly one head and B the event of getting no heads at all. List the sample space and give the compositions of A and B.

Solution and Discussion.   For two tosses of a coin, the elementary outcomes can be conveniently identified by means of a **tree diagram.**

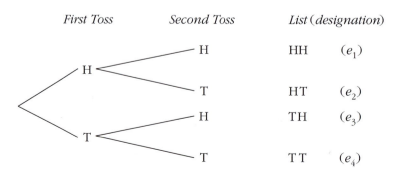

First Toss	Second Toss	List (designation)
	H	HH (e_1)
H	T	HT (e_2)
	H	TH (e_3)
T	T	T T (e_4)

The sample space can then be listed as $S = \{HH, HT, TH, TT\}$. With this designation, we can also write

$$S = \{e_1, e_2, e_3, e_4\}$$

Consider the event A of getting exactly one head. Scanning the list, we see that only the elements HT (e_2) and TH (e_3) satisfy this requirement. Therefore, the event A has the composition

$$A = \{e_2, e_3\}$$

which is, of course, a subset of S. The event B of getting no heads at all consists of the single element e_4 so $B = \{e_4\}$. That is, B is a simple event as well as an event.

The order in which the elements of the sample space are listed is inconsequential. It is the collection that matters. Also, the term *event* is a general term that includes simple events.

EXAMPLE 5.2   The Sample Space for Speeding Violations

On a Saturday morning, 143 cars passing a highway repair zone will be monitored for possible violation of the posted speed limit, and the number of violators will be recorded. Identify

a.   The sample space

b.   The event that more than 60% of the cars violate the speed limit

Solution and Discussion.

a.   Since the number of violators could be any of the numbers $0, 1, 2, \ldots, 143$, the sample space can be listed simply as

$$S = \{0, 1, 2, \ldots, 143\}$$

Using the notation e for elementary outcome, we can also write

$$S = \{e_0, e_1, e_2, \ldots, e_{143}\}$$

b.   Let A stand for the event that more than 60% of the monitored cars violate the speed limit. Calculating $.60 \times 143 = 85.8$, we identify

$$A = \{86, 87, 88, \ldots, 143\}$$

EXAMPLE 5.3   The Sample Space for Type of Advertising

Small business owners will be contacted about their most effective type of advertising. The response will be one of the types listed at the top of page 218:

Mailing flyers

Newspaper

Radio

Telephone book (Yellow Pages)

Television

Trade magazine

For a single, small business owner selected from the association membership:

a. List the sample space.

b. Identify the events $A =$ [printed advertisement] and $B =$ [audio advertisement].

Solution and Discussion.

a. $S =$ [mailing flyers, newspaper, radio, telephone book, television, trade magazine] or $S = \{e_1, e_2, e_3, e_4, e_5, e_6\}$ in the elementary outcome notation.

b. In elementary outcome notation, $A = \{e_1, e_2, e_4, e_6\}$ and $B = \{e_3, e_5\}$.

Examples 5.1, 5.2, and 5.3 illustrate sample spaces that have a finite number of elements. There are also sample spaces with infinitely many elements. For instance, suppose a telemarketer will continue making phone calls until the first sale is made. The first sale could occur on the first, second, third, or even the 1000th call. The conceivable number of attempts does not have a natural upper limit so the list never terminates. That is, $S = \{1, 2, 3, \ldots\}$ has an infinite number of elements. However, we notice that the elements could be arranged one after another in a sequence. An infinite sample space where such an arrangement is possible is called *countably infinite*.

Each sample space in Examples 5.1, 5.2, 5.3, and the telemarketer situation is called a **discrete sample space.** The elements of a discrete sample space can be counted with integers. Examples 5.1, 5.2, and 5.3 each display a discrete sample space with a finite number of elements. The telemarketer sample space is a discrete sample space with a countably infinite number of elements.

Another type of infinite sample space is also important. Suppose a car with a full tank of gasoline is driven until its fuel runs out, and the distance traveled is recorded. Since distance is measured on a continuous scale, any nonnegative number is a possible outcome. Denoting the distance traveled by d, we can describe this sample space as $S = \{d : d \geq 0\}$—that is, the set of all real numbers greater than or equal to zero. Here the elements of S form a continuum and cannot be arranged in a sequence. This is an example of a **continuous sample space.**

We have stated that the probability of an event is a numerical measure of the chance that the event will occur. Intuitively, this quantification can be determined as the proportion, or fraction, of times the event would occur in many repeated trials of the experiment.

An assessment of the probabilities of events and their consequences can help to guide decisions. [CALVIN AND HOBBES © Watterson. Dist. by UNIVERSAL PRESS SYNDICATE. Reprinted with permission. All rights reserved.]

> The **probability of an event** is a numerical value that represents the proportion of times the event is expected to occur when the experiment is repeated under identical conditions.

The probability of event A is denoted by $P(A)$.

Since a proportion must lie between 0 and 1, the probability of an event is a number between 0 and 1. To explore a few other important properties of probability, let us refer to the experiment in Example 5.1 of tossing a coin twice. The event A of getting exactly one head consists of the elementary outcomes HT (e_2) and TH (e_3). Consequently, A occurs if either of these outcomes occurs. Because

$$\begin{bmatrix} \text{Proportion of times} \\ A \text{ occurs} \end{bmatrix} = \begin{bmatrix} \text{Proportion of times} \\ \text{HT occurs} \end{bmatrix} + \begin{bmatrix} \text{Proportion of times} \\ \text{TH occurs} \end{bmatrix}$$

the number that we assign as $P(A)$ must be the sum of the two numbers $P(HT)$ and $P(TH)$. Guided by this example, we state some general properties of probability.

> The probability of an event is the sum of the probabilities assigned to all the elementary outcomes contained in the event.

Next, since the sample space S includes all conceivable outcomes, in every trial of the experiment, some element of S must occur. Viewed as an event, S is certain to occur, and therefore its probability is 1.

> The sum of the probabilities of all the elements of S must be 1.

EXAMPLE 5.4   Determining the Probability of an Event

If a recently purchased building can be resold before the closing date, a large profit will be realized. If it can be sold within six months of closing, a moderate profit will be realized, and a loss will result if the building is not sold within those six months. An expert in real estate investments assigns the probabilities

$$P(\text{large profit}) = .7 \qquad P(\text{moderate profit}) = .2 \qquad P(\text{loss}) = .1$$

a. Let $A = [\text{make a profit}]$. Determine $P(A)$.
b. Check that $P(S) = 1$.

Solution and Discussion.

a. Set $e_1 = [\text{large profit}]$, $e_2 = [\text{moderate profit}]$, and $e_3 = [\text{loss}]$. Then $A = \{e_1, e_2\}$. Summing the probabilities for all the outcomes in A, we obtain

$$P(A) = P(e_1) + P(e_2) = .7 + .2 = .9$$

b. $P(S) = P(e_1) + P(e_2) + P(e_3) = .7 + .2 + .1 = 1.0$

> In summary, **probability** must satisfy:
>
> 1. $0 \le P(A) \le 1$ for all events A
> 2. $P(A) = \sum_{\text{all } e \text{ in } A} P(e)$
> 3. $P(S) = \sum_{\text{all } e \text{ in } S} P(e) = 1$

We have deduced these basic properties of probability by reasoning from the definition that the probability of an event is the proportion of times the event is expected to occur in many repeated trials of the experiment.

EXERCISES

5.1 Match the proposed probability of *A* with the appropriate written description. (More than one description may apply.)

Probability	Written Description
(a) .95	(i) No chance of happening
(b) .02	(ii) Very likely to happen
(c) 3.0	(iii) As much chance of happening as not
(d) − .3	(iv) Very little chance of happening
(e) .4	(v) May occur but by no means certain
(f) .5	(vi) An incorrect assignment
(g) 0	

5.2 For each numerical value assigned to the probability of an event, identify the written statements that are appropriate.

(a) .01   (b) .7   (c) $\frac{1}{186}$ (d) 1.1   (e) $\frac{1}{2}$ (f) $\frac{43}{45}$

Written statements: (i) cannot be a probability, (ii) the event is very unlikely to happen, (iii) 50–50 chance of happening, (iv) sure to happen, (v) more likely to happen than not.

5.3 Identify the statement that best describes each $P(A)$.

(a) $P(A) = .04$ (i) $P(A)$ is incorrect.

(b) $P(A) = .40$ (ii) *A* rarely occurs.

(c) $P(A) = 4.0$ (iii) *A* occurs moderately often.

5.4 Construct a sample space for each of the following experiments.

a. Someone claims to be able to taste the difference between the same brand of bottled, tap, and canned draft beer. A glass of each is poured and given to the subject in unknown order. The subject is asked to identify the contents of each glass. The number of correct identifications will be recorded.

b. The number of traffic fatalities in a state next year will be recorded.

c. The length of time a new video recorder will continue to work satisfactorily without service will be observed.

5.5 Refer to the corresponding parts of Exercise 5.4. Identify the following events.

a. No more than one correct identification

b. Fewer accidents than last year (If last year's value is unknown, use 345.)

c. Longer than the 90-day warranty but less than 425.4 days

5.6 When bidding on two projects, the president and vice president of a construction company make the following assessments for winning the contracts:

President	Vice President
$P(\text{win none}) = .2$	$P(\text{win none}) = .1$
$P(\text{win only one}) = .5$	$P(\text{win Project 1}) = .2$
$P(\text{win both}) = .3$	$P(\text{win Project 2}) = .4$
	$P(\text{win both}) = .3$

For both cases, determine whether the probability assignment is permissible.

5.7 Two potential customers will be contacted. If both contacts result in sales, the experiment will stop. If one sale is obtained in the two contacts, a third potential customer will be contacted. Finally, in the case where both of the first two potential customers fail to purchase, two additional customers will be contacted.

a. Make a tree diagram and list the sample space.

b. Give the composition of the events

$$A = [\text{two sales}] \qquad B = [\text{two do not purchase}]$$

5.8 There are four elementary outcomes in the sample space. If $P(e_1) = .1$, $P(e_2) = .5$, $P(e_3) = .1$, what is the probability of e_4?

5.9 Suppose $S = \{e_1, e_2, e_3\}$. If the simple events e_1, e_2, and e_3 are all equally likely, what are the numerical values of $P(e_1)$, $P(e_2)$, and $P(e_3)$?

5.10 The sample space for the response of one person's attitude toward a balanced budget amendment consists of the three elementary outcomes: $e_1 = [\text{unfavorable}]$, $e_2 = [\text{favorable}]$, and $e_3 = [\text{undecided}]$. Are the following assignments of probabilities permissible?

a. $P(e_1) = .4$, $P(e_2) = .5$, $P(e_3) = .1$

b. $P(e_1) = .4$, $P(e_2) = .4$, $P(e_3) = .4$

c. $P(e_1) = .5$, $P(e_2) = .5$, $P(e_3) = 0$

5.11 One of four persons, Ann, Ben, Chris, or Dan, will be promoted next month. Consequently, the sample space consists of the four elementary outcomes $e_1 = [\text{Ann}]$, $e_2 = [\text{Ben}]$, $e_3 = [\text{Chris}]$, $e_4 = [\text{Dan}]$. You are told that e_1 and e_4 are equally likely, e_2 is twice as likely as e_1, and e_3 is four times as likely as e_1.

a. Determine $P(e_1)$, $P(e_2)$, $P(e_3)$, and $P(e_4)$.

b. If $A = \{e_1, e_3\}$, find $P(A)$.

5.12 The owner of a small business is contemplating the introduction of a new product next year. A sample space for the market conditions at the time the product is launched consists of four elementary outcomes: $e_1 = [\text{very favorable}]$, $e_2 = [\text{somewhat favorable}]$, $e_3 = [\text{somewhat unfavorable}]$, and $e_4 = [\text{very unfavorable}]$. The probabilities are in the ratios $9 : 6 : 4 : 1$. If $A = \{e_1, e_2\}$, find the probability of A.

5.13 *Probability and Odds.* The probability of an event is often expressed in terms of odds. Specifically, when we say that the odds are k to m that an event will occur, we mean that the probability of the event is $k/(k + m)$. For instance, "the odds are 4 to 1 that candidate Jones will win" means that $P(\text{Jones will win}) = \frac{4}{5} = .8$. Express the following statements in terms of probability.

a. The odds are 2 to 1 that Nancy will be promoted to partner this year.

b. The odds are 5 to 2 that the city council will delay the funding of a new sports arena.

5.14 *Probability and Odds (continued).* If the odds are k to m that an event A will occur, the subjective probability that the event will occur is $p = k/(k + m)$, and the **odds ratio** is $p/(1 - p)$. Answer the following questions.

a. What are the odds of completing the audit on time if the probability is $\frac{2}{3}$?

b.   What are the odds of giving a timely response to a customer inquiry if the probability is $\frac{3}{5}$?

c.   What is the probability of being assigned to a new job if the odds are 3 to 1?

5.3   METHODS OF ASSIGNING PROBABILITY

An assignment of probabilities to all the events in a sample space determines a probability model. To be a valid probability model, the probability assignment must satisfy the properties stated in the previous section. Any assignment of numbers $P(e_i)$ to the elementary outcomes will satisfy the three conditions of probability provided these numbers are nonnegative, and their sum over all the outcomes e_i in S is 1. However, to be of any practical import, the probability assigned to an event must also be in agreement with the concept of probability as the proportion of times the event is expected to occur. A company that greatly overestimates the probability that a new product will be successful could suffer serious financial consequences.

Next we discuss the determination of probabilities in two important situations.

EQUALLY LIKELY ELEMENTARY OUTCOMES—THE UNIFORM PROBABILITY MODEL

Often the description of an experiment ensures that each elementary outcome is as likely to occur as any other. For example, consider the experiment of rolling a fair die and recording the top face. The sample space can be listed as

$$S = \{e_1, e_2, e_3, e_4, e_5, e_6\}$$

where e_1 stands for the elementary outcome of getting the face 1, and similarly for $e_2, e_3, \ldots, e_6$.

Without actually rolling a die, we can deduce the probabilities. Because a fair die is a symmetric cube, each of its six faces is equally likely to appear. In other words, each face is expected to occur one-sixth of the time. The probability assignments should therefore be

$$P(e_1) = P(e_2) = P(e_3) = P(e_4) = P(e_5) = P(e_6) = \frac{1}{6}$$

and any other assignment would contradict the statement that the die is fair. We say that rolling a fair die conforms to a uniform probability model because the total probability 1 is evenly apportioned to all the elementary outcomes.

What is the probability of getting a number higher than 4? Letting A denote this event, we have the composition $A = \{e_5, e_6\}$, so

$$P(A) = P(e_5) + P(e_6) = \frac{1}{6} + \frac{1}{6} = \frac{1}{3}$$

When the elementary outcomes are modeled as equally likely, we have a uniform probability model. If there are k elementary outcomes in S, each is assigned the probability of $1/k$.

Uniform Probability Model

Let S have k equally likely elementary outcomes.

An event A consisting of m elementary outcomes is then assigned probability

$$P(A) = \frac{m}{k} = \frac{\text{number of elementary outcomes in } A}{\text{number of elementary of outcomes in } S}$$

EXAMPLE 5.5   A Fair Coin and Equally Likely Outcomes

Find the probability of getting exactly one head in two tosses of a fair coin.

Solution and Discussion.   In Example 5.1, there are four elementary outcomes in the sample space: $S = \{HH, HT, TH, TT\}$. A fair coin means there is no reason to believe that getting a Head is more likely than getting a Tail. Thus, the four elementary outcomes in S are equally likely. We therefore assign the probability $\frac{1}{4}$ to each of them. The event $A = $ [one head] has two elementary outcomes—namely, HT and TH. Hence,

$$P(A) = \frac{2}{4} = .5$$

EXAMPLE 5.6   Random Selection and Equally Likely Outcomes

Suppose that among 50 potential customers, 8 will sign a service contract and 42 will not. If one of these potential customers is randomly selected, what is the probability that the selected customer will sign a service contract?

Solution and Discussion.   The intuitive notion of random selection is that each customer is as likely to be selected as any other. If we view the selection of each individual potential customer as an elementary outcome, the sample space consists of 50 e's, of which 8 are in the event, sign a contract. Consequently,

$$P(\text{sign a contract}) = \frac{8}{50} = .16$$

Warning: Considering that the selected person will either sign the service contract (C) or not (N), we can write the sample space as $S = \{C, N\}$, but we should be aware that the elements C and N are not equally likely.

PROBABILITY AS LONG-RUN RELATIVE FREQUENCY

In many situations, it is not possible to construct a sample space where the elementary outcomes are equally likely. If one corner of a die is cut off, it would be unreasonable to assume that the faces remain equally likely. In this case, the assignments of probability to various faces can no longer be made by deductive reasoning. When speaking of the probability (or risk) that a man will die during a given decade of his life, we may choose to identify the occurrence of death at each decade or even at each year of age as an elementary outcome. However, no sound reasoning can support a uniform probability model. In fact, from extensive mortality studies, actuaries have found considerable disparity in the risk of death at different age levels.

When the assumption of equally likely outcomes is not tenable, how do we assess the probability of an event? One recourse is to repeat the experiment many times and observe the proportion of times the event occurs. Letting n denote the number of repetitions (or trials) of an experiment, we set

$$\text{Relative frequency of event } A \text{ in } n \text{ trials} = \frac{\text{Number of times } A \text{ occurs in } n \text{ trials}}{n}$$

Let A be the event of getting a 6 when rolling a die. Our first ten rolls gave 5, 6, 2, 1, 3, 1, 2, 5, 1, and 2. For simplicity, we will calculate the relative frequency at every fifth roll. At the end of the first five rolls, 6 appeared once, so the observed relative frequency of A would be $\frac{1}{5} = .20$. At the end of ten trials, the relative frequency of A is $\frac{1}{10} = .10$. Continuing until the die is rolled 100 times, we found that 6 occurred 16 times, so the relative frequency of A was $\frac{16}{100} = .16$.

Figure 5.1(a) shows a plot of the relative frequency of obtaining a 6 versus the number of trials when the relative frequency is updated at the end of every five trials

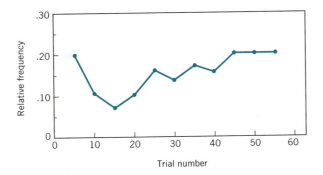

(a) Relative frequency updated after every 5 trials

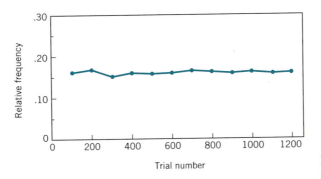

(b) Relative frequency updated after every 100 trials

Figure 5.1   Stabilization of Relative Frequency: Obtaining a 6 in a Roll of a Die

through 55 repetitions of the experiment. Consistent with our previous discussion, the first relative frequency in this plot is .20 and the second is .10. Notice there is considerable variability in the relative frequency when the number of trials, n, is small.

Figure 5.1(b) shows the relative frequency versus the number of trials, with the relative frequency updated at the end of every hundred rolls. The first relative frequency in this plot is .16 as discussed previously. In the second 100 rolls of the die, 6 came up 18 times, so the relative frequency after 200 trials is determined by collecting the first two sets together to give

$$\frac{16 + 18}{200} = \frac{34}{200} = .17$$

This is the second relative frequency plotted in Figure 5.1(b). From Figure 5.1(b), we see that fluctuations in the relative frequency decrease with increasing n. In this case, the relative frequency is relatively stable after about 200 repetitions of the experiment.

For any experiment, two persons separately performing the same experiment n times are not going to get exactly the same results, and therefore the relative frequency graphs will be different. However, the numerical value at which the relative frequency stabilizes in the long run will be the same. This concept, called *long-run stability of relative frequency,* is the key point illustrated in Figure 5.1.

Probability as Long-Run Relative Frequency

We define $P(A)$, the probability of an event A, as the value to which the relative frequency stabilizes with an increasing number of trials.

Although we will never know $P(A)$ exactly, it can be estimated quite accurately by repeating the experiment many times.

The property of the long-run stabilization of relative frequencies is based on the findings of experimenters in many fields who have studied the behavior of the relative frequencies under prolonged repetitions of their experiments. French gamblers, who provided much of the early impetus for the study of probability, performed experiments such as tossing dice and coins, drawing cards, and playing other games of chance thousands and thousands of times. They observed the stabilization property of relative frequency and applied this knowledge to achieve an understanding of the uncertainty involved in these games.

Actuaries have compiled and studied volumes of mortality data to examine the relative frequency of the occurrence of such events as death in particular age groups. In each context, the relative frequencies were found to stabilize at specific numerical values as the number of cases studied increased. Life and accident insurance companies actually depend on the stability property of relative frequencies to determine risks and set premiums.

EXAMPLE 5.7   Control of Expenses and Relative Frequency

For companies, travel and entertainment expenses are the third largest controllable expenses behind salaries and data-processing expenses. Experience has shown that instituting formal written policies can lead to more accurate reporting and better control of travel and entertainment expenses. Based on a large survey of companies, a relative frequency of .63 of the companies have a formal written policy, .35 of the companies have informal guidelines, and .02 have no guidelines for expenses (*Management Review*, June 1993, pp. 61–63). Suppose the same conditions prevail this year.

a. Explain how to use long-run relative frequency to approximate the probabilities that a company will have each of the three control systems—formal policy, informal guidelines, and no guidelines—on expenses.

b. Assign probabilities to each of the elementary outcomes: [formal policy], [informal guidelines], and [no guidelines].

c. Approximate the probability that a company will have some form of guideline or policy.

Solution and Discussion.

a. Since the survey was based on a large number of companies, the long-run relative frequency of each category should have stabilized near its probability.

b. We approximate

$$P(\text{formal policy}) = .63$$
$$P(\text{informal guidelines}) = .35$$
$$P(\text{no guidelines}) = .02$$

c. Since the event [some form of guideline] consists of the two elementary events [formal policy] and [informal guidelines], we add their probabilities to obtain

$$P(\text{some form of guideline}) = P(\text{formal policy}) + P(\text{informal guidelines})$$
$$= .63 + .35 = .98$$

EXAMPLE 5.8   Automobile Accident Claims and Relative Frequency

An insurance company reported the following experience with damage-only claims for automobile accidents (data courtesy of J. Hickman).

Numbers of Damage-Only Claims

	Age		Total
	Under 25	**25 or older**	
Claim	1053	1020	2073
No claim	4139	6087	10226
Total	5192	7107	12299

Suppose this claim history is valid for those insured this year by the company.

a. Explain how to use long-run relative frequency to approximate the probability that a driver insured by the company will make a claim.

b. Approximate the probability that a driver under 25 insured by the company will make a claim.

c. Approximate the probability that a driver over 25 insured by the company will make a claim.

d. Explain, in the context of the long-run relative frequency interpretation of probability, why this company needs to charge more for insurance for drivers under the age of 25.

Solution and Discussion.

a. A large number, 12229, of policies were in effect. Each can be considered an experiment where the outcome is either "no claim" or "claim" (really, one or more claims). Since 2073 drivers made a claim, we approximate

$$P(\text{claim}) = \frac{2073}{12299} = .169$$

b. Restricting our attention to insured drivers under the age of 25, we approximate the probability of a claim as

$$\frac{1053}{5192} = .203$$

c. A similar approximation, for insured drivers over the age of 25, gives

$$\frac{1020}{7107} = .144$$

d. Based on the company's experience, the probability is more than 40% higher that an insured driver under 25 will make a claim. In the long run, the relative frequency of claims would be 40% higher for this group. Money would be lost if persons in both age groups were charged the same premiums, since those in the older age group would likely move to other companies with a competitive rate for their age group.

EXERCISES

5.15 Consider the experiment of tossing a coin three times.

a. List the sample space by drawing a tree diagram.

b. Assign probabilities to the elementary outcomes.

c. Find the probability of getting exactly one head.

5.16   A letter is chosen at random from the word PROFIT. What is the probability that it is a vowel?

5.17   A stack contains eight tickets numbered 1, 1, 1, 2, 2, 3, 3, 3. One ticket will be drawn at random, and its number will be noted.

   a.   List the sample space, and assign probabilities to the elementary outcomes.

   b.   What is the probability of drawing an odd-numbered ticket?

5.18   Research has narrowed the list to five real estate investments of nearly the same cost. Suppose the investor selects one, by lottery, and makes the purchase. Unknown to the investor at this time, three of the investments will ultimately show a profit at the end of the first year and the other two will not.

   a.   List the sample space and assign probabilities to the elementary outcomes.

   b.   What is the probability that the selected investment will show a profit at the end of the first year?

5.19   Suppose you are eating at a pizza parlor with two friends. You have agreed to the following rule to decide who will pay the bill. Each person will toss a coin. The person who gets a result that is different from the other two will pay the bill. If all three tosses yield the same result, the bill will be shared by all. Find the probability that:

   a.   Only you will have to pay.

   b.   All three will share the bill.

5.20   A white and a colored die are tossed. The possible outcomes are shown in the following illustration.

   a.   Identify the events A = [sum = 6], B = [sum = 7], C = [sum is even], and D = [same number on each die].

   b.   If both dice are fair, assign probability to each elementary outcome.

   c.   Obtain $P(A)$, $P(B)$, $P(C)$, and $P(D)$.

5.21   The August 3, 1993, issue of *Business Week* ranked the top 68 companies according to a technological strength index based on the number of patents a company had and how often the company's patents were cited in new applications. We give the first 11 companies, ranked according to the index, along with the number of new patents granted for the year 1991 in the table at the top of page 230.

Company (Headquarters Country)	Number of U.S. Patents (1991)
Toshiba (Japan)	1156
Hitachi (Japan)	1139
Canon (Japan)	828
Mitsubishi Electric (Japan)	959
Eastman Kodak (U.S.)	887
IBM (U.S.)	680
General Motors (U.S.)	863
General Electric (U.S.)	923
Fuji Photo Film (Japan)	742
Motorola (U.S.)	631
AT&T (U.S.)	487
Total	9295

Give a long-run frequency interpretation of the probability that a new patent, filed by one of these companies, will be filed by a company with headquarters in the United States. If one patent is selected at random, find the probability that:

a.   It belongs to IBM.

b.   It belongs to a company with headquarters in Japan.

5.22   The June 14, 1993, issue of *Business Week* listed 46 productivity pacesetters. These were domestic companies whose sales per employee were at least 125% of the industry average. Of these companies, 23 were reported to have fewer employees than five years earlier, 12 had an increase in employees of less than 10%, and 11 had an increase of 10% or more employees. If one of these companies is selected by lottery, use the relative frequencies to determine

a.   The probabilities of

$$e_1 = [\text{fewer employees}]$$

$$e_2 = [\text{increase less than 10\%}]$$

$$e_3 = [\text{increase 10\% or more}]$$

b.   The probability of an increase in the number of employees

5.23   A profile of working persons in the United States is given in the following table (*Statistical Abstract of the United States,* 1992, p. 396).

Working Persons in the United States

Occupation	Total (millions)
Managerial/professional	29.1
Technical/sales/administrative	29.5
Service	11.8
Precision production	11.7
Operators/fabricators	14.0
Farming/forestry/fishing	2.8
Total	98.9

If a worker is selected at random, find the probability of the following occupations:

a.   Managerial/professional

b.   Service

5.24   A corporation will randomly select one of its 15 departments for an audit of travel expenditures to investigate compliance with company policy. Suppose that, unknown to the corporation, 10 of these departments are in compliance, 3 are borderline cases, and 2 are in gross violation.

a.   Formulate the sample space in such a way that a uniform probability model holds.

b.   Find the probability that a gross violator will be detected.

5.25   Explain why the long-run relative frequency interpretation of probability does not apply to the following situations.

a.   The proportion of days the Dow Jones average of industrial stock prices exceeds 5700

b.   The proportion of last year's income tax returns containing improper deductions if the data are collected only in a slack period, for example, January

c.   The proportion of cars that do not meet emission standards if the data are collected from service stations where the mechanics have been asked to check the emissions while attending to other requested services

5.26   One part of a quiz consists of two multiple-choice questions with these suggested answers: True (T), False (F), or Insufficient data to answer (I). An unprepared student randomly marks one of the three answers to each question.

a.   Construct a tree diagram of the sample space, that is, all possible pairs of answers the student might mark.

b.   What is the probability of exactly one correct answer?

5.4   EVENT RELATIONS AND TWO LAWS OF PROBABILITY

Recall that the probability of an event A is the sum of the probabilities of all elementary outcomes that are in A. It often turns out, however, that the event of interest has a complex structure that requires the tedious listing of all of its elementary outcomes. On the other hand, this event may be related to other events that can be handled more easily. The purpose of this section is to introduce the three most basic event relations: complement, union, and intersection. We then show that these event relations are the basis for some laws of probability.

The event operations are conveniently described in graphical terms. First, we represent the sample space as a collection of points in a diagram, each point identified with a specific elementary outcome. The geometric pattern of the plotted points is irrelevant. It is important that each point be clearly tagged to indicate which elementary outcome it represents, and to be sure that no elementary outcome is missed or duplicated in the diagram. To represent an event A, identify the points that correspond to the elementary outcomes in A, enclose them in a boundary line, and attach the tag A. This representation, called a **Venn diagram,** is illustrated in the next example.

EXAMPLE 5.9   A Venn Diagram

A coin is tossed twice. Make a Venn diagram that indicates the following events:

$$A = [\text{Tail at the second toss}]$$

$$B = [\text{At least one head}]$$

Solution and Discussion.   Here the sample space is $S = \{HH, HT, TH, TT\}$, and the two events have the compositions $A = \{HT, TT\}$, $B = \{HH, HT, TH\}$. The Venn diagram is shown in Figure 5.2.

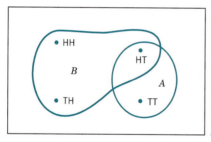

Figure 5.2   Venn Diagram of the Events in Example 5.9

We now define the three basic event operations and introduce the corresponding symbols.

Complement of the event A: Denoted by $\overline{A}$. The set of all elementary outcomes that are *not* in A. The occurrence of $\overline{A}$ means that A *does not occur.*

Union of two events A and B: Denoted by $A \cup B$. The set of all elementary outcomes that are in A, and B, or in both. The occurrence of $A \cup B$ means that *either A or B or both occur.*

> **Intersection of two events A and B:** Denoted by $A \cap B$. The set of all elementary outcomes that are in A and in B. The occurrence of $A \cap B$ means *both A and B occur.*

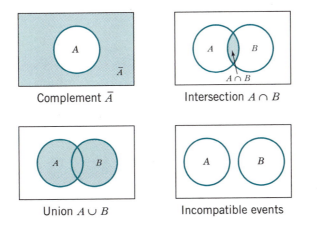

Complement $\bar{A}$ Intersection $A \cap B$

Union $A \cup B$ Incompatible events

Notice that $A \cup B$ is a larger set containing A as well as B, whereas $A \cap B$ is the common part of the sets A and B. Also, it is evident from the definitions that $A \cup B$ and $B \cup A$ are both expressions for the union of A and B, and $A \cap B$ and $B \cap A$ are both expressions for the intersection of A and B. The operations of union and intersection can be extended to more than two events. For instance, $A \cup B \cup C$ stands for the set of all elementary outcomes that *occur at least once* in A, B, and C, whereas $A \cap B \cap C$ represents the *simultaneous occurrence* of all three events.

Two events A and B are called **incompatible** or **mutually exclusive** if their intersection $A \cap B$ is empty. Because incompatible events have no elementary outcomes in common, they cannot occur simultaneously.

EXAMPLE 5.10   Complement, Union, and Intersection

A list of possible investment opportunities has been narrowed to four possibilities.

Investment	Industry	Region of Country
1	Medical	West Coast
2	Medical	Midwest
3	Electronics	West Coast
4	Electronics	West Coast

Further research should help to identify the best two opportunities, but suppose you choose two by lottery. Let $A =$ [same industry], $B =$ [same region], and $C =$ [different industries]. Determine the composition of the events

$$C \quad \overline{A} \quad A \cup B \quad A \cap B \quad B \cap C$$

Solution and Discussion.   The elements of the sample space are the six possible pairs of investments selected from investments $\{1, 2, 3, 4\}$. The pairs consisting of different industries are $\{1, 3\}$, $\{1, 4\}$, $\{2, 3\}$, and $\{2, 4\}$. To simplify the notation, let the pairs be denoted by

$$\{1, 2\} = e_1 \quad \{1, 3\} = e_2 \quad \{1, 4\} = e_3$$
$$\{2, 3\} = e_4 \quad \{2, 4\} = e_5 \quad \{3, 4\} = e_6$$

Thus $C = \{e_2, e_3, e_4, e_5\}$. The event $\overline{A}$ is the same as the event C. Using the definitions of union and intersection, with $A = \{e_1, e_6\}$ and $B = \{e_2, e_3, e_6\}$, we obtain

$$A \cup B = \{e_1, e_2, e_3, e_6\}$$
$$A \cap B = \{e_6\}$$
$$B \cap C = \{e_2, e_3\}$$

EXAMPLE 5.11   Elementary Outcomes, Events, and a Venn Diagram

The Valhalla Valley Country Club is well known for its quality golf course and highly regarded dining facilities. An outdoor pool and tennis courts are also available to members. In spite of being well respected for many years, the club's applications for membership were declining. Board members contracted a market research firm to conduct a survey of its members, as well as members of other country clubs in the area. To determine factors that influenced their decision to join the club, one of the questions was:

Did the quality of the dining facilities influence your decision to join? *Yes/No.*

The Board also wanted to know whether demographic factors, such as age, gender, or income, had any bearing on the decision to join. Age was recorded in the categories:

30 and under   31 to 50   over 50

a.   For a person selected from the Valhalla Valley membership, list all elementary outcomes consisting of the responses that include the influence of the dining facilities and the age category.

b.   Display the elementary outcomes in the form of a table that can also be used to record the counts for each outcome, based on a sample of members.

c.   Define the events $A =$ [yes, dining was influential] and $B =$ [age 31–50], and construct a Venn diagram indicating these events.

d.   Specify the events $A \cap B$ and $\overline{A}$. Also, describe these two events in words.

Solution and Discussion.

a. Each elementary outcome consists of a pair, [dining response, age group]. Using e to denote an elementary outcome, we list the six elementary outcomes as follows:

$$e_1 = \text{[not influential, 30 or under]} \qquad e_2 = \text{[not influential, 31 to 50]}$$
$$e_3 = \text{[not influential, over 50]} \qquad e_4 = \text{[influential, 30 or under]}$$
$$e_5 = \text{[influential, 31 to 50]} \qquad e_6 = \text{[influential, over 50]}$$

b. The table for recording the number of each outcome would have the form

		Age		
		30 or under	31 to 50	over 50
Dining	Not influential			
	Influential			

c. The events are $A = \{e_4, e_5, e_6\}$ and $B = \{e_2, e_5\}$. The Venn diagram is shown in Figure 5.3.

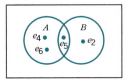

Figure 5.3   Venn Diagram of the Events in Example 5.11

d. $A \cap B = \{e_5\}$ is the event consisting of the single elementary outcome e_5; that is, dining facilities were an influential factor for a person in the 31–50 age group. $\overline{A} = \{e_1, e_2, e_3\}$ is the event that dining facilities were not influential in the decision to join for a person of any age group.

Let us now examine how probabilities behave as the operations of complementation, union, and intersection are applied to events. (It would be worthwhile for you to review the properties of probability discussed in Section 5.2. In particular, recall that $P(A)$ is the sum of the probabilities of the elementary outcomes that are in event A, and $P(S) = 1$ where S is the entire collection of elementary outcomes, that is, the sample space.)

First, let us examine how $P(\overline{A})$ is related to $P(A)$. Now $\overline{A}$ is the set of all elementary outcomes not in A. Together, the two sets A and $\overline{A}$ comprise S. Consequently, the sum of the probabilities of all the elementary outcomes that are in A plus the sum of the probabilities of all the elementary outcomes in $\overline{A}$ must be the sum of the probabilities of all the elementary outcomes or, equivalently, the elementary outcomes in S. We have $P(A) + P(\overline{A}) = P(S) = 1$, and we arrive at the following law:

Law of the Complement: $P(A) = 1 - P(\overline{A})$

This law or formula is useful for calculating $P(A)$ when $\overline{A}$ is of a simpler form than A and thus $P(\overline{A})$ is easier to calculate.

Recall that $A \cup B$ is composed of elementary outcomes that are in A, B, or in both A and B. Thus, $P(A \cup B)$ is the sum of the probabilities assigned to these elementary outcomes, each probability counted *just once*. On the other hand, $P(A) + P(B)$ includes contributions from all the elementary outcomes, but it counts those in $A \cap B$ twice (see the figure of $A \cap B$). To adjust for this double counting, we must subtract $P(A \cap B)$ from $P(A) + P(B)$. This results in the following law:

Addition Law: $P(A \cup B) = P(A) + P(B) - P(A \cap B)$

If the events A and B are incompatible, their intersection, $A \cap B$, is empty, so $P(A \cap B) = 0$. Therefore, for the union of incompatible events, we obtain:

Addition Law for Incompatible Events: $P(A \cup B) = P(A) + P(B)$

The addition law expresses the probability of a larger event, $A \cup B$, in terms of the probabilities of the smaller events, A, B, and $A \cap B$. Applications of these two laws are given in the following examples.

EXAMPLE 5.12   Illustrating the Law of the Complement

One consequence of the random walk model for stock prices is that, in the short run, prices are unpredictable in the sense that prices are as likely to go up as they are to go down. Changes from one period to another will also be unrelated. Consider a sequence of three weekly changes in the Standard and Poor's (S&P) 500 Index. What is the probability of observing at least one *increase* under the random walk model?

Solution and Discussion.   Let us denote an increase by I and a decrease by D. The elementary outcomes can be conveniently enumerated by means of a tree diagram.

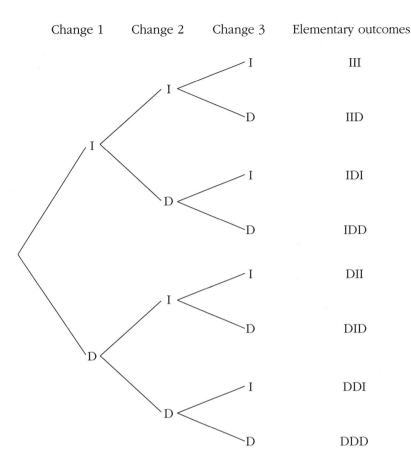

| Change 1 | Change 2 | Change 3 | Elementary outcomes |

There are 8 elementary outcomes in the sample space, and, according to the random walk model of stock prices, they are equally likely, so each has probability $\frac{1}{8}$. Let A denote the event of observing at least one increase. Scanning our list, we see that A contains 7 elementary outcomes, all except DDD. A direct calculation yields $P(A) = \frac{7}{8}$.

Now let us see how this probability calculation could be considerably simplified. First, making a complete list of the sample space is unnecessary. Since the elementary outcomes are equally likely, we need only determine that there are a total of 8 outcomes in S. How can we obtain this count without making a list? Note that an outcome is represented by three letters. There are two choices for each letter: I or D. We then have $2 \times 2 \times 2 = 8$ ways of filling the three slots. The tree diagram illustrates this multiplicative rule of counting. Evidently the event A contains many elementary outcomes. Alternatively, $\overline{A}$ is the event of observing all decreases. It consists of the single elementary outcome DDD, so $P(\overline{A}) = \frac{1}{8}$. According to the law of the complement

$$P(A) = 1 - P(\overline{A}) = 1 - \frac{1}{8} = \frac{7}{8}$$

EXAMPLE 5.13   Illustrating the Addition Law

Refer to Example 5.10, where two investment opportunities are selected from four by lottery. What is the probability that the selected investment opportunities are either in the same industry or in the same region?

Solution and Discussion.   We listed the 6 elementary outcomes that comprise the sample space in Example 5.10. The lottery selection makes all choices equally likely, so the uniform probability model applies. The two events of interest are

$$A = [\text{same industry}] = \{e_1, e_6\}$$
$$B = [\text{same region}] = \{e_2, e_3, e_6\}$$

Because A consists of two elementary outcomes and B consists of three,

$$P(A) = \frac{2}{6} \quad \text{and} \quad P(B) = \frac{3}{6}$$

We must calculate $P(A \cup B)$. To use the addition law, we also need to calculate $P(A \cap B)$. From Example 5.10, $A \cap B = \{e_6\}$, so $P(A \cap B) = \frac{1}{6}$. Therefore,

$$P(A \cup B) = P(A) + P(B) - P(A \cap B)$$
$$= \frac{2}{6} + \frac{3}{6} - \frac{1}{6} = \frac{4}{6} = \frac{2}{3}$$

which is confirmed by the observation that $A \cup B = \{e_1, e_2, e_3, e_6\}$ has four elementary outcomes.

EXAMPLE 5.14   More Probability Calculations

The accompanying Venn diagram shows three events, A, B, and C, and also the probabilities of the various intersections (for instance, $P(A \cap B) = .07$, $P(A \cap \bar{B}) = .13$). Determine

a. $P(A)$
b. $P(A \cap \bar{C})$
c. $P(A \cup B)$

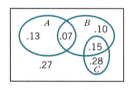

Solution and Discussion.   To calculate a probability, first identify the set in the Venn diagram. Then add the probabilities of those intersections that together form the stated event. Consequently,

a. $P(A) = .13 + .07 = .20$

b. $P(B \cap \overline{C}) = .10 + .07 = .17$

c. $P(A \cup B) = .13 + .07 + .10 + .15 = .45$

EXAMPLE 5.15   Events in Set Notation and Their Probabilities

Refer to Example 5.14. Express the following events in set notation and find their probabilities.

a.   Both B and C occur.

b. C occurs and B does not.

c.   Exactly one of the three events occurs.

Solution and Discussion.   The stated events and their probabilities are:

a. $B \cap C$, $P(B \cap C) = .15$

b. $\overline{B} \cap C$, $P(\overline{B} \cap C) = .28$

c. $(A \cap \overline{B} \cap \overline{C}) \cup (\overline{A} \cap B \cap \overline{C}) \cup (\overline{A} \cap \overline{B} \cap C)$
probability $= .13 + .10 + .28 = .51$

EXERCISES

5.27   Suppose the sample space of an experiment has 7 elementary outcomes $e_1, e_2, \ldots, e_7$. Suppose event $A = \{e_2, e_4, e_5, e_7\}$ and event $B = \{e_1, e_2, e_5\}$.

   a.   Draw a Venn diagram and show the events A and B.

   b.   Express the following events in terms of the sets of elementary outcomes: (i) $A \cap B$, (ii) $\overline{B}$, (iii) $A \cap \overline{B}$, and (iv) $A \cup B$.

5.28   A sample space consists of 8 elementary outcomes with the following probabilities.

$$P(e_1) = .16 \qquad P(e_2) = P(e_3) = P(e_4) = .08$$
$$P(e_5) = P(e_6) = P(e_7) = P(e_8) = .15$$

Three events are defined as $A = \{e_1, e_2, e_5, e_6, e_7\}$, $B = \{e_2, e_3, e_6, e_7\}$ and $C = \{e_6, e_8\}$.

   a.   Draw a Venn diagram and show the events.

   b.   Give the compositions, and determine the probabilities of (i) $\overline{B}$, (ii) $B \cap C$, (iii) $A \cup C$, and (iv) $\overline{A} \cup C$.

5.29   Refer to Exercise 5.28. For each of the following written descriptions, write the event in set notation, give its composition in terms of elementary outcomes, and find its probability.

   a. C does not occur.

   b.   Both A and B occur.

   c. A occurs and B does not occur.

   d.   Neither A nor C occurs.

5.30 Suppose you have had interviews for summer jobs at a grocery store, a department store, and a lumber yard. Let G, D, and L denote the events of getting an offer from the grocery store, the department store, and the lumber yard, respectively. Express the following events in set notation.

a. You get offers from the grocery store and the lumber yard.

b. You get offers from the grocery store and the lumber yard but fail to get an offer from the department store.

c. You do not get offers from the department store and the lumber yard.

5.31 Four applicants will be interviewed for a position with an oil company. They have the following characteristics:

1. Accounting major, female, GPA 3.5
2. Marketing major, female, GPA 3.8
3. Finance major, male, GPA 3.7
4. Finance major, female, GPA 3.2

One of the candidates will be hired.

a. Draw a Venn diagram and show the events:

   A: A finance major is hired.

   B: The GPA of the selected candidate is higher than 3.6.

   C: A female candidate is hired.

b. Give the composition of the events $A \cup B$ and $A \cap B$.

5.32 Refer to Exercise 5.31. Give a written description of each of the following events and also state the composition of the events.

a. $\overline{C}$

b. $C \cap \overline{A}$

c. $A \cup \overline{C}$

5.33 The probabilities are .7, .3, and .2 that a potential investor will purchase shares in European stock funds, Asian stock funds, or both. Find the probability the potential investor will purchase shares in

a. At least one of the funds

b. Neither of the two funds

5.34 Out of 120 members of the Valhalla Valley Country Club who responded to a survey, 67% felt the golfing facilities were influential in their decision to join, 44% felt the dining facilities were influential, and 21% felt that both were influential factors in their decision to join the club. Using the results of the survey as the probabilities for a potential new member, determine the probability that the potential new member

a. Would consider the golfing facilities, the dining facilities, or both as influential factors when making a decision to join

b. Would consider neither the golf facilities nor the dining facilities as influential factors when making a decision to join

5.35 A sample space consists of 9 elementary outcomes $e_1, e_2, \ldots, e_9$ whose probabilities are:

$$P(e_1) = P(e_2) = .08 \qquad P(e_3) = P(e_4) = P(e_5) = .1$$
$$P(e_6) = P(e_7) = .2 \qquad P(e_8) = P(e_9) = .07$$

Suppose $A = \{e_1, e_5, e_8\}$ and $B = \{e_2, e_5, e_8, e_9\}$.

a.   Calculate $P(A)$, $P(B)$, and $P(A \cap B)$.

b.   Using the addition law of probability, calculate $P(A \cup B)$.

c.   List the composition of the event $A \cup B$, and calculate $P(A \cup B)$ by adding the probabilities of the elementary outcomes.

d.   Calculate $P(\overline{B})$ from $P(B)$. Calculate $P(\overline{B})$ directly from the elementary outcomes of $\overline{B}$.

5.36   Refer to Exercise 5.27. Suppose the elementary outcomes are assigned the probabilities:

$$P(e_1) = P(e_2) = P(e_3) = .1 \qquad P(e_4) = P(e_5) = .08$$
$$P(e_6) = .3 \qquad P(e_7) = .24$$

a.   Find $P(A)$, $P(B)$, and $P(A \cap B)$.

b.   Using the laws of probability, and the results of part **a,** calculate $P(\overline{A})$ and $P(A \cup B)$.

c.   Verify your answers to part **b** by adding the probabilities of the elementary outcomes in each of $\overline{A}$ and $A \cup B$.

5.37   Explain why there must be a mistake in each of the following statements.

a.   A computer repair person claims that the probability is .8 that the hard disk is working properly, .7 that the RAM is working properly, and .3 that they are both working properly.

b.   An accountant claims that the probability is .95 that there are no significant errors in her analysis and the probability is .08 that there are one or two significant errors.

5.38   Explain why there must be a mistake in each of the following statements.

a.   A real estate investor claims that the probability is .6 that a certain property can be sold for a profit within one year and .3 that it cannot.

b.   The manager of a civic center claims that the probability is .7 that a magic show will make money for the center, .3 that a dance program will make money, and .4 that they both will make money.

5.39   For two events A and B, the following probabilities are specified:

$$P(A) = .52 \qquad P(B) = .36 \qquad P(A \cap B) = .20$$

a.   Enter these probabilities in the following table.

	B	$\overline{B}$
A		
$\overline{A}$		

b. Determine the probabilities of $A \cap \overline{B}$, $\overline{A} \cap B$, and $\overline{A} \cap \overline{B}$, and fill in the remainder of the table.

5.40 Refer to Exercise 5.39. Express the following events in set notation and find their probabilities.

a. B occurs and A does not occur.

b. Neither A nor B occurs.

c. Either A occurs or B does not occur.

5.41 The following table shows the probabilities concerning two events A and B.

	B	$\overline{B}$
A	.25	.12
$\overline{A}$		
	.40	

a. Determine the missing probabilities in the table.

b. What is the probability that A occurs and B does not occur?

c. Find the probability that either A or B occurs.

d. Find the probability that one of these events occurs and the other does not.

5.42 A profile of working persons in the United States is given in the following table.

Working Persons in the United States

Occupation	Men	Women	Total (millions)
Managerial/professional	15.8	13.3	29.1
Technical/sales/administrative	10.6	18.9	29.5
Service	4.5	7.3	11.8
Precision production	10.7	1.0	11.7
Operators/fabricators	10.2	3.7	13.9
Farming/forestry/fishing	2.3	.5	2.8
Total (millions)	54.1	44.7	98.8

SOURCE: *Statistical Abstract of the United States,* 1992, p. 396.

If a worker is selected at random, find the probability that the worker's occupation is

a. Managerial/professional

b. Service or precision production

c. Not in service

5.43 If $P(A) = .6$ and $P(B) = .5$, can A and B be incompatible (mutually exclusive)? Why or why not?

5.44 From the probabilities shown in this Venn diagram,

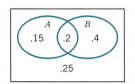

determine the probabilities of the following events:

a. A does not occur.

b. A occurs and B does not occur.

c. Exactly one of the events A and B occurs.

5.45 Of the 19 nursing homes in the city, 6 are in violation of sanitary standards, 8 are in violation of security standards, and 5 are in violation of both. If a nursing home is chosen at random, what is the probability that it is in compliance with both security and sanitary standards?

5.46 Given the probability that A occurs is $\frac{1}{3}$, the probability that B does not occur is $\frac{1}{4}$, and the probability that either A or B occurs is $\frac{8}{9}$, find the following probabilities:

a. A does not occur.

b. Both A and B occur.

c. A occurs and B does not occur.

5.47 One insurance company's yearly experience with automobile damage-only claims is summarized in terms of two risk factors, the age of driver and the type of car, in the table shown here.

	High Performance		Sedan		
	Under 25	**25 or older**	**Under 25**	**25 or older**	**Total**
Claim	390	213	663	807	2073
No claim	1232	1068	2907	5019	10226
Total	1622	1281	3570	5826	12299

SOURCE: Data courtesy of James Hickman.

Suppose an insured person is chosen at random from this group, and the events A, B, and C are defined as

A: High-performance car

B: Under 25 years old

C: Claim

a. Determine these probabilities:

    i. $P(A)$ ii. $P(C)$ iii. $P(B \cap C)$ iv. $P(A \cap B \cap C)$

b. Provide a written description of the following events and find their probabilities.

    i. $\overline{A} \cap \overline{B}$ ii. $\overline{A} \cup \overline{C}$ iii. $\overline{A} \cap \overline{B} \cap \overline{C}$

5.48 A large magazine publisher makes most of its profits from mail order sales of items to persons on its subscription list. Because only a small percentage of readers purchase any one particular item, large-scale test mailings are a must for any items under consideration. If certain demographic characteristics can help identify those who are likely to purchase, those segments can be targeted in a full-scale mailing. The frequency table at the top of page 244 shows a typical classification, but with income and age collapsed to two categories.

	Purchase		No Purchase	
	Less than $40K	≥ $40K	Less than $40K	≥ $40K
Under 30	1	3	5	9
30 or over	4	8	10	18

If a person is selected at random from this group, find the probability that he or she

a. Made a purchase

b. Did not make a purchase but is under 30 years of age and has an income of $40K or more

c. Either made a purchase or has an income of $40K or more

5.5   CONDITIONAL PROBABILITY AND INDEPENDENCE

The probability of an event A must often be modified after information is obtained as to whether a related event B has taken place. The revised probability of A when it is known that B has occurred is called the **conditional probability** of A given B and is denoted by $P(A|B)$. To illustrate how such a modification is made, we consider an example that will lead us to the formula for conditional probability.

EXAMPLE 5.16   Calculating a Conditional Probability

Refer to Example 5.8, which presents an insurance company's experience with damage-only claims on automobile insurance policies. The claim experience organized according to the age of the driver is shown in the following table with proportions rather than frequencies in each category.

Proportions of Damage-Only Claims

	Under 25	25 or older	Total
Claim	.09	.08	.17
No claim	.34	.49	.83
Total	.43	.57	1.00

a. What is the probability that a person selected at random from this group of insured persons made a claim?

b. The person selected at random is found to be under 25 years of age. What is the probability that this person also made a claim?

Solution and Discussion.   Let A denote the event that an insured person makes a claim, and let B denote the event that the person is under 25 years of age.

a. Since 17% of this group of insured persons made a claim and the individual is selected at random from this group, we conclude that $P(A) = .17$. This is the unconditional probability of A.

b.   When we are given the information that the selected person is under age 25, the categories in the second (25 or older) column of the table are not relevant to this person. The first column shows that among the subgroup of insured persons under age 25, the proportion making a claim is $.09/.43$. Therefore, given the information that the insured is under 25 years of age, the probability that he or she makes a claim is

$$P(A|B) = \frac{.09}{.43} = .21$$

The probability of making a claim has risen from .17 to .21 when we are told the insured is under 25 years of age.

Noting that $P(A \cap B) = .09$ and $P(B) = .43$, we have derived $P(A|B)$ by taking the ratio $P(A \cap B)/P(B)$. In other words, $P(A|B)$ is the proportion of the population having the characteristic A among all those having the characteristic B.

The conditional probability of A given B is denoted by $P(A|B)$ and is defined by the formula $P(A \cap B)/P(B)$, provided $P(B) > 0$.

Conditional Probability of A Given B

$$P(A|B) = \frac{P(A \cap B)}{P(B)}$$

Equivalently, this formula can be written

$$P(A \cap B) = P(B)P(A|B)$$

The latter expression is called the multiplication law of probability.

In the same way, the conditional probability of B given A can be written as

$$P(B|A) = \frac{P(A \cap B)}{P(A)}$$

which gives the relation $P(A \cap B) = P(A)P(B|A)$. Thus, there are two forms of the multiplication law, but both state that the conditional probability of an event multiplied by the probability of the conditioning event produces the probability of the intersection. To summarize,

---

Multiplication Law: $P(A \cap B) = P(B)P(A|B) = P(A)P(B|A)$

The multiplication law can be used in two ways depending on convenience. When it is easy to compute $P(A)$ and $P(B|A)$ directly, these values can be used to evaluate $P(A \cap B)$. Alternatively, if it is easy to calculate $P(B)$ and $P(A|B)$ directly, these values can be used to compute $P(A \cap B)$.

EXAMPLE 5.17   Using the Multiplication Law

A list of important customers contains 25 names. Among them, 20 have their accounts in good standing, whereas 5 are delinquent. Two persons will be selected at random from this list, and the status of their accounts checked. Calculate the probability that:

a.   Both accounts are delinquent.

b.   One account is delinquent and the other is in good standing.

Solution and Discussion.   We will use the symbols D for delinquent and G for good standing and attach subscripts to identify the order of selection. For instance, $G_1 \cap D_2$ will represent the event that the first account checked is in good standing and the second delinquent.

a.   The problem is to calculate $P(D_1 \cap D_2)$. Since $D_1 \cap D_2$ is the intersection of the two events D_1 and D_2, we can use the multiplication law and write

$$P(D_1 \cap D_2) = P(D_1)P(D_2|D_1)$$

To calculate $P(D_1)$, we need only consider selecting one delinquent account at random from 20 good and 5 delinquent accounts. Clearly, $P(D_1) = \frac{5}{25}$. The next step is to evaluate $P(D_2|D_1)$. Given that D_1 has occurred, there will remain 20 good and 4 delinquent accounts at the time the second selection is made. Therefore, the conditional probability of D_2 given D_1 is $P(D_2|D_1) = \frac{4}{24}$. Multiplying these two probabilities, we get

$$P(\text{both delinquent}) = P(D_1 \cap D_2) = \frac{5}{25} \times \frac{4}{24} = \frac{1}{30} = .033$$

b.   The event [exactly one delinquent account] is the union of the two incompatible events $G_1 \cap D_2$ and $D_1 \cap G_2$. The probability of each of these can be calculated by the multiplication law as in part **a**. Specifically,

$$P(G_1 \cap D_2) = P(G_1)P(D_2|G_1) = \frac{20}{25} \times \frac{5}{24} = \frac{1}{6}$$

$$P(D_1 \cap G_2) = P(D_1)P(G_2|D_1) = \frac{5}{25} \times \frac{20}{24} = \frac{1}{6}$$

The required probability is

$$P((G_1 \cap D_2) \cup (D_1 \cap G_2)) = P(G_1 \cap D_2) + P(D_1 \cap G_2) = \frac{1}{6} + \frac{1}{6} = \frac{2}{6} = .333$$

Remark

In solving the problems in this example, we have avoided listing the sample space corresponding to the selection of two accounts from a list of 25 accounts. A judicious use of the multiplication law has made it possible to focus attention on one draw at a time, thus simplifying the probability calculations.

A situation that merits special attention occurs when the conditional probability $P(A|B)$ turns out to be the same as the unconditional probability $P(A)$. Information about the occurrence of B then has no bearing on the assessment of the probability of A. Consequently, when the equality $P(A|B) = P(A)$ holds, we say the events A and B are independent.

Independent Events

Two events A and B are **independent** if $P(A|B) = P(A)$. Equivalent conditions are

$$P(B|A) = P(B)$$

or

$$P(A \cap B) = P(A)P(B)$$

The general expression for conditional probability is $P(A|B) = P(A \cap B)/P(B)$, so the independence condition $P(A|B) = P(A)$ is equivalent to $P(A \cap B) = P(A)P(B)$, which is the last expression. The formula $P(A \cap B) = P(A)P(B)$ may be used as an alternative definition of independence and applies even when $P(A)$ or $P(B)$ is 0. This form shows that the definition of independence is symmetric in events A and B. The other equivalent condition is obtained from

$$P(B|A) = \frac{P(A \cap B)}{P(A)} = \frac{P(A)P(B)}{P(A)} = P(B)$$

EXAMPLE 5.18 Determining Whether Two Events Are Independent

In Example 5.16, are the two events $A = $ [claim] and $B = $ [under 25] independent?

Solution and Discussion.   Referring to Example 5.16, we have

$$P(A) = .17$$

$$P(A|B) = \frac{P(A \cap B)}{P(B)} = \frac{.09}{.43} = .21$$

so the two events are not independent. The probability of making a claim depends on the age of the driver. (For the events to be independent, we must have $P(A|B) = P(A)$.)

Caution

Do not confuse the terms *incompatible events* and *independent events*. Recall events are incompatible if their intersection $A \cap B$ is empty so that $P(A \cap B) = 0$. That is, both events cannot occur simultaneously. On the other hand, if A and B are independent, $P(A \cap B) = P(A)P(B) \neq 0$ as long as A and B have nonzero probabilities. Incompatible events are necessarily dependent since knowing that one event has occurred precludes the occurrence of the other event, that is, changes its nonzero probability to 0.

The independence of two events has been introduced in the context of checking a given assignment of probabilities to see whether the formula $P(A|B) = P(A)$ holds. If it does, events A and B are independent. A second use of the condition of independence occurs in the assignment of probability when the experiment consists of two physically unrelated parts. When events A and B refer to unrelated parts of an experiment, $A \cap B$ is assigned the probability $P(A \cap B) = P(A)P(B)$.

EXAMPLE 5.19   Sampling with Replacement

In the context of Example 5.17, suppose that a box contains 25 cards identifying the accounts, of which 5 are delinquent and 20 are in good standing. One card is drawn at random. It is returned to the box, and then another card is drawn at random. What is the probability that both cards that are drawn represent delinquent accounts?

Solution and Discussion.   As before, we use the letters D for delinquent and G for good standing. Because the first card is returned to the box, the contents of the box remain unchanged. Hence, with each draw, $P(D) = \frac{5}{25}$, and the results of the two draws are independent. Instead of working with conditional probability as we did in Example 5.17, we use the independence condition to calculate

$$P(D_1 \cap D_2) = P(D_1)P(D_2) = \frac{5}{25} \times \frac{5}{25} = .04$$

Remark 1

Evidently, this method of probability calculation extends to any number of draws if, after each draw, the selected card is returned to the box. For instance, the probability that the first draw produces a D and the next two draws produce G's is

$$P(D_1 \cap G_2 \cap G_3) = \frac{5}{25} \times \frac{20}{25} \times \frac{20}{25} = .128$$

Remark 2

Sampling with replacement is seldom used in practice but it serves as a conceptual frame for simple probability calculations when a problem is concerned with sampling from a large population. For example, consider drawing 3 cards from a box containing cards representing 2500 accounts of which 2000 are G's and 500 are D's. Whether a selected card is returned to the box before the next draw makes little difference in the probabilities, since the composition of the box from draw to draw is essentially unchanged. The model of independent draws serves as a reasonable approximation to reality in this case.

THE RULE OF TOTAL PROBABILITY

The general multiplication rule leads to an alternative rule called the rule of total probability. An event A can occur either when an event B occurs or when it does not occur. That is, A can be written as the disjoint union of $A \cap B$ and $A \cap \overline{B}$. Consequently,

---

Rule of Total Probability

$$P(A) = P(A \cap B) + P(A \cap \overline{B})$$
$$= P(A|B)P(B) + P(A|\overline{B})P(\overline{B})$$

---

by the general multiplication rule applied to each of the two terms involving the probabilities of intersections.

As an example, let A be the event that a person tests positive for a serious virus, and let B be the event that a person actually has the virus. Suppose the virus is present in about 1.2% of the population. Because medical tests are sometimes incorrect, we could model the uncertainty by giving the conditional probability of .999 for a correct positive test (when the person has the virus) and the conditional probability of .01 for a false positive test. That is, we are given the conditional probabilities $P(A|B) = .999$ and $P(A|\overline{B}) = .01$, as well as the probability of prevalence $P(B) = .012$, so $P(\overline{B}) = 1 - .012 = .988$. Consequently, by the law of total probability,

$$P(A) = P(A \cap B) + P(A \cap \overline{B}) = P(A|B)P(B) + P(A|\overline{B})P(\overline{B})$$

$$= .999 \times .012 + .01 \times .988 = .022$$

is the probability that a randomly selected person tests positive for the virus.

BAYES' THEOREM

Suppose we have two events A and B that can occur together, and we know the probabilities $P(B)$ (and hence $P(\overline{B}) = 1 - P(B)$), $P(A|B)$, and $P(A|\overline{B})$. Now suppose we are told the event A has occurred. How does this knowledge affect the initial probabilities associated with B (and $\overline{B}$)?

The probabilities $P(B)$ and $P(\overline{B})$ are called *prior probabilities* since they represent the probabilities associated with these events without knowing the status of event A, or any other event for that matter. Once we know that A has occurred, the updated or *posterior probability* of B is given by the conditional probability

$$P(B|A) = \frac{P(A \cap B)}{P(A)}$$

The numerator can be written as $P(A \cap B) = P(A|B)P(B)$ by the multiplication rule. The denominator can be written as $P(A) = P(A|B)P(B) + P(A|\overline{B})P(\overline{B})$ by the rule of total probability. Substituting for the numerator and denominator in the conditional probability formula, we obtain

---

Bayes' Theorem

$$P(B|A) = \frac{P(A|B)P(B)}{P(A|B)P(B) + P(A|\overline{B})P(\overline{B})}$$

The posterior probability of $\overline{B}$ is then $P(\overline{B}|A) = 1 - P(B|A)$.

Referring to the example discussed in conjunction with the Rule of Total Probability, we find that the updated or posterior probability of having the virus given that the test is positive is

$$P(B|A) = \frac{P(A|B)P(B)}{P(A|B)P(B) + P(A|\overline{B})P(\overline{B})} = \frac{.999 \times .012}{.999 \times .012 + .01 \times .988} = .548$$

The computation of the probabilities of having and not having the virus given the test is positive is summarized in Table 5.1.

The probability of having the virus has increased from .012 (the prior probability) to .548 (the posterior probability). But even though a person has tested positive, the probability is just over $\frac{1}{2}$ that he or she has the virus.

TABLE 5.1   Bayes' Theorem Calculations for the Virus Problem

Events B_i	Prior probability $P(B_i)$	Conditional probability $P(A\|B_i)$	$P(A \cap B_i) =$ $P(A\|B_i)P(B_i)$	Posterior probability $P(B_i\|A)$
$B_1 = B = $ [has virus]	.012	.999	.01199	$.01199/.02187 = \quad .548 = P(B\|A)$
$B_2 = \overline{B} = $ [does not have virus]	.988	.01	.00988	$.00988/.02187 = \quad .452 = P(\overline{B}\|A)$
			.02187	1.000

EXERCISES

5.49 Suppose that $P(A) = .68$, $P(B) = .55$, and $P(A \cap B) = .32$. Find:
  a.   The conditional probability that B occurs given that A occurs.
  b.   The conditional probability that B does not occur given that A occurs.
  c.   The conditional probability that B occurs given that A does not occur.

5.50 Suppose that $P(A) = .4$, $P(B) = .6$, and the probability that either A occurs or B occurs is .7. Find:
  a.   The conditional probability that A occurs given that B occurs.
  b.   The conditional probability that B occurs given that A does not occur.

5.51 The following events relate to a population of drivers:

$$A = \text{[defensive driving last year]}$$
$$B = \text{[accident in current year]}$$

The probabilities (proportions of population) are given in the following Venn diagram. Find $P(B|A)$. Are events A and B independent?

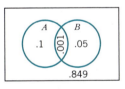

5.52 Suppose $P(A) = .45$, $P(B) = .32$, and $P(\overline{A} \cap B) = .20$.
  a.   Determine all the probabilities needed to fill in the following table.

	B	$\overline{B}$	
A			.45
$\overline{A}$	.20		
	.32		

  b.   Find the conditional probability of A given that B does not occur.

5.53 For two events A and B, the following probabilities are given.

$$P(A) = .5 \qquad P(B) = .25 \qquad P(A|B) = .8$$

Use the appropriate laws of probability to calculate each of the following:

a. $P(\overline{A})$

b. $P(A \cap B)$

c. $P(A \cup B)$

5.54   In a certain country, men constitute 58% of the labor force. The rates of unemployment are 6.2% and 4.3% among males and females, respectively.

a.   Suppose a worker is selected at random from the country's labor force. What probabilities do these percentages represent? (Use symbols such as M for male, E for employed, and so forth.)

b.   What is the overall rate of unemployment in the country?

c.   If a worker, selected at random, is found to be unemployed, what is the probability that the worker is a woman?

5.55   Given $P(A) = .5$, $P(B) = .5$, and $P(A \cup B) = .8$.

a.   Are A and B independent? Why or why not?

b.   Can A and B be incompatible? Why or why not?

5.56   Suppose $P(A) = .50$ and $P(B) = .22$.

a.   Determine $P(A \cup B)$ if A and B are independent.

b.   Determine $P(A \cup B)$ if A and B are incompatible.

c.   Find $P(A|\overline{B})$ if A and B are incompatible.

5.57   Refer to Exercise 5.42.

a.   Suppose a worker will be chosen at random from those workers who are female. What is the probability that this worker will be a precision production worker? Explain how this can be interpreted as a conditional probability.

b.   Define the events $A = $ [precision production], $B = $ [female], and $C = $ [service]. Calculate the following conditional probabilities and interpret them.

i. $P(A|B)$ ii. $P(\overline{A}|B)$ iii. $P(C|A)$

c.   Are the events $A = $ [precision production] and $B = $ [female] independent? Explain.

5.58   Refer to Exercise 5.45.

a.   If a nursing home, selected at random, is found to comply with security standards, what is the probability that it violates sanitary standards?

b.   If a nursing home, selected at random, is found to violate at least one of the two standards, what is the probability that it complies with security standards?

5.59   In a shipment of 15 room air conditioners, there are 4 with defective thermostats. Two air conditioners will be selected at random and inspected one after the other. Find the probability that:

a.   The first is defective.

b.   The first is defective and the second is good.

c.   Both are defective.

d.   The second one is defective.

e.   Exactly one is defective.

5.60 Refer to Exercise 5.59. Now suppose 3 air conditioners will be selected at random and checked one after another. Find the probability that:

    a.   All three are good.

    b.   The first two are good and the third is defective.

    c.   Two are good and one is defective.

5.61 An accountant screens large batches of bills according to the following sampling inspection plan. He inspects 4 bills chosen at random from each batch and passes the batch if, among the 4, none is irregular. Find the probability that a batch will be passed if, in fact,

    a.   5% of its bills are irregular.

    b.   20% of its bills are irregular.

5.62 The probability that a customer will rate the service at the bank excellent, as opposed to not excellent, is .3. Three customers will be asked to rate the service at the bank. Assume the 3 ratings are independent.

    a.   List the sample space and assign probabilities to the simple events.

    b.   Find the probability that at least two of the three customers give an excellent rating.

5.63 Items coming off a production line are categorized as good (G), slightly blemished (B), and defective (D), and the percentages are 75%, 15%, and 10%, respectively. Suppose that 2 items are randomly selected for inspection, and the selections are independent.

    a.   List all outcomes and assign probabilities to each outcome.

    b.   Find the probability that at least one of the items is slightly blemished.

    c.   Find the probability that neither of the items is good.

5.64 A firm has 80% of its service calls made by a contractor, and 10% of these calls result in customer complaints. The other 20% of the service calls are made by their own employees, and these calls have a 5% complaint rate. Find the probability of a complaint.

5.65 A mail order firm sends 60% of its orders by a parcel service that delivers late 2% of the time. It sends the other 40% by a combination bus service and local transportation that delivers late 7% of the time. Find the probability that an order will be delivered late.

5.66 Refer to Exercise 5.64. Use Bayes' theorem to find the probability that a complaint was from a customer whose service was provided by the contractor.

5.67 Refer to Exercise 5.65. Use Bayes' theorem to find the probability that an order delivered late was sent by the parcel service.

5.6   RANDOM SAMPLING FROM A FINITE POPULATION

We introduced the phrase *randomly selected* in Chapter 4. Intuitively, the notion of random selection means equally likely; that is, one selection of items is not favored over another selection. How do we determine what an equally likely selection is, and what implications does this have for computing probabilities?

Equally likely implies equal probability. In general, to determine what we mean by an equally likely choice, we have to enumerate all the elementary outcomes in the sample space. This is not difficult when both the population size and the sample size are small numbers. With larger numbers, making a list of all possible choices becomes a tedious job. However, a counting rule is available that greatly simplifies computations.

We begin with an example that illustrates the equally likely concept and associated probability calculations where the population size and the sample size are small numbers, so all possible samples can be easily listed.

EXAMPLE 5.20 Random Sampling from a Small Finite Population

There are five qualified applicants for two editorial positions on a college newspaper. Two of these applicants are men and three are women. If the positions are filled by randomly selecting two of the five applicants, what is the probability that neither of the men is selected?

Solution and Discussion.   Suppose the three women are identified as a, b, and c, and the two men as d and e. Two applicants are selected at random from the

$$\text{Population:} \quad \{ \underbrace{a, b, c,}_{\text{women}} \ \underbrace{d, e}_{\text{men}} \}$$

The possible samples of size two are

$$
\begin{array}{llll}
\{a, b\} & \{b, c\} & \{c, d\} & \{d, e\} \\
\{a, c\} & \{b, d\} & \{c, e\} & \\
\{a, d\} & \{b, e\} & & \\
\{a, e\} & & &
\end{array}
$$

As the list shows, our sample space has 10 elementary outcomes. The notion of random selection dictates that these are all equally likely, so each outcome is assigned the probability $\frac{1}{10}$. Let A represent the event that two women are selected. Scanning our list, we see that A consists of the three elementary outcomes

$$\{a, b\} \quad \{a, c\} \quad \{b, c\}$$

Consequently,

$$P(A) = \frac{\text{Number of elements in } A}{\text{Number of elements in } S} = \frac{3}{10} = .3$$

Our probability calculation in Example 5.20 required knowledge of only two counts: the number of elements in A and the number of elements in S. It is possible to arrive at these counts without formally listing the sample space. An important counting rule comes to our aid.

Rule of Combinations

The number of possible choices of r objects from a group of N distinct objects is denoted by $\binom{N}{r}$, which is read "N choose r." We have the following formula:

Combination formula:
$$\binom{N}{r} = \frac{N \times (N-1) \times \cdots \times (N-r+1)}{r \times (r-1) \times \cdots \times 2 \times 1}$$

The numerator of the formula for $\binom{N}{r}$ is the product of r consecutive integers starting with N and proceeding downward. The denominator is also the product of r consecutive integers but starting with r and proceeding down to 1.

To explain the combination formula, we consider the number of possible choices (or collections) of three letters from the seven letters $\{a, b, c, d, e, f, g\}$. This number is denoted by $\binom{7}{3}$.

Initially, consider the number of *ordered* selections. (That is, we shall count the selection (a, b, c) as being different from the selection (b, a, c) even though the same three letters are involved.) The first letter selected can be any one of the 7 letters, the second letter chosen can be any one of the remaining 6 letters, and the third choice can be any one of the remaining 5 letters. Thinking of a tree diagram, we multiply the possibilities to arrive at the following count.

The number of ordered selections of 3 letters from 7 is given by the product $7 \times 6 \times 5$.

Now a particular unordered collection, say, $\{a, b, c\}$, can produce $3 \times 2 \times 1$ ordered triplets as you can verify by constructing a tree diagram. The number of collections of three letters, ignoring order, is denoted by $\binom{7}{3}$. Each of these collections produces $3 \times 2 \times 1$ orderings for a total of $\binom{7}{3} \times 3 \times 2 \times 1$ orderings. Because the total number of ordered triplets is $7 \times 6 \times 5$, we must have

$$\binom{7}{3} \times 3 \times 2 \times 1 = 7 \times 6 \times 5$$

or

$$\binom{7}{3} = \frac{7 \times 6 \times 5}{3 \times 2 \times 1}$$

This explains the formula for $\binom{N}{r}$ for the case $N = 7$ and $r = 3$.

Although not immediately apparent, there is a certain symmetry in the counts $\binom{N}{r}$. The process of selecting r objects is the same as choosing $N - r$ objects to leave behind. Because every choice of r objects corresponds to a choice of $N - r$ objects,

$$\binom{N}{r} = \binom{N}{N-r}$$

Schematically,

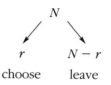

The symmetry relation above often simplifies calculations. Since $\binom{N}{N} = 1$, we take $\binom{N}{0} = 1$.

EXAMPLE 5.21   Calculating Possible Choices of r Objects from N Objects

Calculate the values of $\binom{5}{2}$, $\binom{15}{4}$, and $\binom{15}{11}$.

Solution and Discussion.

$$\binom{5}{2} = \frac{5 \times 4}{2 \times 1} = 10 \qquad \binom{15}{4} = \frac{15 \times 14 \times 13 \times 12}{4 \times 3 \times 2 \times 1} = 1365$$

Using the relation $\binom{N}{r} = \binom{N}{N-r}$, we have

$$\binom{15}{11} = \binom{15}{4} = 1365$$

EXAMPLE 5.22   Evaluating Probabilities Using the Rule of Combinations

Refer to Example 5.20 concerning the random selection of two persons from a group of three women and two men. Let A be the event that neither person selected is a man. Calculate the probability of A without listing the sample space.

Solution and Discussion.   The number of ways 2 people can be selected from 5 is given by

$$\binom{5}{2} = \frac{5 \times 4}{2 \times 1} = 10$$

Random selection means that the 10 outcomes are equally likely. Next we count the outcomes that are favorable to A, that is, that both people selected are women. Two women can be selected from 3 women in

$$\binom{3}{2} = \frac{3 \times 2}{2 \times 1} = 3$$

ways. Since all outcomes are equally likely, the ratio of the number of outcomes in A to the number of outcomes in S gives

$$P(A) = \frac{3}{10} = .3$$

which agrees with the result in Example 5.20.

The notion of a random sample from a finite population is crucial to statistical inference. To generalize from a sample to a population (enumerative studies), it is imperative that the sampling process be impartial. This criterion is met if the selection process is such that all possible samples of a given size have equal opportunity to be selected. This is the idea behind random sampling. A formal definition follows.

Random Sample from a Finite Population

A sample of size n from a population of N distinct objects is said to be a **random sample** if each collection of size n has the same probability $1/\binom{N}{n}$ of being selected.

Notice that this is a conceptual rather than an operational definition of a random sample. We have not discussed how we actually select a random sample. On the surface, it might seem that a haphazard selection by the experimenter would result in a random sample. Unfortunately, a seemingly haphazard selection may have hidden bias. For instance, when asked to select an integer between 1 and 9 at random, more people select 7 than any other number. Also, odd integers are more popular than even integers. Therefore, asking an individual to select an integer between 1 and 9 does not result in a random sample of size 1. The nine integers do not have the same probability of being selected. The selection of objects must be done by some device that cannot think. In other words, some sort of mechanization of the selection process is required to make it truly haphazard.

Self-selection also results in samples that are not random. A radio personality may ask listeners to call in with their opinions on an important issue to be put before the voters. The population of listeners is not the population of people who can vote. Even if the population is restricted to listeners, it is only those with strong opinions who will trouble themselves to make a call. A relatively small proportion of listeners having one extreme opinion may outweigh a majority who share an opposite opinion but do not hold it so strongly.

Therefore, choosing a random sample from a finite population is not always as easy as it may seem. Recording the response of every 20th person who enters the grounds of a summer theater should provide a reasonably representative opinion about the kind of advertising that brought the show to the attention of the customers. It avoids the difficulty of asking the same question to two people who came together, but it fails to meet the strict requirements of a random sample because not all pairs of persons entering the grounds have the same chance of being selected. The same is true for triplets of people, and so forth.

Any formal procedure for selecting a random sample starts with a list of the finite population. One may then make a card for each of the N numbers of the population, shuffle the cards, and draw n cards. The sample then consists of the items in the list located at the positions corresponding to the n numbers selected. This method is easy to understand but awkward to implement for large populations. It is easier to use a table of random digits, such as Table 1 in Appendix B, or computer-generated random numbers.

EXAMPLE 5.23   Selecting a Random Sample Using a Table of Random Digits

A company has 20 franchises in a state. The company wants to select two and investigate the friendliness of the service. Use the random number table (Table 1, Appendix B) to select two franchises.

Solution and Discussion.   Ideally, the starting point in the table should be selected at random. Suppose we select the first page of Table 1 and we read two digits at a time from columns 9 and 10 beginning in row 1. We continue reading, ignoring duplicates, until we have two numbers 20 or less. This gives 82 85 02 12. Consequently, we select franchises 2 and 12 as our random sample.

Random samples are most conveniently selected by using a computer to generate random numbers. We illustrate one method in Exercise 5.82.

EXERCISES

5.68   Evaluate:

a. $\binom{8}{2}$ b. $\binom{10}{4}$ c. $\binom{20}{3}$

d. $\binom{20}{17}$ e. $\binom{30}{4}$ f. $\binom{30}{26}$

5.69   List all the samples from $\{a, b, c, d, e\}$ when
a.   2 out of 5 are selected.
b.   3 out of 5 are selected.

Count the number of samples in each case.

5.70   Of the 9 available candidates for membership on a university committee, 5 are men and 4 are women. The committee is to consist of 4 people.
a.   How many different selections of the committee are possible?
b.   How many selections are possible if the committee must have 2 men and 2 women?

5.71   If a coin is tossed 12 times, the outcome can be recorded as a 12-character sequence of H's and T's according to the results of the successive tosses. In how many ways can there be 4 H's and 8 T's? (In other words, in how many ways can one choose 4 positions out of 12 to put the letter H?)

5.72   Out of 12 people applying for an assembly job, 3 cannot do the work. Suppose 2 people will be hired.

   a.   How many distinct pairs are possible?

   b.   In how many of the pairs will 0 or 1 people not be able to do the work?

   c.   If 2 people are chosen in a random manner, what is the probability that neither will be able to do the job?

5.73   After a preliminary screening, the list of qualified jurors consists of 10 males and 7 females. The 5 jurors the judge selects from this list are all males. Did the selection process seem to discriminate against females? Answer the question by calculating the probability of having no female members of the jury if the selection is random.

5.74   A shipment of 18 computers contains 4 with minor defects. If 3 computers are selected at random, find the probability of the following events:

   a. A = [none of these computers has a minor defect]

   b. B = [exactly two of these computers have a minor defect]

5.75   *Ordered Sampling Versus Unordered Sampling.* Refer to Exercise 5.74. Suppose the sampling of the three computers is done by randomly choosing one computer after another and without replacement. The event A can then be described as $G_1G_2G_3$, where G denotes good and the subscripts refer to the order of the draws. Use the method of Example 5.17 to calculate $P(A)$ and $P(B)$. Verify that you get the same results as in Exercise 5.74. [*Remark:*   To arrive at a random sample, we may randomly draw one item at a time without replacement and then disregard the order of the draws.]

5.76   A college senior is selected at random from each state. Next, one senior is selected at random from the group of 50. Does this procedure produce a senior selected at random from those in the United States? Explain.

5.77   Are the following methods of selection likely to produce a random sample of 5 students from your school? Explain.

   a.   Pick 5 students throwing flying discs on the mall.

   b.   Pick 5 students who are studying in the library on Friday night.

   c.   Pick 5 students sitting near you in your statistics course.

5.78   In how many ordered ways can four different commercials be played on TV during a single commercial break?

5.79   In how many ways can 5 of 30 companies be selected for a special audit if order is not important?

5.80   In how many ways can 3 of 25 company branches be selected for special first-, second-, and third-place quality awards?

5.81   Use the table of random digits in Table 1 of Appendix B to select 5 insurance companies among the 35 that insure in a city.

5.82 (*Minitab or similar program recommended*) The Minitab commands

```
SET C1
1:85
END
SAMPLE 10 OBSERVATIONS FROM C1 SET IN C2
```

will select 10 random numbers between 1 and 85 without replacement. The results of one call to this command gave

27   81   35   63   48   44   57   77   47   37

To select random numbers with replacement, use the Minitab commands

```
SET C1
1:85
END
SAMPLE 10 OBSERVATIONS FROM C1 SET IN C2;
REPLACE.
```

The results of one call to this command gave

17   22   4   13   50   53   61   6   17   70

Select 15 random digits between 1 and 120:

a. With replacement
b. Without replacement

5.7 STATISTICS IN CONTEXT

Conditional probabilities provide the basis for determining life insurance premiums. The government provides tables of survival probabilities, based on census information, arranged in steps of one-year intervals. Table 5.2 is a portion of the government table used by actuaries. Each major company has its own version of Table 5.2, modified according to its own experience, the type of insurance involved, and such grouping factors as smoker/nonsmoker.

The first column of Table 5.2 lists the interval of ages. For example, 20–21 is for all persons who reach their 20th birthday but who have not reached their 21st birthday. The second column gives the conditional probabilities of not surviving one additional year. For the age interval 20–21,

$$P(\text{life} < 21 \,|\, \text{life} \geq 20) = \frac{P(\text{life} < 21 \cap \text{life} \geq 20)}{P(\text{life} \geq 20)}$$

$$= \frac{P(20 \leq \text{life} < 21)}{P(\text{life} \geq 20)} = .00120$$

according to the entry in the second column.

Reading down the second column further, we get the following probabilities:

$$P(\text{life} < 22 \,|\, \text{life} \geq 21) = .00127 \qquad P(\text{life} < 23 \,|\, \text{life} \geq 22) = .00132$$

$$P(\text{life} < 24 \,|\, \text{life} \geq 23) = .00134 \qquad P(\text{life} < 25 \,|\, \text{life} \geq 24) = .00133$$

TABLE 5.2   Part of the Life Table for the Total Population of the United States, 1979–1981

Age Interval	Proportion Dying	Of 100,000 Born Alive	Age Interval	Proportion Dying	Of 100,000 Born Alive
Period of Life Between Two Ages (1)	Proportion of Persons Alive at Beginning of Age Interval Dying During Interval (2)	Number Living at Beginning of Age Interval (3)	Period of Life Between Two Ages (1)	Proportion of Persons Alive at Beginning of Age Interval Dying During Interval (2)	Number Living at Beginning of Age Interval (3)
Years			Years		
0–1	.01260	100000	30–31	.00133	96477
1–2	.00093	98740	31–32	.00134	96350
2–3	.00065	98648	32–33	.00137	96220
3–4	.00050	98584	33–34	.00142	96088
4–5	.00040	98535	34–35	.00150	95951
5–6	.00037	98495	35–36	.00159	95808
6–7	.00033	98459	36–37	.00170	95655
7–8	.00030	98426	37–38	.00183	95492
8–9	.00027	98396	38–39	.00197	95317
9–10	.00023	98370	39–40	.00213	95129
10–11	.00020	98347	40–41	.00232	94926
11–12	.00019	98328	41–42	.00254	94706
12–13	.00025	98309	42–43	.00279	94465
13–14	.00037	98285	43–44	.00306	94201
14–15	.00053	98248	44–45	.00335	93913
15–16	.00069	98196	45–46	.00366	93599
16–17	.00083	98129	46–47	.00401	93256
17–18	.00095	98047	47–48	.00442	92882
18–19	.00105	97953	48–49	.00488	92472
19–20	.00112	97851	49–50	.00538	92021
20–21	.00120	97741	50–51	.00589	91526
21–22	.00127	97623	51–52	.00642	90986
22–23	.00132	97499	52–53	.00699	90402
23–24	.00134	97370	53–54	.00761	89771
24–25	.00133	97240	54–55	.00830	89087
25–26	.00132	97110	55–56	.00902	88348
26–27	.00131	96982	56–57	.00978	87551
27–28	.00130	96856	57–58	.01059	86695
28–29	.00130	96730	58–59	.01151	85776
29–30	.00131	96604	59–60	.01254	84789

These probabilities peak at 23–24 and then drop a little until the end of the twenties where they begin a steady rise.

For further comparison, we see that

$$P(\text{life} < 41 \mid \text{life} \geq 40) = .00232$$

This probability, of death in the next year, is nearly twice the value for a 20-year-old. Clearly, a different premium must be charged to a 40-year-old than a 20-year-old for the same amount of coverage. The conditional probabilities in Table 5.2 are well determined because each is based on a large number of people. The long-run frequencies are very stable.

The third column of Table 5.2 contains the entries that can be converted to probabilities of survival. The table starts with 100,000 persons born alive. For the age group 20–21, the third column entry 97,741 represents the estimated number who reach their 20th birthday. Since 97,741 out of 100,000 reach 20 years of age, the survival probability is approximated by

$$P(\text{life} \geq 20) = \frac{97{,}741}{100{,}000} = .97741$$

Further,

$$P(\text{life} \geq 21) = .97623$$
$$P(\text{life} \geq 22) = .97499$$
$$P(\text{life} \geq 23) = .97370$$
$$P(\text{life} \geq 24) = .97240$$
$$P(\text{life} \geq 25) = .97110$$

The survival probabilities could be used to determine the entries in column 2 since $P(20 \leq \text{life} < 21) = P(\text{life} \geq 20) - P(\text{life} \geq 21)$ and so forth. We shall not pursue this argument, but instead we illustrate how insurance companies figure the cost to set premiums.

What premium should be set on a life insurance policy for a randomly selected 20-year-old? To simplify the discussion, we consider a single payment premium for a 2-year term policy that pays \$1 at the end of the year in which death occurs.

Because the applicant is 20 years of age, it is appropriate to condition on the event [life $\geq$ 20]. In addition to the probability

$$P(20 \leq \text{life} < 21 \mid \text{life} \geq 20) = \frac{P(20 \leq \text{life} < 21)}{P(\text{life} \geq 20)} = .00120$$

of death in the first year, we must know the probabilities of death in the next year. For example,

$$P(21 \leq \text{life} < 22 \mid \text{life} \geq 20) = \frac{P(21 \leq \text{life} < 22 \cap \text{life} \geq 20)}{P(\text{life} \geq 20)}$$
$$= \frac{P(21 \leq \text{life} < 22)}{P(\text{life} \geq 20)}$$

Although this probability can be expressed in terms of survival probabilities, actuaries prefer to also include the 1-year-ahead probability terms from column 2. Multiplying and dividing by $P(\text{life} \geq 21)$, we have

$$P(21 \leq \text{life} < 22 \,|\, \text{life} \geq 20) = \frac{P(21 \leq \text{life} < 22)}{P(\text{life} \geq 21)} \frac{P(\text{life} \geq 21)}{P(\text{life} \geq 20)}$$

$$= P(21 \leq \text{life} < 22 \,|\, \text{life} \geq 21)\frac{P(\text{life} \geq 21)}{P(\text{life} \geq 20)}$$

$$= .00127 \times \frac{.97623}{.97741} = .00127$$

The calculation of cost becomes somewhat complicated because one needs to know the present value of a $1 payment in the year of death. A dollar one year from now is worth less than a dollar today. If the current interest rate is 5%, next year's dollar has a present value of $(1/1.05) = \$.9524$. A dollar paid out in two years would have a present value of $(.9524) \times (.9524) = (.9524)^2 = .9071$ dollar.

Since life length is random, death can occur at any time and cannot be predicted with certainty, the present value of a $1 payoff at death is random. We call the present value a random variable. To obtain a single number for the present value of a future $1 payoff, that is, the premium, we multiply each conditional probability of death by the present value of the payoff and sum. The result is called the expected present value and is the basis for the premium.

For the 2-year term life insurance of $1, the expected present value, for a purchaser of age 20, is

$$\text{Expected present value} = \$1(.9524 \times .00120 + (.9524)^2 \times .00127)$$

$$= \$.00229$$

or .229 cent.

To cover its expected payout in current dollars, the company would require a premium of .229 cent. An additional amount must be added to cover the cost of salaries, overhead, and profit, as well as something to account for the fact that the payout is random. When a large number of 20-year-olds are insured, the average payout will be close to .229 cent, but the total payout may still have quite a bit of variability that must be taken into account.

To make these premium calculations work, Table 5.2 must be based on a very large number of people—ideally, the whole population. Other complications arise because the interest (discount) rate seldom remains constant for 1 year let alone the period covering the life of the policy.

5.8 CHAPTER SUMMARY

In this chapter, we have learned:

- **Probability** is a numerical measure of uncertainty with values from 0 to 1. A value close to 0 indicates an event is extremely unlikely and a value close to 1 indicates an event is very likely, with the intermediate values interpreted accordingly.

- An **experiment** is the process of observing a phenomenon that has variation in its outcomes.

    1. The **sample space** associated with an experiment is the collection of all possible distinct outcomes of the experiment.
    2. Each outcome is called an **elementary event,** a **simple event,** or an **element** of the sample space.
    3. An **event** is the collection of elementary outcomes possessing a designated feature.

- An event occurs when any one of the elementary outcomes in the event occurs.
- The elements of a discrete sample space may be counted with the integers.
- The elements of a continuous sample space form a continuum and cannot be counted with the integers.
- The probability of an event is a numerical value that represents the proportion of times the event is expected to occur when the experiment is repeated under identical conditions.
- The probability of an event is the sum of the probabilities assigned to all the elementary outcomes contained in the event.
- The sum of the probabilities of all the elements of the sample space S must be 1.
- When the elementary outcomes are modeled as equally likely, the probability of an event A is

$$P(A) = \frac{\text{Number of elementary outcomes in } A}{\text{Number of elementary outcomes in } S}$$

- When the elementary outcomes are not equally likely, one recourse for determining the probability of an event is to take the **probability** as the **long-run relative frequency.** Thus, for large n,

$$P(A) = \frac{\text{Number of times } A \text{ occurs in } n \text{ trials}}{n}$$

- The **complement** of the event A, denoted by $\overline{A}$, is the set of all elementary outcomes that are not in A. The occurrence of $\overline{A}$ means that A does not occur.
- The **union** of two events A and B, denoted by $A \cup B$, is the set of all elementary outcomes that are in A, in B, or in both. The occurrence of $A \cup B$ means that either A or B or both occur.
- The **intersection** of two events A and B, denoted by $A \cap B$, is the set of all elementary outcomes that are in A and in B. The occurrence of $A \cap B$ means that both A and B occur.
- Two events A and B are called **incompatible** or **mutually exclusive** if their intersection $A \cap B$ is empty. Incompatible events cannot occur simultaneously.
- The revised probability of an event A when it is known that an event B has occurred is called the **conditional probability of A given B,** and is denoted by $P(A|B)$. We have

$$P(A|B) = \frac{P(A \cap B)}{P(B)}$$

Also

$$P(B|A) = \frac{P(A \cap B)}{P(A)}$$

- Two events A and B are **independent** if $P(A|B) = P(A)$. Equivalent conditions are $P(B|A) = P(B)$ and $P(A \cap B) = P(A)P(B)$.
- Events that are not independent are said to be **dependent.**
- If two events A and B can occur together and we are told that A has occurred, then the initial probability of B is related to the revised probability of B given A by **Bayes' theorem:**

$$P(B|A) = \frac{P(A|B)P(B)}{P(A|B)P(B) + P(A|\overline{B})P(\overline{B})}$$

Here $P(B)$ is called the **prior probability** of B, and $P(B|A)$ is called the **posterior probability** of B.

- Some probability calculations are simplified by using the **Rule of Combinations** that gives the possible choices of r objects from N objects. The number of possible choices is denoted by $\binom{N}{r}$. We have

$$\binom{N}{r} = \frac{N \times (N-1) \times \cdots \times (N-r+1)}{r \times (r-1) \times \cdots \times 2 \times 1}$$

- A sample of size n from a finite population of N distinct objects is said to be a **random sample** if each collection of size n has the same probability $1/\binom{N}{n}$ of being selected.

5.9   IMPORTANT CONCEPTS AND TOOLS

CONCEPTS

TOOLS

5.10   KEY FORMULAS

Probability must satisfy:

(i) $0 \le P(A) \le 1$, for all events A

(ii) $P(A) = \sum_{\text{all } e \text{ in } A} P(e)$

(iii) $P(S) = \sum_{\text{all } e \text{ in } S} P(e) = 1$

For a uniform probability model:

$$P(A) = \frac{m}{k} = \frac{\text{Number of elementary outcomes in } A}{\text{Number of elementary outcomes in } S}$$

$$\text{Relative frequency of event } A \text{ in } n \text{ trials} = \frac{\text{Number of times } A \text{ occurs in } n \text{ trials}}{n}$$

Law of the Complement: $P(A) = 1 - P(\overline{A})$

Addition Law: $P(A \cup B) = P(A) + P(B) - P(A \cap B)$

Addition Law for Incompatible Events: $P(A \cup B) = P(A) + P(B)$

Multiplication Law: $P(A \cap B) = P(B)P(A|B) = P(A)P(B|A)$

For independent events: $P(A|B) = P(A)$ or $P(A \cap B) = P(A)P(B)$

Rule of total probability:

$$P(A) = P(A \cap B) + P(A \cap \overline{B})$$
$$= P(A|B)P(B) + P(A|\overline{B})P(\overline{B})$$

Bayes' Theorem:

$$P(B|A) = \frac{P(A|B)P(B)}{P(A|B)P(B) + P(A|\overline{B})P(\overline{B})}$$

Combination formula: $\dbinom{N}{r} = \dfrac{N \times (N-1) \times \cdots \times (N-r+1)}{r \times (r-1) \times \cdots \times 2 \times 1}$

REVIEW EXERCISES

5.83 Describe the sample space for each of the following experiments:
  a. The record of your football team after its first game next season
  b. The number of franchise locations out of 20 that will receive an excellent rating for friendly service
  c. In an unemployment survey, 1000 persons will be asked to answer "yes" or "no" to the question, "Are you employed?" Only the number answering "no" will be recorded.
  d. A geophysicist wants to determine the natural gas reserve in a particular area. The volume will be given in cubic feet.

5.84 For the sample spaces in Exercise 5.83, identify those that are discrete and those that are continuous.

5.85 Identify the following events in parts **a** and **b,** respectively, of Exercise 5.83.

a. Do not lose.

b. At least half of the locations are rated excellent.

5.86 A driver is stopped for erratic driving, and the alcohol content of his blood is checked. Specify the sample space and the event A = [level exceeds legal limit] if the legal limit is .10.

5.87 The Wimbledon men's tennis championship ends when one player wins three sets.

a. How many elementary outcomes end in three sets? In four sets?

b. If the players are evenly matched, what is the probability that the tennis match ends in four sets?

Hint: Let $AABA$ be the event that player A wins the first, second, and fourth sets. By independence,

$$P(AABA) = \frac{1}{2} \times \frac{1}{2} \times \frac{1}{2} \times \frac{1}{2}$$

5.88 Does the uniform probability model apply to the following observations? Explain.

a. The day of the week on which the maximum pollution reading for nitrous oxides occurs downtown in a large city

b. The day of the week on which the monthly maximum temperature occurs

c. The week of the year for peak retail sales of new cars

5.89 A three-digit number is formed by arranging the digits 1, 5, and 6 in random order.

a. List the sample space.

b. Find the probability of getting a number larger than 400.

c. What is the probability that an even number is obtained?

5.90 Mr. Hope, a character apprehended by Sherlock Holmes, was driven by revenge to commit two murders. He presented two seemingly identical pills, one containing a deadly poison, to an adversary who selected one while Mr. Hope took the other. The entire procedure was then to be repeated with a second victim. Mr. Hope felt that Providence would protect him. What is the probability of the success of his endeavor?

5.91 Partnership has become a classic term in economic development. Government, especially state government, has played a key support role in helping small- and medium-size companies expand their exports. The National Governors Association provided the following list of state offices around the world.

Country	Number of State Offices
Belgium	14
Germany	16
Hong Kong	11
Japan	39
Mexico	9
South Korea	16
Taiwan	18
United Kingdom	18
Other	15

If an office is selected at random, give the probability for the following:

a. It is located in Japan.

b. It is not located in Japan.

c. It is located in Japan or Hong Kong.

d. It is located in Hong Kong given that it is not in Japan.

5.92 In a marketing experiment, a subject shows keen interest (K), some interest (I), or no interest at all (N) in a proposed advertisement. The experiment will be performed on two subjects.

a. Using a tree diagram, list the sample space.

b. Suppose, for each subject, $P(K) = .4$, $P(I) = .3$, $P(N) = .3$, and the responses of different subjects are independent. Assign probabilities to the elementary outcomes. In addition,

    i. Find the probability that at least one of the subjects shows a keen interest.

    ii. Find the probability that both of the subjects have at least some interest.

5.93 Advertising expenditure totals (millions of dollars) during a recent year are given here for the top 10 spenders.

Company	Ad Spending	Industry
AT&T	35.5	Communications (including computers)
Hewlett-Packard Co.	32.2	Computer
IBM Corp.	31.0	Computer
Microsoft	28.9	Computer
ZEOS Intl. Ltd.	28.7	Computer
NEC Corp.	26.6	Electrical
Digital Equipment Corp.	25.4	Computer
Intel Corp.	22.4	Computer
General Motors Corp.	18.4	Automotive
Dell Computer Corp.	18.3	Computer

SOURCE: *Business Marketing*, Oct. 1992, p. 42.

For a company selected at random from these ten, find the probability that

a.   It is in the computer business.

b.   It is not in the computer business.

c.   General Motors is selected given that a computer company is not selected.

5.94   A bank interested in expanding its customer base requested a market survey. Customers were asked to rate overall service on a 5-point scale from excellent to unsatisfactory. The results are summarized in the following table, where we have also included the age of the respondents.

	Excellent	**Good**	**Average**	**Poor**	**Unsatisfactory**	**Total**
Under 40	115	151	52	3	1	322
40 and over	203	77	18	1	2	301
Total	318	228	70	4	3	623

Source: Data courtesy of Gilbert Churchill, Jr.

a.   Explain how a long-run frequency interpretation can be applied to approximate the probability of receiving a rating of excellent for overall service.

b.   Approximate the probability of a rating of excellent.

5.95   Refer to Exercise 5.94. Suppose a person is selected at random from those whose responses are summarized in the table. Let A = [excellent rating] and B = [40 or over]. Determine the following:

a. $P(A \cup B)$

b. $P(\overline{A} \cup \overline{B})$

c. $P(A \mid B)$

d.   Are A and B independent? Explain.

5.96   Refer to Exercise 5.47. Calculate the probability

a. $P(C \cup B)$

b. $P(C \cup \overline{B})$

c. $P(A \cup B \cup C)$

5.97   Refer to Exercise 5.47. Calculate the conditional probability of a claim given that the person drives a high-performance car. Are these two events independent? Discuss.

5.98   To help control travel and entertainment expenses, many companies require receipts for all meal claims over $25. An accountant has estimated that only 40% of the unreceipted meal claims are accurate. Find the probability that:

a.   An unreceipted meal claim is accurate.

b.   Two unreceipted meal claims are both accurate if the claims can be treated as independent.

5.99   Based on a current population survey, it is estimated that 32.3% of working males and 46% of working females use the computer at work (*Statistical Abstract of the United States,* 1992, p. 366).

a. For a working person selected at random, convert both of these figures to conditional probabilities.

b. Another table in the same source gives the percentage of females among people working as 45.2%. Combine this information with that of part **a** to obtain the probability that the selected person is a female who uses a computer at work.

c. Calculate all the probabilities necessary to fill all the positions in the following table.

	Use computer	Do not use computer	Total
Male			
Female			
Total			1.000

5.100 Referring to Exercise 5.99, calculate the probability of being female given that the person uses a computer at work. Are these two events independent? Explain.

5.101 In how many ways can 2 of 16 prospective locations be selected for placing new automatic teller machines?

5.102 An IRS agent receives a batch of 15 tax returns that were flagged by a computer for possible tax violations. Suppose, unknown to the agent, 6 of these returns have illegal deductions and the other 9 are in good standing. If the agent randomly selects 4 of these returns for audit, what is the probability that:

a. None of the returns that contain illegal deductions is selected?

b. At least 2 returns have illegal deductions?

5.103 Refer to Exercise 5.102. Suppose the agent will randomly select 4 returns for audit, one after another. What is the probability that the first 2 returns audited are in good standing and the last 2 have illegal deductions?

5.104 Two production lines contribute to the total amount of a company's product. Line 1 provides 30% of the total, and 15% of its products are defective. Line 2 provides 70% of the total, and 5% of its products are defective.

a. What percentage of the items in the total collection of products are defective?

b. Suppose an item is randomly selected from the total and found to be defective. What is the probability that it came from Line 1? [*Hint:* See the Rule of Total Probability and Bayes' Theorem.]

5.105 It is somewhat surprising to learn the probability that 2 people in a class share the same birthday. As an approximation, assume that the 365 days in a year are equally likely birthdays.

a. What is the probability that, among 3 people, at least 2 have the same birthday? [*Hint:* Imagine a tree diagram. For 3 people, there are $365 \times 365 \times 365$ possible birthday outcomes. Of these, $365 \times 364 \times 363$ outcomes correspond to no common birthdays.]

b. Generalize the reasoning in part **a** to N people. Show that

$$P(\text{no common birthday}) = \frac{365 \times 364 \times \cdots \times (365 - N + 1)}{(365)^N}$$

c. Using the result in part **b**, verify $P(\text{no common birthday})$ for the five values of N in the following table:

N	5	9	18	22	23
$P(\text{no common birthday})$	.973	.905	.653	.524	.493

We see that with $N = 23$ people, the probability is greater than $\frac{1}{2}$ that at least 2 share a common birthday.

5.106 Refer to Table 5.2 (page 261), which contains survival probabilities.

a. Calculate $P(\text{life} \geq 30 \mid \text{life} \geq 20)$.

b. Calculate $P(25 \leq \text{life} < 30 \mid \text{life} \geq 20)$.

c. Are the events [life $\geq$ 30] and [life $\geq$ 20] independent? Explain.

After reading this chapter, you should be able to:

- Distinguish between discrete and continuous random variables.
- Recognize a probability distribution.
- Define a probability distribution for a discrete random variable.
- Compute the mean, variance, and standard deviation of a discrete random variable.
- Express the mean and variance of a linear function of a random variable in terms of the mean and variance of the random variable.
- Determine the mean of the sum or difference of two random variables.
- Determine the variance of the sum or difference of two random variables.
- Define a Bernoulli trial.
- Describe the binomial probability distribution and determine its mean, variance, and standard deviation.
- Use the binomial probability distribution to model the number of successes in n Bernoulli trials.
- Use a table of binomial probabilities.
- Define and compute cumulative probabilities.

CHAPTER SIX

Random Variables and Probability Distributions

6.1 INTRODUCTION

The probability model of an experiment contains two basic ingredients:

1. The sample space containing all the elementary outcomes
2. An assignment of probability to each elementary outcome

Calculating probabilities from elementary outcomes and from the events derived from them can be cumbersome when the outcomes have only qualitative descriptions rather than numerical values. This is true even though counting rules are available to simplify the process.

For experiments like the toss of two coins with qualitative outcomes, HH, HT, TH, and TT, or the rating of service with qualitative outcomes, Excellent, Good, Average, Poor, and Unsatisfactory, we are often interested in characteristics that are numerical. In the coin tossing experiment, we may be interested in the number of heads in two tosses, in which case only the numbers 0, 1, and 2 are relevant. If 100 customers rate service, the only information required for evaluating service may be the number of responses in each of the five categories. Once we have compiled this summary, we can dispense with the detailed record of the 100 respondents.

Of course, outcomes of some experiments are naturally numerical: the starting salaries of graduating seniors, the daily number of burglaries in a city, tomorrow's stock prices, and so forth. But even in these situations, interest often centers on other related numerical aspects of the experiments. We may be interested in the *median* salary of next May's graduates, the *proportion* of daily burglaries after 10 P.M., and tomorrow's *expected* stock price.

Although the original outcome may be qualitative or quantitative, in the final analysis it is some numerical aspect or *numerical summary* of the experiment that often forms the basis for improving a process, launching a new product, strengthening inadequate accounting controls, raising capital, and many other business decisions. As we will see, a numerical summary of observations (outcomes) forms a natural basis for drawing inferences.

6.2   RANDOM VARIABLES

Focusing our attention on the numerical features of the elementary outcomes, we introduce the idea of a random variable.

> A **random variable** X associates a numerical value with each elementary outcome of an experiment.

The numerical value is determined by some characteristic of the elementary outcome, and typically it will vary from outcome to outcome. The word *random* serves to emphasize the fact that before the experiment is performed, we do not know the specific outcome and, consequently, its associated value of X. The following examples illustrate the concept of a random variable.

EXAMPLE 6.1   The Number of Heads in Three Tosses of a Coin

Suppose X is the number of heads obtained in three tosses of a coin. List the numerical values of X and the corresponding elementary outcomes.

Solution and Discussion.   First, X is a variable since the number of heads in three tosses of a coin can have any of the values 0, 1, 2, or 3. In fact, X is a discrete variable. Second, this variable is random in the sense that its value before the coin is tossed cannot be predicted with certainty. We can, however, make a list of the elementary outcomes and the associated values of X.

Outcome	Value of X
HHH	3
HHT	2
HTH	2
HTT	1
THH	2
THT	1
TTH	1
TTT	0

For each elementary outcome, there is only one value for X. However, several elementary outcomes may yield the same value. Scanning our list, we now identify the events (the collections of elementary outcomes) that correspond to distinct values of X.

Numerical Value of X as an Event	Composition of the Event
$[X = 0]$ =	$\{TTT\}$
$[X = 1]$ =	$\{HTT, THT, TTH\}$
$[X = 2]$ =	$\{HHT, HTH, THH\}$
$[X = 3]$ =	$\{HHH\}$

The random variable X, the number of heads in three tosses of a coin, defines a correspondence between the collections of elementary outcomes and the real numbers 0, 1, 2, and 3.

Guided by this example, we have two general facts:

1. The events corresponding to the distinct values of X are incompatible; that is, any two of these events cannot occur together.

2. The union of these events is the entire sample space.

Typically, the possible values of a random variable X can be determined directly from the description of the random variable without listing the sample space. But to assign probabilities to these values, it is sometimes helpful to refer to the sample space.

EXAMPLE 6.2   The Number of Tasters Who Prefer a Generic Brand

A panel of 12 tasters is asked to compare the crispiness of a name brand cornflakes with a cheaper generic brand. Let X denote the number of tasters who rate the generic brand at least as crisp as the name brand. Determine the values for X.

Solution and Discussion.   Here X can take any of the values $0, 1, \ldots, 12$.

EXAMPLE 6.3   The Number of Cars Passing an Intersection

At an intersection, an observer will count the number X of cars passing by until a new Mercedes is spotted. Determine the values for X.

Solution and Discussion.   The possible values for X are $1, 2, 3, \ldots$, where the list never terminates.

As we have implied, a random variable is said to be a **discrete random variable** if it takes either a finite number of values or an infinite number of values that can be arranged in a sequence that can be counted with the positive integers 1, 2, 3, ..., and so forth. On the other hand, if the random variable represents some characteristic that is measured on a continuous scale and, therefore, is capable of assuming any of the values in an interval of numbers, it is called a **continuous random variable.** Some examples of continuous random variables are the time a person will stay in his or her first job after graduation, the height of a newly planted seedling after a year, and the distance a golf ball will travel when it is struck for the first time.

The definitions of discrete and continuous random variables are analogous to the definitions of discrete and continuous variables discussed in Chapter 2. A variable becomes random when it is explicitly associated with an experiment and its values determined by the elementary outcomes.

Since the values of a random variable are directly linked to (collections of) elementary outcomes, we can associate probabilities with these values. A list of the values of the random variable and their associated probabilities is called the **probability distribution of the random variable.** In this chapter, we concentrate on probability distributions of discrete random variables since the development parallels the development of probability in Chapter 5. Probability distributions of continuous random variables, such as the normal density function introduced in Chapter 2, require a little different perspective. The general development of continuous probability distributions and the concept of a sampling distribution are considered in Chapter 7.

EXERCISES

6.1   Identify each of the following as a discrete or continuous random variable.

    a.   Number of cars serviced at a garage during a day

    b.   Amount of precipitation produced by a rainstorm

    c.   Number of new businesses started in the state during the next year

    d.   Length of time it takes for a mail order clerk to complete a phone call from a customer

    e.   Number of correct answers a student will get on a quiz containing 20 questions

    f.   Number of cars ticketed for illegal parking on campus today

6.2   Identify each of the following as a discrete or continuous random variable.

    a.   The loss of weight following a diet program

    b.   The magnitude of an earthquake as measured on the open-ended Richter scale

   c.   The number of filled seats on an airplane for a particular flight

   d.   The number of cars sold at a dealership in a day

   e.   The percentage of fruit juice in a drink mix

6.3   Two of the integers $\{2, 4, 6, 7, 8\}$ are selected at random without replacement. Let X denote the difference between the larger and smaller numbers.

   a.   List all elementary outcomes and the corresponding values of X.

   b.   List the distinct values of X, and determine their probabilities by summing the probabilities associated with the appropriate elementary outcomes consisting of 10 pairs of integers.

6.4   Three brands of frozen pizza, A, B, and C, are rated by two judges. Each judge assigns the ratings 1 for best, 2 for intermediate, and 3 for worst. Let X denote the total score (the sum of the ratings received from the two judges) for Pizza A.

   a.   List all pairs of ratings that A can receive.

   b.   List the distinct values of X.

6.5   Refer to Exercise 6.4. Suppose there are two brands of frozen pizza, A and B, and four judges. Each judge gives the ratings 1 for better and 2 for worse of the two pizzas.

   a.   List all possible assignments of ratings for Pizza A by the four judges.

   b.   List the distinct values of X, the total score of A.

6.6   Suppose that a factory supervisor records whether the day or the night shift has a higher production rate for each of the next three days. List the possible outcomes and, for each outcome, record the number of days X that the night shift has a higher production rate. (Assume there are no ties.)

6.7   Each week a grocery shopper buys either canned (C) or bottled (B) soft drinks. The type of soft drink purchased in three consecutive weeks will be recorded. If a different type of soft drink is purchased this week than the previous week, we say that there is a switch.

   a.   List the sample space.

   b.   Let X denote the number of switches. Determine the value of X for each elementary outcome. (For example, for BBB, $X = 0$; for BCB, $X = 2$.)

6.8   A psychologist interested in group dynamics in the workplace studied groups of three people. For one group, Ann, Barbara, and Carol, each is asked which of the other two she likes to work with more.

   a.   Using A, B, and C to denote the three women, list the possible outcomes.

   b.   Let X be the number of times Carol is chosen. List the values of X.

6.3 PROBABILITY DISTRIBUTION OF A DISCRETE RANDOM VARIABLE

We are now in a position to formally define the probability distribution of a discrete random variable. The examples in this section show how these probability distributions arise naturally from an experiment once the characteristic of interest is identified and the probabilities for the elementary outcomes are determined.

> The **probability distribution,** or simply the **distribution,** of a discrete random variable X is a list of the distinct numerical values of X along with their associated probabilities. Often a formula can be used in place of a detailed list to specify the probability distribution of X.

EXAMPLE 6.4   The Probability Distribution of the Number of Heads in Three Tosses of a Coin

If X represents the number of heads in three tosses of a fair coin, find the probability distribution of X.

Solution and Discussion.   We have already listed the eight elementary outcomes and the corresponding values of X in Example 6.1. The distinct values of X are 0, 1, 2, and 3. We now calculate their probabilities.

The model of a fair coin implies that the eight elementary outcomes are equally likely, so each is assigned probability $\frac{1}{8}$. The event $[X = 0]$ corresponds to the single outcome TTT so its probability is necessarily $\frac{1}{8}$. (The only way $X = 0$ can occur is if outcome TTT occurs.) Consider the event $[X = 1]$. This corresponds to the event $A = \{HTT, THT, TTH\}$, which has probability $\frac{1}{8} + \frac{1}{8} + \frac{1}{8} = \frac{3}{8}$, so $[X = 1]$ has probability $\frac{3}{8}$. In the same way, $[X = 2]$ has probability $\frac{3}{8}$ and $[X = 3]$ has probability $\frac{1}{8}$. We display the probability distribution of X in Table 6.1. Since the values of X correspond to nonoverlapping collections of all the elementary outcomes in the sample space S, the sum of their probabilities is 1.

TABLE 6.1   The Probability Distribution of X, the Number of Heads in Three Tosses of a Coin

Value of X	Probability
0	$\frac{1}{8}$
1	$\frac{3}{8}$
2	$\frac{3}{8}$
3	$\frac{1}{8}$
Total	1

In general, we will use the notation x_1, x_2, and so on to denote the distinct values of a random variable X. The probability that a particular value x_i occurs will be denoted by $f(x_i)$. As in Example 6.4, if X can take k possible values $x_1, x_2, \ldots, x_k$ with the corresponding probabilities $f(x_1), f(x_2), \ldots, f(x_k)$, the probability distribution of X can be displayed in the format of Table 6.2.

TABLE 6.2 The Tabular Form of a Discrete Probability Distribution

Value x	Probability $f(x)$
x_1	$f(x_1)$
x_2	$f(x_2)$
$\vdots$	$\vdots$
x_k	$f(x_k)$
Total	1

Since the quantities $f(x_i)$ represent probabilities, they must all be numbers between 0 and 1. Furthermore, when summed over all possible values of X, these probabilities must add up to 1.

The probability distribution of a discrete random variable X is given by the function

$$f(x_i) = P(X = x_i)$$

which satisfies:

1. $f(x_i) \geq 0$, for each value x_i of X
2. $\sum_{i=1}^{k} f(x_i) = 1$

The probability distribution or the probability function describes the manner in which the total probability 1 gets apportioned to the individual values of the random variable.

A picture of a probability distribution helps reveal any pattern in the distribution of probabilities. We consider a display, called a **probability histogram,** that is similar in form to the relative frequency histogram discussed in Chapter 2.

To draw a probability histogram, we first mark the values of X on the horizontal axis. With each value x_i as the center, a vertical rectangle is constructed whose area equals the probability $f(x_i)$. The probability histogram for the distribution of Example 6.4 is shown in Figure 6.1.

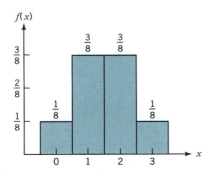

Figure 6.1 The Probability Histogram of X, the Number of Heads in 3 Tosses of a Coin

EXAMPLE 6.5 The Probability Distribution of the Number of Viewers Remembering a Product

Suppose 30% of the people who view a commercial remember the product two hours later. Four persons who viewed the commercial are randomly selected from a much larger group. Let X denote the number of viewers in the sample who remember the product two hours later. Obtain the probability distribution of X, and plot the probability histogram.

Solution and Discussion. Because each person either remembers (R) or does not remember (N) the product, the number of elementary outcomes for the sample of size four is $2 \times 2 \times 2 \times 2 = 16$. These outcomes are listed here according to the values of X.

$X = 0$	$X = 1$	$X = 2$	$X = 3$	$X = 4$
NNNN	NNNR	NNRR	NRRR	RRRR
	NNRN	NRNR	RNRR	
	NRNN	NRRN	RRNR	
	RNNN	RNNR	RRRN	
		RNRN		
		RRNN		

To complete the probability distribution, we must calculate the probability of each value of X. We first consider the assignment of probabilities to the elementary outcomes. For a single viewer selected at random, we obviously have $P(R) = .3$ and $P(N) = .7$ since 30% of the population of viewers remembered the product. Since the sample is much smaller than the population, observing one sample outcome will not appreciably affect the chances associated with the next sample outcome, and, consequently, the observations on the four viewers can be treated as independent.

Using independence and the multiplication law of probabilities, we have $P(\text{NNNN}) = .7 \times .7 \times .7 \times .7 = .2401$ so $P(X = 0) = .2401$. The event $[X = 1]$ corresponds to four elementary outcomes, each containing three N's and one R. Since, for example, $P(\text{NNNR}) = (.7)^3 \times (.3) = .1029$, and the same probability holds for the remaining three outcomes of this type, $P(X = 1) = .1029 + .1029 + .1029 + .1029 = 4 \times .1029 = .4116$. In the same manner,

$$P(X = 2) = 6 \times (.7)^2 \times (.3)^2 = .2646$$

$$P(X = 3) = 4 \times (.7) \times (.3)^3 = .0756$$

$$P(X = 4) = (.3)^4 = .0081$$

Collecting these results, we get the probability distribution of X given in Table 6.3 and the probability histogram plotted in Figure 6.2.

The probability histogram is skewed, or has a long tail, to the right. But the bulk of the probability is associated with the smaller values of X.

TABLE 6.3 The Probability Distribution of X in Example 6.5

x	$f(x)$
0	.2401
1	.4116
2	.2646
3	.0756
4	.0081
Total	1.0000

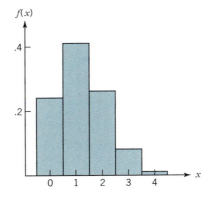

Figure 6.2   Probability Histogram of X in Example 6.5

At this point, it is informative to consider the role of probability distributions in statistical inference. Probability concepts and appropriate probability distributions serve as the foundation for many of the methods we will introduce to generalize random sample information to the larger population.

To calculate the probabilities associated with the values of a random variable, we need to know everything about the uncertainties of the experimental outcomes. In Example 6.5, for example, the chances of observing the various values of X were calculated under the assumptions that the responses of the individual viewers were independent and that the proportion of all viewers who remembered the product was .3. In practice, this population proportion is rarely known. Suppose the letter p stands for the unknown proportion of viewers who remembered the product. Statistical inference attempts to determine the values of p that are plausible given the value of X actually observed in the random sample.

To fix ideas, suppose all four of the sampled viewers remembered the product. Based on this observation, is .3 a plausible value for p? Table 6.3 shows that if p were indeed .3, the chance of observing the extreme value $X = 4$ is only .0081. This very low probability (highly unlikely sample outcome) casts doubt on the hypothesis that $p = .3$. This kind of statistical reasoning will be explored further in later chapters.

The probability distributions in Examples 6.4 and 6.5 were obtained by first assigning probabilities to the elementary outcomes using a process of logical deduction. When this cannot be done, we must turn to an empirical determination of the distribution. This involves repeating the experiment a large number of times (observing a large number of occurrences) and using the relative frequencies of the various values of X as approximations of the corresponding probabilities.

EXAMPLE 6.6   The Probability Distribution of the Number of Magazine Subscriptions

Let X denote the number of magazines to which a college senior subscribes. A survey of 400 college seniors produced the frequency distribution in Table 6.4 at the top of page 282. Approximate the probability distribution of X.

TABLE 6.4   **Frequency Distribution of the Number X of Magazine Subscriptions**

Magazine Subscriptions x	Frequency	Relative Frequency
0	61	.15
1	153	.38
2	106	.27
3	56	.14
4	24	.06
Total	400	1.00

Solution and Discussion.   Viewing the relative frequencies as empirical estimates of the probabilities, we have obtained an approximate determination of the probability distribution of X. The true probability distribution would emerge if a vast number (ideally, the entire population) of seniors were surveyed.

The probability distribution of X can be used to calculate the probabilities defined in terms of X.

EXAMPLE 6.7   Using a Probability Distribution

Consider the probability distribution in Table 6.5. What is the probability that X is equal to or larger than 2?

TABLE 6.5   **A Probability Distribution**

Value x	Probability $f(x)$
0	.02
1	.23
2	.40
3	.25
4	.10

Solution and Discussion.   The event $[X \geq 2]$ is composed of $[X = 2]$, $[X = 3]$, and $[X = 4]$. Thus

$$P(X \geq 2) = f(2) + f(3) + f(4)$$
$$= .40 + .25 + .10 = .75$$

Similarly, we can also calculate

$$P(X \leq 2) = f(0) + f(1) + f(2)$$
$$= .02 + .23 + .40 = .65$$

It is important to keep in mind the distinction between a relative frequency distribution and the probability distribution. The former is a sample-based entity and is therefore susceptible to variation as the sampling occasion changes. By contrast, the probability distribution is a stable entity that refers to the entire population. It is a theoretical construct that serves as a model for describing the variation in a population characteristic. At times, as in Example 6.6, a relative frequency distribution may be used as an approximation (an estimate) of the probability distribution.

> The **probability distribution** is a **model** for describing variation in a population.

EXERCISES

6.9 Listed here are the elementary outcomes of an experiment, their probabilities, and the value of a random variable X at each outcome.

Elementary Outcome	Probability	Value of X
e_1	.08	2
e_2	.29	0
e_3	.15	2
e_4	.08	0
e_5	.16	4
e_6	.11	0
e_7	.13	0

Obtain the probability distribution of X.

6.10 Two of the integers $\{1, 2, 6, 7, 9\}$ are selected at random without replacement. Let X denote the sum of the two integers.
   a. List all pairs and the corresponding values of X.
   b. List the distinct values of X.
   c. Obtain the probability distribution of X.

6.11 As part of a project to improve customer service, a person has been assigned to respond quickly to inquiries arriving by phone, fax, or e-mail. Long delays still occur when nonroutine requests arrive. Suppose 0, 1, 2, 3, 4, 5, and 6 nonroutine inquiries in a week have probabilities .05, .10, .15, .20, .25, .15, and .10, respectively. What is the probability that, in the next week, the company will receive the following?
   a. At most 3 nonroutine requests
   b. At least 5 nonroutine requests
   c. Between 2 and 5, inclusive, nonroutine requests

6.12 Determine whether each of the following is a legitimate probability distribution. If not, explain why not.

(a)		(b)		(c)		(d)	
x	$f(x)$	x	$f(x)$	x	$f(x)$	x	$f(x)$
2	.2	1	.4	-2	.25	0	.3
8	.6	3	.5	0	.50	1	$-.1$
13	.1	9	.3	2	.25	2	.8
15	.1	10	.2	4	0		

6.13 For each of the following cases, list the values of x and $f(x)$ and determine whether the specification represents a probability distribution. If not, state the properties that are violated.

    a. $f(x) = \frac{1}{10}(x-2)$ for $x = 3, 4, 5, 6$

    b. $f(x) = \frac{1}{2}(x-2)$ for $x = 1, 2, 3, 4$

    c. $f(x) = \frac{1}{20}(2x+4)$ for $x = -2, -1, 0, 1, 2$

    d. $f(x) = 3/2^x$ for $x = 2, 3, 4, 5$

6.14 The probability distribution of X is given by the function

$$f(x) = \frac{1}{15}\binom{4}{x} \quad \text{for } x = 1, 2, 3, 4$$

Find:

    a. $P(X = 2)$

    b. $P(X \text{ is odd})$

6.15 Refer to Exercise 6.7. Suppose that for each purchase, $P(B) = \frac{1}{2}$, and the decisions in different weeks are independent. Assign probabilities to the elementary outcomes and obtain the distribution of X.

6.16 Refer to Exercise 6.8. Assuming each choice is equally likely, determine the probability distribution of X.

6.17 One card will be drawn at random from five cards bearing the numbers -2, -1, 0, 1, 2. Determine the probability distribution of the square of the number that appears on the selected card.

6.18 Two marbles will be drawn at random, without replacement, from the six marbles numbered as shown.

① ① ① ① ② ②

Let X denote the sum of the numbers on the selected marbles. List the possible values of X, and determine the probability distribution.

6.19 A surprise quiz contains three multiple-choice questions. Question 1 has three suggested answers, Question 2 has three suggested answers, and Question 3 has two. A completely unprepared student decides to choose the answers at random. Let X denote the number of questions the student answers correctly.

    a. List the possible values of X.

    b. Find the probability distribution of X.

c. Find $P(\text{at least one correct}) = P(X \geq 1)$.

d. Construct the probability histogram.

6.20 A probability distribution is given in the accompanying table with the additional information that the even values of X are equally likely. Determine the missing entries in the table.

x	$f(x)$
1	.2
2	
3	.2
4	
5	.3
6	

6.21 Consider the following setting for a random experiment: A box contains 100 cards, of which 25 are numbered 1, 28 are numbered 2, 30 are numbered 3, and 17 are numbered 4. One card will be drawn from the box and its number X observed. Determine the probability distribution of X.

6.22 Two probability distributions are shown in the following tables. For each case, describe a setting of random selection (like the one in Exercise 6.21) that yields the given probability distribution.

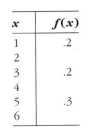

(a)		**(b)**	
x	$f(x)$	x	$f(x)$
2	.36	-2	$\dfrac{3}{11}$
4	.42	0	$\dfrac{4}{11}$
6	.22	4	$\dfrac{2}{11}$
		5	$\dfrac{2}{11}$

6.23 As part of a marketing analysis, 200 students were asked the question, "How many times did you order pizza from Double Dave's last week?" The numbers of responses were 70, 84, 36, and 10 for 0, 1, 2, and 3 times, respectively. Let X be the number of times a randomly selected student would order. Use the survey data to approximate

a. The probability distribution of X

b. The probability that X is greater than or equal to 2

6.24 In a study of job mobility upon entering the job market, 203 new accounting graduates were followed after taking jobs with a large firm. The numbers staying in their initial position beyond the first, second, third, and fourth years are 106, 72, 25, and 0, respectively. Let X denote the time in the initial position (in discrete units of whole years) for these graduates. Using these data, approximate the probability distribution of X.

6.25 Use the probability distribution

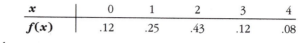

x	0	1	2	3	4
$f(x)$	.12	.25	.43	.12	.08

to calculate:

a. $P(X \leq 3)$

b. $P(X \geq 2)$

c. $P(1 \leq X \leq 3)$

6.26 Of seven candidates seeking three positions in customer relations, four have degrees in business and three do not. If three candidates are selected at random, find the probability distribution of X, the number of people among the selected candidates with business degrees.

6.27 Based on recent records, the manager of a car-painting center has determined the following probability distribution for the number of customers per day.

x	$f(x)$
0	.05
1	.20
2	.30
3	.25
4	.15
5	.05

a. If the center has the capacity to serve two customers per day, what is the probability that one or more customers will be turned away on a given day?

b. What is the probability that the center's capacity will not be fully utilized on a day?

c. How much must the center's capacity increase so that the probability of turning away a customer is no more than .10?

6.28 Suppose X denotes the number of telephones in a single-family residential dwelling. An examination of the phone subscription records of 381 residences in a city gives the following relative frequency distribution.

Number of Phones (x)	Number of Residences (frequency)
0	2
1	82
2	161
3	89
4	47
Total	381

a. Using these data, obtain an approximate determination of the probability distribution of X.

b. Why is this distribution regarded as an approximation?

c. Construct the probability histogram.

6.4 EXPECTATION (MEAN) AND STANDARD DEVIATION OF A PROBABILITY DISTRIBUTION

We introduced the sample mean, $\bar{x}$, and sample standard deviation, s, in Chapter 1. Recall that these quantities measure location and spread for a set of data. We can also define a numerical measure for the center of a probability distribution and a numerical measure for its spread. Probability distributions are theoretical models in which the probabilities can be viewed as long-run relative frequencies. That is, because the probabilities are approximated by the relative frequencies from very large data sets, the measures for location and spread of probability distributions can be viewed as the population counterparts of the corresponding sample quantities.

Before defining a measure of location for a probability distribution, we first review the calculation of the mean of a data set. Suppose a die is tossed 20 times with the following results:

4	3	4	2	5	1	6	6	5	2
2	6	5	4	6	2	1	6	2	4

The sample mean is

$$\bar{x} = \frac{\text{Sum of the observations}}{\text{Sample size}} = \frac{76}{20} = 3.8$$

Alternatively, we could count the frequencies at each value and use the relative frequencies to calculate the sample mean. This gives

$$\bar{x} = 1\left(\frac{2}{20}\right) + 2\left(\frac{5}{20}\right) + 3\left(\frac{1}{20}\right) + 4\left(\frac{4}{20}\right) + 5\left(\frac{3}{20}\right) + 6\left(\frac{5}{20}\right) = \frac{76}{20} = 3.8$$

The second calculation illustrates the formula

Sample mean: $\bar{x} = \sum (\text{Value} \times \text{Relative frequency})$

If we imagine a very large number of tosses of a die (many more than 20), the relative frequencies will approach the probabilities, each of which is $\frac{1}{6}$ for a fair die. The mean of the (infinite) collection of tosses of a fair die should then be calculated as

$$1\left(\frac{1}{6}\right) + 2\left(\frac{1}{6}\right) + 3\left(\frac{1}{6}\right) + 4\left(\frac{1}{6}\right) + 5\left(\frac{1}{6}\right) + 6\left(\frac{1}{6}\right) = \sum (\text{Value} \times \text{Probability}) = 3.5$$

Motivated by the fair die example and the stability of a long-run relative frequency, it is natural to define the **mean** of a random variable X or of its probability distribution as

$$\sum (\text{Value} \times \text{Probability}) \quad \text{or} \quad \sum_{i=1}^{k} x_i f(x_i)$$

where the x_i's denote the k distinct values of X. The mean of the probability distribution is also called the population mean for the variable X and is denoted by the Greek letter μ (mu).

The mean of a random variable X is also called its **expected value.** The notation $E(X)$ is used to denote the expected value. Thus, the mean μ and expected value $E(X)$ are the same quantity and will be used interchangeably.

The **mean** of the discrete random variable X or the population mean is

Mean: $E(X) = \mu = \sum(\text{Value} \times \text{Probability}) = \sum x_i f(x_i)$

Here the sum extends over all the distinct values of X.

EXAMPLE 6.8   Calculating the Mean of a Probability Distribution

Let X denote the number of heads in three tosses of a fair coin. Calculate the mean of X.

Solution and Discussion.   The probability distribution of X is recorded in Table 6.1 of Example 6.4. The calculations leading to the mean are given in Table 6.6.

TABLE 6.6 Mean of the Distribution in Table 6.1

x	$f(x)$	$xf(x)$
0	$\frac{1}{8}$	0
1	$\frac{3}{8}$	$\frac{3}{8}$
2	$\frac{3}{8}$	$\frac{6}{8}$
3	$\frac{1}{8}$	$\frac{3}{8}$
Total	1	$\frac{12}{8} = 1.5 = \mu$

From the calculations in Table 6.6, we see that the mean is 1.5.

When a data set is plotted as a dot diagram or a frequency histogram, the sample mean is the balancing point or the center of gravity of the figure. In the same way, the mean or expected value is the balancing point of the probability distribution when pictured as a probability histogram. Consequently, a probability histogram with a long right-hand tail will tend to have a mean toward the right. A symmetric probability histogram will have a mean in the center, and so forth. The mean μ measures center in the same way the sample mean measures center in a set of data.

Like many concepts of probability, the idea of the mean or expected value originated from studies of gambling. When the random variable X refers to the financial gain in a game of chance, such as playing poker or participating in a state lottery, the term *expected gain* is more appealing than *mean gain*. In statistical studies, both terms—mean and expected value—are widely used.

EXAMPLE 6.9   The Mean as an Expected Value

A trip insurance policy pays $1000 to the customer in case of a loss due to theft or damage on a five-day trip. If the risk of such a loss is assessed to be 1 in 200, what is a fair premium for this policy?

Solution and Discussion.   The probability that the company will be liable to pay $1000 to a customer is $\frac{1}{200}$ = .005. Therefore, the probability distribution of X, the payment per customer, is:

Payment (x)	Probability $f(x)$
$0	.995
$1000	.005

We calculate

$$E(X) = \$0 \times .995 + \$1000 \times .005 = \$5.00$$

The company's expected cost per customer is $5 and, therefore, a premium equal to this amount is viewed as a fair premium. If this premium is charged, and no other costs are involved, then the company will neither make a profit nor lose money in the long run. In practice, the premium is set at a higher price because it must include administrative costs and intended profit.

The concept of expected value also leads to a numerical measure for the spread of a probability distribution—namely, the standard deviation. The reasoning behind the definition of the standard deviation of a probability distribution parallels that for the sample standard deviation of a data set introduced in Chapter 1.

We take the mean μ as the center of the distribution of X and express variation of X in terms of the deviation $(X - \mu)$. The **variance** of X is defined as the expected value of the squared deviation $(X - \mu)^2$. Let $x_1, x_2, \ldots, x_k$ be the distinct values of X. To calculate this expected value, we note that

$(X - \mu)^2$ Takes Value	With Probability
$(x_1 - \mu)^2$	$f(x_1)$
$(x_2 - \mu)^2$	$f(x_2)$
$\vdots$	$\vdots$
$(x_k - \mu)^2$	$f(x_k)$

The expected value of $(X - \mu)^2$ is obtained by multiplying each value $(x_i - \mu)^2$ by the probability $f(x_i)$ and then summing these products. This shows the reasoning behind the definition

$$\text{Variance of } X = \sum (\text{Deviation})^2 \times (\text{Probability})$$

$$= \sum_{i=1}^{k} (x_i - \mu)^2 f(x_i)$$

F. Stuart Westmorland/Tony Stone Images/New York, Inc.

No Casino Game Has a Positive Expected Profit

Each year, thousands of visitors go to casinos to gamble. Although all count on being lucky and a few indeed return with a smiling face, most leave the casino with a light purse. But, what should be a gambler's expectation?

Consider a simple bet on the red of a roulette wheel that has 18 red, 18 black, and 2 green slots. This bet is at even money, so a $10 wager on red has as an expected profit

$$E(\text{Profit}) = (10)(\tfrac{18}{38}) + (-10)(\tfrac{20}{38}) = -.526$$

The negative expected profit says we expect to lose an average of 52.6¢ on every $10 bet. Over a long series of bets, the relative frequency of winning will approach the probability $\tfrac{18}{38}$ and that of losing will approach $\tfrac{20}{38}$, so a player will lose a substantial amount of money.

Other bets against the house have a similar negative expected profit. How else could a casino stay in business?

The variance of X is abbreviated as var(X) and is also denoted by σ^2 (sigma squared). The **standard deviation** of X is the positive square root of the variance and is denoted by sd(X) or σ (sigma).

Variance: $\qquad\qquad\qquad \sigma^2 = \text{var}(X) = \sum (x_i - \mu)^2 f(x_i)$

Standard deviation: $\quad \sigma = \text{sd}(X) = +\sqrt{\text{var}(X)}$

The variance of X is also called the population variance, and the standard deviation of X is frequently called the population standard deviation.

EXAMPLE 6.10   Calculating the Variance and Standard Deviation of a Probability Distribution

Calculate the variance and the standard deviation of the distribution of X that appears in the left two columns of Table 6.7.

TABLE 6.7   Calculation of Variance and Standard Deviation

x	$f(x)$	$xf(x)$	$(x - \mu)$	$(x - \mu)^2$	$(x - \mu)^2 f(x)$
0	.1	0	-2	4	.4
1	.2	.2	-1	1	.2
2	.4	.8	0	0	0
3	.2	.6	1	1	.2
4	.1	.4	2	4	.4
Total	1.0	$2.0 = \mu$			$1.2 = \sigma^2$

Solution and Discussion.   The details of the calculation of σ^2 and σ are shown in the last four columns of Table 6.7. Since the variance (and standard deviation) measure spread with the mean as the center of the distribution, we must first calculate μ. This calculation occurs in column 3 of the table. We see that

$$\text{var}(X) = \sigma^2 = 1.2$$

and, consequently,

$$\text{sd}(X) = \sigma = \sqrt{1.2} = 1.095$$

An alternative formula for σ^2 often simplifies the numerical work. With a little algebra, we have

$$\sigma^2 = \sum_{i=1}^{k} x_i^2 f(x_i) - \mu^2$$

EXAMPLE 6.11   Calculating the Variance with the Alternative Formula

Illustrate the alternative formula for σ^2 using the probability distribution in Example 6.10.

Solution and Discussion.   The probability distribution is reproduced in Table 6.8, along with columns for $xf(x)$ and $x^2f(x)$.

TABLE 6.8   Calculation of Variance by Alternative Formula

x	$f(x)$	$xf(x)$	$x^2f(x)$
0	.1	0	0
1	.2	.2	.2
2	.4	.8	1.6
3	.2	.6	1.8
4	.1	.4	1.6
Total	1.0	$2.0 = \mu$	$5.2 = \sum x^2f(x)$

Therefore

$$\sigma^2 = 5.2 - (2.0)^2 = 1.2$$

$$\sigma = \sqrt{1.2} = 1.095$$

which agree with the results in Example 6.10.

The standard deviation σ, rather than the variance σ^2, is the appropriate measure of spread. Its unit is the same as that of the random variable X. For example, if X is income in dollars, σ will have the unit (dollar) whereas σ^2 has the rather artificial unit (dollar)^2.

SOME RULES FOR MEANS AND VARIANCES

A linear transformation, or linear function, is represented by a formula whose graph is a straight line. We can also change the scale and location of a random variable X by considering a new random variable Y related to X by a linear transformation of the form $Y = a + bX$, where a and b are any constants.

Once we multiply X by a constant b, we change the relative positions of the values of X and their locations with respect to the origin. Consequently, the multiplicative constant affects both the mean and the variance (or standard deviation) of X. Adding a constant a to the random variable does not change the relative positions of its values— they all increase or decrease by the same amount—but it does change their locations with respect to the origin. The additive constant affects the mean but not the variance (or standard deviation).

Let μ_X and σ_X^2 be the mean and variance of X and define a new random variable $Y = a + bX$. Then the mean and variance (standard deviation) of Y are related to the mean and variance (standard deviation) of X.

The random variable $Y = a + bX$ has

$$\mu_Y = \mu_{a+bX} = a + b\mu_X$$
$$\sigma_Y^2 = \sigma_{a+bX}^2 = b^2\sigma_X^2 \quad \text{so } \sigma_{a+bX} = |b|\sigma_X$$

To summarize, if a random variable is multiplied by a constant b, the mean is multiplied by the same constant. The variance is multiplied by the square of the constant and the standard deviation by its absolute value. If a constant a is added to a random variable, the same constant is added to the mean but the variance remains unchanged.

EXAMPLE 6.12   Calculating the Mean and Variance of a Linear Function of a Random Variable

An investigator concerned with job safety asked a large number of workers to respond to the question, "How often do you suffer mental lapses on the job?" The responses were recorded on a 5-point scale from Never to Very often. The categories were coded 0, 1, 2, 3, and 4, respectively, and the probability distribution for X, the response of a worker selected at random, is given here. This probability distribution was derived from the relative frequencies associated with the response categories in the initial survey.

Probability Distribution of X

x	$f(x)$
0	.10
1	.40
2	.25
3	.20
4	.05
Total	1.00

Suppose we create a new random variable $Y = -4 + 2X = 2X - 4$. Then, for example, when $X = 0$, $Y = 2(0) - 4 = -4$ and $.10 = P(X = 0) = P(Y = -4)$. Continuing in this fashion, we create the probability distribution for Y, as follows.

Probability Distribution of Y

y	$f(y)$
−4	.10
−2	.40
0	.25
2	.20
4	.05
Total	1.00

a. Find the mean and variance of X.

b. Find the mean and variance of Y.

c. Since $Y = 2X - 4$, verify that $\mu_Y = \mu_{2X-4} = 2\mu_X - 4$ and $\sigma_Y^2 = \sigma_{2X-4}^2 = 2^2 \sigma_X^2$.

Solution and Discussion.

a. $\mu_X = 0 \times .10 + 1 \times .40 + 2 \times .25 + 3 \times .20 + 4 \times .05 = 1.70$

$\sigma_X^2 = 0^2 \times .10 + 1^2 \times .40 + 2^2 \times .25 + 3^2 \times .20 + 4^2 \times .05 - (1.70)^2$
$= 1.11$

b. $\mu_Y = (-4) \times .10 + (-2) \times .40 + 0 \times .25 + 2 \times .20 + 4 \times .05 = -.60$

$\sigma_Y^2 = (-4)^2 \times .10 + (-2)^2 \times .40 + 0^2 \times .25 + 2^2 \times .20 + 4^2 \times .05 - (-.60)^2$
$= 4.44$

c. Clearly, $\mu_Y = -.60 = 2(1.70) - 4 = 2\mu_X - 4$ and $\sigma_Y^2 = 4.44 = 2^2(1.11) = 2^2 \sigma_X^2$.

Multiplying the random variable by 2 increases the variance by a factor of $2^2 = 4$. The additive constant -4 does not change the variance but it does contribute to a change in the mean.

On occasion it is necessary to consider the mean and variance of the sum of two random variables X and Y. For example, X and Y may be the rates of return over the next year on two current investments. We may want to know the total expected return and its variance (or risk) to compare it with another opportunity which, say, is inherently very risky but has the potential to yield a large return.

As another example, X may be the number of households watching a college football bowl game next January 1 on a particular television network, and Y may be the number of households watching a later bowl game on the same network. To negotiate prices for commercial minutes, the network is interested in the total number of households $X + Y$ tuned to its college football offerings on January 1 and, in particular, the expected total number of households.

It should not be surprising that the mean of $X + Y$ will always be the sum of the two individual means, $\mu_X + \mu_Y$. (Similarly, the mean of the difference $X - Y$ is the difference between the individual means, $\mu_X - \mu_Y$.) The case of the variance is more complicated. To see why this might be so, suppose X is the percentage correct and Y is the percentage incorrect for an Accounting major taking a CPA exam. We must have $X + Y = 100\%$ for every instance. That is, even though X may vary and, consequently, Y may vary, the sum $X + Y$ has zero variance. This extreme case illustrates that it is necessary to know how the two variables vary together, or jointly, before the variance of the sum can be determined. However, unlike the CPA exam example, if the two random variables are completely unrelated, or *independent,* the variances simply add.

Mean of the sum or difference of two random variables:

$$\mu_{X+Y} = \mu_X + \mu_Y$$
$$\mu_{X-Y} = \mu_X - \mu_Y$$

Variance of the sum or difference of two *independent* random variables:

$$\sigma^2_{X+Y} = \sigma^2_X + \sigma^2_Y$$
$$\sigma^2_{X-Y} = \sigma^2_X + \sigma^2_Y$$

EXAMPLE 6.13 Calculating the Mean of the Sum of Two Random Variables

Suppose a store manager has modeled next week's sales X of their smaller hot tub unit with the probability distribution given here:

x	$f(x)$	
0	.1	
1	.2	$\mu_X = 1.9$
2	.4	$\sigma^2_X = .89$
3	.3	
Total	1.00	

The manager models the weekly sales Y of the larger hot tub unit with the following probability distribution:

y	$f(y)$	
0	.6	
1	.3	$\mu_Y = .5$
2	.1	$\sigma^2_Y = .45$
Total	1.00	

a. Find the mean of the total number $X + Y$ of hot tub units sold next week.

b. Suppose the sale of a small unit yields a $500 profit and the profit on a large unit is $900. Determine an expression for total profit and find its expected value.

Solution and Discussion.

a. To find the mean of a sum of two random variables, we simply add the individual means. Therefore

$$\mu_{X+Y} = \mu_X + \mu_Y = 1.9 + .5 = 2.4 \text{ units}$$

b. In this case, the expression for total profit is $500X + 900Y$. The mean of $500X$ is $500\mu_X = 500(1.9) = 950$ by the rule for the mean of a linear transformation. Similarly, the mean of $900Y$ is $900\mu_Y = 900(.5) = 450$. The mean of $500X + 900Y$, or the expected total profit, is

$$\$500\mu_X + \$900\mu_Y = \$950 + \$450 = \$1400$$

Because the sales of the two units are likely to be related, we do not have enough information to calculate the variance of total sales. The simple rule for adding individual variances does not apply.

EXERCISES

6.29 Given the following probability distribution:

x	$f(x)$
0	.4
1	.3
2	.2
3	.1

a. Construct the probability histogram.

b. Find $E(X)$, σ^2, and σ.

6.30 Find the mean and standard deviation of the following distribution:

x	$f(x)$
0	.3
1	.5
2	.1
3	.1

6.31 In bidding for a remodeling project, a contractor determines that she will have a net profit of $50,000 if she gets the contract and a net loss of $500 if her bid fails. If the probability of getting the contract is $\frac{1}{4}$, calculate the contractor's expected return.

6.32 A book club announces a sweepstakes to attract new subscribers. The prizes and corresponding chances are listed here. (Typically, the prizes are listed in bold print in an advertising flyer, whereas the chances are listed in fine print.)

Prize	Chance
$50000	1 in one million
$5000	1 in 250,000
$100	1 in 5000
$20	1 in 500

Suppose you have just mailed your sweepstakes tickets and X stands for your winnings.

    a. List the probability distribution of X. (*Caution:* The chance of winning nothing is not given, but you can figure that out from the information provided.)

    b. Calculate your expected winnings.

6.33 Calculate the mean and standard deviation for the probability distribution given in Example 6.5 (see Table 6.3).

6.34 An insurance policy pays $800 for the loss due to theft of a canoe. If the probability of a theft is taken to be .05, find the expected payment. If the insurance company charges $50 for the policy, what is the expected profit per policy?

6.35 A construction company submits bids for two projects. Listed here are the profit and the probability of winning each project. Assume that the outcomes of the two bids are independent.

	Profit	Chance of Winning Bid
Project A	$75,000	.50
Project B	$120,000	.65

    a. List the possible outcomes (win, not win) for the two projects and find their probabilities.

    b. Let X denote the company's total profit from the two contracts. Determine the probability distribution of X.

    c. If it costs the company $2000 for preparatory surveys and paperwork for the two bids, what is the expected net profit?

6.36 Refer to Exercise 6.35, but suppose that the projects are scheduled consecutively with A in the first year and B in the second year. The company's chance of winning Project A is still .50. Instead of the assumption of independence, now assume that if the company wins Project A, its chance of winning B becomes .80 because of a boost in its image, but its chance drops to .40 in case it fails to win A. Under this premise, do parts **a–c** of Exercise 6.35.

6.37 Upon examination of the claims records of 280 policyholders over a period of five years, an insurance company makes an empirical determination of the probability distribution of X = number of claims per policyholder in five years.

x	$f(x)$
0	.307
1	.286
2	.204
3	.114
4	.064
5	.018
6	.007

    a. Calculate the expected value of X.

    b. Calculate the standard deviation of X.

6.38 Suppose the probability function of a random variable X is given by the formula

$$f(x) = \frac{60}{77}\frac{1}{x} \quad \text{for } x = 2, 3, 4, 5$$

Calculate the mean and standard deviation of this distribution.

6.39 The probability distribution of a random variable X is given by the function

$$f(x) = \frac{1}{84}\binom{5}{x}\binom{4}{3-x} \quad \text{for } x = 0, 1, 2, 3$$

a. Calculate the numerical probabilities and list the distribution.
b. Calculate the mean and standard deviation of X.

6.40 Refer to Exercise 6.11. Using the probability distribution for the number of nonroutine requests, find:

a. The mean number of nonroutine requests
b. The variance of the number of nonroutine requests
c. The standard deviation of the number of nonroutine requests

6.41 Refer to the probability distribution for the capacity of the car-painting center in Exercise 6.27. Find the

a. Mean number of customers per day
b. Variance of the number of customers per day
c. Standard deviation of the number of customers per day

6.42 The probability distributions of two random variables X and Y are given here.

x	$f(x)$		y	$f(y)$
0	.1		2	.2
1	.3		4	.4
2	.4		6	.3
3	.2		8	.1

a. From the X distribution, determine the distribution of the random variable $8 - 2X$, and verify that it coincides with the Y distribution.
b. Calculate the mean μ_X and standard deviation σ_X of X.
c. From the Y distribution, calculate the mean μ_Y and standard deviation σ_Y of Y.
d. If $Y = a + bX$, then according to theory we must have the relations $\mu_Y = a + b\mu_X$ and $\sigma_Y = |b|\sigma_X$. Verify these relations using your results in parts **b** and **c**.

6.43 A developer of electronic games is planning a major investment. The profit from this investment is a random variable X whose distribution is estimated in the following table.

Profit (millions)	Probability
0	.1
1.0	.5
1.5	.2
2.0	.2

a. Find the mean profit and the standard deviation of profit.

b. Suppose the company will have to pay a $100,000 source of capital fee plus 5% of the profits. The investment will then yield

$$Y = .95X - .1$$

millions of dollars. Find the mean and standard deviation of Y.

6.44 A person selling personal computers for home office use will contact four customers during a week. Each contact can result in either a sale, with probability .2, or no sale, with probability .8. Assume the customer contacts are independent.

a. List the elementary outcomes and assign probabilities.

b. If X denotes the number of computers sold during the week, obtain the probability distribution of X.

c. Calculate the expected value of X.

6.45 Refer to Exercise 6.44. Suppose the computers are priced at $2000 each, and let Y denote the salesman's total sales (in dollars) during a week.

a. Determine the probability distribution of Y.

b. Calculate $E(Y)$. Note that it is the same as $2000 \times E(X)$.

6.46 *Median of a Probability Distribution.* The **median** of a distribution is the value m_0 such that $P(X \le m_0) \ge .5$ and $P(X \ge m_0) \ge .5$. In other words, the probability at or below m_0 is at least .5, and the probability at or above m_0 is at least .5. Find the median of the distribution given in Exercise 6.29.

6.5   BERNOULLI TRIALS AND THE BINOMIAL DISTRIBUTION

As illustrated in Examples 6.1, 6.2, and 6.5, there are numerous statistical investigations where the outcomes are only two possible categories, and the relevant random variable is the number of times, or frequency, one category occurs when the experiment is repeated several times. The probability distribution of X, the number of elements in the specified category, is calculated under the assumption that the population proportion of the category is known. For instance, the probability distribution in Table 6.3 of Example 6.5 was determined from the specification that 30% of all viewers of a commercial remembered the product after two hours.

In a practical situation, however, the population proportion is usually an unknown quantity. When this is so, the probability distribution of X cannot be numerically determined. Yet it is often possible to construct a model for the probability distribution of X that contains the unknown population proportion as a constant quantity or parameter. This probability model then allows us to make inferences about the population proportion from observations on the random variable X. As we shall see, this general approach is not limited to a population proportion; but, in this section, we focus on a population proportion.

A **probability model** is an assumed form of the probability distribution that describes the chance behavior for a random variable X.

Probabilities are expressed in terms of relevant population quantities, called **parameters.**

We now develop a quite versatile probability model that can be applied in many situations where the population can be conceived as a collection of items that fall in one of only two categories. It is convenient to label the two categories as "success" and "failure."

BERNOULLI TRIALS—SUCCESSES AND FAILURES

Sampling situations where the elements of a population have a dichotomy abound in virtually all walks of life. A few examples are:

- Inspecting a specified number of items coming off a production line and counting the number of defective items
- Surveying a sample of voters and observing the number favoring a reduction in public spending on welfare
- Examining a sample of checks for a period and determining the number processed in compliance with stated accounting procedures
- Questioning a number of a bank's customers and counting the number who would use a home computer to do their banking

Selecting a single element of the population is envisioned as a trial of the (sampling) experiment, so each trial can result in one of two possible outcomes. Our goal is to develop a probability model for the number of outcomes in one category when trials are repeated, say, n times.

Suppose each repetition of the experiment, each trial, can result in one of two possible outcomes labeled success (S) or failure (F). Customarily, the outcome that we are primarily interested in is called success (even if it is a disastrous event, for example, "unemployed"). To arrive at our probability model, we need some additional conditions on the repeated trials. Trials that satisfy these conditions are called Bernoulli trials after the Swiss mathematician Jacob Bernoulli.

Bernoulli Trials

1. Each trial yields one of two outcomes, conveniently called success (S) and failure (F).
2. For each trial, the probability of success $P(S)$ is the same and is denoted by $p = P(S)$. The probability of failure is then $P(F) = 1 - p$ for each trial and is denoted by q, so that $p + q = 1$.
3. Trials are independent. The probability of success in a trial does not change given any information about the outcomes of other trials.

Perhaps the simplest example of Bernoulli trials is the prototype model of tossing a coin where the occurrences *head* and *tail* can be labeled S and F, respectively. For a fair coin, we have $p = q = \frac{1}{2}$.

EXAMPLE 6.14   Sampling from a Finite Population with Two Categories of Elements

Show whether sampling from a finite population with two categories of elements can be regarded as a sequence of Bernoulli trials when

a.   Sampling with replacement

b.   Sampling without replacement

from a population of 15 items of which 5 are defective.

Solution and Discussion.   Consider a lot (population) of items in which each item can be classified as either defective or nondefective and that the lot consists of 15 items of which 5 are defective and 10 are nondefective.

a.   *Sampling with Replacement.* An item is drawn at random, that is, in a manner such that all items in the lot are equally likely to be selected. The quality of the item is recorded and it is returned to the lot before the next drawing. The conditions for Bernoulli trials are satisfied. If the occurrence of a defective is labeled S, we have $P(S) = \frac{5}{15}$.

b.   *Sampling Without Replacement.* In the situation in part **a,** suppose that three items are drawn one at a time but without replacement; that is, they are not put back into the lot after they are drawn. Then the condition concerning the independence of trials is violated. For the first drawing, $P(S) = \frac{5}{15}$. If the first draw produces S, the lot then contains 14 items, 4 of which are defective. Given this information about the result of the first draw, the conditional probability of obtaining an S on the second draw is then $\frac{4}{14} \neq \frac{5}{15}$, which establishes the lack of independence.

   The violation of the condition of independence illustrated in part **b** loses its impact when the population is very large and only a small fraction of it is sampled. Consider sampling 3 items without replacement from a lot of 1500 items, 500 of which are defective. With S_1 denoting the occurrence of S on the first draw, and S_2 the occurrence of S on the second draw, we have

$$P(S_1) = \frac{500}{1500} = \frac{5}{15}$$

and

$$P(S_2|S_1) = \frac{499}{1499}$$

For most practical purposes, the latter fraction can be approximated by $\frac{5}{15}$. Strictly speaking, consecutive trials are not independent, but the violation of independence is almost negligible, and the model of Bernoulli trials can be assumed as a good approximation.

The following remarks summarize the important points illustrated in Example 6.14.

Remarks

If elements are sampled from a dichotomous population at random and with replacement, the conditions for Bernoulli trials are satisfied. When the sampling is made without replacement, the condition of independent trials is violated. However, if the population is large and only a small fraction of it (less than 10% as a rule of thumb) is sampled, the effect of this violation is negligible, and the model of Bernoulli trials can be used as an approximation.

The next example illustrates the kinds of approximations that are sometimes employed when using the Bernoulli trials model.

EXAMPLE 6.15   **Market Testing a New Product**

A fast food chain is considering a new chicken product for its menu. From its thousands of stores nationwide, 10 are selected for test marketing. The possible outcomes for each store are that the product will sell successfully (S) or that it will not (F). Can we regard the results at the 10 stores as 10 repetitions of a Bernoulli trial?

Solution and Discussion.   Each store has a particular type of clientele that to some extent differs in several characteristics from store to store. Also, variables like the local weather may affect what people order. Therefore, strictly speaking, it may not be possible to regard the trials made at 10 different locations as 10 repetitions of an experiment under identical conditions, as the definition of Bernoulli trials demands. We must remember that the conditions of a probability model are abstractions that help to realistically simplify the complex mechanism governing the outcomes of an experiment. Identifying the results at the 10 stores as Bernoulli trials must be viewed as an approximation of the real world. The merit of the approximation ultimately rests on how successfully the model explains chance variations in the outcomes.

THE BINOMIAL DISTRIBUTION

Consider a fixed number n of Bernoulli trials with the success probability p in each trial. The number of successes in n trials is a random variable that we denote by X. The probability distribution of this random variable X is called a **binomial distribution.**

The binomial distribution depends on two quantities, n and p. For instance, the distribution appearing in Table 6.1 in Example 6.4 is precisely the binomial distribution with $n = 3$ and $p = .5$. The distribution in Table 6.3 in Example 6.5 is the binomial distribution with $n = 4$ and $p = .3$.

The Binomial Distribution

Denote

$$n = \text{a fixed number of Bernoulli trials}$$
$$p = \text{the probability of success in each trial}$$
$$X = \text{the (random) number of successes in } n \text{ trials}$$

The random variable X is called a **binomial random variable.** Its distribution is called a binomial distribution.

To summarize, the binomial distribution associates probabilities with the number of successes in n Bernoulli trials, where the probability of success on a single trial is p. A review of the developments in Example 6.5 will help motivate the general formula for the binomial distribution.

EXAMPLE 6.16   Determining the Probabilities for the Number of Viewers Who Remember a New Product

Refer to Example 6.5. The random variable X represents the number of viewers who remember the product among a sample of size $n = 4$ people who viewed the commercial. Instead of the numerical value .3, we now denote the population proportion of viewers who remembered the product by the symbol p, and those who did not by the symbol $q = 1 - p$. Furthermore, we relabel the outcome "remember the product" as a success (S) and the outcome "do not remember" as a failure (F). Construct the probability model for X.

Solution and Discussion.   The elementary outcomes of sampling 4 viewers, the associated probabilities, and the value of X are listed here.

	FFFF	SFFF	SSFF	SSSF	SSSS
		FSFF	SFSF	SSFS	
		FFSF	SFFS	SFSS	
		FFFS	FSSF	FSSS	
			FSFS		
			FFSS		

Value of X	0	1	2	3	4
Probability of Each Outcome	q^4	pq^3	p^2q^2	p^3q	p^4
Number of Outcomes	$1 = \binom{4}{0}$	$4 = \binom{4}{1}$	$6 = \binom{4}{2}$	$4 = \binom{4}{3}$	$1 = \binom{4}{4}$

Because the population is vast, the trials can be treated as independent. Also, for an individual trial, $P(S) = p$ and $P(F) = q = 1 - p$. The event $[X = 0]$ is equivalent to the single outcome FFFF whose probability is

$$P(X = 0) = P(\text{FFFF}) = q \times q \times q \times q = q^4$$

To arrive at an expression for $P(X = 1)$, we consider the outcomes listed in the second column of the previous display. The probability of, for example, SFFF is

$$P(\text{SFFF}) = p \times q \times q \times q = pq^3$$

and the same result holds for every outcome in this column. There are 4 incompatible outcomes, so we obtain $P(X = 1) = 4pq^3$. The factor 4 is the number of outcomes with one S and three F's. Notice we can obtain this count without making a complete list of the outcomes. Every outcome has four places. The 1 place where S occurs can be selected from the 4 places in $\binom{4}{1}$ ways, whereas the remaining places must be filled with F's.

Continuing with this reasoning, we find that the value $X = 2$ occurs with $\binom{4}{2} = 6$ outcomes, each of which has probability p^2q^2. Therefore, $P(X = 2) = \binom{4}{2}p^2q^2$. After working out the probabilities for the remaining values of X, we get the binomial distribution for $n = 4$ trials that is given in Table 6.9.

TABLE 6.9 Binomial Distribution for $n = 4$ Trials

Value x	0	1	2	3	4
Probability $f(x)$	$\binom{4}{0}p^0q^4$	$\binom{4}{1}p^1q^3$	$\binom{4}{2}p^2q^2$	$\binom{4}{3}p^3q^1$	$\binom{4}{4}p^4q^0$

You should verify that the numerical probabilities appearing in Table 6.3 in Example 6.5 are obtained by substituting $p = .3$ and $q = .7$ in the entries of Table 6.9.

Extending the argument in Example 6.16 to the case of a general number n of Bernoulli trials, we observe that there are $\binom{n}{x}$ outcomes that have exactly x successes and $n - x$ failures. The probability of every such outcome is $p^x q^{n-x}$. Therefore,

$$f(x) = P(X = x) = \binom{n}{x}p^x q^{n-x} \quad \text{for } x = 0, 1, \ldots, n$$

is the formula for the binomial distribution with n trials.

The **binomial distribution** with n Bernoulli trials and success probability p is described by the equation

$$f(x) = P(X = x) = \binom{n}{x}p^x q^{n-x}$$

where $q = 1 - p$ and $x = 0, 1, \ldots, n$.

EXAMPLE 6.17 Using the Binomial Distribution

The Securities and Exchange Commission has mandated that public companies include a management's discussion and analysis section in their annual reports. One of the goals was to make public predictable events and trends that may affect the business. (See Pava, M., and Epstein, M. "How good is MD & A as an investment tool?" *Journal of Accounting,* pp. 51–53, Mar. 1993.)

Based on a survey of companies' annual reports and subsequent events that affect the industry, the probability is approximately .25 that management will correctly anticipate industry-specific events. Suppose 5 public companies in one industry are randomly selected and their last year's annual report checked to see whether it correctly anticipated this year's decline in demand. What is the probability that, among these 5 companies,

a. None of the companies anticipated the decline?

b. Four or more of the companies anticipated the decline?

Solution and Discussion.   Because there are different companies involved, we will treat the 5 trials as independent. Let the random variable X be the number of companies that correctly anticipated the decrease in demand among the 5 selected. If we identify the occurrence of correctly anticipating the decrease as a success S, then X has the binomial distribution with $n = 5$ and $p = .25$. The required probabilities are

a. $P(X = 0) = f(0) = (.75)^5 = .237$

b. $P(X \geq 4) = f(4) + f(5) = \binom{5}{4}(.25)^4(.75)^1 + \binom{5}{5}(.25)^5(.75)^0$

$$= .015 + .001 = .016$$

PEANUTS reprinted by permission of United Feature Syndicate, Inc.

Poor Linus. Chance did not even favor him with half correct.

To illustrate the manner in which the values of p influence the shape of the binomial distribution, the probability histograms for three binomial distributions with $n = 6$ and $p = .5, .3,$ and $.7$ are shown in Figure 6.3.

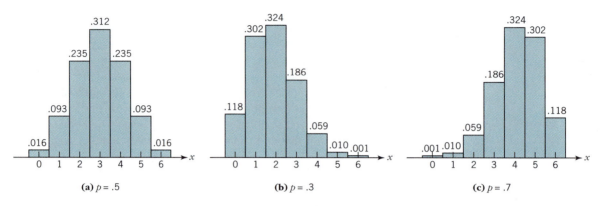

(a) $p = .5$ (b) $p = .3$ (c) $p = .7$

Figure 6.3   Binomial Distributions for $n = 6$

When $p = .5$, the binomial distribution is symmetric with the highest probability occurring at the center. For values of p smaller than .5, more probability is shifted toward smaller values of x and the distribution has a longer tail to the right. Figure 6.3(b), where the binomial distribution with $p = .3$ is plotted, illustrates this tendency. On the other hand, Figure 6.3(c) with $p = .7$ illustrates the opposite tendency; the value of p is larger than .5 and more probability is shifted toward higher values of x. This distribution has a longer tail to the left.

Considering the histograms in Figures 6.3(b) and 6.3(c), we note that the value of p in one histogram is the same as the value of q in the other. The probabilities in one histogram are exactly the same as those in the other, but their order is reversed. This illustrates a general property of the binomial distribution: When p and q are interchanged, the distribution of probabilities is reversed.

THE BINOMIAL TABLE

Although the binomial distribution is easily calculated on a computer and some hand calculators, a short table of binomial probabilities is provided in Table 2, Appendix B. It covers sample sizes from 1 to 25 and several values of p. For a given (n, p) pair, the table entry corresponding to each c represents the **cumulative probability** $P(X \leq c) = \sum_{x=0}^{c} f(x)$, as explained in the following tables.

The Binomial Distribution

Value x	Probability $f(x)$
0	$f(0)$
1	$f(1)$
2	$f(2)$
$\vdots$	$\vdots$
n	$f(n)$
Total	1

Appendix 2, Table B, provides $P(X \leq c)$

c	Table Entry $\sum_{x=0}^{c} f(x) = P(X \leq c)$
0	$f(0)$
1	$f(0) + f(1)$
2	$f(0) + f(1) + f(2)$
$\vdots$	$\vdots$
n	1.000

The probability of an individual value x can be obtained from this table by a subtraction of two consecutive entries. For example,

$$P(X = 2) = f(2) = \left(\begin{matrix}\text{Table entry at} \\ c = 2\end{matrix}\right) - \left(\begin{matrix}\text{Table entry at} \\ c = 1\end{matrix}\right)$$

EXAMPLE 6.18   Using the Binomial Table

Suppose two new luxury cars, Car C and Car L, give equally comfortable rides. If 15 customers are blindfolded and given a ride in each, the probability is .5 that a customer would say Car C gives a more comfortable ride. Find the probability that:

a.   At most, 6 customers will prefer Car C.

b.   The number of customers who prefer Car C will be no fewer than 6 and no more than 10.

c.   Twelve or more customers will prefer Car C.

Solution and Discussion.   Designating the choice of Car C by S and assuming the results for different customers are independent, X = the number who prefer the ride of Car C has a binomial distribution with $n = 15$ and $p = .5$. To compute the required probabilities, we use the binomial table for $n = 15$ and $p = .5$.

a. $P(X \leq 6) = .304$, which is obtained directly from the table by reading from the row $c = 6$.

b.   We must calculate

$$P(6 \leq X \leq 10) = f(6) + f(7) + f(8) + f(9) + f(10)$$

$$= \sum_{x=6}^{10} f(x)$$

The table entry corresponding to $c = 10$ gives

$$P(x \leq 10) = \sum_{x=0}^{10} f(x) = .941$$

and the entry corresponding to $c = 5$ gives

$$P(x \leq 5) = \sum_{x=0}^{5} f(x) = .151$$

Because their difference represents the sum $\sum_{x=6}^{10} f(x)$, we obtain

$$P(6 \leq X \leq 10) = P(X \leq 10) - P(X \leq 5)$$
$$= .941 - .151 = .790$$

c.   To find $P(X \geq 12)$, we use the law of the complement and compute

$$P(X \geq 12) = 1 - P(X \leq 11) = 1 - .982 = .018$$

Note that $[X < 12]$ is the same event as $[X \leq 11]$. (Recall the example of the blindfold test ride in Section 5.1 of Chapter 5. The mystery surrounding the numerical probability .018 is now resolved.)

THE MEAN AND STANDARD DEVIATION OF THE BINOMIAL DISTRIBUTION

We have a general formula that gives the binomial probabilities for any n and p. In later chapters, we will need to know the mean and standard deviation of the binomial distribution. These quantities can be computed using the general expressions for the mean and standard deviation of a discrete probability distribution, but the algebra is somewhat tedious and we simply quote the results. The expression for the mean, however, is apparent from the following intuitive reasoning: Suppose a fair coin will be tossed 100 times. The number of heads X in 100 tosses is a binomial random variable with $n = 100$ and $p = .5$. The expected number of heads is $100 \times .5 = 50$ or, equivalently, np. Alternatively, if the probability of an event is p, then in n Bernoulli trials the event is expected to happen np times. Again, this gives np as the mean of the binomial distribution.

The binomial distribution with n trials and success probability p has

$$\text{Mean} = np$$
$$\text{Variance} = npq$$
$$\text{Standard deviation} = \sqrt{npq}$$

where $q = 1 - p$.

EXAMPLE 6.19   Calculating the Mean and Standard Deviation of a Binomial Distribution

Calculate the mean and standard deviation for a binomial distribution with $n = 3$ and $p = .5$.

Solution and Discussion.   Using the formulas, we obtain

$$\text{Mean} = np = 3 \times .5 = 1.5$$
$$\text{Standard deviation} = \sqrt{npq} = \sqrt{3 \times .5 \times .5} = \sqrt{.75} = .866$$

The mean agrees with the results in Example 6.8. The standard deviation can be checked by numerical calculations using Table 6.6 in Example 6.8 and the definition of the standard deviation σ.

EXERCISES

6.47 Is the model for Bernoulli trials plausible in each of the following situations? If not, discuss the nature of the violation of the model assumptions.

a.   For each of 40 customers at a grocery store, record whether they purchased ketchup.

b.   Record whether each of 10 franchise locations in Los Angeles had an increase in sales over the last year.

c.   Items coming off an assembly line are inspected and classified as defective or nondefective.

d.   Visit several consecutive houses on a block and record whether today's newspaper was delivered on time.

6.48 In each of the following cases, examine whether repetitions of the stated experiment conform to the model of Bernoulli trials. When the model is appropriate, determine the numerical value of p or indicate how it can be determined.

a.   Roll a fair die and observe the number that shows up.

b.   Roll a fair die and observe whether the number 5 shows up.

c.   Roll two fair dice and observe the total of the points that show up.

d.   Roll two fair dice and observe whether a total of 7 is obtained.

e.   Roll a loaded (unfair) die and observe whether the number 5 shows up.

6.49 A jar contains 25 candies of which 7 are brown, 10 are yellow, and 8 are other colors. Consider 4 successive draws of 1 candy at random from the jar, and suppose the appearance of a yellow candy is the event of interest. For each of the following situations, indicate whether the model of Bernoulli trials is reasonable and, if so, determine the numerical value of p.

a.   After each draw, the selected candy is returned to the jar.

b.   After each draw, the selected candy is not returned to the jar.

c.   After each draw, the selected candy is returned to the jar and one new candy of the same color is added to the jar.

6.50 Refer to Exercise 6.49. Suppose the candy mix consists of 2500 candies, of which 700 are brown, 1000 are yellow, and 800 are other colors. Repeat parts **a–c** of Exercise 6.49 in this setting.

6.51 A market researcher intends to study the consumer preference for regular or decaffeinated coffee. Examine the plausibility of the model of Bernoulli trials in the following situations.

a.   One hundred customers are randomly selected, and each is asked to report the types of coffee (regular or decaffeinated) purchased on the five most recent occasions. Considering each purchase as a trial, this inquiry deals with 500 trials.

b.   Five hundred consumers are randomly selected, and each is asked about the most recent purchase of coffee. Here again the inquiry deals with 500 trials.

6.52 A backpacking party carries three emergency signal flares, each of which will light with a probability of .99. Assuming the flares operate independently of one another, find:

    a. The probability that at least one flare lights

    b. The probability that exactly two flares light

6.53 Consider Bernoulli trials with success probability $p = \frac{1}{4}$.

    a. Find the probability that four trials result in all failures.

    b. Given that the first four trials result in all failures, what is the conditional probability that the next four trials are all successes?

    c. Find the probability that the first success occurs on the fourth trial.

6.54 A new driver, who did not take driver's education, has probability .8 of passing the driver's license examination. If tries are independent, find the probability that the driver

    a. Will not pass in two attempts

    b. Will not pass in three attempts

6.55 A presentation designed to attract venture capital funds results either in a commitment (C) or in no commitment (N). As a first step, the presentation is to be given to two different investment groups. If both make a commitment to invest, no further presentations will be made. If exactly one group commits, then the presentation will be made to one more group. If neither of the first two groups commits, then the presentation will be made to two more groups.

    a. List the sample space.

    b. Assume that the groups make their decisions independently of one another and that the probability is $\frac{1}{3}$ that any one group will make a commitment. Assign probabilities to the elementary outcomes.

    c. Let X be the number of commitments. Obtain the probability distribution of X using the information in part **b.**

6.56 For each situation, state whether a binomial distribution holds for the random variable X. Also, identify the numerical values of n and p for those cases for which a binomial distribution is appropriate.

    a. Ten people are randomly selected, called, and asked to answer all the questions in a market survey. The random variable X denotes the number of people who answer all the questions.

    b. People are randomly selected and called until one is willing to answer all the questions in a market survey. The random variable X denotes the number of people called.

6.57 For each situation, state whether a binomial distribution holds for the random variable X. Also, identify the numerical values of n and p for those cases for which a binomial distribution is appropriate.

    a. A fair die is rolled 9 times, and X denotes the number of times 5 turns up.

    b. A fair coin is tossed until a head appears, and X denotes the number of tosses.

    c. A jar contains ten marbles; three are numbered 1, three are numbered 2, two are numbered 3, and two are numbered 4. Three marbles are drawn at random, one after another and with replacement. The random variable X denotes the count of the selected marbles that are numbered either 1 or 2.

d. Repeat the experiment described in part **c,** but let X denote the sum of the numbers on the selected marbles.

6.58 Construct a tree diagram for three Bernoulli trials—each trial yielding either a success (S) or a failure (F). Attach probabilities in terms of $p = P(S)$ and $q = 1-p = P(F)$ to each elementary outcome. Construct a table of the resulting binomial distribution for $n = 3$.

6.59 In each case, find the probability of x successes in n Bernoulli trials with success probability p for each trial.

a. $x = 2, n = 4, p = \frac{1}{3}$

b. $x = 3, n = 6, p = .25$

c. $x = 2, n = 6, p = .75$

6.60 Plot the probability histograms for the binomial distributions for $n = 5$ and $p = .2, .5, .8$. Locate the means on these histograms. Find $P(X \geq 4)$ for each of the three cases.

6.61 Suppose X has a binomial distribution with $n = 5$ and $p = .35$. Calculate the probabilities $f(x) = P(X = x)$ for $x = 0, 1, \ldots, 5$, and find:

a. $P(X \leq 2)$

b. $P(X \geq 2)$

c. $P(X = 2 \text{ or } 4)$

6.62 *Mode of a Probability Distribution.* The **mode** of a probability distribution is the most probable value of the random variable X. Determine the mode of the binomial distribution in Exercise 6.61.

6.63 Among people in the managerial or professional occupations in the United States, about 46% are female. For three people selected at random from these occupations, use the binomial distribution to find the probability that:

a. All three are female.

b. Exactly one is female.

6.64 Human error has been given as the primary cause of error in 70% of the accidents in an industry. Assuming errors are independent of one another, find the probability that human error will be the primary cause of error in

a. Fewer than 4 of the next 7 accidents

b. At least 4 of the next 7 accidents

c. Exactly 4 of the next 7 accidents

6.65 The probability is .3 that the downtime of an automated teller will exceed five minutes. If downtimes are independent, find the probability that:

a. The next 3 downtimes will all exceed five minutes.

b. Exactly 3 of the next 6 downtimes will exceed five minutes.

6.66 A coffee distributor claims that at most 10% of their privately labeled one-pound packages contain less than one pound of coffee. Fifteen packages will be randomly selected, and their contents weighed. The claim will be upheld if three or fewer of the packages weigh less than one pound; otherwise it will be rejected.

a.   What is the probability of rejecting the claim if, in fact, the population proportion of underweight packages is .10? (Assume the package weights are independent of one another.)

b.   What is the probability of rejecting the claim if the population proportion is .30?

6.67   The probability that a voter will believe a rumor about a politician is .2. Suppose that 20 voters will be told the rumor individually, and let X denote the number of these voters who believe the rumor.

a.   Find the probability that none of the 20 voters believes the rumor.

b.   Find the probability that 7 or more believe the rumor.

c.   Determine the mean and standard deviation of X.

6.68   The following table shows the proportions of managers in a large company cross-classified according to gender and level of management. Suppose that the selection of a manager is considered a trial and that the level "upper management" is a success.

	Upper Management	Not Upper Management
Male	.16	.36
Female	.09	.39

For each case of the following cases, identify the numerical value of p and find the required probability.

a.   Four managers are selected at random. What is the probability that none is from upper management?

b.   Four males are selected at random. What is the probability that none is from upper management?

c.   Two males and two females are selected at random. What is the probability that none are from upper management?

6.69   Refer to the table in Exercise 6.68, which shows the proportions of managers in a large company cross-classified according to gender and level of management. For parts **a–c,** find the mean and standard deviation of the specified random variable.

a. X is the number of upper-level managers in a random sample of 10 managers.

b. Y is the number of male upper-level managers in a random sample of 40 males.

c. Z is the number of female managers not at the upper level in a random sample of 40 females.

6.70   Find the mean and variance of the binomial distribution with

a. $n = 24$ and $p = .4$

b. $n = 24$ and $p = .6$

c. $n = 96$ and $p = .4$

6.71 For the binomial distribution with $n = 3$ and $p = .6$,

a. List the probability distribution, x, $f(x)$, in a table.

b. Calculate the mean and standard deviation numerically from the table in part **a** using the definitions in Section 6.4.

c. Check your results in part **b** with the formulas mean $= np$ and standard deviation $= \sqrt{npq}$.

6.72 *Geometric Distribution.* Suppose that, instead of performing a fixed number of Bernoulli trials, an investigator performs trials until the first success occurs. The number of successes is now fixed at 1, but the number of trials Y is now random. The random variable Y can assume any of the values 1, 2, 3, and so on with no upper limit.

a. Show that $f(y) = q^{y-1}p$, $y = 1, 2, \ldots$ (This probability distribution is known as the *geometric distribution*.)

b. Find the probability of 3 or fewer trials to the first success (S) if $p = P(S) = .5$.

6.73 *Poisson Distribution for Rare Events.* The Poisson distribution is often appropriate when the probability of an event (success) is small. It has served as a probability model for the number of calls per hour to an answering service, the number of incorrect invoices reported by customers, and the number of earthquakes in a year. The Poisson distribution also approximates the binomial distribution when the mean or expected value np is small but the number of trials n is large. The Poisson distribution with mean m has the form

$$f(x) = e^{-m}\frac{m^x}{x!} \quad \text{for } x = 0, 1, 2, \ldots$$

where e is the exponential number or 2.718 (rounded) and $x!$ is the number $x(x-1)(x-2)\cdots 1$ with $0! = 1$. Given $m = 3$ and $e^{-3} = .05$, find:

a. $P(X = 0)$

b. $P(X = 1)$

6.74 Let X have a binomial distribution with $n = 100$ and $p = .03$.

a. Evaluate $P(X = 0) = (1 - .03)^{100}$.

b. Evaluate $P(X = 1) = 100(.03)(1 - .03)^{99}$.

c. Compare your answers in parts **a** and **b** to those obtained in Exercise 6.73 using the Poisson distribution with $m = np = 100(.03) = 3$.

6.75 Given a binomial distribution.

a. If $n = 80$ and $p = .35$, find the mean and standard deviation.

b. If the mean is 54 and the standard deviation is 6, determine the numerical values of n and p.

6.76 (*Minitab or similar program recommended*) Many computer packages produce binomial probabilities. The single Minitab command

```
CDF;
BINOMIAL WITH N = 5, P = 0.25.
```

produces the following cumulative probabilities:

```
BINOMIAL WITH N = 5, P = 0.25000
     K P(X LESS OR = K)
     0          0.2373
     1          0.6328
     2          0.8965
     3          0.9844
     4          0.9990
     5          1.0000
```

The command

```
PDF;
BINOMIAL WITH N = 5, P = 0.25.
```

produces the individual probabilities

```
BINOMIAL WITH N = 5, P = 0.25000
        K          P(X = K)
        0           0.2373
        1           0.3955
        2           0.2637
        3           0.0879
        4           0.0146
        5           0.0010
```

Using the computer, calculate the following binomial probabilities:

a. $P(X \leq 8)$ and $P(X = 8)$ when $n = 12$ and $p = .64$

b. $P(10 \leq X \leq 15)$ when $n = 30$ and $p = .42$

6.6   STATISTICS IN CONTEXT

Probability distributions enable us to predict future outcomes that are subject to chance variation. As we discussed in the Statistics in Context section of Chapter 5, insurance companies must accurately account for chance variation when setting premiums. Previously, we considered the problem of setting life insurance premiums based on the information in life tables. In this section, we discuss the role probability distributions play in setting premiums for automobile insurance.

Because a few drivers make more than one claim a year, it is necessary to be able to estimate the probabilities associated with multiple claims. An insurance company reported the following damage-only claims from automobile accidents based on one year's experience:

Number of Damage-Only Claims

Number of Claims	Number of Policies
0	10226
1	1846
2	208
3	19
Total	12299

SOURCE: Data courtesy of James Hickman.

Converting the counts to relative frequencies, for instance, 10226/12299 = .831, we approximate the probability distribution of the number of damage-only claims.

Probability Distribution of the Number of Damage-Only Claims per Policy

Number of Claims x	Probability $f(x)$
0	.831
1	.150
2	.017
3	.002
Total	1.000

We have set the probability of four or more claims to 0 because that number did not appear in the large data set. We could also argue that some small probability should be assigned since the event is not impossible.

The population mean number of claims per policy is

$$\mu = E(X) = 0 \times .831 + 1 \times .150 + 2 \times .017 + 3 \times .002 = .190 \text{ claim}$$

Continuing with the calculation of the variance, we first obtain

$$\sum x^2 f(x) = 0^2 \times .831 + 1^2 \times .150 + 2^2 \times .017 + 3^2 \times .002 = .236$$

so the variance is

$$\sigma^2 = \text{var}(X) = .236 - (.190)^2 = .200 \text{ (claim)}^2$$

The standard deviation of the number of claims per policy is

$$\sigma = \text{sd}(X) = \sqrt{.200} = .447 \text{ claim}$$

More precise information can be obtained from claim experience that is separated according to the risk factor, the age of the insured.

Number of Damage-Only Claims

Number of Claims	Under Age 25 Number of Policies	Age 25 or Older Number of Policies	Total
0	4139	6087	10226
1	926	920	1846
2	116	92	208
3	11	8	19
Total	5192	7107	12299

Converting to separate relative frequencies for each age group (for example, 4139/5192 = .797 is the relative frequency of 0 claims for an insured driver under age 25), we obtain the following two approximate probability distributions:

Under Age 25		**Age 25 or Older**	
Probability Distribution of the Number of Damage-Only Claims per Policy		**Probability Distribution of the Number of Damage-Only Claims per Policy**	
Number of Claims x	**Probability f(x)**	**Number of Claims x**	**Probability f(x)**
0	.797	0	.856
1	.179	1	.130
2	.022	2	.013
3	.002	3	.001
Total	1.000	Total	1.000

For the under-25 age group, you may verify (see Exercise 6.78) that

$$\mu = E(X) = .229 \text{ claim}$$

and

$$\sigma^2 = \text{var}(X) = .285 - (.229)^2 = .233 \text{ (claim)}^2$$

Consequently,

$$\sigma = \text{sd}(X) = \sqrt{.233} = .483 \text{ claim}$$

For age 25 or older drivers, the mean number of claims per policy is

$$\mu = E(X) = .159 \text{ claim}$$

which is quite a bit smaller than the mean number of claims for the under-25 age group. The variance is

$$\sigma^2 = \text{var}(X) = .191 - (.159)^2 = .166 \text{ (claim)}^2$$

The standard deviation of the number of claims per policy for the 25 and over group is

$$\sigma = \text{sd}(X) = \sqrt{.166} = .407 \text{ claim}$$

To further emphasize the role of chance variation, suppose that the probability distribution for all policies is valid for next year and that the company will have 10,000 policies in effect. As we have seen, the mean number of claims on one policy is .190, so, for example, with two policies in effect we would expect $.190 + .190 = 2(.190) = .380$ claim. For three policies, the expected number of claims is $3(.190) = .570$, and, for 10,000 policies, the expected number of claims is $10,000(.190) = 1900$.

If the claims for different policies are independent, we can extend our results for the variance of the sum of two random variables and argue that the variances for the number of claims per policy can be added together. This gives $10,000(.200) = 2000$ for the variance of the number of claims with 10,000 policies. The standard deviation is $\sqrt{2000} = 44.72$ claims.

How much should the company charge for a premium? One might argue that, in addition to overhead and other administrative costs, a prudent company should charge enough to cover a total number of claims 3 standard deviations above the expected value. (As we have learned from our discussions in previous chapters, the expected value or mean plus or minus 3 standard deviations generally captures very nearly all of the data subject to chance variation.) Thus the company should be able to cover $1900 + 3(44.72) = 2034$ claims.

Planning to allow for 2034 claims might, at first sight, seem too restrictive a requirement to someone unfamiliar with chance behavior. But, it is precisely the kind of reasoning that must be followed if a company is to remain solvent and pay the legitimate claims of those drivers it insures.

Finally, insurance companies set premiums not only to allow for claims substantially above the expected number but also to protect themselves against various risk factors, like the age of the driver. (Our analysis in this section has shown that drivers under 25 years of age have a different claim history than those drivers 25 and over.) This recognition produces the various rate classes that govern the charges for automobile insurance.

6.7 CHAPTER SUMMARY

In this chapter, we have learned:

- A **random variable** associates a numerical value with each elementary outcome of an experiment.

  1. A **discrete random variable** takes either a finite number of values or an infinite number of values that can be arranged in a sequence that can be counted with the positive integers 1, 2,..., and so forth.

  2. A **continuous random variable** can assume any of the values in an interval of numbers.

- A **probability distribution** of the random variable is a list of the values of the random variable and their associated probabilities of occurrence. Often a formula can be used in place of a detailed list to specify the probability distribution of the random variable. A probability distribution is a model for describing variation in a population.

- The probability distribution of a discrete random variable X is given by the function $f(x_i) = P(X = x_i)$, $i = 1, 2, \ldots, k$, which satisfies:

  1. $f(x_i) \geq 0$ for each value x_i of X
  2. $\sum_{i=1}^{k} f(x_i) = 1$

- A **probability histogram** is a picture of a probability distribution. To draw a probability histogram, first mark the values of the random variable X on the horizontal axis. Next, with each value x_i as the center, construct a vertical rectangle whose area equals the probability $f(x_i)$.

- The **mean** of the discrete random variable X, or the **population mean,** is

$$E(X) = \mu = \sum (\text{Value} \times \text{Probability}) = \sum_{i=1}^{k} x_i f(x_i)$$

- The **variance** of X is abbreviated as var(X) and is also denoted by σ^2 (sigma squared). The **standard deviation** of X is the positive square root of the variance and is denoted by sd(X) or σ (sigma). The variance of X is also called the **population variance** and the standard deviation of X is frequently called the **population standard deviation.** In symbols,

$$\sigma^2 = \text{var}(X) = \sum_{i=1}^{k}(x_i - \mu)^2 f(x_i)$$

$$\sigma = \text{sd}(X) = +\sqrt{\text{var}(X)}$$

- To relate the mean and variance of $Y = a + bX$ to the mean and variance of X:

1. $\mu_{a+bX} = a + b\mu_X$
2. $\sigma_{a+bX}^2 = b^2\sigma_X^2$ so $\sigma_{a+bX} = |b|\sigma_X$

- The mean of the sum or difference of two random variables can be expressed as

$$\mu_{X+Y} = \mu_X + \mu_Y$$

$$\mu_{X-Y} = \mu_X - \mu_Y$$

- The variance of the sum or difference of two independent random variables can be expressed as

$$\sigma_{X+Y}^2 = \sigma_X^2 + \sigma_Y^2$$

$$\sigma_{X-Y}^2 = \sigma_X^2 + \sigma_Y^2$$

- A **probability model** is an assumed form of the probability distribution that describes the chance behavior for a random variable X. Probabilities are expressed in terms of relevant population quantities, called **parameters.**

- A **Bernoulli trial** has the following characteristics:

1. Each trial yields one of two outcomes, conveniently called success (S) and failure (F).
2. For each trial, the probabilitiy of success $P(S)$ is the same and is denoted by $p = P(S)$. The probability of failure is then $P(F) = 1 - p$ for each trial and is denoted by q, so that $p + q = 1$.
3. Trials are independent. The probability of success in a trial does not change given any information about the outcomes of other trials.

- If X represents the number of successes in n Bernoulli trials with probability p of success on any one trial, then X is called a **binomial random variable.**

- The **binomial probability distribution** is given by

$$f(x) = P(X = x) = \binom{n}{x}p^x q^{n-x}$$

where $q = 1 - p$ and $x = 0, 1, \ldots, n$.

1. For $p = .5$, the binomial distribution is symmetric. For $p > .5$, the binomial distribution is skewed to the left. For $p < .5$, the binomial distribution is skewed to the right.

2. The binomial distribution has

$$\text{Mean} = np$$
$$\text{Variance} = npq$$
$$\text{Standard deviation} = \sqrt{npq}$$

3. The **binomial table** gives the cumulative probabilities

$$P(X \le c) = \sum_{x=0}^{c} f(x)$$

for selected values of n and p.

6.8 IMPORTANT CONCEPTS AND TOOLS

CONCEPTS

Bernoulli trials, 300
Continuous random variable, 276
Cumulative probability, 306
Discrete random variable, 276
Expected value, 288
Mean of a probability distribution, 288
Parameter, 299

Probability distribution, 278
Probability histogram, 279
Probability model, 299
Random variable, 274
Standard deviation of a probability distribution, 291
Variance of a probability distribution, 291

TOOLS

Binomial distribution, 304
Binomial table, 306

6.9 KEY FORMULAS

The probability distribution of a discrete random variable X is given by the function

$$f(x_i) = P(X = x_i)$$

which satisfies:

1. $f(x_i) \ge 0$ for each value x_i, $i = 1, 2, \ldots, k$, of X
2. $\sum_{i=1}^{k} f(x_i) = 1$

For a discrete random variable:

Mean: $E(X) = \mu = \sum(\text{Value} \times \text{Probability}) = \sum_{i=1}^{k} x_i f(x_i)$

Variance: $\sigma^2 = \text{var}(X) = \sum_{i=1}^{k} (x_i - \mu)^2 f(x_i)$

Standard deviation: $\sigma = \mathrm{sd}(X) = +\sqrt{\mathrm{var}(X)}$

Alternative formula for variance: $\sigma^2 = \displaystyle\sum_{i=1}^{k} x_i^2 f(x_i) - \mu^2$

Let μ_X and σ_X^2 be the mean and variance of X, and let the random variable $Y = a + bX$. Then the mean and variance (standard deviation) of Y are related to the mean and variance (standard deviation) of X as follows:

$$\mu_{a+bX} = a + b\mu_X$$
$$\sigma_{a+bX}^2 = b^2 \sigma_X^2 \quad \text{so } \sigma_{a+bX} = |b|\sigma_X$$

Mean of the sum or difference of two random variables:

$$\mu_{X+Y} = \mu_X + \mu_Y$$
$$\mu_{X-Y} = \mu_X - \mu_Y$$

Variance of the sum or difference of two independent random variables:

$$\sigma_{X+Y}^2 = \sigma_X^2 + \sigma_Y^2$$
$$\sigma_{X-Y}^2 = \sigma_X^2 + \sigma_Y^2$$

The binomial distribution with n Bernoulli trials and success probability p is described by the equation

$$f(x) = P(X = x) = \binom{n}{x} p^x q^{n-x}$$

where $q = 1 - p$ and $x = 0, 1, \ldots, n$.

The binomial distribution has

$$\text{Mean} = np$$
$$\text{Variance} = npq$$
$$\text{Standard deviation} = \sqrt{npq}$$

where $q = 1 - p$.

Cumulative probability: $F(c) = P(X \le c) = \sum_{x=0}^{c} f(x)$

REVIEW EXERCISES

6.77   Refer to Section 6.6, Statistics in Context. Using the table with the probability distribution for the number of damage-only claims for the Under Age 25 group, evaluate the probability that the number of claims will be 2 or more. Evaluate this same probablity using the probability distribution for the Age 25 and Older group. Compare the two probabilities. Are older drivers likely to have fewer claims per policy? Explain.

6.78 Refer to Section 6.6, Statistics in Context. Using the table with the probability distribution for the number of damage-only claims for the Under Age 25 group, verify that $\mu = .229$ and $\sigma^2 = .233$.

6.79 Let X denote the difference (number of heads $-$ number of tails) in three tosses of a coin.

a. List the possible values of X.

b. List the elementary outcomes associated with each value of X.

6.80 Suppose there are two boxes: Box 1 contains 20 articles of which 6 are defective, and Box 2 contains 30 articles of which 5 are defective. One article is randomly selected from each box, and the selections from the two boxes are independent. Let X denote the total number of defective articles obtained.

a. List the possible values of X, and identify the elementary outcomes associated with each value.

b. Determine the probability distribution of X.

6.81 Refer to Exercise 6.80. Suppose the contents of the two boxes are pooled together into a single larger box. Two articles are then drawn at random and without replacement. Let W denote the number of defective articles in the sample. Obtain the probability distribution of W.

6.82 The probability distribution of a random variable X is given by the formula

$$f(x) = \frac{32}{31}\left(\frac{1}{2^x}\right) \quad \text{for } x = 1, 2, 3, 4, 5$$

a. Calculate the numerical value of $f(x)$ for each x, and make a table of the probability distribution.

b. Plot the probability histogram.

6.83 Given the following probability distribution:

x	$f(x)$
0	.3
1	.4
2	.3

a. Calculate μ.

b. Calculate σ^2 and σ.

c. Plot the probability histogram and locate μ.

6.84 Given the following probability distribution:

x	$f(x)$
2	.1
3	.3
4	.3
5	.2
6	.1

a.   Calculate $E(X)$.

b.   Calculate sd(X).

c.   Plot the probability histogram and locate the mean.

6.85   Refer to Exercise 6.84.

a.   List the x values that lie in the interval $\mu - \sigma$ to $\mu + \sigma$, and calculate $P(\mu - \sigma \leq X \leq \mu + \sigma)$.

b.   List the x values that lie in the interval $\mu - 2\sigma$ to $\mu + 2\sigma$, and calculate $P(\mu - 2\sigma \leq X \leq \mu + 2\sigma)$.

6.86   A student buys a lottery ticket for $1. For every 1000 tickets sold, a drawing will be held and two tickets will be selected at random with replacement. The owner of each ticket selected will receive a bicycle.

a.   What is the probability that the student will win a bicycle?

b.   If each bicycle is worth $260, determine the student's expected gain.

6.87   A lawyer believes that the probability is .3 that she can win a wage discimination suit. If she wins the case, she will make $15,000, but if she loses, she gets nothing.

a.   What is the lawyer's expected gain?

b.   If the lawyer has to spend $2500 preparing the case, what is her expected net gain?

6.88   The number of overnight emergency calls, X, to the answering service of a heating and air conditioning firm has the probabilities .05, .10, .15, .35, .20, and .15, for 0, 1, 2, 3, 4, and 5 calls, respectively.

a.   Find the probability of fewer than 3 calls.

b.   Determine $E(X)$ and sd(X).

6.89   A store conducts a lottery with 5000 cards. The prizes and corresponding numbers of cards are listed in the table. Suppose you have received one of the cards (presumably, selected at random), and let X denote your prize.

Prize	Number of Cards
$4000	1
1000	3
100	95
5	425
0	4476

a.   Obtain the probability distribution of X.

b.   Calculate the expected value of X.

c.   If you have to pay $6 to get a card, find the probability that you will lose money.

6.90   A roulette wheel has 38 slots: 18 red, 18 black, and 2 green. A gambler will play three times, each time betting $5 on red. The gambler gets $10 if red occurs and loses the bet otherwise. Let X denote the net gain of the gambler after three plays (for instance, if he loses all three times, then $X = -\$15$).

a. Obtain the probability distribution of X.

b. Calculate the expected value of X.

c. Will the expected net gain be different if the player alternates his bets between red and black? Explain.

6.91 Suppose that X can take the values 0, 1, 2, 3, and 4, and the probability distribution of X is *incompletely* specified by the function

$$f(x) = \frac{1}{4}\left(\frac{3}{4}\right)^x \quad \text{for } x = 0, 1, 2, 3$$

Find:

a. $f(4)$

b. $P(X \geq 2)$

c. $E(X)$

d. $sd(X)$

6.92 Recall that the cumulative probability is the sum of the probabilities at or below each value of X. Specifically,

$$F(c) = P(X \leq c) = \sum_{x \leq c} f(x)$$

or

$$\frac{\text{Cumulative distribution}}{\text{function at c}} = \frac{\text{Sum of probabilities}}{\text{of all values } x \leq c}$$

For the probability distribution given here

x	$f(x)$	$F(x)$
1	.07	.07
2	.12	.19
3	.25	
4	.28	
5	.18	
6	.10	

we calculate

$$F(1) = P(X \leq 1) = f(1) = .07$$
$$F(2) = P(X \leq 2) = f(1) + f(2) = .19$$

a. Complete the $F(x)$ column in the previous table.

b. Now cover the $f(x)$ column. From the $F(x)$ column, reconstruct the probability function $f(x)$. [*Hint:* $f(x) = F(x) - F(x-1)$.]

6.93 An internal auditor evaluating the revenue process checks to see whether (i) the order was properly billed, (ii) credit was approved before shipping, and (iii) the goods were shipped. Let X be the total number of mistakes in the billing process. For example, if the billing was not proper and credit approval was not obtained in advance, then $X = 2$. Suppose the possible values 0, 1,

2, and 3 of X have probabilities .90, .05, .03, and .02, respectively. Give the probability that, for a new order, the billing process will contain

a. 0 mistakes

b. At least 2 mistakes

c. 1 or 2 mistakes

6.94 Refer to the sales of hot tubs in Example 6.13. Suppose the profit is $300 for small units and $800 for large units. Determine

a. The expected profit

b. The standard deviation of total profit

6.95 According to *Fortune* magazine, 30% of the world's supply of gold comes from South Africa. If you order a gold brick, you might argue the probability that it came from South Africa is .3. The same would be true for the second brick and subsequent bricks that you order from the same dealer. Suppose success corresponds to South Africa as the source of a gold brick. Does ordering bricks from the same dealer represent a sequence of Bernoulli trials? Explain.

6.96 Is the model of Bernoulli trials plausible in each of the following situations? Identify any serious violations of the Bernoulli trials assumptions.

a. A dentist records the presence or absence of a cavity in each tooth in the lower jaw.

b. People applying for a driver's license will be recorded as writing right- or left-handed.

c. Each day of the first week of April is recorded as being either clear or cloudy.

d. The time it takes to be served is observed for each person taking a seat at a lunch counter.

e. Cars selected at random will or will not pass a state safety inspection.

6.97 Give an example (different from those in Exercise 6.96) of repeated trials with two possible outcomes where:

a. The model of Bernoulli trials is reasonable.

b. The condition of independent trials is violated.

c. The condition of equal $P(\text{success})$ is violated.

6.98 For each of the following situations, is a binomial distribution reasonable for the random variable X? Justify your answer.

a. A multiple-choice examination has 10 questions, each of which has 5 suggested answers. A student selects each answer to the questions by guessing (that is, one answer is chosen at random from the 5 possibilities). Let X be the number of marked answers that are wrong.

b. A multiple-choice examination has two parts: Part I has 8 problems, each with 5 suggested answers, and Part II has 10 problems, each with 4 suggested answers. A student selects each answer by guessing. Let X denote the number of problems that the student answers correctly.

c. Twenty married couples are interviewed about exercise. Let X be the number of people (out of the 40 people interviewed) who are joggers.

6.99 A basketball team scores 40% of the time it gets the ball. Find the probability that the first basket occurs on the team's third possession. (Assume independent trials.)

6.100 According to *Road and Track* magazine, 51% of the cars starting Grand Prix races in 1990 finished the race. A team will start two cars in a race next year. Using .51 as the probability that a car will finish a race, and assuming independent trials, find the probability that at least one of the two cars will finish the race.

6.101 A school newspaper claims that 80% of the students support its view on a campus issue. A random sample of 20 students is selected, and 12 students agree with the newspaper. Determine $P(12 \text{ or fewer agree})$ if 80% of the students agree with the newspaper's view. Is the newspaper's claim plausible? Explain.

6.102 For a binomial distribution with $n = 14$ and $p = .4$, calculate:
a. $P(4 \leq X \leq 9)$ b. $P(4 < X \leq 9)$ c. $P(4 < X < 9)$
d. $E(X)$ e. $sd(X)$

6.103 Using the binomial table,
a.   List the probability distribution for $n = 5$ and $p = .4$.
b.   Plot the probability histogram for the distribution in part **a.**
c.   Calculate $E(X)$ and $var(X)$ from the entries in the list in part **a.**
d.   Calculate $E(X) = np$ and $var(X) = npq$, and compare your answers with those in part **c.**

6.104 Using the binomial table, find the probability of:
a.   Three successes in 8 trials when $p = .4$
b.   Seven failures in 16 trials when $p = .6$
c.   Three or fewer successes in 9 trials when $p = .4$
d.   More than 12 successes in 16 trials when $p = .7$
e.   The number of successes between 8 and 13 (both inclusive) in 16 trials when $p = .6$

6.105 Using the binomial table, find the probability of:
a.   Three or fewer successes for $p = .1, .2, .3, .4,$ and $.5$ when $n = 12$
b.   Three or fewer successes for $p = .1, .2, .3, .4,$ and $.5$ when $n = 18$

6.106 Jones claims to have extrasensory perception (ESP). To test this claim, a psychologist shows Jones five cards that carry different pictures. Then Jones is blindfolded, and the psychologist selects one card and asks Jones to identify the picture. This process is repeated 16 times. Suppose, in reality, that Jones has no ESP and selects a picture by guessing. What is the probability that Jones' guesses are
a.   Correct at most 3 times?
b.   Wrong at least 10 times?

6.107 Refer to Exercise 6.106. Find the expected value and standard deviation of the number of correct identifications.

After reading this chapter, you should be able to:

- Distinguish probability models for continuous random variables from those for discrete random variables.

- Discuss the concepts of probability density curves and probability density functions.

- Use probability density curves to evaluate probabilities for continuous random variables.

- Evaluate probabilities for normal random variables and use the normal distribution to approximate the binomial distribution.

- Construct normal-scores plots and use them to assess the degree to which data correspond to a normal distribution.

- Transform the measurement scale for data whose distribution is clearly nonnormal to give data that are more nearly normally distributed.

- Discuss the difference between a population parameter and a sample-based quantity called a statistic.

- Understand the concept of a sampling distribution.

- Discuss the nature of the sampling distribution of the sample average $\overline{X}$, including its mean and variance.

- Discuss and use the central limit theorem.

CHAPTER SEVEN

Continuous Random Variables and Sampling Distributions

7.1 INTRODUCTION

Outcomes that can be represented by the values of a discrete random variable are relatively easy to handle. Since a discrete random variable assumes only some isolated values, usually integers representing a count, probabilities can be directly assigned to these values. Probability statements and summary measures, like the mean and standard deviation, can be obtained with straightforward numerical calculations.

However, as we have seen, many variables of interest in business are essentially continuous; that is, they can take on any value in an interval. Examples that we have mentioned previously include the time it takes for equipment to fail, weight of a package, the rate of return on an investment, and paper strength. Manipulating continuous random variables is not quite as easy as manipulating discrete random variables, although the computer makes the mathematical work much less forbidding.

What does it mean to assign probabilities to the values of a continuous random variable? There are so many of them in an interval (too many to be counted with the positive integers) that the chance of any particular value occurring must be incredibly small. How do we deal with a bunch of extremely small numbers? The answer is, we do not. It makes more sense with continuous random variables to assign probabilities to (perhaps small) intervals rather than to single values. For example, when we ask for the probability that next year's rate of return will be .0345682117..., we are really asking for the probability that next year's rate of return will be around .035, say, from .033 to .037, since we never record rates of return to an unlimited number of decimal places.

7.2   PROBABILITY MODEL FOR A CONTINUOUS RANDOM VARIABLE

Our development of probability models for continuous random variables, and their use in assigning probabilities, draws on our discussion of density histograms in Chapter 2. In Section 2.5, we talked about grouping data into class intervals and recording the relative frequencies associated with these intervals. We mentioned that as the number of observations in a data set increases, histograms can be constructed with class intervals having smaller widths. A relative frequency histogram can be converted to a density histogram (see Table 2.3) with the following properties:

1.   The total area under the density histogram is 1.

2.   For two points a and b representing the left- and right-hand endpoints, respectively, of some class, the proportion of measurements in the interval a to b is the *area* under the histogram above this interval.

In the remaining discussion, let's consider the transaction time X for an employee to complete a call and enter the order in the computer system at a large mail order firm. How do we think about the distribution of X? Initially, suppose that we have recorded 100 transaction times (in seconds), grouped the data into 10 class intervals each 10 seconds in length, and constructed the density histogram shown in Figure 7.1(a). Figure 7.1(a) shows, for example, that the interval from 175 to 195 seconds contains a proportion .28 + .25 = .53 of the measurements.

Next, suppose that the number of measurements is increased to 5000 and that they are grouped into class intervals of 2.5 seconds. The resulting density histogram appears in Figure 7.1(b). This is a refinement of the histogram in Figure 7.1(a) because it is constructed from a larger set of observations and exhibits densities for finer class intervals. (Narrowing the class interval without increasing the number of observations would obscure the overall shape of the distribution.)

Continuing in this manner, we can imagine further refinements of the density histogram with larger numbers of observations and smaller class intervals. (In pursuing this conceptual argument, we ignore the difficulty that results from the limited accuracy

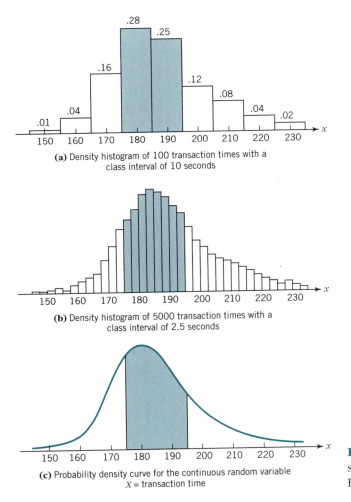

(a) Density histogram of 100 transaction times with a class interval of 10 seconds

(b) Density histogram of 5000 transaction times with a class interval of 2.5 seconds

(c) Probability density curve for the continuous random variable X = transaction time

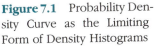

Figure 7.1 Probability Density Curve as the Limiting Form of Density Histograms

of the measuring device.) As the density histogram is refined, the jumps between consecutive rectangles tend to flatten out and the top of the histogram approximates the shape of a smooth curve, as illustrated in Figure 7.1(c).

Interpreting probability as long-run relative frequency, the curve obtained as the limiting form of the density histogram represents the manner in which the total probability 1 is distributed over the interval of possible values of the random variable X. This curve is called the *probability density curve* of the continuous random variable X. The mathematical function $f(x)$ whose graph produces this curve is called the **probability density function** of the continuous random variable X.

We have already encountered plots of probability density functions. The bell-shaped normal density curve was introduced in Chapter 2 and, at that time, we referred to this curve as the normal distribution. We paid particular attention to determining areas under a normal density curve. As we shall see, these areas can be interpreted as probabilities. The normal density curve, for example, gives the distribution of probabilities over intervals of values of a particular continuous random variable.

The properties that we listed previously for a density histogram are shared by a probability density curve that is, after all, a limiting smooth form of a histogram. Also, since a histogram can never go below the x-axis, it must be the case that $f(x)$ is nonnegative for all x.

The **probability density function** $f(x)$ describes the distribution of probability for a continuous random variable. It has these properties:

1. The total area under the probability density curve is 1.
2. $P(a \leq X \leq b)$ = area under the probability density curve between a and b
3. $f(x) \geq 0$ for all x

Unlike the description of a discrete probability distribution, the probability density $f(x)$ for a continuous random variable does not give a nonzero probability for $X = x$. Instead, a probability density function relates the probability of an interval (a, b) of values to the area under the density curve in a strip over this interval. A single point x interpreted as an interval with a width of 0, supports 0 area, so $P(X = x) = 0$.

Intuitively, although any value in an interval is theoretically possible (with a measuring instrument of unlimited accuracy), the chance of getting a specific value is vanishingly small. Consider again the transaction time example. The statement $P(X = 185) = 0$ might seem shocking. This does not mean that no transaction time can be recorded to last exactly 185 seconds. It does mean that with a device that measures transaction times to the nearest second, 185 is indistinguishable from all numbers in an interval immediately surrounding it, say, 184.5 to 185.5 seconds. However, the area under the probability density curve from 184.5 to 185.5 is no longer 0, so it makes sense to talk about the probability associated with an interval of values surrounding 185. As the interval around 185 gets smaller and smaller, the probability associated with the interval gets smaller and smaller, eventually becoming 0. This is consistent with the impossible chance of distinguishing 185 from numbers very, very, very close to it.

With a continuous random variable, the probability that $X = x$ is *always* 0. It is meaningful to speak only about the probability that X lies in an interval.

When determining the probability of an interval a to b, we need not be concerned if either or both endpoints are included in the interval. Since the probabilities of $X = a$ and $X = b$ are both equal to 0,

$$P(a \leq X \leq b) = P(a < X \leq b) = P(a \leq X < b) = P(a < X < b)$$

In contrast, these probabilities may not be equal for a discrete random variable.

For continuous random variables, probabilities are given by areas under probability density curves. Fortunately, for important distributions like the normal, areas have been extensively tabled. Most tables list the entire area to the left of each point. To obtain the probabilities of other intervals, we apply the following rules.

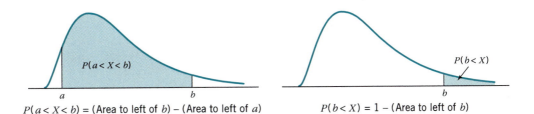

$P(a < X < b) = $ (Area to left of b) $-$ (Area to left of a) $P(b < X) = 1 - $ (Area to left of b)

A probability model for a continuous random variable is specified by giving the mathematical form of the probability density function. If a fairly large number of observations of a continuous random variable is available, we may try to approximate the top of the staircase silhouette of the density histogram by a mathematical curve.

In the absence of a large data set, we may tentatively assume a reasonable model that may have been suggested by data from a similar source. Of course, any model obtained in this way must be closely scrutinized to verify that it conforms to the data at hand.

FEATURES OF A CONTINUOUS DISTRIBUTION

As is true for density histograms, the probability density curves of continuous random variables could possess a wide variety of shapes. A few of these are illustrated in Figure 7.2. The term *skewed* is used to indicate a long tail in one direction.

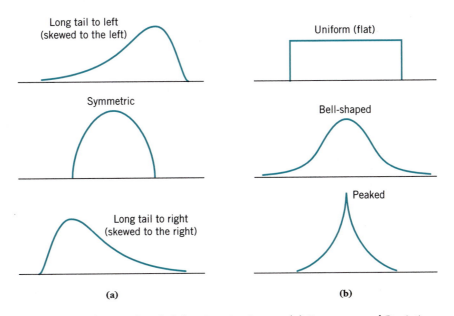

Figure 7.2   Shapes of Probability Density Curves. (a) Symmetry and Deviations from Symmetry. (b) Different Peakedness

A continuous random variable X also has a mean, or expected value $E(X)$, as well as a variance and standard deviation. Their interpretations are the same as in the case of discrete random variables, but their formal definitions involve integral calculus and are therefore not pursued here. However, it is instructive to see in Figure 7.3 that the mean $\mu = E(X)$ marks the center of gravity or balance point of the probability mass. The median, another measure of center, is the value of X that divides the area under the density curve into halves.

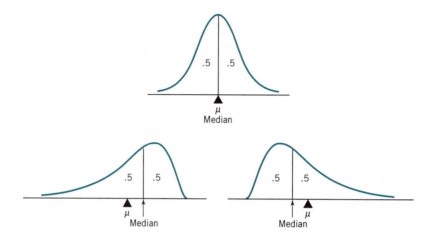

Figure 7.3   Mean as the Balance Point and Median as the Point of Equal Division of Probability Mass

In addition to the median, we can also define the quartiles and other percentiles of a continuous probability distribution.

The **population 100pth percentile** is an x value that has area p to its left and area $1 - p$ to its right.

$$\text{Lower (first) quartile} = \text{25th percentile}$$
$$\text{Second quartile (or median)} = \text{50th percentile}$$
$$\text{Upper (third) quartile} = \text{75th percentile}$$

The quartiles for two distributions are shown in Figure 7.4.

As we mentioned in Chapter 2, it is often convenient to convert random variables to a dimensionless scale. Recall that the standardized variable

$$Z = \frac{X - \mu}{\sigma} = \frac{\text{Variable} - \text{Mean}}{\text{Standard deviation}}$$

has no units and has mean 0 and standard deviation 1. If the probability density function for X is known, the probability density function for Z can be determined.

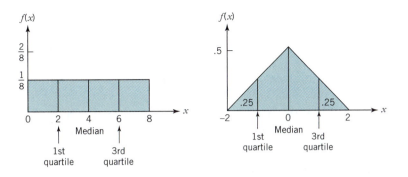

Figure 7.4   Quartiles of Two Continuous Distributions

EXERCISES

7.1   Which of the functions sketched in (a)–(d) in the accompanying figure could be a probability density function for a continuous random variable? Why or why not?

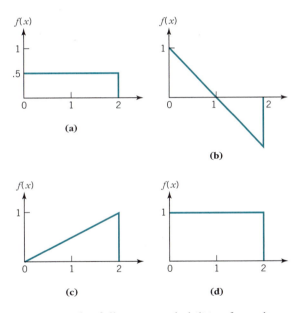

7.2   Determine the following probabilities from the curve diagrammed in Exercise 7.1(a):

a. $P(0 < X < .5)$ b. $P(.5 < X < 1)$

c. $P(1.5 < X < 2)$ d. $P(X = 1)$

7.3   For the curve graphed in Exercise 7.1(c), which of the two intervals is assigned a higher probability: $(0 < X < .5)$ or $(1.5 < X < 2)$? Why?

7.4   Determine the median and the quartiles for the probability distribution given in Exercise 7.1(a).

7.5   Determine the median and the quartiles for the probability distribution given in Exercise 7.1(c).

7.6   Determine the 10th percentile of the curve in Exercise 7.1(a).

7.7   If a student is more likely to be late than on time for the 1:20 P.M. accounting class:

   a.   Determine whether the median of the student's arrival time is earlier than, equal to, or later than 1:20 P.M.

   b.   On the basis of the information provided, can you determine whether the mean of the student's arrival time distribution is earlier than, equal to, or later than 1:20 P.M.? Discuss.

7.8   Which of the distributions in Figure 7.3 are compatible with the following statements?

   a.   The distribution of starting salaries for information system specialists has a mean of $35,000, but half of the newly employed specialists make less than $30,000 annually.

   b.   In spite of recent large increases in salary, half of all professional football players still make less than the mean salary.

7.9   Find the standardized variable Z if X has:

   a.   Mean 15 and standard deviation 4

   b.   Mean -9 and standard deviation 7

   c.   Mean 151 and variance 25

7.10   Find the standardized variable Z if X has:

   a.   Mean 8 and standard deviation 2

   b.   Mean 350 and standard deviation 25

   c.   Mean -67 and variance 100

7.11   The heights of males 18–24 years old have a mean of 70 inches and a standard deviation of 2.8 inches. The heights of females 18–24 years old have a mean of 65 inches and a standard deviation of 2.4 inches (*Statistical Abstract of the United States 1990*, Table 201).

   a.   Find the standardized variable for the heights of the males.

   b.   Find the standardized variable for the heights of the females.

   c.   For a person 66 inches tall, find the value of the standardized variable for the males.

   d.   For a person 66 inches tall, find the value of the standardized variable for the females. Compare your answer with part **c** and discuss.

7.3   THE NORMAL DISTRIBUTION REVISITED

In Chapter 2, we introduced the normal distribution and learned how to find areas under the bell-shaped normal curve using Table 3 in Appendix B. Recall that a normal distribution is completely specified once its mean, μ, and standard deviation, σ, are known. Consequently, we also introduced the shorthand notation $N(\mu, \sigma)$ to represent a normal distribution with a given mean and standard deviation.

An area under a normal density curve over some interval of values can now be interpreted as a probability. Moreover, you will remember that if the random variable X has a $N(\mu, \sigma)$ distribution, then the standardized variable $Z = (X - \mu)/\sigma$ has a $N(0, 1)$ distribution. This fact enables us to calculate any normal probability from the table of standard normal probabilities.

EXAMPLE 7.1   Review of Normal Probability Calculations

The number of calories in a salad on the lunch menu is normally distributed with mean 200 and standard deviation 5. Find the probability that the salad you select will contain:

a.   More than 208 calories

b.   Between 190 and 200 calories

Solution and Discussion.   Let X denote the number of calories in a salad. Then X has a $N(200, 5)$ distribution and the standardized variable

$$Z = \frac{X - \mu}{\sigma}$$

has a $N(0, 1)$ distribution.

a.   Since the z value corresponding to $x = 208$ is

$$z = \frac{208 - 200}{5} = 1.6$$

we have

$$P(X > 208) = P\left(\frac{X - 200}{5} > \frac{208 - 200}{5}\right)$$

$$= P(Z > 1.6)$$
$$= 1 - P(Z \le 1.6)$$
$$= 1 - .9452 = .0548$$

or approximately 5%.

b.   The z values corresponding to $x = 190$ and $x = 200$ are

$$\frac{190 - 200}{5} = -2.0 \quad \text{and} \quad \frac{200 - 200}{5} = 0$$

respectively. Consequently,

$$P(190 \le X \le 200) = P(-2.0 \le Z \le 0)$$
$$= .5 - .0228 = .4772$$

or approximately 48%.

EXAMPLE 7.2   Rates of Return and the Normal Distribution

Table 7.1 contains the monthly rates of return on the S&P 500 Stock Index for a period of $n = 47$ consecutive months. The February rate of return, .0410, for example, is calculated by subtracting the value of the S&P 500 Index at the end of January from its value at the end of February, and then dividing by the end of January number. In other words, the monthly rate of return measures the relative change in the index over a particular month.

TABLE 7.1   Monthly Rates of Return (read across) on the S&P 500 Index

—	.0410	−.0339	.0094	.0032	.0423	−.0054
−.0394	.0390	.0256	−.0191	.0146	.0687	−.0294
.0206	.0489	.0345	−.0080	.0847	.0154	−.0066
−.0255	.0164	.0212	−.0713	.0085	.0240	−.0273
.0880	−.0089	−.0052	−.0991	−.0525	−.0067	.0582
.0245	.0407	.0651	.0220	.0003	.0379	−.0491
.0439	.0195	−.0193	.0118	−.0449	.1058	

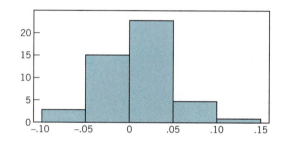

The frequency histogram of the rates of return in Table 7.1 approximates a normal distribution. The near normality of S&P monthly returns is further confirmed by the normal-scores plot in Section 7.5. Expressed in terms of percentage rate of return, a future rate of return X might be modeled as a normal random variable with mean 1.03% and standard deviation 4.16%. Assuming this model holds today,

a. Calculate the probability the monthly rate of return twelve months from now will be between 1.5% and 5.5%.

b. What proportion of the future monthly returns are smaller than 0?

c. Find the 30th percentile of the rates of return distribution.

Solution and Discussion.

a. In terms of the standardized variable

$$Z = \frac{X - 1.03}{4.16}$$

we must find the probability

$$P\left(\frac{1.5 - 1.03}{4.16} < Z < \frac{5.5 - 1.03}{4.16}\right) = P(.113 < Z < 1.075)$$

Interpolating in the standard normal table, we obtain the probability .8588 − .5450 = .3138.

b. The z value corresponding to 0 is

$$z = \frac{0 - 1.03}{4.16} = -.248$$

so

$$P(X \leq 0) = P(Z \leq -.248) = .4021$$

Thus, approximately 40% of the rates of return would be less than 0. In other words, the rate 0 nearly locates the 40th percentile.

c. We first find the 30th percentile on the z-scale and then convert it to the x-scale. Interpolating by eye in the standard normal table, we find

$$P(Z \leq -.524) = .30$$

The standardized value $z = -.524$ corresponds to

$$x = 1.03 + 4.16(-.524) = -1.150$$

Therefore, the 30th percentile of the rates of return distribution is approximately −1.15. The minus sign implies a loss of 1.15%.

EXERCISES

7.12 The time for workers to assemble a component for an automobile steering mechanism has a normal distribution with a mean of 25 seconds and a standard deviation of 2.2 seconds. For a randomly selected worker, find the probability that the time to assemble a component will be

a. Greater than 29 seconds

b. Longer than 24 seconds but less than 27 seconds

7.13 The time it takes a symphony orchestra to play Beethoven's *Ninth Symphony* has a normal distribution with a mean of 64.3 minutes and a standard deviation of 1.15 minutes. The next time it is played, what is the probability that it will take between 62.5 minutes and 67.7 minutes?

7.14 The weights of apples harvested at an orchard are normally distributed with a mean of 5 oz and a standard deviation of 1.1 oz. What is the probability that the next apple, selected at random for inspection, will weigh over 4 oz?

7.15 The monthly rate of return on an investment has a normal distribution with a mean of .5% and a standard deviation of .2%.

a. What is the probability that next month's rate of return will be larger than .75%?

b. Find the probability that the next two monthly rates of return will both be larger than .6%. (Assume the two rates of return are independent.)

c. Suppose conditions remain stable so the same distribution applies for a long period of time. What proportion of the monthly rates of return exceed .75%?

7.16 According to government reports, the heights of adult male residents of the United States are approximately normally distributed with a mean of 69.0 inches and a standard deviation of 2.8 inches. If a clothing manufacturer wants to limit her market to the central 80% of the adult male population, what range of heights should be targeted?

7.17 At a plant making high-quality laser printing paper, an instrument measuring paper weight has an error of measurement that is normally distributed with a mean of .05 and a standard deviation of 1.5. That is, in repeated measurements, the distribution of the difference (Recorded weight − True weight) is $N(.05, 1.5)$.

a. What percentage of the measurements overstate the true weight?

b. Suppose a measurement error is regarded as serious when the recorded value differs from the true value by more than 2.8. What percentage of the measurements will be serious errors?

c. Find the 80th percentile of the error distribution.

7.18 The time for an emergency medical squad to arrive at a sports center at the edge of town is distributed as a normal variable with $\mu = 17$ minutes and $\sigma = 3$ minutes.

a. Determine the probability that the time to arrival is:

  i. More than 22 minutes

  ii. Between 13 and 21 minutes

  iii. Between 15.5 and 18.5 minutes

b. Determine the arrival time interval of length 1 minute that has the highest probability.

7.19 The force required to puncture a cardboard mailing tube with a sharp object has a $N(32, 4)$ distribution. What is the probability that a tube will puncture if it is struck by

a. A 25-pound blow with the object?

b. A 35-pound blow with the object?

7.4   THE NORMAL APPROXIMATION TO THE BINOMIAL DISTRIBUTION

The binomial distribution, introduced in Chapter 6, associates probabilities with the number of successes X in n independent trials of a random experiment with two mutually exclusive outcomes, success and failure. When the success probability p is not too near 0 or 1, and the number of trials is large, areas under an appropriate normal distribution serve as good approximations to binomial probabilities. Bypassing the mathematical proof, we concentrate on illustrating the manner in which this approximation works.

Figure 7.5 shows the binomial distributions for $p = .4$ and the number of trials $n = 5$, 12, and 25. Notice how the distribution begins to assume the distinctive bell shape as n increases. Even though the binomial distribution with $p = .4$ is not symmetric, the lack of symmetry becomes negligible for large n.

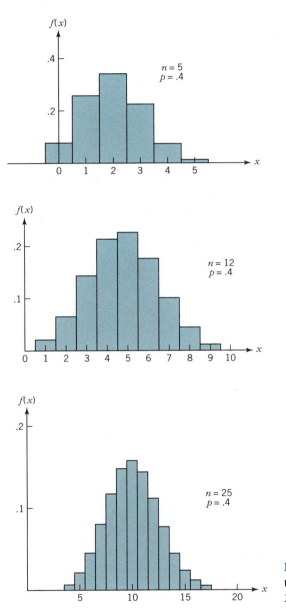

Figure 7.5   The Binomial Distribution for $p = .4$ and $n = 5$, 12, and 25

How do we approximate the binomial probability

$$f(x) = P(X = x) = \binom{n}{x} p^x (1 - p)^{n-x}$$

by a normal probability? The normal probability assigned to a single value x is 0. However, when x is an integer, we can mark off an interval, centered on x, of length 1 and assign a probability to this interval. Figure 7.6 contains a schematic display of the normal probability assigned to the interval $x - \frac{1}{2}$ to $x + \frac{1}{2}$. This normal probability will be used to approximate the binomial probability above. The addition and subtraction of $\frac{1}{2}$ is called the **continuity correction.**

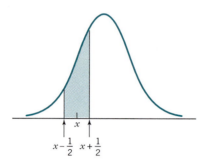

Figure 7.6   The Continuity Correction

For $n = 15$ and $p = .4$, the binomial distribution gives

$$P(X = 7) = .787 - .610 = .177$$

Recall from Chapter 6 that the binomial distribution has

$$\mu = np = 15(.4) = 6 \quad \text{and} \quad \sigma = \sqrt{np(1-p)} = \sqrt{15(.4)(.6)} = 1.897$$

To approximate the binomial probability, we select a normal distribution with the same mean, $\mu = 6$, and standard deviation, $\sigma = 1.897$, and compute the probability assigned to the interval $7 - \frac{1}{2}$ to $7 + \frac{1}{2}$. Thus

$$P(6.5 < X < 7.5) = P\left(\frac{6.5 - 6}{1.897} < \frac{X - 6}{1.897} < \frac{7.5 - 6}{1.897}\right)$$

$$\approx P(.264 < Z < .791) = .7855 - .6041 = .1814$$

Considering that $n = 15$ is small, the approximation .1814 is reasonable compared to the exact value .177. More important, the accuracy of the approximation improves as n increases.

The normal approximation to the binomial applies when n is large and the success probability p is not too close to 0 or 1. The binomial probability of $(a \leq X \leq b)$ is approximated by the normal probability over the same interval $(a \leq X \leq b)$ where the endpoints are included in both intervals. (For simplicity, we will ignore the continuity correction when we approximate binomial probabilities for an *interval of values.*)

The Normal Approximation to the Binomial

When np and $n(1-p)$ are both large, say, greater than 15, the binomial distribution is well approximated by the normal distribution having mean $\mu = np$ and standard deviation $\sigma = \sqrt{np(1-p)}$. That is,

$$Z = \frac{X - np}{\sqrt{np(1-p)}} \quad \text{is approximately } N(0,1).$$

EXAMPLE 7.3   Approximating Binomial Probabilities

Let X have a binomial distribution with $p = .6$ and $n = 150$. Approximate the following probabilities:

a. X is between 82 and 101 inclusive.

b. X is greater than 97.

Solution and Discussion.   We first calculate the mean and standard deviation of X.

$$\text{Mean} = np = 150(.6) = 90$$

$$\text{Standard deviation} = \sqrt{np(1-p)} = \sqrt{150(.6)(.4)} = 6$$

Since $np = 90$ and $n(1-p) = 60$ are both large, the standardized variable

$$Z = \frac{X - 90}{6}$$

is approximately normally distributed with mean 0 and standard deviation 1.

a.   The event $(82 \leq X \leq 101)$ includes both endpoints. The normal approximation is then

$$P(82 \leq X \leq 101) = P\left(\frac{82 - 90}{6} \leq \frac{X - 90}{6} \leq \frac{101 - 90}{6}\right)$$

$$= P(-1.33 \leq Z \leq 1.83)$$

Using the normal table, we get

$$P(-1.33 \leq Z \leq 1.83) = .9664 - .0918 = .8746$$

The approximate value of the binomial probability $P(82 \leq X \leq 101)$ is .8746.

b. Notice for $(X > 97)$ that 97 is not included so, from a normal approximation perspective, $(X \geq 98)$ is the event of interest. Consequently,

$$P(X \geq 98) = P\left(\frac{X - 90}{6} \geq \frac{98 - 90}{6}\right)$$

$$= P(Z \geq 1.33) = 1 - .9082 = .0918$$

The normal approximation to the binomial gives $P(X > 97) = .0918$.

EXAMPLE 7.4   An Advertising Application

Based on a recent nationwide poll, a seller of printed advertisements estimates that 56% of all adults usually open all the mail they receive. If this is still the current rate at which adults open mail, what is the probability that, in a random sample of 1000 adults, the number who usually open all of their mail will be

a. Less than 541?
b. 570 or more?

Solution and Discussion.   Let X be the number of people who usually open all of their mail among the random sample of 1000 adults. With the assumption that the proportion of the population that usually opens all of their mail is .56, X has a binomial distribution with $n = 1000$ and $p = .56$. Since

$$np = 1000(.56) = 560 \quad \text{and} \quad \sqrt{np(1 - p)} = \sqrt{1000 \times .56 \times .44} = 15.697$$

the distribution of X is approximately $N(560, 15.697)$.

a. Because X is a count, the event $[X < 541]$ is the same as the event $[X \leq 540]$. Using the normal approximation,

$$P(X \leq 540) \approx P\left(Z \leq \frac{540 - 560}{15.697}\right) = P(Z \leq -1.27) = .1020$$

There is about a .10 probability that fewer than 541 adults in the sample usually open all of the mail they receive.

b. Similarly,

$$P(X \geq 570) \approx P\left(Z \geq \frac{570 - 560}{15.697}\right) = P(Z \geq .64) = 1 - .7389 = .2611$$

The probability is about .26 that 570 or more adults in the sample usually open all their mail.

EXAMPLE 7.5   An Accounting Application

An accountant decides to sample paid invoices to perform a control evaluation of the cash disbursement system. Initially, he will only count the total number of payments made in error and disregard the type of error. (The types of error are: The goods were not received, the invoice amount was incorrect, or the bill was paid previously.) At the worst, the accountant expects only about 6% of the payments to be made in error. Discuss the normal approximation to the distribution of X = number of payments made in error when

a.   100 invoices are selected at random for the sample.

b.   500 invoices are selected at random for the sample.

Solution and Discussion.   We assume the probability that a particular invoice contains an error is $p = .06$.

a.   When $n = 100$ and $p = .06$, $np = 100(.06) = 6$ is too small for the normal approximation to give accurate results. Instead, we must use computer software to calculate the exact binomial probabilities associated with values of X.

b.   With $n = 500$, $np = 500(.06) = 30$ and $n(1 - p) = 500(.94) = 470$ are both large, so the normal approximation can be employed even though p is close to 0. The very large sample size compensates for the small "success" probability to give large values for np and $n(1 - p)$. For this situation, the normal approximation works well.

Remark

If the object is to calculate binomial probabilities, the best practice today is to evaluate them directly using an established statistical software package. However, the fact that

$$\frac{X - np}{\sqrt{np(1 - p)}} \quad \text{is approximately } N(0, 1)$$

when np and $n(1 - p)$ are both large is important. Since the normal density function closely approximates the binomial distribution under certain circumstances, it will be used in later chapters when we discuss inferences about proportions.

EXERCISES

7.20   Let the number of successes X have a binomial distribution with $n = 25$ and $p = .6$.

   a.   Find the exact probabilities of:

$$X = 17 \qquad 11 \leq X \leq 18 \qquad 11 < X < 18$$

   b.   Find the probabilities of each event in part **a** using the normal approximation to the binomial distribution.

7.21   Let the number of successes X have a binomial distribution with $n = 25$ and $p = .7$.

a. Find the exact probabilities of
$$X = 15 \qquad 13 \le X \le 19 \qquad 13 < X < 19$$

b. Find the probabilities of each event in part **a** using the normal approximation to the binomial distribution.

7.22 Let the number of successes X have a binomial distribution with $n = 300$ and $p = .25$. Approximate the probability of

a. $X = 80$

b. $X \le 65$

c. $68 \le X \le 89$

7.23 Let the number of successes X have a binomial distribution with $n = 200$ and $p = .75$. Approximate these probabilities:

a. $X = 140$

b. $X \le 160$

c. $137 \le X \le 162$

7.24 Determine whether the normal approximation to the binomial distribution is appropriate in each of the following situations.

a. $n = 90, p = .23$

b. $n = 100, p = .02$

c. $n = 71, p = .4$

d. $n = 120, p = .97$

7.25 Determine whether the normal approximation to the binomial distribution is appropriate in each of the following situations.

a. $n = 500, p = .33$ b. $n = 10, p = .5$

c. $n = 400, p = .01$ d. $n = 200, p = .98$

e. $n = 100, p = .61$

7.26 Copy Figure 7.5 and add the standard scale $z = (x - np)/\sqrt{np(1 - p)}$ beneath the x-axis for $n = 5$, 12, and 25. Notice how the distributions center on 0 and that most of the probability lies between $z = -2$ and $z = 2$.

7.27 The median age of residents in the United States is 32.3 years. If a survey of 200 residents is taken, approximate the probability that at least 110 will be under 32.3 years of age.

7.28 The unemployment rate in a city is 7.9%. A random sample of 300 persons is selected from the labor force. Approximate the probability that:

a. Fewer than 18 unemployed persons are in the sample.

b. More than 30 unemployed persons are in the sample.

7.29 Of the customers visiting the stereo section of a large electronics store, only 25% make a purchase. If 70 customers visit the stereo section tomorrow, approximate the probability that more than 20 will make a purchase.

7.30 The weekly amount spent by a company for travel has approximately a normal distribution with mean $2500 and standard deviation $400. If $3000 is budgeted to cover next week's travel expenses, what is the probability that the actual expenses will exceed the budgeted amount?

7.31 Refer to Exercise 7.30. How much should be budgeted each week so that the probability is only .05 that the actual expenses will exceed the budgeted amount?

7.32 In a large midwestern university, 30% of the students live in apartments. If 200 students are randomly selected, find the probability that the number of them living in apartments will be between 50 and 75 inclusive.

7.33 According to a study of mobility, 35.2% of United States residents in the age group 20–24 years moved to different housing in 1988 from where they lived in 1987 (*Statistical Abstract of the United States 1990,* Table 25). If the same percentage holds today, determine the approximate probability that, in a random sample of 100 residents 20–24 years old, there will be 41 or more persons who have moved in the past year.

7.34 At one large company, it is estimated that 20% of all expense claims for business lunches are incorrectly documented.

    a. If a random sample of 300 claims are audited, approximate the probability that the number of incorrectly documented claims will be between 49 and 71 inclusive.

    b. After 300 claims are sampled, suppose that 72 claims are found to be incorrectly documented. Does this contradict the hypothesis that 20% of all claims are incorrectly documented? Give a reason for your answer based on the (small) probability of obtaining 72 or more incorrect claims in a sample of 300 claims.

7.5   CHECKING THE PLAUSIBILITY OF A NORMAL DISTRIBUTION AND TRANSFORMATIONS TO NEAR NORMALITY

Does a normal distribution serve as a reasonable model for a population of observations? This question is of interest because many commonly used statistical procedures require that the parent population be nearly normal. If a normal distribution is tentatively assumed to be a plausible model, we must still check this assumption once the sample data are in hand.

Although they involve judgment, graphical procedures are useful in detecting serious departures from normality. Stem-and-leaf plots, boxplots, and density histograms can be checked for lack of symmetry and outliers. In addition, the bell-shaped appearance of the normal density can be checked by comparing the proportions of sample observations in the intervals $\bar{x} \pm s$, $\bar{x} \pm 2s$, and $\bar{x} \pm 3s$ with the corresponding areas under the normal curve provided by the 68–95–99.7 rule (see Chapter 2).

A more effective graphical procedure for checking normality is the **normal-scores plot.** The normal-scores plot provides an assessment of the assumption of normality even for moderate sample sizes that are not large enough to construct histograms. However, as a practical matter, at least 15 to 20 observations are necessary to reveal meaningful patterns in the data. To simplify the discussion, we introduce the ideas behind a normal-scores plot in the context of a small sample of size 4.

The term **normal scores** refers to an idealized sample from a standard normal distribution. Basically, normal scores are the particular quantiles, the z values, that divide the standard normal distribution into intervals of equal probability. For example, the $n = 4$ normal scores are the z values that divide the standard normal distribution into 5 segments of equal probability $\frac{1}{5} = .2$. In general, n normal scores divide the $N(0, 1)$ distribution into $n + 1$ equal-probability intervals. The normal scores, denoted by q_1, q_2, q_3, and q_4, for a sample of size 4 are shown in Figure 7.7.

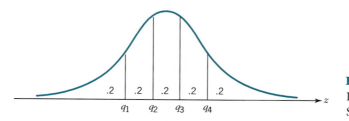

Figure 7.7 The $N(0, 1)$ Distribution and Normal Scores for $n = 4$

Using Table 3 in Appendix B, we find that

$$q_1 = -.84$$
$$q_2 = -.25$$
$$q_3 = .25$$
$$q_4 = .84$$

Once the normal scores are determined, they can be paired with the ordered sample observations. A plot of these ordered pairs should resemble a straight line if a normal distribution is an appropriate model for the data. This follows because any normal variable X is linearly related to a standard normal variable Z by the expression $X = \mu + \sigma Z$. Here μ and σ are the mean and standard deviation, respectively, of the presumed normal population from which the sample observations were selected.

To construct a normal-scores plot:

1. Order the sample data from smallest to largest.
2. Obtain the normal scores.
3. Pair the ith largest observation with the ith largest normal score, and plot the pairs in a graph.

EXAMPLE 7.6 Constructing a Normal-Scores Plot

Suppose a random sample of size $n = 4$ has produced the observations $x_1 = 68$, $x_2 = 82$, $x_3 = 44$, and $x_4 = 75$. Construct a normal-scores plot.

Solution and Discussion. The ordered observations and the normal scores are given in Table 7.2, and the normal-scores plot of these data is shown in Figure 7.8.

How do we interpret the plot? Let μ and σ denote the mean and standard deviation of the population from which the sample was obtained. The normal scores that are the idealized z-observations can then be converted to the x-scale by the usual relation $x = \mu + \sigma z$. The actual x-observations and the corresponding idealized observations are given in Table 7.3.

TABLE 7.2

Normal Scores	Ordered Sample
$q_1 = -.84$	44
$q_2 = -.25$	68
$q_3 = .25$	75
$q_4 = .84$	82

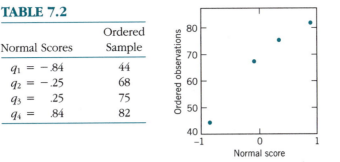

TABLE 7.3

Observed x Values	Idealized x Values
44	$\mu + \sigma q_1$
68	$\mu + \sigma q_2$
75	$\mu + \sigma q_3$
82	$\mu + \sigma q_4$

Figure 7.8   Normal-Scores Plot for Data in Table 7.2

If the population were indeed normal, we would expect the two columns in Table 7.3 to be close. In other words, a plot of the observed x values versus the normal scores would produce a straight-line pattern with the intercept of the line indicating the value of μ and the slope of the line indicating σ. The pattern in Figure 7.8 is reasonably straight, although with $n = 4$ observations, it is difficult to argue convincingly for or against normality.

A straight-line pattern in a normal-scores plot supports the plausibility of a normal model. A curved appearance indicates a departure from normality.

Normal-scores plots are easily constructed using a computer. The Minitab commands

```
NAME C1 'OBS' C2 'NSCORE'
NSCORE C1 C2
PLOT C1*C2
```

will create a normal-scores plot of the data in column C1. Most statistical software programs, including Minitab, use slightly different variants of the normal scores described here, but the plots are very similar if 20 or more observations are plotted.

EXAMPLE 7.7   **Normal-Scores Plot of S&P 500 Index**

Monthly rates of return of the S&P 500 Index are given in Table 7.1 (page 336). Construct a normal-scores plot of these data.

Solution and Discussion.   The normal-scores plot is shown in Figure 7.9 (page 348).

The straight-line pattern is very evident. The underlying distribution of monthly returns is nearly normal.

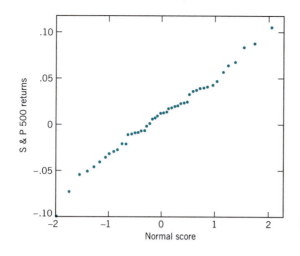

Figure 7.9 Normal-Scores Plot of S&P 500 Monthly Returns

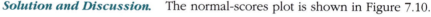

EXAMPLE 7.8   Normal-Scores Plot of Insurance Claims

Construct a normal-scores plot of the insurance claims data set given in Table 2.5.

Solution and Discussion.   The normal-scores plot is shown in Figure 7.10.

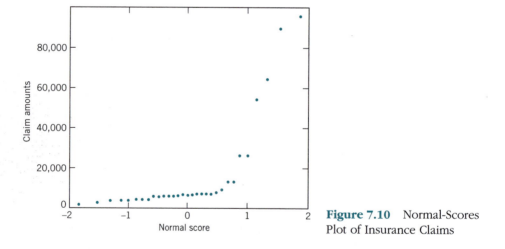

Figure 7.10 Normal-Scores Plot of Insurance Claims

There is a very strong bend in the normal-scores plot. These data are far from normal. The 6 to 8 largest claims are too large.

TRANSFORMING OBSERVATIONS TO NEAR NORMALITY **(OPTIONAL)**

A valid application of many powerful techniques of statistical inference, especially those suited to small or moderate samples, requires that the population distribution be reasonably close to normal. When the sample measurements appear to have been taken from a population that departs drastically from normality, an appropriate conversion to a new variable may bring the distribution close to normal. Efficient techniques can then be applied to the converted or *transformed* data, whereas their application to the original data would have been questionable. Inferential methods requiring the assumption of normality are discussed in later chapters. The goal of our discussion here is to show how a transformation can improve the approximation to a normal distribution.

There is no rule for determining the best transformation in a given situation. For any data set that does not have a symmetric histogram, we consider a variety of transformations.

Some Useful Transformations

Make large values larger: Make large values smaller:

$$x^3 \quad x^2 \qquad\qquad \sqrt{x} \quad \sqrt[4]{x} \quad \ln(x) \quad \frac{1}{x}$$

You may recall that $\ln(x)$ is the natural logarithm. Fortunately, computers easily calculate and order the transformed values, so that several transformations in a list can be quickly tested. Note, however, that the observations must all be positive if we intend to use $\sqrt{x}$, $\sqrt[4]{x}$, and $\ln(x)$.

The selection of a good transformation is largely a matter of trial and error. If the data set contains a few numbers that appear to be detached far to the right, $\sqrt{x}$, $\sqrt[4]{x}$, $\ln(x)$, or negative powers of x will pull these stragglers closer to the other observations and should be considered.

EXAMPLE 7.9   Transformation of Turnaround Times to Process Insurance Claims

The turnaround times in days required to process health insurance claims are given in Table C.4, Appendix C. These data will be discussed more extensively in the Statistics in Context section. At this point,

a. Make a normal-scores plot of these data.

b. Make a normal-scores plot of the natural logarithms of the turnaround times.

c. Approximate the probability that the turnaround time will be greater than 14 days using a normal probability calculation based on part **b**.

Solution and Discussion.

a. The normal-scores plot of the original data is shown in Figure 7.11(a) on page 350. There is a very strong bend in the plot, indicating that these data are far from normal. A histogram of the data is shown in Figure 7.12(a). Note that this histogram is strongly skewed to the right.

b. The normal-scores plot of the natural logarithms of the data is shown in Figure 7.11(b). The pattern is nearly that of a straight line, and the approximation to normality is much better. This is reinforced by the histogram of the natural logarithms displayed in Figure 7.12(b).

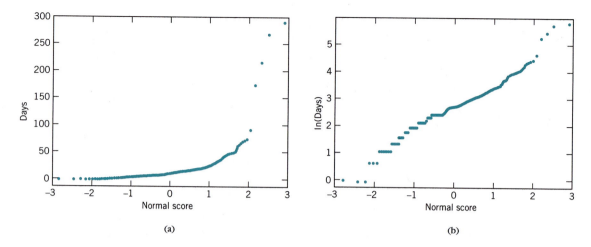

Figure 7.11   (a) Normal-Scores Plot of Turnaround Times. (b) Normal-Scores Plot of Natural Logarithms of Turnaround Times

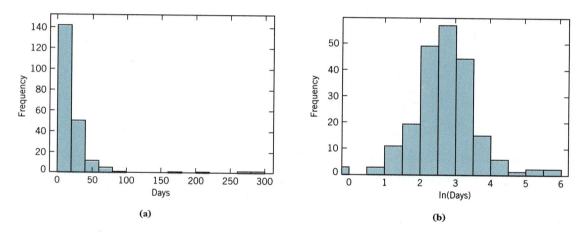

Figure 7.12   (a) Histogram of Turnaround Times. (b) Histogram of Natural Logarithms of Turnaround Times

c.   A computer calculation provides the sample mean, 2.700, and the sample standard deviation, .873, for $Y = \ln(\text{turnaround time})$. On the log scale, more than 14 days becomes more than $\ln(14) = 2.639$. Assuming then that Y has a $N(2.700, .873)$ distribution, the z value is

$$z = \frac{2.639 - 2.700}{.873} = -.070$$

and the required probability is $P(Z > -.070) = .528$. About 53% of the claims take longer than 14 days to process.

EXAMPLE 7.10   **Transformation of Microwave Oven Radiation Data**

The amounts of radiation emitted through the closed doors of $n = 42$ microwave ovens were given in Table 2.8. Summary plots of the original data and the radiation measurements after taking their fourth roots (square root twice) are shown in Panels 2.1 and 2.2 in the Statistics in Context section of Chapter 2. Construct normal-scores plots of the original measurements and the transformed (fourth roots) measurements.

Solution and Discussion.   The normal-scores plots of the original and transformed microwave radiation data are displayed in Figure 7.13.

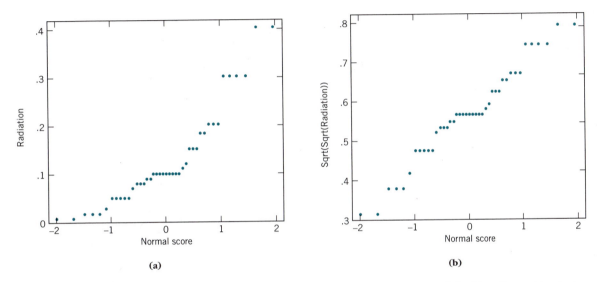

Figure 7.13   (a) Normal-Scores Plot of Radiation Data. (b) Normal-Scores Plot of the Transformed Radiation Data

The normal-scores plot of the radiation data has an upward bend. These data are nonnormal and, as the plots in Panel 2.1 indicate, are skewed to the right.

The normal-scores plot of the transformed radiation measurements is fairly straight, indicating that these data are nearly normal (see the stem-and-leaf plot and boxplot in Panel 2.2). However, there is some curvature near the center of this normal-scores plot. This curvature indicates that there are a few more transformed observations around the middle of the distribution than we would expect from a normal distribution.

EXERCISES

7.35   The normal scores for a sample of size 10 are

$$-1.34 \quad -.91 \quad -.60 \quad -.35 \quad -.11 \quad .11 \quad .35 \quad .60 \quad .91 \quad 1.34$$

In one study of bus routes, the investigator recorded the number of riders who paid cash as opposed to those who used a pass. Make a normal-scores plot of the following numbers of riders who paid cash during 10 weekday mornings on one bus route in Madison, Wisconsin.

27	13	22	11	18	19	14	23	24	25

7.36 Refer to Exercise 7.35. Make a normal-scores plot of the square roots of the numbers of riders who paid cash.

7.37 A sample of size $n = 10$ has produced the ordered observations

7	10	11	13	17	20	21	27	32	34

Construct a normal-scores plot of these data. Interpret the plot.

7.38 (*Minitab or similar program recommended*) The R&D expenditures as a percentage of sales for 12 of the world's largest automobile manufacturers are given in Example 2.2. Construct a normal-scores plot of these data. Interpret the plot.

7.39 (*Minitab or similar program recommended*) The 1984 national 800-meter dash records for women are given in Example 2.3. Construct a normal-scores plot of these data. Interpret the plot.

Nat800m.dat

7.40 (*Minitab or similar program recommended*) Consider the actual costs of $n = 36$ construction projects in Example 2.13.

ConsCost.dat

a. Construct and interpret the normal-scores plot of these data.

b. Let x denote a construction cost. Transform these data by taking their square root, $\sqrt{x}$. Construct and interpret the normal-scores plot of the transformed data.

c. Refer to part **b.** Transform the cost data by taking their natural logarithms, $\ln(x)$. Show and interpret the normal-scores plot of the transformed data.

d. Given the results in parts **a–c,** which representation of the data appears to be best approximated by a normal curve? Explain.

7.41 (*Optional*) (*Minitab or similar program recommended*) Consider the $n = 31$ death claim amounts given in Table 2.5. A normal-scores plot of these insurance claims is shown in Figure 7.10 (page 348). Let x denote a claim amount.

DeathClm.dat

a. Try several transformations of x, including $\sqrt{x}$, $\ln(x)$, $\frac{1}{\sqrt{x}}$, and others, to see whether you can improve on the normal-scores plot in Figure 7.10.

b. Remove the four largest claim amounts from the data set. Generate a normal-scores plot of the remaining $n = 27$ observations. Interpret the plot. Try several transformations of the data to see whether you can improve the "straightness" of the normal-scores plot for the reduced data set.

7.42 (*Optional*) (*Minitab or similar program recommended*) Make a normal-scores plot of the media revenue data in Table C.7, Appendix C, and comment on any departure from normality. If necessary, try some simple transformations of the data to see whether you can improve the approximation to normality as judged by a normal-scores plot.

SportFrn.dat

7.43 (*Optional*) (*Minitab or similar program recommended*) Make a normal-scores plot of the current interest rate data for life insurance policies in Table C.5, Appendix C. Comment on any departure from normality. If necessary, try some simple transformations of the data to see whether you can improve the approximation to normality as judged by a normal-scores plot.

LifeIns.dat

SportFrn.dat

7.44   (*Optional*) (*Minitab or similar program recommended*) Make normal-scores plots of the gate revenues of the Major League Baseball and National Football League franchises in Table C.7, Appendix C. If necessary, try some simple transformations of the data to see whether you can improve the approximations to normality as judged by normal-scores plots.

HealthTu.dat

7.45   (*Optional*) (*Minitab or similar program recommended*) Refer to the turnaround times for handling health insurance claims in Table C.4, Appendix C. Delete the four largest observations that are greater than 100 days. Construct a normal-scores plot for the reduced data set. Compare the result with the normal-scores plot in Figure 7.11(a). Is the nonnormality of the full data set due primarily to the effect of the four largest observations? Explain.

HealthTu.dat

7.46   (*Optional*) (*Minitab or similar program recommended*) Refer to Exercise 7.45. After dropping the four largest observations, make a normal-scores plot of

a.   ln (turnaround time)

b.   (turnaround time)$^{.2}$

Which transformed variable appears to be more nearly normal? Discuss.

7.47   (*Optional*) Refer to Exercise 7.46. The transformed variable (turnaround time)$^{.2}$ is nearly normal with mean $\mu = 1.719$ and standard deviation $\sigma = .263$. Determine the probability that the turnaround time is greater than 14 days or, equivalently, that the transformed time is greater than $(14)^{.2}$. Compare the result with the probability in Example 7.9. Which probability do you think is "correct?" Explain. (See also Statistics in Context, Section 7.8.)

7.6   STATISTICS AND THEIR SAMPLING DISTRIBUTIONS

The ideas underlying inferences are at the heart of statistical inquiry. These ideas enable an investigator to argue from the particular observations that occur in a sample to general conclusions about the population. These generalizations, or inferences, are founded on an understanding of the way in which variation in the population is transmitted, via sampling, to variation in sample quantities like the sample mean. The way in which population variation is transmitted to sample quantities is the subject of this section. This is often a difficult concept to grasp but it forms the basis for many of the methods to follow.

When we collect data to make decisions, we are typically interested in learning about some numerical feature of the population. Examples include the proportion of the population with a particular characteristic, the mean and standard deviation of the population, the population total, or some other numerical measure of location or variability.

> **Parameter:**   A numerical feature of the population

The true value of a population parameter is ordinarily an unknown constant. It can be correctly determined only by a census or complete study of the population. The concepts of statistical inference arise whenever a census is impossible or not practically feasible.

When only a sample is available, our inferences about a population parameter must depend on an appropriate sample-based quantity. Although a parameter refers to some numerical characteristic of the population, a sample-based quantity is called a statistic.

Statistic: A numerical valued function of the sample observations

---

The sample mean

$$\overline{X} = \frac{X_1 + X_2 + \cdots + X_n}{n}$$

is a statistic because its numerical value can be computed once the sample data consisting of the values of $X_1, X_2, \ldots, X_n$ are available. Likewise, the sample median and the sample standard deviation are also sample-based quantities, so each is a statistic.

A sample-based quantity (statistic) then must serve as our source of information about the value of a parameter. Three points are crucial:

1. Because a sample is only a part of the population, the numerical value of a statistic cannot be expected to give us the exact value of the parameter.

2. The observed value of a statistic depends on the particular sample that happens to be selected.

3. There will be some variability in the values of a statistic over different occasions of sampling.

To illustrate these points, consider the following example. An urban planner wishes to study the average commuting distance of workers from their homes to their principal places of business. Here the appropriate population consists of the commuting distances of all the workers in the city. The mean of this finite but large and unrecorded set of numbers is the population mean, which we denote by μ. Suppose we want to learn about the parameter μ by collecting data from a sample of workers. Consequently, 80 workers are randomly selected (think about how this might be done), and the sample mean of their commuting distances is found to be $\overline{x} = 8.3$ miles. Clearly, the population mean μ cannot be claimed to be exactly 8.3 miles. Why?

If one were to observe another random sample of 80 workers, the sample mean would almost surely be something other than 8.3 miles. Because the commuting distances are different (vary) in the population of workers, the sample mean would also vary on different occasions of sampling. Different samples contain, in general, different workers. In practice, of course, we observe only one sample and correspondingly a single value of the sample mean, such as $\overline{x} = 8.3$. However, the variability of the $\overline{x}$ values in repeated sampling contains the clue as to how precisely we can hope to determine μ from the information about $\overline{x}$.

The previous example illustrates the important concept that the value of a statistic varies in repeated sampling. In other words, a statistic is itself a random variable and, consequently, has its own probability distribution. The variability of a statistic in repeated sampling is described by this probability distribution.

> **Sampling distribution:** The probability distribution of a statistic

The qualifier *sampling* indicates that the distribution is conceived in the context of repeated sampling from a population. We often drop the qualifier and simply say the distribution of a statistic.

Although in any given situation we are limited to one sample and the corresponding single value for a statistic, over different samples the statistic varies according to its sampling distribution. The sampling distribution of a statistic is determined from the distribution $f(x)$ that governs the population, and it also depends on the sample size n. The next example illustrates the sampling distribution of $\overline{X}$ when the sample size is 2 and the population consists of 4 units.

EXAMPLE 7.11   A Sampling Distribution of $\overline{X}$

A population consists of 4 housing units. The value of X, the number of telephones per unit, is indicated by the large number in each of the schematic houses shown here.

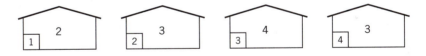

Consider drawing a random sample of size 2 with replacement. That is, we select a unit at random, replace it, and select another unit at random. Let X_1 and X_2 denote the value of X obtained on the first and second drawing, respectively. Find the sampling distribution of $\overline{X} = (X_1 + X_2)/2$.

Solution and Discussion.   The population distribution of X is given in Table 7.4 (page 356), which simply reflects the fact that the value 3 for X occurs in $\frac{1}{2}$ of the population, whereas the values 2 and 4 occur in $\frac{1}{4}$ of the population of housing units.

Because each unit is equally likely to be selected, the observation X_1, the result of the first draw, has the same distribution as given in Table 7.4. Since the sampling is with replacement, the second observation X_2 also has this same distribution.

We identify the units in the sample by their house numbers given in boxes. The sixteen possible samples (x_1, x_2), which are equally likely, are given in Table 7.5 along with the sample mean $\overline{x}$.

Six of the sixteen samples give $\overline{x} = 3$, so the probability that $\overline{X} = 3$ is $\frac{6}{16}$. Continuing in this manner, we get the probability distribution of $\overline{X}$ given in Table 7.6.

The distribution in Table 7.6 refers to the behavior of $\overline{X}$ in repeated samples of size 2 with replacement. If the sampling is repeated a large number of times, in about $\frac{4}{16}$ or 25% of the cases the sample mean will equal 2.5. It will equal 4 about $\frac{1}{16}$ or 6.25% of the time.

TABLE 7.4 Population Distribution

x	$f(x)$
2	$\dfrac{1}{4}$
3	$\dfrac{1}{2}$
4	$\dfrac{1}{4}$

TABLE 7.5 The Possible Samples and the Value of $\overline{X}$

First House	Second House	(x_1, x_2)	$(x_1 + x_2)/2 = \overline{x}$
1	1	(2,2)	2
1	2	(2,3)	2.5
1	3	(2,4)	3
1	4	(2,3)	2.5
2	1	(3,2)	2.5
2	2	(3,3)	3
2	3	(3,4)	3.5
2	4	(3,3)	3
3	1	(4,2)	3
3	2	(4,3)	3.5
3	3	(4,4)	4
3	4	(4,3)	3.5
4	1	(3,2)	2.5
4	2	(3,3)	3
4	3	(3,4)	3.5
4	4	(3,3)	3

TABLE 7.6 The Probability Distribution of $\overline{X} = (X_1 + X_2)/2$

Value of $\overline{X}$	Probability
2.0	$\dfrac{1}{16}$
2.5	$\dfrac{4}{16}$
3.0	$\dfrac{6}{16}$
3.5	$\dfrac{4}{16}$
4.0	$\dfrac{1}{16}$

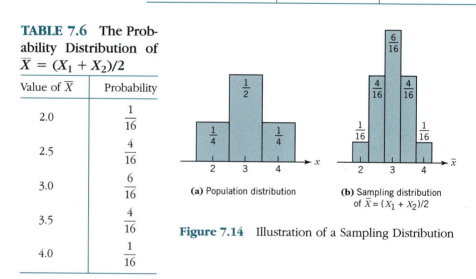

(a) Population distribution

(b) Sampling distribution of $\overline{X} = (X_1 + X_2)/2$

Figure 7.14 Illustration of a Sampling Distribution

The relationship between the population distribution and the sampling distribution of $\overline{X}$ is illustrated graphically in Figure 7.14. Notice that the two distributions have the same mean, 3, but the sampling distribution of $\overline{X}$ is more tightly concentrated about this mean. As we shall see, this is no accident.

The key conditions for a random sample can be summarized as follows. *The observations $X_1, X_2, \ldots, X_n$ are a random sample of size n from the population distribution if they result from independent selections and each has the same distribution as the population.*

Suppose, in the context of Example 7.11, that the population consists of 400 housing units of which 200 have 3 phones, 100 have 2 phones, and 100 have

4 phones. When sampling two units from this larger population, it would make very little difference whether we replace the first unit selected before selecting the second. To a high degree of approximation, each observation would still have the same distribution—namely, $P(X = 3) = .5$ and $P(X = 2) = P(X = 4) = .25$, the distribution that characterizes the population.

When the population is very large and the sample size relatively small, it is inconsequential whether a unit is replaced before the next unit is selected. Therefore, under these conditions too, we will refer to the observations as a random sample.

Because of variation in the population, random samples vary and so does the value of $\overline{X}$ or any other statistic. We illustrated the notion of a sampling distribution using a small population with only three values of X and a small sample of size $n = 2$. The calculations leading to a sampling distribution get more tedious and extensive when the population has many values of X and n is large. The basic procedure, however, remains the same. Once the population and sample size are specified:

1. List all possible samples of size n.

2. Calculate the value of the statistic for each sample.

3. List the distinct values of the statistic obtained in Step 2. Calculate the corresponding probabilities by identifying all the samples that give the same value of the statistic.

Sampling distributions in complicated cases can often be derived with the help of advanced mathematical methods. Alternatively, sampling distributions can frequently be approximated using a computer. The idea is to program the computer to draw a random sample and calculate the statistic. This procedure is then repeated a large number of times, and a relative frequency or density histogram is constructed from the values of the statistic. This histogram is an approximation to the sampling distribution of the statistic (see Exercise 7.54).

EXERCISES

7.48 Identify each of the following as either a parameter or a statistic.

    a. Sample standard deviation

    b. Sample range

    c. Population 10th percentile

    d. Sample first quartile

    e. Population median

7.49 Identify the parameter, statistic, and population when they appear in each of the following statements.

    a. There were 11 persons who served on the U.S. Supreme Court in the decade of the 1980s.

    b. A survey of 1000 minority persons living in Chicago revealed that 185 were out of work.

    c. Out of a sample of 100 females, 46 said they usually read advertisements that they receive in the mail.

7.50 A random sample of size 2 will be selected, with replacement, from the set of numbers (1, 3, 5).

   a. List all possible samples and evaluate $\bar{x}$ for each.

   b. Determine the sampling distribution of $\overline{X}$.

7.51 A random sample of size 2 will be selected, with replacement, from the set of numbers (2, 4, 6).

   a. List all possible samples and evaluate $\bar{x}$ and s^2 for each.

   b. Determine the sampling distribution of $\overline{X}$.

   c. Determine the sampling distribution of S^2.

7.52 A consumer wants to study the size of strawberries for sale at the Farm Patch. If a sample of size 4 is taken from the top of a basket of berries, will the berry sizes be a random sample? Explain.

7.53 To determine the time a cashier spends on a customer in the express lane, the manager decides to record the time at the checkout for a customer who is being served at 10 past the hour, 20 past the hour, and so on. Will measurements collected in this manner be a random sample of the times a cashier spends on a customer? Explain.

CapExFa.dat

7.54 (*Minitab or similar program recommended*) Refer to the capital expenditures on machinery and equipment for 588 farms given in Table 4.2 (see Exercise 4.20).

   a. Determine the mean and standard deviation for this population of capital expenditures. Construct a relative frequency histogram for the expenditure data.

   b. Select 50 simple random samples of size $n = 10$ from the population of capital expenditures. Calculate the sample mean $\bar{x}$ for each of the 50 samples. Calculate the mean of the sample means and the standard deviation of the sample means. Compare these numbers with the mean and standard deviation in part **a.**

   c. Construct a relative frequency histogram for the sample means in part **b.** (This histogram approximates the sampling distribution of $\overline{X}$ for samples of size $n = 10$ from the population of capital expenditures.)

   d. Compare the histograms in parts **a** and **b.** Comment on their shapes, locations, and spreads.

7.7 DISTRIBUTION OF THE SAMPLE MEAN AND THE CENTRAL LIMIT THEOREM

Inferences about the population mean are of prime practical importance, since the mean often represents the center of a population. Not surprisingly, inference procedures are based on the sample mean

$$\overline{X} = \frac{X_1 + X_2 + \cdots + X_n}{n}$$

and its sampling distribution. Consequently, we now explore the sampling distribution of $\overline{X}$ in some detail. Our discussion will highlight the role of the normal distribution as a useful approximation to the sampling distribution of $\overline{X}$.

To proceed, we must relate the sampling distribution of $\overline{X}$ to the population from which the random sample was selected. Using our customary notation, let

$$\text{Population mean} = \mu$$
$$\text{Population standard deviation} = \sigma$$

The mean and standard deviation of the sampling distribution of $\overline{X}$ are then determined in terms of μ and σ.

Mean and Standard Deviation of $\overline{X}$

The distribution of the sample mean, based on a random sample of size n, has

$$E(\overline{X}) = \mu \quad (= \text{Population mean})$$

$$\text{var}(\overline{X}) = \frac{\sigma^2}{n} \quad \left(= \frac{\text{Population variance}}{\text{Sample size}} \right)$$

$$\text{sd}(\overline{X}) = \frac{\sigma}{\sqrt{n}} \quad \left(= \frac{\text{Population standard deviation}}{\sqrt{\text{Sample size}}} \right)$$

These results suggest the following. First, the distribution of $\overline{X}$ is centered at the population mean in the sense that expectation serves as a measure of the center of the distribution. Second, the standard deviation of $\overline{X}$ is the population standard deviation divided by the square root of the sample size. Thus the variability of the sample mean is governed by two factors: the population variability σ and the sample size n. Large variability in the population induces large variability in $\overline{X}$, thus making the sample information about μ less dependable. However, this can be countered by choosing a large n. For instance, with $n = 100$, the standard deviation of $\overline{X}$ is $\sigma/\sqrt{100} = \sigma/10$, one-tenth the population standard deviation. With increasing sample size, the standard deviation $\sigma/\sqrt{n}$ decreases and the distribution of $\overline{X}$ tends to become more concentrated around the population mean μ.

To summarize, the sample average for random samples varies about the population mean μ whatever its value, and the deviations of $\overline{X}$ from μ tend to decrease with increasing sample size. This is good news, for it means the value of the sample mean is likely to be close to that of the population mean, particularly for large random samples.

EXAMPLE 7.12   Calculating the Mean and Standard Deviation of $\overline{X}$

Calculate the mean and standard deviation for the population distribution given in Table 7.4 (page 356) and for the distribution of $\overline{X}$ given in Table 7.6 (page 356). Verify the relations $E(\overline{X}) = \mu$ and $\text{sd}(\overline{X}) = \sigma/\sqrt{n}$.

Solution and Discussion.   The calculations are summarized in the following tables:

Population Distribution

x	$f(x)$	$xf(x)$	$x^2f(x)$
2	$\frac{1}{4}$	.5	1.0
3	$\frac{1}{2}$	1.5	4.5
4	$\frac{1}{4}$	1.0	4.0
Total	1	3	9.5

$$\mu = 3$$
$$\sigma^2 = 9.5 - 3^2 = .5 \quad \text{so } \sigma = \sqrt{.5}$$

Distribution of $\overline{X} = (X_1 + X_2)/2$

x	$f(x)$	$xf(x)$	$x^2f(x)$
2	$\frac{1}{16}$	$\frac{2}{16}$	$\frac{4}{16}$
2.5	$\frac{4}{16}$	$\frac{10}{16}$	$\frac{25}{16}$
3	$\frac{6}{16}$	$\frac{18}{16}$	$\frac{54}{16}$
3.5	$\frac{4}{16}$	$\frac{14}{16}$	$\frac{49}{16}$
4	$\frac{1}{16}$	$\frac{4}{16}$	$\frac{16}{16}$
Total	1	3	$\frac{148}{16} = 9.25$

$$E(\overline{X}) = 3 = \mu$$
$$\text{var}(\overline{X}) = 9.25 - 3^2 = .25 \quad \text{so } \text{sd}(\overline{X}) = \sqrt{.25}$$

We have shown directly from the distribution of $\overline{X}$ that $\text{sd}(\overline{X}) = \sqrt{.25} = .50$. This confirms the general relation

$$\text{sd}(\overline{X}) = \frac{\sigma}{\sqrt{n}} = \frac{\sqrt{.5}}{\sqrt{2}} = \sqrt{.25} = .5$$

Two important results deal with the *shape* of the sampling distribution of $\overline{X}$. The result in the next box gives the exact form of the distribution of $\overline{X}$ when the population distribution is normal.

In random sampling from a normal population with mean μ and standard deviation σ, the sample mean $\overline{X}$ has a normal distribution with mean μ and standard deviation $\sigma/\sqrt{n}$. That is, $\overline{X}$ has distribution $N(\mu, \sigma/\sqrt{n})$.

When sampling from a nonnormal population, the distribution of $\overline{X}$ depends on the particular form of the population distribution that prevails. However, a surprising result, known as the **central limit theorem,** states that when the sample size is large, the distribution of $\overline{X}$ is approximately normal regardless of the shape of the population distribution. In practice, the normal approximation is usually adequate when n is greater than 30.

The Central Limit Theorem

In random sampling from an arbitrary population with mean μ and standard deviation σ, when n is large, the distribution of $\overline{X}$ is approximately normal with mean μ and standard deviation $\sigma/\sqrt{n}$. Consequently,

$$Z = \frac{\overline{X} - \mu}{\sigma/\sqrt{n}} \quad \text{is approximately } N(0,1).$$

The population distribution may be continuous, discrete, symmetric, or asymmetric. Whatever its form, the central limit theorem asserts that as long as the population standard deviation is finite, the distribution of the sample mean $\overline{X}$ is nearly normal if the sample size is large. This is important, because later we will use this result to make inferences about a population mean.

For example, we can estimate the average length of time to complete an audit assignment, the average number of telephone calls per shift, and the average monthly salary for supervisory personnel in the airline industry using techniques based on the fact that the sample mean in each of these cases behaves like a normal random variable if the sample size is large. In this sense, the normal distribution plays a central role in the development of statistical methods. Although a proof of the central limit theorem is beyond the scope of this book, we can empirically demonstrate how this result works.

EXAMPLE 7.13   Demonstration of the Central Limit Theorem

Consider a population having a discrete uniform distribution that places probability .1 on each of the integers $0, 1, \ldots, 9$. This may be an appropriate model for the distribution of the last digit in telephone numbers or the first overflow digit in computer calculations. A diagram of this distribution appears in Figure 7.15. The population has $\mu = 4.5$ and $\sigma = 2.872$.

Construct the sampling distribution of the sample mean for random samples of size 5 from the population represented by the distribution in Figure 7.15.

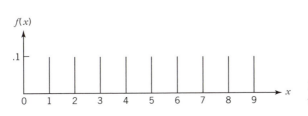

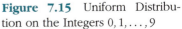
Figure 7.15 Uniform Distribution on the Integers $0, 1, \ldots, 9$

Solution and Discussion.   A computer was used to generate 100 random samples of size 5 from this distribution, and $\bar{x}$ was computed for each sample. The results of this repeated random sampling are given in Table 7.7. The density histogram in Figure 7.16 is constructed from 100 observed values of $\bar{x}$. Although the population distribution (Figure 7.15) is far from normal, the top of the histogram of the $\bar{x}$ values (Figure 7.16) has the appearance of a bell-shaped curve, even for the small sample size of 5. For larger sample sizes, the normal distribution would give an even closer approximation.

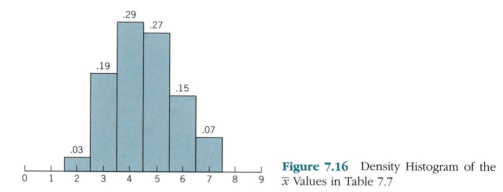

Figure 7.16   Density Histogram of the $\bar{x}$ Values in Table 7.7

Using the 100 simulated $\bar{x}$ values in Table 7.7, we find the sample mean and standard deviation of these quantities to be 4.54 and 1.215, respectively. These numbers are in close agreement with the theoretical values for the mean and standard deviation of $\overline{X}$, specifically, $\mu = 4.5$ and $\sigma/\sqrt{n} = 2.872/\sqrt{5} = 1.284$.

Figure 7.17 is another graphic example of the central limit theorem. The population distribution represented by the solid curve is a continuous asymmetric distribution with $\mu = 2$ and $\sigma = 1.41$. The distributions of the sample mean for samples of sizes $n = 3$ and $n = 10$ are plotted as dashed curves on the graph. The dashed curves indicate that with increasing n, the distributions of the sample mean become more concentrated about μ and look more like a normal distribution.

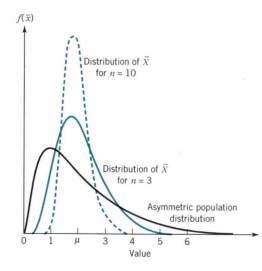

Figure 7.17   The Population Distribution and the Distributions of $\overline{X}$ for $n = 3$ and $n = 10$

TABLE 7.7 Samples of Size 5 from a Discrete Uniform Distribution

Sample Number	Observations	Sum	Mean $\overline{x}$	Sample Number	Observations	Sum	Mean $\overline{x}$
1	4, 7, 9, 0, 6	26	5.2	51	4, 7, 3, 8, 8	30	6.0
2	7, 3, 7, 7, 4	28	5.6	52	2, 0, 3, 3, 2	10	2.0
3	0, 4, 6, 9, 2	21	4.2	53	4, 4, 2, 6, 3	19	3.8
4	7, 6, 1, 9, 1	24	4.8	54	1, 6, 4, 0, 6	17	3.4
5	9, 0, 2, 9, 4	24	4.8	55	2, 4, 5, 8, 9	28	5.6
6	9, 4, 9, 4, 2	28	5.6	56	1, 5, 5, 4, 0	15	3.0
7	7, 4, 2, 1, 6	20	4.0	57	3, 7, 5, 4, 3	22	4.4
8	4, 4, 7, 7, 9	31	6.2	58	3, 7, 0, 7, 6	23	4.6
9	8, 7, 6, 0, 5	26	5.2	59	4, 8, 9, 5, 9	35	7.0
10	7, 9, 1, 0, 6	23	4.6	60	6, 7, 8, 2, 9	32	6.4
11	1, 3, 6, 5, 7	22	4.4	61	7, 3, 6, 3, 6	25	5.0
12	3, 7, 5, 3, 2	20	4.0	62	7, 4, 6, 0, 1	18	3.6
13	5, 6, 6, 5, 0	22	4.4	63	7, 9, 9, 7, 5	37	7.4
14	9, 9, 6, 4, 1	29	5.8	64	8, 0, 6, 2, 7	23	4.6
15	0, 0, 9, 5, 7	21	4.2	65	6, 5, 3, 6, 2	22	4.4
16	4, 9, 1, 1, 6	21	4.2	66	5, 0, 5, 2, 9	21	4.2
17	9, 4, 1, 1, 4	19	3.8	67	2, 9, 4, 9, 1	25	5.0
18	6, 4, 2, 7, 3	22	4.4	68	9, 5, 2, 2, 6	24	4.8
19	9, 4, 4, 1, 8	26	5.2	69	0, 1, 4, 4, 4	13	2.6
20	8, 4, 6, 8, 3	29	5.8	70	5, 4, 0, 5, 2	16	3.2
21	5, 2, 2, 6, 1	16	3.2	71	1, 1, 4, 2, 0	8	1.6
22	2, 2, 9, 1, 0	14	2.8	72	9, 5, 4, 5, 9	32	6.4
23	1, 4, 5, 8, 8	26	5.2	73	7, 1, 6, 6, 9	29	5.8
24	8, 1, 6, 3, 7	25	5.0	74	3, 5, 0, 0, 5	13	2.6
25	1, 2, 0, 9, 6	18	3.6	75	3, 7, 7, 3, 5	25	5.0
26	8, 5, 3, 0, 0	16	3.2	76	7, 4, 7, 6, 2	26	5.2
27	9, 5, 8, 5, 0	27	5.4	77	8, 1, 0, 9, 1	19	3.8
28	8, 9, 1, 1, 8	27	5.4	78	6, 4, 7, 9, 3	29	5.8
29	8, 0, 7, 4, 0	19	3.8	79	7, 7, 6, 9, 7	36	7.2
30	6, 5, 5, 3, 0	19	3.8	80	9, 4, 2, 9, 9	33	6.6
31	4, 6, 4, 2, 1	17	3.4	81	3, 3, 3, 3, 3	15	3.0
32	7, 8, 3, 6, 5	29	5.8	82	8, 7, 7, 0, 3	25	5.0
33	4, 2, 8, 5, 2	21	4.2	83	5, 3, 2, 1, 1	12	2.4
34	7, 1, 9, 0, 9	26	5.2	84	0, 4, 5, 2, 6	17	3.4
35	5, 8, 4, 1, 4	22	4.4	85	3, 7, 5, 4, 1	20	4.0
36	6, 4, 4, 5, 1	20	4.0	86	7, 4, 5, 9, 8	33	6.6
37	4, 2, 1, 1, 6	14	2.8	87	3, 2, 9, 0, 5	19	3.8
38	4, 7, 5, 5, 7	28	5.6	88	4, 6, 6, 3, 3	22	4.4
39	9, 0, 5, 9, 2	25	5.0	89	1, 0, 9, 3, 7	20	4.0
40	3, 1, 5, 4, 5	18	3.6	90	2, 9, 6, 8, 5	30	6.0
41	9, 8, 6, 3, 2	28	5.6	91	4, 8, 0, 7, 6	25	5.0
42	9, 4, 2, 2, 8	25	5.0	92	5, 6, 7, 6, 3	27	5.4
43	8, 4, 7, 2, 2	23	4.6	93	3, 6, 2, 5, 6	22	4.4
44	0, 7, 3, 4, 9	23	4.6	94	0, 1, 1, 8, 4	14	2.8
45	0, 2, 7, 5, 2	16	3.2	95	3, 6, 6, 4, 5	24	4.8
46	7, 1, 9, 9, 9	35	7.0	96	9, 2, 9, 8, 6	34	6.8
47	4, 0, 5, 9, 4	22	4.4	97	2, 0, 0, 6, 8	16	3.2
48	5, 8, 6, 3, 3	25	5.0	98	0, 4, 5, 0, 5	14	2.8
49	4, 5, 0, 5, 3	17	3.4	99	0, 3, 7, 3, 9	22	4.4
50	7, 7, 2, 0, 1	17	3.4	100	2, 5, 0, 0, 7	14	2.8

EXAMPLE 7.14   Probability Calculations with the Sample Mean

Consider a population with mean 82 and standard deviation 12.

a.   If a random sample of size 64 is selected, what is the probability that the sample mean will lie between 80.8 and 83.2?

b.   With a random sample of size 100, what is the probability that the sample mean will lie between 80.8 and 83.2?

Solution and Discussion.

a.   Since $n = 64$ is large, the central limit theorem tells us that the distribution of $\overline{X}$ is approximately normal with

$$\text{Mean} = \mu = 82$$

$$\text{Standard deviation} = \frac{\sigma}{\sqrt{n}} = \frac{12}{\sqrt{64}} = 1.5$$

To calculate $P(80.8 < \overline{X} < 83.2)$, we convert to the standardized variable

$$Z = \frac{\overline{X} - \mu}{\sigma/\sqrt{n}} = \frac{\overline{X} - 82}{1.5}$$

The z values corresponding to 80.8 and 83.2 are

$$\frac{80.8 - 82}{1.5} = -.8 \quad \text{and} \quad \frac{83.2 - 82}{1.5} = .8$$

The $\overline{x}$- and corresponding z-scales are shown here:

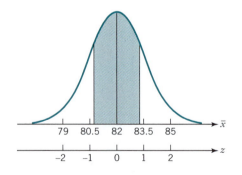

Consequently,

$$P(80.8 < \overline{X} < 83.2) = P(-.8 < Z < .8)$$
$$= .7881 - .2119$$
$$= .5762$$

b. We now have $n = 100$, so $\sigma/\sqrt{n} = 12/\sqrt{100} = 1.2$, and

$$Z = \frac{\overline{X} - 82}{1.2}$$

Therefore,

$$P(80.8 < \overline{X} < 83.2) = P\left(\frac{80.8 - 82}{1.2} < Z < \frac{83.2 - 82}{1.2}\right)$$

$$= P(-1.0 < Z < 1.0)$$

$$= .8413 - .1487$$

$$= .6826$$

Note that the interval $(80.8, \ 83.2)$ is centered at $\mu = 82$. The probability that $\overline{X}$ will lie in this interval is larger for $n = 100$ than for $n = 64$.

EXAMPLE 7.15   Additional Probability Calculations with the Sample Mean

The population distribution of gripping strengths of industrial workers is known to have a mean of 110 and a standard deviation of 10. For a random sample of 75 workers, what is the probability that the sample mean gripping strength will be:

a. Between 109 and 112?

b. Greater than 111?

Solution and Discussion.   The population mean and standard deviation are $\mu = 110$ and $\sigma = 10$, respectively. The sample size $n = 75$ is large, so the central limit theorem ensures that the distribution of $\overline{X}$ is approximately normal with

$$\text{Mean} = 110$$

$$\text{Standard deviation} = \frac{\sigma}{\sqrt{n}} = \frac{10}{\sqrt{75}} = 1.155$$

a. To find $P(109 < \overline{X} < 112)$, we form the standardized variable

$$Z = \frac{\overline{X} - 110}{1.155}$$

and calculate the z values:

$$\frac{109 - 110}{1.155} = -.866 \quad \text{and} \quad \frac{112 - 110}{1.155} = 1.732$$

The required probability is

$$P(109 < \overline{X} < 112) = P(-.866 < Z < 1.732)$$

$$= .958 - .193$$

$$= .765$$

b. $P(\overline{X} > 111) = P\left(Z > \dfrac{111 - 110}{1.155}\right)$

$\qquad\qquad\qquad = P(Z > .866)$

$\qquad\qquad\qquad = 1 - P(Z \le .866)$

$\qquad\qquad\qquad = 1 - .807$

$\qquad\qquad\qquad = .193$

How large should n be for the normal approximation to be used for the distribution of $\overline{X}$? The adequacy of the approximation depends on the extent to which the population distribution deviates from the normal distribution. If the population distribution is normal, then $\overline{X}$ is exactly normally distributed for all n, small or large. As the population increasingly departs from normality, larger values of n are required for a good approximation. Ordinarily, $n > 30$ provides a satisfactory approximation.

EXERCISES

7.55 A population has mean 99 and standard deviation 7. Calculate $E(\overline{X})$ and sd$(\overline{X})$ for a random sample of size

   a. 4

   b. 25

7.56 A population has mean 250 and standard deviation 12. Calculate the expected value and standard deviation of $\overline{X}$ for a random sample of size

   a. 3

   b. 16

7.57 A population has standard deviation 10. What is the standard deviation of $\overline{X}$ for a random sample of the following sizes?

   a. $n = 25$

   b. $n = 100$

   c. $n = 400$

7.58 A population has standard deviation 84. What is the standard deviation of $\overline{X}$ for a random sample of the following sizes?

   a. $n = 36$

   b. $n = 144$

7.59 Using the sampling distribution for $\overline{X} = (X_1 + X_2)/2$ in Exercise 7.50, verify that $E(\overline{X}) = \mu$ and sd$(\overline{X}) = \sigma/\sqrt{2}$.

7.60 Using the sampling distribution for $\overline{X} = (X_1 + X_2)/2$ in Exercise 7.51, verify that $E(\overline{X}) = \mu$ and sd$(\overline{X}) = \sigma/\sqrt{2}$.

7.61 A normal population has $\mu = 27$ and $\sigma = 3$. For a random sample of size $n = 4$, determine the

a. Mean of $\overline{X}$

b. Standard deviation of $\overline{X}$

c. Distribution of $\overline{X}$

7.62 A normal population has $\mu = 20$ and $\sigma = 5$. For a random sample of size $n = 6$, determine the

a. Mean of $\overline{X}$

b. Standard deviation of $\overline{X}$

c. Distribution of $\overline{X}$

7.63 The amount of sulfur in the daily emissions from a power plant has a normal distribution with a mean of 134 pounds and a standard deviation of 22 pounds. For a random sample of 5 days, find the probability that the total amount of sulfur emissions will exceed 700 pounds. [*Hint:* Saying that a total of 5 measurements exceed 700 pounds is the same as saying that their mean exceeds 140 pounds.]

7.64 To avoid difficulties with governmental consumer protection agencies, a manufacturer must be reasonably certain that its bags of potato chips actually contain 16 ounces of chips. One recognized way of monitoring the amount of chips in a bag is to take a random sample of a few bags from each hour's production. The sample mean $\overline{X}$ of the contents of the bags then provides important information about whether the process is meeting the weight requirement. Records for one packaging machine indicate that its fill weights are nearly normally distributed with a standard deviation of .122 ounce. If this machine is set so that the mean fill weight is 16.08 ounces per bag:

a. What is the probability that the sample mean contents of 9 bags, selected at random, will be less than 16.0 ounces?

b. In the long run, what proportion of the bags filled by this machine will contain less than 16.0 ounces of potato chips?

7.65 For the packaging machine in Exercise 7.64:

a. What should the setting for the mean fill rate be so that the probability is only .02 that the mean contents of a sample of 9 bags will be less than 16.0 ounces?

b. Assume that the setting of the machine is as determined in part **a.** In the long run, what proportion of the bags filled by the machine will contain less than 16.0 ounces of potato chips?

7.66 The number of days between receipt of an order and shipment of the goods for in-stock items is normally distributed with mean 3.0 days and standard deviation .5 day. Data will be collected for a random sample of 16 orders. Let $\overline{X}$ denote the sample mean of the 16 times from receipt of order to shipment of goods.

a. What is the distribution of $\overline{X}$? Is it the exact or an approximate distribution?

    b.   What is the probability that:

       i. $\overline{X}$ will exceed 3.7 days?

       ii. $\overline{X}$ will be between 2.84 and 3.16?

7.67   The distribution of personal income of persons working in a large Eastern city has $\mu = \$31,000$ and $\sigma = \$5000$.

    a.   What is the approximate distribution of $\overline{X}$ based on a random sample of 100 persons?

    b.   Evaluate $P(\overline{X} > \$31,500)$.

7.68   A random sample of size 100 is taken from a population having a mean of 20 and a standard deviation of 5. The shape of the population distribution is unknown.

    a.   What can you say about the sampling distribution of the sample mean $\overline{X}$?

    b.   Find the probability that $\overline{X}$ will exceed 20.75.

7.69   As part of a market survey on how Cap Comics customers make decisions, comic store owners will be asked to allocate 100 points for the following five factors:

Price   Timely   Reputation of   Product   Other
delivery   Cap Comics   selection

In an earlier survey, the square root of the score for Price is approximately normally distributed with mean 6 and standard deviation 2. What is the probability that the sample mean of 12 customers' scores for Price will be less than 25 so that the square root is less than 5?

7.70   The heights of male students at a university have a nearly normal distribution with mean 70 inches and standard deviation 2.8 inches. If 5 male students are randomly selected to make up an intramural basketball team, what is the probability that the heights of the team will average over 72 inches?

7.71   According to the growth chart that doctors use as a reference, the heights of two-year-old boys are normally distributed with mean 34.5 inches and standard deviation 1.3 inches. For a random sample of 6 two-year-old boys, find the probability that the sample mean will be between 34.1 and 35.2 inches.

7.72   The weight of an almond is normally distributed with mean .05 ounce and standard deviation .015 ounce. Find the probability that a package of 100 almonds will weigh between 4.8 ounces and 5.3 ounces. That is, find the probability that $\overline{X}$ will be between .048 ounce and .053 ounce.

7.73   Refer to Table 7.7 (page 363).

    a.   Calculate the sample median for each sample.

    b.   Construct a frequency table and make a density histogram.

    c.   Compare the histogram for the median with that given in Figure 7.16 (page 362) for the sample mean. Does your comparison suggest that the sampling distribution of the mean or the median has the smaller variance?

7.74   Explain how the central limit theorem expresses the fact that the probability distribution of $\overline{X}$ concentrates more and more probability near μ as the sample size n increases.

7.8   STATISTICS IN CONTEXT

The ideas of quality and productivity improvement apply equally to service processes. A large church-owned insurance organization noted that one area of major dissatisfaction identified by consumers was the length of time to receive payment on health claims. As a first step in addressing this difficulty, it was decided to collect data to quantify the magnitude of the current problem. A random sample of 212 claims was followed through the health claims processing procedure, and the times needed to complete the procedure were recorded. These data on turnaround times are given in Table C.4, Appendix C.

Computer calculations for the turnaround times data give:

N	MEAN	MEDIAN	STDEV
212	22.82	15.00	34.09

MIN	MAX	Q1	Q3
1.00	292.00	10.00	23.00

The histogram in Figure 7.18 has a long tail to the right.

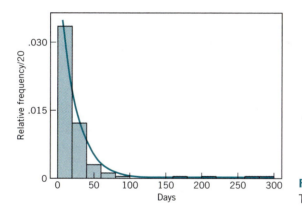

Figure 7.18   Density Histogram of Turnaround Times

If these data are to be used to predict future data, they must be smoothed or otherwise used to estimate a probability density function. (We skip the details that need not concern us here.) An actuarial scientist proposed the smooth curve for the density function that is also shown in Figure 7.18. Its equation is given by

$$f(x) = \frac{1}{22.8} e^{-x/22.8} \quad \text{for } x > 0$$

The delay in response is always nonnegative, so all of the probability is assigned to positive values x. The constant e is approximately 2.7183. It can be shown that the mean of the random variable X having this probability distribution is $\mu = 22.8$, which matches the sample mean of the turnaround times.

Areas under the probability density curve are the probabilities assigned to intervals. Fortunately, a simple formula is available for the area under the curve that is to the left of any $x > 0$. That is, the probability $P(X \leq x)$ is given by

$$P(X \leq x) = 1 - e^{-x/22.8} \quad \text{for } x > 0$$

Our particular model of a probability distribution allows for the possibility of a delay time larger than that encountered in the data set. However, it does assign a small probability to that event. For example,

$$P(X > 300) = 1 - P(X \leq 300) = 1 - (1 - e^{-300/22.8}) = e^{-300/22.8} = .000002$$

The industry standard states that 90% of the checks should be issued within 14 days of receipt of claim. Given the results shown here, we can easily calculate the probability that a response will require more than 14 days to process for our company. We have

$$P(X > 14) = 1 - P(X \leq 14) = e^{-14/22.8} = .541$$

We can also obtain percentiles of the probability distribution. Recall, the median or 50th percentile $x_{.50}$ is the value such that the probability is one-half that it will not be exceeded. That is,

$$P(X \leq x_{.50}) = 1 - e^{-x_{.50}/22.8} = .50$$

or $.50 = e^{-x_{.50}/22.8}$. Taking the natural logarithm gives $x_{.50} = -22.8 \ln(.50) = 15.8$ days. According to the model, the probability is .5 that the time to respond to a claim is 15.8 days or more. This is clearly unacceptable and improvements need to be made. These data and the probability density function will provide a benchmark against which any improved claims process can be measured and evaluated.

The next step for the quality improvement team is to construct a flowchart of the claims process, construct a Pareto chart, and generally to look for opportunities for improvement. That is exactly what was done in this case.

7.9   CHAPTER SUMMARY

In this chapter, we have learned:

● The probability distribution for a continuous random variable X is specified by a **probability density function.**

● The probability that X lies in an interval from a to b is determined by the area under the probability density curve between a and b. The total area under the curve is 1, and the curve is never negative.

● When the number of trials n is large and the success probability p is not too near 0 or 1, the binomial distribution is well approximated by a normal distribution with mean $= np$ and standard deviation $= \sqrt{np(1 - p)}$. Specifically, the probabilities for a binomial random variable X can be approximately calculated by treating

$$Z = \frac{X - np}{\sqrt{np(1 - p)}}$$

as a standard normal random variable.

● The **normal-scores plot** of a data set provides a diagnostic check for possible departure from a normal distribution.

- **Transformation** of the measurement scale often helps to convert a long-tailed (skewed) distribution to one that resembles a normal distribution.

- A **parameter** is a numerical characteristic of the population. It is a constant, although its value is typically unknown to us. The object of a statistical analysis of sample data is to learn about the parameter.

- A numerical characteristic of a sample is called a **statistic.** The value of a statistic varies in repeated sampling.

- A statistic is a random variable. The probability distribution of a statistic is called its **sampling distribution.**

- The sampling distribution of $\overline{X}$ has mean μ and standard deviation $\sigma/\sqrt{n}$, where μ is the population mean, σ is the population standard deviation, and n is the sample size.

- With increasing n, the distribution of $\overline{X}$ is more concentrated about μ.

- If the population distribution is $N(\mu, \sigma)$, the distribution of $\overline{X}$ is $N(\mu, \sigma/\sqrt{n})$.

- Regardless of the shape of the population distribution, the distribution of $\overline{X}$ is approximately $N(\mu, \sigma/\sqrt{n})$ provided n is large. This result is called the **central limit theorem.**

7.10   IMPORTANT CONCEPTS AND TOOLS

CONCEPTS

Continuity correction, 340
Normal scores, 345
Parameter, 353
Population percentile, 332

Probability density function, 330
Sampling distribution, 355
Statistic, 354

TOOLS

Central limit theorem, 361
Normal approximation to the
   binomial, 341
Normal-scores plot, 345
Transformations, 349

7.11   KEY FORMULAS

Standardized variable:

$$Z = \frac{X - \mu}{\sigma} = \frac{\text{Variable} - \text{Mean}}{\text{Standard deviation}}$$

The normal approximation to the binomial:

When np and $n(1 - p)$ are both large, say, greater than 15, the binomial distribution is well approximated by a normal distribution having mean $\mu = np$ and standard deviation $\sigma = \sqrt{np(1 - p)}$. That is,

$$Z = \frac{X - np}{\sqrt{np(1 - p)}} \quad \text{is approximately } N(0, 1).$$

Some useful transformations:

Makes large values larger: x^2, x^3

Makes large values smaller: $\sqrt{x}, \quad \sqrt[4]{x}, \quad \ln(x), \quad \frac{1}{x}$

The distribution of the sample mean, based on a random sample of size n, has

$$E(\overline{X}) = \mu \quad (= \text{Population mean})$$

$$\text{var}(\overline{X}) = \frac{\sigma^2}{n} \quad \left(= \frac{\text{Population variance}}{\text{Sample size}} \right)$$

$$\text{sd}(\overline{X}) = \frac{\sigma}{\sqrt{n}} \quad \left(= \frac{\text{Population standard deviation}}{\sqrt{\text{Sample size}}} \right)$$

The central limit theorem:

In random sampling from an arbitrary population with mean μ and standard deviation σ, when n is large, the distribution of $\overline{X}$ is approximately normal with mean μ and standard deviation $\sigma/\sqrt{n}$. Consequently,

$$Z = \frac{\overline{X} - \mu}{\sigma/\sqrt{n}} \quad \text{is approximately } N(0, 1).$$

REVIEW EXERCISES

7.75 Determine the median and quartiles for the distribution shown in the following diagram.

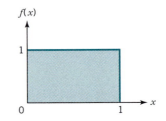

7.76 For the random variable X having the density in Exercise 7.75, find:
   a. $P(X > .8)$
   b. $P(.5 \le X \le .8)$
   c. $P(.5 < X < .8)$

7.77 For a standard normal random variable Z, find:
   a. $P(Z < 1.31)$ b. $P(Z > 1.205)$
   c. $P(.67 < Z < 1.98)$ d. $P(-1.32 < Z < 1.055)$

7.78 The distribution of raw scores in a college qualification test has mean 582 and standard deviation 75.
   a. If a student's raw score is 696, what is the corresponding standardized score?
   b. If the standardized score is $-.8$, what is the raw score?
   c. Find the interval of standardized scores corresponding to raw scores of 380 to 560.

d. Find the interval of raw scores corresponding to the interval of standardized scores of -1.2 to 1.2.

7.79 If X is normally distributed with $\mu = 100$ and $\sigma = 8$, find:

a. $P(X < 107)$ b. $P(X < 97)$

c. $P(X > 110)$ d. $P(X > 90)$

e. $P(95 < X < 106)$ f. $P(103 < X < 114)$

g. $P(88 < X < 100)$ h. $P(60 < X < 108)$

7.80 If X has a normal distribution with $\mu = 200$ and $\sigma = 5$, find b such that:

a. $P(X < b) = .670$

b. $P(X > b) = .011$

c. $P(|X - 200| < b) = .966$

7.81 The bonding strength of a drop of plastic glue is normally distributed with mean 100 pounds and standard deviation 8 pounds. A broken plastic strip is repaired with a drop of this glue and then subjected to a test load of 98 pounds. What is the probability that the bonding will fail?

7.82 *Grading on a Curve.* The scores on an examination are normally distributed with mean $\mu = 70$ and standard deviation $\sigma = 8$. Suppose that the instructor decides to assign letter grades according to the following scheme (left endpoint included):

Scores	Grade
Less than 58	F
58 to 66	D
66 to 74	C
74 to 82	B
82 and above	A

Find the percentage of students in each grade category.

7.83 Suppose the duration of trouble-free operation of a new vacuum cleaner is normally distributed with mean 530 days and standard deviation 100 days.

a. What is the probability that the vacuum cleaner will work for at least two years without trouble?

b. The company wishes to set the warranty period so that no more than 10% of the vacuum cleaners would need repair services while under warranty. How long a warranty period must be set?

7.84 An aptitude test administered to aircraft pilot trainees requires a series of operations to be performed in quick succession. Suppose that the time needed to complete the test is normally distributed with mean 90 minutes and standard deviation 20 minutes.

a. To pass the test, a candidate must complete it within 80 minutes. What percentage of the candidates will pass the test?

b. If the top 5% of the candidates are to be given a certificate of commendation, how fast must a candidate complete the test to be eligible for a certificate?

7.85 Let X denote the number of successes in n Bernoulli trials with a success probability of p.

a. Find the exact probabilities of each of the following:
    i. $X \leq 5$ when $n = 25$, $p = .4$
    ii. $11 \leq X \leq 17$ when $n = 20$, $p = .7$
    iii. $X \geq 11$ when $n = 16$, $p = .5$

b. Use a normal approximation for each situation in part **a.**

7.86 It is known from past experience that 9% of tax bills are paid late. If 20,000 tax bills are sent out, find the probability that:

a. Fewer than 1750 are paid late

b. 2000 or more are paid late

7.87 A particular television program, say, Program A, previously drew 30% of the viewing audience. To determine whether a recent rescheduling of the programs on a competing channel has adversely affected the audience of Program A, a random sample of 400 viewers is to be asked whether they currently watch this program.

a. If the percentage of viewers watching Program A has not changed, what is the probability that fewer than 105 out of the sample of 400 will be found to watch the program?

b. If the number of viewers of the program is actually found to be less than 105, will this strongly support the suspicion that the population percentage has decreased?

7.88 The number of successes X has a binomial distribution. State whether the normal approximation is appropriate in each of the following situations.

a. $n = 400$, $p = .28$ b. $n = 20$, $p = .04$

c. $n = 90$, $p = .99$

7.89 Because 10% of the reservation holders are "no-shows," an airline sells 400 tickets for a flight that can accommodate 370 passengers.

a. Find the probability that one or more reservation holders will not be accommodated on the flight.

b. Find the probability of fewer than 350 passengers on the flight.

7.90 A population consists of four numbers $\{2, 4, 6, 8\}$. Consider drawing a random sample of size 2 with replacement.

a. List all possible samples, and calculate the value of $\overline{X}$ for each sample.

b. Determine the sampling distribution of $\overline{X}$.

c. Write down the population distribution, and calculate its mean μ and standard deviation σ.

d. Calculate the mean and standard deviation of the sampling distribution of $\overline{X}$ obtained in part **b,** and verify that these agree with μ and $\sigma/\sqrt{2}$, respectively.

7.91 Refer to Exercise 7.90. Instead of $\overline{X}$, consider the statistic

Sample range R = Largest observation − Smallest observation

For instance, if the sample observations are 2 and 6, then $R = 6 - 2 = 4$.

a.   Calculate the sample range for all possible samples.

b.   Determine the sampling distribution of R.

7.92   A random sample is to be selected from a population with mean 550 and standard deviation 70. Find the mean and standard deviation of $\overline{X}$ for

a.   Sample size 16

b.   Sample size 160

7.93   What sample size is required for the standard deviation of $\overline{X}$ to be:

a. $\frac{1}{4}$ of the population standard deviation

b. $\frac{1}{8}$ of the population standard deviation

c.   15% of the population standard deviation

7.94   Suppose a population distribution is normal with mean 80 and standard deviation 10. For a random sample of size $n = 9$:

a.   What are the mean and standard deviation of $\overline{X}$?

b.   What is the distribution of $\overline{X}$? Is this distribution exact or approximate?

c.   Find the probability that $\overline{X}$ lies between 76 and 84.

7.95   The weights of pears in an orchard are normally distributed with mean .32 pound and standard deviation .08 pound.

a.   If one pear is selected at random, what is the probability that its weight will be between .28 and .34 pound?

b.   If $\overline{X}$ denotes the average weight of a random sample of 4 pears, what is the probability that $\overline{X}$ will be between .28 and .34 pound?

7.96   A random sample of size 150 is taken from a population with mean 60 and standard deviation 8. The population is not normal.

a.   Is it reasonable to assume a normal distribution for the sample mean $\overline{X}$? Discuss.

b.   Find the probability that $\overline{X}$ lies between 59 and 61.

c.   Find the probability that $\overline{X}$ exceeds 62.

7.97   The distribution for the time that it takes a student to complete the fall class registration has a mean of 94 minutes and a standard deviation of 10 minutes. For a random sample of 81 students:

a.   Determine the mean and standard deviation of $\overline{X}$.

b.   What can you say about the distribution of $\overline{X}$?

7.98   Refer to Exercise 7.97. Evaluate

a. $P(\overline{X} > 96)$ b. $P(92.3 < \overline{X} < 96.0)$

c. $P(\overline{X} < 95)$

7.99   The mean and standard deviation of the strength of a packaging material are 55 pounds and 7 pounds, respectively. If 40 pieces of this material are tested:

a.   What is the probability that the sample mean strength $\overline{X}$ will be between 54 and 56 pounds?

b.   Find the interval, centered at 55, where $\overline{X}$ will lie with probability .95.

7.100 Consider a random sample of size $n = 100$ from a population that has a standard deviation of $\sigma = 20$.

    a. Find the probability that the sample mean $\overline{X}$ will lie within 2 units of the population mean; that is, find $P(-2 \leq \overline{X} - \mu \leq 2)$.

    b. Find the number k so that $P(-k \leq \overline{X} - \mu \leq k) = .90$.

    c. What is the probability that $\overline{X}$ will differ from μ by more than 4 units?

7.101 The time that customers take to complete their transactions at a money machine is a random variable with mean 2 minutes and standard deviation .6 minute. Find the probability that a random sample of 50 customers will take between 90 and 112.5 minutes to complete all their transactions. That is, find the probability that $\overline{X}$ will be between 1.8 and 2.25 minutes.

7.102 *Class Project.*

    a. Each student counts the number of occupants X, including the driver, in each of 20 passing cars. Calculate the mean $\overline{X}$ of the sample.

    b. Repeat part **a** 10 times for a total of 200 occupant counts and 10 sample means.

    c. Collect the data sets of the individual occupant counts x from the entire class, and construct a relative frequency histogram.

    d. Collect the sample mean values $\overline{x}$ from the entire class (10 from each student), and construct a relative frequency histogram for $\overline{x}$ choosing appropriate class intervals.

    e. Plot the two relative frequency histograms, and comment on the closeness of their shapes to the normal distribution.

7.103 *Class Project.* Pick something that can be measured fairly easily. For example, you might record daily soft-drink consumption, hours of sleep for different students, or the amount of money spent on textbooks for the academic year.

    a. Each student collects a sample of size 7 and computes the sample mean $\overline{X}$ and the sample median M.

    b. Repeat part **a** 30 times for a total of 210 individual measurements and 30 sample means and medians.

    c. Plot dot diagrams for the values of the two statistics in part **b.** These plots reflect the individual sampling distributions.

    d. Compare the amounts of variation in $\overline{X}$ and M.

7.104 (*Minitab or similar program recommended*) Conduct a computer simulation experiment to verify the central limit theorem. Generate $n = 6$ observations from the continuous uniform distribution on the interval $[0, 1)$. Calculate the value of $\overline{X}$. Repeat this experiment 150 times. Make a histogram of the $\overline{x}$'s and construct a normal-scores plot. Does the distribution of $\overline{X}$ appear to be normal for $n = 6$? Repeat the procedure for $n = 20$. Comment on the effect of sample size on the shape of the distribution of $\overline{X}$.

The Minitab commands:

```
RANDOM 150 C1-C6;
 UNIFORM 0 1.
ADD C1-C6 SET C10
LET C11 = C10/6.0
```

will generate random samples of size $n = 6$ from the uniform distribution on $[0, 1)$ in each of 150 rows of columns C1 through C6. Column C11 contains the 150 sample means.

The normal-scores plot and other descriptive summaries of the $\bar{x}$ values are given by the Minitab commands:

```
HISTOGRAM C11
DESCRIBE C11
NSCORE C11 SET C12
PLOT C11*C12
```

To make this exercise more interesting, replace the **UNIFORM 0 1** command by a command that generates observations from a different distribution. For example, try a discrete distribution like the uniform distribution on the integers $0, 1, \ldots, 9$.

CompAtti.dat

7.105 (*Minitab or similar program recommended*) Make a normal-scores plot of the computer anxiety scores data in Table C.2, Appendix C. Comment on the appearance of the plot.

7.106 Refer to the data on turnaround times for processing health care claims in Table C.4, Appendix C. From the histogram in Figure 7.18, it could be argued that the four largest observations are unusually large. Suppose these four observations are dropped. The sample mean then becomes 18.65. Suppose the probability model having $P(X \leq x) = 1 - e^{-x/18.65}$ is used to represent the reduced set of turnaround times. Find:

a. The probability that a claim takes longer than 14 days to process

b. The median x_{50} of this probability distribution

7.107 Refer to Exercise 7.106 and Section 7.8. Does dropping the four largest observations change the distribution of turnaround times very much? Discuss.

CHAPTER OBJECTIVES

After reading this chapter, you should be able to:

- Discuss the concept of statistical inference.
- Distinguish between a point estimator and an interval estimator of a population parameter.
- Construct a point estimate of a population mean and its associated standard error.
- Determine the sample size required to estimate the mean μ within a desired error margin.
- Construct a confidence interval for a population mean.
- Understand the general steps in testing statistical hypotheses.
- Carry out tests of hypotheses concerning population means.
- Calculate P-values or significance probabilities.
- Understand the relation between confidence intervals and two-sided tests of hypotheses.
- Discuss Student's t distribution and the use of the t statistic in small sample inferences for normal populations.

CHAPTER EIGHT

From Samples to Populations: Inferences About Means

8.1 INTRODUCTION

Statistical inferences are generalizations about a population that are made on the basis of a sample. For example, a mail order company, planning its staffing requirements, decides to collect data on the number of calls handled by each operator who takes phone orders and enters them on the computer. On one occasion, the number of calls per 8-hour shift was recorded for 75 workers. These data could be described by the methods presented in Chapter 2, but there is a wider purpose to this study, namely, learning about the collection of the number of calls handled by a particular operator, or even the number of all potential calls that could be handled by a particular operator during a shift. Attention is not confined to just the 75 numbers that are included in the sample but extends to this much larger collection of number of calls. This is what we mean by a statistical inference. That is, given the specific sample of the 75 calls that were handled and recorded, we need to generalize to the population of all potential numbers of calls. Typically, the generalization would be a statement about the mean number of calls or some other feature of the population.

The methods of statistical inference discussed in this chapter take two forms. First, we discuss *estimation,* or guessing the value of some population quantity from sample information. Second, we discuss *testing hypotheses,* or checking to see whether a specified value for a population quantity (a hypothesis) is consistent with the sample evidence. As we will see, the two general methods of inference are related.

The inferential procedures that we develop depend on an assumed form for the population distribution of the sample observations. In fact, inferences are often framed in terms of the characteristics, such as the mean, of this population distribution. As we develop the methods of inference, we will come to understand why the central limit theorem is so important.

How do statistical inferences relate to business decisions? Several brief examples may help to clarify the relationship.

A company negotiating a price for a 60-second commercial on television is concerned with the commercial's effectiveness and the number of viewers it will reach. Two versions of the commercial are available. As we pointed out in Example 1.3, random samples of viewers can be used to view the two commercials, and the proportion of viewers in each sample who remember a key message can be determined. From this information, it is possible to decide whether the two commercials are equally effective, or alternatively, if one commercial is likely to be more effective than the other (a statistical inference). Also, the A. C. Nielsen Company maintains a sample of households to collect data on the TV programs watched by members of the households. From these data, the total number of households viewing a particular TV program can be estimated (a statistical inference). The company can contract with A. C. Nielsen to determine the number of viewers their TV commercial is likely to reach. The company can then decide what to pay for the TV spot.

In Example 1.4, we discussed the problem of substantial losses of cheese solids during the manufacture of processed cheese forms. Cheese manufacturers were paying for more cheese solids than they were actually receiving in the 500-pound barrels they purchased from suppliers. In this case, the sampling method used to estimate the amount of cheese solids in 500-pound barrels was demonstrated to produce inaccurate results. The National Cheese Institute supported a decision to develop a new sampling method that would allow accurate estimation (a statistical inference) of the amount of cheese solids in a 500-pound barrel based on a small sample collected from the barrel. The new sampling procedure saved the manufacturers of processed cheese forms millions of dollars.

Hardwood trees are harvested in a selective manner for the manufacture of fine furniture. The volume of lumber in a selected tree determines the worth of the tree to the buyer and determines the price paid to the grower. Volume is not easily measured before the tree is harvested. Volume can be estimated (a statistical inference) from two common measurements made before cutting down a tree: the diameter of the tree 4.5 feet off the ground (chest height) and the height of the tree from sighting instruments. A sample of trees can be used to develop a procedure for estimating the volume of a selected tree from these two measurements. A decision to harvest the tree based on its estimated dollar value can then be made.

A manufacturer of electronic printed circuit boards for radar units in aircraft routinely samples the production output to determine the number and type of defects on individual boards. The number of defects on sampled boards is monitored by means of a control chart to determine whether the production process is producing printed circuit boards with acceptable—we hope zero—numbers of defects (a statistical inference). If not, corrective action will be taken.

Companies are increasingly turning to temporary employees to satisfy staffing requirements, particularly during peak periods. A sample of records relating to the number of employees hired over previous time periods can be used to estimate (a statistical inference) the temporary staffing requirements for the coming period. Resources can then be allocated to hire the required number of temporary employees.

A company treasurer must decide among several short-term investment opportunities. The decision is influenced by the future movement of interest rates. Historical short-term interest rates (90-day T-bill rates, high-grade commercial paper rates, and so forth) are available for selected time periods. Based on a sample of historical rates, the level of interest rates for several investment opportunities can be estimated (a statistical inference). Funds can then be allocated to these opportunities on the basis of anticipated returns.

The TV commercial, amount of cheese solids, and lumber volume examples involve enumerative studies. In each of these cases, the inferences apply to an existing population at a particular point in time. The printed circuit board, temporary employee, and interest rate examples involve analytic studies in the sense that the inferences involve characteristics of a process that occurs over time. In each case, we assume that the process is stable (the same cause-and-effect system remains in place), and the inference refers to a hypothetical population of possible values at a future point in time.

When the population is described by a probability distribution or probability density function, parameters such as the mean, variance, and median are generally of interest. As we have indicated in our brief examples, most of the time we want to *estimate the value* of a parameter (the mean number of households watching a TV program, the mean demand for temporary employees, and so forth). A single number estimate is called a **point estimate.** An interval of numbers that is likely to contain the value of the parameter is called an **interval estimate.** Later, we will see why interval estimates are more desirable than point estimates.

On some occasions, we may have a value for the population parameter in mind and want to know whether it is appropriate (the proportion of people who prefer Commercial 1 is greater than .5, the mean number of defectives on the printed circuit boards is less than 1, and so forth). We will learn how to use the sample evidence to decide whether our hypothesized value for the parameter is appropriate or not. The procedure for checking hypothesized values is referred to as **testing hypotheses.**

Estimation and hypothesis testing are examples of statistical inference.

Statistical inference deals with drawing conclusions about population parameters from an analysis of the sample data.

The following examples illustrate the estimation part of statistical inference.

EXAMPLE 8.1   Estimating the Number of Calls per Shift

Mail order companies do a large volume of business during the weeks leading up to the holidays. They may receive a few thousand calls a day and need to add sufficient staff to handle that volume of business. The computer system for recording orders also monitors each worker's activity. The number of calls per eight-hour shift handled by 75 different workers at one company are:

97	118	91	102	118	117	104	57	96	95	92
87	102	127	105	71	109	83	96	96	84	114
68	76	94	73	51	88	69	101	120	106	110
78	91	81	76	93	81	93	94	94	107	102
70	110	105	77	76	100	92	111	104	74	108
80	87	92	50	86	82	96	59	55	82	74
57	72	91	94	108	80	72	73	96		

(Courtesy of Lands' End)

Estimate the mean number of calls, μ, handled by one operator during an eight-hour shift.

Solution and Discussion.   Let us proceed under the assumption that the workers included in the sample and the calls on the days on which the data were collected are representative. That is, we assume the 75 numbers are a random sample from the population of interest. Consequently, it is reasonable to use the sample values to make inferences about the population mean number of calls, μ, that could be handled by an operator during one shift.

A computer calculation yields

```
N     MEAN      STDEV
75    89.60     17.32
```

and it would seem reasonable to take the sample value $\bar{x} = 89.6$ calls as an estimate of the population mean μ. This value is our point estimate of the population mean.

EXAMPLE 8.2   Estimating Percent Earnings

A large construction company was trying to establish a useful way to view typical profits from jobs obtained from competitive bidding. Because the jobs vary substantially in size and the final amount of the successful bid, the company decided to express profits as the percent earnings:

$$\text{Percent earnings} = 100 \times \frac{\text{Earnings}}{\text{Actual construction costs}}$$

When money is lost on a project, the earnings are negative and so is the resulting net profit. A sample of 30 jobs yielded the percent earnings:

15.9	21.3	−1.8	6.6	.4	53.6	19.7	−.5	6.7	−2.3
11.9	−.3	19.0	12.8	−9.6	26.8	21.0	32.0	−.4	10.9
6.9	−8.5	3.5	3.5	−1.9	4.0	13.0	15.1	9.7	33.9

Given these data, what is a plausible value for the mean percent earnings for the population of jobs or even all potential jobs?

Solution and Discussion.   Because the data were collected from a random sample of jobs completed, it is reasonable to assume that they are representative, and therefore, we can use the sample values to make inferences about the population mean. A computer calculation gives

$$\bar{x} = 10.76\% \quad \text{and} \quad s = 13.71\%$$

It would seem reasonable to take the sample value $\bar{x} = 10.76\%$ as an estimate of the population mean μ. However, we would not expect the population mean percent earnings to exactly equal 10.76. We must develop some additional statistical reasoning before we can provide an indication of the uncertainty associated with making this generalization.

8.2 POINT ESTIMATION OF A POPULATION MEAN

Because inference proceeds from the specific sample to the general case of the population and because any sample will be different from other samples taken from the same population, there must inevitably be some uncertainty connected with an inference. Nevertheless, in the context of point estimation, the goal is to provide a single number as the estimate of the population value. What sample quantity should we use to estimate the population mean μ? More formally, beginning with a random sample $X_1, X_2, \ldots, X_n$ of size n from the population, we must specify a sample statistic whose value is related to the unknown value of the population parameter, in this case, μ. This statistic is the estimator of the population parameter.

> A statistic whose value gives an estimate of a parameter is called a **point estimator** or, simply, an **estimator.**
>
> The standard deviation of the estimator is called its **standard error** or s.e.

Intuitively, the sample mean

$$\bar{X} = \frac{X_1 + X_2 + \cdots + X_n}{n}$$

could be a good statistic for estimating the population mean. For instance, when estimating the mean number of calls in Example 8.1, we got the result $\bar{x} = 89.6$ calls. The estimate 89.6 is called a point estimate, or simply an estimate of μ. Some uncertainty is associated with this estimate and it must be quantified.

To quantify the uncertainty associated with using the sample mean to estimate the population mean, we turn to the sampling distribution of $\bar{X}$ introduced in Chapter 7. Recall that the sampling distribution of $\bar{X}$ has the following properties:

1. $E(\overline{X}) = \mu$

2. $sd(\overline{X}) = \dfrac{\sigma}{\sqrt{n}}$ so s.e.$(\overline{X}) = \dfrac{\sigma}{\sqrt{n}}$

3. With a large sample size n, the distribution of $\overline{X}$ is nearly normal with mean μ and standard deviation $\dfrac{\sigma}{\sqrt{n}}$.

The first result states that $\overline{X}$ is centered about μ, in the sense of expectation. The second states that its standard deviation is equal to the population standard deviation divided by the square root of the sample size. From the third result, as shown in Figure 8.1, we can understand how closely $\overline{X}$ is expected to estimate the population mean μ.

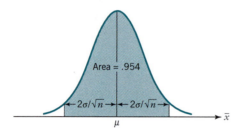

Area = .954

$\leftarrow 2\sigma/\sqrt{n} \rightarrow \!\leftarrow 2\sigma/\sqrt{n} \rightarrow$

μ $\bar{x}$

Figure 8.1   Approximate Normal Distribution of $\overline{X}$

For any normal distribution, the interval extending 2 standard deviations on each side of the mean is assigned probability .954. Consequently, prior to selecting the sample, the probability is about .95 that the estimator $\overline{X}$ will be within $2\sigma/\sqrt{n}$ units of the true population mean μ. This can be rephrased in terms of the bound on the error: *When $\overline{X}$ is taken as the estimator for μ, its 95.4% error bound is $2\sigma/\sqrt{n}$.*

The choice of probability .954 is convenient but arbitrary. We can specify an error bound corresponding to any symmetric interval about μ with a specified probability content.

Let $1 - \alpha$ denote the desired high probability, such as .95 or .90. The following notation enables us to write the expression for the $100(1 - \alpha)\%$ error margin.

$z_{\alpha/2}$ **Notation**

We define $z_{\alpha/2}$ to be the upper $\alpha/2$ point of the standard normal distribution. Similarly, $z_{1-\alpha/2}$ is the upper $1 - \alpha/2$ point of the standard normal distribution.

The area under the normal curve to the right of $z_{\alpha/2}$ is $\alpha/2$. Since $z_{1-\alpha/2} = -z_{\alpha/2}$, the area between $-z_{\alpha/2}$ and $z_{\alpha/2}$ is $1 - \alpha$ (see Figure 8.2).

A few values of $z_{\alpha/2}$ obtained from the normal table, for common values of $1 - \alpha$, appear in Table 8.1 for easy reference.

Since the population standard deviation, σ, is usually unknown, the standard error of $\overline{X}$ must be estimated. When the sample size is large, we can estimate σ by the sample standard deviation

$$S = \sqrt{\dfrac{\sum_{i=1}^{n}(X_i - \overline{X})^2}{n - 1}}$$

and the effect on the probability is negligible.

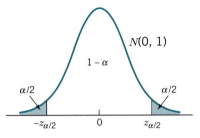

Figure 8.2   An Illustration of the $z_{\alpha/2}$ Notation

TABLE 8.1   Values of $z_{\alpha/2}$

$1-\alpha$	.80	.85	.90	.95	.99
$z_{\alpha/2}$	1.28	1.44	1.645	1.96	2.58

In summary:

Point Estimation of the Population Mean

Parameter: Population mean μ

Data: $X_1, X_2, \ldots, X_n$ (a random sample of size n)

Estimator: $\overline{X}$ (the sample mean) with estimated $\text{s.e.}(\overline{X}) = \dfrac{s}{\sqrt{n}}$

For a large sample size n, the $100(1-\alpha)\%$ **error margin** is $z_{\alpha/2}\dfrac{\sigma}{\sqrt{n}}$. If σ is unknown, use s in place of σ.

EXAMPLE 8.3   Calculating a Point Estimate and Error Margin for the Mean Number of Calls per Shift

Refer to the 75 measurements on the number of calls in Example 8.1. Give a point estimate of the population mean number of calls and the associated 95% error margin.

Solution and Discussion.   The sample mean and standard deviation, computed from the 75 measurements, are

$$\overline{x} = \frac{\sum x_i}{75} = 89.60 \text{ calls}$$

$$s = \sqrt{\frac{\sum (x_i - \overline{x})^2}{74}} = 17.32 \text{ calls}$$

To calculate the 95% error bound, we set $1 - \alpha = .95$ so that $\alpha/2 = .025$. The normal table gives $z_{.025} = 1.96$. Consequently, the 95% error margin is

$$1.96 \times \frac{s}{\sqrt{n}} = 1.96 \times \frac{17.32}{\sqrt{75}} = 3.92 \text{ calls}$$

How do we interpret the error margin in this case? Prior to sampling, the probability is approximately .95 that the sample mean will be within $\pm 1.96\ S/\sqrt{n}$ of the population mean. Consequently, we are quite certain that $\overline{x} = 89.60$ is within ± 3.92 of the unknown value of the population mean number of calls per shift.

Remarks

(a) The standard error should *not* be interpreted as the expected or "typical" error as the term *standard* may suggest. For instance, if s.e.$(\overline{X}) = 6.0$, it is not the case that the error of estimation $\overline{X} - \mu$ is likely to be 6.0. Rather, prior to observing the data, the probability is .954 that this error will be less than 2 s.e.$(\overline{X}) = 12.0$ and the probability is .6826 that it will be less than s.e.$(\overline{X}) = 6.0$ (see Exercise 8.13).

(b) A point estimate and its variability are often reported in either of two forms:

$$\text{estimate} \pm \text{s.e.} \quad \text{or} \quad \text{estimate} \pm 2\,\text{s.e.}$$

When reporting a numerical result as 27.3 ± 3.8, you must specify whether 3.8 represents s.e. or 2 s.e.

DETERMINING THE SAMPLE SIZE

The selection of sample size should be done in the planning stage of any investigation. Of course, the larger the sample, the more information that will be available about the value of the parameter. However, because sampling can be costly and time consuming, an investigator needs to know the sample size required to give the desired precision in advance. No absolute bound can be given for the error of estimation, so we base our calculations on a bound that will hold with high probability prior to taking the sample.

When using $\overline{X}$ for estimating a population mean, the first step is to specify e, the desired error margin and $1 - \alpha$, the probability associated with the error margin. The desired error bound is then equated to the expression for the $100(1 - \alpha)\%$ error margin. Consequently, we set

$$e = z_{\alpha/2}\frac{\sigma}{\sqrt{n}}$$

Solving this equation for n, we obtain the required sample size,

$$n = \left[\frac{z_{\alpha/2}\sigma}{e}\right]^2$$

The solution is rounded up to the next integer because a sample size cannot be fractional.

This procedure is valid for determining a sample size as long as the resulting sample size is greater than 30, so that the normal approximation to $\overline{X}$ is satisfactory.

> The **required sample size** is
>
> $$n = \left[\frac{z_{\alpha/2}\sigma}{e} \right]^2$$
>
> to be $100(1 - \alpha)\%$ sure that the error of estimation $|\overline{X} - \mu|$ does not exceed e.

If σ is completely unknown, a small pilot sample could be collected and the sample standard deviation used to estimate σ in the equation for sample size. Otherwise, the sample size selection can be made by evaluating the solutions for several plausible values for σ.

EXAMPLE 8.4   Determining the Sample Size, σ Known

Because of unavoidable delays between the time an invoice is sent and payment is received from foreign customers, fluctuating exchange rates can lead to increased or decreased profits. An accountant decides to evaluate the magnitude of this component of profit during the current year. From the previous year's experience, she thinks it is reasonable to assume that the standard deviation σ is $150 per transaction. How many transactions must the accountant review to have a 90% error margin less than $20 when estimating the mean?

Solution and Discussion.   Here $\sigma = 150$ and $1 - \alpha = .90$, so $\alpha/2 = .05$. The upper .05 point of the standard normal is $z_{.05} = 1.645$. Since the tolerable bound is $e = 20$,

$$n = \left[\frac{1.645 \times 150}{20} \right]^2 = 152.2$$

Rounding up, we get the required sample size of 153 transactions.

EXAMPLE 8.5   Determining the Sample Size, σ Unknown

A society of travel service providers would like to learn about the amount a traveler spends on local tours at destination cities. Because the mean and standard deviation of the distribution of expenditures are unknown, it was necessary to first collect a small random sample of values. Twenty travelers recorded their expenditures. These data have a sample standard deviation of $143. Using this estimate from the pilot sample, determine the number of travelers to include to have a 95% error margin less than $10 when estimating the mean.

Solution and Discussion.   Here σ is estimated as 143 and $1 - \alpha = .95$, so $\alpha/2 = .025$. The upper .025 point of the standard normal is $z_{.025} = 1.96$. Since the tolerable bound is $e = 10$,

$$n = \left[\frac{1.96 \times 143}{10}\right]^2 = 785.6$$

After rounding up, the required sample size is 786 travelers.

EXERCISES

8.1 For estimating a population mean with the sample mean $\overline{X}$, find (i) the standard error of $\overline{X}$ and (ii) the $100(1 - \alpha)\%$ error margin in each case.

   a. $n = 175, \sigma = 20, 1 - \alpha = .95$
   b. $n = 103, \sigma = 5.4, 1 - \alpha = .92$
   c. $n = 200, \sigma = 63, 1 - \alpha = .99$

8.2 For estimating a population mean with the sample mean $\overline{X}$, find (i) the point estimate of μ, (ii) its estimated standard error, and (iii) the $100(1 - \alpha)\%$ error margin in each case.

   a. $n = 75, \overline{x} = 83.6, s = 31, 1 - \alpha = .98$
   b. $n = 64, \overline{x} = 427, s = 3.9, 1 - \alpha = .975$
   c. $n = 82, \overline{x} = .724, s = 7.7, 1 - \alpha = .90$

8.3 Consider the problem of estimating a population mean μ based on a random sample of size n. Compute the point estimate of μ and its estimated standard error in each of the following situations:

   a. $n = 68, \sum x_i = 1506, \sum(x_i - \overline{x})^2 = 327$
   b. $n = 52, \sum x_i = 792, \sum(x_i - \overline{x})^2 = 102$
   c. $n = 73, \sum x_i = 1124, \sum(x_i - \overline{x})^2 = 209$

8.4 Determine a 95.4% error margin for the estimation of μ in each of the three cases in Exercise 8.3.

8.5 Data on the average weekly earnings were obtained from a survey of 50 nonsupervisory personnel in the insurance industry. The sample mean and standard deviation were found to be \$624 and \$44, respectively. Estimate the population mean weekly earnings, and determine the 95% error margin.

8.6 When estimating μ from a large sample, suppose that the 95% error margin of $\overline{X}$ is 4.83. From this information, determine the

   a.   Estimated s.e. of $\overline{X}$
   b.   90% error margin

8.7 For each case, determine the sample size n that is required for estimating the population mean with the specified error margin.

   a. $\sigma = 4.7$, 95% error margin $= .85$
   b. $\sigma = 315$, 97% error margin $= 10.0$
   c. $\sigma = .44$, 80% error margin $= .02$

8.8 When estimating the mean of a population using $\overline{X}$, how large a sample is required so that the 95.4% error margin is

a.   One-sixth of the population standard deviation?

b.   12% of the population standard deviation?

8.9   Refer to Exercise 8.5. Suppose that the survey of 50 workers was, in fact, a pilot study intended to provide information on the population standard deviation. On the basis of the sample information, $s = \$44$ would be the estimate of σ. Determine the sample size required for estimating the mean weekly earnings with a 98% error margin of $4.50.

8.10   Seasonal employees at a large mail order company request the help of an experienced supervisor when difficulties arise with phone orders. Data on the activities of a supervisor covering 10 seasonal operators for a total of $n = 48$ hours yielded a mean of 12.7 requests for help per hour and a standard deviation of 5.2.

a.   From these data, estimate the mean number of requests for help in an hour, and give the 90% error margin.

b.   Suppose the supervisor is assigned to twice the number of original phone operators. Estimate the mean number of requests for help in an hour, and give the 90% error margin.

c.   Is your 90% error margin in part **b** larger than that in part **a?** Explain by comparing the variance of $\overline{X}$ with the variance of $2\overline{X}$.

8.11   Daily usage of the office copy machines was monitored for 56 working days. The daily number of copies had mean 382.7 and standard deviation 61.28 copies.

a.   From these data, estimate the mean number of copies in a day, and give the 90% error margin.

b.   Estimate the mean number of copies in a five-day working week, and give the 90% error margin.

c.   Is your 90% error margin in part **b** larger than that in part **a?** Explain by comparing the variance of $\overline{X}$ with the variance of $5\overline{X}$.

8.12   An insurance company finds that 340 automobile property-only accident claims had a mean of $1790 and a standard deviation of $635. Assuming these claims can be treated as a random sample of size 340 from the population of all possible automobile property-only accident claims, estimate the mean value of an automobile property-only accident claim and give the 95% error margin.

8.13   Verify that the probability is .6826 that the error of estimation $\overline{X} - \mu$ will be smaller, in absolute value, than the s.e.$(\overline{X}) = \sigma/\sqrt{n}$.

8.14   *Estimating the Mean of a Finite Population.* Suppose the population of interest consists of a finite number of units N. As described in Section 5.6, a random sample of size n can be obtained by sampling without replacement. The sample mean $\overline{x}$ and standard deviation s are calculated from the sample by the usual formulas. It is still true that $E(\overline{X}) = \mu$, so the expectation of $\overline{X}$ is equal to the population mean. That is, $\overline{X}$ will be a reasonable point estimator of μ. However, the variance of $\overline{X}$ is no longer σ^2/n but is modified by the finite population correction factor $(N - n)/(N - 1)$ so that

$$\operatorname{var}(\overline{X}) = \frac{\sigma^2}{n} \frac{N - n}{N - 1}$$

When $\overline{x}$ is chosen as the point estimate of μ, its estimated standard error is

$$\frac{s}{\sqrt{n}}\sqrt{\frac{N-n}{N-1}}$$

where s is the sample standard deviation.

a. A random sample of 40 accounting majors, taken from the 350 accounting majors in the junior class, provided the sample values $\overline{x} = 1.73$ and $s = .62$ for the number of memberships in professional societies. Give a point estimate of the population mean, and estimate its standard error.

b. Change orders can substantially increase the profits when building homes. A random sample of 20 homes is selected, among the 82 recently built in an area, and the ratio (dollar amount of change orders/initial construction bid) recorded. The sample mean was $\overline{x} = .19$ and the standard deviation was $s = .06$. Give a point estimate of the population mean, and estimate its standard error.

8.3 CONFIDENCE INTERVAL FOR μ

Instead of a point estimate, it is usually more informative to produce an interval of plausible values for the true value of any unknown parameter. Ideally, we would like to obtain a sample and then determine an interval that would, for instance, definitely contain the population mean μ. However, because of sample-to-sample variability, this goal is unattainable. Instead, we specify a high probability, typically .90, .95, or .99, that a proposed interval will cover the true value of the unknown mean. Because this probability pertains to the interval before the sample is observed, it is called the **level of confidence.** An interval obtained by a procedure satisfying the probability requirement is called a **confidence interval.**

We first develop a confidence interval for the mean of a normal distribution when the standard deviation σ is *known*. Once the concepts are presented, we will proceed to more realistic cases where σ is unknown.

When the underlying population is normal, we know from the discussion in Section 7.7 that the distribution of $\overline{X}$ is normal with mean μ and standard deviation $\sigma/\sqrt{n}$. This normal sampling distribution is also a good approximation, whatever the underlying population distribution, provided that the sample size n is large. Because we have assumed that σ is known, and the sample size is also known, the standard deviation $\sigma/\sqrt{n}$ of $\overline{X}$ is known. We now show how probability calculations based on the normal distribution lead to confidence intervals for the unknown population mean μ.

The normal table shows that the probability is .95 that a normal random variable will be within 1.96 standard deviations of its mean. For $\overline{X}$, this probability becomes

$$P\left[\mu - 1.96\frac{\sigma}{\sqrt{n}} < \overline{X} < \mu + 1.96\frac{\sigma}{\sqrt{n}}\right] = .95$$

as shown in Figure 8.3.

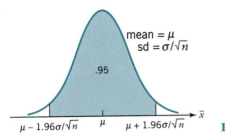

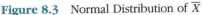

Figure 8.3   Normal Distribution of $\overline{X}$

Transposing $\sigma/\sqrt{n}$ from one side of the inequality to the other, the left-hand inequality in the probability statement

$$\mu - 1.96\frac{\sigma}{\sqrt{n}} < \overline{X} \quad \text{becomes} \quad \mu < \overline{X} + 1.96\frac{\sigma}{\sqrt{n}}$$

and the right-hand inequality

$$\overline{X} < \mu + 1.96\frac{\sigma}{\sqrt{n}} \quad \text{becomes} \quad \overline{X} - 1.96\frac{\sigma}{\sqrt{n}} < \mu$$

Together, these two event relations establish that the event

$$\left\{ \mu - 1.96\frac{\sigma}{\sqrt{n}} < \overline{X} < \mu + 1.96\frac{\sigma}{\sqrt{n}} \right\}$$

is equivalent to the event

$$\left\{ \overline{X} - 1.96\frac{\sigma}{\sqrt{n}} < \mu < \overline{X} + 1.96\frac{\sigma}{\sqrt{n}} \right\}$$

Both events state that $\overline{X} - \mu$ will lie between $-1.96\sigma/\sqrt{n}$ and $1.96\sigma/\sqrt{n}$. Consequently, the statement connected with probability .95

$$P\left[\mu - 1.96\frac{\sigma}{\sqrt{n}} < \overline{X} < \mu + 1.96\frac{\sigma}{\sqrt{n}} \right] = .95$$

can also be expressed as

$$P\left[\overline{X} - 1.96\frac{\sigma}{\sqrt{n}} < \mu < \overline{X} + 1.96\frac{\sigma}{\sqrt{n}} \right] = .95$$

This last form of the probability statement has an important interpretation. Before we observe the sample, the probability is .95 that the random interval from $\overline{X} - 1.96\sigma/\sqrt{n}$ to $\overline{X} + 1.96\sigma/\sqrt{n}$ will cover the unknown mean μ. Because the standard deviation σ

was assumed to be known, the upper and lower endpoints can be calculated when the sample data become available. We call the interval

$$\left(\bar{x} - 1.96\frac{\sigma}{\sqrt{n}}, \ \bar{x} + 1.96\frac{\sigma}{\sqrt{n}} \right)$$

a **95% confidence interval for** μ when the population is normal and its standard deviation σ is known.

EXAMPLE 8.6   Constructing a Confidence Interval for μ When σ Is Known

A random sample of size 25 is obtained from a normal population having known standard deviation $\sigma = 14.3$. The sample mean is found to be 31.5. Obtain a 95% confidence interval for the unknown population mean μ.

Solution and Discussion.   Using the observed value $\bar{x} = 31.5$ and the given value $\sigma = 14.3$, the 95% confidence interval

$$\left(\bar{x} - 1.96\frac{\sigma}{\sqrt{n}}, \ \bar{x} + 1.96\frac{\sigma}{\sqrt{n}} \right)$$

becomes

$$\left(31.5 - 1.96\frac{14.3}{\sqrt{25}}, \ 31.5 + 1.96\frac{14.3}{\sqrt{25}} \right) \quad \text{or} \quad (25.9, \ 37.1)$$

Keep in mind that the 95% confidence interval $(25.9, \ 37.1)$ developed in Example 8.6 either contains the mean μ or it does not, and we will never know which is the case. However, there is a good chance that it does since we are using a procedure with a 95% probability of success. The probability refers to the *procedure* for constructing the interval, not to the probability content of the particular interval $(25.9, \ 37.1)$. Once the interval is constructed, nothing is random, since the interval and the mean μ are both fixed.

We need not restrict our attention to 95% confidence intervals. Rather than probability .95, the investigator can specify a high probability $1 - \alpha$. The only change to obtain the resulting $100(1 - \alpha)\%$ confidence interval is to replace 1.96 by $z_{\alpha/2}$. As shown in Figure 8.2, the probability to the right of $z_{\alpha/2}$ is $\alpha/2$.

In summary, a $100(1 - \alpha)\%$ confidence interval for the mean μ of a normal distribution with known σ is given by

$$\left(\bar{x} - z_{\alpha/2}\frac{\sigma}{\sqrt{n}}, \ \bar{x} + z_{\alpha/2}\frac{\sigma}{\sqrt{n}} \right)$$

INTERPRETATION OF CONFIDENCE INTERVALS

To gain some insight into the interpretation of confidence intervals, we use a computer to generate repeated random samples, each of size 8, from a normal distribution with mean $\mu = 10$ and standard deviation $\sigma = 3$. Although we actually know the mean, we will treat it as unknown, and calculate the 95% confidence interval

$$\left(\bar{x} - 1.96\frac{3}{\sqrt{8}}, \quad \bar{x} + 1.96\frac{3}{\sqrt{8}} \right)$$

from each random sample. For the first sample, $\bar{x} = 9.8$, so the 95% confidence interval is (7.72, 11.88). This interval does cover the true mean. This interval, and those for 14 additional samples, are graphed as lines in Figure 8.4. The center of each interval, indicated by a dot, is the value of $\bar{x}$. Note that all of the intervals have the same length, $2(1.96\sigma/\sqrt{n}) = 4.16$.

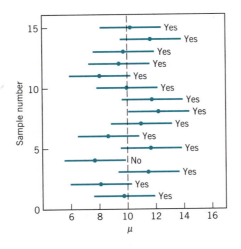

Figure 8.4   Interpretation of Confidence Interval for μ, σ Known

When a confidence interval covers the true mean, the horizontal line crosses the dotted line through $\mu = 10$. Note that $\frac{14}{15}$ or .96 of the intervals cover the true value of the mean. This is quite close to the specified probability .95, which is the long-run limit for the relative frequency of covering the true value in a large number of repetitions.

We summarize the key ideas in confidence interval construction in terms of 95% confidence intervals for a normal population mean:

1. Before the sample is taken,

$$\left(\overline{X} - 1.96\frac{\sigma}{\sqrt{n}}, \quad \overline{X} + 1.96\frac{\sigma}{\sqrt{n}} \right)$$

    is a random interval that attempts to cover the true value of the mean μ.

2. We interpret the probability

$$P\left[\overline{X} - 1.96\frac{\sigma}{\sqrt{n}} < \mu < \overline{X} + 1.96\frac{\sigma}{\sqrt{n}} \right] = .95$$

as the long-run relative frequency. Over many repetitions of the sampling, the true mean will be covered by approximately 95% of the intervals.

3. Once the value $\bar{x}$ is obtained from a sample, the interval

$$\left(\bar{x} - 1.96\frac{\sigma}{\sqrt{n}}, \ \bar{x} + 1.96\frac{\sigma}{\sqrt{n}} \right)$$

is a realization of the random interval. Once the numerical value for the interval is determined, it is no longer proper to talk about probability .95. Rather, we use the term *confidence*.

Even if the same problem is not repeated, the confidence interval approach is sound. For instance, if 95% confidence intervals are calculated in *all* applications, then approximately 95% of the time the true mean will be contained in its respective confidence interval. It is this long-run coverage property that leads to the use of the term *confidence*.

A LARGE SAMPLE CONFIDENCE INTERVAL FOR μ

What happens if the population standard deviation is unknown or the population is not normal? When the sample size n is large, the central limit theorem tells us that the distribution of $\overline{X}$ is nearly normal whatever the form of the population distribution. Consequently, for large samples, we can still make the probability statement

$$P\left[\overline{X} - z_{\alpha/2}\frac{\sigma}{\sqrt{n}} < \mu < \overline{X} + z_{\alpha/2}\frac{\sigma}{\sqrt{n}} \right] = 1 - \alpha$$

The probability $1 - \alpha$ is approximate when the population is not normal. Although, prior to sampling, the interval

$$\left(\overline{X} - z_{\alpha/2}\frac{\sigma}{\sqrt{n}}, \ \overline{X} + z_{\alpha/2}\frac{\sigma}{\sqrt{n}} \right)$$

will include μ with probability $1 - \alpha$, it cannot serve as a confidence interval since σ is unknown. However, because the sample size is large, replacing $\sigma/\sqrt{n}$ by the estimate $s/\sqrt{n}$ does not appreciably affect the probability statement.

Large Sample Confidence Interval for μ

When the sample size n is large, a $100(1 - \alpha)\%$ confidence interval for μ is given by

$$\left(\bar{x} - z_{\alpha/2}\frac{s}{\sqrt{n}}, \ \bar{x} + z_{\alpha/2}\frac{s}{\sqrt{n}} \right)$$

where s is the sample standard deviation.

EXAMPLE 8.7   Constructing Large Sample Confidence Intervals for μ

A researcher presented 43 experienced accountants with an audit situation and asked each of them to make a decision on the case. The total time each accountant took to read the materials, consult any references, and come to the decision was recorded. The mean and standard deviation for the decision times were calculated to be 7.40 hours and 1.2 hours, respectively. Determine (a) 95% and (b) 80% confidence intervals for the mean time to complete the audit task.

Solution and Discussion.   The sample size is $n = 43$, so a normal approximation to the distribution of $\overline{X}$ is appropriate. We have the observed values

$$\overline{x} = 7.40 \quad \text{and} \quad s = 1.2$$

a.   With $1 - \alpha = .95$, we have $\alpha/2 = .025$ and $z_{.025} = 1.96$. Moreover,

$$1.96 \frac{s}{\sqrt{n}} = 1.96 \frac{1.2}{\sqrt{43}} = .36$$

so the 95% confidence interval for the population mean μ is

$$\left(\overline{x} - 1.96 \frac{s}{\sqrt{n}}, \; \overline{x} + 1.96 \frac{s}{\sqrt{n}} \right) \quad \text{or} \quad (7.40 - .36, \; 7.40 + .36) \quad \text{or} \quad (7.04, \; 7.76)$$

The investigator is 95% confident that the mean time to complete the task, μ, is between 7.04 and 7.76 hours. That is, about 95% of the time, random samples of 43 accountants would produce intervals $\overline{x} \pm 1.96 s/\sqrt{n}$ that contain μ, the mean decision time.

b.   With $1 - \alpha = .80$, we have $\alpha/2 = .10$ and $z_{.10} = 1.28$, so

$$1.28 \frac{s}{\sqrt{n}} = 1.28 \frac{1.2}{\sqrt{43}} = .23$$

and the 80% confidence interval for the population mean μ is

$$(7.40 - .23, \; 7.40 + .23) \quad \text{or} \quad (7.17, \; 7.63)$$

Comparing the two confidence intervals, we see that the 80% confidence interval is shorter. Although the shorter interval seems to be giving more precise information about μ, it has a smaller long-run relative frequency of being correct.

EXAMPLE 8.8   Calculating a Confidence Interval for the Mean Number of Calls per Shift

Refer to Example 8.1, where the number of calls handled per shift is given for each of 75 workers. Obtain a 90% confidence interval for the mean number of calls. Also comment on the shape of the distribution of calls per shift.

Solution and Discussion. The computer calculation, presented in Example 8.1, gives $n = 75$, $\bar{x} = 89.60$, and $s = 17.32$. Since $1 - \alpha = .90$, $\alpha/2 = .05$ and $z_{.05} = 1.645$. The large sample 90% confidence interval for μ is given by

$$\left(\bar{x} - 1.645\frac{s}{\sqrt{n}}, \ \bar{x} + 1.645\frac{s}{\sqrt{n}} \right)$$

or $\left(89.60 - 1.645\frac{17.32}{\sqrt{75}}, \ 89.60 + 1.645\frac{17.32}{\sqrt{75}} \right)$

or $(86.31, \ 92.89)$ calls per shift.

A large sample also contains information on the shape of the distribution that can be exhibited by graphical displays. Figure 8.5 gives the stem-and-leaf display, accompanied by the box plot and a table of descriptive statistics.

```
Stem-and-leaf of C1          N   = 75
Leaf Unit = 1.0

     2      5 01
     6      5 5779
     6      6
     8      6 89
    16      7 01223344
    21      7 66678
    29      8 00112234
    33      8 6778
   (12)     9 111222334444
    30      9 5666667
    23     10 0122244
    16     10 5567889
     9     11 0014
     5     11 788
     2     12 0
     1     12 7
```

	N	MEAN	MEDIAN	TRMEAN	STDEV	SEMEAN
	75	89.60	92.00	89.91	17.32	2.00

	MIN	MAX	Q1	Q3
	50.00	127.00	76.00	102.00

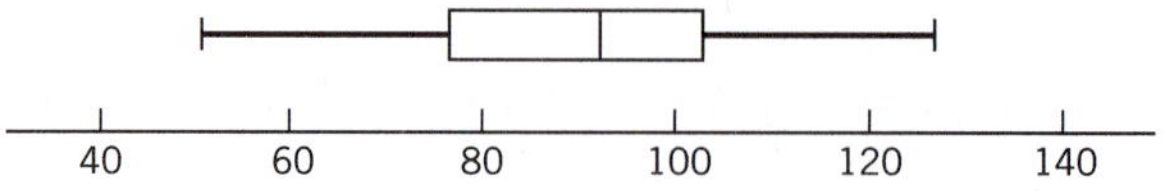

Figure 8.5 Stem-and-Leaf Display, Box Plot, and Descriptive Statistics for the Calls per Shift

These displays suggest that the population of calls per shift may have a long left-hand tail, that is, may be skewed to the left. However, the form of the population distribution is not crucial in this case because the large sample size (and the central limit theorem) allows us to treat $\overline{X}$ as a normal random variable. This leads directly to the form for the large sample confidence interval for μ given earlier.

EXERCISES

8.15 Determine a 90% confidence interval for μ if $n = 49$, $\overline{x} = 38.4$, and $s = 6.1$.

8.16 Determine a 95% confidence interval for μ if $n = 64$, $\overline{x} = 7.3$, and $s = 2.8$.

8.17 A quality monitoring procedure specifies that a 90% confidence interval be determined for the mean each time a sample is selected. After 400 instances, approximately how many of these intervals will cover their respective true means?

8.18 An inventory planning procedure specifies that a 95% confidence interval be determined for mean daily sales of an item based on sales at a random sample of retail stores. After 300 instances, approximately how many of these intervals will cover their respective true daily mean sales?

8.19 Each day during the year, a manager takes a large sample of cellular phone calls and determines a 95% confidence interval for the mean length of all cellular phone calls that day. Of these 365 confidence intervals, approximately how many would cover their respective population means?

8.20 An accountant samples 100 travel reimbursement claims for undocumented expenses and finds $\overline{x} = 37.60$ dollars and $s = 14.30$ dollars. He reports that a 95% confidence interval for the mean undocumented expenses per claim is

$$37.60 - 1.96 \times \frac{14.30}{10} \quad \text{to} \quad 37.60 + 1.96 \times \frac{14.30}{10} \quad \text{or} \quad (34.80, \ 40.40)$$

a. Is the statement correct?

b. Does the interval $(34.80, \ 40.40)$ cover the true mean? Explain.

8.21 A market researcher asks a sample of 400 potential customers to try a new snack product and to rate taste on a 5-point scale from awful (1) to delicious (5). He finds $\overline{x} = 3.93$ and $s = .94$. He reports that a 90% confidence interval for the mean taste rating is

$$3.93 - 1.645 \times \frac{.94}{20} \quad \text{to} \quad 3.93 + 1.645 \times \frac{.94}{20} \quad \text{or} \quad (3.85, \ 4.01)$$

a. Is the statement correct?

b. Does the interval $(3.85, \ 4.01)$ cover the true mean? Explain.

8.22 A study for a shipping company of a sample $n = 48$ trips gave a mean shipment weight of 2.83 thousand pounds and a standard deviation of 1.2 thousand pounds. Use these data to construct a 95% confidence interval for the true mean weight of all shipments.

8.23 A manager at a power company monitored the time required to process high-efficiency lamp bulb rebates. A random sample of $n = 58$ applications gave a mean time of 2.7 minutes and a standard deviation of .92 minute. Use these data to construct a 95% confidence interval for the population mean time to process a rebate application.

8.24 Refer to Exercise 8.5. Determine a 98% confidence interval for the mean weekly earnings of nonsupervisory personnel in the insurance industry.

8.25 From data on a large sample from a population of sales receipts, a small business owner reports that a point estimate of the population mean dollar sales per transaction, μ, is $\bar{x} = 1234$ dollars and its 95% error margin is 75.2 dollars. Use this information to construct a

a. 95% confidence interval for the mean μ

b. 90% confidence interval for the mean μ

8.26 A company wishing to improve its customer service randomly selected 81 incoming calls to its hot line that have been put on hold. The total hold time for each of these calls was recorded. The company determined that a point estimate of the population mean hold time, μ, is $\bar{x} = 3.4$ minutes and its 95% error margin is 1.2 minutes. Use this information to construct a

a. 95% confidence interval for the mean μ

b. 90% confidence interval for the mean μ

8.27 From data on a large sample of sales transactions, a small business owner reports that a 95% confidence interval for the mean profit per transaction, μ, is $(23.41, \ 102.59)$. Use these data to determine

a. A point estimate of the mean μ and its 95% error margin

b. A 90% confidence interval for the mean μ

8.28 A credit company selects a sample of 55 contested items and records their amounts. The company reports that a 95% confidence interval for the mean amount contested, μ, is $(43.7, \ 162.3)$ dollars. Use these data to determine

a. A point estimate of the mean μ and its 95% error margin

b. A 90% confidence interval for the mean μ

8.29 On the basis of a random sample of size $n = 144$, someone proposes that

$$(\bar{x} - .13s, \ \bar{x} + .13s)$$

is a large sample confidence interval for μ. What is the level of confidence associated with this interval?

8.30 An accounting company selected a random sample of 75 franchise offices from among the thousands it needed to audit and recorded the time to complete an audit of each franchise office in the sample. The company determined that a 95% confidence interval for the population mean time μ to audit a franchise office is (58.2 hours, 109.6 hours). Answer the following questions "Yes," "No," or "Cannot tell" and justify your answer.

a. Does the population mean lie in the interval $(58.2, 109.6)$?

b. Does the sample mean lie in the interval $(58.2, 109.6)$?

c. For a future sample of 75 franchises, will the sample mean fall in the interval $(58.2, 109.6)$?

d. Do 95% of the sample data lie in the interval $(58.2, 109.6)$?

e.   For a higher level of confidence, say, 98%, will the confidence interval calculation produce an interval narrower than $(58.2, 109.6)$?

8.31   A stockbroker measured the number of customer buy/sell orders that she handled per day over the course of 58 working days. She determined that a 90% confidence interval for the population mean number of buy/sell orders per day, μ, is $(12.6, 18.7)$. Answer the following questions "Yes," "No," or "Cannot tell" and justify your answer.

a.   Does the population mean lie in the interval $(12.6, 18.7)$?

b.   Does the sample mean lie in the interval $(12.6, 18.7)$?

c.   For a future sample of buy/sell orders on 58 days, will the sample mean fall in the interval $(12.6, 18.7)$?

d.   Do 90% of the sample data lie in the interval $(12.6, 18.7)$?

e.   For a lower level of confidence, say, 88%, will the confidence interval calculation produce an interval narrower than $(12.6, 18.7)$?

8.4   TEST OF HYPOTHESES

Populations are described by probability distributions or probability density functions. A statement such as

The population mean is greater than 23.7

The population standard deviation is less than 12.6

or

At least 75% of the probability is assigned to values larger than 9.1

that concerns a feature of the population is called a statistical hypothesis. The term *statistical* serves to remind us that chance variation has been modeled by a distribution, and that the hypotheses are made about its features. In some cases, the population is very real, as the population of current values of cars owned by residents of California. In other cases, such as the population of ratings of taste on all possible packages of a new high-fiber breakfast cereal, the population is more abstract, although it can be modeled with a probability distribution.

> **Statistical hypothesis** or **Hypothesis:** A statement about a feature of the population

A problem of testing a statistical hypothesis arises when a claim or conjecture about a population parameter must be demonstrated or refuted on the basis of data collected as a sample from the population. Because the ideas are somewhat involved, we will introduce the formulation of statistical hypotheses and the sequence of steps for testing them in the context of a specific problem.

Problem: *Does a simplified reporting form speed up the handling of consumers' requests for information?*

As part of the continuing commitment to quality and productivity improvement, a manufacturer decided to concentrate on the time it takes to process consumer requests for further information. From extensive records on a very large number of earlier requests, the distribution of time to respond has mean 8.3 days and standard deviation 3.1 days. The mean was clearly unacceptable, and a study of the existing process led to several suggestions for improvement.

One major change was suggested: Have an experienced person sort the incoming requests, handle the simple ones as soon as possible, and route the others to appropriate sources. The quality team responsible for this project thinks that this will reduce the mean response time to less than 8.3 days. As experimental verification for this claim, the new procedure will be put into effect for a couple of months. Then a random sample of 60 requests will be selected, and the sample mean $\bar{x}$ calculated. How should the result be used to obtain a statistical verification of the claim that the true (population) mean is less than 8.3 days?

We develop our answer beginning with some intuitive reasoning. Let μ denote the population mean. This is the mean of the entire collection of possible times to process consumer requests. The collection of 60 times in the sample cannot provide a definite answer to whether μ is now less than 8.3 days. In the absence of any absolute proof that the hypothesis holds or that it does not hold, we must settle for "strong evidence." The weight of evidence is anchored on a probability calculation.

Since the sample size $n = 60$ is large, we know that the sampling distribution of $\overline{X}$ is approximately normal with mean μ. If $\mu = 8.3$, then $\overline{X} - 8.3$ will have mean 0. On the other hand, if μ is less than 8.3, as specified in the hypothesis, then $\overline{X} - 8.3$ will have a negative mean. That is, $\overline{X}$ will tend to be smaller than 8.3.

How far must $\overline{X}$ fall below 8.3 to provide strong evidence in favor of the hypothesis? For large samples, we know that, when $\mu = 8.3$,

$$Z = \frac{\overline{X} - \mu}{\sigma/\sqrt{n}} = \frac{\overline{X} - 8.3}{\sigma/\sqrt{60}}$$

has, approximately, a standard normal distribution according to the central limit theorem. If it can be assumed that $\sigma = 3.1$, which agrees with the earlier study, Z can provide information about the value of μ. A large negative value for Z occurs when $\overline{X}$ is several standard deviations, or several $\sigma/\sqrt{60}$, below 8.3—a highly unlikely event. Consequently, a large negative value for Z suggests that the mean μ is not 8.3 but a smaller value.

Evidently, any decision about the strength of evidence for the hypothesis must be tied to a low probability of making a wrong decision. This probability must be specified in advance of recording the observations.

We are now ready for a detailed discussion of the testing procedure.

THE HYPOTHESES AND THE DECISIONS

Whenever we seek to establish a claim or conjecture on the basis of information contained in a sample, the problem is called a problem of testing hypotheses. The claim or hypothesis that we wish to establish is called the **alternative hypothesis** (H_1). The opposite hypothesis, the one that nullifies the original claim or hypothesis, is called the **null hypothesis** (H_0).

In the context of the problem of testing the claim that the mean time to process customer requests is less than 8.3 days, we take the alternative hypothesis to be a **one-sided hypothesis.** It specifies that the value of μ is below, or on one side of, 8.3, and we write

$$H_1: \quad \mu < 8.3$$

The opposite hypothesis, the mean is greater than or equal to 8.3 days, is then the null hypothesis. However, according to the description of the problem, the quality improvement committee does not distinguish between no change, $\mu = 8.3$, and an even longer mean time to respond, $\mu > 8.3$, since the assertion about an improved mean response time is false in either case. Consequently, it is customary to simply have the null hypothesis specify that there is no difference. The notation is

$$H_0: \quad \mu = 8.3$$

Throughout our introduction to testing hypotheses, we will formulate all null hypotheses with equality.

Formulation of H_0 and H_1

When the goal of the study is to establish an assertion on the basis of a sample:

H_0 is taken as the negation of the assertion.

H_1 is taken as the assertion itself.

Once the hypotheses H_0 and H_1 are specified, it is time to consider the possible decisions that can be reached on the basis of a sample. Hypothesis testing requires a yes/no conclusion, so there are only two possible decisions.

The Two Possible Decisions

Either

Reject H_0 and conclude that H_1 is substantiated

or

Fail to reject H_0 and conclude that H_1 has not been substantiated.

When $\mu = 8.3$, so that H_0: $\mu = 8.3$ prevails, an error will occur if the data lead us to reject H_0 and conclude that H_1 has been substantiated. The second decision, fail to reject H_0, will be the correct decision. On the other hand, if $\mu = 7.6$ days, say, so that H_1: $\mu < 8.3$ holds, then the decision to reject H_0 is correct. It is now the decision where we fail to reject H_0 that is in error. Notice that, for any fixed state of nature μ, only one kind of error is possible. The following table summarizes the possible consequences of these decisions.

	Unknown True Situation	
Decision	**H_0 True** $\mu = 8.3$	**H_1 True** $\mu < 8.3$
Reject H_0	Wrong rejection of H_0 (Type I error)	Correct decision
Fail to reject H_0	Correct decision	Wrong retention of H_0 (Type II error)

It is customary to call the incorrect rejection of H_0 a Type I error and the incorrect decision not to reject H_0, when H_1 is true, a Type II error. To summarize,

---

The Two Possible Types of Error

Type I error: Rejection of H_0 when H_0 is true
Type II error: Failure to reject H_0 when H_1 is true

The next example illustrates the construction of a **two-sided hypothesis.**

EXAMPLE 8.9   Illustrating Hypotheses and Decision Errors

A committee on compensation wants to show that there has been a change in the mean number of hours worked by persons in junior management positions. The old established value is 55 hours per week.

a. Formulate the null and alternative hypotheses for establishing this claim.
b. What error can possibly be made if $\mu = 55$?
c. What error can possibly be made if $\mu = 68$?
d. What error can possibly be made if $\mu = 43$?

Solution and Discussion.

a. According to the guidelines for setting the hypotheses, the claim we wish to establish should be taken as the alternative. Consequently, the alternative hypothesis states that the mean is different from 55 hours. That is, values of μ above 55 or below 55 constitute the two-sided alternative hypothesis. The appropriate notation is

$$H_1: \quad \mu \neq 55$$

The null hypothesis is then H_0: $\mu = 55$.

b. When $\mu = 55$, the null hypothesis is true. The only possible error occurs when we incorrectly reject H_0, a Type I error.

c. When $\mu = 68$, the alternative hypothesis is true. The only possible error occurs when we fail to reject H_0, a Type II error.

d. When $\mu = 43$, the alternative hypothesis is true. The only possible error occurs when we fail to reject H_0, a Type II error.

Procedures for testing hypotheses have much in common with a court trial. The jury clings to the null hypothesis of "not guilty" unless there is very convincing evidence of guilt. Further, the intent of the proceedings is to establish the assertion that the defendant is guilty, not to establish innocence.

Let us return to our initial problem of attempting to show that the new procedure for handling consumer requests for information leads to a mean response rate less than 8.3 days. According to our guidelines, the claim became the alternative hypothesis H_1: $\mu < 8.3$ days, and the null hypothesis was that of no difference or H_0: $\mu = 8.3$ days. A structure for deciding between the two hypotheses will be developed that favors the null hypothesis, unless the statistical evidence in favor of the alternative hypothesis is very strong.

TEST STATISTICS AND THE PROBABILITIES OF ERROR

Continuing with our problem of consumer requests for information, a sample of times to respond to requests under the new procedure must be collected to help us decide between the two hypotheses. We will calculate the value of $\overline{X}$ for this sample. If it is far enough below the null value 8.3 days, we will reject the null hypothesis in favor of the alternative hypothesis. If it is realistic to assume that the population standard deviation is 3.1, we could, for example, reject H_0 if

$$Z = \frac{\overline{X} - 8.3}{3.1/\sqrt{60}} < -1.645$$

With this choice, the observed $\overline{x}$ would have to be 1.645 standard deviations below the null hypothesis value before H_0 could be rejected.

Before proceeding, we introduce the following terminology.

> **Test statistic:** A statistic whose value is used to determine the action
>
> **Test of hypotheses:** A specification of values of the test statistic for which the null hypothesis should be rejected
>
> **Rejection region** or **Critical region:** The set of values for which the null hypothesis should be rejected

A test is completely specified by a test statistic and the rejection region.

The alternative hypothesis H_1 is the hypothesis to be substantiated on the basis of the information in the sample. If H_0 is true and the sample data lead to its rejection in favor of H_1, a Type I error occurs. Since we do not want to conclude H_1 true unless there is substantial support for it, we must keep the chance of a Type I error small.

That is, we must specify a small probability, denoted by α, that H_0 will be rejected when, in fact, it is true. The probability of a Type I error, α, is called the **level of significance** or simply the **significance level** of the test.

Similarly, there is a probability of making a Type II error when H_1 is true. The probability of failing to reject H_0 when H_1 is true is denoted by β. Its value depends on the particular value of μ that prevails under H_1.

Two Probabilities of Error

α = Probability of a Type I error. Called the **level of significance.**

β = Probability of a Type II error

EXAMPLE 8.10   Illustrating Errors, Rejection Region, and Significance Level

Refer to the problem of testing

$$H_0: \quad \mu = 8.3 \quad \text{versus} \quad H_1: \quad \mu < 8.3$$

where μ is the mean time to respond to requests. Suppose it can be assumed that the standard deviation is 3.1 days, so a test can be based on the statistic Z whose value is

$$z = \frac{\bar{x} - 8.3}{3.1/\sqrt{60}}$$

a. What error can be made if $\mu = 8.3$?
b. What error can be made if $\mu = 6.7$?
c. Suppose the level of significance, α, must be less than .06. Does the rejection region

$$z = \frac{\bar{x} - 8.3}{3.1/\sqrt{60}} < -1.645$$

satisfy this condition? If so, what is the actual level of significance?

Solution and Discussion.

a. When $\mu = 8.3$, the null hypothesis is true, so the rejection of H_0, or a Type I error, is the only error that it is possible to make. The other action, failure to reject H_0, is not an error.

b. When $\mu = 6.7$ is true, the alternative hypothesis holds, so failure to reject H_0, or a Type II error, is the only error that it is possible to make. The other action, rejection of H_0, is not an error.

c. Since the sample size is large, the distribution of Z is approximately standard normal under H_0. From the standard normal table (Table 3, Appendix B), we find $P(Z < -1.645) = .05$. Consequently, the proposed rejection region, shown in Figure 8.6, has level of significance $\alpha = .05$.

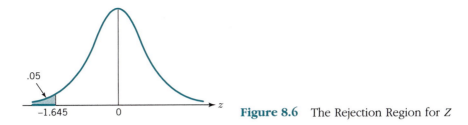

Figure 8.6   The Rejection Region for Z

The significance level for the rejection region satisfies the specification that it be less than .06.

The next example illustrates the calculation of the probability of a Type II error, or of a failure to reject H_0 when it is false.

EXAMPLE 8.11   Calculating the Probability of a Type II Error

Refer to Example 8.10, where the level $\alpha = .05$ rejection region is

$$z = \frac{\bar{x} - 8.3}{3.1/\sqrt{60}} < -1.645$$

Determine the probability of a Type II error if $\mu = 7.4$.

Solution and Discussion.   When $\mu = 7.4$, the mean of $\bar{X} - 8.3$ is negative and Z also has a negative mean. An error will be made when $Z \geq -1.645$, for then we will fail to reject H_0. The calculation of the error probability, β, is based on the fact that $(\bar{X} - 7.4)/(3.1/\sqrt{60})$ has a standard normal distribution when $\mu = 7.4$. The probability of error is

$$\beta = P(Z \geq -1.645) = P\left(\frac{\bar{X} - 8.3}{3.1/\sqrt{60}} \geq -1.645\right)$$

$$= P\left(\bar{X} \geq 8.3 - \frac{3.1}{\sqrt{60}} \times 1.645\right)$$

$$= P\left(\bar{X} - 7.4 \geq 8.3 - 7.4 - \frac{3.1}{\sqrt{60}} \times 1.645\right)$$

$$= P\left(\frac{\bar{X} - 7.4}{3.1/\sqrt{60}} \geq 2.249 - 1.645\right)$$

$$= 1 - P\left(\frac{\bar{X} - 7.4}{3.1/\sqrt{60}} < .604\right) = .2729$$

For a fixed sample size, both errors cannot be made simultaneously small. If we insist on strong evidence before we reject H_0, we must choose α small. In our examples dealing with the time to respond to requests for information, "strong evidence" may mean replacing -1.645 by -2.00 or an even more extreme value for Z. When that is the case, it is more difficult to reject H_0 even when H_1 is true, so the probability, β, will become larger.

This point about the relative magnitudes of the errors is illustrated in Figure 8.7. The figure shows the distribution of $\overline{X}$ where the rejection region $\overline{x} \leq c = 8.3 - 1.645(3.1/\sqrt{60})$ is equivalent to $z \leq -1.645$. The Type I error probability α is shown as the area under the normal curve centered at $\mu = 8.3$, which is the approximate distribution of $\overline{X}$ under the null hypothesis. The Type II error probability β is shown as the shaded area under the normal curve with $\mu = 7.4$. If c is increased, β will decrease but α will increase. Both error probabilities cannot be made smaller by changing c. We will not pursue the calculation of the probabilities of Type II errors, but you should be aware of their existence.

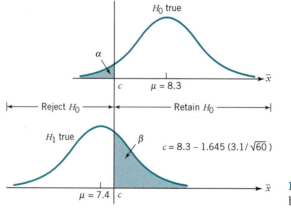

Figure 8.7 The Two Error Probabilities α and β

The choice of the level α is not a statistical problem but rather must be determined by the strength of evidence required by the investigator to reject H_0. One traditional choice is $\alpha = .05$. For this choice, the long-run interpretation of probability implies that a true null hypothesis H_0 would be wrongly rejected in about 5 out of 100 independent applications.

CONDUCTING A TEST OF HYPOTHESES

The steps that we followed to test the hypotheses in the previous example are common to all testing situations. For ease of reference, we set them out in a formal list. The level α should be chosen by the investigator—the person in a position to weigh the consequences of the two types of error. The typical values for α are .01, .05, and .10. In any case, α should be determined when the hypotheses are specified and before the data are collected.

The Steps for Testing Hypotheses

1. *Formulate the hypotheses.* Specify the null hypothesis H_0 and the alternative hypothesis H_1. Specify α.

2. *Select a test statistic.* Choose the test statistic and identify the form of the rejection region.

3. *Determine the rejection region.* For the specified level α, determine the rejection region.

4. *Calculate the test statistic.* Calculate the value of the test statistic from the sample.

5. *Draw a conclusion.* State whether, at the specified level of significance α, H_0 should be rejected in favor of H_1. Interpret the conclusion in the context of the application.

THE CONCEPT OF *P*-VALUE

If it is difficult to specify a meaningful value for α beforehand, you may skip Step 3. Your conclusion can be based on the *P*-value.

P-Value

The **P-value** or **significance probability** is the probability of getting at least as extreme a sample result as the one actually observed if H_0 is true. Equivalently, the *P*-value may be regarded as the smallest α for which the observed test statistic leads to the rejection of H_0.

A small *P*-value means a strong rejection of H_0.

In other words, the *P*-value is the probability under H_0 of the occurrence of the particular observed value or more extreme values. The significance probability gauges the strength of evidence against H_0 on a numerical scale. A small *P*-value indicates strong support of H_1. *It is good statistical practice to record the significance probability when performing a test of hypotheses even if the decision is based on a predetermined α.* Quoting the significance probability allows people with different notions of "strength of evidence" to reach different conclusions. A *P*-value of .071 may be convincing to some people but not to others.

Examples showing the calculation of the *P*-value are given in the next section.

STATISTICAL SIGNIFICANCE AND PRACTICAL SIGNIFICANCE

A test statistic based on a large sample will likely fall in the rejection region (be statistically significant) under even a small deviation from a hypothesized population value. If such a small deviation from a hypothesized value has no useful practical implication, then a decision based on the statistical result must be carefully considered. We must understand the process under study well enough to know what constitutes a practically important deviation. Typically, estimating the magnitude of the deviation from the hypothesized value directly using a confidence interval will provide the most useful information from the data. This issue is explored in Section 8.6. Any practical action must be based on more than statistical significance.

EXERCISES

8.32 Claims or research hypotheses that must be substantiated by sample data are presented here. In each case, identify the null hypothesis (H_0) and the alternative hypothesis (H_1) in terms of the population mean μ.

a. The average verbal score of students who took a management aptitude test in California in 1995 is greater than 24.

b. The mean hospital bill for a birth in the city is less than $2000.

c. The mean dinner expenses for an employee's out-of-state travel is different from $31.80, the amount used for the previous year's planning.

d. The mean number of pages in a statistical consulting firm's fax transmissions is less than 4.7 pages.

8.33 Claims or research hypotheses that must be substantiated by sample data are given here. In each case, identify the null hypothesis (H_0) and the alternative hypothesis (H_1) in terms of the population mean μ.

a. The mean number of days to process a refund after returns are received at the mail order company is less than 9.5 days.

b. The mean hourly rate for temporary office workers in the city is more than $7.40.

c. The mean number of hours a salesperson works per sale of a copier machine is different from 3.4 hours, the mean determined by an earlier study.

d. The mean time between purchases of a brand of mouthwash, by loyal customers, is more than 35 days.

8.34 Suppose data are collected and the decision is made to reject the null hypothesis. In the context of each part **a–d** of Exercise 8.32, answer the following questions.

Under what circumstances is the decision correct?

When is it an incorrect decision, and what type of error is then made?

8.35 Suppose data are collected and the decision is made to reject the null hypothesis. In the context of each part **a–d** of Exercise 8.33, answer the following questions.

Under what circumstances is the decision correct?

When is it an incorrect decision, and what type of error is then made?

8.36 For each situation in parts **a–d** in Exercise 8.32, state whether the rejection region is one-sided or two-sided. If it is one-sided, specify the direction.

8.37 For each situation in parts **a–d** in Exercise 8.33, state whether the rejection region is one-sided or two-sided. If it is one-sided, specify the direction.

8.5 TESTING HYPOTHESES CONCERNING THE MEAN

Having introduced the reasoning and notations for testing hypotheses, we now apply them to tests concerning the mean. When the sample size is large, tests of hypotheses concerning the sample mean will be based on the test statistic Z, whose value is

$$z = \frac{\overline{x} - \mu_0}{s/\sqrt{n}}$$

where μ_0 is the value of the population mean specified under H_0.

According to the central limit theorem, $(\overline{X} - \mu_0)/(\sigma/\sqrt{n})$ is approximately distributed as a standard normal when the null hypothesis $\mu = \mu_0$ is true. Estimating σ by the sample standard deviation S does not appreciably alter the distribution provided that n is larger than, say, 30.

By working with the standard units, or z values, we are able to set rejection regions for a wide variety of applications. The null hypothesis $H_0: \mu = \mu_0$ can be tested against the alternative $\mu < \mu_0$, the alternatve $\mu > \mu_0$, or the alternative $\mu \neq \mu_0$.

Recall that z_α is the number such that the area under the standard normal curve to its right is α. The form of the rejection region is determined from the form of the alternative hypothesis. A large value for Z corresponds to a value for $\overline{X}$ that is substantially above μ_0. The rejection regions are summarized in the following table.

Rejection Region for Testing $\mu = \mu_0$
(Large Samples, α Level Test)

Test Statistic: $Z = \dfrac{\overline{X} - \mu_0}{S/\sqrt{n}}$

Alternative Hypothesis	Reject Null Hypothesis If
$\mu < \mu_0$	$z < -z_\alpha$
$\mu > \mu_0$	$z > z_\alpha$
$\mu \neq \mu_0$	$z < -z_{\alpha/2}$ or $z > z_{\alpha/2}$

For instance, when $\alpha = .05$, $z_\alpha = z_{.05} = 1.645$ and $z_{\alpha/2} = z_{.025} = 1.96$.

EXAMPLE 8.12 Conducting a One-Sided Test and Calculating the P-Value

At a medical care facility, phone calls from patients are received by the staff and then questions and requests are referred to the doctors who return the call at a later time. From a sample of 84 calls collected over a one-week period, the sample mean time to return the call was $\overline{x} = 2.18$ hours and the standard deviation was $s = .73$ hour.

Test, with $\alpha = .05$, the claim that the mean time to return calls is greater than 2.0 hours. Also calculate the P-value and interpret the result.

Solution and Discussion. Corresponding to our steps in testing a hypothesis, we proceed as follows:

1. *Hypotheses*. The claim is taken as the alternative hypothesis. Consequently,

    Null hypothesis H_0: $\mu = 2.0$
    Alternative hypothesis H_1: $\mu > 2.0$

    We are given $\alpha = .05$.

2. *Test statistic*. The sample size is $n = 84$ and $\mu_0 = 2.0$, so the test statistic Z takes the value

$$z = \frac{\overline{x} - \mu_0}{s/\sqrt{n}} = \frac{\overline{x} - 2.0}{s/\sqrt{84}}$$

The alternative hypothesis is one-sided, so we reject H_0 if Z is large.

3. *Rejection Region*. Since $\alpha = .05$ and, from the normal table, $z_{.05} = 1.645$, the one-sided rejection region is (see Figure 8.8)

$$z = \frac{\overline{x} - 2.0}{s/\sqrt{84}} > 1.645$$

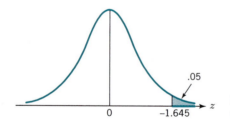

.05

0   −1.645 z

Figure 8.8   A Right-Sided Rejection Region with $\alpha = .05$

4. *Calculation*. We observe $\overline{x} = 2.18$ hours and $s = .73$ hour so the observed value of the test statistic is

$$z = \frac{\overline{x} - 2.0}{s/\sqrt{84}} = \frac{2.18 - 2.0}{.73/\sqrt{84}} = 2.26$$

5. *Conclusion*. The observed value of the test statistic, 2.26, falls in the rejection region. At level $\alpha = .05$, we reject the null hypothesis in favor of the alternative and conclude that the mean time to return a call is greater than 2 hours.

Because the observed value of z is 2.26 and because larger values are more extreme evidence in favor of the alternative hypothesis, the significance probability or P-value is

$$P\text{-value} = P(Z > 2.26) = .0119$$

from the normal table. The probability of getting as extreme a sample result as $\bar{x} = 2.18$ if $H_0 : \mu = 2.0$ is true is about .01. The evidence is quite strong that the mean time to return a call is greater than 2 hours.

EXAMPLE 8.13 Conducting a Two-Sided Test and Calculating the *P*-Value

Over a period of years, a toothpaste has received a mean rating of 5.9, on a 7-point scale, for overall customer satisfaction with the product. Because of a minor unadvertised change in the product, there is concern that the customer satisfaction may have changed. Suppose the satisfaction ratings from a sample of 60 customers have a mean of 5.60 and a standard deviation of .87. Do these data indicate that the mean satisfaction rating is different from 5.9? Test with $\alpha = .05$.

Solution and Discussion. We follow the steps in testing a hypothesis:

1. *Hypotheses.* We are seeking support for the conclusion that a change has occurred. This claim is taken as the alternative hypothesis. Consequently, the hypotheses should be formulated as

   Null hypothesis $\quad H_0 : \quad \mu = 5.9$
   Alternative hypothesis $H_1 : \quad \mu \neq 5.9$

   We are given $\alpha = .05$.

2. *Test Statistic.* The sample size is $n = 60$ and $\mu_0 = 5.9$, so the test statistic Z takes the value

$$ z = \frac{\bar{x} - \mu_0}{s / \sqrt{n}} = \frac{\bar{x} - 5.9}{s / \sqrt{60}} $$

   The alternative hypothesis is two-sided, so we reject if Z is large or if Z takes a large negative value.

3. *Rejection Region.* The specified α is .05, so $\alpha/2 = .025$. From the normal table, $z_{.025} = 1.96$. The two-sided rejection region is (see Figure 8.9)

$$ z = \frac{\bar{x} - 5.9}{s / \sqrt{60}} > 1.96 \quad \text{or} \quad z = \frac{\bar{x} - 5.9}{s / \sqrt{60}} < -1.96 $$

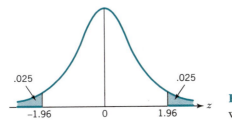

Figure 8.9 A Two-Sided Rejection Region with $\alpha = .05$

4. *Calculation.* We observe $\bar{x} = 5.60$ and $s = .87$, so the observed value of the test statistic Z is

$$z = \frac{\bar{x} - 5.9}{s/\sqrt{60}}$$
$$= \frac{5.60 - 5.9}{.87/\sqrt{60}} = -2.67$$

5. *Conclusion.* The observed value of the test statistic, -2.67, falls in the rejection region. At level $\alpha = .05$, we reject the null hypothesis in favor of the alternative that the mean customer satisfaction rating has changed.

Because the observed value of z is -2.67, values less than -2.67 as well as values greater than 2.67 are considered to provide more extreme evidence in favor of the alternative hypothesis. Consequently, using the normal table, the significance probability or *P*-value is

$$\text{P-value} = P(Z < -2.67) + P(Z > 2.67)$$
$$= .0038 + (1 - .9962) = .0076$$

It is highly unlikely that we would get as extreme a sample result as $\bar{x} = 5.60$ if H_0: $\mu = 5.9$ is true. Consequently, the evidence is quite strong that the mean customer satisfaction rating has changed.

Even though it seems that the mean customer satisfaction rating has decreased, we conducted a *two-sided* test, so the valid conclusion is that there has been a change.

EXERCISES

8.38 A sample of 45 sales receipts from the university bookstore has $\bar{x} = \$147$ and $s = \$12.40$. Use these values to perform a test of H_0: $\mu = 151$ against H_1: $\mu < 151$ with $\alpha = .05$. Calculate the *P*-value.

8.39 Use the values for $\bar{x}$ and s in Exercise 8.38 to perform a test of H_0: $\mu = 151$ against H_1: $\mu \neq 151$ with $\alpha = .05$. Calculate the *P*-value. Why does the *P*-value change from the one in Exercise 8.38?

8.40 In the problem of testing H_0: $\mu = 20$ against H_1: $\mu \neq 20$, the following sample quantities are recorded:

$$n = 65 \qquad \bar{x} = 17.14 \qquad s = 15.6$$

a. Specify the test statistic and determine the rejection region when $\alpha = .05$.

b. Calculate the test statistic and draw a conclusion.

c. Calculate the *P*-value and interpret the result.

8.41 Refer to Example 8.2 concerning percent earnings. Test H_0: $\mu = 15$ against H_1: $\mu \neq 15$ with $\alpha = .10$.

8.42 A sample of 50 graduating seniors was asked about the number of requests for second interviews they received. The mean number was 2.8 and the standard deviation was 3.2. Test H_0: $\mu = 2.0$ against H_1: $\mu \neq 2.0$ with $\alpha = .05$.

8.43 A random sample of 80 companies who announced corrections to their balance sheets took a mean time of 8.1 days longer than in the previous year for the time between balance sheet construction and complete audit. The standard deviation of these times was 1.3. Test H_0: $\mu = 7.5$ days against H_1: $\mu > 7.5$ days. Calculate the P-value and interpret the result.

8.44 A random sample of size 36 yields the statistics $\overline{x} = 70.3$ and $s = 15.9$. In the context of each of the following hypothesis testing problems, determine the P-value and state whether it signifies a strong rejection of H_0.

   a. H_0: $\mu = 64$ versus H_1: $\mu > 64$

   b. H_0: $\mu = 75$ versus H_1: $\mu < 75$

   c. H_0: $\mu = 66$ versus H_1: $\mu \neq 66$

8.45 In a given situation, suppose H_0 was not rejected at $\alpha = .03$. Answer the following questions as "Yes," "No," or "Cannot tell."

   a. Would H_0 also be retained at $\alpha = .02$?

   b. Would H_0 also be retained at $\alpha = .05$?

   c. Is the P-value smaller than .03?

8.46 Refer to Example 8.11. Calculate the Type II error probability when $\mu = 7.1$.

8.6 THE RELATION BETWEEN CONFIDENCE INTERVALS AND TESTS

A confidence interval is a sample-based interval designed to capture the value of a population parameter. An interval is necessary to reflect the uncertainty associated with using incomplete, or sample, information. A test of hypotheses is a procedure for deciding whether a specified value for a population parameter is reasonable, that is, consistent with the sample data. The decision in a hypothesis test is subject to error because, again, it is based on incomplete information.

    Although the two methods of inference appear to be addressing different issues, they are, in fact, both concerned with plausible values for a population parameter. If we focus on the same population parameter and use the same sample, we would hope to make inferences using either procedure that do not contradict one another. We show, by considering the case of a population mean, that this is indeed true.

    We first consider the large sample $100(1 - \alpha)\%$ confidence interval for μ

$$\left(\overline{x} - z_{\alpha/2}\frac{s}{\sqrt{n}}, \ \ \overline{x} + z_{\alpha/2}\frac{s}{\sqrt{n}} \right)$$

Now recall that the level α two-sided test of H_0: $\mu = \mu_0$ versus H_1: $\mu \neq \mu_0$ has the rejection region

$$\frac{\overline{x} - \mu_0}{s/\sqrt{n}} > z_{\alpha/2} \quad \text{or} \quad \frac{\overline{x} - \mu_0}{s/\sqrt{n}} < -z_{\alpha/2}$$

The acceptance region is obtained by reversing the inequalities to obtain the values of $\bar{x}$ and s that do not lead to the rejection of H_0: $\mu = \mu_0$. Thus

$$\text{Acceptance region: } -z_{\alpha/2} < \frac{\bar{x} - \mu_0}{s/\sqrt{n}} < z_{\alpha/2}$$

Rearranging these inequalities by first multiplying by $s/\sqrt{n}$, we find that the acceptance region can be expressed as

$$\text{Acceptance region: } \bar{x} - z_{\alpha/2}\frac{s}{\sqrt{n}} < \mu_0 < \bar{x} + z_{\alpha/2}\frac{s}{\sqrt{n}}$$

Notice that the limits of the acceptance region are identical to the limits of the previous confidence interval. The null hypothesis H_0: $\mu = \mu_0$ will not be rejected at level α when, and only when, the hypothesized value μ_0 lies in the $100(1 - \alpha)\%$ confidence interval for μ. The confidence interval tells us at once the outcomes of the two-sided test for any null hypothesis that specifies a single value μ_0 for μ.

EXAMPLE 8.14   Relation Between a Confidence Interval and a Two-Sided Test

Refer to Example 8.8. We obtained a 90% confidence interval $(86.31, 92.89)$ for the mean number of calls handled per shift. Use the relation between 90% confidence intervals and two-sided tests of level $\alpha = .10$ to test

a. H_0: $\mu = 87.3$ versus H_1: $\mu \neq 87.3$
b. H_0: $\mu = 82.7$ versus H_1: $\mu \neq 82.7$

Solution and Discussion.

a.   In view of the relation just established, the null hypothesis H_0: $\mu = 87.3$ would not be rejected at level .10 since 87.3 lies in the 90% confidence interval for μ.
b.   Because the value 82.7 lies outside of the 90% confidence interval, the null hypothesis H_0: $\mu = 82.7$ would be rejected at level .10.

A confidence interval statement provides more complete information regarding the values of an unknown parameter than a two-sided test of a single null hypothesis H_0: $\mu = \mu_0$. We favor a confidence interval approach when one is available.

The relation between tests and confidence intervals holds quite generally and is not just restricted to large sample tests of the mean. Let θ be any population parameter. If level α tests of H_0: $\theta = \theta_0$ versus H_1: $\theta \neq \theta_0$ are obtained, then a confidence interval can be constructed by collecting all of the values θ_0 that would not be rejected by these tests. This is exactly the relation we described previously for population means.

EXERCISES

8.47 A large sample 95% confidence interval for a population mean is $(-3.4, 12.7)$. Using the relation between confidence intervals and two-sided tests, determine the appropriate action if you were to use the same data to carry out the following tests of hypotheses.

a. H_0: $\mu = -4$ versus H_1: $\mu \neq -4$ $(\alpha = .05)$

b. H_0: $\mu = 1$ versus H_1: $\mu \neq 1$ $(\alpha = .05)$

8.48 In Example 8.7, we obtained the 95% confidence interval $(7.04, 7.76)$ for the mean time (in hours) to complete an audit task. Use the relation between confidence intervals and two-sided tests to determine whether the same data would reject or not reject

a. H_0: $\mu = 7.5$ versus H_1: $\mu \neq 7.5$ $(\alpha = .05)$

b. H_0: $\mu = 7$ versus H_1: $\mu \neq 7$ $(\alpha = .05)$

8.49 Consider the hypotheses H_0: $\mu = 16$ and H_1: $\mu \neq 16$. Suppose the z value for testing H_0 at level $\alpha = .10$ does not fall in the rejection region. If you use the same data to construct a 90% confidence interval for μ, would $\mu = 16$ fall in the interval? Explain.

8.7 STUDENT'S t DISTRIBUTION AND SMALL SAMPLE INFERENCES FOR A NORMAL POPULATION MEAN

To this point, the inferences we have considered about a population mean are based on large samples. If the sample size is large, we can appeal to the central limit theorem for the sampling distribution of $\overline{X}$ and not have to worry about the form of the population from which the sample is selected. If the sample size is small, however, the central limit theorem no longer applies, and the form of the population is important for developing confidence intervals and tests.

If we know the population is normal with mean μ and standard deviation σ, then, for a random sample of size n, $\overline{X}$ is exactly distributed as $N(\mu, \sigma/\sqrt{n})$. Consequently, the standardized variable

$$Z = \frac{\overline{X} - \mu}{\sigma/\sqrt{n}}$$

has the standard normal distribution. Even in this situation, however, we cannot base inferences on $\overline{X}$ or Z because, in most practical situations, the standard deviation σ is unknown. For example, we cannot generate a confidence interval for μ of the form

$$\left(\overline{x} - z_{\alpha/2} \frac{\sigma}{\sqrt{n}}, \ \overline{x} + z_{\alpha/2} \frac{\sigma}{\sqrt{n}} \right)$$

The natural choice of replacing σ with the observed sample standard deviation s is reasonable if the sample size is large, but not if the sample size is small.

Consider the ratio*

$$t = \frac{\overline{X} - \mu}{S/\sqrt{n}}$$

obtained by replacing σ with S. The notation t is used to distinguish this ratio from the standard normal variable Z.

Although estimating σ with S does not appreciably alter the distribution of this ratio in large samples, it does make a substantial difference if the sample size is small. In fact, the ratio t is no longer standardized. Replacing σ by the sample quantity S introduces more variability in the ratio, making its standard deviation larger than 1.

The distribution of the ratio t has been derived for normal populations and is known in the statistical literature as **Student's t distribution.** This distribution was first studied by a British chemist W. S. Gosset, who published his work in 1908 under the pseudonym "Student." The brewery for which he worked apparently did not want the competition to know that it was using statistical techniques to better understand and improve its fermentation process.

Student's t Distribution

If $X_1, X_2, \ldots, X_n$ is a random sample from a normal population $N(\mu, \sigma)$ and

$$\overline{X} = \frac{1}{n} \sum X_i \quad \text{and} \quad S^2 = \frac{\sum (X_i - \overline{X})^2}{n - 1}$$

then the distribution of

$$t = \frac{\overline{X} - \mu}{S/\sqrt{n}}$$

is called Student's t distribution with $n - 1$ degrees of freedom.

The qualification "with $n - 1$ degrees of freedom" is necessary because with each different sample size or value of $n - 1$, there is a different t distribution. The choice $n - 1$ coincides with the divisor for the estimator S^2, which is based on $n - 1$ degrees of freedom.

The t distributions are all symmetric around 0 but have tails that are more spread out than those of the $N(0, 1)$ distribution. This agrees with our previous remark that for large n, the ratio

$$\frac{\overline{X} - \mu}{S/\sqrt{n}}$$

---

*The use of a lowercase t to represent both the random variable and its observed value is so prevalent in the statistical literature that we do not use, for example, the notation T and t to distinguish the two. However, we have tried to maintain this distinction, at least initially, for other statistics such as $\overline{X}$ and $\overline{x}$, and S and s.

is approximately standard normal. The density curves for *t* with 2 and 5 degrees of freedom are plotted in Figure 8.10 along with the $N(0,1)$ curve.

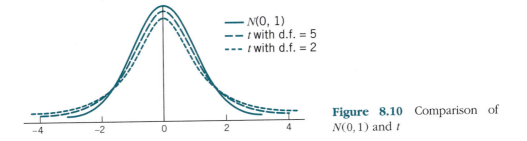

Figure 8.10 Comparison of $N(0,1)$ and *t*

Table 4 in Appendix B gives the upper α points t_α for selected values of α and the degrees of freedom (abbreviated d.f.).

Since the *t* distribution is symmetric around 0, the lower α point is simply $-t_\alpha$. The entries in the last row of the *t* table marked "d.f. = infinity" are exactly the percentage points of the $N(0,1)$ distribution.

EXAMPLE 8.15 Using the *t* Table

a. Using Table 4, Appendix B, determine the upper .10 point of the *t* distribution with 5 degrees of freedom. Also find the lower .10 point.

b. For the *t* distribution with d.f. = 9, find the number *b* such that

$$P(-b < t < b) = .90$$

Solution and Discussion.

a. With d.f. = 5, the upper .10 point of the *t* distribution is found from Table 4, Appendix B, to be $t_{.10} = 1.476$. Since the curve is centered at 0, the lower .10 point is simply $-t_{.10} = -1.476$ (see Figure 8.11).

**Percentage Points of
t distributions**

d.f.	α	$\cdots$	.10
$\vdots$			$\vdots$
5		$\cdots$	1.476

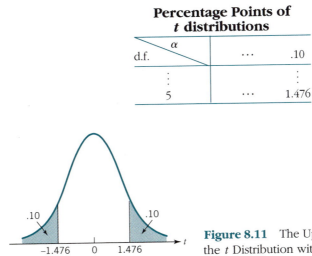

Figure 8.11 The Upper and Lower .10 Points of the *t* Distribution with d.f. = 5

b. For the probability in the interval $(-b, b)$ to be .90, we must have a probability of .05 to the right of b and, consequently, a probability .05 to the left of $-b$ (see the following figure). Thus the number b is the upper $\alpha = .05$ point of the t distribution. Reading Table 4 in Appendix B with $\alpha = .05$ and d.f. $= 9$, we find $t_{.05} = 1.833$, so $b = 1.833$.

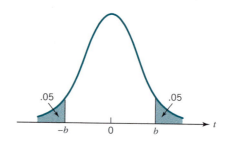

EXAMPLE 8.16   Interpreting a t Value

A manager at a credit card company claims that the mean time to resolve disputed claims is 30 days. To test this claim, data were collected on a sample of fifteen disputed claims. The fifteen claims had a mean time to resolve of 35.9 days and a standard deviation of 10.2 days.

If the data can be regarded as a random sample from a normal population, do they cast suspicion on the manager's claim?

Solution and Discussion.   If the manager's claim is correct, the population mean is $\mu = 30$ and the random variable

$$t = \frac{\overline{X} - \mu}{S/\sqrt{n}}$$

has Student's t distribution with $n - 1 = 15 - 1 = 14$ degrees of freedom. The manager's claim would be suspect if the value of this variable is too large or too small because this occurs when the value of $\overline{x}$ is far from μ. The observed value is

$$t = \frac{\overline{x} - \mu}{s/\sqrt{n}} = \frac{35.9 - 30}{10.2/\sqrt{15}} = 2.240$$

Consulting Table 4, Appendix B, for 14 degrees of freedom, we see that $t_{.025} = 2.145$. Before the sample is obtained, the probability that t will exceed 2.145 is .025. Similarly, the probability is .025 that t will be less than -2.145. Adding these two equal probabilities, the probability is $.025 + .025 = .05$ that t will be larger than 2.145 or less than -2.145. Rather than accept the explanation that an event with small probability has occurred, we question the claim that the mean is 30 days. A larger value for the mean would be more consistent with the data.

Inferences about the mean of a normal distribution are based on Student's t distribution.

CONFIDENCE INTERVALS FOR A NORMAL POPULATION MEAN

To obtain a $100(1 - \alpha)\%$ confidence interval for μ, we first consult the t table (Table 4, Appendix B) to find $t_{\alpha/2}$, the upper $\alpha/2$ point of the t distribution having $n - 1$ degrees of freedom (see Figure 8.12).

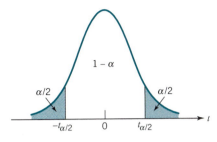

Figure 8.12   The Upper $100\alpha/2$ Percentile, $t_{\alpha/2}$

According to the definition of $t_{\alpha/2}$,

$$P\left[-t_{\alpha/2} < \frac{\overline{X} - \mu}{S/\sqrt{n}} < t_{\alpha/2}\right] = 1 - \alpha$$

The next step is to rearrange the terms in brackets so that the mean, μ, remains alone in the center. The probability statement then becomes

$$P\left[\overline{X} - t_{\alpha/2}\frac{S}{\sqrt{n}} < \mu < \overline{X} + t_{\alpha/2}\frac{S}{\sqrt{n}}\right] = 1 - \alpha$$

This probability statement yields the confidence interval. The probability is $1 - \alpha$ that the random interval from $\overline{X} - t_{\alpha/2}\dfrac{S}{\sqrt{n}}$ to $\overline{X} + t_{\alpha/2}\dfrac{S}{\sqrt{n}}$ will cover μ. The observed value of this interval is called a $100(1 - \alpha)\%$ confidence interval for μ.

A Confidence Interval for a Normal Population Mean

A $100(1 - \alpha)\%$ confidence interval for μ is given by

$$\left(\overline{x} - t_{\alpha/2}\frac{s}{\sqrt{n}}, \ \overline{x} + t_{\alpha/2}\frac{s}{\sqrt{n}}\right)$$

where $t_{\alpha/2}$ is the upper $\alpha/2$ point of the t distribution with $n - 1$ degrees of freedom.

EXAMPLE 8.17   Constructing a Confidence Interval for a Normal Population Mean

One measure of the quality of copier paper is its whiteness. A sample of 15 sheets cut from the production roll had a mean whiteness of 8.2 and a standard deviation of

1.3. Determine a 90% confidence interval for the mean whiteness of the roll. (From considerable experience with whiteness readings on many other rolls, it is reasonable to assume that they have a normal distribution.)

Solution and Discussion. The sample size $n = 15$ is small, but we have related information to support the assumption that the population distribution is normal. Since $\alpha = .10$, we have $\alpha/2 = .05$, and the t table gives $t_{.05} = 1.761$ for $n - 1 = 14$ degrees of freedom. Given the data $\bar{x} = 8.2$ and $s = 1.3$, the 90% confidence interval for the mean whiteness, μ, becomes

$$\left(\bar{x} - t_{\alpha/2}\frac{s}{\sqrt{n}}, \ \bar{x} + t_{\alpha/2}\frac{s}{\sqrt{n}}\right) \quad \text{or} \quad \left(8.2 - 1.761\frac{1.3}{\sqrt{15}}, \ 8.2 + 1.761\frac{1.3}{\sqrt{15}}\right)$$

or $(7.6, 8.8)$. We are 90% confident that the mean whiteness for the roll is between 7.6 and 8.8.

It is instructive to review the general meaning of confidence intervals in the context of the $100(1 - \alpha)\%$ confidence intervals

$$\left(\bar{x} - t_{\alpha/2}\frac{s}{\sqrt{n}}, \ \bar{x} + t_{\alpha/2}\frac{s}{\sqrt{n}}\right)$$

for the mean of a normal population.

This interval is centered at the sample mean $\bar{x}$ so the center varies from sample to sample. Further, the length of the interval is $2t_{\alpha/2}\,s/\sqrt{n}$ and this too varies from sample to sample because it is a multiple of the sample standard deviation s. This contrasts with the fixed length $2z_{\alpha/2}\sigma/\sqrt{n}$ of the intervals shown in Figure 8.4 for the known σ situation.

Although the intervals now have variable centers and variable lengths, they are still $100(1 - \alpha)\%$ confidence intervals. If the sampling is repeated a large number of times and a confidence interval calculated for each sample, approximately a proportion $1 - \alpha$ of the intervals will cover the true population mean μ.

Figure 8.13 shows the result of drawing 15 samples of size 8 from a normal population with $\mu = 10$ and $\sigma = 3.0$, and calculating the 95% confidence intervals. Since $\alpha = .05$, $\alpha/2 = .025$, and the t table gives $t_{\alpha/2} = t_{.025} = 2.365$ for $8 - 1 = 7$ degrees of freedom. The 95% confidence interval has limits $\bar{x} \pm 2.365\,s/\sqrt{8}$. For the first sample, $\bar{x} = 9.8$ and $s = 4.2$, so the interval is $(6.21, 13.41)$. This is shown as the lowest horizontal line segment in Figure 8.13. It covers the mean. Over the 15 samples, the intervals vary both in center and length, but 14 out of 15, or proportion $\frac{14}{15} = .96$, cover the true population mean.

TESTING HYPOTHESES ABOUT A NORMAL POPULATION MEAN

The steps for conducting tests of hypotheses concerning a mean were discussed in Section 8.5. Only the distribution of the test statistic must be modified to account for the fact that the sample size may be small.

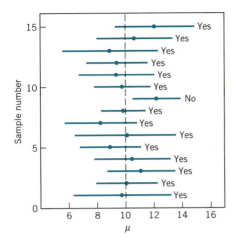

Figure 8.13 Behavior of Confidence Intervals Based on the *t* Distribution

Provided it is reasonable to assume that the population distribution is normal, the test statistic *t* with value

$$t = \frac{\overline{x} - \mu_0}{s/\sqrt{n}}$$

has Student's *t* distribution with $n - 1$ degrees of freedom. The *t* table (Table 4, Appendix B) is used to determine the critical region.

The form of the rejection region is determined from the form of the alternative hypothesis. A large value for *t* corresponds to a value for $\overline{x}$ that is much larger than μ_0 when the distance is measured in estimated standard deviation units. The rejection regions are summarized in the following table.

Rejection Region for Testing $\mu = \mu_0$
$$\left(\begin{array}{c}\textbf{Small Sample from a Normal Population}\\ \boldsymbol{\alpha} \textbf{ Level Test}\end{array}\right)$$

Test Statistic: $t = \dfrac{\overline{X} - \mu_0}{S/\sqrt{n}}$

Alternative Hypothesis	Reject Null Hypothesis If
$\mu < \mu_0$	$t < -t_\alpha$
$\mu > \mu_0$	$t > t_\alpha$
$\mu \neq \mu_0$	$t < -t_{\alpha/2}$ or $t > t_{\alpha/2}$

The test for the mean of a normal population when σ is unknown and the sample size is small is summarized in the box.

Testing Hypotheses About a Mean—Small Samples

When testing H_0: $\mu = \mu_0$ for a *normal distribution,* the test statistic t takes the value

$$t = \frac{\bar{x} - \mu_0}{s/\sqrt{n}}$$

and it has Student's t distribution with $n - 1$ degrees of freedom.

The rejection region is specified in terms of the alternative hypothesis in the previous table. The test is called a **Student's t test,** or simply a **t test.**

EXAMPLE 8.18   A One-Sided Test for a Normal Population Mean

The manager of a frozen yogurt store claims that a medium-size serving contains an average of more than 4 ounces of yogurt. From a random sample of 14 servings, he obtains a mean of 4.31 ounces and a standard deviation of .52 ounce. Test, with $\alpha = .05$, the manager's claim. Assume that the distribution of weight per serving is normal.

Solution and Discussion.   Corresponding to our steps for testing hypotheses, we determine the following:

1. *Hypotheses.* Let μ denote the mean weight of yogurt in a medium-size serving. The claim that the mean is greater than 4 ounces is taken as the alternative hypothesis. Consequently, the null hypothesis is H_0: $\mu = 4.0$ and the alternative hypothesis is H_1: $\mu > 4.0$. We are given $\alpha = .05$.

2. *Test Statistic.* The sample size $n = 14$ is small, but we are told the population is normal. Since $\mu_0 = 4.0$, the test statistic takes the value

$$t = \frac{\bar{x} - \mu_0}{s/\sqrt{n}} = \frac{\bar{x} - 4.0}{s/\sqrt{14}}$$

The alternative hypothesis H_1: $\mu > \mu_0$ is one-sided, so we reject the null hypothesis if the observed value of t is large.

3. *Rejection Region.* The specified α is .05 and the sample size is $n = 14$, so t has $n - 1 = 13$ degrees of freedom. From the t table, $t_{.05} = 1.771$ for 13 degrees of freedom, so the rejection region is (see Figure 8.14)

$$t = \frac{\bar{x} - 4.0}{s/\sqrt{14}} > 1.771$$

4. *Calculation.* We observe $\bar{x} = 4.31$ and $s = .52$, so the observed value of the test statistic is

$$t = \frac{\bar{x} - 4.0}{s/\sqrt{14}} = \frac{4.31 - 4.0}{.52/\sqrt{14}} = 2.23$$

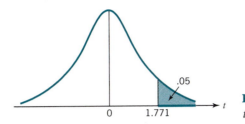

Figure 8.14   Right-Sided Rejection Region for *t* Test with $\alpha = .05$

5. *Conclusion.* The observed value of the test statistic, 2.23, falls in the rejection region. At level $\alpha = .05$, we reject the null hypothesis in favor of the alternative that the mean weight of yogurt in medium-size servings is greater than 4 ounces.

The conclusion of a test can be strengthened by calculating the *P*-value or significance probability. Here, the observed value of *t* is 2.23. Values greater than $t = 2.23$ are considered to provide more extreme evidence in favor of the alternative hypothesis. From the *t* table, for 13 degrees of freedom, $t_{.025} = 2.160$ and $t_{.01} = 2.650$, so it can be determined only that the *P*-value is between .01 and .025. However, a computer calculation gives the significance probability

$$P\text{-value} = P(t > 2.23) = .022$$

Observing a value as extreme as $\bar{x} = 4.31$ with $s = .52$, if H_0: $\mu = 4.0$ is true, is about .02. Thus, the evidence is relatively strong that the mean serving weight is greater than 4 ounces.

EXERCISES

8.50   Using the table for the *t* distributions, find the
  a.   Upper .05 point when d.f. = 5
  b.   Lower .025 point when d.f. = 18
  c.   Lower .01 point when d.f. = 11
  d.   Upper .10 point when d.f. = 16

8.51   Name the *t* percentiles shown, and find their values from Table 4, Appendix B.

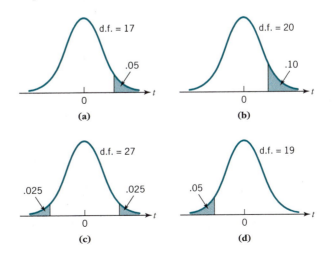

8.52 Using the table for the t distributions, find:
  a.   The 90th percentile of t when d.f. $= 11$
  b.   The 99th percentile of t when d.f. $= 3$
  c.   The 5th percentile of t when d.f. $= 26$
  d.   The lower and upper quartiles of t when d.f. $= 19$

8.53 Find the probability of
  a. $t < -1.740$ when d.f. $= 17$
  b. $|t| > 3.143$ when d.f. $= 6$
  c. $-1.330 < t < 1.330$ when d.f. $= 18$
  d. $-1.372 < t < 2.764$ when d.f. $= 10$

8.54 In each case, find the number b so that:
  a. $P(t < b) = .95$ when d.f. $= 6$
  b. $P(-b < t < b) = .95$ when d.f. $= 15$
  c. $P(t > b) = .01$ when d.f. $= 8$
  d. $P(t > b) = .99$ when d.f. $= 11$

8.55 Record the $t_{.05}$ values for d.f. $= 5, 10, 15, 20$, and 29. Does this percentile increase or decrease with increasing degrees of freedom?

8.56 Using the table for the t distributions, make an assessment for the probability of the stated event. (The answer to part **a** is provided.)
  a. $t > 2.6$ when d.f. $= 7$
  (*Answer:* $P(t > 2.6)$ is between .01 and .025 because 2.6 lies between $t_{.025} = 2.365$ and $t_{.01} = 2.998$.)
  b. $t > 1.9$ when d.f. $= 15$
  c. $t < -1.5$ when d.f. $= 17$
  d. $|t| > 1.9$ when d.f. $= 15$
  e. $|t| < 2.8$ when d.f. $= 20$

8.57 What can you say about the number c in each case? Justify your answer. (The answer to part **a** is provided.)
  a. $P(t > c) = .03$ when d.f. $= 5$
  (*Answer:* c is between 2.015 and 2.571 because $t_{.05} = 2.015$ and $t_{.025} = 2.571$.)
  b. $P(t > c) = .016$ when d.f. $= 9$
  c. $P(t < -c) = .004$ when d.f. $= 12$
  d. $P(|t| > c) = .03$ when d.f. $= 5$
  e. $P(|t| < c) = .96$ when d.f. $= 21$

8.58 Given the random sample of five observations 25, 31, 22, 26, 21 from a normal population, obtain a 95% confidence interval for the population mean.

8.59 Given the random sample of four observations 12, 7, 16, 9 from a normal population, obtain a 90% confidence interval for the population mean.

8.60 A random sample of size 12 from a normal population yields $\bar{x} = 35.7$ and $s = 4.2$. Obtain a 95% confidence interval for the population mean.

8.61 Refer to Exercise 8.60. Obtain a 90% confidence interval for the population mean.

8.62 A random sample of size 8 from a normal population has mean $\bar{x} = 21.4$ and standard deviation $s = 7.3$. Obtain a 95% confidence interval for the population mean.

8.63 Refer to Exercise 8.62. Obtain a 90% confidence interval for the population mean.

8.64 (*Minitab or similar program recommended*) The number of pieces of mail received and delivered by one employee in a large office, for 10 days, was collected to help determine workload. Use the 10 observations

| 247 | 46 | 72 | 147 | 198 | 288 | 83 | 133 | 161 | 136 |

to obtain a 95% confidence interval for the population mean number of pieces of mail handled. Construct a normal-scores plot. Is the assumption you made to construct the confidence interval warranted? Discuss.

8.65 (*Minitab or similar program recommended*) Purchasers of bicycles also purchase several accessories including helmets, racks, and water bottles. A random sample of 12 invoices, from extensive records available, gave the following dollar amounts for sales of accessory equipment:

| 38 | 65 | 82 | 114 | 77 | 19 |
| 142 | 93 | 63 | 107 | 58 | 76 |

Obtain a 95% confidence interval for the population mean sales of accessory equipment. Construct a normal-scores plot. Is the assumption you made to construct the confidence interval warranted? Discuss.

8.66 Assuming a fixed sample of size 10 from a normal population, compare the lengths of a 90% and a 95% confidence interval for μ by calculating the ratio of the lengths.

8.67 To gather information about the need for expertise on computer graphics software, the consultants record the number of help requests per week for 10 weeks. These data give $\bar{x} = 8.2$ and $s = 4.1$ requests. Determine a 95% confidence interval for the mean number of requests per week for help with graphics software. Specify any assumption(s) you made to construct the confidence interval.

8.68 Specify the null hypothesis and the alternative hypothesis if a manager wants to establish that the mean number of customer contacts per day for salespersons is different from 6.3.

8.69 A random sample of size 9 from a normal population has mean $\bar{x} = 324.5$ and standard deviation $s = 15.2$. Does this evidence support the claim that the population mean is less than 335? Test with $\alpha = .05$. Calculate the *P*-value and interpret this number.

8.70 A random sample of size 15 from a normal population has mean $\bar{x} = 4.32$ and standard deviation $s = 1.63$. Does this evidence support the claim that the population mean is greater than 3.5? Test with $\alpha = .025$. Calculate the *P*-value and interpret this number.

8.71 Refer to Exercise 8.70. Test $H_0: \mu = 3.5$ versus $H_1: \mu \neq 3.5$ with $\alpha = .05$. Calculate the *P*-value and interpret this number.

8.72 Given a random sample of 7 quarts of ice cream selected from different production runs for the same flavor, an inspector wants to verify that the mean fat content is less than 8%. Experience with similar sets of measurements suggests that the population distribution is normal. Calculate the *P*-value if the sample has mean $\bar{x}$ = 7.1% and standard deviation s = 1.3%. Using the *P*-value, determine the result of the test at α = .05.

8.73 An accounting firm wishes to set a guideline for the time required to complete a certain audit operation. A sample of times from 18 different junior auditors has mean $\bar{x}$ = 3.2 hours and standard deviation s = 1.6 hours. Experience with similar sets of measurements suggests that the population distribution is normal. Test H_0: μ = 2.6 hours versus H_1: μ > 2.6 hours using α = .025. Determine the *P*-value and interpret this number.

8.74 Refer to Exercise 8.73. Test H_0: μ = 2.6 versus H_1: $\mu \neq$ 2.6 with α = .05. Determine the *P*-value and interpret this number.

8.75 Follow the steps in Section 8.6 to establish that the 95% confidence interval

$$\left(\bar{x} - t_{.025}\frac{s}{\sqrt{n}}, \quad \bar{x} + t_{.025}\frac{s}{\sqrt{n}}\right)$$

contains exactly those values μ_0 for the mean that would not be rejected by a two-sided t test of H_0: $\mu = \mu_0$ versus H_1: $\mu \neq \mu_0$ at level α = .05.

8.76 Combustion efficiency measurements were made on six home heating furnaces of a new model. The sample mean and standard deviation were found to be 93.6% and 2.75%, respectively. Experience with similar sets of measurements suggests that the population distribution is normal. Do these data provide strong evidence that the mean efficiency for this model is greater than 90%? Test with α = .05. Also, determine the *P*-value and comment on its size.

8.77 (*Minitab or similar program recommended*) Refer to Exercise 8.65 concerning the purchase of accessories for bicycles. Test H_0: μ = 60 versus H_1: $\mu \neq$ 60 with α = .05. Is your conclusion consistent with the 95% confidence interval constructed in Exercise 8.65? Discuss. Construct a normal-scores plot of the data, and comment on the assumption of a normal population.

CompAtti.dat
FuelCost.dat

8.78 (*Minitab or similar program recommended*) The statistical package Minitab can be used to calculate t tests. With the data on number of calls per shift from Example 8.1 stored in column C1, the command

```
TTEST MU = 93.0 C1
```

produces the output

```
TEST OF MU = 93.00 VS MU N.E. 93.00
```

	N	MEAN	STDEV	SE MEAN	T	P VALUE
C1	75	89.60	17.32	2.00	−1.70	0.093

You must still compare your preselected level α with the printed *P*-value to obtain the conclusion of your test. On the basis of these calculations, we would reject H_0: μ = 93.0 at level .10. Would we reject H_0: μ = 93 at level α = .05? Explain. Also

a. Using the computer anxiety data in Table C.2, Appendix C, test H_0: $\mu = 3.0$ at level .05. Would we reject H_0 at level .10? Explain.

b. Using the fuel cost per mile for 23 diesel trucks given in Exercise 2.10, test H_0: $\mu = 10.5$ at level $\alpha = .05$. Would you reject H_0 at level .10? Explain.

8.79 (*Minitab or similar program recommended*) The statistical package Minitab will calculate the small sample confidence interval for μ. With the number of calls per shift data from Example 8.1 stored in column C1, the command

TINTERVAL 95 PERCENT C1

produces the output

```
          N     MEAN   STDEV   SE MEAN   95.0 PERCENT C.I.
C1       75    89.60   17.32    2.00    ( 85.61,   93.59)
```

a. Obtain a 90% confidence interval for μ.

b. Using the fuel cost per mile for 23 diesel trucks given in Exercise 2.10, construct a 95% confidence interval for the population mean μ. Is the test of hypotheses at level .05 in Exercise 8.78 part **b** consistent with this 95% confidence interval? Explain.

8.80 (*Minitab or similar program recommended*) You can simulate the coverage properties of the small sample confidence intervals for μ by generating 20 samples of size 10 from a normal distribution having mean $\mu = 15$ and standard deviation $\sigma = 3$. The small sample confidence interval is calculated for each of the 20 samples. The Minitab commands are

```
RANDOM 10 C1-C20;
 NORMAL MU=15 SIGMA=3.
TINTERVAL 95 PERCENT C1-C20
```

a. From your output, determine the proportion of the 20 intervals that cover the true mean $\mu = 15$. Is the result consistent with the confidence level associated with these intervals?

b. Repeat part **a** using samples of size 5.

8.8 STATISTICS IN CONTEXT

Many smaller credit unions do not have sufficient assets to sustain a credit card program for their individual members. This is particularly true for some international credit unions. However, the association of credit unions can provide the necessary assets. Consequently, the central office for the association is in charge of processing credit card applications, including credit checks, approvals, data entry, and marketing.

Ordinarily, several applications are collected at a local credit union and these are sent to the central office in a single file. Problems were indicated when several association members expressed dissatisfaction with the total time taken to complete the processing of application folders.

A quality team was formed to study the process. As a first step, data were gathered on each of the component processes. The mean time to complete each process, in days, was then estimated for each component process. The results are summarized next.

Estimated Mean Processing Time

Component Process	Mean (days)
Application data entry	.8
Application review	.9
Recommendation	4.9
Account data entry	1.0
Account posting	1.8
Plastic card generation	3.9
Postal handling	4.1

The estimated mean times for the component processes, graphed in Figure 8.15, reveal that the recommendation process was taking an average of almost 5 working days to complete. This step merited further scrutiny.

By law, the local credit union issuing the card must sign off on each individual card. This also allows them to use any additional information they might have about their own member's creditworthiness. This signing off to extend credit is called the recommendation process.

Data on the recommendation cycle time, that is, the time to complete the recommendation process, were collected on 241 files. These data, already ordered from smallest to largest, are

0	0	0	0	0	0	0	0	0	0	0	0	0
0	0	0	0	0	0	0	0	0	0	0	0	0
0	0	0	0	0	0	0	0	0	0	0	0	0
0	0	0	0	0	0	0	0	0	0	0	0	0
0	0	0	0	0	0	0	0	0	0	1	1	1
1	1	1	1	1	1	1	1	1	1	1	1	1
1	1	1	1	1	1	1	1	1	1	1	1	1
1	1	1	1	1	1	1	1	1	1	1	1	1
1	1	1	1	1	1	1	2	2	2	2	2	2
2	2	2	2	2	2	2	2	2	2	2	2	2
2	2	3	3	3	3	3	3	3	4	4	4	4
4	4	4	4	4	4	4	4	4	4	4	5	5
5	5	5	5	5	5	5	5	5	5	6	6	6
6	6	6	6	6	6	6	6	6	6	6	7	7
7	7	7	7	7	7	7	8	8	8	8	8	8
8	8	8	8	8	8	9	9	9	9	9	9	9
9	10	11	11	11	11	11	11	11	12	12	12	12
12	12	12	13	13	13	13	13	14	15	15	17	19
21	22	22	24	26	27	28						

(Data courtesy of Joseph Haefner)

Notice that 31 out of 241, or about 13%, of the folders took longer than 10 working days, or two weeks, to be processed. The median time is only 2.0 days. As suspected, the histogram (Figure 8.16) exhibits a long right-hand tail.

It is a good idea to check that the recommendation process is stable over time. The first 40 process times are plotted in chronological order in Figure 8.17. We have drawn a center line at $\bar{x} = 4.29$ and the two control limits at $\bar{x} + 2s = 4.29 + 2 \times 5.38 = 15.05$ and $\bar{x} - 2s = 4.29 - 2 \times 5.38$ or 0 since negative times are impossible.

The level of the process appears to be stable, but there are a few very large process times. The plot for the remainder of the data is similar.

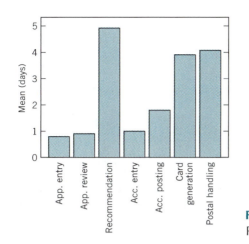

Figure 8.15 Mean Times for the Component Processes

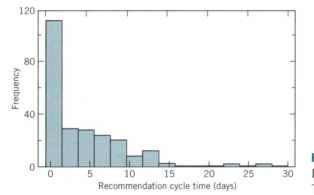

Figure 8.16 Histogram of the Initial Recommendation Cycle Times

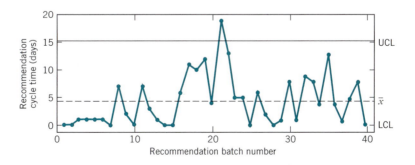

Figure 8.17 Time Plot of the First (Unordered) Recommendation Cycle Times

The sample size $n = 241$ is large, and we could calculate a large sample 95% confidence interval for the mean recommendation time under the current process. Since $z_{.025} = 1.96$, the 95% confidence interval is

$$\left(\bar{x} - 1.96\frac{s}{\sqrt{n}}, \ \bar{x} + 1.96\frac{s}{\sqrt{n}} \right)$$

or

$$\left(4.29 - 1.96\frac{5.38}{\sqrt{241}}, \ 4.29 + 1.96\frac{5.38}{\sqrt{241}} \right) = (3.61, \ 4.97) \text{ days}$$

At this stage, the quality team held regular meetings to review the recommendation process and to propose theories to explain the

WHEN   WHO   WHAT   WHERE

questions concerning the lengthy times to complete the recommendation process. These are displayed as fishbone diagrams in Figure 8.18. Fishbone, or cause-and-effect, diagrams are used in brainstorming sessions to examine factors that may influence a given situation. An "effect" is a desirable or undesirable situation, or condition, produced by a system of "causes." In a fishbone diagram, the horizontal line or backbone represents the effect, and the angled lines (bones) attached to the horizontal line represent the potential causes.

It was decided to look at what effect the day of the week had on the time to complete the recommendation process. Data were collected but a particular day of the week did not seem to be important.

Next, data were collected to show that the mode of communication was a possible cause for the slow recommendation times. Some folders were handled by communicating with the local credit union by phone and others by communicating by fax. This was fortuitous, since the use of a fax was new at a few local credit unions. When the data were divided according to the method of communication, as shown in Figure 8.19, the quality team decided that fax was the preferred method of communication.

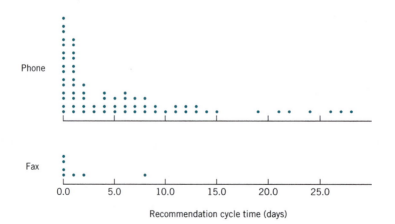

Each dot represents 4 points in the phone data.

Figure 8.19   Comparison of Cycle Times for Phone Versus Fax

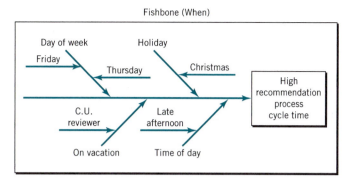

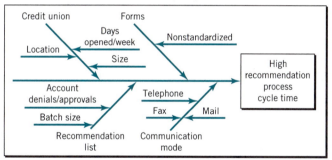

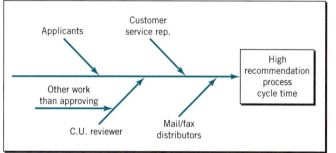

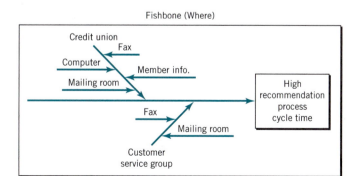

Figure 8.18 Fishbone Diagrams of Possible Factors that Influence High Recommendation Cycle Times

When communication by fax was used, workers at the member organizations were able to see the questions raised by the central office in front of them and write the answers down and return the information with little delay. Thus it became department policy always to use fax communication.

After the new policy was implemented, data were collected to verify that, indeed, there was an improvement. These data were recorded in hours during working days because it was recognized that a finer time scale would be more useful. There were still a few folders being handled by phone over this period. Looking only at the recommendation cycle times handled by fax communication, and ignoring a cycle time of 135.87 hours that occurred when the local credit union was undergoing a merger, we obtain this summary:

```
 N     MEAN   MEDIAN    STDEV
140    15.91   16.10    16.43

 MIN    MAX     Q1       Q3
0.14   88.55   1.37    23.92
```

A 95% confidence interval for the new mean recommendation cycle time, in hours, is given by

$$\left(\bar{x} - 1.96 \frac{s}{\sqrt{n}}, \ \bar{x} + 1.96 \frac{s}{\sqrt{n}} \right)$$

or

$$\left(15.91 - 1.96 \frac{16.43}{\sqrt{140}}, \ 15.91 + 1.96 \frac{16.43}{\sqrt{140}} \right) \quad \text{or} \quad (13.19, \ 18.63) \text{ hours}$$

Notice that even the upper limit is less than 19 hours or about 2.4 working days.

Once the correct data were collected and graphed according to the phone/fax groupings, an important improvement was made, which led to savings of tens of thousands of dollars and a large improvement in member satisfaction.

8.9   CHAPTER SUMMARY

In this chapter, we have learned:

- **Statistical inference** is concerned with drawing conclusions about population parameters from an analysis of the sample data.

- A sample quantity designed to provide a single number guess for a population parameter is called a **point estimator.** The value of a point estimator, computed once the sample is in hand, is called a **point estimate.**

- The standard deviation of a point estimator is called its **standard error** or **s.e.**

- A point estimator of the population mean is the sample mean $\overline{X}$. The standard error of $\overline{X}$ is $\sigma/\sqrt{n}$, where σ is the population standard deviation and n is the sample size. The estimated standard error is $s/\sqrt{n}$, where s is the sample standard deviation.

- For large samples, $\overline{X}$ has the $N(\mu, \sigma/\sqrt{n})$ distribution. If $z_{\alpha/2}$ is the upper $\alpha/2$ percent point of the standard normal distribution, the $100(1 - \alpha)\%$ **error margin** associated with the point estimator $\overline{X}$ is $e = z_{\alpha/2}(\sigma/\sqrt{n})$. If σ is unknown, use the observed sample standard deviation s in place of σ.

- The required simple random sample size is

$$n = \left[\frac{z_{\alpha/2}\sigma}{e} \right]^2$$

  to be $100(1 - \alpha)\%$ sure that the error of estimation $|\overline{X} - \mu|$ does not exceed the desired error margin e. If σ is unknown, use s, determined from a small pilot study, in place of σ. Alternatively, the sample size selection can be made by evaluating the solutions for several plausible values for σ.

- A **confidence interval** is an interval, computed from the sample, of plausible values for the true value of a population parameter. The **level of confidence** is the probability, before the sample is observed, that the proposed interval will contain the true value of the population parameter.

- A $100(1 - \alpha)\%$ confidence interval for the mean μ of a normal distribution with known standard deviation σ is

$$\left(\overline{x} - z_{\alpha/2}\frac{\sigma}{\sqrt{n}}, \ \overline{x} + z_{\alpha/2}\frac{\sigma}{\sqrt{n}} \right)$$

  This interval can be used as an approximate $100(1 - \alpha)\%$ confidence interval for the mean μ of practically any population if the sample size n is large. If the sample size is large and σ is unknown, replace σ with the sample standard deviation s.

- A **statistical hypothesis** or **hypothesis** is a statement about a feature of the population. The claim or hypothesis we wish to establish is called the **alternative hypothesis** or H_1. The opposite hypothesis, the one that nullifies the original claim, is called the **null hypothesis** or H_0.

- Hypotheses may be **one-sided** or **two-sided.** Decisions about the null and alternative hypotheses are made on the basis of sample evidence. We can either reject H_0 and conclude that H_1 is substantiated or fail to reject H_0 and conclude that H_1 has not been substantiated.

- A **Type I error** is made when we reject a true null hypothesis. A **Type II error** is made when we fail to reject a false null hypothesis.

- The statistic whose value is used to determine the decision (action) is called the **test statistic. A test of hypotheses** is a specification of values of the test statistic for which the null hypothesis should be rejected. The set of values for which the null hypothesis should be rejected is called the **rejection region** or **critical region** of the test.

- The probability of a Type I error is denoted by α and is called the **significance level** or, simply, **level** of the test. The probability of a Type II error is denoted by β.

- The steps for testing hypotheses can be summarized as follows:

  1. Formulate the hypotheses.

  2. Select a test statistic.

3. Determine the rejection region.

4. Calculate the test statistic.

5. Draw a conclusion.

- The **P-value** or **significance probability** of a test statistic is the probability of getting as extreme a sample result as the one actually observed if the null hypothesis H_0 is true. It is the smallest α for which this observation leads to the rejection of H_0. A small P-value means a strong rejection of H_0.

- Large sample tests of a population mean are based on the test statistic

$$Z = \frac{\overline{X} - \mu_0}{S/\sqrt{n}}$$

1. For a test of the hypotheses H_0: $\mu = \mu_0$ and H_1: $\mu \neq \mu_0$ at level α, the rejection region consists of the values of Z where

$$z < -z_{\alpha/2} \quad \text{or} \quad z > z_{\alpha/2}$$

2. For the hypotheses H_0: $\mu = \mu_0$ and H_1: $\mu > \mu_0$, the rejection region at level α is

$$z > z_{\alpha}$$

3. For a test of the hypotheses H_0: $\mu = \mu_0$ and H_1: $\mu < \mu_0$, the rejection region at level α is

$$z < -z_{\alpha}$$

- A relation exists between confidence intervals and two-sided tests of hypotheses. The large sample $100(1 - \alpha)\%$ confidence interval for, say, a population mean may be regarded as the set of values μ_0 that would not be rejected by an α level test of H_0: $\mu = \mu_0$ versus H_1: $\mu \neq \mu_0$. That is, given the sample, the confidence interval may be viewed as the set of "acceptable" values for μ.

- For small samples, inferences about a normal population mean with unknown standard deviation σ are based on the t statistic

$$t = \frac{\overline{X} - \mu}{S/\sqrt{n}}$$

which has Student's t distribution with $n - 1$ degrees of freedom.

- A $100(1 - \alpha)\%$ confidence interval for the mean μ of a normal population when σ is unknown and the sample size n is small (say, $n < 30$) is

$$\left(\overline{x} - t_{\alpha/2} \frac{s}{\sqrt{n}}, \ \overline{x} + t_{\alpha/2} \frac{s}{\sqrt{n}} \right)$$

where $t_{\alpha/2}$ is the upper $\alpha/2$ point of the t distribution with $n - 1$ degrees of freedom.

- The small sample α level t tests for a normal population mean μ with unknown standard deviation σ are:

a. H_0: $\mu = \mu_0$, H_1: $\mu \neq \mu_0$
Reject H_0 if $t < -t_{\alpha/2}$ or $t > t_{\alpha/2}$.

b. H_0: $\mu = \mu_0$, H_1: $\mu > \mu_0$
Reject H_0 if $t > t_\alpha$.

c. H_0: $\mu = \mu_0$, H_1: $\mu < \mu_0$
Reject H_0 if $t < -t_\alpha$.

8.10   IMPORTANT CONCEPTS AND TOOLS

CONCEPTS

Alternative hypothesis, 400
Confidence interval, 390
Critical region, 403
Error margin, 385
Interval estimate, 381
Level of confidence, 390
Level of significance, 404
Null hypothesis, 401
One-sided hypothesis, 401
Point estimate, 381
Point estimator, 383
Rejection region, 403

Relation between confidence intervals and tests, 413
Significance probability, 407
Standard error, 383
Statistical hypothesis, 399
Statistical inference, 381
Student's t distribution, 416
Test statistic, 403
Test of hypotheses, 403
Two-sided hypothesis, 402
Type I error, 402
Type II error, 402
z_α notation, 384

TOOLS

Large sample confidence interval for μ, 394
Large sample tests for μ, 409
P-value, 407
Required sample size, 387
Small sample confidence interval for a normal population mean, 419
Small sample tests for a normal population mean, 421

8.11   KEY FORMULAS

The sample size required to be $100(1-\alpha)\%$ sure that the error of estimation $|\overline{X} - \mu|$ does not exceed e:

$$n = \left[\frac{z_{\alpha/2}\sigma}{e}\right]^2$$

Large sample $100(1-\alpha)\%$ confidence interval for a population mean μ (σ unknown):

$$\left(\overline{x} - z_{\alpha/2}\frac{s}{\sqrt{n}}, \ \overline{x} + z_{\alpha/2}\frac{s}{\sqrt{n}}\right)$$

Large sample test statistic Z for a population mean μ (σ unknown) takes the value

$$z = \frac{\overline{x} - \mu_0}{s/\sqrt{n}}$$

and has a $N(0,1)$ distribution.

Small sample confidence interval for a normal population mean μ (σ unknown):

$$\left(\overline{x} - t_{\alpha/2}\frac{s}{\sqrt{n}}, \ \overline{x} + t_{\alpha/2}\frac{s}{\sqrt{n}}\right)$$

Small sample test statistic t for a normal population mean μ (σ unknown) takes value

$$t = \frac{\overline{x} - \mu_0}{s/\sqrt{n}}$$

and has Student's t distribution with $n - 1$ degrees of freedom.

REVIEW EXERCISES

8.81   Consider the problem of estimating a population mean μ based on a random sample of size n. Compute the point estimate of μ and its estimated standard error in each of the following situations.

   a. $n = 75$, $\sum x_i = 1235$, $\sum (x_i - \overline{x})^2 = 249$

   b. $n = 48$, $\sum x_i = 88.6$, $\sum (x_i - \overline{x})^2 = 307.2$

8.82   By what factor must the sample size be increased to reduce the standard error of $\overline{X}$ to one-third its original value?

8.83   For each case, determine the sample size n that is required for estimating the population mean with the specified error margin.

   a. $\sigma = 8.5$, 95% error margin $= .6$

   b. $\sigma = 103$, 97% error margin $= 12.0$

   c. $\sigma = .14$, 85% error margin $= .03$

8.84   Calculate a $100(1 - \alpha)\%$ confidence interval for the population mean in each of the following cases.

   a. $n = 65$, $\sum x_i = 3022$, $\sum (x_i - \overline{x})^2 = 2406$, $1 - \alpha = .95$

   b. $n = 50$, $\sum x_i = 7225$, $\sum (x_i - \overline{x})^2 = 408.2$, $1 - \alpha = .90$

8.85   In a given situation, suppose H_0 was rejected at $\alpha = .05$. Answer the following questions as "Yes," "No," or "Cannot tell."

   a.   Would H_0 also be rejected at $\alpha = .03$?

   b.   Would H_0 also be rejected at $\alpha = .08$?

   c.   Is the P-value larger than .05?

8.86   Give the test statistic and determine the rejection region at the specified level of significance. Assume the sample size is large.

   a. H_0: $\mu = 21.6$ versus H_1: $\mu \neq 21.6$, $\alpha = .05$

   b. H_0: $\mu = 45.7$ versus H_1: $\mu < 45.7$, $\alpha = .03$

8.87   Give the test statistic and determine the rejection region at the specified level of significance. Assume the sample size is large.

   a. H_0: $\mu = 102$ versus H_1: $\mu \neq 102$, $\alpha = .10$

   b. H_0: $\mu = 6.4$ versus H_1: $\mu > 6.4$, $\alpha = .09$

8.88   A random sample of size 50 yields the statistics $\overline{x} = 27.3$ and $s = 6.4$. In the context of each of the following hypothesis testing problems, determine the P-value and state whether it signifies a strong rejection of H_0.

   a. H_0: $\mu = 29$ versus H_1: $\mu > 29$

b. H_0: $\mu = 31$ versus H_1: $\mu < 31$

c. H_0: $\mu = 29$ versus H_1: $\mu \neq 29$

8.89 Refer to Section 8.8, Statistics in Context, and the data on the recommendation cycle times after the almost complete change to fax communication. Obtain a 90% confidence interval for the mean cycle time for those 140 cases where fax communication was used (see the descriptive statistics on page 432).

8.90 Refer to the data on the number of calls per shift in Example 8.1. Obtain a 95% confidence interval for the mean number of calls.

8.91 Refer to the data on the number of calls per shift in Example 8.1. Test the null hypothesis that the mean is 85 against a two-sided alternative. Take $\alpha = .05$. Determine the P-value and comment on its size.

8.92 A large sample 95% confidence interval for the mean μ is found to be (102.4, 110.6). Use the relation between confidence intervals and two-sided tests to determine the conclusion for testing

a. H_0: $\mu = 100$ versus H_1: $\mu \neq 100$ ($\alpha = .05$)

b. H_0: $\mu = 110$ versus H_1: $\mu \neq 110$ ($\alpha = .05$)

8.93 A large sample 95% confidence interval for the mean μ is found to be (4.25, 9.25). Use the relation between confidence intervals and two-sided tests to determine the conclusion for testing

a. H_0: $\mu = 9.0$ versus H_1: $\mu \neq 9.0$ ($\alpha = .05$)

b. H_0: $\mu = 9.4$ versus H_1: $\mu \neq 9.4$ ($\alpha = .05$)

8.94 Given the random sample of five observations 22, 35, 27, 46, 30 from a normal population, obtain a 90% confidence interval for the population mean.

8.95 A random sample of size 21 from a normal population yields $\overline{x} = 8.72$ and $s = 2.2$. Obtain a 95% confidence interval for the population mean.

8.96 A random sample of size 15 from a normal population has mean $\overline{x} = 41.6$ and standard deviation $s = 9.32$. Obtain a 95% confidence interval for the population mean.

8.97 The daily number of returns handled by one employee at a large mail order company were recorded for ten days. These data are given here:

28	35	32	19	48	29	30	43	36	21

Stating any assumption(s) you make, obtain a 95% confidence interval for the population mean number of returns.

8.98 Refer to Exercise 8.97. Test H_0: $\mu = 25$ versus H_1: $\mu \neq 25$ with $\alpha = .05$. What assumption(s) must you make to carry out this test? Determine the P-value and comment on its size.

8.99 A national sales firm monitors operators taking orders by phone. The average time for a phone call, in seconds, is used as one summary of the activity for the shift. The average talk times, for 15 persons, are

195	223	230	237	271	239	275	262
226	275	179	214	176	208	189	

Stating any assumption(s) you make, obtain a 95% confidence interval for the population mean.

8.100   Refer to Exercise 8.99. Test H_0: $\mu = 205$ versus H_1: $\mu \neq 205$ with $\alpha = .05$. What assumption(s) must you make to carry out this test? Determine the P-value and comment on its size.

8.101   Specify the null hypothesis and the alternative hypothesis if a manager wants to establish that the mean time to process an order and ship goods is less than 1.5 working days.

8.102   The air quality in one area of a large office complex was sampled on eight different days. The mean carbon dioxide measurement was 4.5 parts per million (ppm) and the standard deviation was 2.1. Experience with similar sets of measurements suggests that the population distribution is normal. Test, with $\alpha = .05$, that the population mean exceeds the recommended upper limit of 2.4 ppm. Determine the P-value and comment on its size.

After reading this chapter, you should be able to:

- Construct a confidence interval for the difference in two means using independent random samples.

- Carry out tests of hypotheses for the difference in two population means using independent random samples.

- Discuss the concept of pairing or blocking.

- Construct confidence intervals and conduct tests of hypotheses for the mean difference using paired observations.

- Carry out an analysis of variance.

- Test for the equality of several population means using independent random samples and the F test.

- Construct simultaneous confidence intervals for pairwise differences in means.

- Conduct a graphical residual analysis to check model assumptions.

CHAPTER NINE

Comparing Means

9.1 INTRODUCTION

In our discussion of the design of experiments in Chapter 4, we indicated that advances often involve comparisons and that an appropriately chosen experimental design is crucial to making valid comparisons. For example, luxury car manufacturers want to know why consumers purchase their cars rather than those of their competitors. Surveys of recent purchasers of German, Japanese, and American luxury cars can produce data that allow comparisons of attributes (or perceived attributes) that influenced the purchase decisions. Do German luxury car owners value fun and excitement more than American luxury car owners? Which group of car owners puts a higher value on comfort? As another example, the workforce in many countries is becoming more diverse. Do managerial values differ dramatically in different parts of the world? Will Americans have a hard time working for Hong Kong managers? Will foreign nationals have a hard time working for American managers? Data from surveys of managers in various countries with respect to measures of managerial values can be used to check for differences. Are Hong Kong managers more intolerant of ambiguity than American managers? Which country has managers that are the most dogmatic?

An experimental design specifies the manner in which the experimental units are selected and assigned to treatments. For comparing two treatments there are two basic designs:

1. Independent samples
2. Matched pairs or related pair samples

Both of these designs produce stronger conclusions when randomization is possible.

Under the independent samples design, the available units are randomly divided into groups using, say, a table of random digits. One group is assigned the first treatment and the other group is assigned the second treatment, and so forth. Alternatively, experimental units may be randomly selected from naturally distinct populations. For example, random samples might be selected from different countries or different firms.

In a study of brand loyalty, consumers could be randomly assigned to two product classes: soft drinks and beer. The responses to the first treatment (amount of brand switching among soft drinks) are independent of the responses to the second treatment (amount of brand switching among beers) since they are measured on separate and unrelated groups of units. Moreover, the collection of responses from the first treatment (soft drinks) can be considered as a random sample from one population and the collection of responses from the second treatment (beers) as a random sample from another population. Questions of comparison can then be formulated as questions comparing these two population distributions of numbers of different brands purchased.

In a matched pairs design, units in each pair are alike, whereas units in different pairs may be dissimilar. Randomization occurs within a pair. For each pair, one unit is chosen at random to receive Treatment 1; the other unit receives Treatment 2. In a comparative test of two preliminary versions of a motivational management tape, pairs of individuals are selected who are as alike as possible (same gender, same age, same amount of education, and so forth). One member of the pair is chosen at random to listen to Tape 1; the other member listens to Tape 2. The response (rating of the message) of an experimental unit is influenced not only by the treatment but also by the conditions prevailing in the pair. By taking the difference between the two responses in each pair (Treatment 1 response − Treatment 2 response, for example), we can filter out the conditions common to each member of the pair. In addition, the differences in response from pair to pair are independent since they are measured on separate and unrelated pairs. The collection of differences can be considered a random sample from a population distribution, and questions of comparison can be formulated in terms of questions about the nature of this distribution.

Our brand loyalty study can also be conceived as a matched pairs design. A random sample of consumers can be selected, and each consumer asked to keep track of his or her purchases of soft drinks and beer for a period of time. The number of different brands of soft drinks purchased and the number of different brands of beer purchased can be recorded for each consumer. The difference in these two numbers for each consumer provides information on the amount of brand switching for soft drinks relative to that for beer. Are beer drinkers more brand loyal?

The choice of an independent samples or a matched pairs sample design depends on the resources available to conduct the study and the required generalizability of the results. A matched pairs design typically involves a smaller sample but can be quite effective at detecting real differences if they exist. An independent samples design typically involves large samples, but can allow more diversity of sampling units and, consequently, inferences about broader populations.

The importance of randomization cannot be stressed enough. Unfortunately, there are many situations where the investigator cannot randomize the application of the treatments. If we were to record the percentage of patients who die at large research hospitals and compare these numbers with those of typical hospitals, the research hospitals would seem to be more dangerous. But the patients were not randomly assigned to hospitals, and the most seriously ill persons tend to select the research hospitals.

The hospital example illustrates that, when randomization is not possible, we must be cautious before attributing any apparent differences to the treatments. The differences may well be due to some other uncontrolled factor.

> **Randomization** helps prevent uncontrolled sources of variation from influencing the responses in a systematic manner.

The point to keep in mind is that making comparisons comes down to comparing population distributions. Moreover, the population distributions are typically compared by examining their means.

9.2   INDEPENDENT RANDOM SAMPLES FROM TWO POPULATIONS

With the design of independent random samples, a collection of $n_1 + n_2$ subjects is randomly divided into two groups—n_1 in the first group and n_2 in the second—and the responses are recorded. We conceptualize Population 1 as the collection of responses that would result if a vast number of subjects were given Treatment 1. Similarly, Population 2 refers to the population of responses under Treatment 2. The design of independent samples can then be viewed as one that produces unrelated random samples from two populations (see Figure 9.1 on page 444).

In other situations, the populations to be compared may be quite real entities. For instance, we may wish to compare the residential property values in the east suburb of a city with those in the west suburb. Here the issue of assigning experimental units to treatments does not arise. The collection of all residential properties in each suburb constitutes a population from which a sample will be drawn at random.

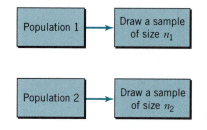

Figure 9.1 Independent Random Samples

With the design of independent random samples, we obtain:

Sample	Summary Statistics	
$X_1, X_2, \ldots, X_{n_1}$ from Population 1	$\overline{x} = \dfrac{1}{n_1} \displaystyle\sum_{i=1}^{n_1} x_i$	$s_1^2 = \dfrac{\sum_{i=1}^{n_1}(x_i - \overline{x})^2}{n_1 - 1}$
$Y_1, Y_2, \ldots, Y_{n_2}$ from Population 2	$\overline{y} = \dfrac{1}{n_2} \displaystyle\sum_{i=1}^{n_2} y_i$	$s_2^2 = \dfrac{\sum_{i=1}^{n_2}(y_i - \overline{y})^2}{n_2 - 1}$

To construct confidence intervals or to test hypotheses, we specify a statistical model for the data.

Statistical Model: Independent Random Samples

$X_1, X_2, \ldots, X_{n_1}$ is a random sample of size n_1 from Population 1 whose mean is denoted by μ_1 and whose standard deviation is denoted by σ_1.

$Y_1, Y_2, \ldots, Y_{n_2}$ is a random sample of size n_2 from Population 2 whose mean is denoted by μ_2 and whose standard deviation is denoted by σ_2.

The samples are independent; i.e., response measurements under one treatment are unrelated to response measurements under the other treatment.

We make comparisons by comparing the mean responses of the two treatments or populations. That is, we are interested in making inferences about the parameter

$$\mu_1 - \mu_2 = (\text{Mean of population 1}) - (\text{Mean of population 2})$$

INFERENCES FROM LARGE SAMPLES

It seems natural to base inferences about the difference $\mu_1 - \mu_2$ on its estimator $\overline{X} - \overline{Y}$, the difference in the sample means. When both sample sizes n_1 and n_2 are large (say, greater than 30), $\overline{X}$ and $\overline{Y}$ are each approximately normal, and their difference $\overline{X} - \overline{Y}$ is approximately normal with

Mean: $\quad E(\overline{X} - \overline{Y}) = \mu_1 - \mu_2$

Variance: $\quad \text{var}(\overline{X} - \overline{Y}) = \dfrac{\sigma_1^2}{n_1} + \dfrac{\sigma_2^2}{n_2}$

Standard error: $\quad \text{s.e.}(\overline{X} - \overline{Y}) = \sqrt{\dfrac{\sigma_1^2}{n_1} + \dfrac{\sigma_2^2}{n_2}}$

Note: Because the entities $\overline{X}$ and $\overline{Y}$ vary in repeated sampling and they vary independently of each other, the distance between them becomes more variable than the individual members. This explains the mathematical fact that the variance of the difference $(\overline{X} - \overline{Y})$ equals the *sum* of the variances of $\overline{X}$ and $\overline{Y}$.

When n_1 and n_2 are both large, the normal approximation remains valid if σ_1^2 and σ_2^2 are replaced by their estimates

$$s_1^2 = \frac{\sum_{i=1}^{n_1}(x_i - \overline{x})^2}{n_1 - 1} \quad \text{and} \quad s_2^2 = \frac{\sum_{i=1}^{n_2}(y_i - \overline{y})^2}{n_2 - 1}$$

We conclude that, when the sample sizes n_1 and n_2 are large, the variable Z with value

$$z = \frac{(\overline{x} - \overline{y}) - (\mu_1 - \mu_2)}{\sqrt{\dfrac{s_1^2}{n_1} + \dfrac{s_2^2}{n_2}}} \quad \text{is approximately } N(0, 1).$$

A confidence interval for $\mu_1 - \mu_2$ is constructed from this sampling distribution. Using the same arguments as for the case of a single population mean, we get this form for the confidence interval:

Estimate of parameter $\pm$ (z value)(Estimated standard error)

Large Sample Confidence Interval for $\mu_1 - \mu_2$

When n_1 and n_2 are greater than 30, an approximate $100(1 - \alpha)\%$ confidence interval for $\mu_1 - \mu_2$ is given by

$$\left(\overline{x} - \overline{y} - z_{\alpha/2}\sqrt{\frac{s_1^2}{n_1} + \frac{s_2^2}{n_2}}, \ \overline{x} - \overline{y} + z_{\alpha/2}\sqrt{\frac{s_1^2}{n_1} + \frac{s_2^2}{n_2}} \right)$$

where $z_{\alpha/2}$ is the upper $\alpha/2$ point of the $N(0, 1)$ distribution.

EXAMPLE 9.1 Constructing a Confidence Interval for $\mu_1 - \mu_2$

As part of an investigation of employee turnover, an industry-wide survey of people in sales management positions gave the number of years of experience in sales-related positions. These data are summarized in the following table.

	Males	Females
Sample size	80	70
Mean years	21.7	18.5
Std. dev. of years	9.3	4.8

Construct a 95% confidence interval for the difference of means $\mu_1 - \mu_2$.

Solution and Discussion.   We are given that

$$n_1 = 80 \qquad \overline{x} = 21.7 \qquad s_1 = 9.3$$
$$n_2 = 70 \qquad \overline{y} = 18.5 \qquad s_2 = 4.8$$

so the difference of sample means is

$$\overline{x} - \overline{y} = 21.7 - 18.5 = 3.2 \text{ years}$$

and its estimated standard deviation is

$$\sqrt{\frac{s_1^2}{n_1} + \frac{s_2^2}{n_2}} = \sqrt{\frac{(9.3)^2}{80} + \frac{(4.8)^2}{70}} = 1.19$$

We use $z_{.025} = 1.96$ for the 95% confidence interval, so

$$z_{.025}\sqrt{\frac{s_1^2}{n_1} + \frac{s_2^2}{n_2}} = 1.96 \times 1.19 = 2.33$$

and the 95% confidence interval for $\mu_1 - \mu_2$ is given by

$$(3.2 - 2.33, \ 3.2 + 2.33) \quad \text{or} \quad (.87, \ 5.33) \text{ years}$$

Males have an average of .87 to 5.33 years more experience in sales-related positions.

A test of the null hypothesis that the two population means are the same, $H_0: \mu_1 - \mu_2 = 0$, is based on the test statistic Z with value

$$z = \frac{\overline{x} - \overline{y}}{\sqrt{\dfrac{s_1^2}{n_1} + \dfrac{s_2^2}{n_2}}}$$

When the samples sizes n_1 and n_2 are large and $\mu_1 - \mu_2 = 0$, Z is approximately standard normal.

EXAMPLE 9.2   Testing the Equality of Two Population Means

Do the data on experience in sales positions in Example 9.1 provide strong evidence that the mean years of sales experience for males is different from that of females? Test with $\alpha = .02$.

Solution and Discussion.   We follow the steps for testing hypotheses discussed in Chapter 8.

1. *Hypotheses*. Our goal is to establish that the population means μ_1 and μ_2 are different, that is, $\mu_1 - \mu_2 \neq 0$. Consequently, with the goal as the alternative hypothesis, the hypotheses are formulated as

    Null hypothesis H_0: $\mu_1 - \mu_2 = 0$
    Alternative hypothesis H_1: $\mu_1 - \mu_2 \neq 0$

    We are given $\alpha = .02$.

2. *Test Statistic*. The value of the test statistic is

$$z = \frac{\overline{x} - \overline{y}}{\sqrt{\dfrac{s_1^2}{n_1} + \dfrac{s_2^2}{n_2}}}$$

    The alternative hypothesis is two-sided, so we reject H_0 if Z is large or if Z takes a large negative value.

3. *Rejection Region*. The specified α is .02, so $\alpha/2 = .01$ and, from the normal table, $z_{.01} = 2.33$. The two-sided rejection region is $z > 2.33$ or $z < -2.33$.

4. *Calculation*. From Example 9.1,

$$n_1 = 80 \quad \overline{x} = 21.7 \quad s_1 = 9.3$$
$$n_2 = 70 \quad \overline{y} = 18.5 \quad s_2 = 4.8$$

    so the observed value of the test statistic is

$$z = \frac{\overline{x} - \overline{y}}{\sqrt{\dfrac{s_1^2}{n_1} + \dfrac{s_2^2}{n_2}}} = \frac{21.7 - 18.5}{\sqrt{\dfrac{(9.3)^2}{80} + \dfrac{(4.8)^2}{70}}} = \frac{3.2}{1.19} = 2.69$$

5. *Conclusion*. The observed value of the test statistic, 2.69, falls in the rejection region. At level $\alpha = .02$, we reject the null hypothesis in favor of the alternative that the mean years of sales experience is different for males and females.

    Because the observed value is $z = 2.69$, values less than -2.69 as well as values greater than 2.69 are considered to provide more extreme evidence in favor of the alternative hypothesis. Consequently, the significance probability, or *P*-value, is

$$P\text{-value} = P(Z < -2.69) + P(Z > 2.69) = .0036 + (1 - .9964) = .0072$$

    from the normal table. The probability is about .007 of observing as extreme a sample result as the one observed if H_0 is true. We conclude that the evidence is quite strong that the mean years of sales experience are different.

    The test statistic in Example 9.2 can be modified to test a claim that, say, μ_1 is more than 2.4 years larger than μ_2. Then the alternative hypothesis is H_1: $\mu_1 - \mu_2 > 2.4$, and the null hypothesis is H_0: $\mu_1 - \mu_2 = 2.4$. In general, we can make the difference in means under the null hypothesis any number. Denoting this number by δ_0, we summarize the procedure for testing H_0: $\mu_1 - \mu_2 = \delta_0$ against possible alternatives. The case $\mu_1 = \mu_2$ corresponds to $\delta_0 = 0$.

Testing H_0: $\mu_1 - \mu_2 = \delta_0$ with Large Samples

Test statistic Z with value

$$z = \frac{\overline{x} - \overline{y} - \delta_0}{\sqrt{\dfrac{s_1^2}{n_1} + \dfrac{s_2^2}{n_2}}}$$

Alternative Hypothesis	Level α Rejection Region
H_1: $\mu_1 - \mu_2 > \delta_0$	$z > z_\alpha$
H_1: $\mu_1 - \mu_2 < \delta_0$	$z < -z_\alpha$
H_1: $\mu_1 - \mu_2 \neq \delta_0$	$z > z_{\alpha/2}$ or $z < -z_{\alpha/2}$

EXAMPLE 9.3   Testing a Null Hypothesis Specifying a Nonzero Difference in Two Population Means

Do the data on years of sales experience in Example 9.1 provide strong evidence that the mean for males is more than 1 year larger than the mean for females? Test with $\alpha = .05$.

Solution and Discussion.   We use the following steps for testing hypotheses:

1. *Hypotheses.* Our goal is to establish that the population mean μ_1 is more than 1 year larger than μ_2. Because the claim should be taken as the alternative hypothesis, the hypotheses are formulated as

    Null hypothesis H_0: $\mu_1 - \mu_2 = 1$
    Alternative hypothesis H_1: $\mu_1 - \mu_2 > 1$

    We are given $\alpha = .05$.

2. *Test Statistic.* The test statistic Z has the value

    $$z = \frac{\overline{x} - \overline{y} - 1}{\sqrt{\dfrac{s_1^2}{n_1} + \dfrac{s_2^2}{n_2}}}$$

    Since the alternative hypothesis is right-sided, we reject H_0 if Z is large.

3. *Rejection Region.* The specified α is .05 and, from the normal table, $z_{.05} = 1.645$, so the rejection region is $z > 1.645$.

4. *Calculation.* We are given

$$n_1 = 80 \qquad \bar{x} = 21.7 \qquad s_1 = 9.3$$
$$n_2 = 70 \qquad \bar{y} = 18.5 \qquad s_2 = 4.8$$

so the value of the test statistic is

$$z = \frac{\bar{x} - \bar{y} - 1}{\sqrt{\dfrac{s_1^2}{n_1} + \dfrac{s_2^2}{n_2}}} = \frac{21.7 - 18.5 - 1}{\sqrt{\dfrac{(9.3)^2}{80} + \dfrac{(4.8)^2}{70}}} = \frac{2.2}{1.19} = 1.85$$

5. *Conclusion.* The observed value of the test statistic, 1.85, falls in the rejection region. At level $\alpha = .05$, we reject the null hypothesis in favor of the alternative that the mean sales experience for males is more than 1 year longer than that for females.

Because the observed value is $z = 1.85$, values greater than 1.85 are considered to provide more extreme evidence in favor of the alternative hypothesis. Consequently, the significance probability, or *P*-value, is

$$P\text{-value} = P(Z > 1.85) = (1 - .9678) = .0322$$

from the normal table. If H_0 is true, the probability of getting a sample result as extreme as the one we observed is about .03. Consequently, the evidence is strong that the mean number of years of sales experience for males is more than 1 year longer than the mean for females.

INFERENCES FROM SMALL SAMPLES

Not surprisingly, more structure is required to formulate appropriate inference procedures for small samples. We will introduce the small sample procedures for comparing two population means that are valid under the following assumptions about the population distributions. The usefulness of these procedures depends on how closely the sample observations follow the assumptions made about the population distributions. If the assumptions are not warranted, the conclusions reached as a result of a confidence interval or a test of hypotheses may be grossly misleading.

Additional Assumptions When the Sample Sizes Are Small

Both populations are normal.

The population standard deviations σ_1 and σ_2 are equal.

The restriction to normal populations is not new. It was previously introduced for small sample inferences about the mean of a single population. The second restriction, of equal standard deviations, is somewhat artificial, and we shall deal with it later.

For the moment, however, we let σ denote the common population standard deviation and summarize the small sample assumptions and notation.

Small Sample Assumptions

$X_1, X_2, \ldots, X_{n_1}$ is a random sample from $N(\mu_1, \sigma)$.

$Y_1, Y_2, \ldots, Y_{n_2}$ is a random sample from $N(\mu_2, \sigma)$.

$X_1, X_2, \ldots, X_{n_1}$ and $Y_1, Y_2, \ldots, Y_{n_2}$ are independent.

With the small sample assumptions, the statistic $\overline{X} - \overline{Y}$ has

$$\textbf{Mean:} \quad E(\overline{X} - \overline{Y}) = \mu_1 - \mu_2$$

$$\textbf{Variance:} \quad \mathrm{var}(\overline{X} - \overline{Y}) = \frac{\sigma^2}{n_1} + \frac{\sigma^2}{n_2} = \sigma^2\left(\frac{1}{n_1} + \frac{1}{n_2}\right)$$

We assume that the two normal populations have the same variance σ^2. This common variance can be estimated by combining the information provided by both samples. In view of the constraint that the deviations $x_i - \overline{x}$ sum to zero, the quantity $\sum_{i=1}^{n_1}(x_i - \overline{x})^2$ incorporates $n_1 - 1$ pieces of information about σ^2 from the first sample. Independently of this, and with the constraint $\sum_{i=1}^{n_2}(y_i - \overline{y}) = 0$, the quantity $\sum_{i=1}^{n_2}(y_i - \overline{y})^2$ contains $n_2 - 1$ pieces of information about σ^2 from the second sample. These two quantities can be combined as

$$\sum_{i=1}^{n_1}(x_i - \overline{x})^2 + \sum_{i=1}^{n_2}(y_i - \overline{y})^2$$

to obtain a *pooled estimate* of the common σ^2. The proper divisor is the sum of the component degrees of freedom, or $(n_1 - 1) + (n_2 - 1) = n_1 + n_2 - 2$.

Pooled Estimate of the Common σ^2

$$\begin{aligned}
s^2_{\text{pooled}} &= \frac{\sum_{i=1}^{n_1}(x_i - \overline{x})^2 + \sum_{i=1}^{n_2}(y_i - \overline{y})^2}{n_1 + n_2 - 2} \\[2mm]
&= \frac{(n_1 - 1)s_1^2 + (n_2 - 1)s_2^2}{n_1 + n_2 - 2}
\end{aligned}$$

Notice that the pooled estimator of the common population variance is a *weighted average* of the two sample variances. That is, the pooled estimator can be written

$$s^2_{\text{pooled}} = w_1 s_1^2 + w_2 s_2^2$$

where

$$w_1 = \frac{n_1 - 1}{n_1 + n_2 - 2} \qquad w_2 = \frac{n_2 - 1}{n_1 + n_2 - 2}$$

and $w_1 + w_2 = 1$. The sample variance from the larger sample has more influence, or receives the larger weight, in the calculation of s^2_{pooled}.

EXAMPLE 9.4   Calculating s^2_{pooled}

Calculate s^2_{pooled} from the two samples:

Sample from population   1:   7   3   8
Sample from population   2:   2   6   9   3

Solution and Discussion.   The sample means are

$$\bar{x} = \frac{\sum_{i=1}^{3} x_i}{3} = \frac{18}{3} = 6$$

$$\bar{y} = \frac{\sum_{i=1}^{4} y_i}{4} = \frac{20}{4} = 5$$

so that

$$(3 - 1)s_1^2 = (7 - 6)^2 + (3 - 6)^2 + (8 - 6)^2 = 14$$
$$(4 - 1)s_2^2 = (2 - 5)^2 + (6 - 5)^2 + (9 - 5)^2 + (3 - 5)^2 = 30$$

Consequently, $s_1^2 = 7$, $s_2^2 = 10$, and the pooled variance is

$$s^2_{pooled} = \frac{\sum(x_i - \bar{x})^2 + \sum(y_i - \bar{y})^2}{n_1 + n_2 - 2} = \frac{14 + 30}{3 + 4 - 2} = 8.80$$

The pooled sample variance is closer to 10 than 7 because the second sample size is larger than the first.

If, for example, a calculator gives the standard deviations directly so that $s_1 = \sqrt{7} = 2.646$ and $s_2 = \sqrt{10} = 3.162$, these quantities can be inserted in the formula for the pooled variance to give

$$s^2_{pooled} = \frac{(n_1 - 1)(s_1)^2 + (n_2 - 1)(s_2)^2}{n_1 + n_2 - 2} = \frac{2(2.646)^2 + 3(3.162)^2}{3 + 4 - 2} = 8.80$$

Under the assumption that the two population variances are equal and the populations normal, the random variable Z with value

$$z = \frac{\bar{x} - \bar{y} - (\mu_1 - \mu_2)}{\sigma\sqrt{\dfrac{1}{n_1} + \dfrac{1}{n_2}}}$$

has a standard normal distribution.

We can use s_{pooled}^2 to estimate the common variance σ^2 and obtain a Student's t variable that provides the basis for making small sample inferences about $\mu_1 - \mu_2$.

The random variable t whose value is

$$t = \frac{\overline{x} - \overline{y} - (\mu_1 - \mu_2)}{s_{pooled}\sqrt{\dfrac{1}{n_1} + \dfrac{1}{n_2}}}$$

has the Student's t distribution with $n_1 + n_2 - 2$ degrees of freedom.

Confidence intervals for $\mu_1 - \mu_2$, obtained from this distribution, are of the form

Estimate of parameter $\pm (t_{\alpha/2})$(Estimated standard error)

Confidence Interval for $\mu_1 - \mu_2$ with Small Normal Samples

A $100(1 - \alpha)\%$ confidence interval for $\mu_1 - \mu_2$ is

$$\left(\overline{x} - \overline{y} - t_{\alpha/2}s_{pooled}\sqrt{\frac{1}{n_1} + \frac{1}{n_2}}, \quad \overline{x} - \overline{y} + t_{\alpha/2}s_{pooled}\sqrt{\frac{1}{n_1} + \frac{1}{n_2}} \right)$$

where

$$s_{pooled}^2 = \frac{(n_1 - 1)s_1^2 + (n_2 - 1)s_2^2}{n_1 + n_2 - 2}$$

and $t_{\alpha/2}$ is the upper $\alpha/2$ point of the t distribution with $n_1 + n_2 - 2$ degrees of freedom.

EXAMPLE 9.5 Constructing a Confidence Interval for the Difference in Two Population Means

A large consulting company estimates several components of job cost when preparing a bid. A sample of 8 bids for government projects and a sample of 8 bids for private projects provided the data on the management cost component (as a percentage of the total bid).

Government	.3	.9	1.4	2.2	2.4	3.9	3.5	1.8
Private	4.2	1.2	2.5	2.7	3.7	5.2	4.0	1.9

Treat these data as independent random samples, and obtain a 95% confidence interval for the difference in the mean management cost components. Also comment on the assumptions.

Solution and Discussion.   The sample means and standard deviations are

	Government	**Private**
Sample size	8	8
Mean cost	2.050	3.175
Std. dev. of cost	1.227	1.326

We have $\bar{x} - \bar{y} = 2.050 - 3.175 = -1.125$, and the value of the pooled variance is

$$s_{\text{pooled}}^2 = \frac{(n_1 - 1)(s_1)^2 + (n_2 - 1)(s_2)^2}{n_1 + n_2 - 2} = \frac{7(1.227)^2 + 7(1.326)^2}{8 + 8 - 2} = 1.632$$

Taking the square root, we obtain $s_{\text{pooled}} = 1.278$.

Since $\alpha = .05$, $\alpha/2 = .025$ and $t_{.025} = 2.145$ for $8 + 8 - 2 = 14$ degrees of freedom. Thus

$$t_{\alpha/2}\, s_{\text{pooled}} \sqrt{\frac{1}{n_1} + \frac{1}{n_2}} = 2.145(1.278)\sqrt{\frac{1}{8} + \frac{1}{8}} = 1.371$$

and the 95% confidence interval for $\mu_1 - \mu_2$ becomes

$$(-1.125 - 1.371, \ -1.125 + 1.371) \quad \text{or} \quad (-2.50, \ .25)$$

The mean management cost component, as a percentage of total bid, is .25% lower to 2.50% higher for private than for government projects. Notice that 0 is a plausible value for the difference of means. What does this suggest?

Because the two standard deviations are nearly equal, the assumption of equal population variances is not contradicted. The sample sizes are too small to assess the assumption of normal distributions. Ordinarily, we would look for evidence of lack of normality in dotplots and normal-scores plots.

We now turn to testing for differences in two population means when the sample sizes are small.

Testing H_0: $\mu_1 - \mu_2 = \delta_0$ with Small Normal Samples

Test statistic t with value

$$t = \frac{\bar{x} - \bar{y} - \delta_0}{s_{\text{pooled}}\sqrt{\dfrac{1}{n_1} + \dfrac{1}{n_2}}}$$

Alternative Hypothesis	**Level α Rejection Region**
H_1: $\mu_1 - \mu_2 > \delta_0$	$t > t_\alpha$
H_1: $\mu_1 - \mu_2 < \delta_0$	$t < -t_\alpha$
H_1: $\mu_1 - \mu_2 \neq \delta_0$	$t > t_{\alpha/2}$ or $t < -t_{\alpha/2}$

EXAMPLE 9.6   Testing for a Difference in Two Population Means

Refer to the data on management costs in Example 9.5. Test, with $\alpha = .10$, the assertion that the mean is larger for private projects than for government projects.

Solution and Discussion.   The steps for testing hypotheses are summarized here.

1. *Hypotheses.* The assertion is that μ_2 is larger than μ_1 or, equivalently, that $\mu_1 - \mu_2 < 0$. This claim is the alternative hypothesis so, with $\delta_0 = 0$, we have

    Null hypothesis $H_0: \mu_1 - \mu_2 = 0$
    Alternative hypothesis $H_1: \mu_1 - \mu_2 < 0$

    We are given $\alpha = .10$.

2. *Test Statistic.* The value of the test statistic is

$$t = \frac{\overline{x} - \overline{y}}{s_{\text{pooled}}\sqrt{\dfrac{1}{n_1} + \dfrac{1}{n_2}}}$$

    and the alternative hypothesis is one-sided. In this case, we reject H_0 if t takes a large negative value.

3. *Rejection Region.* We have $\alpha = .10$, and there are $8 + 8 - 2 = 14$ degrees of freedom so, using the t table, $t_{.10} = 1.345$. Consequently, the one-sided rejection region is the set $t < -1.345$.

4. *Calculation.* From Example 9.5,

$$n_1 = 8 \qquad \overline{x} = 2.050 \qquad s_1 = 1.227$$
$$n_2 = 8 \qquad \overline{y} = 3.175 \qquad s_2 = 1.326$$

    and $s_{\text{pooled}} = 1.278$, so the test statistic takes the value

$$t = \frac{\overline{x} - \overline{y}}{s_{\text{pooled}}\sqrt{\dfrac{1}{n_1} + \dfrac{1}{n_2}}} = \frac{2.050 - 3.175}{1.278\sqrt{\dfrac{1}{8} + \dfrac{1}{8}}} = -1.761$$

5. *Conclusion.* The observed value of the test statistic, -1.761, falls in the rejection region. At level $\alpha = .10$, we reject the null hypothesis in favor of the alternative that the mean management cost is higher for private projects than for government projects.

Because the observed value of the test statistic is $t = -1.761$, the significance probability is

$$P\text{-value} = P(t < -1.761) = .05$$

according to the t table. Consequently, we would reject the null hypothesis at the $\alpha = .05$ level.

In any practical situation, the two sample standard deviations s_1 and s_2 will not be equal, even if the population values are nearly equal, so how can we decide whether to pool them? As a rule of thumb, we suggest that the pooled estimate of variance should not be calculated if the ratio of standard deviations is greater than 2.0. If pooling is not reasonable, there is an approximate procedure for testing the equality of two normal population means with small samples. This procedure, due to Satterthwaite, is given in Exercise 9.19.

EXERCISES

9.1 Independent random samples from two populations have provided these summary statistics:

Sample 1	Sample 2
$n_1 = 55$	$n_2 = 45$
$\bar{x} = 72$	$\bar{y} = 64$
$s_1^2 = 150$	$s_2^2 = 142$

a. Obtain a point estimate of $\mu_1 - \mu_2$ and give an estimate of its standard error.

b. Obtain a 95% confidence interval for $\mu_1 - \mu_2$.

9.2 Luxury car manufacturers want to know why consumers purchase their cars. A survey, conducted of recent purchasers of luxury cars, included a question asking how important owners value

fun, enjoyment, and excitement

in their daily lives. The response was measured on a 7-point scale, with the endpoints labeled "very important" and "very unimportant." The value 1 corresponds to very important, and 7 to very unimportant. The results for American luxury car owners and German luxury car owners are:

American car owners: $n_1 = 58$, $\bar{x} = 2.97$, $s_1^2 = 2.36$

German car owners: $n_2 = 38$, $\bar{y} = 2.17$, $s_2^2 = 2.07$

Source: Private communication from A. Sukhdial based on an article by A. Sukhdial and G. Chakraborty that appeared in the *Journal of Advertising Research*, Jan./Feb. 1995.

a. Do these data confirm that German luxury car owners value fun, enjoyment, and excitement more than American luxury car owners? Test with $\alpha = .05$.

b. Construct a 95% confidence interval for the difference in the population means. Is the confidence interval consistent with the result of the test of hypotheses in part **a?** Explain.

9.3 Refer to Exercise 9.2. Luxury car owners were asked to respond (using the same 7-point scale as in Exercise 9.2) to how they feel about comfort as an attribute of a car. The results for American luxury car owners and German luxury car owners are:

American car owners: $n_1 = 58$, $\bar{x} = 1.05$, $s_1^2 = .35$

German car owners: $n_2 = 38$, $\bar{y} = 1.52$, $s_2^2 = .51$

a. Do these data confirm that German luxury car owners differ from American luxury car owners with respect to the mean response on the importance of the attribute comfort? Test with $\alpha = .05$.

b. Construct a 95% confidence interval for the difference in the population means. Which group of car owners appears to place a higher value on comfort? Explain.

9.4 In a study of the differences in managerial values in different parts of the world,*

intolerance of ambiguity

was quantified by responses to 8 questions. Each question was recorded on a 5-point scale, so the total score ranged from 5 to 40. The top score indicated the highest desire for more certainty. These data are summarized for American and People's Republic of China managers:

American managers: $n_1 = 62$, $\bar{x} = 19.8$, $s_1 = 4.59$

People's Republic of China managers: $n_2 = 82$, $\bar{y} = 24.7$, $s_2 = 4.78$

a. Do these data confirm that Chinese managers differ from American managers with respect to the mean response on the intolerance of ambiguity scale? Test with $\alpha = .05$.

b. Construct a 95% confidence interval for the difference in the population means. Which group of managers is more tolerant of ambiguity? Explain.

CompAtti.dat

9.5 (*Minitab or similar program recommended*) Refer to Table C.2 of Appendix C, and test for the equality of mean computer anxiety scores (CARS) for male and female accounting students. Use significance level $\alpha = .05$. Determine the *P*-value and comment on its size.

CompAtti.dat

9.6 (*Minitab or similar program recommended*) Refer to Table C.2 of Appendix C, and obtain a 90% confidence interval for the difference of mean computer anxiety scores (CARS) for male and female accounting students.

CompAtti.dat

9.7 (*Minitab or similar program recommended*) Refer to Table C.2 of Appendix C, and test for the equality of mean computer attitude scores (CAS) for male and female accounting students. Use significance level $\alpha = .05$. Determine the *P*-value and comment on its size.

CompAtti.dat

9.8 (*Minitab or similar program recommended*) Refer to Table C.2 of Appendix C, and obtain a 90% confidence interval for the difference of mean computer attitude scores (CAS) for male and female accounting students.

9.9 A group of 141 subjects is used in an experiment to compare two treatments. Treatment 1 is given to 79 subjects selected at random, and the remaining 62 subjects are given Treatment 2. The means and standard deviations of the responses follow:

	Treatment 1	Treatment 2
Mean	109	128
Standard deviation	46.2	53.4

---

*D. Ralston, D. Gustafson, F. Cheung, and R. Terpstra, "Differences in Managerial Values: A study of U.S., Hong Kong, and PRC managers." *Journal of International Business Studies,* Vol. 24, No. 2, 1993, p. 261.

Determine a 98% confidence interval for the difference in mean treatment effects.

9.10   Refer to Exercise 9.9. Suppose the investigator wishes to establish that Treatment 2 has a higher mean response than Treatment 1.

a.   Formulate H_0 and H_1.

b.   State the test statistic and the rejection region with $\alpha = .05$.

c.   Perform the test at $\alpha = .05$. Also, determine the P-value and comment on its size.

9.11   A national equal employment opportunities committee is conducting an investigation to determine whether female employees are as well paid as their male counterparts in comparable jobs. Random samples of 75 males and 64 females in junior academic positions are selected, and the following annual salary data are obtained:

	Male	**Female**
Mean	$45,530	$44,620
Standard deviation	$780	$750

Construct a 95% confidence interval for the difference between the mean salaries of males and females in junior academic positions. Interpret the result.

9.12   Refer to the confidence interval obtained in Exercise 9.11. If you were to test the null hypothesis that the mean salaries are equal versus the two-sided alternative that the mean salaries are unequal, what would be the conclusion of your test with $\alpha = .05$? (See Section 8.6.)

9.13   Suppose that, with independent random samples of sizes 52 and 67 from two populations, a 95% confidence interval for $\mu_1 - \mu_2$ has been found to be $(6.88, 9.26)$. Using this result determine:

a.   A point estimate of $\mu_1 - \mu_2$ and its estimated standard error

b.   A 90% confidence interval for $\mu_1 - \mu_2$

9.14   You are given

$$n_1 = 15 \qquad \bar{x} = 20 \qquad \sum (x_i - \bar{x})^2 = 28$$
$$n_2 = 12 \qquad \bar{y} = 17 \qquad \sum (y_i - \bar{y})^2 = 22$$

a.   Obtain s_{pooled}^2.

b.   Test H_0: $\mu_1 = \mu_2$ against H_1: $\mu_1 > \mu_2$ with $\alpha = .05$. Determine the P-value and comment on its size.

c.   Construct a 95% confidence interval for $\mu_1 - \mu_2$.

9.15   The following summary statistics are recorded for independent random samples from two populations:

Sample 1	**Sample 2**
$n_1 = 9$	$n_2 = 6$
$\bar{x} = 16.18$	$\bar{y} = 4.22$
$s_1 = 1.54$	$s_2 = 1.37$

Stating any assumptions you make,

a. Calculate a 95% confidence interval for $\mu_1 - \mu_2$.

b. Test the null hypothesis $H_0: \mu_1 - \mu_2 = 10$ versus the alternative hypothesis $H_1: \mu_1 - \mu_2 > 10$ with $\alpha = .01$. Determine the P-value and interpret this number.

9.16 Suppose that, for a random sample of size 5 from Population 1, the sample mean and standard deviation were 10.6 and 3.62, respectively, while a random sample of size 8 from Population 2 yielded a sample mean of 14.9 and a sample standard deviation of 4.17.

a. Determine a 90% confidence interval for the difference between the population means.

b. Test the null hypothesis $\mu_1 = \mu_2$ versus the alternative $\mu_1 < \mu_2$ at $\alpha = .025$. Determine the P-value and comment on its size.

9.17 To compare two programs for training industrial workers to perform a skilled job, 20 workers are included in an experiment. Of these, 10 are selected at random and trained by Method 1; the remaining 10 workers are trained by Method 2. After completion of training, all the workers are subjected to a time-and-motion test that records the speed of performance of a skilled job. The following data are obtained.

					Time (minutes)					
Method 1	15	20	11	23	16	21	18	16	27	24
Method 2	23	31	13	19	23	17	28	26	25	28

a. Can you conclude from the data that the mean job time is significantly less after training with Method 1 than after training with Method 2? (Test with $\alpha = .05$.)

b. State the assumptions you make for the population distributions.

c. Construct a 95% confidence interval for the population mean difference in job times between the two methods.

9.18 Based on the data of independent random samples of sizes 6 and 5 from two populations, we report the following:

"Under the assumption of normal populations with equal but unknown standard deviations, the 90% confidence interval for $\mu_1 - \mu_2$ is (76, 102)."

From this report,

a. Determine the 98% confidence interval for $\mu_1 - \mu_2$.

b. State the conclusion of testing $H_0: \mu_1 - \mu_2 = 100$ versus $H_1: \mu_1 - \mu_2 \neq 100$ at $\alpha = .10$.

9.19 *Satterthwaite Test.* When the sample sizes are small and the populations are normal, the population standard deviations may still be quite different. If the sample standard deviations s_1 and s_2 differ by more than a factor of 2, we have stated that it is usually not advisable to pool the variances. Instead, the test is based on the statistic that takes the value

$$\frac{\overline{x} - \overline{y} - \delta_0}{\sqrt{\dfrac{s_1^2}{n_1} + \dfrac{s_2^2}{n_2}}}$$

and whose distribution is approximated by a Student's t distribution where the degrees of freedom are estimated from the sample variances:

$$\text{degrees of freedom} = \frac{\left(\dfrac{s_1^2}{n_1} + \dfrac{s_2^2}{n_2}\right)^2}{\dfrac{\left(\dfrac{s_1^2}{n_1}\right)^2}{n_1 - 1} + \dfrac{\left(\dfrac{s_2^2}{n_2}\right)^2}{n_2 - 1}}$$

Apply the Satterthwaite procedure to test equality of the two population means in the following problems.

a. Independent samples are obtained from two normal distributions. For the first sample $n_1 = 6$, $\bar{x} = 7.5$, and $s_1 = 2.3$; for the second sample, $n_2 = 5$, $\bar{y} = 11.4$, and $s_2 = 5.1$.

b. Independent samples are obtained from two normal distributions. For the first sample, $n_1 = 9$, $\bar{x} = 12.4$, and $s_1 = 4.7$, for the second sample, $n_2 = 7$, $\bar{y} = 9.6$, and $s_2 = 2.2$.

9.20 (*Minitab or similar program recommended*) A two-sample analysis can be done using Minitab. The commands

```
SET C1
4 6 2 7
SET C2
7 9 5
TWOSAMPLE 95 C1 C2;
POOLED.
```

produce the pooled t test and a 95% confidence interval for $\mu_1 - \mu_2$.

```
TWOSAMPLE-T 95 PERCENT FOR C1 VS C2

       N    MEAN   STDEV      SE MEAN
C1     4    4.75   2.22         1.1
C2     3    7.00   2.00         1.2
95 PCT CI FOR MU C1 - MU C2:  (-6.4, 1.9)
TTEST MU C1 = MU C2 (VS NE):  T = -1.38  P = 0.23  DF = 5.0
```

a. Find the P-value and comment on its magnitude.

b. Is -3 a plausible value for the difference $\mu_1 - \mu_2$? Explain.

c. Using the Minitab commands, find a 97% confidence interval for the difference in population means corresponding to the data in Exercise 9.17.

9.3 MATCHED PAIRS COMPARISONS

When making comparisons, it is often desirable to select experimental units that are as much alike as possible. Then, any difference in the response between members of a pair can be attributed to the particular treatments applied, and not to differences in the experimental units themselves. However, the condition that all experimental units be alike can severely limit the number that are available for a comparative experiment. For instance, to compare two different sales training programs, it may be impractical to look for subjects of the same sex, amount of experience, level of intelligence, and similar personalities. Aside from the practical limitations, we would rarely want to confine the comparison to such a narrow group. Any inferences that are gleaned from the experiment must apply to both sexes, various levels of experience, and so forth.

The concept of **matching** or **pairing** provides a compromise between the two conflicting demands that the experimental units be alike to detect treatment effects yet also be of different kinds to generalize the findings.

For example, when market researchers want to determine which of two versions of a new cereal is preferred, they may gather 100 persons at a time and try both versions. A taste rating of 1 to 5 is given to each. Both cereals are tasted by each subject, so the two ratings are naturally paired. The difference of ratings would then reflect subjects' preferences. It would not be influenced by uncontrolled variables. By using a large number of subjects, conclusions will apply to a population having a wide variety of individual taste preferences.

The matched pairs design is reviewed here. Keep in mind that one member of the pair of like experimental units is selected at random to receive Treatment 1, the other unit receives Treatment 2.

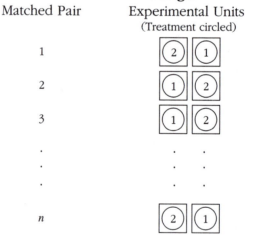

Matched Pairs Design

A pair of like experimental units is called a **block.** Units within a block are similar. Units in different blocks may be quite dissimilar.

In a matched pairs design, the response of an experimental unit is influenced by:

The conditions prevailing in the block (pair)

A treatment effect

By taking the difference between the two observations in a block, we can eliminate the common block effect. These differences then permit us to focus on the effects of treatments, eliminating the possibility of contamination from unwanted sources of variation.

> ### Pairing (or Blocking)
>
> **Pairing** like experimental units according to some identifiable characteristic(s) serves to remove this source of variation from the experiment.

The structure of the observations in a paired comparison is given in the box, where x and y denote the responses to Treatment 1 and Treatment 2, respectively. The difference between the responses in each pair is recorded in the last column, and the summary statistics are also presented.

Structure of Data for a Matched Pairs Comparison

Pair	Treatment 1	Treatment 2	Difference
1	x_1	y_1	$d_1 = x_1 - y_1$
2	x_2	y_2	$d_2 = x_2 - y_2$
$\vdots$	$\vdots$	$\vdots$	$\vdots$
n	x_n	y_n	$d_n = x_n - y_n$

The differences $d_1, d_2, \ldots, d_n$ are a random sample.

Summary statistics:

$$\overline{d} = \frac{1}{n} \sum_{i=1}^{n} d_i \qquad s_d^2 = \frac{\sum_{i=1}^{n} (d_i - \overline{d})^2}{n - 1}$$

Although we assume the pairs (X_i, Y_i) are independent of one another, X_i and Y_i within the ith pair will usually be dependent. In fact, if the pairing of experimental units is effective, we would expect X_i and Y_i to be relatively large or small together. Expressed in another way, we would expect (X_i, Y_i) to have a high positive correlation. Because the differences $D_i = X_i - Y_i, i = 1, 2, \ldots, n$ are free of the block effects, it is reasonable to assume that they constitute a random sample from a population with mean $= \delta$ and variance $= \sigma_d^2$, where δ represents the mean difference of the treatment effects. In other words,

$$E(D_i) = \delta$$
$$\mathrm{var}(D_i) = \sigma_d^2 \qquad i = 1, 2, \ldots, n$$

If the mean difference δ is zero, then the two treatments can be considered equivalent. A positive δ signifies that Treatment 1 has a higher mean response than Treatment 2. Considering $D_1, D_2, \ldots, D_n$ to be a random sample from a population, we can immediately apply the techniques discussed in Chapter 8 to learn about the population mean δ.

As we learned in Chapter 8, the assumption of an underlying normal distribution can be relaxed when the sample size is large. The central limit theorem applied to the differences $D_1, D_2, \ldots, D_n$ suggests that when n is large, say, greater than 30, the random variable whose value is

$$\frac{\overline{d} - \delta}{s_d / \sqrt{n}} \quad \text{is approximately } N(0, 1).$$

The inferences can then be based on the percentage points of the $N(0, 1)$ distribution or, equivalently, on the percentage points of the t distribution, with the degrees of freedom marked "infinity."

Small Sample Inferences About the Mean Difference δ

Assume the observed differences $d_i = x_i - y_i$ are a random sample from a $N(\delta, \sigma_d)$ distribution. Let

$$\overline{d} = \frac{\sum_{i=1}^{n} d_i}{n} \quad \text{and} \quad s_d = \sqrt{\frac{\sum_{i=1}^{n} (d_i - \overline{d})^2}{n - 1}}$$

Then,

A $100(1 - \alpha)\%$ confidence interval for δ is given by

$$\left(\overline{d} - t_{\alpha/2} \frac{s_d}{\sqrt{n}}, \ \overline{d} + t_{\alpha/2} \frac{s_d}{\sqrt{n}} \right)$$

where $t_{\alpha/2}$ is based on $n - 1$ degrees of freedom.
A test of $H_0: \delta = \delta_0$ is based on the test statistic t with value

$$t = \frac{\overline{d} - \delta_0}{s_d / \sqrt{n}}$$

and the Student's t distribution has $n - 1$ d.f.

EXAMPLE 9.7 Making Inferences About a Mean Difference

As part of an internal audit of its bidding process, a company selected a sample of 20 recently completed cases for review. One aspect concerned the procedure for estimating labor costs on projects. Data were collected on the estimated labor hours and the actual labor hours (recorded in thousands of hours) for these projects.

a. Obtain a 95% confidence interval for the mean difference between estimated and actual labor.

b. Do these data provide evidence that the mean difference is not zero? Test with $\alpha = .02$.

Solution and Discussion.

a.   The paired differences (Estimated − Actual) are calculated in the last rows of Table 9.1. The mean and standard deviation of the $n = 20$ differences are

$$\bar{d} = -.505 \qquad s_d = .615$$

TABLE 9.1   Estimated and Actual Labor (thousands of hours)

Project no.	1	2	3	4	5	6	7	8	9	10
Estimated (x)	2.8	.9	2.3	4.6	3.1	59.0	2.1	.5	48.5	4.5
Actual (y)	3.2	1.3	2.5	6.7	3.2	59.6	2.0	.5	49.8	4.8
$d = x - y$	−.4	−.4	−.2	−2.1	−.1	−.6	.1	0	−1.3	−.3

Project no.	11	12	13	14	15	16	17	18	19	20
Estimated (x)	8.5	2.9	2.5	1.6	13.8	3.6	5.0	2.0	1.1	8.5
Actual (y)	9.6	2.9	3.1	1.5	15.6	3.7	5.6	2.2	1.3	8.8
$d = x - y$	−1.1	0	−.6	.1	−1.8	−.1	−.6	−.2	−.2	−.3

Assuming the differences are a random sample from a normal distribution having mean δ, a 95% confidence interval for δ is

$$\left(\bar{d} - t_{.025} \frac{s_d}{\sqrt{20}}, \ \bar{d} + t_{.025} \frac{s_d}{\sqrt{20}} \right)$$

where $t_{.025}$ is based on $20 - 1 = 19$ degrees of freedom. Substituting the appropriate numbers, the 95% confidence interval is

$$\left(-.505 - 2.093 \frac{.615}{\sqrt{20}}, \ -.505 + 2.093 \frac{.615}{\sqrt{20}} \right) \quad \text{or} \quad (-.793, \ -.217)$$

We are 95% confident that, on average, the estimate of the number of labor hours for a project is 217 to 793 hours below the actual number of labor hours spent on a job. The process of estimating labor hours should be revised given this systematic underestimation.

b.   The steps for testing hypotheses follow.

1.   *Hypotheses.* The alternative hypothesis is $\delta \neq 0$ so

Null hypothesis $\qquad H_0: \delta = \mu_1 - \mu_2 = 0$
Alternative hypothesis $H_1: \delta = \mu_1 - \mu_2 \neq 0$

We are given $\alpha = .02$.

2.   *Test Statistic.* The test statistic t has the value

$$t = \frac{\bar{d}}{s_d / \sqrt{n}}$$

and the alternative hypothesis is two-sided, so we reject H_0 if t takes a large positive or a large negative value.

3. *Rejection Region.* Since $\alpha = .02$ and the Student's t distribution has $20-1 = 19$ degrees of freedom, from the t table, $t_{.01} = 2.539$. The two-sided rejection region is $t > 2.539$ or $t < -2.539$.

4. *Calculation.* The observed value of the test statistic is

$$t = \frac{\overline{d}}{s_d/\sqrt{n}} = \frac{-.505}{.615/\sqrt{20}} = -3.672$$

5. *Conclusion.* The observed value of the test statistic, -3.672, falls in the rejection region. At level $\alpha = .02$, we reject the null hypothesis in favor of the alternative that the mean difference is not zero.

Because the observed value of t is -3.672, the significance probability is P-value $= P(t < -3.672) + P(t > 3.672)$. Consulting the t table for 19 degrees of freedom, we determine that the P-value is less than .01. A computer calculation gives

$$P\text{-value} = P(t < -3.672) + P(t > 3.672) = 2(.0008) = .0016$$

so the evidence against the null hypothesis is very strong.

The dot diagram of the differences in Figure 9.2 gives some indication of a longer lower tail than would be expected with a normal distribution. However, with a sample size of 20, the evidence is not conclusive, and the t distribution is still a good approximation to the sampling distribution of the test statistic.

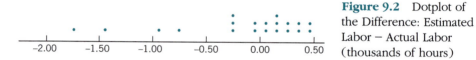

Figure 9.2   Dotplot of the Difference: Estimated Labor − Actual Labor (thousands of hours)

EXERCISES

9.21 Given the following paired sample data,

x	y
6	7
10	9
8	11
13	11

a. Evaluate the t statistic, $t = \dfrac{\overline{d}}{s_d/\sqrt{n}}$.

b. How many degrees of freedom does this t statistic have?

9.22 Given the following paired sample data,

x	y
5	4
3	2
7	4
5	6
8	8
7	9

a. Evaluate the t statistic, $t = \dfrac{\overline{d}}{s_d/\sqrt{n}}$.

b. How many degrees of freedom does this t statistic have?

9.23 To compare two treatments, a matched pairs experiment was conducted with 12 pairs of subjects. The paired differences, the response to Treatment A minus the response to Treatment B, were recorded:

2	5	6	8	−6	4
18	−12	17	−7	16	12

a. Is there strong evidence that Treatment A produces a larger mean response than Treatment B? Test with $\alpha = .05$. Determine the P-value and comment on its size.

b. Construct a 95% confidence interval for the mean difference of the responses to the two treatments.

9.24 A manufacturer claims his boot waterproofing is better than the major brand. Five pairs of boots are available for a test.

a. Explain how you would conduct a paired sample test.

b. Write down your assignment of waterproofing to each boot. How did you randomize?

9.25 It is claimed that an industrial safety program is effective in reducing the loss of working hours resulting from factory accidents. The following data are collected concerning the weekly loss of working hours resulting from accidents in six plants both before and after the safety program is initiated.

			Plant			
	1	2	3	4	5	6
Before	12	29	16	37	28	15
After	10	28	17	35	25	16

Do the data substantiate the claim? Use $\alpha = .05$.

9.26 A study is to be made of the relative effectiveness of two kinds of cough medicines in increasing sleep. Six people with colds are given Medicine A the first night and Medicine B the second night. Their hours of sleep each night are recorded. The data are given at the top of page 466.

	Subject					
	1	2	3	4	5	6
Medicine A	4.8	4.1	5.8	4.9	5.3	7.4
Medicine B	3.9	4.2	5.0	4.9	5.4	7.1

a. Establish a 95% confidence interval for the mean change in hours of sleep when switching from Medicine A to Medicine B.

b. How and what would you randomize in this study? Briefly explain your reason for randomization.

9.27 Two methods of memorizing difficult material are being tested to determine whether one produces better retention. Nine pairs of students are included in the study. The students in each pair are matched according to IQ and academic background and then assigned to the two methods at random. A memorization test is given to all the students, and the following scores are obtained:

	Pair								
	1	2	3	4	5	6	7	8	9
Method A	90	86	72	65	44	52	46	38	43
Method B	85	87	70	62	44	53	42	35	46

At $\alpha = .05$, test to determine whether there is a significant difference in the effectiveness of the two methods. Determine the P-value and comment on its size.

9.28 (*Minitab or similar program recommended*) A controlled study was conducted to examine brand loyalty.* Consumers in the sample were given the products free in exchange for keeping a complete record of both their soft drink and beer purchases. The study lasted 24 weeks. The data related to the number of purchases and brand switching are given here for 13 consumers.

BrandLoy.dat

Subject	Number of Soft Drink Purchases	Number of Soft Drink Brands	Number of Beer Purchases	Number of Beer Brands
1	98	3	93	5
2	180	6	93	4
3	92	6	95	4
4	97	3	92	4
5	87	5	91	4
6	91	4	92	4
7	87	5	88	5
8	89	5	180	5
9	327	6	95	5
10	213	7	92	4
11	96	4	91	4
12	80	6	94	3
13	162	6	94	5

*M. Trivedi, F. Bass, and R. Rao, "A Model for Stochastic Variety-Seeking," *Marketing Science*, **13**, 1994, p. 287.

a. Calculate the difference

d = (Number of brands of soft drinks purchased) − (Number of brands of beer purchased)

for each of the 13 consumers. Construct a normal-scores plot of these differences. Do the differences appear to be normally distributed? Explain.

b. Construct a 90% confidence interval for the mean difference of

(Number of brands of soft drinks purchased) − (Number of brands of beer purchased)

Do consumers seek more brand variety in their purchases of soft drinks or beer? Answer using the confidence interval just constructed.

BrandLoy.dat

9.29 (*Minitab or similar program recommended*) Refer to Exercise 9.28. Test the assertion that consumers seek more brand variety in their soft drink purchases than in their beer purchases. That is, conduct an appropriate test of hypotheses concerning the population mean difference. Use α = .05. Calculate the P-value. Would the null hypothesis be rejected with α = .02? Explain.

9.30 (*Minitab or similar program recommended*) Refer to Exercise 9.28. Using some additional data not displayed in Exercise 9.28, we can measure brand loyalty by calculating the proportion of times a consumer purchases their favorite brand. The differences

(Proportion for favorite soft drink) − (Proportion for favorite beer)

for the 13 consumers in the study were

.162	− .073	− .195	.079	− .033	.036	.003
.036	− .041	− .081	− .014	− .139	− .024	

a. Construct a normal-scores plot of the differences. Do these data appear to be normally distributed? Explain.

b. Construct a 95% confidence interval for the mean difference. Is there a difference in brand loyalty between soft drinks and beer? Explain.

9.31 In an experiment conducted to see whether electrical pricing policies can affect consumer behavior, 10 homeowners in Wisconsin had to pay a premium for power use during the peak hours. They were offered lower off-peak rates. For each home, the July on-peak usage (kilowatt hours) last year was compared to the July usage two years ago.

Two Years Ago	Last Year
200	160
180	175
240	210
425	370
120	110
333	298
418	368
380	250
340	305
516	477

a. Find a 95% confidence interval for the mean decrease.

b. Test H_0: $\delta = 0$ against H_1: $\delta \neq 0$ at level $\alpha = .05$.

c. Comment on the feasibility of randomization of treatments.

d. Without randomization, in what way could the results in parts **a** and **b** be misleading? [*Hint:* What if air conditioning is a prime factor in electrical use and July of last year was cooler than July two years ago?]

9.32 Measurements of the left- and right-hand gripping strengths of 10 left-handed writers are recorded.

	Person									
	1	2	3	4	5	6	7	8	9	10
Left hand	140	90	125	130	95	121	85	97	131	110
Right hand	138	87	110	132	96	120	86	90	129	100

a. Do the data provide strong evidence that people who write with the left hand have a greater gripping strength in the left hand than they do with the right hand?

b. Construct a 90% confidence interval for the mean difference.

9.4 COMPARISON OF SEVERAL MEANS

When we want to compare several populations, we can use a powerful tool called the **analysis of variance (ANOVA)**. This versatile statistical tool breaks up the total variation in a data set into separate pieces that are attributable to the *sources* of variation that are present. When k population means are being compared, the two sources of variation are:

1. differences *between* means

2. *within* population variation or error

In this section, we restrict our discussion to the comparison of k means, although ANOVA techniques apply to much more general comparisons. For example, in Chapters 11 and 12, we will use ANOVA to assess the significance of regression models.

In the context of our discussion in Section 9.1, comparisons among several populations occur when we want to compare the value placed on comfort for American luxury car owners, German luxury car owners, and Japanese luxury car owners. Here the three populations correspond to owners of American, German, and Japanese luxury cars, respectively.

THE COMPLETELY RANDOMIZED DESIGN AND THE ANOVA TABLE

It is usually more expedient, both in terms of time and expense, to simultaneously compare several treatments than it is to conduct several comparative trials two at a time. The term **completely randomized design** is synonymous with selecting independent random samples from several populations, where each population is identified as the population of responses under a particular treatment.

Consider a comparison among k treatments or populations. Let Treatment 1 be applied to n_1 experimental units, Treatment 2 to n_2 units, ..., and Treatment k to n_k units. In a completely randomized design, the n_1 experimental units scheduled to receive Treatment 1 are selected at random from the $n = n_1 + n_2 + \cdots + n_k$ available units. Then n_2 units are randomly selected from the remaining lot to receive Treatment 2, and proceeding in this manner, the final n_k units receive Treatment k. The special case of this design for a comparison of $k = 2$ treatments has already been discussed in Section 9.2. The data structure for the response measurements can be represented by the format shown in Table 9.2, where y_{ij} is the jth observation on Treatment i. The summary statistics appear in the last two columns.

TABLE 9.2   Data Structure for the Completely Randomized Design with k Treatments

	Observations	Mean	Sum of Squares
Treatment 1	$y_{11}, y_{12}, \ldots, y_{1n_1}$	$\bar{y}_1$	$\sum_{j=1}^{n_1}(y_{1j} - \bar{y}_1)^2$
Treatment 2	$y_{21}, y_{22}, \ldots, y_{2n_2}$	$\bar{y}_2$	$\sum_{j=1}^{n_2}(y_{2j} - \bar{y}_2)^2$
$\vdots$	$\vdots$	$\vdots$	$\vdots$
Treatment k	$y_{k1}, y_{k2}, \ldots, y_{kn_k}$	$\bar{y}_k$	$\sum_{j=1}^{n_k}(y_{kj} - \bar{y}_k)^2$

$$\text{Grand mean} = \frac{\text{Sum of all observations}}{n_1 + n_2 + \cdots + n_k} = \frac{n_1\bar{y}_1 + \cdots + n_k\bar{y}_k}{n_1 + \cdots + n_k}$$

Before proceeding with the general case of k treatments, it is instructive to explain the reasoning behind the analysis of variance and the associated calculations in terms of a numerical example.

EXAMPLE 9.8   Summarizing Data from Four Treatments

Suppose that, a few months after opening four new stores, a company records the number of bad checks received per month at each of them. The data and summary statistics are given in Table 9.3.

TABLE 9.3   Numbers of Bad Checks

Store	Observations	Mean	Sum of Squares
A	8 13 6 10 13	$\bar{y}_1 = 10$	$\sum_{j=1}^{5}(y_{1j} - \bar{y}_1)^2 = 38$
B	12 16 19 13	$\bar{y}_2 = 15$	$\sum_{j=1}^{4}(y_{2j} - \bar{y}_2)^2 = 30$
C	15 14 12 13 15 13 16	$\bar{y}_3 = 14$	$\sum_{j=1}^{7}(y_{3j} - \bar{y}_3)^2 = 12$
D	10 13 15 13 14 13	$\bar{y}_4 = 13$	$\sum_{j=1}^{6}(y_{4j} - \bar{y}_4)^2 = 14$
	Grand mean $\bar{y} = 13$		

Solution and Discussion.   Given data of this kind, we would like to be able to determine whether there is a significant difference between the mean number of bad checks for stores. If there is a difference, confidence intervals should be given for the mean differences.

An analysis of the results like those in Example 9.8 essentially consists of decomposing the observations into contributions from different sources of variation. Reasoning that the deviation of an individual observation from the grand mean, $y_{ij} - \bar{y}$, is partly due to differences among the mean differences among stores and partly due to random variation in measurements within the same group, we suggest the following decomposition:

$$\text{Observation} = \binom{\text{Grand}}{\text{mean}} + \binom{\text{Deviation due}}{\text{to treatment}} + (\text{Residual})$$

$$y_{ij} \quad = \quad \bar{y} \quad + \quad (\bar{y}_i - \bar{y}) \quad + (y_{ij} - \bar{y}_i)$$

For the data given in Table 9.3, the decomposition of all the observations can be presented in the form of the following arrays:

Observation y_{ij}

$$\begin{bmatrix} 8 & 13 & 6 & 10 & 13 \\ 12 & 16 & 19 & 13 \\ 15 & 14 & 12 & 13 & 15 & 13 & 16 \\ 10 & 13 & 15 & 13 & 14 & 13 \end{bmatrix}$$

Mean $\bar{y}$ ⟶ **Treatment $\bar{y}_i - \bar{y}$**

$$= \begin{bmatrix} 13 & 13 & 13 & 13 & 13 \\ 13 & 13 & 13 & 13 \\ 13 & 13 & 13 & 13 & 13 & 13 & 13 \\ 13 & 13 & 13 & 13 & 13 & 13 \end{bmatrix} + \begin{bmatrix} -3 & -3 & -3 & -3 & -3 \\ 2 & 2 & 2 & 2 \\ 1 & 1 & 1 & 1 & 1 & 1 & 1 \\ 0 & 0 & 0 & 0 & 0 & 0 \end{bmatrix}$$

Residual $y_{ij} - \bar{y}_i$

$$+ \begin{bmatrix} -2 & 3 & -4 & 0 & 3 \\ -3 & 1 & 4 & -2 \\ 1 & 0 & -2 & -1 & 1 & -1 & 2 \\ -3 & 0 & 2 & 0 & 1 & 0 \end{bmatrix}$$

For instance, the entries in the upper left-hand corner of the arrays show that

$$8 = 13 + (-3) + (-2)$$
$$y_{11} = \bar{y} + (\bar{y}_1 - \bar{y}) + (y_{11} - \bar{y}_1)$$

If there really is no difference in means, we would expect the entries $\bar{y}_i - \bar{y}$ in the second array on the right-hand side to be near zero. The sum of the squares of all of the entries in this array gives an overall measure of differences due to treatments. The calculation is:

$$\underbrace{(-3)^2 + \cdots + (-3)^2}_{n_1 = 5} + \underbrace{2^2 + \cdots + 2^2}_{n_2 = 4} + \underbrace{1^2 + \cdots + 1^2}_{n_3 = 7} + \underbrace{0^2 + \cdots + 0^2}_{n_4 = 6}$$

$$= 5(-3)^2 + 4(2)^2 + 7(1)^2 + 6(0)^2 = 68$$

The sum of squares due to differences in the treatment means is called the **treatment sum of squares** or **between sum of squares** and is given by the expression

$$\text{Treatment Sum of Squares} = \sum_{i=1}^{4} n_i(\bar{y}_i - \bar{y})^2 = 68$$

The last array consists of the entries $(y_{ij} - \bar{y}_i)$ that are the deviations of individual observations from the corresponding treatment means. These deviations reflect inherent variabilities in the experimental material and the measuring device and are called the **residuals.** The overall variation due to random errors is measured by the sum of squares of all these residuals

$$(-2)^2 + 3^2 + (-4)^2 + \cdots + 1^2 + 0^2 = 94$$

Thus we obtain

$$\text{Error Sum of Squares} = \sum_{i=1}^{4}\sum_{j=1}^{n_i}(y_{ij} - \bar{y}_i)^2 = 94$$

The double summation indicates that the elements are summed within each row and then over different rows. Alternatively, referring to the last column in Table 9.3, we obtain

$$\text{Error Sum of Squares} = \sum_{j=1}^{5}(y_{1j} - \bar{y}_1)^2 + \sum_{j=1}^{4}(y_{2j} - \bar{y}_2)^2$$

$$+ \sum_{j=1}^{7}(y_{3j} - \bar{y}_3)^2 + \sum_{j=1}^{6}(y_{4j} - \bar{y}_4)^2$$

$$= 38 + 30 + 12 + 14 = 94$$

Finally, the deviations of individual observations from the grand mean $y_{ij} - \bar{y}$ are given by the array

$$\begin{bmatrix} -5 & 0 & -7 & -3 & 0 & & \\ -1 & 3 & 6 & 0 & & & \\ 2 & 1 & -1 & 0 & 2 & 0 & 3 \\ -3 & 0 & 2 & 0 & 1 & 0 & \end{bmatrix}$$

The total variation present in the data is measured by the sum of squares of all these deviations. Thus

$$\text{Total Sum of Squares} = \sum_{i=1}^{4}\sum_{j=1}^{n_i}(y_{ij} - \bar{y})^2$$

$$= (-5)^2 + 0^2 + (-7)^2 + \cdots + 0^2$$

$$= 162$$

Notice that the total sum of squares, 162, is the sum of the treatment sum of squares, 68, and the error sum of squares, 94.

It is time to turn our attention to another property of this decomposition, the **degrees of freedom*** associated with the sums of squares.

In our present example, the treatment sum of squares is the sum of four terms, $n_1(\bar{y}_1 - \bar{y})^2 + n_2(\bar{y}_2 - \bar{y})^2 + n_3(\bar{y}_3 - \bar{y})^2 + n_4(\bar{y}_4 - \bar{y})^2$, where the elements satisfy the single requirement

$$n_1(\bar{y}_1 - \bar{y}) + n_2(\bar{y}_2 - \bar{y}) + n_3(\bar{y}_3 - \bar{y}) + n_4(\bar{y}_4 - \bar{y}) = 0$$

This equality holds because the grand mean $\bar{y}$ is a weighted average of the treatment means, or

$$\bar{y} = \frac{n_1 \bar{y}_1 + n_2 \bar{y}_2 + n_3 \bar{y}_3 + n_4 \bar{y}_4}{n_1 + n_2 + n_3 + n_4}$$

Consequently, the number of degrees of freedom associated with the treatment sum of squares is $4 - 1 = 3$. To determine the degrees of freedom for the error sum of squares, we note that the entries $(y_{ij} - \bar{y}_i)$ in each row of the residual array sum to zero and that there are 4 rows. The number of degrees of freedom for the error sum of squares is then $(n_1 + n_2 + n_3 + n_4) - 4 = 22 - 4 = 18$. Finally, the number of degrees of freedom for the total sum of squares is $(n_1 + n_2 + n_3 + n_4) - 1 = 22 - 1 = 21$, because the 22 entries $(y_{ij} - \bar{y})$ whose squares are summed satisfy the single requirement that their total is zero. Notice that the degrees of freedom for the total sum of squares is the sum of the degrees of freedom for treatment and error.

We summarize the calculations thus far in Table 9.4.

TABLE 9.4 **Partial ANOVA Table for Bad Checks Data**

Source	Sum of Squares	d.f.
Treatment	68	3
Error	94	18
Total	162	21

Guided by this numerical example, we now present the general formulas for the analysis of variance for a comparison of k treatments, using the data structure given in Table 9.2. Beginning with the basic decomposition

$$(y_{ij} - \bar{y}) = (\bar{y}_i - \bar{y}) + (y_{ij} - \bar{y}_i)$$

and squaring each side of the equation, we obtain

$$(y_{ij} - \bar{y})^2 = (\bar{y}_i - \bar{y})^2 + (y_{ij} - \bar{y}_i)^2 + 2(\bar{y}_i - \bar{y})(y_{ij} - \bar{y}_i)$$

---

*The degrees of freedom is the number of quantities needed to calculate a sum of squares that are free to vary, that is, whose values are not determined by some numerical requirement, such as, for example, $\sum(x_i - \bar{x}) = 0$.

When summed over $j = 1, \ldots, n_i$, the last term on the right-hand side of this equation reduces to zero because of the relation $\sum_{j=1}^{n_i}(y_{ij} - \bar{y}_i) = 0$. Therefore, summing each side of the preceding relation over $j = 1, \ldots, n_i$ and $i = 1, \ldots, k$ provides the decomposition

$$\sum_{i=1}^{k}\sum_{j=1}^{n_i}(y_{ij} - \bar{y})^2 = \sum_{i=1}^{k} n_i(\bar{y}_i - \bar{y})^2 + \sum_{i=1}^{k}\sum_{j=1}^{n_i}(y_{ij} - \bar{y}_i)^2$$

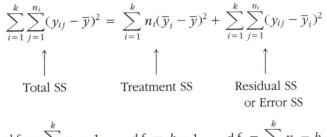

| Total SS | Treatment SS | Residual SS or Error SS |

$$\text{d.f.} = \sum_{i=1}^{k} n_i - 1 \qquad \text{d.f.} = k - 1 \qquad \text{d.f.} = \sum_{i=1}^{k} n_i - k$$

It is customary to display the decomposition of the sum of squares and the degrees of freedom in a tabular form called the **analysis of variance table,** abbreviated as **ANOVA table.** This table contains the sums of squares and degrees of freedom columns, and an additional column for the **mean square** associated with a component. The mean square is defined as

$$\text{Mean Square} = \frac{\text{Sum of Squares}}{\text{d.f.}}$$

Table 9.5 is the general ANOVA table for comparing k treatments.

TABLE 9.5   ANOVA Table for Comparing k Treatments

Source	Sum of Squares	d.f.	Mean Square
Treatment	$\text{SST} = \sum_{i=1}^{k} n_i(\bar{y}_i - \bar{y})^2$	$k - 1$	$\text{MST} = \dfrac{\text{SST}}{k - 1}$
Error	$\text{SSE} = \sum_{i=1}^{k}\sum_{j=1}^{n_i}(y_{ij} - \bar{y}_i)^2$	$\sum_{i=1}^{k} n_i - k$	$\text{MSE} = \dfrac{\text{SSE}}{\sum_{i=1}^{k} n_i - k}$
Total	$\sum_{i=1}^{k}\sum_{j=1}^{n_i}(y_{ij} - \bar{y})^2$	$\sum_{i=1}^{k} n_i - 1$	

THE POPULATION MODEL AND INFERENCES

As we shall see, the relative sizes of the mean square for treatments and the mean square for error provide information about the equality of the population means. However, to decide whether the variation in sample means is due to chance, we must introduce a statistical model. To this end, we assume that the response measurements with the ith treatment constitute a random sample from a normal population with a mean of μ_i and a *common variance* of σ^2. The samples are assumed to be mutually independent.

Population Model for Comparing k Treatments

$$Y_{ij} = \mu_i + \varepsilon_{ij} \qquad j = 1, \ldots, n_i \quad \text{and} \quad i = 1, \ldots, k$$

where $\mu_i = i$th treatment mean. The errors ε_{ij} are all independently distributed as $N(0, \sigma)$.

F DISTRIBUTION

The null hypothesis that no difference exists among the k treatment (population) means can now be phrased as follows:

$$H_0: \quad \mu_1 = \mu_2 = \cdots = \mu_k$$

The alternative hypothesis is that not all the μ_i's are equal. Seeking a criterion to test the null hypothesis, we observe that when the population means are all equal, each $(\bar{y}_i - \bar{y})$ is expected to be small, and consequently, the treatment mean square $\sum n_i (\bar{y}_i - \bar{y})^2/(k - 1)$ is expected to be small. On the other hand, it is likely to be large when the means differ markedly. The error mean square, which provides an estimate of σ^2, can be used as a yardstick for determining how large a treatment mean square should be before it indicates significant differences. If all the means are equal (H_0 is true), the ratio

$$F = \frac{\text{Treatment Mean Square}}{\text{Error Mean Square}} = \frac{\text{Treatment SS}/(k - 1)}{\text{Error SS}/(\sum_{i=1}^{k} n_i - k)}$$

has an F distribution* with d.f. $= (k - 1, n - k)$ where $n = \sum n_i$.

An F distribution is specified in terms of its numerator degrees of freedom $\nu_1 = k - 1$ and denominator degrees of freedom $\nu_2 = n - k$. We denote

$$F_\alpha(\nu_1, \nu_2) = \text{upper } \alpha \text{ point of the } F \text{ with } (\nu_1, \nu_2) \text{ d.f.}$$

The upper $\alpha = .05$ and $\alpha = .10$ points are given in Table 6, Appendix B, for several pairs of d.f. With $\nu_1 = 7$ and $\nu_2 = 15$, for $\alpha = .05$, we read from column $\nu_1 = 7$ and row $\nu_2 = 15$ to obtain $F_{.05}(7, 15) = 2.71$ (see Table 9.6).

TABLE 9.6 **Percentage Points of $F(\nu_1, \nu_2)$ Distributions, $\alpha = .05$**

ν_2 \ ν_1	$\cdots$	7	$\cdots$
$\vdots$		$\vdots$	
15	$\cdots$	2.71	
$\vdots$			

---

*The F distribution is named in honor of Sir Ronald A. Fisher, a giant in the development and application of statistical methodology.

We summarize the F test in the following box.

F Test for Equality of Means

Reject H_0: $\mu_1 = \mu_2 = \cdots = \mu_k$ if

$$F = \frac{\text{Treatment SS}/(k-1)}{\text{Error SS}/(n-k)} > F_\alpha(k-1, n-k)$$

where $n = \sum_{i=1}^{k} n_i$ and $F_\alpha(k-1, n-k)$ is the upper α point of the F distribution with d.f. $= (k-1, n-k)$.

The computed value of the F ratio is usually presented in the last column of the ANOVA table.

EXAMPLE 9.9   Constructing an ANOVA Table and F Test for the Bad Checks Data

Construct the full ANOVA table for the bad checks data given in Example 9.8, and test the null hypothesis that the means for the four stores are equal. Use $\alpha = .05$.

Solution and Discussion.   Using the results in Table 9.4, we construct the ANOVA table that appears in Table 9.7.

TABLE 9.7   ANOVA Table for the Data Given in Example 9.8

Source	Sum of Squares	d.f.	Mean Square	F ratio
Treatment	68	3	22.67	$\frac{22.67}{5.22} = 4.34$
Error	94	18	5.22	
Total	162	21		

A test of the null hypothesis H_0: $\mu_1 = \mu_2 = \mu_3 = \mu_4$ is performed by comparing the observed F value 4.34 with the tabulated value of F with d.f. $= (3, 18)$. At the .05 level of significance, the tabulated value is found to be 3.16. Because $F = 4.34 > 3.16$, we conclude that there is a significant difference among the mean number of bad checks at the four stores.

The next questions, of course, are: Which stores are different? What causes the differences? How can we reduce the number of bad checks at all stores? We will see how to deal with the first question when we discuss confidence intervals for estimating the differences in pairs of population means. The remaining questions must be addressed by other methodology and people familiar with the operations of the stores.

EXAMPLE 9.10 Testing for the Equality of Population Means with Absenteeism Data

A large transportation company has many employees who are on call. However, if an employee is not called by 10 A.M., he or she can decline to work that day. On-call employees who refuse to work are one component of the total number of employees absent. A quality team was formed to study the problem of absenteeism. The team consulted company records and obtained daily data on the number of employees absent for a total of 68 weeks. A time series plot of the daily number of employees absent suggested that weekdays, weekends, and special holidays should be treated separately. Absenteeism appeared to be higher on weekends than on weekdays and holidays. (Employees receive overtime pay for holidays.)

The following table gives the summary statistics for the numbers of employees absent, grouped according to weekdays, weekends, and holidays.

Period	Number	Mean	Std. dev.
Weekday	308	60.3	10.8
Weekend	126	159.7	10.5
Holiday	7	25.7	20.6

Create the ANOVA table and test for the equality of treatment means. Use $\alpha = .05$.

Solution and Discussion. Since $(n_1 - 1)s_1^2 = \sum_{j=1}^{n_1} n_1(y_{1j} - \bar{y}_1)^2$ with similar expressions for s_2^2 and s_3^2, the sum of squares error is

$$\begin{aligned} \text{SSE} &= (n_1 - 1)s_1^2 + (n_2 - 1)s_2^2 + (n_3 - 1)s_3^2 \\ &= 307(10.8)^2 + 125(10.5)^2 + 6(20.6)^2 = 52{,}135.89 \end{aligned}$$

The SSE has $441 - 3 = 438$ degrees of freedom so MSE $= 52{,}135.89/438 = 119.03$. The grand mean is

$$\bar{y} = \frac{n_1\bar{y}_1 + n_2\bar{y}_2 + n_3\bar{y}_3}{n_1 + n_2 + n_3} = \frac{308(60.3) + 126(159.7) + 7(25.7)}{308 + 126 + 7} = 88.15$$

and the treatment sum of squares is

$$\text{SST} = 308(60.3 - 88.15)^2 + 126(159.7 - 88.15)^2 + 7(25.7 - 88.15)^2 = 911{,}236.46$$

The treatment sum of squares has $3 - 1 = 2$ degrees of freedom, so the mean square for treatments is $911{,}236.46/2 = 455{,}618.23$.

The F statistic is

$$F = \frac{\text{SST}/(k - 1)}{\text{SSE}/(n - k)} = \frac{911{,}236.46/2}{52{,}135.89/438} = 3828$$

The ANOVA table is given in Table 9.8.

With $(2, 438)$ degrees of freedom, $F_{.05}$ is approximately 3.00, so the null hypothesis H_0: $\mu_1 = \mu_2 = \mu_3$ is rejected. We conclude the mean number of absentees is different for weekdays, weekends, and holidays.

TABLE 9.8   ANOVA Table for Absenteeism Data

Source	Sum of Squares	d.f.	Mean Square	F ratio
Treatment	911,236.46	2	4,555,618.23	3828
Error	52,135.89	438	119.03	
Total	963,372.35	440		

It is helpful to display the k samples in an analysis of variance with *simultaneous boxplots,* that is, boxplots aligned vertically like the boxplots representing GRE scores in Figure 2.11 in Chapter 2. This provides a graphical check on the assumption of constant variance, as well as indicating visually the sizes of the differences in means the F test may detect.

SIMULTANEOUS CONFIDENCE INTERVALS

The ANOVA F test is only the initial step in our analysis. It determines whether significant differences exist among the treatment means. Our goal should be more than to conclude merely that treatment differences are indicated by the data. Rather, we must detect likenesses and differences among the treatments. Can we say that Treatment 1 is better than the rest? Is there no difference between Treatments 2 and 3? The problem of estimating differences in treatment means is of even greater interest than the overall F test.

Referring to the comparison of k treatments using the data structure given in Table 9.2, we examine how a confidence interval can be established for $\mu_1 - \mu_2$, the mean difference between Treatment 1 and Treatment 2. The statistic whose value is

$$t = \frac{(\bar{y}_1 - \bar{y}_2) - (\mu_1 - \mu_2)}{\sqrt{\dfrac{\text{SSE}}{n-k}} \sqrt{\dfrac{1}{n_1} + \dfrac{1}{n_2}}}$$

has a t distribution with d.f. $= n - k$, and this can be used to construct a confidence interval for $\mu_1 - \mu_2$. More generally,

---

Confidence Interval for a Single Difference

A $100(1 - \alpha)\%$ confidence interval for $(\mu_i - \mu_{i'})$, the mean difference between Treatment i and Treatment i', is given by

$$\left(\bar{y}_i - \bar{y}_{i'} - t_{\alpha/2}\, s \sqrt{\frac{1}{n_i} + \frac{1}{n_{i'}}}, \quad \bar{y}_i - \bar{y}_{i'} + t_{\alpha/2}\, s \sqrt{\frac{1}{n_i} + \frac{1}{n_{i'}}} \right)$$

where

$$s = \sqrt{\text{MSE}} = \sqrt{\frac{\text{SSE}}{n-k}}$$

and $t_{\alpha/2}$ is the upper $\alpha/2$ point of t with d.f. $= n - k$.

If the F test first shows a significant difference in means, then some statisticians believe that it is reasonable to compare means pairwise according to the preceding intervals. However, many statisticians prefer a more conservative procedure based on the following reasoning.

Without the provision that the F test is significant, the preceding method provides *individual* confidence intervals for pairwise differences. For instance, with $k = 4$ treatments, there are $\binom{4}{2} = 6$ pairwise differences $(\mu_i - \mu_{i'})$, and this procedure applied to all pairs yields six confidence statements, each having a $100(1 - \alpha)\%$ level of confidence. It is difficult to determine what level of confidence will be achieved for claiming that *all* six of these statements are correct. To overcome this dilemma, procedures have been developed for several confidence intervals to be constructed in such a manner that the joint probability that all the statements are true is guaranteed not to fall below a predetermined level. Such intervals are called **multiple confidence intervals** or **simultaneous confidence intervals.** Numerous methods proposed in the statistical literature have achieved varying degrees of success. We present one that can be used simply and conveniently in general applications.

The procedure, called the **multiple-t confidence intervals,** consists of setting confidence intervals for the differences $(\mu_i - \mu_{i'})$ in much the same way we just did for the individual differences except that a different percentage point is read from the t table.

Multiple-t Confidence Intervals

A set of $100(1 - \alpha)\%$ simultaneous confidence intervals for m pairwise differences $(\mu_i - \mu_{i'})$ is given by

$$\left(\bar{y}_i - \bar{y}_{i'} - t_{\alpha/(2m)}\, s\sqrt{\frac{1}{n_i} + \frac{1}{n_{i'}}}, \quad \bar{y}_i - \bar{y}_{i'} + t_{\alpha/(2m)}\, s\sqrt{\frac{1}{n_i} + \frac{1}{n_{i'}}} \right)$$

where $s = \sqrt{\text{MSE}}$, $m =$ the number of confidence statements, and $t_{\alpha/(2m)} =$ upper $\alpha/(2m)$ point of t with d.f. $= n - k$.

Using this procedure, the probability of all the m statements being correct is at least $(1 - \alpha)$.

Operationally, the construction of these confidence intervals does not require any new concepts or calculations, but it usually involves some nonstandard percentage point of t. For example, with $k = 3$ and $(1 - \alpha) = .95$, if we want to construct simultaneous intervals for all $m = \binom{k}{2} = 3$ pairwise comparisons, we need the upper $\alpha/(2m) = .05/6 = .00833$ point of a t distribution.

EXAMPLE 9.11   Constructing Multiple-t Confidence Intervals with the Absenteeism Data

Using the absenteeism data introduced in Example 9.10 and reproduced here,

Period	Number	Mean	Std. dev.
Weekday	308	60.3	10.8
Weekend	126	159.7	10.5
Holiday	7	25.7	20.6

construct the 95% multiple-t confidence intervals for the pairwise differences of the means.

Solution and Discussion.   From Example 9.10, MSE = 119.03 and the estimated standard deviation is

$$s = \sqrt{\text{MSE}} = \sqrt{119.03} = 10.91$$

Since $\alpha = .05$ and we require $m = 3$ pairwise comparisons, we need the upper $\alpha/(2m) = .05/(2 \times 3) = .00833$ point of the t distribution with 438 degrees of freedom. With this many degrees of freedom, the t distribution is indistinguishable from the standard normal distribution. Using the last row of the t table, we find $t_{.00833} = 2.394$. The three confidence intervals become

$$\text{Weekday} - \text{Weekend:} \quad 60.3 - 159.7 \pm 2.394(10.91)\sqrt{\frac{1}{308} + \frac{1}{126}}$$

$$\text{or} \quad (-102.2, \ -96.6)$$

$$\text{Weekday} - \text{Holiday:} \quad 60.3 - 25.7 \pm 2.394(10.91)\sqrt{\frac{1}{308} + \frac{1}{7}}$$

$$\text{or} \quad (24.6, \ 44.6)$$

$$\text{Weekend} - \text{Holiday:} \quad 159.7 - 25.7 \pm 2.394(10.91)\sqrt{\frac{1}{126} + \frac{1}{7}}$$

$$\text{or} \quad (123.9, \ 144.1)$$

All the population means are different. The mean absenteeism for holidays is considerably lower than even the weekend mean. Recall, there are special pay incentives that apply on holidays.

GRAPHICAL DIAGNOSTICS AND DISPLAYS

In addition to testing hypotheses and setting confidence intervals, an analysis of data must include a critical examination of the assumptions involved in the model. When comparing several treatments using the methods of this section, we assume the responses to the treatments can be modeled as independent observations from normal populations with the same standard deviation but possibly different means. This is expressed by the population model

$$Y_{ij} = \mu_i + \varepsilon_{ij}$$

where the errors ε_{ij} are all independently distributed as $N(0, \sigma)$.

Using the sample mean $\bar{y}_i$ to estimate μ_i, and constructing the identity

$$y_{ij} = \bar{y}_i + (y_{ij} - \bar{y}_i)$$

we see that the **residuals** $(y_{ij} - \bar{y}_i)$ are estimates of the errors ε_{ij}. Consequently, if the assumptions are correct, the residuals should look like independent observations from a $N(0, \sigma)$ distribution, where σ can be estimated by $s = \sqrt{MSE}$. The residuals should be examined for evidence of serious violations of the assumptions. This aspect of the analysis is ignored in the ANOVA table summary.

Simple graphical techniques are often helpful in highlighting violations of the assumptions. Dotplots, stem-and-leaf diagrams, boxplots, and normal-scores plots can all be used to analyze residuals.

EXAMPLE 9.12   Plotting Residuals Using the Bad Checks Data

Determine the residuals for the bad checks data given in Table 9.3 in Example 9.8. Graphically examine them for possible violations of the assumptions.

Solution and Discussion.   The residuals are given in Table 9.9.

TABLE 9.9   Residuals $y_{ij} - \bar{y}_i$ for the Data Given in Table 9.3

Store	Residuals						
A	-2	3	-4	0	3		
B	-3	1	4	-2			
C	1	0	-2	-1	1	-1	2
D	-3	0	2	0	1	0	

Residual plots of these data are shown in Figures 9.3 and 9.4. Figure 9.3 shows a normal-scores plot of all of the residuals combined. Figure 9.4(a) is a dotplot of the combined residuals, and Figure 9.4(b) contains dotplots of residuals corresponding to the individual stores (treatments).

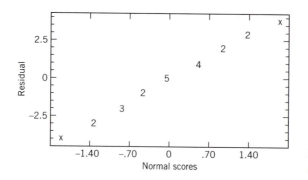

Figure 9.3 Normal-Scores Plot of All Residuals from Table 9.9

The normal-scores plot and the combined residual plot indicate no apparent departure from normality. The individual dotplots corresponding to each treatment do not depict any clear violations of the assumptions. The spread of the residuals for Stores C and D is a little less than that for Stores A and B, but the number of observations is small

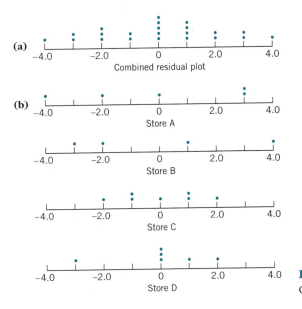

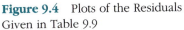

Figure 9.4 Plots of the Residuals Given in Table 9.9

in all cases. Therefore, it is difficult to argue against a common population standard deviation σ. Similarly, with so few observations, it is difficult to check the normality of the individual treatment observations. However, there is no compelling reason to believe the responses for each store (treatment) are not approximately normally distributed.

If the number of observations for each treatment is sufficiently large, boxplots can be constructed and aligned on a common scale. These boxplots provide a direct graphical comparison of treatments.

EXERCISES

9.33 Consider the following responses from the application of four treatments.

Treatment	Observations	
1	6	10
2	9	5
3	9	7
4	4	6

a. Construct the arrays that show a decomposition of the observations according to the grand mean, deviation due to treatment, and residual.

b. Find the sum of squares for each array.

c. Determine the degrees of freedom for each sum of squares.

d. Summarize the data in an ANOVA table.

9.34   Consider the following responses from the application of three treatments.

Treatment	Observations			
1	35	24	28	21
2	19	14	14	13
3	21	16	21	14

a. Construct the arrays that show a decomposition of the observations according to grand mean, deviation due to treatment, and residual.
b. Find the sum of squares for each array.
c. Determine the degrees of freedom for each sum of squares.
d. Summarize the data in an ANOVA table.

9.35   Repeat Exercise 9.34 for the following data:

Treatment	Observations			
1	5	3	2	2
2	5	0	1	
3	2	1	0	1

9.36   Use the relations for sum of squares and degrees of freedom to complete the following ANOVA table.

Source	Sum of Squares	d.f.
Treatment	36	5
Error		
Total	92	30

9.37   Provide a decomposition of the following observations, and obtain the ANOVA table.

Treatment	Observations			
1	2	1	3	
2	1	5		
3	9	5	6	4
4	3	4	5	

9.38   Summary statistics from three independent samples are as follows:

$$n_1 = 10 \quad \bar{y}_1 = 5 \quad (n_1 - 1)s_1^2 = \sum_{j=1}^{10}(y_{1j} - \bar{y}_1)^2 = 30$$

$$n_2 = 6 \quad \bar{y}_2 = 2 \quad (n_2 - 1)s_2^2 = \sum_{j=1}^{6}(y_{2j} - \bar{y}_2)^2 = 16$$

$$n_3 = 9 \quad \bar{y}_3 = 7 \quad (n_3 - 1)s_3^2 = \sum_{j=1}^{9}(y_{3j} - \bar{y}_3)^2 = 16$$

Create the ANOVA table.

9.39 Using the table of percentage points for the F distribution, find:
   a. The upper 5% point when $\nu_1 = 5$ and $\nu_2 = 10$
   b. The upper 5% point when $\nu_1 = 10$ and $\nu_2 = 5$

9.40 Using Table 6 in Appendix B, find the upper 10% point of F for:
   a. d.f. = $(3, 5)$ b. d.f. = $(3, 10)$
   c. d.f. = $(3, 15)$ d. d.f. = $(10, 3)$

9.41 Given the following ANOVA table:

Source	Sum of Squares	d.f.
Treatment	104	5
Error	109	20
Total	213	25

   Carry out the F test for equality of means taking $\alpha = .10$.

9.42 Given the following ANOVA table:

Source	Sum of Squares	d.f.
Treatment	24	5
Error	57	35
Total	81	40

   Carry out the F test for equality of means taking $\alpha = .05$.

9.43 Using the data in Exercise 9.33, construct the ANOVA table and test for equality of means using $\alpha = .05$.

9.44 Using the data in Exercise 9.34, construct the ANOVA table and test for equality of means using $\alpha = .05$.

9.45 Using the data in Exercise 9.35, construct the ANOVA table and test for equality of means using $\alpha = .05$.

9.46 Three bread recipes are to be compared with respect to density of the loaf. Five loaves will be baked using each recipe.
   a. If one loaf is made and baked at a time, how would you determine the order? That is, how would you assign loaves to recipes?
   b. Given the following loaf density data, conduct an F test for equality of means. Take $\alpha = .05$. Interpret the result.

Recipe	Observations				
1	.95	.86	.71	.72	.74
2	.71	.85	.62	.72	.64
3	.69	.68	.51	.73	.44

9.47 Taking $\alpha = .05$ and $n - k = 26$, determine the appropriate percentile of the t distribution when calculating the multiple-t confidence intervals with
   a. $m = 3$
   b. $m = 5$

9.48 Construct the 90% multiple-t confidence intervals using the bad checks data in Example 9.8.

9.49 Given the following summary statistics,

$$n_1 = 30 \qquad \bar{y}_1 = 10.2$$
$$n_2 = 18 \qquad \bar{y}_2 = 8.1 \qquad\qquad s = 3.2$$
$$n_3 = 24 \qquad \bar{y}_3 = 9.7$$
$$n_4 = 8 \qquad \bar{y}_4 = 6.2$$

Use $\alpha = .10$ and determine

a. t intervals for each of the six differences of means

b. The six multiple-t intervals

Discuss the difference between the two sets of intervals in parts **a** and **b.**

9.50 Refer to Exercise 9.2. A survey of owners of luxury cars included a question asking how important owners value

fun, enjoyment, and excitement

in their daily lives. The response was measured on a 7-point scale. The value 1 corresponds to "very important," and the value 7 corresponds to "very unimportant." The summary results for American luxury car owners, German luxury car owners, and Japanese luxury car owners are:

American car owners: $n_1 = 58, \quad \bar{y}_1 = 2.97, \quad s_1^2 = 2.36$

German car owners: $n_2 = 38, \quad \bar{y}_2 = 2.17, \quad s_2^2 = 2.07$

Japanese car owners: $n_3 = 59, \quad \bar{y}_3 = 2.88, \quad s_3^2 = 2.17$

a. Do these data confirm that there is a difference in the population mean values of fun, enjoyment and excitement for these groups? Test with $\alpha = .05$.

b. Construct multiple-t 95% confidence intervals for the paired differences of population means. Interpret these intervals.

9.51 Refer to Exercise 9.4. In a study of differences in managerial values in different parts of the world,

intolerance of ambiguity

was quantified by responses to 8 questions, and each question was recorded on a 5-point scale, so the total score ranged from 5 to 40. The top score indicated the highest desire for more certainty. These data are summarized for American managers, People's Republic of China managers, and Hong Kong managers.

American managers: $n_1 = 62, \quad \bar{y}_1 = 19.8, \quad s_1 = 4.59$

People's Republic of China managers: $n_2 = 82, \quad \bar{y}_2 = 24.7, \quad s_2 = 4.78$

Hong Kong managers: $n_3 = 182, \quad \bar{y}_3 = 22.1, \quad s_3 = 4.68$

a. Do these data indicate that managers differ from country to country with respect to the mean response on the intolerance of ambiguity scale? Test with $\alpha = .05$.

b. Construct multiple-t 95% confidence intervals for the paired differences of the population means. Interpret these intervals.

9.52 Minitab or a similar program can be used to do analysis of variance. Data on the times required to return patient phone calls are presented in the next section, Statistics in Context. These data organized by day of the week were placed in columns C1, C2, C3, C4, and C5 by the SET command in Minitab. The Minitab commands

```
NAME C1 'MON' C2 'TUE' C3 'WED' C4 'THU' C5 'FRI'
AOVONEWAY C1-C5
```

produced the labeled output

```
ANALYSIS OF VARIANCE
SOURCE     DF        SS        MS       F        P
FACTOR      4      18974     4743     1.26    0.290
ERROR     110     414074     3764
TOTAL     114     433048
                             INDIVIDUAL 95 PCT CI'S FOR MEAN
                             BASED ON POOLED STDEV
 LEVEL   N      MEAN    STDEV  -----+---------+---------+---------+-
MON      31    97.26   60.07        (--------*--------)
TUE      25    98.16   52.02        (--------*---------)
WED      20   128.75   67.82                  (----------*---------)
THU      21    90.19   65.52   (----------*----------)
FRI      18    95.72   63.07      (----------*-----------)
                             -----+---------+---------+---------+-
POOLED STDEV =      61.35       75        100       125       150
```

a. Identify the SSE and its degrees of freedom. Also locate s.

b. Check the calculation of F from the given sum of squares and degrees of freedom. Interpret the F statistic and its corresponding P-value.

c. Interpret the individual 95% confidence intervals for the mean time to return calls for the various weekdays. If 95% multiple-t intervals were constructed for the means, how would their locations and lengths compare with the individual 95% intervals?

9.5   STATISTICS IN CONTEXT

Supervisory personnel at a primary health care facility became aware that there was a problem with responding in a timely manner to phone calls received from patients. With the current informal process, calls are taken by a designated pool of employees on the second floor, or, if they are all busy, by people on the third floor who have other health care assignments. The essential details of any call are then relayed by written request to medical personnel who determine whether it is necessary to pull a chart and consult a doctor to obtain the information required to return the call. Once the information is gathered, a nurse returns the call.

A quality team was formed to study the process with the goal of reducing the time to return a patient's call.

The first step was to collect data on the number of calls received in a day and the location where the calls were answered. A summary of the times to return the calls, in minutes, confirms that there is a rather high volume of calls and that the mean time to return calls, 101.4 minutes, is quite large. The calls could be about children with high fevers or from adults with serious symptoms trying to decide whether they need to come in for immediate care. The complete summary statistics are:

N	MEAN	MEDIAN	STDEV	SEMEAN
115	101.40	100.00	61.63	5.75

MIN	MAX	Q1	Q3
5.00	305.00	50.00	145.00

The data appear to be stable across the days of the week in which they were collected. A simplified fishbone chart indicating where delays occur is shown in Figure 9.5.

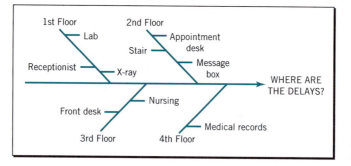

Figure 9.5   Fishbone Chart Indicating Where Delays Occur

As part of the answer to the first round of *what, where, who,* and *when* questions concerning the delays, it was decided to split the data according to the location where the call was received.

The return times for calls, ordered according to magnitude, received by members of the second floor pool are

8	10	30	40	45	50	51	58	60	61	64
65	65	75	75	90	93	100	100	100	100	100
105	105	110	110	115	115	115	118	120	120	125
130	130	135	140	140	145	145	145	148	150	150
155	160	160	165	170	170	175	180	180	185	200
220	230	255	305							

and those received by the backup persons on the third floor are

5	10	10	10	10	10	15	15	15	15	20
20	25	25	25	30	35	35	40	45	45	45
50	50	55	60	65	70	80	85	85	90	95
95	95	95	100	100	110	110	120	125	130	135
135	145	150	150	150	155	155	155	170	190	195
240										

These data have the summary statistics:

	N	MEAN	MEDIAN	STDEV
SECOND	59	121.46	118.00	58.04
THIRD	56	80.27	75.00	58.61

	MIN	MAX	Q1	Q3
SECOND	8.00	305.00	75.00	155.00
THIRD	5.00	240.00	25.00	128.75

It is clear that calls received on the third floor are handled more efficiently. There may be something to learn here, or there may just be a simpler line of communication.

Using the procedure discussed in Section 9.2, we can test for equality of the two population mean times to return a call. Using Minitab, and the pooled procedure, we have

```
TWOSAMPLE T FOR SECOND VS THIRD
             N       MEAN      STDEV
SECOND      59      121.5       58.0
THIRD       56       80.3       58.6

95 PCT CI FOR MU SECOND - MU THIRD: (19.6, 62.7)

TTEST MU SECOND = MU THIRD (VS NE): T = 3.79 P = 0.0002 DF = 113
```

Stem-and-leaf diagrams, with five repeated stems, for the times rounded to 10 minutes follow:

```
Stem-and-leaf of C1    N  = 59        Stem-and-leaf of C2    N  = 56
Leaf Unit = 10 (SECOND FLOOR)         Leaf Unit = 10 (THIRD FLOOR)

    2      0 01                           10     0 0111111111
    3      0 3                            18     0 22222333
    8      0 44555                        25     0 4444555
   15      0 6666677                      28     0 667
   17      0 99                           28     0 88899999
  (13)     1 0000000111111               20     1 0011
   29      1 222333                       16     1 22333
   23      1 444444555                    11     1 4555555
   14      1 666777                        4     1 7
    8      1 888                           3     1 99
    5      2 0                             1     2
    4      2 23                            1     2
    2      2 5                             1     2 4
    1      2
    1      2
    1      3 0
```

It is clear that the mean time to respond depends on the location where the call was received. The stem-and-leaf diagrams show the distribution of response times. The response times for calls answered on the third floor are more concentrated near 0 (measured in 10-minute units) and not as symmetric as those for calls answered on the second floor.

The information presented here represents only the first step in a project to improve the quality of the responses to patient telephone inquiries. Additional fishbone charts dealing with identifying the types of delays (what), the people involved in the process (who), and the time periods in which the delays occurred (when) were constructed and interpreted. Decisions were made to collect more data. Analyses of the data suggested certain changes would lead to an improved process. The changes were made and monitored, and satisfactory improvements were achieved.

9.6   CHAPTER SUMMARY

In this chapter we have learned:

- We can compare means with independent random samples from two populations. A comparison involves making inferences about the difference $\mu_1 - \mu_2$.

1. For large samples ($n_1 > 30$ and $n_2 > 30$), a $100(1 - \alpha)\%$ confidence interval for $\mu_1 - \mu_2$ has the form

$$(\overline{x} - \overline{y}) \pm z_{\alpha/2} \sqrt{\frac{s_1^2}{n_1} + \frac{s_2^2}{n_2}}$$

where $z_{\alpha/2}$ is the upper $\alpha/2$ point of $N(0, 1)$. To test the hypothesis H_0: $\mu_1 - \mu_2 = \delta_0$, we use the statistic whose value is

$$z = \frac{\overline{x} - \overline{y} - \delta_0}{\sqrt{\dfrac{s_1^2}{n_1} + \dfrac{s_2^2}{n_2}}}$$

With significance level α, H_0 is rejected if

$z > z_{\alpha/2}$ or $z < -z_{\alpha/2}$ for the two-sided alternative H_1: $\mu_1 - \mu_2 \neq \delta_0$
$z > z_\alpha$ for the one-sided alternative H_1: $\mu_1 - \mu_2 > \delta_0$
$z < -z_\alpha$ for the one-sided alternative H_1: $\mu_1 - \mu_2 < \delta_0$

2. For small samples, inferences are based on a t statistic. To use this statistic, we make two assumptions:

   Both populations are normal.
   The population standard deviations σ_1 and σ_2 are equal.

   With these assumptions, a $100(1 - \alpha)\%$ confidence interval for the mean difference is

$$(\overline{x} - \overline{y}) \pm t_{\alpha/2} s_{\text{pooled}} \sqrt{\frac{1}{n_1} + \frac{1}{n_2}}$$

where $t_{\alpha/2}$ is the upper $\alpha/2$ point of the t distribution with d.f. $= n_1 + n_2 - 2$ and s_{pooled} is the pooled estimate of the common population standard deviation σ. To test the hypothesis H_0: $\mu_1 - \mu_2 = \delta_0$, we use the statistic whose value is

$$t = \frac{\overline{x} - \overline{y} - \delta_0}{s_{\text{pooled}} \sqrt{\dfrac{1}{n_1} + \dfrac{1}{n_2}}}$$

With significance level α, H_0 is rejected if

$t > t_{\alpha/2}$ or $t < -t_{\alpha/2}$ for the two-sided alternative H_1: $\mu_1 - \mu_2 \neq \delta_0$

$t > t_\alpha$ for the one-sided alternative H_1: $\mu_1 - \mu_2 > \delta_0$

$t < -t_\alpha$ for the one-sided alternative H_1: $\mu_1 - \mu_2 < \delta_0$

where the t percentage point has d.f. $= n_1 + n_2 - 2$.

● When comparing two populations (or treatments), it is often advantageous to **pair** or **block** similar experimental units and randomly assign the two treatments to members of each pair. Pairing or blocking like experimental units according to some identifiable characteristic(s) serves to remove this source of variation from the experiment.

● For a **matched pairs comparison** of means, observations from the second population or treatment are subtracted from those from the first population or treatment to get the differences $d_i = x_i - y_i$, $i = 1, 2, \ldots, n$. With $\delta = \mu_1 - \mu_2$, inferences about δ are based on the statistic with value

$$\frac{\overline{d} - \delta}{s_d / \sqrt{n}}$$

where

$$\overline{d} = \frac{\sum_{i=1}^{n} d_i}{n} \quad \text{and} \quad s_d^2 = \sum_{i=1}^{n} (d_i - \overline{d})^2$$

1. For large samples ($n > 30$), the statistic with value

$$z = \frac{\overline{d} - \delta}{s_d / \sqrt{n}} \quad \text{is approximately } N(0, 1),$$

and a $100(1 - \alpha)\%$ confidence interval for δ is

$$\overline{d} \pm z_{\alpha/2} \frac{s_d}{\sqrt{n}}$$

To test the hypothesis H_0: $\delta = \delta_0$, we use the observed quantity

$$z = \frac{\overline{d} - \delta_0}{s_d / \sqrt{n}}$$

With significance level α, H_0 is rejected if

$z > z_{\alpha/2}$ or $z < -z_{\alpha/2}$ for the two-sided alternative H_1: $\delta \neq \delta_0$

$z > z_\alpha$ for the one-sided alternative H_1: $\delta > \delta_0$

$z < -z_\alpha$ for the one-sided alternative H_1: $\delta < \delta_0$

2. For small samples, we make the assumption that the differences $d_i = x_i - y_i$ come from a normal distribution, in which case, a $100(1 - \alpha)\%$ confidence interval for δ is given by

$$\overline{d} \pm t_{\alpha/2} \frac{s_d}{\sqrt{n}}$$

where $t_{\alpha/2}$ is based on $n - 1$ degrees of freedom. A test of H_0: $\delta = \delta_0$ is based on the test statistic t with value

$$t = \frac{\bar{d} - \delta_0}{s_d/\sqrt{n}}$$

The statistic has Student's t distribution with d.f. $= n - 1$. With significance level α, H_0 is rejected if

$t > t_{\alpha/2}$ or $t < -t_{\alpha/2}$ for the two-sided alternative H_1: $\delta \neq \delta_0$

$t > t_\alpha$ for the one-sided alternative H_1: $\delta > \delta_0$

$t < -t_\alpha$ for the one-sided alternative H_1: $\delta < \delta_0$

- A powerful technique called the **analysis of variance** (ANOVA) can be used to compare several population means. When comparing k population means, the two sources of variation are (1) differences between means and (2) within population variation or error.

- A **completely randomized design** is synonymous with independent random sampling from several populations when each population is identified as the population of responses under a particular treatment.

- The observations from a completely randomized design can be used to compute a **treatment sum of squares,** an **error sum of squares,** and a **total sum of squares.** The treatment sum of squares measures the variation arising from differences between means. The error sum of squares measures the within population or error variation. Each sum of squares has associated degrees of freedom.

- The sums of squares and their associated degrees of freedom can be displayed in a convenient format called an **ANOVA table.**

- If the independent random samples are each from normal populations and these have a common standard deviation σ, an **F test** can be used to test for equality of population means. The null hypothesis H_0: $\mu_1 = \mu_2 = \cdots = \mu_k$ is rejected if

$$F = \frac{\text{Treatment SS}/(k - 1)}{\text{Error SS}/(n - k)} > F_\alpha(k - 1, n - k)$$

where $n = \sum_{i=1}^{k} n_i$ and $F_\alpha(k - 1, n - k)$ is the upper α point of the F distribution with d.f. $= (k - 1, n - k)$.

- A $100(1 - \alpha)\%$ confidence interval for $(\mu_i - \mu_{i'})$, the mean difference between treatment i and treatment i', is given by

$$(\bar{y}_i - \bar{y}_{i'}) \pm t_{\alpha/2} s \sqrt{\frac{1}{n_i} + \frac{1}{n_{i'}}}$$

where

$$s = \sqrt{\text{MSE}} = \sqrt{\frac{\text{SSE}}{n - k}}$$

and $t_{\alpha/2}$ is the upper $\alpha/2$ point of t with d.f. $= n - k$.

- **Multiple-t confidence intervals** can be used to make simultaneous comparisons of pairwise differences in means. A set of $100(1 - \alpha)\%$ simultaneous confidence intervals for m pairwise differences $(\mu_i - \mu_{i'})$ is given by

$$(\overline{y}_i - \overline{y}_{i'}) \pm t_{\alpha/(2m)} \, s \sqrt{\frac{1}{n_i} + \frac{1}{n_{i'}}}$$

where $s = \sqrt{\text{MSE}}$, $m =$ the number of confidence statements, and $t_{\alpha/(2m)} =$ upper $\alpha/(2m)$ point of t with d.f. $= n - k$. Using this procedure, the confidence associated with all the m statements being correct is at least $(1 - \alpha)$.

- **Graphical displays** are useful for checking the assumptions underlying a comparison of means or treatments. Dotplots, stem-and-leaf diagrams, boxplots, and normal-scores plots can all be used to analyze the residuals, $(y_{ij} - \overline{y}_i)$.

9.7   IMPORTANT CONCEPTS AND TOOLS

CONCEPTS

Analysis of variance, 468
Block, 460
Completely randomized design, 468
Degrees of freedom associated with a sum of squares, 472
Error sum of squares, 471
F distribution, 474
F ratio, 474
Matched pairs design, 461

Mean square, 473
Multiple-t confidence intervals, 478
Pairing, 461
Pooled estimator of the common σ^2, 450
Population model for comparing k treatments, 474
Randomization, 443
Residuals, 480

Simultaneous confidence intervals, 478
Small sample assumptions for comparing two means, 450
Statistical model for independent random samples, 444
Total sum of squares, 471
Treatment sum of squares, 471

TOOLS

Analysis of variance table, 473
Confidence interval for a mean difference δ (paired observations), 462
Confidence interval for a single pairwise difference $(\mu_i - \mu_{i'})$, 477

Confidence interval for $\mu_1 - \mu_2$ with small normal samples, 452
F test for equality of means, 475
Large sample confidence interval for $\mu_1 - \mu_2$, 445
Simultaneous confidence interval for a pairwise difference $(\mu_i - \mu_{i'})$, 478

Tests of H_0: $\delta = \delta_0$ for small normal samples (paired observations), 462
Tests of H_0: $\mu_1 - \mu_2 = \delta_0$ with large samples, 448
Tests of H_0: $\mu_1 - \mu_2 = \delta_0$ with small normal samples, 453

9.8   KEY FORMULAS

INFERENCES WITH TWO INDEPENDENT RANDOM SAMPLES

a. *Large Samples*. When n_1 and n_2 are both greater than 30, inferences about $\mu_1 - \mu_2$ are based on the fact that the random variable with value

$$\frac{(\overline{x} - \overline{y}) - (\mu_1 - \mu_2)}{\sqrt{\dfrac{s_1^2}{n_1} + \dfrac{s_2^2}{n_2}}} \quad \text{is approximately } N(0, 1).$$

A $100(1 - \alpha)\%$ confidence interval for $(\mu_1 - \mu_2)$ is

$$(\overline{x} - \overline{y}) \pm z_{\alpha/2} \sqrt{\frac{s_1^2}{n_1} + \frac{s_2^2}{n_2}}$$

To test H_0: $\mu_1 - \mu_2 = \delta_0$, we use the normal test statistic Z with value

$$z = \frac{(\overline{x} - \overline{y}) - \delta_0}{\sqrt{\frac{s_1^2}{n_1} + \frac{s_2^2}{n_2}}}$$

No assumptions are needed in regard to the shape of the population distributions.

b. *Small Samples.* When n_1 and n_2 are small, inferences using the t distribution require the assumptions:

Both populations are normal.

$\sigma_1 = \sigma_2$

The common σ^2 is estimated by

$$s_{pooled}^2 = \frac{(n_1 - 1)s_1^2 + (n_2 - 1)s_2^2}{n_1 + n_2 - 2}$$

Inferences about $\mu_1 - \mu_2$ are based on the t statistic with value

$$t = \frac{(\overline{x} - \overline{y}) - (\mu_1 - \mu_2)}{s_{pooled}\sqrt{\frac{1}{n_1} + \frac{1}{n_2}}}, \quad \text{and d.f.} = n_1 + n_2 - 2.$$

A $100(1 - \alpha)\%$ confidence interval for $\mu_1 - \mu_2$ is

$$(\overline{x} - \overline{y}) \pm t_{\alpha/2}s_{pooled}\sqrt{\frac{1}{n_1} + \frac{1}{n_2}}$$

To test H_0: $\mu_1 - \mu_2 = \delta_0$, we use the test statistic t with value

$$t = \frac{(\overline{x} - \overline{y}) - \delta_0}{s_{pooled}\sqrt{\frac{1}{n_1} + \frac{1}{n_2}}}, \quad \text{and d.f.} = n_1 + n_2 - 2.$$

INFERENCES WITH A MATCHED PAIRS SAMPLE

With a paired sample $(x_1, y_1), (x_2, y_2), \ldots, (x_n, y_n)$, calculate the differences $d_i = x_i - y_i$, their mean $\overline{d}$, and standard deviation s_d. If n is small, we assume the d_i's come from the normal distribution $N(\delta, \sigma_d)$. Inferences are based on a t statistic with value

$$t = \frac{\overline{d} - \delta}{s_d/\sqrt{n}}, \quad \text{and d.f.} = n - 1.$$

A $100(1 - \alpha)\%$ confidence interval for δ is

$$\overline{d} \pm t_{\alpha/2} \frac{s_d}{\sqrt{n}}$$

The test of H_0: $\delta = \delta_0$ is performed with the test statistic having the value

$$t = \frac{\overline{d} - \delta_0}{s_d/\sqrt{n}}, \quad \text{and d.f.} = n - 1.$$

If n is large, the assumption of a normal distribution for the d_i's is not required. Inferences are based on the fact that the statistic Z with value

$$z = \frac{\overline{d} - \delta_0}{s_d/\sqrt{n}} \quad \text{is approximately } N(0, 1).$$

COMPARING SEVERAL POPULATIONS USING THE ANALYSIS OF VARIANCE (ANOVA)

The jth observation on the ith treatment is y_{ij}. The total variation in the observations y_{ij} is given by

$$\text{Total Sum of Squares} = \sum_{i=1}^{k} \sum_{j=1}^{n_i} (y_{ij} - \overline{y})^2 \quad \text{with d.f.} = \left(\sum_{i=1}^{k} n_i\right) - 1$$

The total sum of squares can be partitioned into two components:
    Treatment Sum of Squares

$$\text{SST} = \sum_{i=1}^{k} n_i (\overline{y}_i - \overline{y})^2 \quad \text{with d.f.} = k - 1$$

and
    Error Sum of Squares

$$\text{SSE} = \sum_{i=1}^{k} \sum_{j=1}^{n_i} (y_{ij} - \overline{y}_i)^2 \quad \text{with d.f.} = n - k$$

where $n = \sum_{i=1}^{k} n_i$.

$$\text{Mean Square} = \frac{\text{Sum of Squares}}{\text{Degrees of Freedom}}$$

$$F \text{ statistic} = \frac{\text{Treatment Mean Square}}{\text{Error Mean Square}}$$

Assuming the observations on each treatment are normally distributed with a common standard deviation σ, a test of H_0: $\mu_1 = \mu_2 = \cdots = \mu_k$ is performed using

$$F = \frac{\text{Treatment Mean Square}}{\text{Error Mean Square}} \quad \text{with d.f.} = (k - 1, n - k)$$

Simultaneous confidence intervals for population mean differences $\mu_i - \mu_{i'}$ are given by the multiple-t intervals

$$(y_i - y_{i'}) \pm t_{\alpha/(2m)}\, s\, \sqrt{\frac{1}{n_i} + \frac{1}{n_{i'}}}$$

where $s = \sqrt{MSE}$, m = number of confidence statements, and $t_{\alpha/(2m)}$ = upper $\alpha/(2m)$ point of t with d.f. = $n - k$. These intervals have an overall confidence level of at least $(1 - \alpha)$.

REVIEW EXERCISES

9.53 A bank processes loan applications at two sites, and it is recognized that the approval process must be speeded up. To obtain a reference for the current procedures and to compare the handling of applications at the two sites, you must run an experiment. Thirty new applications are available. Explain how you would split the applications in half and assign 15 to the first processing site and 15 to the second.

9.54 Refer to the loan application processing at two sites described in Exercise 9.53. Explain how you could conduct a matched pairs experiment by making a second copy of each application folder and its contents.

9.55 The following summary is recorded for independent samples from two populations.

Sample 1	Sample 2
$n_1 = 65$	$n_2 = 60$
$\bar{x} = 194$	$\bar{y} = 165$
$s_1^2 = 86$	$s_2^2 = 137$

a. Construct a 98% confidence interval for $\mu_1 - \mu_2$.

b. Test H_0: $\mu_1 - \mu_2 = 35$ versus H_1: $\mu_1 - \mu_2 \neq 35$ with $\alpha = .02$.

c. Test H_0: $\mu_1 - \mu_2 = 35$ versus H_1: $\mu_1 - \mu_2 < 35$ with $\alpha = .05$.

9.56 Two sets of values for the standard deviations of independent random samples, each of size 52, from two populations are given here. For each case, determine whether an observed difference of 10 between the sample means is statistically significant at $\alpha = .05$.

a. $s_1 = 21$, $s_2 = 29$

b. $s_1 = 11$, $s_2 = 14$

9.57 A group of 88 subjects is used in an experiment to compare two treatments. From this group, 40 subjects are randomly selected and assigned to Treatment 1, and the remaining 48 subjects are assigned to Treatment 2. The means and standard deviations of the responses are:

	Treatment 1	Treatment 2
Mean	15.62	27.25
Standard deviation	2.88	4.32

Determine a 95% confidence interval for the mean difference of the treatment responses.

9.58 Refer to Exercise 9.57. Suppose that the investigator wishes to establish that the mean response of Treatment 2 is larger than that of Treatment 1 by more than 10 units.

    a. Formulate the null hypothesis and the alternative hypothesis.

    b. Determine the value of the test statistic, and describe the rejection region with $\alpha = .10$.

    c. Perform the test with $\alpha = .10$. Also, find the P-value and comment on its magnitude.

9.59 The following data are from two samples:

$$8 \quad 10 \quad 7 \quad 9 \quad 8 \quad \text{and} \quad 6 \quad 2 \quad 4 \quad 8$$

Obtain

    a. s^2_{pooled}

    b. The value of the t statistic for testing H_0: $\mu_1 - \mu_2 = 2$ and its degrees of freedom

9.60 Two work designs are being considered for possible adoption in an assembly plant. A time study is conducted with 10 workers using Design 1 and 12 workers using Design 2. The means and standard deviations of their assembly times (in minutes) are:

	Design 1	Design 2
Mean	78.3	85.6
Standard deviation	4.8	6.5

Is the mean assembly time significantly higher for Design 2? Defend your position.

9.61 Refer to Exercise 9.60. Construct 95% confidence intervals for the mean assembly times for Design 1 and Design 2 individually (see Chapter 8).

9.62 The following summary statistics are recorded for two independent random samples from two populations.

Sample 1	Sample 2
$n_1 = 11$	$n_2 = 13$
$\bar{x} = 10.7$	$\bar{y} = 9.6$
$s^2_1 = 1.36$	$s^2_2 = 2.17$

    a. Construct a 95% confidence interval for $\mu_1 - \mu_2$.

    b. What assumptions (if any) must you make about the population distributions to use the interval in part **a** with the stated level of confidence?

9.63 Refer to Exercise 9.62. Is there strong evidence that Population 1 has a higher mean than Population 2? Explain.

9.64 In each of the following cases, how would you select the experimental units and conduct the experiment?

a. Compare the mileage obtained from two different gasolines; 16 cars are available for the experiment.

b. Test two varnishes; 12 birch boards are available for the experiment.

c. Compare two methods of teaching basic ice skating; 40 seven-year-old boys are available for the experiment.

9.65 To compare two treatments, a matched pairs experiment was conducted with 9 pairs of subjects. The differences

$$(\text{Response to Treatment 1}) - (\text{Response to Treatment 2})$$

were recorded. The differences are

−1.26	−.82	1.32	3.16	2.18
4.62	.60	−.55	1.54	

a. Is there strong evidence of a difference between the mean responses of the two treatments? Test with $\alpha = .02$.

b. Construct a 90% confidence interval for the mean difference of the response to the two treatments. Interpret this interval.

9.66 A trucking firm wishes to choose between two alternate routes for transporting merchandise from one depot to another. One major concern is the travel time. In a study, 5 drivers were randomly selected from a group of 10 and assigned to Route A, the other 5 were assigned to Route B. The following data were obtained.

	Travel Time (hours)				
Route A	18	24	30	21	32
Route B	22	29	34	25	35

a. Is there a significant difference between the mean travel times of the two routes? State the assumptions about the population distributions you have made in answering this question.

b. Suggest an alternative design for this study that would make a comparison more effective.

9.67 It is anticipated that a new instructional method will more effectively improve the reading ability of elementary-school children than the standard method currently in use. To test this conjecture, 16 children are divided at random into two groups of 8 each. One group is instructed using the standard method and the other group is instructed using the new method. The children's scores on a reading test are as follows:

Standard	65	70	76	63	72	71	68	68
New	75	80	72	77	69	81	71	78

a. Test for a difference in the population mean scores. Take $\alpha = .05$.

b. Construct a 95% confidence interval for the difference in the population mean scores. Is the confidence interval consistent with the results of the test of hypotheses in part **a?** Explain.

9.68 Provide a decomposition of the following observations from a completely randomized design with three treatments into grand mean, deviation due to treatment, and residual components.

Treatment 1	Treatment 2	Treatment 3
19	16	13
18	11	16
21	13	18
18	14	11
	11	15
		11

9.69 Refer to Exercise 9.68. Compute the sums of squares, and construct the ANOVA table (including the mean square column).

9.70 Using the table of percentage points for the F distribution, find:
   a. The upper 5% point when d.f. $= (8, 12)$
   b. The upper 5% point when d.f. $= (8, 20)$
   c. The upper 10% point when d.f. $= (8, 12)$

9.71 Refer to Exercise 9.51. In a study of differences in managerial values in different parts of the world, the Eastern developed value

human-heartedness

a measure of compassion toward others, was quantified by responses to a group of survey questions, and scored on a scale of 1 to 9. Higher scores indicate a stronger belief in this value. These data are summarized for American managers, People's Republic of China managers, and Hong Kong managers:

American managers: $n_1 = 62$, $\bar{y}_1 = 5.9$, $s_1 = .78$
People's Republic of China managers: $n_2 = 82$, $\bar{y}_2 = 4.9$, $s_2 = .53$
Hong Kong managers: $n_3 = 182$, $\bar{y}_3 = 5.5$, $s_3 = .73$

   a. Do these data confirm that managers differ from country to country with respect to the mean response on the human-heartedness scale? Test with $\alpha = .05$.
   b. Construct multiple-t 95% confidence intervals for the paired differences of the population means. Interpret these intervals.

BurnTime.dat

9.72 (*Minitab or similar program recommended*) As part of a multilab study, four fabrics are tested for flammability by the National Institute for Standards and Technology. The following burn times in seconds are recorded after a paper tab is ignited on the hem of a dress made of each fabric.

Fabric 1	Fabric 2	Fabric 3	Fabric 4
17.8	11.2	11.8	14.9
16.2	11.4	11.0	10.8
17.5	15.8	10.0	12.8
17.4	10.0	9.2	10.7
15.0	10.4	9.2	10.7

   a. State the statistical model underlying these data, and construct the ANOVA table. With $\alpha = .05$, test the null hypothesis of no difference in degree of flammability for the four fabrics.

b. If the null hypothesis is rejected, construct multiple-t confidence intervals to determine the fabric(s) with the lowest mean burn time.

c. Plot the residuals and comment on the plausibility of the model assumptions.

d. If the tests had been conducted one at a time on a single mannequin, how would you have randomized the fabrics in this experiment?

Thicknes.dat

9.73 (*Minitab or similar program recommended*) Integrated circuits (ICs) are produced on silicon wafers, which are ground to a target thickness at an early stage of production. The wafers are positioned on so-called *frits* on a grinding table and located under the grindstone as pictured in the figure. They are kept in place by means of vacuum decompression.

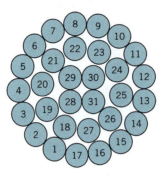

Positions of Silicon Wafers on Grinder

For current control of the process, the thickness of the wafers on Positions 1 and 2 (outer circle), 18 and 19 (middle circle) and 28 (inner circle) is measured. The target thickness is 244 μm. Data from 30 successive batches from the grinding process are displayed in Table 9.10.

TABLE 9.10   Thickness Measurements (μm)

| | Position | | | | | | Position | | | |
Batch	1	2	18	19	28	Batch	1	2	18	19	28
1	240	243	250	253	248	16	237	239	242	247	245
2	238	242	245	251	247	17	242	244	246	251	248
3	239	242	246	250	248	18	243	245	247	252	249
4	235	237	246	249	246	19	243	245	248	251	250
5	240	241	246	247	249	20	244	246	246	250	246
6	240	243	244	248	245	21	241	239	244	250	246
7	240	243	244	249	246	22	242	245	248	251	249
8	245	250	250	247	248	23	242	245	248	243	246
9	238	240	245	248	246	24	241	244	245	249	247
10	240	242	246	249	248	25	236	239	241	246	242
11	240	243	246	250	248	26	243	246	247	252	247
12	241	245	243	247	245	27	241	243	245	248	246
13	247	245	255	250	249	28	239	240	242	243	244
14	237	239	243	247	246	29	239	240	250	252	250
15	242	244	245	248	245	30	241	243	249	255	253

SOURCE: K. C. B. Roes and R. J. M. Does, "Shewhart-type charts in nonstandard situations." *Technometrics*, Vol. 37, No. 1, 1995, pp. 15–24.

a. Consider the data for Positions 1, 18, and 28 only. Use Minitab or a similar program to conduct an analysis of variance. Test for differences in the mean thickness at the three positions. Use $\alpha = .05$.

b. State the statistical model underlying the data in Table 9.10. Are the model assumptions reasonable in this case? Discuss by constructing diagnostic plots (dotplots, boxplots, normal-scores, and so forth) of the residuals from part **a.**

c. Using the data in part **a,** construct 95% multiple-t confidence intervals for the mean thickness at the three positions. Can we conclude the target thickness is being achieved for the wafers subjected to this grinding process? Comment.

After reading this chapter, you should be able to:

- Identify categorical data.
- Construct a confidence interval for a population proportion.
- Determine the sample size required to achieve a specified error margin when estimating a population proportion.
- Conduct tests of hypotheses involving a single population proportion.
- Construct a confidence interval for the difference between two population proportions.
- Test for the equality of two population proportions.
- Read a chi-square table and determine percentage points of a chi-square distribution.
- Test for homogeneity of populations using categorical data organized as a two-way table.
- Test for the independence of two simultaneously observed characteristics using categorical data organized as a two-way table.
- Understand the difference between a test of homogeneity and a test of independence.

CHAPTER TEN

Analyzing Count Data

10.1 INTRODUCTION

As we pointed out in Chapter 3, when the outcomes for variables are categories, as will be the case if we measure traits or characteristics of experimental units, the data come in the form of counts. Examples include the number of graduate school applications accepted, the number of customer complaints, and the number of copiers sold in a week. Often, responses to survey questions are classified into categories, or the responses are directly recorded on, say, a 5-point scale.

Because the observations are associated with categories, they are called **categorical data.** These observations produce a data set consisting of the frequency counts for each category.

EXAMPLE 10.1   Inferences for a Single Population Proportion

A survey of 200 executives revealed that 115 of them would rather leave a message with a voice mail system than a person.* Does this provide convincing information that over half of all executives would prefer voice mail systems? What are the plausible values for the population proportion of executives who prefer voice mail systems?

Solution and Discussion.   As we shall see, statistical tests and confidence intervals can answer these questions. Moreover, for purposes of comparison, samples can be taken from different populations and the distributions, across the categories, examined for differences.

Often it is convenient to organize count data in the form of a two-way table. Situations producing data that can be organized as a two-way table are of two kinds. We can sample separate populations and record the counts that fall in the categories for a single characteristic. This case is illustrated in Example 10.2. The idea is to determine whether the populations are the same with respect to the characteristic.

Alternatively, we can sample a single population and record the counts that fall in the categories defined by two characteristics. This case is illustrated in Example 10.3, where the idea is to determine whether the two characteristics are independent or unrelated.

EXAMPLE 10.2   Two Samples Categorized According to the Same Characteristic

Before commercials are placed on national TV, they undergo testing and modification. Technology has now made it easy to show one version of a commercial to half the audience and a second version to the other half. A follow-up telephone survey is conducted and the responses are categorized as

Don't remember, Remember seeing, or *Able to remember key point*

In one such situation, 80 viewers of Commercial A were interviewed, as were 70 viewers of Commercial B. The data are presented in Table 10.1.

TABLE 10.1   Remembering a Commercial

	Don't Remember	Remember Seeing	Remember Key Point	Total
Commercial A	19	24	37	80
Commercial B	24	28	18	70
Total	43	52	55	150

---

*The sample size and proportions are the same as those reported in *Fortune,* April 4, 1994, p. 76.

Calculating the proportions for each row separately, as suggested in Chapter 3, we obtain the results in Table 10.2.

TABLE 10.2 Relative Frequencies by Commercial

	Don't Remember	Remember Seeing	Remember Key Point	Total
Commercial A	.238	.300	.463	1.001
Commercial B	.343	.400	.257	1.000
Total	.287	.347	.367	1.001

Are the two versions of the commercial equally well remembered? If they are, is there a common distribution across categories?

Solution and Discussion. Again, a statistical test based on these data can answer the question of whether the two versions of the commercial are equally well remembered. If they are equally well remembered, there is a common distribution across the categories that would be estimated by the proportions in the last row of Table 10.2.

EXAMPLE 10.3 One Sample Simultaneously Classified According to Two Characteristics

What is the duration of union contracts? Do the durations depend on the type of industry, say, manufacturing or nonmanufacturing, or are the durations independent of the type of industry?

   A sample of 400 contracts was selected from about 4000 on file and classified according to the two characteristics: (1) duration of contract and (2) type of industry. Among those contracts selected in the survey, 245 contracts were in manufacturing and 155 contracts were classified as nonmanufacturing. The contracts, organized by duration (in years) and type of industry (manufacturing/nonmanufacturing) are given in Table 10.3, a two-way table.

TABLE 10.3 Union Contracts by Duration and Type of Industry*

	2 yr. or less	3 yr.	4 yr. or more	Total
Manufacturing	10	187	48	245
Nonmanufacturing	13	107	35	155
Total	23	294	83	400

*These data give the relative frequencies provided in *Basic Patterns in Union Contracts,* 13th ed., by the editors of Collective Bargaining Negotiations and Contracts, The National Bureau of Affairs, Inc., Washington D.C.

Is the duration of union contracts independent of the type of industry?

Solution and Discussion. A statistical test, based on these data, can answer the question of whether the duration of union contracts is independent of type of industry. We will revisit this question later in the chapter.

In all of the situations discussed in these examples, the goal of the suggested statistical procedure is to draw conclusions about the probability of each category, represented by the population proportion.

10.2   INFERENCES ABOUT PROPORTIONS

When a single response is classified into only two categories, such as employed/not employed, male/female, defective/not defective, we can call the category of interest *success* and the other category *failure*. The population probability of success, or, equivalently, the population proportion of successes, is p, and the corresponding quantity for failures is $q = 1 - p$. When the responses for different subjects or experimental units can be treated as independent and each has the same probability of success, the total number of successes X in a fixed number of trials n has the binomial distribution

$$P(X = x) = \binom{n}{x} p^x q^{n-x} \quad \text{for } x = 0, 1, \ldots, n$$

as described in Section 6.5.

When n items are randomly selected from a population, the data will consist of the count X of the number in the sample that possess the characteristic. The sample proportion*

$$\hat{p} = \frac{X}{n}$$

is an estimator of the population proportion p. The "hat" above p reminds us that this random quantity is a statistic that provides an estimate of the population parameter p.

Recall from Section 7.4 that when the sample size n is large, the binomial distribution is well approximated by a normal distribution with mean np and standard deviation $\sqrt{npq}$. That is,

$$Z = \frac{X - np}{\sqrt{npq}}$$

is approximately standard normal.

Dividing the numerator and denominator in the standard normal variable by n, we have

$$Z = \frac{(X - np)/n}{(\sqrt{npq})/n} = \frac{\hat{p} - p}{\sqrt{pq/n}}$$

---

*It is common practice to use a lowercase $\hat{p}$ to represent both the random variable and its observed value.

We conclude that, for large samples, the sample proportion $\hat{p}$ is approximately normal with mean p and standard deviation $\sqrt{pq/n}$. This fact, illustrated in Figure 10.1, is crucial to making inferences about the population proportion p.

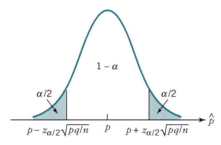

Figure 10.1   Approximate Normal Distribution for $\hat{p}$ When n Is Large

POINT ESTIMATION OF p

When the count X has a binomial distribution for n trials,

$$\mu = E(X) = np \quad \text{and} \quad \sigma = \text{sd}(X) = \sqrt{npq}$$

Since the sample proportion $\hat{p} = X/n$ is the constant $a = 1/n$ times X, by the properties of expectation given in Section 6.4, $\hat{p}$ has mean and standard deviation

$$\mu_{\hat{p}} = \frac{1}{n}\mu_X = \frac{1}{n}np = p$$

$$\sigma_{\hat{p}} = \frac{1}{n}\text{sd}(X) = \frac{1}{n}\sqrt{npq} = \sqrt{\frac{pq}{n}}$$

The first result states that the sampling distribution of $\hat{p}$ has the population proportion p as its mean. The second result says that the standard error of the estimator $\hat{p}$ is

$$\text{s.e.}(\hat{p}) = \sqrt{\frac{pq}{n}}$$

If $\hat{p}$ is used as an estimate of p, its estimated standard error is obtained by replacing p by $\hat{p}$ and q by $\hat{q} = 1 - \hat{p}$ in the formula for standard error:

$$\text{estimated s.e.}(\hat{p}) = \sqrt{\frac{\hat{p}\hat{q}}{n}}$$

When the sample size n is large, prior to sampling, the probability is approximately .954 that the value of the sample proportion will be within $\pm 2(\text{estimated s.e.})$ of the population proportion. That is, there is high probability that the difference or error of estimation, $|\hat{p} - p|$, will be less than $2(\text{estimated s.e.})$. Consequently, we say that $2\sqrt{\hat{p}\hat{q}/n}$ is a 95.4% error margin.

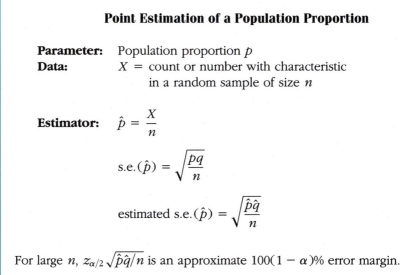

Point Estimation of a Population Proportion

Parameter: Population proportion p
Data: X = count or number with characteristic
in a random sample of size n

Estimator: $\hat{p} = \dfrac{X}{n}$

$$\text{s.e.}(\hat{p}) = \sqrt{\dfrac{pq}{n}}$$

$$\text{estimated s.e.}(\hat{p}) = \sqrt{\dfrac{\hat{p}\hat{q}}{n}}$$

For large n, $z_{\alpha/2}\sqrt{\hat{p}\hat{q}/n}$ is an approximate $100(1 - \alpha)\%$ error margin.

EXAMPLE 10.4   Calculating a Point Estimate for the Proportion of Managers Who Are PC Users

To obtain information about members' personal computer usage, a random sample of 300 managers was selected from the several thousand members of a large national management organization. Among the 300 managers selected, 242 reported that they regularly use a personal computer. Give a single number best guess, or point estimate, of the proportion of members who regularly use a personal computer. Also, give the approximate 95.4% error margin.

Solution and Discussion.   The 300 managers in the sample represent only a small fraction of the total membership, so the count can be treated as if it were a binomial random variable.

Here, $n = 300$ and $x = 242$, so the estimate of the population proportion is

$$\hat{p} = \frac{242}{300} = .807$$

We estimate that 80.7% of the membership of the national management organization regularly use a personal computer.

We have

$$\text{estimated s.e.}(\hat{p}) = \sqrt{\frac{\hat{p}\hat{q}}{n}} = \sqrt{\frac{.807 \times .193}{300}} = .023$$

Consequently, the estimate $\hat{p} = .807$ has an approximate 95.4% error margin of $2 \times .023 = .046$. There is a fairly strong reason to believe that our sample proportion, .807, is within .046 of the unknown population proportion.

EXAMPLE 10.5   **Rating the Taste of a New Breakfast Cereal**

Producers of breakfast cereals continually experiment with new products. Each promising new cereal must be market tested on a sample of potential purchasers. An added twist here is that youngsters are a major component of the market. To elicit accurate information from young people, one firm developed a smiling face scale:

After tasting a new product, respondents are asked to check one box to rate the taste. A good product should have most of the youngsters responding in the two boxes farthest to the right. By grouping these into a single top category and the three left-hand boxes into a lower category, we can estimate the proportion of the market population who would rate taste in the top category.

Out of a sample of 42 youngsters, 30 rated a new cereal in the top category. Determine a point estimate of the population proportion of youngsters who would rate taste in the top category. Also, give the approximate 95.4% error margin.

Solution and Discussion.   Here, $n = 42$ and $x = 30$, so the estimate of the population proportion is

$$\hat{p} = \frac{30}{42} = .714$$

That is, we estimate that about 71% of the population would rate the taste of the new product in the top category.

Also

$$\text{estimated s.e.}(\hat{p}) = \sqrt{\frac{\hat{p}\hat{q}}{n}} = \sqrt{\frac{.714 \times .286}{42}} = .070$$

Consequently, the estimate $\hat{p} = .714$ has an approximate 95.4% error margin of $2 \times .07 = .14$. There is a fairly strong reason to believe that the observed sample proportion, .714, is within .14 of the unknown population proportion.

CONFIDENCE INTERVAL ESTIMATION OF p

We can estimate a population proportion with an interval that incorporates, by its construction, the uncertainty associated with our guess determined from the sample. Remember that we call such an interval a confidence interval.

A large sample confidence interval for a population proportion p follows from the approximate normality of the sample proportion $\hat{p}$. Because $\hat{p}$ is approximately normal with mean p and standard deviation $\sqrt{pq/n}$, the interval from $\hat{p} - z_{\alpha/2}\sqrt{pq/n}$ to $\hat{p} + z_{\alpha/2}\sqrt{pq/n}$ is a candidate. However, the standard deviation involves the unknown parameter p, so we must use the estimated standard deviation $\sqrt{\hat{p}\hat{q}/n}$ to set the endpoints of the interval. Again, the confidence interval takes the form

$$\text{Estimate} \pm (z \text{ value})(\text{Estimated standard error})$$

Large Sample Confidence Interval for a Population Proportion

For large n, a $100(1 - \alpha)\%$ confidence interval for p is given by

$$\left(\hat{p} - z_{\alpha/2}\sqrt{\frac{\hat{p}\hat{q}}{n}}, \ \hat{p} + z_{\alpha/2}\sqrt{\frac{\hat{p}\hat{q}}{n}} \right)$$

EXAMPLE 10.6   Constructing a Confidence Interval for a Population Proportion

In Section 9.5, Statistics in Context, data for the initial reference set showed that 73 out of 115 calls to the health facility were returned within two hours. Find a 90% confidence interval for the population proportion, p, of calls that are returned within two hours.

Solution and Discussion.   Since $\alpha = .10$, $\alpha/2 = .05$. From the normal table, $z_{.05} = 1.645$. Further,

$$\hat{p} = \frac{73}{115} = .635$$

and we calculate

$$z_{.05}\sqrt{\frac{\hat{p}\hat{q}}{n}} = 1.645\sqrt{\frac{.635 \times .365}{115}} = .074$$

Consequently, a 90% confidence interval for the proportion of calls that will be returned within two hours is

$$(.635 - .074, \ .635 + .074) \quad \text{or} \quad (.561, \ .709)$$

Because the interval produced by this procedure will cover the true proportion, p, 90% of the time, we are 90% confident that the proportion of calls that will be returned within two hours is between .561 and .709. This proportion is still quite low and is further indication that the handling of calls must be improved, as indeed it was following the continuous application of quality improvement techniques.

The analysis of a matched pairs experimental design often involves inferences about a single proportion. The next example illustrates this point in the context of a taste-testing study.

EXAMPLE 10.7   Estimating a Population Proportion Using a Matched Pairs Design

Television viewers are periodically exposed to comparative trials for two major brands of cola. A collection of persons, supposedly selected at random but quite likely selected to represent important market segments and to look good on TV, is given a sample of each cola.

In a good statistical design, the colas would be in identical containers and the order in which they were drunk would be determined by a separate flip of a coin for each person. It is also preferable that the experimenter not know which cola is which so that nonverbal signals cannot systematically influence the choice of the preferred cola. When both the subject and the experimenter do not know the cola in any container, the experiment is called a **double-blind** experiment.

In one such experiment, 72 out of 100 persons preferred Cola C. Find a 95% confidence interval for the proportion of persons who prefer Cola C to the other major brand.

Solution and Discussion.   Although two colas are being compared in this matched pairs designed experiment, there is just a single proportion of interest. Let p_C be the proportion of persons in the population who prefer Cola C. The 95% confidence interval has limits $\hat{p} \pm z_{.025} \sqrt{\hat{p}\hat{q}/n}$. Thus

$$\frac{72}{100} \pm 1.96 \sqrt{\frac{.72 \times .38}{100}} \quad \text{gives} \quad (.668, .772)$$

for a 95% confidence interval for the proportion who prefer Cola C. The proportions within the interval are all greater than 2 out of 3, so Cola C is quite strongly preferred. The nature of the experimental design helps rule out explanations other than taste preference.

DETERMINING THE SAMPLE SIZE FOR ESTIMATING p

If we want to estimate a population proportion with a certain precision, how large should the sample be? If $\hat{p}$ is used to estimate a population proportion p, its $100(1 - \alpha)$% error margin is $z_{\alpha/2} \sqrt{pq/n}$. Setting this quantity equal to a specified error margin e, and solving for the sample size n, we obtain

$$n = pq \left(\frac{z_{\alpha/2}}{e} \right)^2$$

If the value of p is known to be approximately equal to some value p_0, then n can be determined from

$$n = p_0(1 - p_0) \left(\frac{z_{\alpha/2}}{e} \right)^2$$

If there is no strong prior information regarding the value of p, the product pq can be replaced by its maximum value $\frac{1}{4}$. Then n can be determined from the relation

$$n = \frac{1}{4}\left(\frac{z_{\alpha/2}}{e}\right)^2$$

EXAMPLE 10.8   Determining the Sample Size to Estimate a Proportion

A market researcher is interested in determining what proportion of current users of her company's best-selling household product are likely to try a new related product. How many persons should be included in a sample if the market researcher wants to be 98% certain that the error of estimation does not exceed .06 if

a. There is no substantial knowledge about the value of p.

b. p is known to be about .7.

Solution and Discussion.   The tolerable error is $e = .06$. Also, $(1 - \alpha) = .98$, so $\alpha/2 = .01$. From the normal table, we find that $z_{.01} = 2.33$.

a. Since p is essentially unknown, the conservative bound on n yields

$$n = \frac{1}{4}\left(\frac{2.33}{.06}\right)^2 = 377.01$$

so a sample of size 378 will suffice whatever the value of p.

b. If $p_0 = .7$, the required sample size is

$$n = (.7 \times .3)\left(\frac{2.33}{.06}\right)^2 = 316.69$$

or, rounding up, $n = 317$.

This example illustrates the striking fact that a sample size of several hundred is required to estimate a proportion accurately.

LARGE SAMPLE TESTS CONCERNING p

Consider testing H_0: $p = p_0$. When the null hypothesis prevails and the number of trials n is large, the sample proportion

$$\hat{p} = \frac{X}{n}$$

is approximately normally distributed with mean p_0 and standard deviation $\sqrt{p_0 q_0/n}$. Consequently,

$$Z = \frac{\hat{p} - p_0}{\sqrt{p_0 q_0/n}}$$

has, approximately, a standard normal distribution.

If the alternative hypothesis is two-sided, H_1: $p \neq p_0$, the rejection region is the set of values $z < -z_{\alpha/2}$ or $z > z_{\alpha/2}$. One-sided alternatives have the same one-tailed rejection regions as those for large sample tests of means given in Section 8.5.

EXAMPLE 10.9 Conducting a One-Sided Test of a Proportion

Refer to Example 10.1. Test the claim that more than half of all executives prefer voice mail systems to leaving a message with a person. Use $\alpha = .05$.

Solution and Discussion

1. *Hypotheses.* The claim becomes the alternative hypothesis $p > .5$, so

   Null hypothesis $\quad\quad H_0$: $\quad p = .5$
   Alternative hypothesis H_1: $\quad p > .5$

   We are given $\alpha = .05$.

2. *Test Statistic.* Since the sample size $n = 200$ is large and the boundary value is $p_0 = .5$, the test statistic Z has the value

$$z = \frac{\hat{p} - .5}{\sqrt{.5 \times .5/200}}$$

   The alternative hypothesis is one-sided, so we reject H_0 if Z takes a large positive value.

3. *Rejection Region.* The specified $\alpha = .05$ and, from the z table, $z_{.05} = 1.645$, so the one-tailed rejection region is

$$z = \frac{\hat{p} - .5}{\sqrt{.5 \times .5/200}} > 1.645$$

4. *Calculation.* In Example 10.1, 115 of the 200 executives preferred voice mail, so $\hat{p} = \frac{115}{200} = .575$. The observed value of the test statistic is

$$z = \frac{\hat{p} - .5}{\sqrt{.5 \times .5/200}} = \frac{.575 - .5}{\sqrt{.5 \times .5/200}} = 2.121$$

5. *Conclusion.* The observed value of the test statistic, 2.121, falls in the rejection region. At level $\alpha = .05$, we reject the null hypothesis in favor of the alternative that the population proportion p is greater than .5.

   The *P*-value is

$$P(Z > 2.121) = .017$$

   or, equivalently, only about 2 times in 100 would we observe a value of $\hat{p}$ as large as .575 if H_0 were true. The evidence against H_0: $p = .5$ is quite strong. The claim that more than half of all executives prefer voice mail to leaving a message with a person is substantiated.

EXERCISES

10.1 Suppose n units are randomly selected from a population and x is the number that are found to have the characteristic of interest. In each case, provide a point estimate of p and determine its 95% error margin.

    a. $n = 60,\quad x = 35$

    b. $n = 420,\quad x = 51$

    c. $n = 1600,\quad x = 942$

10.2 For each case in Exercise 10.1, obtain the 98% error margin.

10.3 For each case in Exercise 10.1, obtain a 95% confidence interval for the population proportion.

10.4 An analyst wishes to determine the market share of an oat cereal, Cereal C, that is, the proportion of Cereal C sales among all sales of cereals. From data from several stores, the analyst finds that out of 393 cereal boxes sold, 103 were Cereal C.

    a. Estimate the market share of Cereal C.

    b. Estimate the s.e. of your estimate in part **a.**

10.5 Refer to Example 10.1. Obtain a 95% confidence interval for the population proportion of executives who prefer voice mail systems to leaving a message with a person.

10.6 Refer to Example 10.2, where 37 out of 80 persons who saw Commercial A remembered a key point. Obtain a 95% confidence interval for the population proportion of viewers of Commercial A who would remember a key point.

10.7 Refer to Example 10.6. Obtain a 95% confidence interval for the population proportion of calls that will be returned within two hours.

10.8 When a customer perceives that the actual quality received is not what was expected, a *quality failure* has occurred. Many companies survey their customers to determine what quality they think was delivered. When a sample of customers was asked about their worst experience when flying, 98 out of 239 said lack of information concerning delays and other problems was a failure. Obtain a 90% confidence interval for the proportion of the population of all passengers who think lack of information was a quality failure during their worst flying experience.

10.9 An insurance executive wants to estimate the proportion of car owners, in a new market area, who purchase at least $1 million of liability coverage in their automobile insurance policies.

    a. How large a sample should be chosen to estimate the proportion with a 95% error margin of .007? Suppose the proportion is known to be about $p_0 = .15$.

    b. How large a sample should be chosen to estimate the proportion with a 95% error margin of .007 if nothing is known about its value?

10.10 A management consulting firm is considering offering a new service and would like to be able to estimate the proportion of businesses in the city that would have a use for the service.

a. How large a sample should be chosen to estimate the proportion with a 90% error margin of .02? Suppose the proportion is known to be about $p_0 = .1$.

b. How large a sample should be chosen to estimate the proportion with a 90% error margin of .02 if nothing is known about its value?

10.11 Travis County maintains a computer list of all employees working for the county. Typically, there are approximately 3000 names on the list. To determine the need for updating the list, a database administrator is interested in the proportion of people on the list who no longer work for Travis County.

a. How large a sample should be chosen to estimate the proportion who no longer work for the county with a 95% error margin of .05 if nothing is known about its value?

b. An initial guess of the proportion who no longer work for the county is .10. How large a sample should be chosen to estimate the proportion with a 95% error margin of .05 with this information?

c. Noting that the sample size needed to achieve the 95% error margin of .05 is highly dependent on the actual, but unknown, value of the population proportion, the administrator decides to select a preliminary sample of 50 names from the list. Suppose in this sample, the administrator finds 4 people no longer employed by the county. With this information, determine the sample size needed to estimate the population proportion with a 95% error margin of .05.

d. Assuming the sample size in part **c** is greater than 50, what should the administrator do to estimate the population proportion—select an entirely new sample of the required size or select enough names so that this new set plus the 50 already selected equal the required size? Discuss.

10.12 Identify the null and the alternative hypotheses in terms of descriptive statements. The type of answer required is illustrated in part **a.**

a. The quality team wants to show that, under the new method for granting approval for projects, a proportion of more than .8 of the projects will complete the approval process within two weeks.
   Answer:

Null hypothesis:	The proportion completed within two weeks is .8.
Alternative hypothesis:	The proportion completed within two weeks is greater than .8.

b. A state department wishes to determine whether the current rate of unemployment varies significantly from the forecast of 6% made the previous quarter.

c. A regional manager for a tax service wants to establish that his company has more than 40% of the commercial accounts in the area.

d. After a change in the procedure for reporting monthly check activity to checking account customers, a bank manager would like to show that more than 75% of its customers would rate the new service as very good or excellent.

10.13 Suppose that, on the basis of a random sample of size 170, you are to verify the claim that a population proportion is larger than .40.

  a. If you set the rejection region $\hat{p} > .453$, what is the level of significance of the test?

  b. Determine the value c so that the rejection region $\hat{p} > c$ has level $\alpha = .025$.

10.14 Suppose that, on the basis of a random sample of size 250, you are to verify the claim that a population proportion is different from .30.

  a. If you set the rejection region $\hat{p} < .24$ or $\hat{p} > .36$, what is the level of significance of the test?

  b. Determine the value c so that the rejection region

$$\hat{p} < .3 - c \quad \text{or} \quad \hat{p} > .3 + c$$

has level $\alpha = .10$.

10.15 Refer to Example 10.2, where 37 out of 80 persons who saw Commercial A remembered a key point.

  a. Formulate the null hypothesis and the alternative hypothesis when the goal is to establish that the population proportion p of viewers of Commercial A who would remember a key point is greater than .35.

  b. Test the hypotheses in part **a** at level $\alpha = .05$.

10.16 Refer to Example 10.6. Let p be the population proportion of calls that will be returned within two hours. Test H_0: $p = .5$ versus H_1: $p > .5$ with $\alpha = .05$. Calculate the P-value and interpret this number.

10.17 Refer to Example 10.6. Let p be the population proportion of calls that will be returned within two hours. Test H_0: $p = .6$ versus H_1: $p > .6$ with $\alpha = .05$. Calculate the P-value and interpret this number.

10.18 Refer to Example 10.7.

  a. Determine a 99% confidence interval for p_C.

  b. Consider the hypotheses H_0: $p_C = .5$ and H_1: $p_C > .5$. Calculate the P-value and comment on its size.

10.19 Refer to the data on turnaround times for processing health claims in Table C.4, Appendix C. In Section 7.8, Statistics in Context, we stated that 90% of the claims should be handled in 14 days or less.

  a. Calculate a point estimate of the population proportion, p, of claims handled in 14 days or less. Give the estimated standard error.

  b. Determine a 95% confidence interval for p.

  c. Show that the current procedure for handling claims does not meet the industry standard by testing H_0: $p = .9$ versus H_1: $p < .9$ with $\alpha = .05$.

10.3 COMPARING TWO PROPORTIONS (OPTIONAL)

Managers frequently must make decisions on which of two procedures or products is better when the only data are categorical. The following example illustrates a survey design for making comparisons on the basis of counts.

EXAMPLE 10.10   A Two Sample Design for Comparing Proportions

A sample of 100 executives from small companies and a sample of 100 executives from large companies were interviewed about having expense-reporting controls in place for employees' use of cellular phones. Of the small companies, 47 had controls in place whereas 79 of the large companies had controls.*

We want to determine whether the population proportions are different and, if so, how different? The answers are forthcoming in Example 10.11.

The statistical reasoning behind making inferences from two independent counts, as in Example 10.10, will now be explained.

COMPARING PROPORTIONS IN TWO DIFFERENT POPULATIONS

Suppose we wish to compare the jobless rate in two cities or the proportion of females in two different types of jobs. The populations are separate, and random samples from each should be independent of one another. To compare the incidence of a characteristic in any two populations, we model the situation by introducing two probabilities:

p_1: the proportion of persons in Population 1 having the characteristic

p_2: the proportion of persons in Population 2 having the characteristic

We will continue to call the presence of the characteristic a success and the absence a failure. The data can then be arranged in the form presented in Table 10.4, where X and Y denote the numbers of successes from independent samples of sizes n_1 and n_2 taken from Population 1 and Population 2, respectively.

TABLE   10.4   Independent Random Samples from Two Dichotomous Populations

	Number of Successes	Number of Failures	Sample Size
Population 1	X	$n_1 - X$	n_1
Population 2	Y	$n_2 - Y$	n_2

From our previous reasoning in Section 10.2, we know that the sample proportion

$$\hat{p}_1 = \frac{X}{n_1} \quad \text{has} \quad \text{var}(\hat{p}_1) = \frac{p_1 q_1}{n_1}$$

$$\hat{p}_2 = \frac{Y}{n_2} \quad \text{has} \quad \text{var}(\hat{p}_2) = \frac{p_2 q_2}{n_2}$$

---

*These are the same proportions as in the Pac Tel Cellular survey "Cellular use and cost management in business," reported in *INC.*, Jan. 1994, p. 112.

where $q_1 = 1 - p_1$ and $q_2 = 1 - p_2$. The difference of the two sample proportions, $\hat{p}_1 - \hat{p}_2$, estimates the difference of the two population proportions, $p_1 - p_2$. Moreover, the two sample proportions are independent, so the variance of $\hat{p}_1 - \hat{p}_2$ is the sum of the variances (see Section 6.4) or

$$\text{var}(\hat{p}_1 - \hat{p}_2) = \text{var}(\hat{p}_1) + \text{var}(\hat{p}_2) = \frac{p_1 q_1}{n_1} + \frac{p_2 q_2}{n_2}$$

and, taking the square root,

$$\text{s.e.}(\hat{p}_1 - \hat{p}_2) = \sqrt{\frac{p_1 q_1}{n_1} + \frac{p_2 q_2}{n_2}}$$

We will restrict our discussion here to situations where both sample sizes are large, say, greater than 30. Then $\hat{p}_1 - \hat{p}_2$ is approximately normally distributed and

$$\frac{(\hat{p}_1 - \hat{p}_2) - (p_1 - p_2)}{\text{Estimated standard error}} \quad \text{is approximately } N(0, 1).$$

Confidence intervals for $p_1 - p_2$ are then of the form $\hat{p}_1 - \hat{p}_2$ plus and minus $z_{\alpha/2}$ times the estimated standard error.

A Large Sample Confidence Interval for $p_1 - p_2$

An approximate $100(1 - \alpha)\%$ confidence interval for $p_1 - p_2$ has endpoints

$$\hat{p}_1 - \hat{p}_2 \pm z_{\alpha/2} \sqrt{\frac{\hat{p}_1 \hat{q}_1}{n_1} + \frac{\hat{p}_2 \hat{q}_2}{n_2}}$$

provided that the sample sizes n_1 and n_2 are both large.

EXAMPLE 10.11 Constructing a Confidence Interval for the Difference of Two Proportions

Refer to the data in Example 10.10, where 47 out of a sample of 100 executives from small companies and 79 out of a sample of 100 executives from large companies had expense-reporting controls in place for employees' use of cellular phones. Determine whether and by how much small companies and large companies differ with regard to the proportion with controls in place by calculating an approximate 95% confidence interval for the difference of proportions.

Solution and Discussion.   Let p_1 be the population proportion of small companies that have expense-reporting controls in place, and let p_2 be the proportion for large companies. The sample sizes $n_1 = 100$ and $n_2 = 100$ are both large, so the large sample confidence interval is applicable. We first find $z_{.025} = 1.96$, from the normal table, and calculate

$$\hat{p}_1 = \frac{47}{100} = .47 \qquad \hat{p}_2 = \frac{79}{100} = .79$$

The 95% confidence interval for $p_1 - p_2$ has endpoints

$$\hat{p}_1 - \hat{p}_2 \pm z_{\alpha/2} \sqrt{\frac{\hat{p}_1 \hat{q}_1}{n_1} + \frac{\hat{p}_2 \hat{q}_2}{n_2}}$$

or

$$(.47 - .79) \pm 1.96 \sqrt{\frac{.47 \times .53}{100} + \frac{.79 \times .21}{100}} = -.32 \pm .126$$

so the 95% confidence interval is $(-.446, \; -.194)$. The proportion of large companies with expense-reporting controls for cellular phone use is .194 to .446 larger than the proportion for small companies.

A test of equality of the two population proportions, H_0: $p_1 = p_2$, employs a modified statistic. Under the null hypothesis, there is a common proportion p for both populations. Consequently, under H_0, the mean of $\hat{p}_1 - \hat{p}_2$ is $p - p = 0$ and its standard deviation is

$$\sqrt{p(1-p)} \sqrt{\frac{1}{n_1} + \frac{1}{n_2}}$$

The common population proportion p in this expression can be estimated by pooling the successes from both populations to give:

$$\text{Pooled estimate} \quad \hat{p} = \frac{X + Y}{n_1 + n_2} = \frac{n_1 \hat{p}_1 + n_2 \hat{p}_2}{n_1 + n_2}$$

$$\text{Estimated s.e. of } \hat{p}_1 - \hat{p}_2 : \sqrt{\hat{p}(1 - \hat{p})} \sqrt{\frac{1}{n_1} + \frac{1}{n_2}}$$

When the two sample sizes are large, $Z = (\hat{p}_1 - \hat{p}_2)/(\text{Estimated s.e.})$ is nearly standard normal.

A Large Sample Test of H_0: $p_1 = p_2$

Test statistic:

$$Z = \frac{\hat{p}_1 - \hat{p}_2}{\sqrt{\hat{p}(1-\hat{p})}\sqrt{\dfrac{1}{n_1} + \dfrac{1}{n_2}}} \quad \text{where} \quad \hat{p} = \frac{X+Y}{n_1+n_2}$$

The level α rejection region are the values of Z where

$$z < -z_\alpha, \quad z > z_\alpha, \quad \text{or} \quad |z| > z_{\alpha/2}$$

according to whether the alternative hypothesis is

$$p_1 < p_2, \quad p_1 > p_2 \quad \text{or} \quad p_1 \neq p_2$$

respectively.

EXAMPLE 10.12   Conducting a Test of Hypotheses for Two Proportions

Refer to the data on cellular phone cost controls in Example 10.11. Do these data show that small businesses are more liberal in their wireless communication management in the sense that the population proportion with controls in place is smaller than the population proportion for large businesses? Test with $\alpha = .05$.

Solution and Discussion.

1. *Hypotheses.* The object of the study is to establish that $p_1 < p_2$, and this statement becomes the alternative hypothesis.

Null hypothesis	H_0: $p_1 = p_2$	or	H_0: $p_1 - p_2 = 0$
Alternative hypothesis	H_1: $p_1 < p_2$	or	H_1: $p_1 - p_2 < 0$

    We are given $\alpha = .05$.

2. *Test Statistic.* Since the sample sizes $n_1 = 100$ and $n_2 = 100$ are large, the test statistic Z has the value

    $$z = \frac{\hat{p}_1 - \hat{p}_2}{\sqrt{\hat{p}(1-\hat{p})}\sqrt{\dfrac{1}{n_1} + \dfrac{1}{n_2}}}$$

    and the alternative hypothesis is one-sided, so we reject H_0 if Z takes a large negative value.

3. *Rejection Region.* The specified $\alpha = .05$ and, from the z table, $z_{.05} = 1.645$, so the one-tailed rejection region is $z < -1.645$.

4.   *Calculation.* We calculate

$$\hat{p}_1 = \frac{47}{100} = .47, \qquad \hat{p}_2 = \frac{79}{100} = .79$$

and

$$\text{Pooled estimate of } p: \quad \hat{p} = \frac{47 + 79}{100 + 100} = .63$$

The observed value of the test statistic is

$$z = \frac{\hat{p}_1 - \hat{p}_2}{\sqrt{\hat{p}(1 - \hat{p})}\sqrt{\dfrac{1}{n_1} + \dfrac{1}{n_2}}} = \frac{.47 - .79}{\sqrt{.63\,(1 - .63)}\sqrt{\dfrac{1}{100} + \dfrac{1}{100}}} = -4.687$$

5.   *Conclusion.* The observed value of the test statistic, -4.687, falls in the rejection region. At level $\alpha = .05$, we reject the null hypothesis in favor of the alternative that the population proportion p_1 is smaller than p_2.

The *P*-value, $P(Z < -4.687)$ is smaller than .0001. The evidence against the null hypothesis H_0: $p_1 = p_2$ is very strong. We conclude that small businesses are more liberal in their wireless communication management than large businesses.

EXERCISES

10.20   Given the data

$$n_1 = 100 \qquad \hat{p}_1 = \frac{45}{100} = .45$$

$$n_2 = 200 \qquad \hat{p}_2 = \frac{130}{200} = .65$$

a.   Find a 95% confidence interval for $p_1 - p_2$.
b.   Perform the large sample Z test for testing the null hypothesis H_0: $p_1 = p_2$ versus the alternative hypothesis H_1: $p_1 < p_2$. Take $\alpha = .05$. Calculate the *P*-value and comment on its size.

10.21   Given the data

$$n_1 = 90 \qquad \hat{p}_1 = \frac{63}{90} = .70$$

$$n_2 = 80 \qquad \hat{p}_2 = \frac{28}{80} = .35$$

a.   Find a 90% confidence interval for $p_1 - p_2$.
b.   Perform the large sample Z test for testing the null hypothesis H_0: $p_1 = p_2$ versus the alternative hypothesis H_1: $p_1 > p_2$. Take $\alpha = .10$. Calculate the *P*-value and comment on its size.

10.22 Those engaged in direct-marketing by mail to consumers are interested in what proportion of persons open all of their mail as opposed to screening out everything that is not personal correspondence or bills. From a sample of 800 adult males, 414 said they usually open all of their mail. Among 900 adult females, 532 said they usually open all of their mail. (These proportions are close to those obtained in a Gallup survey.) Find a 95% confidence interval for the difference in the population proportions of adult males and adult females who open all their mail.

10.23 With reference to Example 10.2, consider the population proportion who will remember a key point after viewing Commercial A and the population proportion who will remember a key point after viewing Commercial B. Find a 95% confidence interval for the difference in population proportions.

10.24 Refer to Exercise 10.23. Perform the large sample Z test for testing the null hypothesis of equal proportions versus a two-sided alternative hypothesis. Take $\alpha = .05$. Calculate the P-value and interpret this number.

10.25 A sample of 160 small business owners from City A and a sample of 155 small business owners from City B were interviewed by phone. Each person was asked about the impact on their business of a proposed new piece of legislation. The following counts were obtained.

	Favorable	Not Favorable	
City A	71	89	160
City B	39	116	155

Establish a 95% confidence interval for the difference of population proportions.

10.26 Refer to Exercise 10.25. Test for equality of the two population proportions against a two-sided alternative. Take $\alpha = .05$. Calculate the P-value and interpret this number.

10.4 COMPARING POPULATIONS FROM TWO-WAY TABLES

We discussed arranging categorical or frequency data as two-way tables in Section 3.5. Suppose we draw a random sample of a fixed size from each of several populations, and classify each response into a category. These data can then be summarized as counts in the form of a two-way table, where the columns refer to the categories and the rows to the different populations. Our objective is to test whether the populations are alike or **homogeneous** with respect to the probabilities of the categories. That is, we need to determine whether the observed proportion for each category is nearly the same for all populations. The test is called a **test of homogeneity,** and it applies to two-way contingency tables that have one set of marginal totals fixed. Here, the fixed margin corresponds to the fixed sample size for each population that is displayed as the row total.

To indicate the issues involved in a test of homogeneity, we reproduce the data on commercials introduced in Example 10.2 and given in Table 10.1.

Remembering a Commercial

	Don't Remember	Remember Seeing	Remember Key Point	Total
Commercial A	19	24	37	80
Commercial B	24	28	18	70
Total	43	52	55	150

Now statistical inferences are based on descriptions, or models, for variation. Here, each category in a row of the table has a probability or unknown population proportion. These probabilities are given in Table 10.5.

TABLE 10.5   Probabilities for Categories of Responses to Remembering a Commercial

	Don't Remember	Remember Seeing	Remember Key Point	Total
Commercial A	p_{A1}	p_{A2}	p_{A3}	1
Commercial B	p_{B1}	p_{B2}	p_{B3}	1

The null hypothesis of "no difference in," or "homogeneity," is

$$H_0: p_{A1} = p_{B1}, p_{A2} = p_{B2}, p_{A3} = p_{B3}$$

Under the null hypothesis, let us denote these common probabilities by p_1, p_2, and p_3, respectively. For any given row, the expected cell frequency is obtained by multiplying these probabilities by the sample size. Consequently, for the first row, the expected cell frequencies are $80p_1$, $80p_2$, and $80p_3$, whereas those for the second row are $70p_1$, $70p_2$, and $70p_3$. However, the common probabilities p_1, p_2, and p_3 are not specified under H_0 and must be estimated.

The column totals 43, 52, and 55 in the "Remembering a Commercial" table are the frequency counts for the categories in the combined sample of size $70 + 80 = 150$. Under the null hypothesis that the populations are alike, the estimated probabilities for the categories are

$$\hat{p}_1 = \frac{43}{150} \qquad \hat{p}_2 = \frac{52}{150} \qquad \hat{p}_3 = \frac{55}{150}$$

Using these estimates, we calculate the expected frequencies for the first row:

$$\frac{80 \times 43}{150} \qquad \frac{80 \times 52}{150} \qquad \frac{80 \times 55}{150}$$

We get similar expressions for the second row using the sample size 70 rather than 80. Notice the expected frequency calculation has the pattern

$$\text{Expected cell frequency} = \frac{(\text{Row total}) \times (\text{Column total})}{\text{Grand total}}$$

where the grand total is the sum of all the cell frequencies.

To test the null hypothesis of like populations, we need to compare the expected cell frequencies with the frequencies actually observed. If the differences are too great, we have reason to believe the null hypothesis is false.

Let O represent an *observed* cell frequency and let E represent an *expected* cell frequency. We shall represent the difference between an observed and expected cell frequency with the discrepancy measure

$$\frac{(O - E)^2}{E}$$

The square of the difference $O - E$ in the numerator ensures that our measure is always positive and it increases as the difference increases. However, a difference of, say, $4 = O - E$ is consistent with the null hypothesis when E is large but not when it is small. We overcome this difficulty by dividing the squared difference by E. A smaller difference $O - E$ in a cell with a small expected frequency is then as important as a larger difference in a cell with a large expected frequency.

Table 10.6 gives the observed and expected frequencies for our current example. The expected frequencies are displayed in parentheses below the observed frequencies for each cell in the table. Table 10.7 contains the discrepancy measures $(O - E)^2/E$.

TABLE 10.6   Observed and Expected Frequencies for the Commercial Data

	Don't Remember	Remember Seeing	Remember Key Point	Total
Commercial A	19 (22.93)	24 (27.73)	37 (29.33)	80
Commercial B	24 (20.07)	28 (24.27)	18 (25.67)	70
Total	43	52	55	150

TABLE 10.7   Values of $(O - E)^2/E$

	Don't Remember	Remember Seeing	Remember Key Point
Commercial A	$\dfrac{(19 - 22.93)^2}{22.93} = .674$	$\dfrac{(24 - 27.73)^2}{27.73} = .502$	$\dfrac{(37 - 29.33)^2}{29.33} = 2.006$
Commercial B	$\dfrac{(24 - 20.07)^2}{20.07} = .770$	$\dfrac{(28 - 24.27)^2}{24.27} = .573$	$\dfrac{(18 - 25.67)^2}{25.67} = 2.292$

Summing the discrepancy measures over all the cells in the table gives an overall measure of homogeneity known as the **chi-square statistic,** denoted by χ^2. Thus

$$\chi^2 = \sum_{\text{cells}} \frac{(O - E)^2}{E}$$

The χ^2 value is

$$\chi^2 = .674 + .502 + 2.006$$
$$+ .770 + .573 + 2.292 = 6.817$$

Is this χ^2 value large enough to reject the null hypothesis of homogeneous populations? To answer this question, we must know the sampling distribution of the χ^2 statistic when the distributions for the two rows are the same, that is, when H_0 is true.

Now the χ^2 statistic has a number of degrees of freedom associated with it. The degrees of freedom depend on the dimension of the two-way table. In our example, each row has three categories but the sum of the counts in these categories is the fixed sample size. That is, there are only two frequency counts in each row that are free to vary. We take these to be the first two entries. This total of $(3 - 1) + (3 - 1) = 4$ free counts must be further reduced because the common probabilities were estimated to obtain the expected frequencies E that enter the χ^2 calculation. The sum of the differences $O - E$ in the first column is

$$O_{A1} - \frac{(\text{Row 1 total}) \times (\text{Column 1 total})}{\text{Grand total}} + O_{B1} - \frac{(\text{Row 2 total}) \times (\text{Column 1 total})}{\text{Grand total}}$$
$$= \text{Column 1 total} - \text{Column 1 total} = 0$$

This condition reduces the two free quantities in Column 1 by 1. The same is true for the second column, so we say that there are $(3 - 1) + (3 - 1) - 2 = 2$ degrees of freedom for the χ^2 statistic. Notice the number of degrees of freedom is equal to (No. of rows $- 1$) $\times$ (No. of columns $- 1$).

An approximate sampling distribution for the χ^2 statistic is available. This distribution is called the **chi-square distribution,** and there is a different distribution for each number of **degrees of freedom.** A typical chi-square distribution is shown in Figure 10.2. The upper 100α percentile, χ^2_α, is the value of a chi-square random variable that is exceeded with probability α. Also shown in the figure is the $100(1 - \alpha)$ percentile, $\chi^2_{1-\alpha}$.

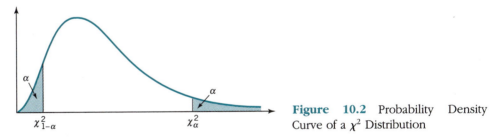

Figure 10.2 Probability Density Curve of a χ^2 Distribution

The values of χ^2_α have been tabulated in Table 5 of Appendix B for various choices of α and degrees of freedom (d.f.).

Returning to our "Remembering a Commercial" example, we see from the table of the chi-square distribution, in the column for $\alpha = .05$ and the row for 2 degrees of freedom, that the upper 5th percentile is $\chi^2_{.05} = 5.99$. Since the observed $\chi^2 = 6.817$ exceeds the upper 5th percentile, we reject the null hypothesis that the distributions are homogeneous at the $\alpha = .05$ level.

Because the large contributions to χ^2 come from the category *Remember key point,* where the relative frequency is $\frac{37}{80} = .463$ for Commercial A and $\frac{18}{70} = .257$ for Commercial B, these data suggest that Commercial A is better. The test itself concludes only that they are different.

We can think of the expected frequencies as the *fit* of the assertion of homogeneous populations to the data. In this context, the χ^2 statistic can be written

$$\sum_{\text{cells}} \frac{(\text{Observation} - \text{Fit})^2}{\text{Fit}}$$

When the expected frequencies reproduce the observed frequencies exactly, the quantity (Observation − Fit) is zero in every case, and $\chi^2 = 0$. Consequently, small values of χ^2 support the homogeneity assertion.

The maximum value of χ^2 depends on the sample size n and the size of the contingency table. The largest value of χ^2 for a table with 2 rows and/or 2 columns is n.

The χ^2 Test of Homogeneity in a Contingency Table

Null hypothesis: In each response category, the probabilities are equal for all the populations.

Test statistic:

$$\chi^2 = \sum_{\text{cells}} \frac{(O - E)^2}{E}$$

where

$O =$ Observed cell frequency

$E = \dfrac{\text{Row total} \times \text{Column total}}{\text{Grand total}}$

d.f. $= (\text{No. of rows} - 1) \times (\text{No. of columns} - 1)$

Rejection region: $\chi^2 > \chi^2_\alpha$

EXAMPLE 10.13   Testing for Homogeneity in a 2 × 2 Contingency Table

In Example 10.10, 47 out of a sample of 100 executives from small companies and 79 out of a sample of 100 executives from large companies had expense-reporting controls in place for employees' use of cellular phones. These data are arranged in Table 10.8 with 2 rows and 2 columns; expected counts are listed below observed counts.

TABLE 10.8   Contingency Table for Expense-Reporting Controls

	With Controls	Without Controls	Total
Small Businesses	47 (63)	53 (37)	100
Large Businesses	79 (63)	21 (37)	100
Total	126	74	200

Test that the populations of large and small businesses are the same with respect to controls for expense reporting. Notice that with only two response categories, testing for the homogeneity of the two populations is equivalent to testing for the equality of the two population proportions of companies that have controls in place. Use the chi-square statistic χ^2 and take $\alpha = .05$.

Solution and Discussion. Let

$$p_1 = \text{proportion of all small businesses with controls}$$
$$p_2 = \text{proportion of all large businesses with controls}$$

1. *Hypotheses.* We test the null hypothesis

$$H_0: p_1 = p_2$$

   against the alternative hypothesis

$$H_1: p_1 \neq p_2$$

   Notice that if $p_1 = p_2$, the probabilities must be equal both for having and not having controls. We are given $\alpha = .05$.

2. *Test Statistic.* For a 2×2 table, the chi-square statistic, χ^2, has $(2 - 1)(2 - 1) = 1$ degree of freedom. The test rejects H_0 for large values of χ^2.

3. *Rejection Region.* $\chi^2 > \chi^2_{.05} = 3.84$

4. *Calculation.* The expected values are already given in parentheses in Table 10.8. We calculate

$$\chi^2 = \frac{(47 - 63)^2}{63} + \frac{(53 - 37)^2}{37} + \frac{(79 - 63)^2}{63} + \frac{(21 - 37)^2}{37}$$
$$= 4.063 + 6.919 + 4.063 + 6.919 = 21.964$$

5. *Conclusion.* The null hypothesis of equality is rejected at the $\alpha = .05$ level. (The P-value is much smaller than .01.)

All four cells, by themselves, have chi-square components that exceed the critical value 3.84. The pattern of frequencies is that large firms are more likely to have expense-reporting controls.

AN EQUIVALENT METHOD OF ANALYZING 2 × 2 TABLES (OPTIONAL)

In Section 10.3, we introduced the test statistic

$$Z = \frac{\hat{p}_1 - \hat{p}_2}{\sqrt{\hat{p}(1 - \hat{p})}\sqrt{\dfrac{1}{n_1} + \dfrac{1}{n_2}}} \qquad \text{where } \hat{p} = \frac{X + Y}{n_1 + n_2}$$

for testing $H_0: p_1 = p_2$ against one- or two-sided alternatives.

Although

$$\chi^2 = \sum_{\text{cells}} \frac{(O - E)^2}{E}$$

and Z appear to be quite different test statistics, it can be shown that an exact relation holds between the two statistics. Namely,

$$Z^2 = \chi^2 \quad (\text{for } 2 \times 2 \text{ tables})$$

For two-sided alternative hypotheses, H_1: $p_1 \neq p_2$, the two procedures are equivalent. However, only Z is appropriate for one-sided alternatives. Notice, from Example 10.12, that $z^2 = (-4.687)^2 = 21.968$, which agrees, within rounding error, with 21.964, the value for the chi-square statistic obtained in Example 10.13.

EXAMPLE 10.14   Testing for the Homogeneity of Three Populations

One approach to protecting intellectual property rights within the United States is by making a challenge of imported goods under Section 337 of a tariff act. Imported goods can be challenged for infringement of a U.S. patent, copyright, or trademark. Once a Section 337 challenge is brought to the International Trade Commission, it can result in the decision that there is no violation, that the product should be excluded from being imported, or that a settlement can be worked out between the parties.* Although we would expect the largest trading partners to be involved in the highest number of cases, it is also of interest to look at the pattern of resolution. The results for 190 challenges, involving three countries, are given in Table 10.9.

TABLE 10.9   A 3 × 3 Contingency Table for Trade Violations

Country	No Violation	Settlement Agreement	Exclusion Order	Total
Germany	10	19	5	34
Japan	27	38	15	80
Taiwan	18	23	35	76

Test the null hypothesis that the distributions for disposition of cases are the same for all three countries. Use $\alpha = .05$.

Solution and Discussion.

1. *Hypotheses.* In words, H_0: The proportions in each category of disposition of cases are the same for all three countries, and H_1: The proportions in at least two of the categories are different.

2. *Test Statistic.* We will use the chi-square statistic, χ^2. There are 3 populations and 3 categories of disposition, so the statistic has $(3-1)(3-1) = 4$ degrees of freedom. We reject H_0 for large values of χ^2.

---

*John Mutti, "Intellectual property protection in the United States under Section 337." *The World Economy,* Vol. 16, 1993, pp. 339–358.

3. *Rejection Region.* From Table 5, Appendix B, $\chi^2_{.05} = 9.49$, so the null hypothesis of equality of the three populations will be rejected if $\chi^2 > 9.49$.

4. *Calculation.* A computer analysis gives the following results:

```
Expected  counts  are  printed  below  observed  counts

              C1          C2          C3      Total
     1        10          19           5         34
            9.84       14.32        9.84

     2        27          38          15         80
           23.16       33.68       23.16

     3        18          23          35         76
           22.00       32.00       22.00

Total        55          80          55        190

ChiSq =  0.003  +   1.533  +   2.382  +
         0.637  +   0.553  +   2.874  +
         0.727  +   2.531  +   7.682  =  18.922

df  =  4
```

5. *Conclusion.* The observed value $\chi^2 = 18.922$ exceeds $\chi^2_{.05} = 9.49$, so we reject the null hypothesis of homogeneity. The largest contribution to the chi-square statistic comes from the Taiwan–Exclusion order cell, where the observed count is high. This is a different pattern from Germany and Japan, which tend to have higher probabilities of settlement agreements.

The *P*-value is less than .01, since $\chi^2_{.01} = 13.21$, so the evidence against homogeneity is very strong. A computer calculation shows the *P*-value is less than .001.

We conclude that knowing the country of origin for the challenged import allows the disposition to be predicted more accurately than just using the category totals for the disposition of cases.

EXERCISES

10.27 Refer to Exercise 10.25. Using the data for Cities A and B, make a 2 × 2 table. Test H_0: $p_A = p_B$ versus H_1: $p_A \neq p_B$ at level $\alpha = .05$ using
  a. The χ^2 test
  b. (*Optional*) The Z test

10.28 Refer to Exercise 10.22. Using the data on mail opening, make a 2 × 2 table, and test for equality of the two population proportions at level $\alpha = .05$ using
  a. The χ^2 test
  b. (*Optional*) The Z test

10.29 As part of a telephone interview, a sample of 500 executives and a sample of 250 MBA students were asked to respond to the question, Should corporations become more directly involved with social problems such as homelessness, education, and drugs?*

	More Involved	Not More Involved	Not Sure
Executives	345	135	20
MBA Students	222	20	8

a. Let p_1 be the probability that an executive will answer More Involved and p_2 be the same probability for an MBA student. Ignore persons who responded Not Sure, and test H_0: $p_1 = p_2$ versus H_1: $p_1 \neq p_2$, using the χ^2 statistic with $\alpha = .05$.

b. Construct a 95% confidence interval for $p_1 - p_2$.

10.30 Refer to Exercise 10.29. Use all three categories of responses, and test for equality of the probabilities for executives and the probabilities for MBA students. Take $\alpha = .01$. Determine the P-value and comment on its size.

10.31 Refer to Example 10.14. The data on intellectual property rights challenges to imports are repeated here, with an additional row for other European countries.

Country	No Violation	Settlement Agreement	Exclusion Order	Total
Germany	10	19	5	34
Japan	27	38	15	80
Taiwan	18	23	35	76
Europe (other)	21	31	19	71

a. Is there strong evidence that the disposition of challenges is different for different countries? Test with $\alpha = .05$. Determine the P-value and comment on its size.

b. Comment on the nature of the differences.

10.32 Refer to Example 10.14. The data on intellectual property rights challenges to imports are repeated here, with an additional row for other Asian countries.

Country	No Violation	Settlement Agreement	Exclusion Order	Total
Germany	10	19	5	34
Japan	27	38	15	80
Taiwan	18	23	35	76
Asia (other)	19	16	27	62

*The resulting percentages are similar to those reported from a Harris poll conducted for *Business Week* in 1995.

    a.   Is there strong evidence that the disposition of challenges is different for different countries? Test with $\alpha = .05$. Determine the *P*-value and comment on its size.

    b.   Comment on the nature of the differences.

10.33   Samples of 50 companies from a large number of companies in each of three industry categories, I, II, and III, were selected. Each company's most recent annual return on equity was determined and the companies were cross-classified according to industry category and the magnitude of return on equity relative to a published average return on equity for all Fortune 500 firms. The results are displayed here.

	Return on Equity		
Industry Type	Above Average	Below Average	Total
I	20	30	50
II	26	24	50
III	35	15	50
Total	81	69	150

    a.   Is there strong evidence that return on equity is different for the different types of industry? Test with $\alpha = .05$.

    b.   (*Optional*) Comment on the nature of any differences, and calculate 95% confidence intervals for the three pairs of differences of the population proportions of above average return.

10.5   TESTS OF INDEPENDENCE WITH TWO-WAY TABLES

When two characteristics are observed on each subject in the sample, the data can be categorized with respect to both characteristics. For instance, a sample of employed persons can be classified according to educational level and type of job, college students can be classified according to year in school and major, and a product can be rated with respect to style and quality.

After the two characteristics are simultaneously categorized, the frequency counts can be expressed as a two-way table, but where only the total sample size is fixed. All the marginal totals are random and will vary from sample to sample. The natural question is whether the two characteristics are independently distributed in the population or whether certain levels of one characteristic tend to be associated with certain levels of the other characteristic. To answer this question, we will develop a **test of independence** for two categorized variables.

EXAMPLE 10.15   Testing for Independence of Political Affiliation and Attitude

The political affiliation–attitude data introduced in Example 3.17 are reproduced in Table 10.10 (page 530), a 2 × 3 table with 6 cells. Recall that 500 persons were questioned regarding their political affiliation and attitude toward a national health care plan.

TABLE 10.10 A 2×3 Contingency Table with Frequencies on Political Affiliation and Attitude

Affiliation	Attitude			Total
	Favor	Indifferent	Oppose	
Democrat	138	83	64	285
Republican	64	67	84	215
Total	202	150	148	500

Is a person's attitude toward the national health care program unrelated to, or statistically independent of, political affiliation? If it is related, we might conclude that Democrats tend to favor the plan, whereas Republicans tend to oppose it.

Solution and Discussion. We first reproduce the relative frequencies, obtained by dividing the cell frequencies by 500, the total number of persons classified, in Table 10.11.

TABLE 10.11 Relative Frequencies for Political Affiliation and Attitude

Affiliation	Attitude			Total
	Favor	Indifferent	Oppose	
Democrat	.276	.166	.128	.570
Republican	.128	.134	.168	.430
Total	.404	.300	.296	1.000

The marginal row totals, .570 and .430, represent the sample proportions of Democrats and Republicans, respectively. Likewise, the column marginal totals, .404, .300, and .296, show the sample proportions in the three categories of attitude.

Imagine a classification of the entire population. The unknown population proportions (i.e., the probabilities of the cells) are represented by the entries in Table 10.12, where the subscripts D and R stand for Democrat and Republican, and 1, 2, and 3 refer to the Favor, Indifferent, and Oppose categories. Table 10.12 is the population analog of Table 10.11 that shows the sample proportions. For instance:

Cell probability	$p_{D1} = P(\text{Democrat and Favor})$
Row marginal probability	$p_D = P(\text{Democrat})$
Column marginal probability	$p_1 = P(\text{Favor})$

TABLE 10.12 Cell Probabilities

	Favor	Indifferent	Oppose	Row Marginal Probability
Democrat	p_{D1}	p_{D2}	p_{D3}	p_D
Republican	p_{R1}	p_{R2}	p_{R3}	p_R
Column Marginal Probability	p_1	p_2	p_3	1

We are concerned with testing the null hypothesis that the two classifications are independent. Recall from Chapter 5 that the probability of the intersection of two independent events is the product of their probabilities. Thus, independence of the two classifications means that $p_{D1} = p_D p_1$, $p_{D2} = p_D p_2$, and so on. The null hypothesis of independence can be formalized as

H_0:   Each cell probability is the product of the corresponding pair of marginal probabilities.

To construct a χ^2 test, we must determine the expected frequencies. Under H_0, the expected cell frequencies are

$$500 p_D p_1 \qquad 500 p_D p_2 \qquad 500 p_D p_3$$
$$500 p_R p_1 \qquad 500 p_R p_2 \qquad 500 p_R p_3$$

These involve the unknown marginal probabilities that must be estimated from the data. From Table 10.10, the estimates are

$$\hat{p}_D = \frac{285}{500} \qquad \hat{p}_R = \frac{215}{500}$$

$$\hat{p}_1 = \frac{202}{500} \qquad \hat{p}_2 = \frac{150}{500} \qquad \hat{p}_3 = \frac{148}{500}$$

Using these estimated probabilities, we compute the expected frequency for each cell of Table 10.10 as

$$\frac{(\text{Row total}) \times (\text{Column total})}{\text{Grand total}}$$

For instance, in the first cell, we have

$$500 \hat{p}_D \hat{p}_1 = 500 \times \frac{285}{500} \times \frac{202}{500}$$

$$= \frac{285 \times 202}{500} = 115.14$$

Table 10.13 gives the observed frequencies with the expected frequencies shown in parentheses. The quantities $(O - E)^2/E$ are given in Table 10.14 (page 532).

TABLE 10.13   **Observed and Expected Cell Frequencies for the Data Given in Table 10.10**

	Favor	Indifferent	Oppose
Democrat	138	83	64
	(115.14)	(85.50)	(84.36)
Republican	64	67	84
	(86.86)	(64.50)	(63.64)

TABLE 10.14   Values of $(O - E)^2/E$

	Favor	Indifferent	Oppose
Democrat	4.539	.073	4.914
Republican	6.016	.097	6.514

The χ^2 value is

$$\chi^2 = \sum_{cells} \frac{(O - E)^2}{E} = 4.539 + .073 + 4.914$$
$$+ 6.016 + .097 + 6.514 = 22.153$$

Having calculated the χ^2 statistic, we must now determine its d.f.

A single random sample is distributed among the 6 cells in the table. Consequently, if we know any 5 frequencies, the 6th is determined because the sum of the cell frequencies is the fixed sample size. We say 5 of the 6 frequencies are free to vary. The total of $6 - 1$ free counts must be further reduced because some of the marginal probabilities required to compute the expected frequencies were estimated. Since $p_D + p_R = 1$ and $p_1 + p_2 + p_3 = 1$, we have really estimated $1 + 2 = 3$ parameters. Hence,

$$\text{d.f. of } \chi^2 = (\text{No. of cells}) - 1 - (\text{No. of parameters estimated})$$
$$= 6 - 1 - 3$$
$$= 2$$

With a level of significance $\alpha = .05$, the tabulated upper 5% point of χ^2 with d.f. $= 2$ is 5.99. Because the observed χ^2 is larger than the tabulated value, the null hypothesis of independence is rejected at $\alpha = .05$. In fact, it would be rejected even for $\alpha = .01$.

The results in Table 10.14 indicate that large contributions to the value of χ^2 have come from the corner cells. Moreover, comparing the observed and expected frequencies in Table 10.13, we see that support for a national health care plan draws more from the Democrats than Republicans.

From our analysis of the contingency table in Example 10.15, the **chi-square test of independence** in a general $r \times c$ contingency table is readily apparent. In fact, it is much the same as the test for homogeneity described in Section 10.4. The expected cell frequencies are determined in the same way—namely,

$$\text{Expected cell frequency} = \frac{(\text{Row total}) \times (\text{Column total})}{\text{Grand total}}$$

and the test statistic is again

$$\chi^2 = \sum_{cells} \frac{(O - E)^2}{E}$$

To determine the d.f. of χ^2 in the general case, we start with $(rc - 1)$ d.f. because there are rc cells into which a single random sample is classified. From this number, we must subtract the number of estimated parameters. The total number of estimated parameters is $(r-1)+(c-1)$ because there are $(r-1)$ free parameters among the row marginal probabilities and $(c-1)$ free parameters among the column marginal probabilities. Therefore

$$
\begin{aligned}
\text{d.f. of } \chi^2 &= rc - 1 - (r-1) - (c-1) \\
&= rc - r - c + 1 \\
&= (r-1)(c-1) \\
&= (\text{No. of rows} - 1) \times (\text{No. of columns} - 1)
\end{aligned}
$$

which is identical with the d.f. of χ^2 for testing homogeneity.

To summarize, the χ^2 test statistic, its d.f., and the rejection region for testing independence are the same as those for testing homogeneity. It is only the statement of the null hypothesis that is different between the two situations.

The Null Hypothesis of Independence

H_0: Each cell probability equals the product of the corresponding row and column marginal probabilities.

EXAMPLE 10.16 Testing for Independence of Type of Industry and Duration of Labor Contracts

In Example 10.3, we considered the duration of union contracts and asked the question, Do the durations depend on the type of industry, manufacturing or nonmanufacturing, or are the contract durations independent of the type of industry?

Recall that a sample of 400 contracts were classified according to two characteristics: duration of contract and type of industry (manufacturing or nonmanufacturing). The data in Table 10.3 are reproduced here.

Union Contracts by Duration and Type of Industry

	2 yr. or less	3 yr.	4 yr. or more	Total
Manufacturing	10	187	48	245
Nonmanufacturing	13	107	35	155
Total	23	294	83	400

Does the duration of a contract depend on the type of industry? Answer by conducting a test for independence with $\alpha = .05$.

Solution and Discussion.

1. *Hypotheses.*

    H_0: Duration of contract and type of industry are independent.

    H_1: Duration of contract and type of industry are dependent.

2. *Test Statistic.* χ^2 with $(2-1)(3-1) = 2$ degrees of freedom

3. *Rejection Region.* Since $\chi^2_{.05} = 5.99$, we reject the null hypothesis if $\chi^2 > 5.99$.

4. *Calculation.* The results of a computer calculation follow:

```
Expected  counts  are  printed  below  observed  counts

              C1          C2          C3      Total
     1        10         187          48        245
            14.09      180.07       50.84

     2        13         107          35        155
             8.91      113.93       32.16

   Total      23         294          83        400

   ChiSq =  1.186  +   0.266  +   0.158  +
            1.875  +   0.421  +   0.250  =  4.157

   df = 2
```

5. *Conclusion.* Since the observed value 4.157 does not exceed 5.99, we cannot reject the null hypothesis of independence.

The *P*-value is greater than .10. Although there is some evidence against independence, it is not strong enough to allow us to relinquish the null hypothesis that the duration of contract does not depend on the industry.

In this situation, the column totals in the last row of the table provide an estimate of the durations of union contracts. For instance, $\frac{294}{400} = .735$ estimates the probability of a 3-year duration in the population of all contracts, regardless of the industry.

SPURIOUS DEPENDENCE

A large χ^2 value suggests association between the two categorical variables; however, as we learned with correlation, we must not conclude that the two characteristics are directly related without supporting evidence. A claim of a cause-and-effect relation must demonstrate *consistency, responsiveness,* and *mechanism,* as discussed in Section 3.3.

Two characteristics may appear to be strongly related because of the common influence of a third factor that is not included in the study. In such cases, the dependence is called a **spurious dependence.** For instance, if a sample of individuals is classified in a 2 × 2 contingency table according to whether they are heavy drinkers and whether they suffer from respiratory trouble, we would probably find a high value for χ^2 and would conclude that a strong statistical association exists between drinking habit and lung condition. But the reason for the association may be that most heavy drinkers are also heavy smokers, and the smoking habit is a direct cause of respiratory trouble. This discussion should remind you of a similar warning given in Chapter 3 regarding the interpretation of a correlation coefficient between two sets of measurements.

EXERCISES

10.34 A large corporation with top end products in both the stereo home systems and musical instruments lines wants to study how the reputation of one line is associated with the reputation of the other. A sample of 543 persons is asked to rate both product lines on a three-point scale: *below average, average, above average*. The data in the form of a 3 × 3 table are given here.

		Stereo			
		Below	Average	Above	Total
Instruments	Below	25	40	65	130
	Average	16	47	98	161
	Above	52	96	114	262
	Total	93	183	277	553

a. Calculate the relative frequencies for each cell in the table. What is the relative frequency of both product lines being rated above average?

b. Perform a test of independence with $\alpha = .05$. If H_0 is rejected, comment on the pattern of dependence.

10.35 Refer to Exercise 10.34. Combine the below average and average categories for both stereo and instruments. Test for independence of the stereo rating and the instruments rating with $\alpha = .05$. Determine the P-value and comment on its size.

10.36 Refer to Example 10.16. Suppose that the sample size for the number of labor contracts was doubled to 800 but all the counts were also doubled so the relative frequencies remained the same. The results are given here.

Union Contracts by Duration and Type of Industry

	2 yr. or less	3 yr.	4 yr. or more	Total
Manufacturing	20	374	96	490
Nonmanufacturing	26	214	70	310
Total	46	588	166	800

a. Verify that the relative frequencies are the same as those in Example 10.16.

b. Calculate the expected frequencies for each cell. How do they compare with those in Example 10.16?

c. Test for independence using $\alpha = .05$. Determine the P-value and comment on its size.

d. Why is your conclusion different from that of Example 10.16?

10.37 Refer to Exercise 3.44. In that exercise a random sample of 500 households is classified according to income, number of cars owned, and household size. The counts are reproduced here.

		Number of cars	
Income	**Household size**	2 or fewer	More than 2
Less than $30,000	4 or fewer	125	100
	More than 4	15	60
$30,000 or more	4 or fewer	100	50
	More than 4	10	40

a. Construct a two-way table of income by number of cars owned for small (4 or fewer) households only. Include the marginal totals and test for independence with $\alpha = .05$.
b. Construct a two-way table of income by number of cars owned for large (more than 4) households only. Include the marginal totals and test for independence with $\alpha = .05$.
c. Discuss the nature of the apparent association between income and number of cars owned for each of the household sizes. Can you think of reasons why the association between these two variables might be different for different size households?

10.38 Refer to Exercise 3.45. A sample of 2900 patients were cross-classified according to Survival after surgery and Hospital where surgery was performed. The data are reproduced here.

Status	Hospital I	Hospital II	Total
Died	88	21	109
Survived	2112	679	2791
Total	2200	700	2900

a. Calculate the expected frequencies for each cell in the table assuming there is no association between hospital and status of patient after surgery.
b. Calculate the χ^2 statistic and test for independence. Use $\alpha = .05$.
c. Interpret your results in part **b.** Do you think the implied dependence may be spurious? (Consider the variable Condition of patient before surgery.)

10.39 A random sample of 130 business executives was classified according to age and the degree of risk aversion as measured by a psychological test. The data are summarized in the following table.

	Degree of Risk Aversion			
Age	Low	Medium	High	Total
Below 45	14	22	7	43
45–55	16	33	12	61
Over 55	5	14	7	26
Total				130

Do these data demonstrate an association between risk aversion and age? Test with $\alpha = .05$. Determine the P-value and comment on its size.

10.40 Here is a cross-tabulation from a survey of 500 women indicating average monthly expenditures on cosmetics and employment (outside the home) status.

	Employment Status			
Spend on Cosmetics	Full-time	Part-time	Not working	Total
Less than $10	30	20	60	
$10–$20	55	60	65	
Over $20	55	80	75	
Total				500

a. Compute the expected frequencies for each cell in the table assuming there is no association between expenditures and employment status.
b. Test for independence with $\alpha = .05$. Identify the two cells that contribute more than 70% to the χ^2 value.
c. Create a 2×3 table by collapsing the first two rows into one row labeled "$20 and under." Examine the association between expenditures on cosmetics and working status. Does the association appear to be stronger or weaker than that of the original table? Discuss.

10.41 Based on interviews of couples seeking divorces, a social worker compiles the following data related to the period of acquaintanceship before marriage and the duration of the marriage:

Acquaintanceship Before Marriage	Duration of Marriage		Total
	≤ 4 years	> 4 years	
Under $\frac{1}{2}$ year	11	8	19
$\frac{1}{2}$–$1\frac{1}{2}$ years	28	24	52
Over $1\frac{1}{2}$ years	21	19	40
Total	60	51	111

Perform a test to determine whether the data substantiate an association between the duration of a marriage and the period of acquaintanceship prior to marriage.

10.42 A campus newspaper polls a random sample of 350 undergraduate students and obtains the following frequency counts regarding a proposed change in dormitory regulations:

	Favor	Indifferent	Oppose	Total
Male	93	72	21	186
Female	55	79	30	164
Total	148	151	51	350

Does the proposal seem to appeal differently to male and female students? Test with $\alpha = .05$.

10.43 Refer to Table C.1 of Appendix C.
a. Construct a two-way table of the individuals who have checking and savings accounts at other banks.
b. Construct a chi-square test of independence with $\alpha = .05$. Interpret the result.

10.6 STATISTICS IN CONTEXT

We introduced a study of the customers of American Trust Bank in Section 4.6, Statistics in Context. Recall that the bank was concerned about meeting customer needs and developing strategies to increase its client base. A mail survey was conducted by the

McGuire Research Agency to collect data on (1) the demographic profiles of current bank customers, (2) customer awareness, use, and overall perception of current bank services, and (3) new bank services desired by customers.

One question, for example, asked customers to rate overall bank services on the 5-point scale

1	2	3	4	5
Excellent	Good	Acceptable	Poor	Unacceptable

As expected, only a few persons rated the service poor or unacceptable. Customers who have these opinions about their banks' service usually change banks. Much of the data from the survey were summarized in Tables 4.3–4.6.

In this section, we take a closer look at these data after reducing the data set to 505 usable responses.* Table C.1 in Appendix C contains a subset of the responses for 150 individuals.

Data on age and service rating for 505 respondents are cross-classified in Table 10.15. As we discussed previously, few respondents rated service as poor or unacceptable; consequently, we grouped the last three categories into a single service category called Acceptable.

TABLE 10.15 Overall Service Rating and Age of Customer

Age Group	Excellent	Good	Acceptable	Total
18–21	7	13	5	25
22–30	56	59	26	141
31–40	34	57	11	102
41–50	22	16	7	45
51–64	51	26	5	82
65+	88	17	5	110
Total	258	188	59	505

We first determine whether there is an association between age and rating of bank service. A computer analysis gives the accompanying printout.

The computer warns us of a low cell frequency (expected count less than 5) in the (age 18–21, acceptable) cell. This may reduce the accuracy of the chi-square distribution approximation to the sampling distribution of the test statistic. However, the value of the test statistic in this case, 73.636, is so high that there is strong evidence of association. Here, $\chi^2_{.05} = 18.31$.

Inspection of the observed values minus the expected values for the large contributions to χ^2 shows that a high proportion of the 65 and over group rate the service excellent, whereas fewer than expected rate the service good. The situation is reversed for the group aged 22 to 30. The bank is evidently doing well with seniors but needs to improve for this other group. This finding is consistent with our discussion of Table 4.6 in Section 4.6.

There is also an interesting feature to the age distribution. A density histogram, with the last age group truncated at 85 years, is given in Figure 10.3. It shows a peak located at the 22–30 age group and a long, thick tail over the older age groups, indicating a large proportion of older customers.

---

*We have eliminated the responses from those under 18 and from some other categories that, upon reflection, were not consistent with the objectives of the study.

```
Expected counts are printed below observed counts

           C1          C2          C3       Total
     1       7          13           5          25
          12.77        9.31        2.92

     2      56          59          26         141
          72.04       52.49       16.47

     3      34          57          11         102
          52.11       37.97       11.92

     4      22          16           7          45
          22.99       16.75        5.26

     5      51          26           5          82
          41.89       30.53        9.58

     6      88          17           5         110
          56.20       40.95       12.85

Total      258         188          59         505

ChiSq =   2.609 +    1.465 +    1.480 +
          3.570 +    0.807 +    5.509 +
          6.294 +    9.535 +    0.071 +
          0.043 +    0.034 +    0.578 +
          1.980 +    0.671 +    2.190 +
         17.996 +   14.008 +    4.797 = 73.636

     df = 10

  1 cells with expected counts less than 5.0.   Age
18--21, acceptable.
```

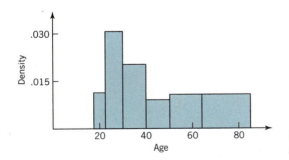

Figure 10.3 Density Histogram of Ages of American Trust's Customers

To determine the adequacy of the customer services the bank offers, data were collected on customer use of bank services at other institutions. A two-way table of the 505 responses to having a regular checking account and having a regular savings account at other institutions is given as Table 10.16 on page 540.

TABLE 10.16   Numbers of Customers with Savings and Checking Accounts at Other Institutions

	Savings	No Savings	Total
Checking	88	61	149
No Checking	184	172	356
Total	272	233	505

The marginal proportions themselves provided important information:

$$\text{Proportion with regular savings} = \frac{272}{505} = .539$$

$$\text{Proportion with regular checking} = \frac{149}{505} = .295$$

A rather high proportion of the bank's customers have savings accounts at other institutions, but a much smaller proportion of these same customers have checking accounts at other institutions.

Somewhat surprisingly, the chi-square test does not reject the null hypothesis of independence between savings and checking at other institutions, at level .05, since $\chi^2 = 2.299 < \chi^2_{.05} = 3.84$. Having a savings account at other institutions is unrelated to having a checking account at other institutions.

Additional analyses of the kind considered in this section provided American Trust with invaluable information about its customer base, use and perceptions of its services, and ideas for improving its long-term viability.

10.7   CHAPTER SUMMARY

In this chapter, we have learned:

- We can use a single response classified into only two categories to make inferences about a population proportion or probability. Inferences are based on the sample proportion

$$\hat{p} = \frac{X}{n}$$

where X is the number of successes in a random sample of size n. The sample proportion is a point estimator of the population proportion of successes, p. For n large, the statistic

$$Z = \frac{X - np}{\sqrt{n\hat{p}\hat{q}}} = \frac{\hat{p} - p}{\sqrt{\hat{p}\hat{q}/n}}$$

has a standard normal distribution, where $\sqrt{\hat{p}\hat{q}/n}$ is the estimated standard error of $\hat{p}$ and $\hat{q} = 1 - \hat{p}$.

1.   Consequently, $e = z_{\alpha/2}\sqrt{\dfrac{\hat{p}\hat{q}}{n}}$ is an approximate $100(1 - \alpha)\%$ error margin. That is, prior to sampling, the probability is approximately $(1 - \alpha)$ that the error of estimation $|\hat{p} - p|$ will be less than the error margin e.

2. The sample size required to achieve a specified error margin $e = z_{\alpha/2}\sqrt{\dfrac{pq}{n}}$ is

$$n = pq\left(\frac{z_{\alpha/2}}{e}\right)^2$$

If there is not strong prior information regarding the value of p, the product $pq = p(1-p)$ can be replaced by its maximum value of $\frac{1}{4}$.

3. A $100(1 - \alpha)\%$ confidence interval for p is given by

$$\left(\hat{p} - z_{\alpha/2}\sqrt{\frac{\hat{p}\hat{q}}{n}}, \hat{p} + z_{\alpha/2}\sqrt{\frac{\hat{p}\hat{q}}{n}}\right)$$

4. To test the hypothesis $H_0\colon p = p_0$, at significance level α, we use the statistic

$$Z = \frac{\hat{p} - p_0}{\sqrt{p_0 q_0/n}}$$

If the alternative hypothesis is two-sided, $H_1\colon p \neq p_0$, the rejection region is $z < -z_{\alpha/2}$ or $z > z_{\alpha/2}$. The one-sided rejection regions are

$$z > z_\alpha \quad \text{for the alternative } H_1\colon p > p_0$$
$$z < -z_\alpha \quad \text{for the alternative } H_1\colon p < p_0$$

● To compare proportions p_1 and p_2 from two different populations, use the difference in the sample proportions $\hat{p}_1 - \hat{p}_2$. Let $\hat{p}_1 = X/n_1$ and $\hat{p}_2 = Y/n_2$ be the sample proportions based on independent random samples of sizes n_1 and n_2 from Populations 1 and 2, respectively. Here, X is the number of successes in the first sample and Y is the number of successes in the second sample. For large samples ($n_1 > 30$ and $n_2 > 30$), the statistic

$$\frac{\hat{p}_1 - \hat{p}_2}{\text{Estimated standard error}} \quad \text{is approximately } N(0, 1),$$

where

$$\text{Estimated standard error} = \sqrt{\frac{\hat{p}_1\hat{q}_1}{n_1} + \frac{\hat{p}_2\hat{q}_2}{n_2}}$$

1. A $100(1 - \alpha)\%$ confidence interval for $p_1 - p_2$ has endpoints

$$\hat{p}_1 - \hat{p}_2 \pm z_{\alpha/2}\sqrt{\frac{\hat{p}_1\hat{q}_1}{n_1} + \frac{\hat{p}_2\hat{q}_2}{n_2}}$$

2. An α level test of $H_0\colon p_1 = p_2$ employs a modified statistic. Under H_0, there is a common population proportion p for both populations. This common proportion is estimated by the pooled estimate

$$\hat{p} = \frac{X + Y}{n_1 + n_2} = \frac{n_1\hat{p}_1 + n_2\hat{p}_2}{n_1 + n_2}$$

When the two sample sizes are large and H_0 is true

$$Z = \frac{\hat{p}_1 - \hat{p}_2}{\text{Estimated s.e.}} = \frac{\hat{p}_1 - \hat{p}_2}{\sqrt{\hat{p}(1 - \hat{p})}\sqrt{\dfrac{1}{n_1} + \dfrac{1}{n_2}}}$$

is approximately standard normal, and the rejection region is

$$z < -z_\alpha, \quad z > z_\alpha \quad \text{or} \quad |z| > z_{\alpha/2}$$

according to whether the alternative hypothesis is

$$p_1 < p_2, \quad p_1 > p_2 \quad \text{or} \quad p_1 \neq p_2$$

respectively.

- Measurements of characteristics or attributes yielding frequency data can be arranged as two-way tables. When we draw a random sample of a fixed size from each of several populations and classify each response into a category, we can test whether the populations are alike or homogeneous with respect to the probabilities of the categories. The test is called a **test of homogeneity** and employs a chi-square statistic that compares observed frequencies with expected frequencies for the cells of the two-way table.

  1. Null hypothesis: In each response category, the probabilities are equal for all the populations. (Populations are homogeneous.)
  2. Test statistic:

  $$\chi^2 = \sum_{\text{cells}} \frac{(O - E)^2}{E}$$

  where O is the observed cell frequency and E is the expected cell frequency with

  $$\text{Expected cell frequency} = \frac{(\text{Row total}) \times (\text{Column total})}{\text{Grand total}}$$

  3. Degrees of freedom (d.f.) associated with the χ^2 test statistic:

  $$\text{d.f.} = (\text{No. of rows} - 1)(\text{No. of columns} - 1)$$

  4. Rejection region: $\chi^2 > \chi_\alpha^2$

- For 2×2 tables with two populations and two response categories, the chi-square test of homogeneity and the test of the equality of two population proportions, $H_0: p_1 = p_2$, based on the Z statistic, are equivalent for two-sided alternatives. In fact, $Z^2 = \chi^2$.

- When two characteristics are observed on each subject in a single sample, the characteristics can be simultaneously categorized and the frequency counts expressed as a two-way table. Only the total sample size is fixed. A **test of independence** can be conducted to determine whether the two characteristics are independently distributed in the population. The test of independence employs a chi-square statistic that compares observed with expected frequencies for the cells of the two-way table.

  1. Null hypothesis: Each cell probability equals the product of the corresponding row and column marginal probabilities. (The characteristics are independent.)
  2. Test statistic:

  $$\chi^2 = \sum_{\text{cells}} \frac{(O - E)^2}{E}$$

  where O is the observed cell frequency and E is the expected cell frequency with

  $$\text{Expected cell frequency} = \frac{(\text{Row total}) \times (\text{Column total})}{\text{Grand total}}$$

3. Degrees of freedom (d.f.) associated with the χ^2 test statistic:

$$\text{d.f.} = (\text{No. of rows} - 1)(\text{No. of columns} - 1)$$

4. Rejection region: $\chi^2 > \chi_\alpha^2$

- The χ^2 test statistic, its d.f., and the rejection region for testing independence are the same as those for testing homogeneity. It is only the statement of the null hypothesis that is different between the two situations.

- A large χ^2 value suggests association between two categorical variables but the two variables may appear to be strongly related because of the common influence of a third factor that is not included in the study. In such cases, the dependence is called **spurious dependence.** We cannot claim two characteristics are directly related without supporting evidence.

10.8 IMPORTANT CONCEPTS AND TOOLS

CONCEPTS

Categorical data, 501
Chi-square distribution, 523
Chi-square statistic, 522
Degrees of freedom (chi-square), 523
Double blind experiment, 509
Null hypothesis of independence, 533
Spurious dependence, 534

TOOLS

Chi-square test of homogeneity, 524
Chi-square test of independence, 532
Confidence interval for a population proportion (large sample), 508
Confidence interval for $p_1 - p_2$ (large samples), 516
Point estimator of a population proportion, 506

Sample size for estimating a population proportion, 510
Tests of H_0: $p = p_0$ (large sample), 510
Tests of H_0: $p_1 = p_2$ (large samples), 518

10.9 KEY FORMULAS

INFERENCES ABOUT A POPULATION PROPORTION WHEN n IS LARGE

Parameter of interest: $p =$ the population proportion of individuals possessing a stated characteristic

Inferences are based on $\hat{p} = \dfrac{X}{n}$, the sample proportion.

i. A point estimator of p is $\hat{p}$.
   Estimated standard error $= \sqrt{\hat{p}\hat{q}/n}$, where $\hat{q} = 1 - \hat{p}$
   $100(1 - \alpha)\%$ error margin $= z_{\alpha/2}\sqrt{\hat{p}\hat{q}/n}$

ii. A $100(1 - \alpha)\%$ confidence interval for p is

$$\left(\hat{p} - z_{\alpha/2}\sqrt{\frac{\hat{p}\hat{q}}{n}}, \ \hat{p} + z_{\alpha/2}\sqrt{\frac{\hat{p}\hat{q}}{n}} \right)$$

iii. To test hypotheses about p, the test statistic is

$$Z = \frac{\hat{p} - p_0}{\sqrt{p_0 q_0/n}}$$

where p_0 is the value of p that is specified by H_0. The rejection region is right-sided, left-sided, or two-sided according to H_1: $p > p_0$, H_1: $p < p_0$, or H_1: $p \neq p_0$, respectively.

The sample size required to achieve a specified error margin $e = z_{\alpha/2}\sqrt{pq/n}$ when estimating p:

$$n = pq\left(\frac{z_{\alpha/2}}{e}\right)^2$$

If there is no strong prior information regarding the value of p, the product pq can be replaced by its maximum value of $\frac{1}{4}$.

COMPARING TWO POPULATION PROPORTIONS FOR LARGE SAMPLES

Data: X = number of successes (S) in sample of size n_1 from Population 1 with $P(S) = p_1$

Y = number of successes (S) in sample of size n_2 from Population 2 with $P(S) = p_2$

Inferences are based on the sample proportions, $\hat{p}_1 = X/n_1$ and $\hat{p}_2 = Y/n_2$, and the pooled estimate $\hat{p} = (X + Y)/(n_1 + n_2)$.

i.   A $100(1 - \alpha)\%$ confidence interval for $\hat{p}_1 - \hat{p}_2$ is

$$\hat{p}_1 - \hat{p}_2 \pm z_{\alpha/2}\sqrt{\frac{\hat{p}_1\hat{q}_1}{n_1} + \frac{\hat{p}_2\hat{q}_2}{n_2}}$$

where $\hat{q}_1 = 1 - \hat{p}_1$ and $\hat{q}_2 = 1 - \hat{p}_2$.

ii. To test H_0: $p_1 = p_2$, use the Z statistic:

$$Z = \frac{\hat{p}_1 - \hat{p}_2}{\sqrt{\hat{p}(1 - \hat{p})}\sqrt{\dfrac{1}{n_1} + \dfrac{1}{n_2}}}$$

For an α level test, the rejection region is

$$z < -z_\alpha, \quad z > z_\alpha, \quad \text{or} \quad |z| > z_{\alpha/2}$$

according to whether the alternative hypothesis is

$$p_1 < p_2, \quad p_1 > p_2, \quad \text{or} \quad p_1 \neq p_2$$

respectively.

TESTING HOMOGENEITY IN AN $r \times c$ TABLE

Data: Independent random samples from r populations, each sample classified in c response categories

Null hypothesis: In each response category, the probabilities are equal for all the populations.

Test statistic:

$$\chi^2 = \sum_{\text{cells}} \frac{(O - E)^2}{E} \qquad \text{d.f.} = (r - 1)(c - 1)$$

where for each cell

$$O = \text{Observed cell frequency}$$

$$E = \frac{(\text{Row total}) \times (\text{Column total})}{\text{Grand total}}$$

Rejection region for α level test: $\chi^2 > \chi_\alpha^2$

TESTING INDEPENDENCE IN AN $r \times c$ TABLE

Data: A random sample of size n is simultaneously classified with respect to two characteristics; one has r categories and the other c categories.

Null hypothesis: The two classifications are independent; that is, each cell probability is the product of the row and column marginal probabilities.

Test statistic and rejection region: Same as those for testing homogeneity.

Limitation: The χ^2 tests are appropriate if no expected cell frequency is too small (≥ 5 is generally required).

REVIEW EXERCISES

10.44 Suppose n units are randomly selected from a large population and x units are found to have the characteristic of interest. For each case, provide a point estimate of the population proportion, p, and determine its 95% error margin.

a. $n = 50$, $x = 32$
b. $n = 250$, $x = 63$
c. $n = 2500$, $x = 1776$

10.45 For each case in Exercise 10.44, determine a 99% error margin.

10.46 For each case in Exercise 10.44, obtain a 95% confidence interval for the population proportion.

10.47 How large a sample must be taken to be 95% sure that the error of estimation does not exceed .03 for estimating a population proportion when

a. p is known to be about .7.
b. p is unknown.

10.48 How large a sample must be taken to be 98% sure that the error of estimation does not exceed .03 when estimating a population proportion if

a. p is known to be about .3.
b. p is unknown.

10.49 Refer to the data regarding customers having checking and savings accounts at other institutions in Table 10.16. Find a 90% confidence interval for the proportion of customers having a savings account at other institutions.

10.50 Refer to the data regarding customers having checking and savings accounts at other institutions in Table 10.16. Find a 90% confidence interval for the proportion of customers having a checking account at other institutions.

10.51 Refer to the data in Table 10.15 concerning bank customers who have been cross-classified according to age and overall service rating. Find a 95% confidence interval for the proportion of customers who rate the service excellent.

10.52 An auditor wonders whether a $238,000 end-of-period balance is correct. There were 5500 transactions during the period, and three attributes are required for each transaction: an invoice for the check, an authorization signature, and a posting to the general ledger. The auditor intends to sample the transactions to verify the dollar amount and the attributes. Of immediate interest is the proportion of transactions, p, that have one or more attributes missing.

a. How large a sample must be selected to achieve a 95% error margin of .01 in estimating the population proportion p? Assume p is no larger than .05 (5%).

b. Construct a 95% confidence interval for p assuming a random sample of size $n = 300$ is selected and $x = 13$ transactions are found to be in error (one or more attributes missing).

10.53 A large university in Texas receives subvention (formula) funding from the state based on the number of students enrolled on the 12th class day of the fall semester. In a 1994 audit of 41,000 student records, 300 registration records were selected at random and 4 records were found to be in error (student reported on 12th class day but fees not paid on time, and so forth).

a. Stating any assumptions you make, construct a 95% confidence interval for the population proportion p of students with registration records in error. Is there a breakdown in an assumption that may invalidate the 95% confidence interval?

b. Calculate a point estimate of the *number* of student records in error using your estimate of the population proportion.

10.54 Local community papers, which carry few stories but lots of advertising, are circulated without charge in most areas of the country. The publishers make their money by charging the advertisers. To sell advertising space at profitable rates, the publishers must be able to verify circulation figures. One Spanish language paper was delivered to numerous sites in the San Francisco Bay area. Fifty papers were left at most drop boxes. One approach to verifying the circulation at these sites is to select a random sample of drop sites from the total of 225 drop sites and see what happens at the sample sites. The sample sites could be visited just after delivery to verify that 50 papers arrived, and visited again 3 days later to count the number of papers remaining. A random sample of 4 drop sites gives the following information.

	Papers Delivered	Papers Remaining
Site 1	50	17
Site 2	47	12
Site 3	48	7
Site 4	50	21

a. Pool the data and estimate the overall proportion, p_D, of papers that were actually delivered. Calculate an estimate of the standard error.

b. Estimate the overall proportion, p_C, of delivered papers that were circulated (removed from the box). Construct a 95% confidence interval for p_C.

c. Give a point estimate of the total circulation using

$$(\text{Number of papers for delivery}) \times \hat{p}_D \times \hat{p}_C$$

where the publisher's records show $50 \times 225 = 11{,}250$ papers were scheduled for delivery.

10.55 Refer to Exercise 5.34. Out of 120 members of the Valhalla Country Club who responded to a survey, 80 or 67% said the golfing facilities were influential, 53 or 44% said the dining facilities were influential, and 25 or 21% said that both were influential factors in their decision to join the club. Construct a two-way table of respondents' frequencies with two categories, influential and not influential, for each of the variables: golf facilities and dining facilities. Test for independence of these variables at level $\alpha = .05$. Interpret your results.

10.56   A recent *Wall Street Journal* article chronicled the trials and tribulations of ProCyte Corporation in its attempt to gain approval for a new drug, informally called BlueGoo, that seemed effective in healing nasty wounds on the feet of diabetic patients who otherwise faced amputation. Finally, ProCyte disclosed that the drug failed to outperform a placebo in its definitive Phase III clinical trial, the last step before a drug is submitted for federal approval. Within minutes, ProCyte's stock fell 68% to less than $3 a share. Some of the Phase II data ProCyte presented to get to the Phase III trial are given in the following table. Of 81 patients in the Phase II trial, 53 had large ulcers on their feet or legs and were randomly assigned to BlueGoo or the placebo, and their progress was evaluated by doctors who were "blinded"—that is, unaware of who was getting a placebo and who was getting BlueGoo. (Twenty-eight patients with smaller wounds or ulcers were ignored. Inexplicably, these people responded as well as or, in some cases, much better to a placebo.)

	BlueGoo	Placebo	Total
Healed	7	0	7
Not healed	21	25	46
Total	28	25	53

a.   Ignoring the fact that some expected frequencies may be less than 5, test for independence of Treatment and Status after treatment. Use $\alpha = .05$.

b.   Interpret the result in part **a.** Several clinical-trial experts said ProCyte should have tested these findings in a follow-up Phase II trial or abandoned the line of research altogether. Do you agree? Discuss.

BankSamp.dat

10.57   (*Minitab or similar program recommended*) Refer to the banking data in Table C.1 of Appendix C. Combine the ages into three groups, 18 to 30, 31 to 64, and 65 and over. Create a two-way table for overall service rating and age, similar to Table 10.15. Conduct a χ^2 test for independence with $\alpha = .05$. Interpret your result. (Omit the one data point with the poor (4) rating for service.)

10.58   (*Minitab or similar program recommended*) Refer to the banking data in Table C.1 of Appendix C. Construct a 90% confidence interval for the proportion of customers who rate the service excellent.

10.59   Explain the difference in the sampling schemes and classifications leading to the chi-square test for homogeneity and the chi-square test for independence.

CHAPTER OBJECTIVES

After reading this chapter, you should be able to:

- Formulate and analyze a straight-line or simple linear regression model.
- Understand the relationship between correlation and simple linear regression.
- Formulate and analyze an autoregressive model with one lagged variable.
- Model and analyze exponential growth.
- Articulate a useful model building strategy.
- Use the residuals to check the assumptions underlying the simple linear regression model.

CHAPTER ELEVEN

Simple Linear Regression

11.1 INTRODUCTION

We introduced the idea of a linear relationship between two variables in Chapter 3. Recall that the correlation coefficient measures the strength of the linear association between two variables but tells us little about its form. To describe the nature of the relationship, we proposed a mathematical expression (model) that plots as a straight line and relates a dependent or response variable y to an independent or explanatory variable x. We called the expression a simple linear regression model, and we looked at several examples of bivariate data sets for which this model seemed appropriate.

There are generally two reasons why we might be interested in expressing the relation between two (or more) variables as a statistical model. First, the magnitude(s) of the coefficient(s) in the model may be of interest for planning purposes. For example, a factory manufactures items in batches, and the production manager wishes to relate the production cost (y) of a batch to the batch size (x). Certain costs are essentially constant or fixed, regardless of batch size x. Administrative and supervisory salaries, debt service, and heating/cooling costs are some examples of fixed costs. Depreciation of plant and equipment already owned is also a fixed cost in the accounting sense. We denote the fixed costs collectively by F. Certain other costs may be directly proportional to the number of units produced—that is, variable costs. For example, the costs of raw materials and labor required to make the product fall in this category. Let C denote the variable cost of producing a single item. In the absence of any other factors, we can then expect to have the relation

$$y = F + Cx$$

or

$$y = (\text{Fixed costs}) + (\text{Variable cost})x$$

Knowing the cost coefficient C may lead to a study of the contributors to variable cost.

A second reason for developing a statistical model is that we may want to forecast the value of the response variable corresponding to a particular value of the explanatory variable. Suppose the sales (y) of a microwave dinner are to be studied in relation to its price (x), while the effects of other factors, including the prices of competing products, are to remain as constant as possible. Without any logical argument to guide us, we would collect data. An experiment may consist of setting different prices at different times and in different stores for the microwave dinner and then recording the sales of the product at these stores over a period of time. Different prices will typically produce different sales. A plot of sales versus price may indicate a downward-sloping function, with sales falling off rather dramatically as price increases. Aside from unpredictable chance variation caused by factors other than price that affect sales, the underlying form of the relation may well be represented by a straight line with a negative slope. Once this line is determined, we might be interested in predicting the sales, y, of microwave dinners at a particular store if the price, x, were increased by 5%.

As we saw in Chapter 3 and as we shall see in the following examples, scatterplots of real bivariate data sets rarely fall exactly along a straight line. The deviations from a line represent *noise*, that is, variation in y due to factors other than x. When the points in a scatterplot have the appearance of a band of roughly uniform thickness oriented with either a positive or negative slope, we need to augment the *deterministic component* $y = a + bx$ by introducing a *random component* to account for deviations from the line.

In this chapter, we emphasize the development of the simple linear, or straight-line, regression model, and discuss model-based inferences.

11.2 REGRESSION WITH A SINGLE PREDICTOR

With two variables, the observations are made in pairs of x and y values. The variable x acts as an independent or predictor variable whose values are either set by the experimenter or recorded without error from operating records, questionnaires, invoices, and so forth. The variable y depends on x but, as we have discussed in the previous examples, is subject to unaccountable variation or error.

Variable Notation

$x = $ **independent variable,** also called **predictor,** causal, or input **variable**

$y = $ **dependent** or **response variable**

It is helpful to introduce the main ideas of regression in the context of the data presented in Example 11.1. This data set will be referred to throughout this chapter.

EXAMPLE 11.1 Constructing a Model for Sales and Advertising Expenditures

A company is interested in the effectiveness of its advertising expenditures. An experiment is conducted to study how the amount spent on advertising affects the sales of a soft drink the company produces. Ten sales areas are included in the experiment. Each area spends its allocated advertising budget (in 10,000's of dollars) on a prime-time television commercial. The observations are recorded in Table 11.1, which shows the expenditures (x) and sales (y) for the 10 areas.

TABLE 11.1 Advertising Expenditures (x) in \$10,000 and Sales (y) in 1000's Units

Advertising Expenditures x	Sales y
2	8
2	4
3	10
4	7
5	11
5	15
6	19
7	16
7	23
8	20

Notice that 7 different amounts of spending are used in the experiment, and some of these are repeated for more than one area. Is there a simple model for the relation linking y with x?

Solution and Discussion.   A glance at Table 11.1 shows that y generally increases with x. A scatterplot of the data is given in Figure 11.1. The scatterplot reveals that the relationship between sales and advertising expenditures is approximately linear; that is, the points seem to cluster around a straight line with a positive slope. It is clear, however, that the points do not lie exactly on a straight line. We will return to these data after formally presenting the straight-line regression model.

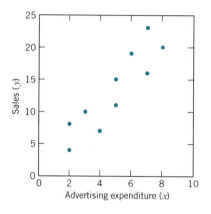

Figure 11.1   Scatterplot for the Data in Table 11.1

A linear, or straight-line, relation is the simplest relationship to handle mathematically, and we begin by presenting the details of a statistical regression analysis for this case. Other situations can often be reduced to this case by applying a suitable transformation to one or both variables, as we noted in Chapter 3 with data that exhibited exponential growth.

A MODEL FOR STRAIGHT-LINE REGRESSION

For a generic experiment, we use n to denote the sample size or the number of runs of the experiment. Each run gives a pair of observations (x, y) in which x is the fixed setting of the independent variable and y denotes the corresponding response. The different runs or pairs of observations are distinguished with a subscript. These data have the structure displayed in Table 11.2.

TABLE 11.2   Data Structure for a Regression with One Predictor

Independent Variable Setting	Response
x_1	y_1
x_2	y_2
$\vdots$	$\vdots$
x_n	y_n

Recall that if the relation between y and x is exactly a straight line, then the variables are connected by the formula

$$y = \beta_0 + \beta_1 x$$

where β_0 is the intercept of the line with the y-axis and β_1 is the slope of the line, or the change in y per unit increase in x.*

Statistical ideas must be introduced in the study of a relation between variables when the points in the scatterplot do not lie perfectly on a line, as in Figure 11.1. We think of the data in the scatterplot as observations on an underlying relation that is being masked by random disturbances or experimental error. From this viewpoint, any observation on the response y consists of the value on the line $\beta_0 + \beta_1 x$ plus a random amount ε that represents the effects of all of the uncontrolled variables and measurement error. That is, the error components ε are the noise that prevents responses y from lying exactly on a straight line. We are now in a position to formulate the straight-line or simple linear regression model.

Statistical Model for Straight-Line Regression

The response Y is a random variable that is related to the controlled, or independent, variable x by

$$Y_i = \beta_0 + \beta_1 x_i + \varepsilon_i \qquad i = 1, 2, \ldots, n$$

where

Y_i denotes the response corresponding to the ith experimental trial in which x is set at value x_i.

$\varepsilon_1, \varepsilon_2, \ldots, \varepsilon_n$ are the unknown error components that represent the deviations of the response from the true linear relation. They are unobservable random variables. We assume that they are independent and each is normally distributed with mean 0 and unknown standard deviation σ.

The coefficients or parameters β_0 and β_1, which together locate the straight line, are unknown.

According to this regression model, the observation Y_i corresponding to level x_i of the independent variable is one observation from the normal distribution with mean $\beta_0 + \beta_1 x_i$ and standard deviation σ. One interpretation of the model is that when we attempt to observe the true value on the line, nature adds the random error ε_i to this quantity. The model is illustrated in Figure 11.2 (page 554), which shows a few normal distributions for the response variable Y. All of the normal distributions have the same standard deviation σ and their means lie on the straight line $\beta_0 + \beta_1 x$. The standard

---

*In Chapter 3, we labeled these coefficients a and b, respectively (see Figure 3.9).

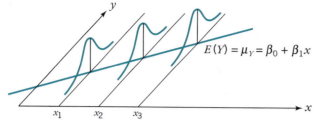

Figure 11.2 Normal Distributions of $Y_i = \beta_0 + \beta_1 x_i + \varepsilon_i$ with Means on a Straight Line

deviation σ is unknown and the line on which the means of these normal distributions are located is also unknown. In fact, one important objective of the statistical analysis is to estimate this line, called the regression line.

EXERCISES

11.1 Plot the line $y = 3 + 2x$ on graph paper by locating the points for $x = 1$ and $x = 4$. What is its intercept? What is its slope?

11.2 Identify the values of the parameters β_0, β_1, and σ in the statistical model

$$Y = 3 + 4x + \varepsilon$$

where ε is a normal random variable with mean 0 and standard deviation 5.

11.3 Identify the values of the parameters β_0, β_1, and σ in the statistical model

$$Y = 7 - 6x + \varepsilon$$

where ε is a normal random variable with mean 0 and standard deviation 4.

11.4 For the straight-line regression model:

a. Determine the mean and standard deviation of Y for $x = 3$, when $\beta_0 = 2$, $\beta_1 = 3$, and $\sigma = 1$.

b. Repeat part **a** with $x = 1$.

11.5 For the straight-line regression model:

a. Determine the mean and standard deviation of Y for $x = 1$, when $\beta_0 = 2$, $\beta_1 = 4$, and $\sigma = 3$.

b. Repeat part **a** with $x = -2$.

11.6 Graph the straight line for the means of the simple linear regression model

$$Y = \beta_0 + \beta_1 x + \varepsilon$$

where $\beta_0 = -2$, $\beta_1 = 4$, and the normal random variable ε has standard deviation 3.

11.7 Graph the straight line for the means of the simple linear regression model

$$Y = \beta_0 + \beta_1 x + \varepsilon$$

where $\beta_0 = 5$, $\beta_1 = 2$, and the normal random variable ε has standard deviation 1.

11.8 Consider the simple linear regression model

$$Y = \beta_0 + \beta_1 x + \varepsilon$$

where $\beta_0 = -2$, $\beta_1 = -1$, and ε has standard deviation 2.

a. What is the mean of the response Y when $x = 3$? When $x = 6$?

b. Will the response at $x = 3$ always be larger than the response at $x = 6$? Explain.

11.9 Consider the simple linear regression model

$$Y = \beta_0 + \beta_1 x + \varepsilon$$

where $\beta_0 = 3$, $\beta_1 = 4$, and ε has standard deviation 5.

a. What is the mean of the response Y when $x = 4$? When $x = 5$?

b. Will the response at $x = 5$ always be larger than the response at $x = 4$? Explain.

11.10 Refer to the example discussed in Section 11.1 regarding fixed and variable costs. An accountant at a manufacturing plant has separated production costs into fixed costs, such as salaries, debt service, and heating and cooling costs, and variable costs that are directly proportional to the number of units produced. Labor and raw material are variable costs. According to this separation of costs, total production cost is the sum of fixed costs plus the variable cost per unit times the number of units produced. However, unexpected variations or circumstances can affect the total production costs. For example, machines can break down, or variation in raw materials can cause production slowdowns.

a. Write a straight-line regression model to relate total costs to the number of items produced.

b. Identify the regression parameters β_0 and β_1 in terms of fixed and variable costs.

c. List one component variable that might be included in the error term ε.

11.11 A real estate investor who owns rental properties wants to update her knowledge of the competition by relating current apartment rent to apartment size in number of square feet. Larger apartments demand more rent, but other factors, such as location and number of bedrooms, contribute to variation in rent even for apartments of the same size.

a. Write a straight-line regression model to relate rent to the number of square feet.

b. Explain the meaning of the regression parameter β_1 in terms of mean rent for an additional square foot of space.

c. List a variable that might affect rent that is not included in the straight line relation and so is a component of the error term ε.

11.3 FITTING A STRAIGHT LINE BY THE METHOD OF LEAST SQUARES

Questions about the slope and intercept coefficients of the regression line can be asked, and forecasts of future values of y can be made once we are confident that the model is correct. To proceed, we first estimate the regression line or, equivalently, the parameters β_0 and β_1. The problem of estimating the regression parameters can be viewed as fitting the best straight line on the scatterplot. As we mentioned in Chapter 3, we can draw a line by eyeballing the scatterplot, but such a judgment may be open to dispute. On the other hand, the method of least squares is an objective and computationally efficient method of determining the best fitting straight line.

To review, suppose an arbitrary line $y = b_0 + b_1x$ is drawn on the scatterplot in Figure 11.3. At the value x_i of the independent variable, the y value predicted by this line is $b_0 + b_1x_i$, whereas the observed value is y_i. The discrepancy between the observed and predicted y values is then $(y_i - b_0 - b_1x_i) = d_i$, which is the vertical distance of the point from the line.

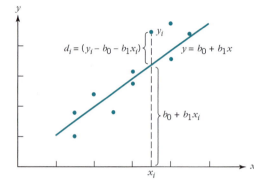

Figure 11.3   Deviations of the Observations from a Line $y = b_0 + b_1x$

Considering the discrepancies d_i at all n points, we take

$$D = \sum_{i=1}^{n} d_i^2 = \sum_{i=1}^{n}(y_i - b_0 - b_1x_i)^2$$

as an overall measure of the discrepancy of the observed points from the trial line $y = b_0 + b_1x$. The magnitude of D obviously depends on the line that is drawn. In other words, it depends on b_0 and b_1, the two quantities that determine the trial line. A good fit will make D as small as possible. We now state the **principle of least squares** in general terms to indicate its usefulness in fitting several other models.

Principle of Least Squares

Determine the values for the model parameters so that the overall discrepancy

$$D = \sum(\text{Observed response} - \text{Predicted response})^2$$

is minimized.

The parameter values thus determined are called the **least squares estimates.**

To fit a straight line then, the least squares principle involves the determination of b_0 and b_1 to minimize*

$$D = \sum_{i=1}^{n}(y_i - b_0 - b_1 x_i)^2$$

The quantities b_0 and b_1 that minimize D are denoted by $\hat{\beta}_0$ and $\hat{\beta}_1$, respectively, and are called the least squares estimates of the parameters β_0 and β_1. The hats indicate that these are estimates of the model parameters. The best fitting straight line is then given by the equation

$$\hat{y} = \hat{\beta}_0 + \hat{\beta}_1 x$$

and the smallest value for D is

$$\text{minimum } D = \sum_{i=1}^{n}(y_i - \hat{y}_i)^2 = \sum_{i=1}^{n}(y_i - \hat{\beta}_0 - \hat{\beta}_1 x_i)^2$$

The algebraic expressions for the least squares estimates of the intercept and slope coefficients of the regression line can be given using the notation introduced in Chapter 3.

Basic Notation

$$\bar{x} = \frac{1}{n}\sum x, \qquad \bar{y} = \frac{1}{n}\sum y$$

$$S_{xx} = \sum(x - \bar{x})^2 = \sum x^2 - \frac{(\sum x)^2}{n}$$

$$S_{yy} = \sum(y - \bar{y})^2 = \sum y^2 - \frac{(\sum y)^2}{n}$$

$$S_{xy} = \sum(x - \bar{x})(y - \bar{y}) = \sum xy - \frac{(\sum x)(\sum y)}{n}$$

The sample means $\bar{x}$ and $\bar{y}$, the sums of squared deviations S_{xx} and S_{yy}, and the sum of cross-products of deviations S_{xy} are the five summary statistics required for calculating the least squares estimates and handling the inference problems associated with the straight-line regression model.

---

*The algebraic expressions for the least squares coefficients can be determined with a little bit of calculus that is beyond the scope of this book.

To summarize:

Least squares estimate of β_1: $\hat{\beta}_1 = \dfrac{S_{xy}}{S_{xx}}$

Least squares estimate of β_0: $\hat{\beta}_0 = \bar{y} - \hat{\beta}_1 \bar{x}$

Fitted (or estimated) **regression line:** $\hat{y} = \hat{\beta}_0 + \hat{\beta}_1 x$

Residuals: $\hat{\varepsilon}_i = y_i - \hat{\beta}_0 - \hat{\beta}_1 x_i = y_i - \hat{y}_i \quad i = 1, 2, \ldots, n$

Recall that the residuals, $\hat{\varepsilon}_i$, are the deviations of the individual observations y_i from the fitted values $\hat{y}_i = \hat{\beta}_0 + \hat{\beta}_1 x_i$ and that a property of the least squares fit is that the sum of the residuals is always zero (see Exercise 11.22).

In Chapter 3, we introduced the identity

$$\text{Observation} = \text{Fit} + \text{Residual}$$

or, in symbols,

$$y = \hat{y} + (y - \hat{y}) = \hat{\beta}_0 + \hat{\beta}_1 x + \hat{\varepsilon}$$

Writing the simple linear regression model

$$y = \beta_0 + \beta_1 x + \varepsilon$$

and comparing the two expressions, we see that the fit may be viewed as an estimate of the deterministic part of the model and the residual as an estimate of the error or random component of the model. Consequently, the residuals can be used to check the model assumptions specified in terms of the properties of the error distribution. This important aspect of regression analysis was introduced in Chapter 3 and is discussed further in Section 11.7. For now, the sum of squares of the residuals and the associated standard deviation of the residuals are quantities of interest because they lead to estimates of the variance σ^2 and standard deviation σ of the normal distributions illustrated in Figure 11.2 (page 554).

The residual sum of squares is also called the sum of squares due to error and is abbreviated SSE. Algebraically,

$$\text{SSE} = \sum_{i=1}^{n} \hat{\varepsilon}_i^2 = S_{yy} - \frac{S_{xy}^2}{S_{xx}}$$

The second expression for SSE is useful for directly calculating SSE (see Exercise 11.20). However, we stress that it is important to determine the individual residuals for their role in checking the adequacy of the regression model.

An estimate of σ^2 is obtained by dividing SSE by its degrees of freedom, $(n - 2)$. The sample size is reduced by two because two degrees of freedom are lost from estimating the two parameters β_0 and β_1. Thus,

Estimate of σ^2: $\quad s^2 = \dfrac{\text{SSE}}{n-2}$

Estimate of σ: $\quad s = \sqrt{s^2} = \sqrt{\dfrac{\text{SSE}}{n-2}}$

In Chapter 3, we introduced s as the standard deviation of the residuals.

Regression analysis is typically done with the help of computer software but it is useful to illustrate the calculations behind some of the computer output. Example 11.2 shows how the algebraic formulas introduced in this section are used to determine the least squares line and an estimate of the error variance σ^2.

EXAMPLE 11.2 Performing a Straight-Line Regression Analysis of the Advertising–Sales Data

Obtain the least squares regression line, the residuals, and the value of SSE for the data listed in Table 11.1 and displayed in Figure 11.1.

Solution and Discussion. The computations leading to the basic quantities $\bar{x}$, $\bar{y}$, S_{xx}, S_{yy}, and S_{xy} are illustrated in Table 11.3. These quantities are then used to determine the coefficients of the least squares line, $\hat{\beta}_0$ and $\hat{\beta}_1$, SSE, and the residuals, $\hat{\varepsilon}$, given in the last column of the table.

TABLE 11.3 Computations for the Least Squares Line, SSE, and Residuals Using the Data in Table 11.1

x	y	x^2	y^2	xy	$\hat{y} = \hat{\beta}_0 + \hat{\beta}_1 x$	$\hat{\varepsilon}$
2	8	4	64	16	5.692	2.308
2	4	4	16	8	5.692	−1.692
3	10	9	100	30	8.315	1.685
4	7	16	49	28	10.939	−3.939
5	11	25	121	55	13.562	−2.562
5	15	25	225	75	13.562	1.438
6	19	36	361	114	16.186	2.814
7	16	49	256	112	18.809	−2.809
7	23	49	529	161	18.809	4.191
8	20	64	400	160	21.433	−1.433
Total 49	133	281	2121	759	132.999[a]	.001[a]

[a]Rounding error. These should be 133 and 0, respectively.

$$\bar{x} = 4.9 \qquad\qquad\qquad \bar{y} = 13.3$$

$$S_{xx} = 281 - \frac{(49)^2}{10} = 40.9 \qquad S_{yy} = 2121 - \frac{(133)^2}{10} = 352.1$$

$$S_{xy} = 759 - \frac{(49)(133)}{10} = 107.3 \qquad \text{SSE} = 352.1 - \frac{(107.3)^2}{40.9} = 70.6015$$

$$\hat{\beta}_1 = \frac{107.3}{40.9} = 2.6235 \qquad\qquad \hat{\beta}_0 = 13.3 - 2.6235 \times 4.9 = .4449$$

The least squares regression line is

$$\hat{y} = .4449 + 2.6235x$$

and the residuals are calculated from the relation

$$\hat{\varepsilon}_i = y_i - \hat{y}_i = y_i - .4449 - 2.6235x_i \qquad i = 1, \ldots, 10$$

The fitted straight line is superimposed on the scatterplot in Figure 11.4.

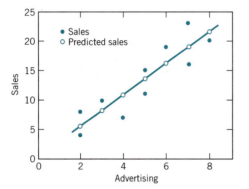

Figure 11.4 The Least Squares Regression Line for the Advertising–Sales Data in Table 11.1

Theoretically,

$$\sum_{i=1}^{n} y_i = \sum_{i=1}^{n} \hat{y}_i = 133 \quad \text{and} \quad \sum_{i=1}^{n} \hat{\varepsilon}_i = 0$$

which agrees with the results presented in Table 11.3, except for the error due to rounding.

The sum of squares of the residuals, SSE, can be calculated directly from the residuals as

$$\sum_{i=1}^{n} \hat{\varepsilon}_i^2 = (2.308)^2 + (-1.692)^2 + \cdots + (-1.433)^2 = 70.6034$$

which agrees, within rounding error, with our previous calculation. Once SSE is available, the estimate of the variance σ^2 is given by

$$s^2 = \frac{\text{SSE}}{n-2} = \frac{70.6015}{8} = 8.825$$

It seems clear from Figure 11.4 that the straight-line regression model does a fairly good job of capturing the relation between advertising expenditures and sales. If so, the fitted straight line can be used to predict sales associated with a new level of expenditure. However, our analysis is not complete until we have thoroughly checked our model.

The calculations involved in a regression analysis become increasingly tedious with larger data sets. For a complete regression analysis, access to a computer with a statistical software package is almost mandatory.

EXERCISES

11.12   Given the five pairs of (x, y) values:

x	0	1	6	3	5
y	5	4	1	3	2

    a.   Construct a scatterplot.
    b.   Calculate $\bar{x}$, $\bar{y}$, S_{xx}, S_{yy}, and S_{xy}.
    c.   Calculate the least squares estimates $\hat{\beta}_0$ and $\hat{\beta}_1$.
    d.   Determine the fitted line and draw the line on the scatterplot.

11.13   Given the six pairs of (x, y) values:

x	1	2	3	3	4	5
y	8	4	5	2	2	0

    a.   Construct a scatterplot.
    b.   Calculate $\bar{x}$, $\bar{y}$, S_{xx}, S_{yy}, and S_{xy}.
    c.   Calculate the least squares estimates $\hat{\beta}_0$ and $\hat{\beta}_1$.
    d.   Determine the fitted line and draw the line on the scatterplot.

11.14   Refer to Exercise 11.12.
    a.   Determine the residuals and verify that they sum to zero.
    b.   Calculate the residual sum of squares SSE by
       i.   adding the squares of the residuals
      ii.   using the formula $SSE = S_{yy} - S_{xy}^2 / S_{xx}$
    c.   Obtain the estimate of σ^2.

11.15   Refer to Exercise 11.13.
    a.   Determine the residuals and verify that they sum to zero.
    b.   Calculate the residual sum of squares SSE by
       i.   adding the squares of the residuals
      ii.   using the formula $SSE = S_{yy} - S_{xy}^2 / S_{xx}$
    c.   Obtain the estimate of σ^2.

11.16   Given the five pairs of (x, y) values:

x	0	1	2	3	4
y	3	2	5	6	9

    a.   Calculate $\bar{x}$, $\bar{y}$, S_{xx}, S_{yy}, and S_{xy}.
    b.   Calculate the least squares estimates $\hat{\beta}_0$ and $\hat{\beta}_1$.
    c.   Determine the fitted line.

11.17 Given the five pairs of (x, y) values:

x	0	2	3	5	7
y	4	3	6	8	9

    a.   Calculate $\bar{x}, \bar{y}, S_{xx}, S_{yy}$, and S_{xy}.

    b.   Calculate the least squares estimates $\hat{\beta}_0$ and $\hat{\beta}_1$.

    c.   Determine the fitted line.

11.18 For a data set of (x, y) values, the following summary statistics were recorded:

$$n = 16 \qquad \bar{x} = 5.4 \qquad \bar{y} = 3.2$$
$$S_{xx} = 10.2 \qquad S_{xy} = 2.76 \qquad S_{yy} = 2.03$$

    a.   Obtain the equation of the best fitting straight line.

    b.   Calculate the residual sum of squares.

    c.   Estimate σ^2.

11.19 For a data set of (x, y) values, the following summary statistics were recorded:

$$n = 15 \qquad \bar{x} = 2.3 \qquad \bar{y} = 5.1$$
$$S_{xx} = 24.15 \qquad S_{xy} = 3.21 \qquad S_{yy} = 4.82$$

    a.   Obtain the equation of the best fitting straight line.

    b.   Calculate the residual sum of squares.

    c.   Estimate σ^2.

11.20 Using the formulas for $\hat{\beta}_1$ and SSE, show that SSE can also be expressed as:

    a. $\text{SSE} = S_{yy} - \hat{\beta}_1 S_{xy}$

    b. $\text{SSE} = S_{yy} - \hat{\beta}_1^2 S_{xx}$

11.21 Referring to the formulas for $\hat{\beta}_0$ and $\hat{\beta}_1$, show that the point $(\bar{x}, \bar{y})$ always lies on the fitted regression line.

11.22 To show that the residuals always sum to zero and to verify the expression for the residual sum of squares, refer to the expressions for $\hat{\beta}_0$ and $\hat{\beta}_1$ and complete the following:

    a.   Show that the predicted values can be expressed as

$$\hat{y}_i = \bar{y} + \hat{\beta}_1(x_i - \bar{x})$$

    b.   Using part **a,** show that the residuals can be written

$$\hat{\varepsilon}_i = y_i - \hat{y}_i = (y_i - \bar{y}) - \hat{\beta}_1(x_i - \bar{x})$$

    c.   Using the second expression for $\hat{\varepsilon}_i$ in part **b,** demonstrate that $\sum \hat{\varepsilon}_i = 0$.

    d.   Squaring the second expression for $\hat{\varepsilon}_i$ in part **b** and summing, show that

$$\sum \hat{\varepsilon}_i^2 = S_{yy} + \hat{\beta}_1^2 S_{xx} - 2\hat{\beta}_1 S_{xy} = S_{yy} - S_{xy}^2 / S_{xx}$$

ApartRen.dat

11.23 (*Minitab or similar program recommended*) Refer to Exercise 11.11. The real estate investor collects the following data on a random sample of apartments on the west side of town.

Rent ($)	Size (sq. ft.)	Rent ($)	Size (sq. ft.)
720	1000	650	800
595	900	748	960
915	1200	685	650
760	810	755	970
1000	1210	815	1000
790	860	745	1000
880	1135	715	1000
845	960	885	1180

a.   Fit a straight-line regression model relating rent to apartment size in square feet.

b.   What is the estimated mean increase in rent for an additional square foot of space?

c.   Determine the error sum of squares and s^2.

11.24   Refer to Exercise 11.23. The real estate investor recorded additional data including the number of bathrooms and the number of bedrooms for the $n = 16$ apartments in Exercise 11.23 (see also Section 12.6). She fit a straight-line regression model relating rent to the number of bathrooms. A portion of the computer output is reproduced here.

```
The regression equation is
Rent = 584 + 139 No.Bath

Predictor        Coef        Stdev      t-ratio          p
Constant       584.38       71.20         8.21      0.000
No.Bath        138.59       47.76         2.90      0.012

s = 85.64          R-sq = 37.6%
```

a.   Identify the fitted line in the output.

b.   What is the change in the mean rent for an additional bathroom?

c.   Calculate s^2.

11.4   INFERENCE FOR SIMPLE LINEAR REGRESSION

By extending the ideas introduced in Chapter 8, we can give confidence intervals and test hypotheses for the slope β_1 and the intercept β_0. Since a regression line is often used for prediction, we will also give a confidence interval for the mean response and an interval estimate for an individual future observation on y, for a given value of the explanatory variable x. The interval used to predict a future observation is called a **prediction interval.**

It is important to remember that, in the straight-line regression model, the response Y is a random variable because the error ε is a random variable. The observed y at each x is simply one of a set of possible values that might have been observed. In this sense, each x defines a different subpopulation of y's. The line $\hat{y} = \hat{\beta}_0 + \hat{\beta}_1 x$ obtained by the principle of least squares is an estimate of the unknown line $E(Y) = \beta_0 + \beta_1 x$ that connects the means of these subpopulations.

In our advertising–sales problem (Example 11.2), the estimated line is

$$\hat{y} = .44 + 2.62x$$

Its slope $\beta_1 = 2.62$ suggests that the mean sales would increase by 2.62 units for each unit increase of spending on advertising. Also, if we were to estimate the mean sales when $x^* = 4.5$, or \$45,000, we would naturally use the least squares line to calculate the estimate, $.44 + 2.62 \times 4.5 = 12.23$, or 12,230 cases. Questions concerning these estimates arise at this point:

1. In light of the value 2.62 for $\hat{\beta}_1$, could the slope β_1 of the true regression line be as much as 4? Could it be 0 so that the true regression line is $E(Y) = \beta_0$, which does not depend on x? What are the plausible values for β_1?

2. How much uncertainty should be attached to the estimated sales of 12.23 corresponding to the given spending $x^* = 4.5$?

To answer these and related questions, we must know something about the **sampling distributions of the least squares estimators.** Because of the presumed normal distribution for the error term in the regression model, the relevant sampling distributions are t distributions. Consequently, interval estimates all take the form

$$\text{Estimate} \pm t_{\alpha/2}(\text{Estimated standard error})$$

where t is a percentage point of an appropriate t distribution and all hypothesis tests are based on a t statistic.

INFERENCES CONCERNING THE SLOPE β_1

Referring to our NHL example (Example 3.9), if total revenue changes, what change can we expect in operating income? For our advertising–sales example, if the amount spent on advertising changes, what change can we expect in dollar sales? Is advertising even related to sales?

If we have a straight-line regression model, these questions concern the slope coefficient. Recall that the slope measures the expected change in the response y for a unit increase in the explanatory variable x. A confidence interval provides an estimate for the magnitude of the slope. It can be constructed using the t distribution.

A $100(1 - \alpha)\%$ **confidence interval for β_1** is

$$\hat{\beta}_1 \pm t_{\alpha/2} \frac{s}{\sqrt{S_{xx}}}$$

where $t_{\alpha/2}$ is the upper $\alpha/2$ point of the t distribution with d.f. $= n - 2$.

EXAMPLE 11.3   Constructing a 95% Confidence Interval for β_1: Advertising–Sales Data

Estimate the magnitude of the slope of the regression line in the model for the advertising–sales data with a 95% confidence interval. Interpret this interval.

Solution and Discussion.   With 8 degrees of freedom, $t_{.025} = 2.306$. Using the results in Example 11.2, $\hat{\beta}_1 = 2.62$, $S_{xx} = 40.9$, and $s = 2.97$, we calculate the 95% confidence interval for β_1:

$$2.62 \pm 2.306 \times \frac{2.97}{\sqrt{40.9}} = 2.62 \pm 2.306(.46) \quad \text{or} \quad (1.56, \ 3.68)$$

We are 95% confident that if advertising spending were increased by one unit, or $10,000, the mean sales would increase somewhere between 1.56 and 3.68 units expressed in 1000's, or between 1560 and 3680 cases.

It may be of special interest to determine whether the expected response varies with the magnitude of the input variable x. If sales is unrelated to advertising, it does not make much sense to increase advertising expenditures with the hope of increasing sales.

According to the simple linear regression model,

$$\text{Expected response} = E(Y) = \mu_Y = \beta_0 + \beta_1 x$$

If $\beta_1 = 0$, the expected response is not related to the explanatory variable x. We can test the null hypothesis H_0: $\beta_1 = 0$ against a one- or a two-sided alternative, depending on the nature of the relation that is anticipated. If we reject H_0, we say the regression is significant.

If H_0: $\beta_1 = 0$ is true, the **test statistic** t with value

$$t = \frac{\hat{\beta}_1}{s/\sqrt{S_{xx}}}$$

has a t distribution with d.f. $= n - 2$.

This result provides us with a way to test H_0, as Example 11.4 illustrates.

EXAMPLE 11.4   Testing H_0: $\beta_1 = 0$ for the Advertising–Sales Data

Do the advertising–sales data in Table 11.1 constitute strong evidence that sales increase with higher levels of advertising expenditures?

Solution and Discussion.   For an increasing relation, we must have $\beta_1 > 0$. Therefore, we can test the null hypothesis H_0: $\beta_1 = 0$ against the one-sided alternative H_1: $\beta_1 > 0$. We select $\alpha = .05$. With d.f. $= 8$, $t_{.05} = 1.860$ and the rejection region is defined by $t > 1.860$. Using the results from Example 11.2, we have

$$\hat{\beta}_1 = 2.62 \qquad S_{xx} = 40.9 \qquad s = 2.97$$

The value of the test statistic is

$$t = \frac{2.62}{2.97/\sqrt{40.9}} = 5.64$$

Since the observed $t = 5.64 > 1.860$, we reject the null hypothesis at the 5% level and conclude that a positive linear relation exists between sales and advertising expenditures. The *P*-value, $P(t \geq 5.64)$, is 0 to three decimal places. There is strong evidence that higher levels of advertising expenditures increase sales.

Warning

We must be careful interpreting the test of H_0: $\beta_1 = 0$. If H_0 is not rejected, we may be tempted to conclude that y does not depend on x. Such an unqualified statement may be erroneous. First, the absence of a straight-line relation has been established only over the range of the x values in the experiment. It may be that x was not varied enough to influence y. Second, the interpretation of lack of dependence on x is valid only if our model formulation is correct. If the scatterplot indicates a relation on a curve, but we inadvertently formulate a straight-line model and test H_0: $\beta_1 = 0$, the conclusion that H_0 is not rejected should be interpreted to mean "no straight-line relation" rather than "no relation." (Recall our discussion of the sample correlation coefficient in Chapter 3.) We elaborate on this point in Section 11.5. In this section, our viewpoint is to assume the regression model is correctly formulated and to discuss the various inference problems associated with it.

To test whether β_1 is equal to a specified value β_{10}, not necessarily zero, the null hypothesis is

$$H_0: \quad \beta_1 = \beta_{10}$$

and we use the test statistic t with value

$$t = \frac{\hat{\beta}_1 - \beta_{10}}{s/\sqrt{S_{xx}}}$$

and d.f. $= n - 2$.

INFERENCES CONCERNING THE INTERCEPT β_0

Inferences similar to the ones for the slope coefficient β_1 can be provided for the intercept parameter β_0. The inference procedures are again based on the t distribution with d.f. $= n - 2$.

A $100(1 - \alpha)\%$ **confidence interval** for β_0 is

$$\hat{\beta}_0 \pm t_{\alpha/2} \, s \sqrt{\frac{1}{n} + \frac{\bar{x}^2}{S_{xx}}}$$

The null hypothesis $H_0: \beta_0 = \beta_{00}$ can be tested using the

$$\textbf{test statistic:} \quad t = \frac{\hat{\beta}_0 - \beta_{00}}{s \sqrt{\dfrac{1}{n} + \dfrac{\bar{x}^2}{S_{xx}}}} \quad \text{with d.f. } = n - 2$$

Inferences for β_0, or the intercept coefficient, are typically of less interest than those for the slope coefficient, because it is β_1, or the slope, that indicates the existence of a relationship and its strength.

EXAMPLE 11.5   Constructing a 95% Confidence Interval for β_0: Advertising–Sales Data

Construct a 95% confidence interval for β_0 using the advertising–sales data in Table 11.1 and the results in Example 11.2.

Solution and Discussion. With 8 degrees of freedom, $t_{.025} = 2.306$. Using $\hat{\beta}_0 = .44$, $\bar{x} = 4.9$, $S_{xx} = 40.9$, and $s = 2.97$, the 95% confidence interval is

$$.44 \pm 2.306 \times 2.97 \sqrt{\frac{1}{10} + \frac{(4.9)^2}{40.9}} = .44 \pm 5.68$$

or $(-5.24, \ 6.12)$.

Examining the range of values covered by the confidence interval, we see that 0 is a plausible value for β_0, suggesting that mean sales is proportional to the level of advertising expenditures. On the other hand, since β_0 represents the mean response corresponding to $x = 0$, the confidence interval also suggests that expected sales can be both positive and negative if there were no advertising expenditures. Here the value for β_0 is not estimated well. This is often the case when a regression model is fit over a set of strictly positive (or strictly negative) input variable values and then extrapolated to the origin $x = 0$. There are no data at the origin to provide information about the y-intercept.

PREDICTING THE MEAN RESPONSE FOR A SPECIFIED x VALUE

From a business perspective, an important objective in a regression study is prediction. What can we say about sales if we know what we will spend on advertising? How much rent should we charge for an apartment with a certain number of square feet if we want to be consistent with the competition? Questions like these can be answered by using the fitted function to estimate the response corresponding to a specified level of the input variable. Initially, we will concentrate on predicting the mean response. Later, we will discuss the problem of predicting a new observation.

According to the straight-line model, the mean response at a value x^* of the input variable x is given by $\beta_0 + \beta_1 x^*$. The expected response is estimated by $\hat{\beta}_0 + \hat{\beta}_1 x^*$, which is the ordinate of the fitted regression line at $x = x^*$. Inferences about the mean response at $x = x^*$ are based on the t distribution with d.f. $= n - 2$.

A $100(1 - \alpha)\%$ **confidence interval for the mean response** $\beta_0 + \beta_1 x^*$ is

$$\hat{\beta}_0 + \hat{\beta}_1 x^* \pm t_{\alpha/2}\, s \sqrt{\frac{1}{n} + \frac{(x^* - \overline{x})^2}{S_{xx}}}$$

In keeping with our general form

$$\text{Estimate} \pm t_{\alpha/2}(\text{Estimated standard error})$$

for a confidence interval, we note that the quantity

$$s \sqrt{\frac{1}{n} + \frac{(x^* - \overline{x})^2}{S_{xx}}}$$

is the estimated standard error associated with our estimate of the mean response.

EXAMPLE 11.6   Constructing Confidence Intervals for Mean Responses: Advertising–Sales Data

Again, consider the data in Table 11.1 and the results in Example 11.2. Construct a 95% confidence interval for the mean sales when the spending on advertising is (a) $x^* = 4.5$ and (b) $x^* = 9$. Interpret the intervals.

Solution and Discussion.

a.   From Example 11.2 with $x^* = 4.5$ ($\$45,000$), we have

$$\hat{\beta}_0 + \hat{\beta}_1 x^* = .44 + 2.62(4.5) = 12.23$$

or 12,230 cases. The estimated standard error associated with this prediction is

$$s \sqrt{\frac{1}{n} + \frac{(x^* - \overline{x})^2}{S_{xx}}} = 2.97 \sqrt{\frac{1}{10} + \frac{(4.5 - 4.9)^2}{40.9}} = .957$$

With 8 degrees of freedom, $t_{.025} = 2.306$, and the 95% confidence interval is

$$12.23 \pm 2.306 \times .957 = 12.23 \pm 2.21$$

or $(10.02, 14.44)$. We are 95% confident that the mean soft drink sales will be between 10,020 and 14,440 cases if $45,000 is spent on television advertising. Here, we can interpret mean sales to be the average sales if each of the population of sales areas spent exactly $45,000 on advertising.

b.   With $x^* = 9$ ($90,000), we have

$$\hat{\beta}_0 + \hat{\beta}_1 x^* = .44 + 2.62(9) = 24.02$$

or 24,020 cases with estimated standard error

$$s\sqrt{\frac{1}{n} + \frac{(x^* - \overline{x})^2}{S_{xx}}} = 2.97\sqrt{\frac{1}{10} + \frac{(9 - 4.9)^2}{40.9}} = 2.123$$

With $t_{.025} = 2.306$, the 95% confidence interval is

$$24.02 \pm 2.306 \times 2.123 = 24.02 \pm 4.90$$

or $(19.12, 28.92)$. We are 95% confident that mean sales will be between 19,120 and 28,920 cases if $90,000 is spent on advertising.

The formula for the estimated standard error of the prediction shows that, every-thing else equal, the size of the standard error increases as $(x^* - \overline{x})^2$ increases. This is confirmed in Example 11.6, where the estimated standard error of our prediction at $x^* = 9$ is more than twice the size of the corresponding quantity at $x^* = 4.5$, which is near the sample mean $\overline{x} = 4.9$. Consequently, the confidence interval associated with the former x^* is also larger. In general, prediction is more precise near the sample mean $\overline{x}$ than it is for values of the x variable that lie far from the mean.

Warning

Extreme caution should be exercised in extending a fitted regression line to make predictions far away from the range of x values covered in the experiment. The confidence interval can become so wide that predictions based on it are extremely unreliable. In addition, the nature of the relationship between the variables may change dramatically for distant values of x, and the current data provide no information with which to detect such a change. Figure 11.5 (page 570) illustrates this situation. A straight-line model may be a useful approximation with x values in the 5–10 range, but if the fitted line were extended to estimate the response at $x^* = 20$, our estimate would drastically miss the mark. (A different model would have to be considered for the larger range of x's.)

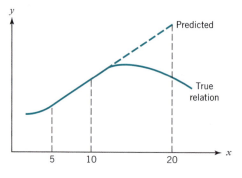

Figure 11.5 Illustration of Potential Danger in Long-range Prediction

PREDICTING A NEW RESPONSE FOR A SPECIFIED x VALUE

Imagine now that we are interested in predicting sales for a single sales area with a given level of advertising x^*. We do not care about the mean sales for all areas, only the sales for this particular area. The prediction is still determined from the fitted straight line; that is, the predicted value of the new response is $\hat{\beta}_0 + \hat{\beta}_1 x^*$. Notice that this is the same value that would be used to predict the mean response at x^*.

A prediction is not of much use without a margin of error to indicate its accuracy. The interval used to predict a new observation is called a **prediction interval.** Its form and interpretation are similar to those of a confidence interval. However, we make a distinction between a prediction interval and a confidence interval: A prediction interval is used to estimate the value of a random variable, in this case, the value of the response y, whereas a confidence interval is used to estimate an unknown constant, such as the mean response or the slope coefficient β_1.

To interpret the prediction interval for a new response, consider the following. Suppose we select a sample of n observations (x_i, y_i) and then one additional observation (x^*, y^*). Calculate, say, a 95% prediction interval for y^* based on the sample. If you were to repeat this procedure many times, 95% of the prediction intervals would contain the additional observation y^*. That is, the probability that this method produces an interval that contains the value of a new observation is .95.

The estimated standard error $s_{\hat{y}}$ used to construct the prediction interval reflects uncertainty that comes from two sources:

1. The uncertainty associated with estimating the mean at x^*, or deterministic part of the model, $\beta_0 + \beta_1 x^*$

2. The uncertainty associated with estimating the error ε

Combining these two sources of uncertainty leads to the expression

$$s_{\hat{y}} = s\sqrt{1 + \frac{1}{n} + \frac{(x^* - \overline{x})^2}{S_{xx}}}$$

Once a prediction and its estimated standard error are available, the prediction interval for the response at x^* can be constructed using a t distribution percentage point with d.f. = $n - 2$.

A $100(1 - \alpha)\%$ **prediction interval for a new response** y^* is

$$\hat{y}^* \pm t_{\alpha/2} s \sqrt{1 + \frac{1}{n} + \frac{(x^* - \overline{x})^2}{S_{xx}}}$$

where

$$\hat{y}^* = \hat{\beta}_0 + \hat{\beta}_1 x^*$$

EXAMPLE 11.7   Constructing a Prediction Interval for a New Response: Advertising–Sales Data

Consider the advertising–sales data in Table 11.1 and Example 11.2. Suppose a single area spends $x^* = 4.5$ or $45,000 dollars on advertising. Construct a 95% prediction interval for the corresponding sales in 1000's of cases. Compare this interval with the 95% confidence interval for population mean sales for this level of advertising.

Solution and Discussion.   The predicted level of sales is

$$\hat{\beta}_0 + \hat{\beta}_1 x^* = .44 + 2.62(4.5) = 12.23$$

With d.f. $= 8$, $t_{.025} = 2.306$ and the 95% prediction interval for the response at $x^* = 4.5$ is

$$12.23 \pm 2.306 \times 2.97 \sqrt{1 + \frac{1}{10} + \frac{(4.5 - 4.9)^2}{40.9}}$$

$$= 12.23 \pm 7.20 \quad \text{or} \quad (5.03, \ 19.43)$$

We estimate that sales for this area will be 5,030 to 19,430 cases if $45,000 is spent on advertising.

From Example 11.6 part **a**, the 95% confidence interval for mean sales at $x^* = 4.5$ is $(10.02, \ 14.44)$. This interval is smaller than the corresponding prediction interval. With the same data, we can estimate the mean more precisely than we can a single observation from the distribution centered at this mean.

If the number of observations is fairly large, the x values are spread out so that S_{xx} is large, and the prediction of a new observation is made at an x value close to the mean $\overline{x}$, the estimated standard error of the prediction is approximately s. In this case, the $100(1 - \alpha)\%$ prediction interval has the simple form

$$\hat{y}^* \pm t_{\alpha/2} s$$

EXAMPLE 11.8 Performing a Simple Linear Regression Analysis with Summary Statistics

In a study to determine the influence of training on the time required to do a complex assembly job, 15 new employees were given amounts of training ranging from 3 to 12 hours. After the training, their times to complete the job were recorded. Let x denote the duration of training (in hours), and let y denote the time to do the job (in minutes). The following summary statistics were obtained:

$$\bar{x} = 7.2 \qquad S_{xx} = 33.6 \qquad S_{xy} = -57.2$$

$$\bar{y} = 45.6 \qquad S_{yy} = 160.2$$

a. Determine the equation of the best fitting straight line for these data.

b. Do the data substantiate the claim that the job time decreases with more hours of training?

c. Estimate the mean job time for 9 hours of training, and construct a 95% confidence interval.

d. Predict the time to do a job y^* for $x^* = 35$ hours, and comment on the result.

Solution and Discussion.

a. The least squares estimates are

$$\hat{\beta}_1 = \frac{S_{xy}}{S_{xx}} = \frac{-57.2}{33.6} = -1.702$$

$$\hat{\beta}_0 = \bar{y} - \hat{\beta}_1\bar{x} = 45.6 - (-1.702) \times 7.2 = 57.854$$

Consequently, the equation of the best fitting line is

$$\hat{y} = 57.854 - 1.702x$$

b. To answer this question, we test H_0: $\beta_1 = 0$ versus H_1: $\beta_1 < 0$. The test statistic is

$$t = \frac{\hat{\beta}_1}{s/\sqrt{S_{xx}}}$$

Suppose we select $\alpha = .01$. With d.f. $= 13$, $t_{01} = 2.650$. In this case, the one-sided rejection region is defined by $t < -2.650$. We calculate

$$SSE = S_{yy} - \frac{S_{xy}^2}{S_{xx}} = 160.2 - \frac{(-57.2)^2}{33.6} = 62.824$$

and

$$s = \sqrt{\frac{SSE}{n-2}} = \sqrt{\frac{62.824}{13}} = 2.198$$

Thus

$$\text{Estimated s.e.}(\hat{\beta}_1) = \frac{s}{\sqrt{S_{xx}}} = \frac{2.198}{\sqrt{33.6}} = .379$$

The t statistic has the value

$$t = \frac{-1.702}{.379} = -4.49$$

Since the observed $t = -4.49 < -2.650$, H_0 is rejected at the 1% level. We conclude that increasing the duration of training significantly reduces the mean job time within the range of training times included in the experiment.

c. The mean time required to complete the assembly job corresponding to $x^* = 9$ hours of training is estimated to be

$$\hat{\beta}_0 + \hat{\beta}_1 x^* = 57.854 - 1.702(9) = 42.54 \text{ minutes}$$

and its estimated standard error is

$$s\sqrt{\frac{1}{n} + \frac{(x^* - \overline{x})^2}{S_{xx}}} = 2.198\sqrt{\frac{1}{15} + \frac{(9 - 7.2)^2}{33.6}} = .888$$

With d.f. $= 13$, $t_{.025} = 2.160$ and the required 95% confidence interval is

$$42.54 \pm 2.160 \times .888 = 42.54 \pm 1.92 \quad \text{or} \quad (40.62, \ 44.46) \text{ minutes}$$

d. Since $x^* = 35$ hours of training is far beyond the experimental range of 3 to 12 hours, predicting y for this x may not be reasonable using the fitted regression line. A formal calculation gives

$$\hat{y}^* = 57.854 - 1.702(35) = -1.72 \text{ minutes}$$

This value for the time required to complete the assembly job does not make much sense. This illustrates the potential danger of using the fitted straight line for prediction beyond the region defined by the sample observations.

Regression analyses are most conveniently done on a computer. Basic output always includes the least squares estimates of the coefficients, their estimated standard errors, the t statistics for testing that the coefficients are 0, and s^2, the estimate of σ^2.

EXERCISES

11.25 Consider a straight-line model for the five pairs of (x, y) values:

x	0	1	6	3	5
y	5	4	1	3	2

a. Calculate the least squares estimates β_0 and β_1. Also, estimate the error variance σ^2.

b. Test H_0: $\beta_1 = 0$ versus H_1: $\beta_1 \neq 0$ with $\alpha = .05$.

c. Construct a 90% confidence interval for the intercept β_0.

d. Provide a point estimate of the mean y value corresponding to $x^* = 2.5$, and construct a 90% confidence interval.

11.26 Refer to Exercise 11.25. Construct a 95% confidence interval for β_1. Interpret this interval.

11.27 Consider a straight-line model for the five pairs of (x, y) values:

x	1	2	3	4	5
y	.9	2.1	2.4	3.3	3.8

a. Calculate the least squares estimates β_0 and β_1. Also, estimate the error variance σ^2.

b. Test H_0: $\beta_1 = 1$ versus H_1: $\beta_1 \neq 1$ with $\alpha = .05$.

c. Construct a 90% confidence interval for the slope β_1.

d. Provide a point estimate of the mean y value corresponding to $x^* = 3.5$, and construct a 95% confidence interval.

11.28 The assessed values (x) and selling prices (y) for a random sample of 7 homes that recently sold in a city suburb are:

x ($1000's)	83.5	90.0	70.5	100.8	110.2	94.6	120.0
y ($1000's)	88.0	91.2	76.2	107.0	111.0	99.0	118.0

a. Construct a scatterplot of these data.

b. Determine the equation of the least squares line, and draw this line on the scatterplot.

c. Construct a 95% confidence interval for the slope of the regression line.

d. Suppose a house in the suburb currently has an assessed value of $140,000. Would you feel comfortable using the least squares line to estimate the selling price of this house? Explain.

11.29 Refer to Exercise 11.28.

a. Estimate the mean selling price of homes that are assessed at $90,000, and construct a 95% confidence interval.

b. For a single home assessed at $90,000, construct a 95% prediction interval for the selling price.

 11.30 (*Minitab or similar program recommended*) A car dealer specializing in Corvettes enlarged his facilities and offered a number of older models for sale during a spring open house. After several months, he collected data from his files on the age and selling price of the Corvettes. The data are reproduced here:

Age (yrs.)	Price ($1000's)
1	39.9
2	32.0
4	25.0
5	20.0
6	16.0
6	20.0
10	13.0
11	13.7
11	11.0
12	12.0
12	20.0
12	9.0
12	9.0
13	12.5
15	7.0

a. Construct a scatterplot of price versus age.

b. Assuming a straight-line model, determine the least squares estimates of the slope and intercept, and the equation for the fitted line.

c. Predict the price of a 19-year-old Corvette. Is there any danger in making this prediction? Explain.

11.31 In Exercise 3.13 of Chapter 3, we listed the number of employees (x) and profits per employee (y) for $n = 16$ publishing firms. Employees were recorded in 1000's and profits per employee in $1000's. The data follow, along with a portion of the computer output from a straight-line regression analysis.

OBS	Profits	Employee
1	33.5	9.4
2	31.4	6.3
3	25.0	10.7
4	23.1	7.4
5	14.2	17.1
6	11.7	21.2
7	10.8	36.8
8	10.5	28.5
9	9.8	10.7
10	9.1	9.9
11	8.5	26.1
12*	8.3	70.5
13	4.8	14.8
14	3.2	21.3
15	2.7	14.6
16	−9.5	26.8

*Dun and Bradstreet.

```
The regression equation is
Profits = 18.0 - 0.271 Employee
```

(continued)

```
Predictor          Coef        Stdev      t-ratio          p
Constant         17.954        4.457         4.03      0.001
Employee        -0.2715        0.1726       -1.57      0.138

s = 10.61          R-sq = 15.0%      R-sq(adj) = 9.0%
```

a. Identify the least squares estimates of the slope and intercept coefficients, and write the equation of the fitted line.

b. Identify s, the estimate of the error term standard deviation. Can you suggest why this quantity is sometimes called the "standard error of the estimate?" [*Hint*: Recall the form of the prediction interval for a new observation when n and S_{xx} are large.]

c. Test the hypothesis H_0: $\beta_1 = 0$ with $\alpha = .10$. Does there appear to be a relationship between profits per employee and number of employees? Discuss.

ProfitPu.dat

11.32 (*Minitab or similar program recommended*) Refer to Exercise 11.31. Observation 12 corresponds to Dun and Bradstreet. Redo the straight-line regression analysis omitting this observation. Does your conclusion in Exercise 11.31(**c**) change? What, if anything, does this imply about the influence of a single observation on a regression analysis when the number of observations is fairly small? Do you think it is reasonable to throw out Dun and Bradstreet? Explain.

11.33 In Example 3.15, we considered data on the number of pairs of telephone wires (x) and the time in hours (y) needed to splice them. An examination of the residuals from a straight-line fit to these data indicated three potential outlying observations. Let "modified x" and "modified y" refer to x and y after removing the three outliers from the data set. The Minitab output from a straight-line fit to the modified data set is shown here.

```
The regression equation is
modif y = 1.65 + 0.00202 modif x

Predictor          Coef          Stdev      t-ratio          p
Constant         1.6527         0.3706         4.46      0.000
modif x       0.0020192      0.0003225         6.26      0.000

s = 1.274          R-sq = 52.8%      R-sq(adj) = 51.5%
```

a. Determine the equation of the fitted least squares line and, consequently, verify the result in Example 3.15.

b. Construct a 90% confidence interval for the regression slope coefficient β_1.

c. You are given that the average of the modified x's is $\bar{x} = 948$. Predict the splicing time for 948 pairs of cables, and construct a 95% prediction interval for a new observation at this value of x.

11.34 (*Minitab or similar program recommended*) Data on estimated cost (x) and actual cost (y) for $n = 26$ construction projects were given in Example 3.2. The Minitab output for a straight-line fit to the bivariate data ($\ln x, \ln y$) is shown here. (See Exercises 3.29 and 3.30 for a reason for using the logarithms of the original data.)

ConsCost.dat

```
The regression equation is
LnActual = 0.003 + 0.968 LnEstim

Predictor          Coef        Stdev      t-ratio         p
Constant         0.0026       0.1625         0.02     0.987
LnEstim         0.96811      0.06583        14.71     0.000

s = 0.4121        R-sq = 90.0%       R-sq(adj) = 89.6%
```

a.   Test the hypothesis $H_0: \beta_0 = 0$ with $\alpha = .05$.

b.   Test the hypothesis $H_0: \beta_1 = 1$ with $\alpha = .05$. Calculate the P-value and comment on its size.

c.   Do your results in parts **a** and **b** suggest a simpler relationship between $\ln y$ and $\ln x$ than the standard straight-line regression model? Explain.

d.   Using the natural logarithms of the data given in Table 3.1, page 103, fit the model

$$\ln y = \beta_1(\ln x) + \varepsilon$$

Is this an adequate model for these data? Discuss.

11.35   Refer to the computer output in Exercise 11.34. You are given $\overline{\ln x} = 2.142$ and $\sum(\ln x_i - \overline{\ln x})^2 = 39.206$.

a.   Predict the actual cost for a project with an estimated cost of 10 (millions $). [*Hint:*   Predict $\ln y$ corresponding to this x and then take the antilog.]

b.   Construct a 90% confidence interval for the actual cost when $x = 10$. [*Hint:*   Construct a 90% confidence interval for $\ln y$ for this x and take the antilogs of the endpoints of the interval.]

11.5   INTERPRETING THE LINEAR RELATION

COEFFICIENT OF DETERMINATION

If all the data points lie very close to the fitted straight line, we say the linear relation is *strong*. On the other hand, if a scatterplot shows that the data points lie in a horizontal band and the slope of the fitted straight line is (approximately) 0, we say there is no linear relation or the linear relation is *weak*. A measure of the strength of the linear relation is called the **coefficient of determination,** denoted by r^2.

Consider the two fitted straight lines in Figure 11.6 (page 578). The fitted straight line in Figure 11.6(a) is horizontal ($\hat{\beta}_1 = 0$) with y-intercept $\hat{\beta}_0 = \overline{y}$. The response is not related to the independent variable. The values of y are roughly the same for all values of x. There is no linear relation, and $r^2 = 0$.

The fitted straight line in Figure 11.6(b) passes through all the data points. The response appears to be perfectly related to the independent variable. As x increases, y decreases in the pattern of a straight line. In this case, there is an exact linear relation and $r^2 = 1$. (The slope of the line is immaterial. If all the data points fell exactly along a fitted line with a positive slope, the linear relation would be perfect and, again, $r^2 = 1$.)

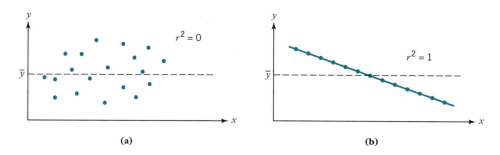

Figure 11.6   (a) Weak Linear Relation (b) Strong Linear Relation

In practice, the fitted straight line ordinarily falls between these two extremes, and r^2 takes on a value between 0 and 1. The closer r^2 is to 1, the stronger the linear relation. We would expect fitted straight lines with high r^2 to be more useful for prediction than those with very small r^2.

The coefficient of determination is developed from the basic identity

$$y = \hat{y} + (y - \hat{y})$$

or

$$\underset{\substack{\text{Observed}\\ y \text{ value}}}{y} = \underset{\substack{\text{Explained by}\\ \text{linear relation}}}{(\hat{\beta}_0 + \hat{\beta}_1 x)} + \underset{\substack{\text{Residual or}\\ \text{deviation from}\\ \text{linear relation}}}{(y - \hat{\beta}_0 - \hat{\beta}_1 x)}$$

In an ideal situation where all the points lie exactly on the line, the residuals are all zero, and the y values are completely accounted for or explained by the linear dependence on x.

Subtracting $\bar{y}$ from both sides of the previous expression, we have

$$(y - \bar{y}) = (\hat{y} - \bar{y}) + (y - \hat{y})$$

We can show algebraically that the sums of squares add:

$$\sum(y_i - \bar{y})^2 = \sum(\hat{y}_i - \bar{y})^2 + \sum(y_i - \hat{y}_i)^2$$

or

$$\text{SST} = \text{SSR} + \text{SSE}$$

where

$$\text{SST} = S_{yy} = \sum(y_i - \bar{y})^2$$

$$\text{SSR} = \sum(\hat{y}_i - \bar{y})^2$$

$$\text{SSE} = \sum(y_i - \hat{y}_i)^2$$

Here, SS stands for *sum of squares* and the T, R, and E represent *total, regression*, and *error*, respectively. We have also called SSE the residual sum of squares. These sums of squares have associated degrees of freedom

$$\text{d.f.}(\text{SST}) = n - 1$$

$$\text{d.f.}(\text{SSR}) = 1$$

$$\text{d.f.}(\text{SSE}) = n - 2$$

Corresponding to the sum of squares, the degrees of freedom are related by

$$n - 1 = 1 + (n - 2)$$

If there is no linear relation, y does not depend on x, and the variation in y is described by the sample variance

$$s_y^2 = \frac{\sum (y_i - \bar{y})^2}{n - 1}$$

If, on the other hand, y is related to x, some of the differences in the y values are due to this relationship.

The regression sum of squares, SSR, measures that part of the variation in y explained by, or due to, the linear relation. The sum of squares of the residuals, SSE, is an overall measure of the departure from linearity. Since

$$\text{SSE} = S_{yy} - \frac{S_{xy}^2}{S_{xx}}$$

we have

$$\text{SSR} = \text{SST} - \text{SSE} = S_{yy} - \left(S_{yy} - \frac{S_{xy}^2}{S_{xx}} \right) = \frac{S_{xy}^2}{S_{xx}}$$

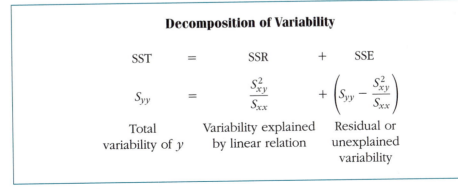

Decomposition of Variability

SST	=	SSR	+	SSE
S_{yy}	=	$\dfrac{S_{xy}^2}{S_{xx}}$	+	$\left(S_{yy} - \dfrac{S_{xy}^2}{S_{xx}} \right)$
Total variability of y		Variability explained by linear relation		Residual or unexplained variability

For the straight-line model to be considered a good fit to the data or, equivalently, for the linear relation to be strong, SSR should be a major portion of SST.

The **coefficient of determination r^2** is the ratio

$$r^2 = \frac{SSR}{SST} = 1 - \frac{SSE}{SST}$$

Since it is the ratio of a part to the whole, necessarily, $0 \le r^2 \le 1$.

If the least squares line is horizontal ($\hat{\beta}_1 = 0$, $\hat{\beta}_0 = \bar{y}$), as in Figure 11.6(a), $\hat{y} = \bar{y}$ for all x and SSR $= 0$. Consequently, $r^2 = 0$. None of the variability in y is explained by the linear relation because y does not depend linearly on x. If all the points lie on the least squares line, as in Figure 11.6(b), SSE $= 0$ and $r^2 = 1$. In this case, the (estimated) linear relationship is solely responsible for the variability in the y values.

Writing

$$r^2 = \frac{SSR}{SST} = \frac{S_{xy}^2/S_{xx}}{S_{yy}} = \frac{S_{xy}^2}{S_{xx}S_{yy}}$$

we have

$$r = \frac{S_{xy}}{\sqrt{S_{xx}S_{yy}}}$$

the sample correlation coefficient introduced in Chapter 3. The square of the sample correlation coefficient is the proportion of variability in y explained by the linear relationship with x.

EXAMPLE 11.9   Calculating r^2

Consider the data related to the influence of training on the time required to complete an assembly job discussed in Example 11.8. From the summary statistics

$$\bar{x} = 7.2 \qquad S_{xx} = 33.6 \qquad S_{xy} = -57.2$$
$$\bar{y} = 45.6 \qquad S_{yy} = 160.2$$

determine the amount of variability in y explained by the linear relationship with x.

Solution and Discussion.   We calculate

$$r^2 = \frac{S_{xy}^2}{S_{xx}S_{yy}} = \frac{(-57.2)^2}{(33.6)(160.2)} = .61$$

This means that 61% of the variability in y is explained by a straight-line model. The model seems reasonable in this respect. Here

$$r = \frac{S_{xy}}{\sqrt{S_{xx}S_{yy}}} = \frac{-57.2}{\sqrt{(33.6)(160.2)}} = -.78 = -\sqrt{r^2}$$

If r is calculated from r^2, it must have the sign of S_{xy}.

When r^2 is small, we can conclude only that a straight-line relation does not give a good fit to the data. This case may arise for the following reasons:

1. There is little relation between the variables in the sense that the scatterplot fails to exhibit any pattern, as illustrated in Figure 11.7(a). In this case, the use of a different regression model is not likely to reduce SSE or to explain a substantial proportion of SST.

2. There is a prominent relation, but it is nonlinear in nature; that is, the scatter is banded around a curve rather than a line. The part of SST explained by the straight-line regression is small because the model is inappropriate. Some other relationship may improve the fit substantially. Figure 11.7(b) illustrates such a case, where SSE can be reduced by fitting a suitable curve to the data.

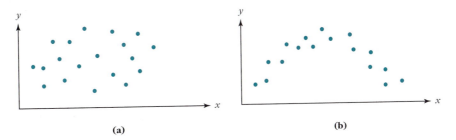

(a)   (b)

Figure 11.7   Scatterplot Patterns: (a) No Relation; (b) A Nonlinear Relation

ANALYSIS OF VARIANCE

In Chapter 9, we introduced the analysis of variance (ANOVA) when we were studying the equality of several population means. The total variability was divided into explained (treatment) and unexplained (error) variability. The sums of squares representing these quantities and their degrees of freedom were set out in an analysis of variance table. The table also contained a mean square (MS) column, where the mean square is given by the general formula

$$MS = \frac{\text{Sum of squares}}{\text{Degrees of freedom}}$$

Finally, an F ratio was listed that could be used to carry out a hypothesis test for the equality of the population means.

The analysis of variance is a general procedure. It can be used in regression analysis to determine whether the response is related to the independent variable(s). If we conclude that a relationship exists, we say that the *regression is significant*. For a straight-line regression model, the significance of the regression is equivalent to testing the null hypothesis H_0: $\beta_1 = 0$ against the alternative, H_1: $\beta_1 \neq 0$. If we reject H_0, we conclude the regression is significant.

The ANOVA procedure for determining the significance of the regression is based on the sums of squares SST, SSR, and SSE, and their degrees of freedom.

Analysis of Variance for Straight-Line Regression

Sum of squares decomposition: SST = SSR + SSE

Degrees of freedom decomposition: $n - 1 = 1 + (n - 2)$

Mean squares: $\text{MSR} = \dfrac{\text{SSR}}{1}$ $\quad$ $\text{MSE} = \dfrac{\text{SSE}}{n - 2} = s^2$

F ratio: $F = \dfrac{\text{MSR}}{\text{MSE}} = \dfrac{\text{MSR}}{s^2}$

Recall that the mean square error, $\text{MSE} = s^2$, estimates σ^2.

The analysis of variance for regression can be organized as a table, called the analysis of variance table, or ANOVA table (see Table 11.4). If a statistical software package is used for regression analysis, an ANOVA table is typically part of the output.

TABLE 11.4 The ANOVA Table for Straight-Line Regression

Source	Sum of Squares	d.f.	Mean Square	F ratio
Regression	SSR	1	MSR = SSR/1	$F = \text{MSR}/\text{MSE}$
Error	SSE	$n - 2$	MSE = SSE/$(n - 2)$	
Total	SST	$n - 1$		

If the assumptions for the error term distribution in the regression model are appropriate and if the null hypothesis H_0: $\beta_1 = 0$ is true, the ratio

$$F = \frac{\text{Regression mean square}}{\text{Error mean square}} = \frac{\text{MSR}}{\text{MSE}}$$

has an F distribution with d.f. $= (1, n - 2)$. Consequently, the F ratio can be used to test for the significance of the regression.

F Test for the Significance of the Regression

In the straight-line regression model, the test of hypotheses

$$H_0: \beta_1 = 0 \quad \text{versus} \quad H_1: \beta_1 \neq 0$$

is based on the F ratio

$$F = \frac{\text{MSR}}{\text{MSE}}$$

with d.f. $= (1, n-2)$. At level α, the rejection region is

$$F > F_\alpha(1, n-2)$$

In our discussion of inferences for the slope coefficient β_1, we presented a t statistic that could be used to test $H_0: \beta_1 = 0$ versus $H_1: \beta_1 \neq 0$. We see that the F ratio tests the same hypotheses. For simple linear regression, the two tests are equivalent. The t version of the test has the advantage of allowing us to more easily test one-sided alternatives. It is also closely related to the confidence interval for β_1. However, as we shall see in Chapter 12, the F test can be extended to check the significance of regression models with more than one independent variable.

P-values associated with both the calculated F and t statistics discussed above are also typically printed as part of the output from software packages that perform regression analyses. Interpreting the P-values as observed significance levels, we can determine at a glance whether the F and t values are large enough to reject H_0.

EXAMPLE 11.10   Interpreting an ANOVA Table

The Minitab output for a straight-line fit to the advertising–sales data in Table 11.1, including the ANOVA table (see Table 11.4), is reproduced here.

```
The regression equation is
Sales = 0.44 + 2.62 Advertis

Predictor         Coef        Stdev     t-ratio          p
Constant         0.445        2.462        0.18      0.861
Advertis        2.6235       0.4645        5.65      0.000

s = 2.971       R-sq = 79.9%      R-sq(adj) = 77.4%

Analysis of Variance
```

SOURCE	DF	SS	MS	F	p
Regression	1	281.50	281.50	31.90	0.000
Error	8	70.60	8.83		
Total	9	352.10			

Show that $r^2 = .799$. Verify that $F = 31.90 = t^2$, and interpret the P-value. Demonstrate that $s = 2.971$.

Solution and Discussion.   From the ANOVA table

$$r^2 = \frac{SSR}{SST} = \frac{281.5}{352.1} = .799 = 1 - \frac{SSE}{SST} = 1 - \frac{70.6}{352.1}$$

$$F = \frac{MSR}{MSE} = \frac{SSR/1}{SSE/8} = \frac{281.5}{8.825} = 31.90$$

Also

$$F = 31.90 = (5.648)^2 = t^2$$

where

$$t = \frac{\text{Coefficient}}{\text{Standard deviation}} = \frac{2.6235}{.4645} = 5.648$$

is the t statistic associated with the slope coefficient.

The P-value $= .000$ following the F ratio is the probability of observing an F value this large if the null hypothesis H_0: $\beta_1 = 0$ is true. This extremely small probability overwhelmingly suggests that $\beta_1 \neq 0$ and, consequently, that the regression is significant.

Finally, the error variance σ^2 in the regression model is estimated by the mean square error $s^2 = MSE = 8.83$. The estimated standard deviation is $s = \sqrt{s^2} = \sqrt{8.83} = 2.97$. The estimated standard deviation provides an indication of the variability of the response, and, if the sample size is large, can be used directly to calculate a prediction interval for a new observation y.

CORRELATION AND REGRESSION (OPTIONAL)

The correlation coefficient measures the strength and direction of the linear association between two variables. However, unlike simple linear regression, correlation does not require that one of the variables be identified as a response variable and the other variable as an explanatory or predictor variable.

An economist may be interested in the strength of the association between the economies of Canada and the United States. Using the major stock exchange indices of the two countries as measures of their economies, the economist calculates the correlation between changes in the Canadian index and changes in the U.S. index. She is interested only in a measure of the association and not in a model that links one index as the response with the other index as the predictor variable.

The owner of a small business is interested in the strength of the association between health care costs per employee and company size as measured by total sales. He wonders whether health care costs per employee tend to decrease as company size increases. He is not interested in modeling the relationship and is concerned only with the correlation.

For these two scenarios, the correlation can be determined from a sample of time periods, in the case of the economist, and from a sample of firms, in the case of the small business owner. The calculation and interpretation of the sample correlation r were discussed in Chapter 3. But what can we say about the correlation in the populations from which the samples were selected?

The correlation between two variables x and y measured for every experimental unit in the population is called the **population correlation,** denoted by the Greek letter ρ. The sample correlation r is an estimate of the population correlation. If $\rho = 0$, there is no linear association in the population, and we would expect the sample correlation r to be close to zero. In general, inferences about ρ can be based on r.

Keep in mind that no correlation means no straight-line association; it does not necessarily mean there is no association of any kind. However, for the special case where the variables X and Y are both normally distributed,* no correlation is equivalent to no association of any kind, that is, X and Y are independent. For this reason, the hypothesis H_0: $\rho = 0$ is of particular interest for two characteristics whose population distributions are normal. A test of H_0: $\rho = 0$ can be based on a t statistic.

---

t Test for Zero Population Correlation

For normal populations, the hypothesis H_0: $\rho = 0$ can be tested using the test statistic with value

$$t = \frac{r\sqrt{n-2}}{\sqrt{1-r^2}}$$

where r is the sample correlation coefficient and n is the sample size. At level α, the rejection regions are defined by

$$H_1: \quad \rho > 0 \qquad t > t_\alpha$$
$$H_1: \quad \rho < 0 \qquad t < -t_\alpha$$
$$H_1: \quad \rho \neq 0 \qquad t > t_{\alpha/2} \quad \text{or} \quad t < -t_{\alpha/2}$$

where the t percentage point is based on d.f. = $n - 2$.

If an explanatory–response relation has been formulated, there is a close connection between correlation and simple linear regression. We have already established that the square of the sample correlation, r^2, is the proportion of variation in the response explained by the estimated linear relation. As we pointed out in Chapter 3, the sample correlation r and the slope $\hat{\beta}_1$ of the least squares line are related. Recall

$$\hat{\beta}_1 = r\frac{\sqrt{S_{yy}}}{\sqrt{S_{xx}}}$$

---

*Actually, the requirement is that X and Y be *jointly normal.* This means that the distribution of X is normal and the conditional distribution of Y for any fixed value of X is normal.

Consequently, since $S_{xx} > 0$ and $S_{yy} > 0$, $\hat{\beta}_1 = 0$ if $r = 0$ and vice versa.

It should not be surprising then that the tests of H_0: $\beta_1 = 0$ and H_0: $\rho = 0$ are related. With a little bit of algebra, one can demonstrate the identity

$$\frac{\hat{\beta}_1}{s/\sqrt{S_{xx}}} = \frac{r\sqrt{n-2}}{\sqrt{1-r^2}}$$

so the t statistics for testing H_0: $\beta_1 = 0$ and H_0: $\rho = 0$ are the same. Testing for the significance of a straight-line relation is equivalent to testing for nonzero linear association.

Significance tests tell us whether there is enough evidence in the data to conclude that β_1 or ρ is different from 0. However, it is the actual sizes of these coefficients that are of most interest. Confidence intervals can be used to estimate the actual sizes of the population coefficients. A confidence interval for β_1 can be easily constructed from the output supplied by most statistical software packages. However, most software packages do not perform the calculations required to construct a confidence interval for the population correlation coefficient. Since it is extremely tedious to calculate by hand, we do not give the method in this book.

EXAMPLE 11.11   Testing for Significant Correlation

In a competitive market, competing brands take market shares from one another. In a study of the effectiveness of a new advertising strategy by a major manufacturer of toothpaste, the weekly market shares for the manufacturer's brand (Crest) and a rival brand (Colgate) were determined for several years. A scatterplot of the weekly changes in Colgate market share and weekly changes in Crest market share is shown here. (The changes or differences in the market share of Colgate are labeled DiffColg, and the changes or differences in the market share of Crest are labeled DiffCres.) The changes in market shares were recorded during a period that included the start of the advertising campaign.

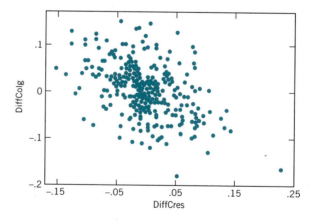

Was the advertising effective? Measure the direction and strength of the association between the market shares. Fit a simple linear regression model with the change (difference) in Colgate market share as the response and the change (difference) in Crest market share as the predictor variable.

Test $H_0: \rho = 0$ versus $H_1: \rho < 0$ with $\alpha = .05$. Demonstrate that the t values for testing $H_0: \rho = 0$ and $H_0: \beta_1 = 0$ are identical.

Solution and Discussion.   Minitab output giving the sample correlation coefficient r and the results of a linear regression analysis* is reproduced here, with $r = -.423$, $n = 275$, $\hat{\beta}_1 = -.44235$, and $s = .05295$.

```
Correlation of DiffColg and DiffCres = -0.423

The regression equation is
DiffColg = -0.00047 - 0.442 DiffCres

275 cases used 1 cases contain missing values

Predictor        Coef        Stdev      t-ratio          p
Constant     -0.000472     0.003194       -0.15      0.883
DiffCres      -0.44235     0.05741        -7.71      0.000

s = 0.05295     R-sq = 17.9%     R-sq(adj) = 17.6%

Analysis of Variance

SOURCE         DF           SS          MS         F         p
Regression      1      0.16647     0.16647     59.37     0.000
Error         273      0.76548     0.00280
Total         274      0.93194
```

The association between the changes in market shares is negative and fairly strong. A positive change in the Crest market share is associated with a negative change in the Colgate market share. Crest seems to be taking market share from Colgate. Since these two brands dominated the toothpaste market at the time of the data collection, the new advertising strategy was effective. This conclusion is reinforced by the fitted straight line with a negative slope coefficient.

The value of the test statistic for testing $H_0: \rho = 0$ is

$$t = \frac{-.423\sqrt{273}}{\sqrt{1 - (-.423)^2}} = -7.71$$

With $n - 2 = 273$ degrees of freedom, the t distribution is indistinguishable from the standard normal distribution. Thus $t_{.05} = z_{.05} = 1.645$. Since

$$t = -7.71 < -1.645 = -z_{.05}$$

---

*The intercept coefficient β_0 is not needed in the regression model. We fit a straight-line model with an intercept to illustrate the relation between a test for a significant slope coefficient and the test for a significant correlation coefficient.

we reject H_0: $\rho = 0$ in favor of H_1: $\rho < 0$ at the 5% level, and conclude that there is a negative linear association between the market shares. The P-value of the observed test statistic is 0 to three decimal places, so the evidence against H_0 is strong.

The value of the t statistic for testing H_0: $\beta_1 = 0$ is

$$t = \frac{\hat{\beta}_1}{s/\sqrt{S_{xx}}} = \frac{-.44235}{.05741} = -7.71$$

which is the t ratio from the Minitab output. This is the value of the test statistic t for testing H_0: $\rho = 0$, and we reach the same conclusion. That is, since

$$t = -7.71 < -1.645 = -z_{.05}$$

we reject H_0: $\beta_1 = 0$ in favor of H_1: $\beta_1 < 0$, and conclude that there is a negative linear relation between the changes in market shares.

EXERCISES

11.36 The following summary statistics were recorded from a data set of (x, y) values:

$$n = 14 \qquad \bar{x} = 1.2 \qquad \bar{y} = 5.1$$
$$S_{xx} = 14.10 \qquad S_{xy} = 2.31 \qquad S_{yy} = 2.01$$

   a. Determine the proportion of the variation in y that is explained by the simple linear regression.
   b. Determine the sample correlation coefficient r.

11.37 Refer to Exercise 11.36. Construct the ANOVA table for the simple linear regression. Include columns for the source, sum of squares, degrees of freedom, mean square, and F ratio.

11.38 A simple linear regression analysis produces the summary statistics:

$$n = 33 \qquad \bar{x} = 22 \qquad \bar{y} = 15$$
$$S_{xx} = 92 \qquad S_{xy} = -160 \qquad S_{yy} = 457$$

   a. Determine the proportion of the variation in y that is explained by the simple linear regression.
   b. Determine the sample correlation coefficient r.

11.39 Refer to Exercise 11.38. Construct the ANOVA table for the simple linear regression. Include columns for the source, sum of squares, degrees of freedom, mean square, and F ratio.

11.40 Given the numbers $S_{xx} = 10.1$, $S_{yy} = 16.5$, and $S_{xy} = 9.3$, determine the proportion of the variation in y that is explained by the simple linear regression. Determine the sample correlation coefficient r.

11.41   (*Optional*) Refer to Exercise 11.25.

    a.   What proportion of the variability in y is explained by the linear regression on x?

    b.   Calculate the sample correlation coefficient.

    c.   Test H_0: $\rho = 0$ versus H_1: $\rho \neq 0$ with $\alpha = .05$.

11.42   (*Optional*) Refer to Exercise 11.28 with the data on assessed values and selling prices for $n = 7$ homes.

    a.   What proportion of the variability in y is explained by the linear regression on x?

    b.   Calculate the sample correlation coefficient.

    c.   Test H_0: $\rho = 0$ versus H_1: $\rho \neq 0$ with $\alpha = .05$.

11.43   (*Minitab or similar program recommended*) Refer to Exercise 11.30 with the data on the age and selling price for $n = 15$ Corvettes.

    a.   What proportion of the variability in y is explained by the linear regression on x?

    b.   Conduct the F test for the significance of the regression with $\alpha = .05$. At what level of α is the regression just significant?

    c.   Demonstrate that $F = t^2$, where t is the value of the t statistic for testing H_0: $\beta_1 = 0$ versus H_1: $\beta_1 \neq 0$.

11.44   Refer to Exercise 11.31 and the Minitab output for the regression analysis of profits per employee and number of employees for $n = 16$ publishing firms.

    a.   Identify r^2 and interpret this number.

    b.   Determine the sample correlation coefficient.

    c.   Is the regression significant at the 10% level? Explain.

11.45   (*Optional*) Refer to Exercise 11.33 and the Minitab output for the regression analysis of time needed to splice pairs of telephone wires and the number of pairs of wires.

    a.   Identify r^2 and interpret this number.

    b.   Determine the sample correlation coefficient.

    c.   Is the regression significant at the 1% level? Explain.

    d.   Test H_0: $\rho = 0$ versus H_1: $\rho \neq 0$ with $\alpha = .01$.

11.46   *Adjusted r^2.* A modified version of r^2, generally denoted by $\bar{r}^2$, is sometimes used to assess the strength of the estimated relationship. This modified coefficient is known as the *adjusted r^2* or r^2 *adjusted for degrees of freedom*. The adjusted r^2 is

$$\bar{r}^2 = 1 - \frac{\text{SSE}/(n-2)}{\text{SST}/(n-1)} = 1 - \left(\frac{n-1}{n-2}\right)(1 - r^2)$$

The adjusted r^2 represents the proportion of the *variance* of y explained by the simple linear regression. Refer to the Minitab output in Example 11.10. Identify $\bar{r}^2$, and verify its value using the entries in the ANOVA table.

11.47   Verify that

$$F = \left(\frac{r^2}{1 - r^2}\right)(n - 2) = \frac{\text{MSR}}{\text{MSE}}$$

for simple linear regression.

11.48   Show that SSE $= (1 - r^2)S_{yy}$, and that the sum of squares due to regression, S_{xy}^2/S_{xx}, can be expressed as $\hat{\beta}_1^2 S_{xx}$.

11.6   SIMPLE LINEAR REGRESSION MODELS AND TIME (OPTIONAL)

An important assumption in a regression model is that the errors, and hence the responses, at different settings of the predictor variable(s) are independent. This means that a y value at one value of x is not related to the y value at another value of x. However, for data collected over time, this is generally not true. Observations in consecutive time periods tend to be related. The amount of earnings this quarter is related to earnings last quarter, employment this month is related to employment last month, market share this week is related to market share last week, and so forth. Inferences from regression models constructed with time series data can be misleading even though the correct "formulas" are used. For example, we might conclude the regression is significant when, in fact, it is not.

Typically, regression models with time series data have to be modified to account for the dependence in the response. The general procedure for doing this is beyond the scope of this book. However, we shall discuss two situations, introduced in Chapter 3, where carefully constructed regression models can be used for representing data collected over time.

First, for time series data that appear to vary about a fixed level, a model relating the current observation to a previous observation may produce good forecasts of future values. If y_t is the observation at time t, a scatterplot of the pairs (y_{t-1}, y_t) and the first-order autocorrelation coefficient r_1 may suggest that observations one time period apart are linearly related. This leads to the simple linear regression model

$$y_t = \beta_0 + \beta_1 y_{t-1} + \varepsilon_t$$

Inferences for this model are exactly the same as those we have discussed previously with y_{t-1} playing the role of the predictor variable x. This model is called a **first-order autoregressive model.** The order refers to the time lag of the predictor variable.

Second, a response that exhibits exponential growth can be transformed to one that exhibits linear growth by taking its logarithm. The logarithm of the response at time t, $\ln y_t$, can then be related to t by a simple linear regression model or **exponential growth model** of the form

$$\ln y_t = \beta_0 + \beta_1 t + \varepsilon_t$$

Inferences about the regression coefficients and the response, $\ln y_t$, again follow the procedures that we have discussed. However, if the growth rate, antilog(β_1) $- 1$, or the original response, y_t, is of interest, then, for example, confidence intervals developed from the linear regression analysis must be transformed by taking antilogs. In both cases, the residuals should be carefully examined to be sure there are no time dependencies remaining in the data.

We begin with a discussion of the autoregressive model.

AUTOREGRESSIVE MODELS WITH ONE LAGGED VARIABLE

Consider the problem of the Canadian importer of cut flowers. He buys from growers in the United States, Mexico, Central, and South America. However, because these sources purchase their growing stock and chemicals from the United States, all the selling prices are quoted in U.S. dollars at the time of the sale. An invoice is not paid immediately, and since the U.S.–Canadian exchange rate fluctuates, the cost to the importer in Canadian dollars is not known at the time of purchase. In fact, an invoice is typically not paid until after the flowers are sold to wholesalers or destroyed. How much risk is associated with this component of the import business? The Friday closing values of the Canadian dollar/U.S. dollar exchange rate for several years are shown in Figure 11.8.

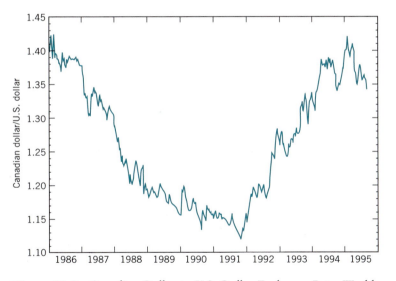

Figure 11.8 Canadian Dollar to U.S. Dollar Exchange Rate, Weekly from 1/3/86 to 8/25/95

Suppose the invoice is paid one week after the purchase of the flowers. If the exchange rate does not change over this period, there is no monetary risk to the importer. If the exchange rate increases from, say, 1.202 to 1.214 for the week, it will cost the importer 1.2 cents more for each U.S. dollar of purchase. If the exchange rate drops, the importer gains.

The importer is interested in the relationship between consecutive weekly exchange rates. A model that relates this week's rate to last week's rate is the first-order autoregressive model

$$y_t = \beta_0 + \beta_1 y_{t-1} + \varepsilon_t \qquad t = 1, 2, \dots, n$$

where y_t is the exchange rate at time (week) t and n is the number of observations. We can fit this model to the exchange rate data in the Data Disk. The result of this fit is summarized in the following Minitab output, where $y_t = $ CN/US Rt is the Canadian/U.S. exchange rate and $y_{t-1} = $ CN/USLg1 is the rate lagged one time period.

```
The regression equation is
CN/US Rt = 0.00720 + 0.994 CN/USLg1

Predictor         Coef        Stdev      t-ratio         p
Constant      0.007204     0.005171        1.39     0.164
CN/USLg1      0.994211     0.004078      243.79     0.000

s = 0.008206      R-sq = 99.2%      R-sq(adj) = 99.2%

Analysis of Variance

SOURCE        DF           SS          MS           F         p
Regression     1       4.0018      4.0018    59432.02     0.000
Error        501       0.0337      0.0001
Total        502       4.0355
```

The regression is significant with $r^2 = .992$. Also, $\hat{\beta}_0 = .007$ with an estimated standard error of .005 and $\hat{\beta}_1 = .994$ with an estimated standard error of .004. We conclude that β_0 is not significantly different from 0. Moreover, the 95% confidence interval for β_1,

$$(.996 - 1.96 \times .004, \quad .996 + 1.96 \times .004) = (.988, \quad 1.004)$$

includes 1.

These results suggest that the exchange rate data may be represented by the "random walk" model

$$y_t = y_{t-1} + \varepsilon_t$$

that yields the fitted function

$$\hat{y}_t = y_{t-1}$$

For this model, the best forecast of next week's exchange rate is this week's exchange rate. An examination of the residuals from a random walk fit suggests that this model is adequate for these data.

EXAMPLE 11.12   Formulating a Seasonal Autoregressive Model

A seasonal event is one that occurs with a more or less regular period. Christmas is a seasonal event whose regularity is disturbed only by leap years. Because of their regularity, seasonal events can be anticipated. In Examples 3.6 and 3.10 of Chapter 3, we discussed a time series consisting of the Wisconsin monthly employment in food and kindred products. This is a seasonal series with a 12-month period. Employment figures in this industry are regularly high in the late summer and early fall but low in the winter and early spring.

With y_t representing current employment and y_{t-12} representing employment 12 months earlier, the autoregressive model with one lagged variable

$$y_t = \beta_0 + \beta_1 y_{t-12} + \varepsilon_t$$

was fit to the employment data. We call this model a seasonal autoregressive model with a seasonal period of 12 (months). For this model, employment in July is related to employment last July, and so forth. Additional Minitab output follows.

```
Predictor              Coef           Stdev         t-ratio          p
Constant              1.209           1.204            1.00      0.317
Lag12 (y_{t-12})    0.98017         0.02043           47.97      0.000

s =  1.722         R-sq =  93.3%       R-sq(adj)  =  93.3%

Analysis of Variance

SOURCE          DF            SS            MS          F          p
Regression       1        6821.1        6821.1    2301.38      0.000
Error          164         486.1           3.0
Total          165        7307.2
```

Based only on this output, does it appear that the model

$$y_t = y_{t-12} + \varepsilon_t$$

might be appropriate for the employment data? What additional factor(s) must be considered before making a final decision?

Solution and Discussion. The t ratio and corresponding P-value indicate that $H_0: \beta_0 = 0$ cannot be rejected. Moreover, you can easily verify that $H_1: \beta_1 = 1$ is not rejected at any reasonable significance level. Therefore, the simple model

$$y_t = y_{t-12} + \varepsilon_t \quad \text{or} \quad y_t - y_{t-12} = \varepsilon_t$$

may be appropriate. This model produces the fitted values

$$\hat{y}_t = y_{t-12}$$

Before adopting this model, however, we must examine the residuals

$$\hat{\varepsilon}_t = y_t - \hat{y}_{t-12}$$

to see whether any information remains that can be used to improve the fit. In this case, as we see in the next section, this simple model does not capture all the information in the data.

A first-order autoregressive model in the seasonal differences $w_t = y_t - y_{t-12}$,

$$w_t = \beta_0 + \beta_1 w_{t-1} + \varepsilon_t$$

seems to represent the employment data well.

A GROWTH MODEL

In Example 3.16 of Chapter 3, we gave the number, y_t, of On the Double copy centers for the years 1983–1996. The natural logarithms of the number of copy centers, $\ln y_t$, were also given. The plots in Figure 3.27 show that the number of centers grows exponentially, while their logarithms grow linearly over time. The output from a straight-line regression analysis for the logarithms, labeled LNCPYCNT, follows.

```
DEP VAR:LNCPYCNT          N: 14
MULTIPLE R: 0.996  SQUARED MULTIPLE R: 0.992
ADJUSTED SQUARED MULTIPLE R: 0.991
STANDARD ERROR OF ESTIMATE:        0.189


   VARIABLE    COEFFICIENT    STD ERROR    STD COEF     T      P(2 TAIL)

CONSTANT         -0.308        0.107        0.000    -2.891     0.014
    TIME          0.483        0.013        0.996    38.564     0.000


                     ANALYSIS OF VARIANCE

  SOURCE     SUM-OF-SQUARES    DF   MEAN-SQUARE    F-RATIO   P

REGRESSION       53.143         1      53.143     1487.164  0.000
RESIDUAL          0.429        12       0.036
```

As we pointed out in Example 3.16, the fitted function is

$$\widehat{\ln y_t} = -.308 + .483t$$

and the annual growth rate is estimated to be

$$100(e^{.483} - 1)\% = 100(1.621 - 1)\% = 62.1\%$$

How do we make inferences when the response variable is a logarithmic transformation? Can we, for example, construct a confidence interval for the annual growth rate or test the hypothesis that the annual growth rate is a specified amount? How do we construct a prediction interval for the number of copy centers in 1997?

First consider inferences about the growth rate. Let the growth rate, in decimal form, be denoted by γ, the Greek letter gamma. The relationship between γ and the slope coefficient β_1 is

$$\gamma = e^{\beta_1} - 1 \quad \text{or} \quad \beta_1 = \ln(\gamma + 1)$$

A value of $\gamma = 0$ corresponds to a value of $\beta_1 = 0$, $\gamma = .5$ corresponds to $\beta_1 = .405$, and so forth.

To test the hypothesis H_0: $\gamma = \gamma_0$, we simply convert γ_0 to a value for β_1 and use the usual test procedures for the regression slope coefficient. Similarly, using the relationship between β_1 and γ, we can convert the endpoints of a confidence interval for β_1 to the endpoints of a confidence interval for γ. The next example illustrates these ideas.

EXAMPLE 11.13　Making Inferences About a Growth Rate

Using the output from the straight-line regression analysis of the On the Double copy center data:

a.　Test the hypothesis H_0: $\gamma = .5$ versus H_1: $\gamma > .5$. Use $\alpha = .05$.

b.　Construct a 95% confidence interval for γ.

Solution and Discussion.

a.　$\gamma = .5$ corresponds to $\beta_1 = .405$. Consequently, testing H_0: $\gamma = .5$ is equivalent to testing H_0: $\beta_1 = .405$. To test the latter, we use the information in the computer output and calculate the t value

$$t = \frac{\hat{\beta}_1 - \beta_{10}}{s/\sqrt{S_{xx}}} = \frac{.483 - .405}{.013} = 6$$

For 12 degrees of freedom, $t_{.05} = 1.782$. Since $t = 6 > 1.782$, we reject H_0 at the 5% level and conclude $\beta_1 > .405$ and, thus, $\gamma > .5$.

b.　A 95% confidence interval for β_1 is given by

$$\hat{\beta}_1 \pm t_{.025} \frac{s}{\sqrt{S_{xx}}}$$

For 12 degrees of freedom, $t_{.025} = 2.179$. Thus

$$(.483 - 2.179 \times .013, \quad .483 + 2.179 \times .013) = (.455, \quad .511)$$

is a 95% confidence interval for β_1. The endpoints of this interval are $\beta_1 = .455$, so that $\gamma = .576$ and $\beta_1 = .511$, so that $\gamma = .667$. Therefore, a 95% confidence interval for γ is ($.576$, $.667$).

A prediction interval for a future response is handled in much the same way as a confidence interval for a growth rate: Generate a prediction interval for the logarithm of a future response and then take the antilogs of the endpoints of this interval.

EXAMPLE 11.14　Constructing a Prediction Interval for an Exponential Growth Response

Use the computer output for the On the Double copy center data to calculate a 95% prediction interval for the number of copy centers in 1997 ($t = 15$).

Solution and Discussion.　We have

$$\widehat{\ln y}_{15} = -.308 + .483(15) = 6.937$$

In addition, $\bar{t} = 7.5$ and $S_{xx} = \sum_{i=1}^{14}(t_i - \bar{t})^2 = 225.5$. With $t_{.025} = 2.179$, the prediction interval for $\ln y_{15}$ is

$$6.937 \pm 2.179(.189)\sqrt{1 + \frac{1}{14} + \frac{(15 - 7.5)^2}{225.5}} \quad \text{or} \quad (6.464, \; 7.410)$$

Taking the antilogs of the endpoints of this interval produces a 95% prediction interval for y_{15}, the number of copy centers in 1997. This prediction interval is

$$(e^{6.464}, \; e^{7.410}) = (642, \; 1652)$$

This interval is not centered at $e^{6.937} = 1030$, the predicted number of copy centers for 1997, because the antilog (exponential) function is nonlinear.

EXERCISES

11.49 The number of connections to an AppleTalk computer network for a ten-year period were given in Exercise 3.40. These data are reproduced here:

Year (x)	1	2	3	4	5	6	7	8	9	10
Connections (y)	20	24	30	32	44	76	90	148	187	220

Refer to Exercise 3.40.

a. Let $y' = \ln y$, and let γ denote the annual growth rate. Using a straight-line fit to the transformed data, test the hypothesis H_0: $\gamma = .3$ versus H_1: $\gamma > .3$ with $\alpha = .10$.

b. Using a straight-line fit to the transformed data, construct a 90% confidence interval for the annual growth rate.

11.50 Refer to Exercise 11.49. Using a straight-line fit to the transformed data, construct a 95% prediction interval for the number of AppleTalk connections in year $x = 11$. Interpret this interval.

S&P500RR.dat

11.51 (*Minitab or similar program recommended*) The monthly rates of return on the S&P 500 Index for the years 1988–1991, which were given in Exercise 3.18, are reproduced here.

	1988	1989	1990	1991
Jan.		6.87	−7.13	4.07
Feb.	4.10	−2.94	.85	6.51
Mar.	−3.39	2.06	2.40	2.20
Apr.	.94	4.89	−2.73	.03
May	.32	3.45	8.80	3.79
June	4.23	−.80	−.89	−4.91
July	−.54	8.47	−.52	4.39
Aug.	−3.94	1.54	−9.91	1.95
Sept.	3.90	−.66	−5.25	−1.93
Oct.	2.56	−2.55	−.67	1.18
Nov.	−1.91	1.64	5.82	−4.49
Dec.	1.46	2.12	2.45	10.58

a. Let y_t be the rate of return for month t. Fit the first-order autoregressive model

$$y_t = \beta_0 + \beta_1 y_{t-1} + \varepsilon_t$$

to the return data. Save the residuals.

b. Refer to the results in part **a.** Are the monthly returns on the S&P 500 Index consistent with the model $y_t = \beta_0 + \varepsilon_t$? Explain.

c. Compute the residual autocorrelation function for lags $k = 1, 2, \ldots, 12$. Is the assumption of independent errors warranted? Explain.

11.7   ANOTHER LOOK AT RESIDUALS

A regression study is not completed by fitting a model by least squares, by providing confidence intervals, and by testing various hypotheses. These steps tell only half the story: the statistical inferences that can be made *when the postulated model is adequate.* In most studies, we cannot be sure that a particular model is correct. Therefore, we suggest the following strategy:

A Model Building Strategy

1. Tentatively entertain a model.
2. Obtain least squares estimates and compute the residuals.
3. Review the model by examining the residuals.
4. If necessary, revise the model and repeat Steps 1–3 until a model is obtained for which the data do not seem to contradict the assumptions made about the model.

Inferences can be seriously misleading if the assumptions made in the model formulation are grossly incompatible with the data. It is, therefore, essential to check the data carefully for indications of any violation of the assumptions. The assumptions for our straight-line regression model are:

1. The underlying relation is linear.
2. The errors are independent.
3. The errors have constant variance.
4. The errors are normally distributed.

Once the model is fitted by least squares, all the information on variation that cannot be explained by the model is contained in the residuals

$$\hat{\varepsilon}_i = y_i - \hat{y}_i \qquad i = 1, 2, \ldots, n$$

where y_i is the observed response and $\hat{y}_i$ is the corresponding value predicted by the fitted model. In the case of simple linear regression, $\hat{y}_i = \hat{\beta}_0 + \hat{\beta}_1 x_i$.

To examine the merits of a tentatively entertained model, we can examine the residuals by plotting them in various ways. Useful plots were illustrated in Chapter 3, where we discussed:

1. Plotting the residuals against the fitted values

2. Plotting the residuals against the explanatory variable

3. Plotting the residuals over time if the data are chronological

If the residual plot indicates that the general nature of the relationship between y and x forms a curve rather than a straight line (see Figure 3.16), a suitable transformation of the data may reduce a nonlinear relation to one that is approximately linear.

An appropriate transformation is often suggested by the pattern of the data. When the scatter diagram exhibits a relationship on a curve in which the y values increase too fast compared to the x values, a plot of $\ln y$ or $\sqrt{y}$ against x may be nearly linear. A simple linear regression model can then be formulated in terms of the transformed variable, and the appropriate analysis can be based on the transformed data. This was the case with the exponential growth data discussed in the previous section.

A transformation may also help to stabilize the variance. Figure 11.9 shows a residual plot that indicates the spread of the residuals increases as the magnitude of the fitted values increases. That is, the variability of the data points about the least squares line is larger for large responses than it is for small responses. This implies that the constant variance assumption may not hold. In this situation, relating the logarithm of y to x may produce residual variation that is more consistent with a constant variance.

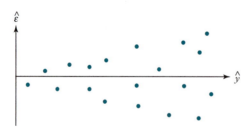

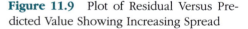

Figure 11.9   Plot of Residual Versus Predicted Value Showing Increasing Spread

Using the t distribution in hypothesis testing and confidence interval estimation is valid as long as the errors are approximately normally distributed. A moderate departure from normality does not impair the conclusions, especially when the data set is large. A violation of the normality assumption alone is typically not as serious as a violation of any of the other assumptions.

We have saved the assumption of independence for last, since it is the most critical. Lack of independence can drastically distort the conclusions drawn from the t tests and the confidence statements associated with interval estimation. The independence assumption is particularly tenuous for time series data—the type of data frequently arising in business and economic applications.

For time series residuals, that is, for residuals produced by using regression methods on time series data, independence can be checked with the procedures introduced in Chapter 3. To review, we can:

1. Plot the residuals against time. There should be no systematic pattern, such as a string of high values followed by a string of low values.

2. Construct scatterplots of pairs of residuals separated by various time periods or lags. Construct a scatterplot of the pairs $(\hat{\varepsilon}_{t-1}, \hat{\varepsilon}_t)$, the pairs $(\hat{\varepsilon}_{t-2}, \hat{\varepsilon}_t)$, and so forth. Independence is suggested if a scatterplot of the pairs of residuals separated by k time periods, $k = 1, 2, \ldots$, is a patternless cluster.

3. Calculate the sample autocorrelation coefficients, r_k, of the residuals. Independence is indicated if the autocorrelation coefficients are uniformly small (in the interval $0 \pm \dfrac{2}{\sqrt{n}}$) for all lags k.

The residual autocorrelation coefficient at lag k, $r_k(\hat{\varepsilon})$, is given by

$$r_k(\hat{\varepsilon}) = \frac{\sum_{t=1}^{n-k} \hat{\varepsilon}_t \, \hat{\varepsilon}_{t+k}}{\sum_{t=1}^{n} \hat{\varepsilon}_t^2} \qquad i = 1, 2, \ldots, K$$

where n is the number of residuals and K is typically taken to be $\frac{n}{4}$. Residual autocorrelation coefficients can be calculated with standard statistical software packages. In general, a plot of the autocorrelation coefficients against the lag k is called the **sample autocorrelation function.**

EXAMPLE 11.15   Interpreting Residual Autocorrelation Functions

In Section 11.6, we fit the weekly Canadian dollar to U.S. dollar exchange rate, y_t, to a first-order autoregressive model, giving

$$\hat{y}_t = .007 + .994 \hat{y}_{t-1}$$

The residual autocorrelation function associated with this fit is displayed in Figure 11.10(a) on page 600.

In Example 11.12 of Section 11.6, a seasonal autoregressive model was fit to the Wisconsin monthly employment in food and kindred products. With y_t representing the current month's employment, the fitted model was

$$\hat{y}_t = 1.209 + .980 \hat{y}_{t-12}$$

The residual autocorrelation function associated with this fit is shown in Figure 11.10(b). Interpret the residual autocorrelation functions in Figure 11.10.

Solution and Discussion.   Approximate 2(standard error) bands have been drawn about 0 on each of diagrams in Figure 11.10. In Figure 11.10(a), the bands are at $\pm \dfrac{2}{\sqrt{n}} = \pm \dfrac{2}{\sqrt{503}} = \pm .09$. In Figure 11.10(b), the bands are at $\pm \dfrac{2}{\sqrt{n}} = \pm \dfrac{2}{\sqrt{166}} = \pm .16$.

```
k    r_k(ε̂) -1.0  -0.8  -0.6  -0.4  -0.2   0.0   0.2   0.4   0.6   0.8   1.0
          --+----+----+----+----+----+--┌-+--┐--+----+----+----+----+-
  1   -0.055                             │ XX │
  2    0.021                               XX
  3   -0.024                             │ XX │
  4    0.032                             │  XX │
  5   -0.082                              XXX
  6    0.041                             │  XX │
  7    0.038                               XX
  8    0.062                               XXX
  9   -0.065                             │XXX │
 10    0.034                               XX
 11   -0.011                               X
 12   -0.036                             │ XX │
 13   -0.002                               X
 14    0.050                               XX
 15   -0.014                             │ X │
 16    0.026                               XX
 17   -0.026                             │ XX │
 18   -0.012                               X
 19    0.011                               X
 20    0.052                             │  XX │
 21   -0.066                             XXX
 22    0.018                               X
 23   -0.018                             │ X │
 24   -0.023                               XX
 25   -0.034                               XX
 26    0.021                             │ XX │
```

(a)

```
k    r_k(ε̂) -1.0  -0.8  -0.6  -0.4  -0.2   0.0   0.2   0.4   0.6   0.8   1.0
          --+----+----+----+----+----+----+----+----+----+----+-
  1    0.645                             │        XXXXX│XXXXXXXXXXXXX
  2    0.324                                      XXXXXXXXX
  3    0.166                                      XXXXX
  4    0.166                             │        XXXXX│
  5    0.164                                      XXXXX
  6    0.158                                      XXXXX
  7    0.177                             │        XXXXX│
  8    0.223                                      XXXXXXX
  9    0.289                                      XXXXXXXX
 10    0.212                             │        XXXXX│X
 11    0.072                                      XXX
 12   -0.126                             │XXXX     │
 13   -0.037                             │ XX     │
 14    0.120                                      XXXX
 15    0.203                                      XXXXX│X
 16    0.205                             │        XXXXX│X
 17    0.202                                      XXXXXX
 18    0.220                                      XXXXX│X
 19    0.166                             │        XXXXX│
 20    0.070                                      XXX
 21   -0.025                             │ XX     │
 22    0.020                                      X
```

(b)

Figure 11.10   Two Residual Autocorrelation Functions

   The uniformly small autocorrelations in Figure 11.10(a) suggest that all the dependencies in the exhange rate data have been captured by the model. There is no reason to doubt the independence assumption. The residual autocorrelation function in Figure 11.10(b), however, suggests that the original model with an assumption of independent errors is not tenable.

   In Figure 11.10(b), there are some large (relative to their approximate standard errors) residual autocorrelations. The largest occurs at lag 1, with some additional large residual autocorrelations at higher lags. The pattern of the residual autocorrelations is also important. Most of the residual autocorrelations are positive, with collections of relatively large values occurring at regular intervals. Clearly, there are dependencies in the employment data not captured by the initial model. What should be done?

As we pointed out in Example 11.12, the original analysis suggests that the estimated regression coefficients are consistent with the model

$$y_t = y_{t-12} + \varepsilon_t \quad \text{or} \quad y_t - y_{t-12} = \varepsilon_t$$

The residual autocorrelations suggest there is (at least) a lag 1 dependency remaining in the data. A next step might be to fit the model

$$w_t = \beta_0 + \beta_1 w_{t-1} + \varepsilon_t$$

with $w_t = y_t - y_{t-12}$. A check of the residuals from this fit would then indicate the need for further modifications of the model (see Section 12.5).

Significant residual autocorrelations suggest that the original model must be modified, but the way to do this is not always obvious. In general, the best model must take into account the nature of the dependence. Sometimes this involves a simple modification of the original regression model. Alternatively, a sophisticated time series model may be developed from first principles.*

It is important to remember that our confidence in statistical inference procedures is related to the validity of the assumptions about them. A mechanically made inference may be misleading if some model assumption is grossly violated. An examination of the residuals is an important part of regression analysis, because it helps to detect any inconsistency between the data and the postulated model.

If no serious violation of the assumptions is uncovered in the process of examining residuals, we consider the model adequate and proceed with the relevant inferences. Otherwise, we must search for a more appropriate model.

EXERCISES

11.52 Given the pairs of (x, y) values

x	.5	1	2	4	5	6	7
y	4.6	3.8	1.8	1.3	.9	.7	.8

a. Plot the scatter diagram.

b. Obtain the best fitting straight line and plot it on the scatter diagram.

c. What proportion of the variability of y is explained by the fitted line?

---

*The development of sophisticated time series models is beyond the scope of this book. The interested reader is referred to Abraham, B., and Ledolter, J., *Statistical Methods for Forecasting,* John Wiley and Sons, New York, 1983.

   d. Examine the residuals. Does the straight-line model appear to be adequate?
       Explain.

11.53 Refer to Exercise 11.52. Consider the reciprocal transformation $y' = 1/y$.
   a. Construct the scatterplot of y' versus x.
   b. Fit a straight-line model to the transformed data.
   c. Calculate r^2 and comment on the adequacy of the fit.
   d. Examine the residuals. Do the transformed data appear to be consistent
       with a straight-line model? Explain.

11.54 To determine the maximum stopping ability of cars when their breaks are
       fully applied, each of 10 cars is driven at a specified speed. The distance each
       requires to come to a complete stop is measured. The various initial speeds
       (x) selected for each of the 10 cars and the stopping distances (y) recorded
       are given here:

x	20	20	30	30	30	40	40	50	50	60
y	16.3	26.7	39.2	63.5	51.3	98.4	65.7	104.1	155.6	217.2

   a. Construct a scatter diagram.
   b. Obtain the best fitting straight line and plot it on the scatter diagram.
   c. Examine the residuals and comment on the appropriateness of the straight-
       line model.

11.55 Refer to Exercise 11.54. Consider the square root transformation $y' = \sqrt{y}$.
   a. Construct a scatterplot of $\sqrt{y}$ versus x.
   b. Fit a straight-line model to the transformed data.
   c. Calculate r^2 and comment on the adequacy of the fit.
   d. Examine the residuals. Do the transformed data appear to be consistent
       with a straight-line model? Explain.

11.8   STATISTICS IN CONTEXT

With the increasing globalization of markets, understanding the behavior of foreign exchange rates is essential for planning strategies for the management of risk. Major unexpected changes in exchange rates can precipitate large losses or gains.

   One theory concerning exchange rates argues that, in a free market, if one country
is experiencing higher inflation than another country, the first country's currency should
become relatively less valuable than the currency of the other country. For instance, if
for some period, the United States has higher inflation than Japan, then the dollar should
buy fewer yen at the end of the period than it did at the beginning.

   To confirm this theory, an international money manager decides to collect quarterly
data on purchasing power (measured by a consumer price index, CPI) and the exchange
rate. These data, along with the values of an explanatory variable x to be defined shortly,
are given in Table 11.5.

TABLE 11.5 Cost of Living Indices and Exchange Rates, 1986 (2nd quarter) through 1992 (2nd quarter)

Quarter	Japan CPI	U.S. CPI	Exchange Rate yen/dollar (y)	x
(1986(2)) 1	100.9	101.3	170.13	—
2	100.4	102.1	155.77	167.961
3	100.4	102.6	160.29	155.011
4	99.5	103.8	153.17	157.017
5	101.1	105.1	142.67	153.708
6	100.9	106.3	146.92	140.780
7	101.1	107.2	135.79	145.975
8	100.6	107.9	128.00	134.242
9	101.3	109.2	125.61	127.356
10	101.5	110.7	133.71	124.153
11	102.2	111.8	125.28	133.307
12	101.7	113.1	128.45	123.234
13	104.1	114.9	138.07	129.421
14	104.2	115.9	142.29	137.010
15	104.9	117.0	143.04	141.899
16	105.3	119.0	147.90	141.172
17	106.7	120.2	155.25	148.370
18	106.9	122.3	145.23	152.870
19	108.7	124.3	130.79	145.299
20	109.2	125.3	133.85	130.343
21	110.3	126.0	138.31	134.447
22	110.3	127.0	137.16	137.221
23	111.7	128.0	129.50	137.816
24	111.3	128.9	128.43	128.135
(1992(2)) 25	112.8	130.9	130.30	128.172

SOURCE: International Financial Statistics 1987–1991, International Monetary Fund.

For his purpose, the money manager quantifies inflation in terms of the consumer price index. In particular, it was decided to measure inflation by the ratio

$$\text{Inflation} = \frac{\text{CPI current}}{\text{CPI previous}}$$

for each country. For instance, from the first to the second numbers, or the second to the third quarter 1986,

$$\text{Japan:} \quad \frac{100.4}{100.9} = .99504 \qquad \text{United States:} \quad \frac{102.1}{101.3} = 1.00790$$

The ratio of the two inflation terms

$$\frac{\text{Japan inflation}}{\text{U.S. inflation}} = \frac{\text{Japan CPI current/Japan CPI previous}}{\text{U.S. CPI current/U.S. CPI previous}}$$

should then indicate the direction that the exchange rate should move. If this latter quantity is less than 1, Japan had smaller inflation and a dollar should buy fewer yen. For the third quarter of 1986,

$$\frac{\text{Japan CPI current/Japan CPI previous}}{\text{U.S. CPI current/U.S. CPI previous}} = \frac{.99504}{1.00790} = .98725$$

so the dollar should buy fewer yen.

To predict the current exchange rate, we consider the explanatory, or predictor, variable

$$x = \text{Previous exchange rate} \times \frac{\text{Japan CPI current/Japan CPI previous}}{\text{U.S. CPI current/U.S. CPI previous}}$$

For the third quarter of 1986, $x = 170.13 \times .98725 = 167.961$. The remaining values for x are given in the last column of Table 11.5.

The plot of $y =$ current exchange rate versus x in Figure 11.11, for the 24 cases where x is available, reveals a moderately strong linear relation.

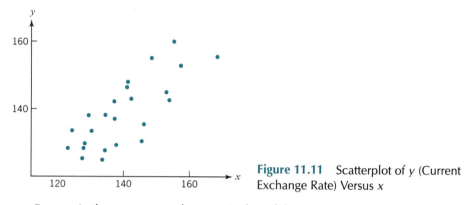

Figure 11.11 Scatterplot of y (Current Exchange Rate) Versus x

Economic theory suggests the statistical model

$$Y = \beta x + \varepsilon$$

where the errors, ε, are independent, have mean 0, and have the same variance, σ^2. For this model, the least squares estimate of the slope is $\hat{\beta} = \sum_{i=1}^{n} x_i y_i / \sum_{i=1}^{n} x_i^2$, as you are asked to verify in Exercise 11.56. The Minitab output follows.

```
The regression equation is
y = 0.992 x

Predictor       Coef        Stdev      t-ratio        p
Noconstant
x            0.99233      0.01059        93.68    0.000

s = 7.278
Analysis of Variance

SOURCE       DF          SS         MS          F         p
Regression    1      464860     464860    8776.52     0.000
Error        23        1218         53
Total        24      466078
```

The Minitab output shows that the estimate $\hat{\beta} = .992$ is less than one estimated standard error from 1.000. The data are compatible with the hypothesis that the coefficient of x is 1, which the economic theory suggests should hold for a free market. The residual autocorrelation function shown in Figure 11.12(a) indicates that the errors from quarter to quarter may be regarded as independent. The normal-scores plot in Figure 11.12(b) is not a straight line, indicating that the errors may not be normally distributed. However, with 24 observations, the departure from normality does not appear to be serious.

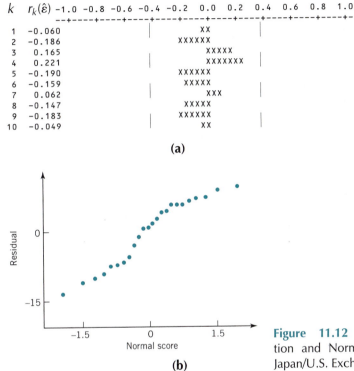

(a)

(b)

Figure 11.12 Residual Autocorrelation and Normal-Scores Plots for the Japan/U.S. Exchange Rate Data

The regression analysis demonstrates the basic soundness of the economic reasoning although it is masked by considerable error. Differing inflation rates really are associated with changes in the exchange rates. However, sources of variation such as interest rates and trade negotiations that would lead to more open Japanese markets, and other planned but unsuccessful interventions to manage the exchange rate, all act to keep the relationship from being perfect.

As we suggested, the data were collected to confirm the economic theory. If, however, the major intent of the study is to predict exchange rates, we have to proceed differently. The new CPI will not be available. Many approaches are possible, but we illustrate one where the ratio of CPIs is calculated for the previous quarter. That is, to predict the exchange rate for the *next* quarter, we choose the predictor variable

$$x = \text{Current exchange rate} \times \frac{\text{Japan CPI current/Japan CPI previous}}{\text{U.S. CPI current/U.S. CPI previous}}$$

The new predictor variable is the lagged inflation ratio times the previous exchange rate.

Fitting the model $y = \beta x + \varepsilon$ to the 23 cases where x is available yields the output

```
The regression equation is
y = 0.997 x

Predictor           Coef        Stdev       t-ratio         p
Noconstant
x                0.99698     0.01029        96.88     0.000

s = 6.853
```

To predict the exchange rate for the third quarter of 1992, we determine the value of the predictor variable

$$x = 130.30 \times \frac{112.8/111.3}{130.9/128.9} = 130.30 \times .99799 = 130.04$$

and compute

$$\hat{y} = .997(130.04) = 129.65$$

The variable x is a useful predictor, although Figure 11.11 indicates the linear relationship is not especially strong.

EXERCISES

11.56 Consider the simple linear regression model

$$Y_i = \beta x_i + \varepsilon_i \qquad i = 1, 2, \ldots, n$$

where the ε_i are independent with mean 0 and variance σ^2.

a. Show that the least squares estimator of the slope is
$\hat{\beta} = \sum_{i=1}^{n} x_i y_i / \sum_{i=1}^{n} x_i^2$.

b. The sum of squares error, SSE $= \sum_{i=1}^{n}(y_i - \hat{\beta}x_i)^2$, has $n - 1$ degrees of freedom since only a single regression parameter is estimated. Use these two quantities to give an estimator of σ^2.

11.57 Refer to Exercise 11.56. Show that the variance of $\hat{\beta}$ is $\sigma^2 / \sum_{i=1}^{n} x_i^2$.

11.58 Using the Minitab output describing the fit of the model $Y = \beta x + \varepsilon$ to the yen/dollar exchange rate, construct a 90% confidence interval for β.

11.59 Using the Minitab output describing the fit of the model $Y = \beta x + \varepsilon$ to the yen/dollar exchange rate, test H_0: $\beta = 1$ versus H_1: $\beta \neq 1$ at level $\alpha = .10$.

11.60 (*Minitab or similar program recommended*) Refer to the data in Table 11.5 (page 603).

USJapInd.dat

a. Fit the model $Y = \beta_0 + \beta_1 x + \varepsilon$ and test for the significance of the regression at level $\alpha = .01$.

b. Give the value of r^2 and comment on the strength of the relation.

c. Test H_0: $\beta_0 = 0$ versus H_1: $\beta_0 \neq 0$ with $\alpha = .05$.

d. Plot the residuals over time and construct the residual autocorrelation function. Is the independence assumption tenable? Explain.

11.61 (*Minitab or similar program recommended*) Table 11.6 is similar to Table 11.5. Table 11.6 contains the CPIs for Mexico and the United States, and the peso/dollar exchange rate for the first quarter of 1986 through the first quarter of 1992.

USMexInd.dat

TABLE 11.6 Cost of Living Indices and Exchange Rates, 1986 (1st quarter) through 1992 (1st quarter)

Quarter	Mexico CPI	U.S. CPI	Exchange Rate peso/dollar (y)	x
(1986(1)) 1	142.1	101.6	423.6	—
2	165.6	101.3	522.2	495.12
3	198.0	102.1	665.7	619.48
4	239.3	102.6	835.6	800.63
5	297.5	103.8	1025.7	1026.82
6	371.4	105.1	1241.7	1264.65
7	463.8	106.3	1460.8	1533.12
8	594.3	107.2	1784.6	1856.11
9	825.4	107.9	2249.4	2462.48
10	920.0	109.2	2281.0	2477.36
11	961.7	110.7	2281.0	2352.08
12	991.3	111.8	2281.0	2328.07
13	1047.3	113.1	2324.2	2382.16
14	1089.6	114.9	2415.5	2380.19
15	1125.1	115.9	2507.0	2472.68
16	1176.5	117.0	2559.2	2596.88
17	1293.3	119.0	2690.0	2765.99
18	1363.7	120.2	2779.3	2808.11
19	1439.8	122.3	2856.4	2884.01
20	1524.7	124.3	2924.7	2976.16
21	1636.4	125.3	2965.0	3113.91
22	1695.6	126.0	3001.2	3055.20
23	1741.8	127.0	3040.1	3058.70
24	1821.6	128.0	3067.4	3154.54
(1992(1)) 25	1920.3	128.9	3066.4	3211.02

SOURCE: International Financial Statistics 1987–1992, International Monetary Fund.

a. Fit the model $Y = \beta x + \varepsilon$.

b. Construct a 95% confidence interval for β. Is $\beta = 1$, which the theory suggests, in the interval? Comment.

c. Is the linear relationship stronger or weaker than it is for Japan and the United States? Discuss.

d. Mexico tries to manage the exchange rate according to the economic ideas behind the curve being fit. A stable planned trend makes it easier for businesspeople to schedule sales and purchases during the year. Explain why this behavior may make the relation appear to be stronger than would be the case if the exchange rate were unmanaged and subject only to free-market forces.

11.62 (*Minitab or similar program recommended*) Refer to Exercise 11.61 and Table 11.6. Fit the model $Y = \beta x + \varepsilon$, where x involves the inflation factor *lagged one quarter*. Using the fitted model:

USMexInd.dat

a. Give an estimate of the exchange rate for the second quarter of 1992.

b. Comment on the strength of the relation used for prediction.

c. Analyze the residuals. Is the model adequate?

d. Examine the observations during a period when Mexico has frozen the exchange rate (for example, Quarters 10–12 in Table 11.6). Does the period of fixed exchange rates appear to be connected to any unusual observations?

11.9 CHAPTER SUMMARY

In this chapter, we have learned:

- How to analyze the **simple linear regression model**

$$Y_i = \beta_0 + \beta_1 x_i + \varepsilon_i \quad i = 1, 2, \ldots, n$$

where

1. Y_i denotes the response corresponding to the ith experimental trial in which x is set at value x_i.

2. $\varepsilon_1, \varepsilon_2, \ldots, \varepsilon_n$ are the unknown error components that represent the deviations of the response from the true linear relation. They are unobservable random variables. We assume the errors are independent and each is normally distributed with mean 0 and unknown standard deviation σ.

3. The coefficients or parameters β_0 and β_1, which together locate the straight line, are unknown.

- The regression model parameters are estimated using the **principle of least squares.** We have:

1. Least squares **estimate of β_1**: $\hat{\beta}_1 = \dfrac{S_{xy}}{S_{xx}}$

2. Least squares **estimate of β_0**: $\hat{\beta}_0 = \bar{y} - \hat{\beta}_1 \bar{x}$

3. **Fitted (or estimated) regression line:** $\hat{y} = \hat{\beta}_0 + \hat{\beta}_1 x$

4. **Residuals:** $\hat{\varepsilon}_i = y_i - \hat{y}_i = y_i - \hat{\beta}_0 - \hat{\beta}_1 x_i, \quad i = 1, 2, \ldots, n$

- The residuals are estimates of the model errors and are analyzed to check the model assumptions.

- Inferences about the slope β_1 are based on the t statistic with d.f. $= n - 2$ taking the value

$$t = \frac{\hat{\beta}_1 - \beta_1}{s/\sqrt{S_{xx}}}$$

where $s = \sqrt{\text{SSE}/(n - 2)}$. The denominator in the t statistic is the estimated standard deviation or estimated standard error (s.e.) of $\hat{\beta}_1$.

1. A $100(1 - \alpha)\%$ **confidence interval for β_1** is

$$\hat{\beta}_1 \pm t_{\alpha/2} \frac{s}{\sqrt{S_{xx}}}$$

2. To test whether β_1 is equal to some specified value β_{10}, not necessarily zero, the null hypothesis is

$$H_0: \beta_1 = \beta_{10}$$

and we use the test statistic with value

$$t = \frac{\hat{\beta}_1 - \beta_{10}}{s/\sqrt{S_{xx}}} \qquad \text{d.f.} = n - 2$$

If the alternative hypothesis is two-sided $H_1: \beta_1 \neq \beta_{10}$, the rejection region is $t < -t_{\alpha/2}$ or $t > t_{\alpha/2}$. The one-sided rejection regions are

$$t > t_\alpha \quad \text{for the alternative } H_1: \beta_1 > \beta_{10}$$
$$t < -t_\alpha \quad \text{for the alternative } H_1: \beta_1 < \beta_{10}$$

● Inferences about the intercept β_0 are based on the t statistic with d.f. $= n - 2$ taking the value

$$t = \frac{\hat{\beta}_0 - \beta_0}{s\sqrt{\dfrac{1}{n} + \dfrac{\bar{x}^2}{S_{xx}}}}$$

The denominator in the t statistic is the estimated standard error of $\hat{\beta}_0$.

1. A $100(1 - \alpha)\%$ **confidence interval for β_0** is

$$\hat{\beta}_0 \pm t_{\alpha/2}\, s\sqrt{\dfrac{1}{n} + \dfrac{\bar{x}^2}{S_{xx}}}$$

2. The null hypothesis $H_0: \beta_0 = \beta_{00}$ can be checked using the test statistic taking value

$$t = \frac{\hat{\beta}_0 - \beta_{00}}{s\sqrt{\dfrac{1}{n} + \dfrac{\bar{x}^2}{S_{xx}}}} \qquad \text{d.f.} = n - 2$$

● A $100(1 - \alpha)\%$ **confidence interval for the mean response $\beta_0 + \beta_1 x^*$** at x^* is

$$\hat{\beta}_0 + \hat{\beta}_1 x^* \pm t_{\alpha/2}\, s\sqrt{\dfrac{1}{n} + \dfrac{(x^* - \bar{x})^2}{S_{xx}}}$$

where the t percentage point is based on d.f. $= n - 2$.

- A $100(1 - \alpha)\%$ **prediction interval for a new response** y^* at x^* is

$$\hat{\beta}_0 + \hat{\beta}_1 x^* \pm t_{\alpha/2}\, s \sqrt{1 + \frac{1}{n} + \frac{(x^* - \bar{x})^2}{S_{xx}}}$$

  where the t percentage point is based on d.f. $= n - 2$.

- The **analysis of variance** for simple linear regression is based on the algebraic identity

$$\sum (y_i - \bar{y})^2 = \sum (\hat{y}_i - \bar{y})^2 + \sum (y_i - \hat{y}_i)^2$$

  or

$$\text{SST} = \text{SSR} + \text{SSE}$$

  We have

1. Sum of squares decomposition: $\text{SST} = \text{SSR} + \text{SSE}$
2. Degrees of freedom decomposition: $n - 1 = 1 + (n - 2)$
3. Mean squares: $\text{MSR} = \text{SSR}/1$, $\text{MSE} = \text{SSE}/(n - 2) = s^2$
4. The mean square error, $\text{MSE} = s^2$, estimates σ^2.
5. The F ratio: $F = \text{MSR}/\text{MSE} = \text{MSR}/s^2$, with d.f. $= (1, n - 2)$, can be used to test the hypothesis $H_0\colon \beta_1 = 0$ versus $H_1\colon \beta_1 \neq 0$. At level α, the rejection region is

$$F > F_\alpha(1, n - 2)$$

6. The strength of the linear relation is measured by the **coefficient of determination**

$$r^2 = \frac{\text{SSR}}{\text{SST}} = 1 - \frac{\text{SSE}}{\text{SST}}$$

- The **correlation coefficient** measures the strength and direction of the linear association between two variables.

1. For normal populations, the hypothesis $H_0\colon \rho = 0$ (zero population correlation) can be tested using the test statistic with value

$$t = \frac{r\sqrt{n - 2}}{\sqrt{1 - r^2}} \qquad \text{d.f.} = n - 2$$

  where r is the sample correlation coefficient and n is the sample size.

2. The tests of $H_0\colon \beta_1 = 0$ and $H_0\colon \rho = 0$ are related. The t statistics for each test are identical, or

$$\frac{\hat{\beta}_1}{s/\sqrt{S_{xx}}} = \frac{r\sqrt{n - 2}}{\sqrt{1 - r^2}}$$

  Testing for no linear relation in the population is equivalent to testing for no linear association.

- **Autoregressive models** with one lagged variable are sometimes useful for modeling a response variable whose values are observed over time. The **first-order autoregressive model** is

$$y_t = \beta_0 + \beta_1 y_{t-1} + \varepsilon_t$$

  Analysis of the first-order autoregressive model follows the analysis of the simple linear regression model with $x = y_{t-1}$.

- A response that exhibits **exponential growth** can be transformed to one that exhibits **linear growth** by taking its logarithm. The logarithm of the response at time t, $\ln y_t$, can be related to t by a model of the form

$$\ln y_t = \beta_0 + \beta_1 t + \varepsilon_t$$

  Inferences about the regression coefficients and the response, $\ln y_t$, again follow the usual procedures. However, if the growth rate, $\text{antilog}(\beta_1) - 1$, or the original response, y_t, is of interest, then, for example, confidence intervals developed from the linear regression analysis must be transformed by taking antilogs.

- A useful **model building strategy** consists of the following steps:

  1. Tentatively entertain a model.

  2. Obtain least squares estimates and compute the residuals.

  3. Review the model by examining the residuals.

  4. If necessary, revise the model and repeat Steps 1–3 until a model is obtained for which the data do not seem to contradict the assumptions made about the model.

- To examine the merits of a tentatively entertained model, we can examine the residuals by plotting them in various ways, as follows:

  1. Construct a histogram or boxplot of the residuals.

  2. Construct a normal-scores plot of the residuals.

  3. Plot the residuals against the fitted values.

  4. Plot the residuals against the explanatory variable.

  5. Plot the residuals over time if the data are chronological.

  6. Construct and plot the residual autocorrelations if the data are chronological.

- **Transformations** can often help to reduce a nonlinear relation to one that is approximately linear, and to help stabilize the variance.

- A moderate departure from normality does not impair the conclusions based on the t distribution, especially when the data set is large.

- Lack of independence can seriously distort the conclusions drawn from the t tests and confidence statements associated with interval estimation. The independence assumption is particularly tenuous for time series data. Lack of independence can best be handled by modifying the original model to account for the nature of the dependence.

11.10 IMPORTANT CONCEPTS AND TOOLS

CONCEPTS

Analysis of variance for straight-line regression, 582
Dependent or response variable, 551
Exponential growth model, 590
First-order autoregressive model, 590
Fitted regression line, 558
Independent or predictor variable, 551
Least squares estimates, 558
Model building strategy, 597
Population correlation, 585
Principle of least squares, 556
Residuals, 558
Sampling distributions of least squares estimators, 564
Straight-line regression model, 553

TOOLS

Analysis of variance table, 582
Coefficient of determination, r^2, 580
Confidence interval for β_0, 567
Confidence interval for β_1, 564
Confidence interval for the mean response, $\beta_0 + \beta_1 x^*$, 568
Estimate of σ^2, 559
F test for the significance of the regression, 583

Prediction interval for a new response, y^*, 571
Sample autocorrelation function, 599
Test statistic for H_0: $\beta_0 = \beta_{00}$, 567
Test statistic for H_0: $\beta_1 = 0$, 566
t test for zero population correlation, 585

11.11 KEY FORMULAS

Basic notation:

$$\bar{x} = \frac{1}{n}\sum x \qquad \bar{y} = \frac{1}{n}\sum y$$

$$S_{xx} = \sum (x - \bar{x})^2 = \sum x^2 - \frac{(\sum x)^2}{n}$$

$$S_{yy} = \sum (y - \bar{y})^2 = \sum y^2 - \frac{(\sum y)^2}{n}$$

$$S_{xy} = \sum (x - \bar{x})(y - \bar{y}) = \sum xy - \frac{(\sum x)(\sum y)}{n}$$

Least squares estimate of β_1: $\hat{\beta}_1 = \dfrac{S_{xy}}{S_{xx}}$

Least squares estimate of β_0: $\hat{\beta}_0 = \bar{y} - \hat{\beta}_1 \bar{x}$

Fitted (or estimated) regression line: $\hat{y} = \hat{\beta}_0 + \hat{\beta}_1 x$

Residuals: $\hat{\varepsilon}_i = y_i - \hat{y}_i = y_i - \hat{\beta}_0 - \hat{\beta}_1 x_i, \qquad i = 1, 2, \ldots, n$

Sum of squares error (SSE): $\text{SSE} = \sum \hat{\varepsilon}_i^2 = S_{yy} - \dfrac{S_{xy}^2}{S_{xx}}$

Estimate of σ^2: $s^2 = \dfrac{\text{SSE}}{n-2}$

Estimate of σ: $s = \sqrt{s^2} = \sqrt{\dfrac{\text{SSE}}{n-2}}$

Inferences concerning the slope β_1:

1. A $100(1 - \alpha)\%$ confidence interval for β_1 is

$$\hat{\beta}_1 \pm t_{\alpha/2} \frac{s}{\sqrt{S_{xx}}}$$

where $t_{\alpha/2}$ is the upper $\alpha/2$ point of the t distribution with d.f. $= n - 2$.

2. To test $H_0: \beta_1 = \beta_{10}$, use the t statistic

$$t = \frac{\hat{\beta}_1 - \beta_{10}}{s/\sqrt{S_{xx}}} \quad \text{with d.f.} = n - 2$$

For an α level test, the rejection region is

$$t < -t_\alpha, \quad t > t_\alpha, \quad \text{or} \quad |t| > t_{\alpha/2}$$

according to whether the alternative hypothesis (H_1) is

$$\beta_1 < \beta_{10}, \quad \beta_1 > \beta_{10}, \quad \text{or} \quad \beta_1 \neq \beta_{10}$$

respectively.

Inferences concerning the intercept β_0:

1. A $100(1 - \alpha)\%$ confidence interval for β_0 is

$$\hat{\beta}_0 \pm t_{\alpha/2} \, s \sqrt{\frac{1}{n} + \frac{\bar{x}^2}{S_{xx}}}$$

where $t_{\alpha/2}$ is the upper $\alpha/2$ point of the t distribution with d.f. $= n - 2$.

2. To test $H_0: \beta_0 = \beta_{00}$, use the t statistic

$$t = \frac{\hat{\beta}_0 - \beta_{00}}{s \sqrt{\dfrac{1}{n} + \dfrac{\bar{x}^2}{S_{xx}}}} \quad \text{with d.f.} = n - 2$$

For an α level test, the rejection regions are of the same form as those for the slope coefficient.

A $100(1 - \alpha)\%$ confidence interval for the mean response $\beta_0 + \beta_1 x^*$ at x^* is

$$\hat{\beta}_0 + \hat{\beta}_1 x^* \pm t_{\alpha/2} \, s \sqrt{\frac{1}{n} + \frac{(x^* - \bar{x})^2}{S_{xx}}}$$

where $t_{\alpha/2}$ is the upper $\alpha/2$ point of the t distribution with d.f. $= n - 2$.

A $100(1 - \alpha)\%$ prediction interval for a new response y^* at x^* is

$$\hat{\beta}_0 + \hat{\beta}_1 x^* \pm t_{\alpha/2} \, s \sqrt{1 + \frac{1}{n} + \frac{(x^* - \bar{x})^2}{S_{xx}}}$$

where $t_{\alpha/2}$ is the upper $\alpha/2$ point of the t distribution with d.f. $= n - 2$.

Decomposition of variability:

$$\text{SST} = \text{SSR} + \text{SSE}$$

$$S_{yy} = \frac{S_{xy}^2}{S_{xx}} + \left(S_{yy} - \frac{S_{xy}^2}{S_{xx}} \right)$$

Coefficient of determination: $r^2 = \text{SSR}/\text{SST} = 1 - \text{SSE}/\text{SST}$

Analysis of variance (ANOVA) table:

Source	Sum of Squares	d.f.	Mean Square	F ratio
Regression	SSR	1	$\text{MSR} = \text{SSR}/1$	$F = \text{MSR}/\text{MSE}$
Error	SSE	$n - 2$	$\text{MSE} = \text{SSE}/(n - 2)$	
Total	SST	$n - 1$		

F test for the significance of the straight-line regression:

To test the hypothesis $H_0: \beta_1 = 0$ versus $H_1: \beta_1 \neq 0$, we can use the F statistic

$$F = \frac{\text{MSR}}{\text{MSE}}$$

with d.f. $= (1, n - 2)$. At level α, the rejection region is

$$F > F_\alpha(1, n - 2)$$

t test for zero population correlation in normal populations:

To test the hypothesis $H_0: \rho = 0$ versus $H_1: \rho \neq 0$, we can use the t statistic with value

$$t = \frac{r\sqrt{n - 2}}{\sqrt{1 - r^2}} \qquad \text{d.f.} = n - 2$$

where r is the sample correlation coefficient and n is the sample size.

For an α level test, the rejection region is

$$t < -t_\alpha, \quad t > t_\alpha, \quad \text{or} \quad |t| > t_{\alpha/2}$$

according to whether the alternative hypothesis H_1 is

$$\rho < 0, \quad \rho > 0, \quad \text{or} \quad \rho \neq 0$$

respectively.

For the exponential growth model

$$\ln y = \beta_0 + \beta_1 t + \varepsilon$$

the relationship between the growth rate γ and the slope coefficient β_1 is

$$\gamma = e^{\beta_1} - 1 \quad \text{or} \quad \beta_1 = \ln(\gamma + 1)$$

The residual autocorrelation at lag k is

$$r_k(\hat{\varepsilon}) = \frac{\sum_{t=1}^{n-k} \hat{\varepsilon}_t \hat{\varepsilon}_{t+k}}{\sum_{t=1}^{n} \hat{\varepsilon}_t^2} \quad i = 1, 2, \ldots, K$$

where n is the number of residuals and K is typically taken to be $n/4$.

REVIEW EXERCISES

11.63 *(Minitab or similar program recommended)* In Exercise 3.38, we explored the relationship between per pupil expenditure on education and Scholastic Assessment Test (SAT) rank for the 50 states. Table 11.7 contains the average total SAT score and the percentage of graduating high school seniors taking the SAT for the 50 states and the District of Columbia. Let y be SAT score and x be the percentage of graduates taking the SAT.

StSATExp.dat

TABLE 11.7   Average SAT Scores and Percentage of High School Graduates Taking SAT

Location	Total SAT Score	Percent Grads Taking SAT	Location	Total SAT Score	Percent Grads Taking SAT
Alabama	1029	8	Montana	1009	21
Alaska	934	47	Nebraska	1050	9
Arizona	944	27	Nevada	917	30
Arkansas	1005	6	New Hampshire	935	70
California	902	45	New Jersey	898	70
Colorado	980	29	New Mexico	1015	11
Connecticut	908	81	New York	892	74
Delaware	897	68	North Carolina	865	60
District of Columbia	857	53	North Dakota	1107	5
Florida	889	48	Ohio	975	23
Georgia	854	65	Oklahoma	1027	9
Hawaii	889	57	Oregon	947	51
Idaho	979	15	Pennsylvania	880	70
Illinois	1048	13	Rhode Island	888	70
Indiana	882	58	South Carolina	844	58
Iowa	1099	5	South Dakota	1069	5
Kansas	1060	9	Tennessee	1040	12
Kentucky	999	11	Texas	893	47
Louisiana	1021	9	Utah	1076	4
Maine	896	68	Vermont	901	68
Maryland	909	64	Virginia	896	65
Massachusetts	907	80	Washington	937	48
Michigan	1033	11	West Virginia	932	17
Minnesota	1085	9	Wisconsin	1073	9
Mississippi	1038	4	Wyoming	1001	10
Missouri	1045	9			

SOURCE: College Board, 1995 as reported in *USA Today,* Aug. 24, 1995.

a. Construct a scatterplot of the data in Table 11.7.

b. Fit the model $Y = \beta_0 + \beta_1 x + \varepsilon$. Give r^2 and comment on the strength of the linear relation.

c. Is the regression significant? Test at the $\alpha = .05$ level.

d. Examine the residuals and comment on the appropriateness of the simple linear regression model.

StSATExp.dat

11.64 (*Minitab or similar program recommended*) Refer to Exercise 11.63.

a. Construct a 95% confidence interval for the mean SAT total score if 35% of a state's graduating high school seniors take the test.

b. Construct a 95% confidence interval for the mean SAT score if 98% of a state's graduating seniors take the test. Comment on the width of this interval relative to the width of the interval in part **a.**

c. Can you explain the apparent negative relationship between mean SAT score and percentage of graduates taking the test? What do you think would happen if, for example, at least 50% of the graduating seniors took the SAT in each state and the District of Columbia?

SportFrn.dat

11.65 (*Optional*) (*Minitab or similar program recommended*) Refer to Exercise 3.35 in Chapter 3. Player costs (x) and operating expenses (y) for $n = 26$ Major League Baseball teams for the 1990–1991 season are given in Table C.7, Appendix C. In Exercise 3.35, you were asked to fit a simple linear regression model to these data and to examine the residuals.

a. Write the equation for the fitted straight line. Determine r^2 and comment on the strength of the linear relation.

b. Test for zero population correlation. Use $\alpha = .01$.

c. Can we conclude that, as a general rule, operating expenses are about twice player costs? Discuss.

d. Estimate operating expenses, with a 95% prediction interval, if player costs are $30.5 million.

e. Using the residuals as a guide, identify any unusual observations. That is, do some teams have unusually low or unusually high player costs as a component of operating expenses?

11.66 (*Optional*) Starbucks Corp., the Seattle-based chain of trendy coffee bars, has enjoyed explosive growth. Based on a graph in the October 24, 1994, issue of *Business Week*, we present the number of Starbuck coffee bars for the 1990–1995 period. (The number for 1995 is an estimate of the number of Starbuck coffee bars.)

Year	1990	1991	1992	1993	1994	1995
Number of Coffee Bars	67	100	167	250	417	633

a. Plot the number of coffee bars against year, with $t = 1$ corresponding to 1990 and so forth. Comment on the appearance of the plot.

b. Plot the logarithms of the number of coffee bars against year. Is this plot consistent with linear growth?

c. Let t denote the year, $t = 1, 2, \ldots, 6$, and let $\ln y$ be the natural logarithm of the number of coffee bars. Fit the model $\ln y = \beta_0 + \beta_1 t + \varepsilon$. Determine r^2, and comment on the strength of the linear relation.

d. Test for the significance of the linear regression. Let $\alpha = .05$.

11.67 (*Optional*) Refer to Exercise 11.66.

a. Construct a 95% confidence interval for the annual growth rate γ. Is .50 a plausible value for γ? Explain.

b. Forecast the number of coffee bars for 1996 with a 95% prediction interval.

c. Predict the number of coffee bars in the year 2000. Do you have much faith in this prediction? Discuss.

11.68 (*Minitab or similar program recommended*) The market shares of Colgate and Crest toothpaste for 276 consecutive weeks are given in the Data Disk. Let y be the market share of Colgate, and let x denote the market share of Crest.

Toothpas.dat

a. Construct a scatterplot of these data.

b. Fit the model $Y = \beta_0 + \beta_1 x + \varepsilon$. Provide an estimate of σ, the standard deviation of the error.

c. Interpret the sign of the estimated slope coefficient. Construct a 95% confidence interval for β_1.

d. Construct a time series plot of the residuals and the residual autocorrelation function. Is the independence assumption for the errors justified? Explain.

After reading this chapter, you should be able to:

- Formulate and analyze multiple linear regression models.
- Understand and use the stepwise regression and all possible regressions procedures.
- Deal with multicollinearity, and interpret certain measures of influence.
- Perform an additive decomposition of a time series.
- Distinguish between stationary and nonstationary time series.
- Identify and analyze autoregressive time series models, and develop forecasts of future observations.

CHAPTER TWELVE

Multiple Linear Regression and Time Series Models

12.1   INTRODUCTION

The Franklin Mint (FM) of Philadelphia, Pennsylvania, is a leading worldwide direct-response marketer of fine quality collectibles and luxury and home decor products. FM offers approximately 200 products, including a full range of specially designed jewelry and its famous Precision Car models, to its collector base through the mail, company-owned retail stores, the print media, and TV, but never in general retail and department stores. About 60% of FM's sales are by mail. The main channel of promotion for FM is through its proprietary collector list, which contains the names and addresses of customers who have purchased at least one item from the company. As of

1992, FM's collector list contained 8.3 million customers worldwide, 6.2 million of them in the United States and Canada, and the remaining 2.1 million in Europe and the Pacific.

In addition to names and addresses, FM's collector list contains accumulated demographic, promotional, purchase, and payment history data. The company uses this information to create a targeted mailing list for each of its promotions. In the late 1980s, the company made a strategic decision to build a brand new promotion selection system based, in part, on a type of *multiple regression model*. The regression model explains purchase decisions in terms of

- the customer's purchase history,
- demographic variables, and
- the product attributes, such as theme, material, artist, sponsor, and product code.

The most challenging part of the new system was the selection of the subset of predictors that "best" explain, in a statistical sense, the customer's choice decisions from among more than 800 potential predictors.

The outputs from the multiple regression model then drive the whole promotional decision process, which includes:

- targeting the "right" audience for each promotion,
- predicting the number of orders to be generated by the mailing,
- determining the number of units to manufacture or procure to meet customer demand,
- offering "personalization," and
- optimizing the number of mailings to a customer.

The new promotional system went into operation in 1992, and net profits attributed to the system have increased each year as this book went to press.

Utility companies in the United States are regulated by state public service or utility commissions. Northern States Power (NSP) Company, headquartered in Minneapolis, Minnesota, services part of the neighboring state of Wisconsin. To build a new power plant that will affect Wisconsin customers, NSP must gain the approval of the Wisconsin Public Service Commission. Part of the argument for the new plant depends on the company's ability to demonstrate growth in the demand for power and to argue convincingly that the growth will continue into the future.

In a case before the Wisconsin Public Service Commission, historical data relating to NSP (Wisconsin) peak, or maximum, monthly demand (see Example 3.18) show that demand has a consistent seasonal pattern (high during the winter heating season, with a secondary peak during the summer air conditioning season) superimposed on an upward sloping linear trend. A *time series model* fit to these data provided an estimate of the annual growth rate in peak demand of about 5% with a ±2% error margin. In addition, the model was used to generate forecasts of future peak demand. This information was presented as evidence for the need for new generating capacity. Although the request for the plant was eventually denied, forecasts of peak demand for the next 24 months made at the time of the NSP hearing proved to be accurate and well within the bounds of their respective 95% prediction intervals.

In this chapter, we study multiple linear regression and time series models. We build on the simple linear regression and first-order autoregressive models introduced in Chapter 11. We focus on the problems of specifying an appropriate model, estimating the model parameters, inference, and model checking or residual analysis. For the most part, we rely on the computer to perform the mathematics, and we simply interpret and use the output from statistical packages like Minitab as necessary.

12.2   THE MULTIPLE LINEAR REGRESSION MODEL

In the simple linear regression model, the response Y depends on the single explanatory variable x according to the linear relation

$$E(Y) = \mu_Y = \beta_0 + \beta_1 x$$

This is the population regression function and defines the mean of Y for each value of x. We assume, for any fixed value of x, the response Y is normally distributed about this mean and has a standard deviation σ that is the same for all values of x.

After a straight line is fit, it may turn out that the unexplained variation is large, so r^2 is small, indicating a poor fit. At the same time, an attempt to transform one or both of the variables may fail to dramatically improve the fit as measured by r^2. This difficulty may well be due to the fact that the response depends not just on x but on other factors as well. When used alone, x fails to be a good predictor of y because of the effect of these other influencing variables. For example, the rent for an apartment is related not only to its size (square feet) but also to its location, the number of bedrooms, and the number of bathrooms.

In the multiple regression model, the response Y depends on p explanatory or predictor variables,* $x_1, x_2, \ldots, x_p$. The mean response is taken to be a linear function of these explanatory variables,

$$E(Y) = \mu_Y = \beta_0 + \beta_1 x_1 + \beta_2 x_2 + \cdots + \beta_p x_p$$

This expression is the *population multiple regression function.* As was the case with simple linear regression, we cannot directly observe the population regression function because the observed values of Y vary about their means. We think of the regression function evaluated at a particular set of values for *all* of the explanatory variables $x_1, x_2, \ldots, x_p$ as the mean of a subpopulation of responses Y. We further assume that the Y's in each of these subpopulations are normally distributed about their means with the same standard deviation σ.

The data for simple linear regression consist of observations (x_i, y_i) on the two variables. In multiple regression, the data on each experimental unit or case consists of an observation on the response and an observation on each of the explanatory variables. We denote the ith observation on the jth explanatory variable by x_{ij}. With this notation, data for multiple regression have the form given in Table 12.1 (page 622). It is convenient to refer to the data for the ith case as simply the ith observation. With

---

*The name *multiple regression* refers to the fact that the response depends on more than one explanatory variable.

TABLE 12.1 Data Structure for Multiple Regression

Experimental Unit or Case	Explanatory Variables				Response
	x_1	x_2	...	x_p	y
1	x_{11}	x_{12}	...	x_{1p}	y_1
2	x_{21}	x_{22}	...	x_{2p}	y_2
.	.	.	...	.	.
.	.	.	...	.	.
i	x_{i1}	x_{i2}	...	x_{ip}	y_i
.	.	.	...	.	.
.	.	.	...	.	.
n	x_{n1}	x_{n2}	...	x_{np}	y_n

this convention, n is the number of observations and p is the number of explanatory variables.

Statistical Model for Multiple Regression

The response Y is a random variable that is related to the independent variables $x_1, x_2, \ldots, x_p$ by

$$Y_i = \beta_0 + \beta_1 x_{i1} + \beta_2 x_{i2} + \cdots + \beta_p x_{ip} + \varepsilon_i \qquad i = 1, 2, \ldots, n$$

where:

1. Y_i denotes the response corresponding to the ith case in which $x_1, x_2, \ldots, x_p$ are set at values $x_{i1}, x_{i2}, \ldots, x_{ip}$.

2. $\varepsilon_1, \varepsilon_2, \ldots, \varepsilon_n$ are the unknown error components that represent the deviations of the response from the true linear relation. They are unobservable random variables. We assume that the errors are independent and each is normally distributed with mean 0 and unknown standard deviation σ.

3. The coefficients or parameters $\beta_0, \beta_1, \beta_2, \ldots, \beta_p$ that together locate the regression function are unknown.

Given the data, the regression parameters can be estimated using the principle of least squares (see Section 11.3). As we mentioned, a multiple regression analysis is easily performed on a computer with the aid of standard statistical packages, such as Minitab, SAS, or SPSS.

EXAMPLE 12.1   A Multiple Regression Model for Newsprint Consumption

A large component of the cost of owning a newspaper is the cost of newsprint. Newspaper publishers are interested in factors that determine annual newsprint consumption. The amount of newsprint used is directly related to the number and size of papers produced, but these quantities depend on newspaper circulation, advertising pages, and, of course, competing papers. Let the response y be newsprint consumption, and let the explanatory variables x_1, x_2, and x_3 denote the number of newspapers in a city, the logarithm* of the number of families in a city, and the logarithm of the total retail sales in a city, respectively. Suppose we collect observations on these variables for 15 cities. Formulate a multiple regression model linking the response to the three explanatory variables.

Solution and Discussion. The multiple regression model is given by

$$Y_i = \beta_0 + \beta_1 x_{i1} + \beta_2 x_{i2} + \beta_3 x_{i3} + \varepsilon_i \qquad i = 1, 2, \ldots, 15$$

The parameters to be estimated in this model are β_0, β_1, β_2, β_3, and σ. Recall that σ is the standard deviation of the error ε_i or, equivalently, of the response Y_i.

EXAMPLE 12.2   A Multiple Regression Model for CEO Compensation

Chief executive officer (CEO) salaries in the United States are of interest because of their relationship to salaries in international firms and to salaries of top professionals outside of corporate America. Also, for an individual firm, the CEO compensation directly, or indirectly, influences the salaries of managers in positions below that of CEO. CEO salary varies greatly from firm to firm, but data suggest that salary can be explained in terms of a firm's sales, the CEO's amount of experience, educational level, and ownership stake in the firm. Suppose 50 firms will be used in a study of CEO compensation. Formulate a multiple linear regression model linking compensation with the explanatory variables sales, experience, educational level, and ownership stake.

Solution and Discussion. Let y denote CEO compensation, and let x_1, x_2, x_3, and x_4 denote firm sales, amount of experience as a CEO, educational level of CEO, and CEO ownership stake in the firm, respectively. The multiple regression model is given by

$$Y_i = \beta_0 + \beta_1 x_{i1} + \beta_2 x_{i2} + \beta_3 x_{i3} + \beta_4 x_{i4} + \varepsilon_i \qquad i = 1, 2, \ldots, 50$$

Here there are five regression function parameters to be estimated, β_0, β_1, \ldots, β_4, and the standard deviation σ of the error term or response.

INFERENCE FOR MULTIPLE REGRESSION MODELS

Inference for multiple regression models is analogous to that for simple linear regression. The least squares estimates of the model parameters, their estimated standard errors, t statistics used to examine the significance of individual terms in the regression model, and an F statistic used to examine the "significance of the regression" are all provided in output from standard software packages. Determining these quantities by hand for a multiple regression model of any size is not practical, and we must rely on the computer for the calculations.

---

*Logarithms of the number of families and the total retail sales are used to make the numbers less positively skewed and more manageable (see Example 12.3).

The estimators of the parameters

$$\beta_0, \beta_1, \beta_2, \ldots, \beta_p$$

are denoted by

$$\hat{\beta}_0, \hat{\beta}_1, \hat{\beta}_2, \ldots, \hat{\beta}_p$$

respectively. Using this notation, we have

$$\text{Observation} = \text{Fit} + \text{Residual}$$

or, for the ith observation,

$$y_i = \hat{y}_i + (y_i - \hat{y}_i)$$

with the fitted value given by

$$\hat{y}_i = \hat{\beta}_0 + \hat{\beta}_1 x_{i1} + \hat{\beta}_2 x_{i2} + \cdots + \hat{\beta}_p x_{ip}$$

Recall that the fit $\hat{y}$ is an estimate of the regression function or deterministic part of the model. It represents that part of y explained by its relation with the x's or predictor variables. The residual $y - \hat{y}$ is an estimate of the error component or random part of the model. It represents that part of y not explained by the predictor variables.

The method of least squares picks the values for $\hat{\beta}_0, \hat{\beta}_1, \ldots, \hat{\beta}_p$ that make the residual (error) sum of squares

$$\text{SSE} = \sum_{i=1}^{n}(y_i - \hat{y}_i)^2 = \sum_{i=1}^{n}(y_i - \hat{\beta}_0 - \hat{\beta}_1 x_{i1} - \cdots - \hat{\beta}_p x_{ip})^2$$

as small as possible. The computations leading to the least squares estimates are beyond the scope of this book but are easily determined with the help of a computer.

The quantity σ^2 is a measure of the variability of the responses about the regression function or, equivalently, about their subpopulation means. As was the case for simple linear regression, an estimator of σ^2 is given by the residual mean square s^2—that is, the residual sum of squares SSE divided by its degrees of freedom. For multiple regression models with p explanatory variables, the residual sum of squares has $n - p - 1$ degrees of freedom.*

Estimator of σ^2: $\qquad s^2 = \dfrac{\text{SSE}}{n - p - 1} = \dfrac{\sum(y_i - \hat{y}_i)^2}{n - p - 1}$

Estimator of σ: $\qquad s = \sqrt{s^2} = \sqrt{\dfrac{\text{SSE}}{n - p - 1}}$

---

*For simple linear regression, $p = 1$ and the residual sum of squares has d.f. $= n - 1 - 1 = n - 2$, the result given in Chapter 11.

Confidence intervals for model parameters and prediction intervals for new responses continue to take the form

$$\text{Estimate} \pm t_{\alpha/2}(\text{Estimated standard error})$$

Tests of the significance of individual terms in the regression model are based on t ratios like

$$t = \frac{\text{Estimate}}{\text{Estimated standard error}}$$

The expressions for the estimated standard errors are complicated, but s is an important component.

Confidence Intervals and Tests of Hypotheses for β_j

A $100(1 - \alpha)\%$ **confidence interval for β_j** is

$$(\hat{\beta}_j - t_{\alpha/2}s_{\hat{\beta}_j}, \ \hat{\beta}_j + t_{\alpha/2}s_{\hat{\beta}_j})$$

where $s_{\hat{\beta}_j}$ is the estimated standard error of $\hat{\beta}_j$ and $t_{\alpha/2}$ is the upper $\alpha/2$ point of a t distribution with d.f. $= n - p - 1$.

To test the hypothesis H_0: $\beta_j = 0$, compute the test statistic

$$t = \frac{\hat{\beta}_j}{s_{\hat{\beta}_j}}$$

For an α level test, reject H_0 if

$$
\begin{aligned}
|t| > t_{\alpha/2} \quad &\text{for} \quad H_1\text{: } \beta_j \neq 0 \\
t > t_{\alpha} \quad &\text{for} \quad H_1\text{: } \beta_j > 0 \\
t < -t_{\alpha} \quad &\text{for} \quad H_1\text{: } \beta_j < 0
\end{aligned}
$$

The P-value is the smallest α for which the observed t value just rejects H_0. Consequently, there is a P-value corresponding to each of these three alternative hypotheses.

Fitted regression functions are often used for prediction so that estimates of the mean response or a new response are required. Confidence intervals for the mean response $E(Y) = \beta_0 + \beta_1 x_1^* + \cdots + \beta_p x_p^*$, or a new response y^*, at the values of the predictor variables $x_1^*, x_2^*, \ldots, x_p^*$ generally require additional input to a computer program. To have the computer generate these interval estimates, we must input the x^*'s and the confidence level $1 - \alpha$. However, the intervals have the general form

$$\hat{y}^* \pm t_{\alpha/2}(\text{Estimated standard error})$$

where

$$\hat{y}^* = \hat{\beta}_0 + \hat{\beta}_1 x_1^* + \hat{\beta}_2 x_2^* + \cdots + \hat{\beta}_p x_p^*$$

At the same settings of the x's, a $100(1 - \alpha)\%$ prediction interval for y^* is wider than a $100(1 - \alpha)\%$ confidence interval for $\beta_0 + \beta_1 x_1^* + \cdots + \beta_p x_p^*$. There is more uncertainty, indicated by the wider interval, in estimating a single response than there is in estimating the mean response.

If n is large and all the x's are quite variable, an approximate $100(1 - \alpha)\%$ prediction interval for the new response y^* is

$$(\hat{y}^* - t_{\alpha/2}s, \ \hat{y}^* + t_{\alpha/2}s)$$

where $t_{\alpha/2}$ is the upper $\alpha/2$ point of a t distribution with d.f. $= n - p - 1$.

As we discussed in Chapter 11, the analysis of variance (ANOVA) is a way to break up the observed variability in the response into two components: one component representing that part of the variability explained by the (estimated) regression and the other component representing the remaining unexplained variability, or error variation. The analysis of variance is based on the algebraic result

$$\sum (y_i - \overline{y})^2 = \sum (\hat{y}_i - \overline{y})^2 + \sum (y_i - \hat{y}_i)^2$$

or

$$\text{SST} = \text{SSR} + \text{SSE}$$

where

$$\text{SST} = \sum (y_i - \overline{y})^2$$
$$\text{SSR} = \sum (\hat{y}_i - \overline{y})^2$$
$$\text{SSE} = \sum (y_i - \hat{y}_i)^2$$

These sums of squares have associated degrees of freedom

$$\text{d.f.(SST)} = n - 1$$
$$\text{d.f.(SSR)} = p$$
$$\text{d.f.(SSE)} = n - p - 1$$

and, corresponding to the sum of squares, the degrees of freedom are related by

$$n - 1 = p + (n - p - 1)$$

Notice that p is the number of explanatory variables in the regression function.

Table 12.2 contains the ANOVA table for multiple regression.

Consider the hypothesis H_0: $\beta_1 = \beta_2 = \cdots = \beta_p = 0$. This hypothesis means that the response y is not related to any of the x's. Thus, a test of H_0 is referred to as a test of the *significance of the regression*. If the regression model assumptions are appropriate and H_0 is true, the ratio

$$F = \frac{\text{MSR}}{\text{MSE}}$$

TABLE 12.2 The ANOVA Table for Multiple Regression

Source	Sum of Squares	d.f.	Mean Square	F ratio
Regression	SSR	p	$\text{MSR} = \text{SSR}/p$	$F = \text{MSR}/\text{MSE}$
Error	SSE	$n - p - 1$	$\text{MSE} = \text{SSE}/(n - p - 1)$	
Total	SST	$n - 1$		

has an F distribution with d.f. $= (p, n - p - 1)$. Thus, the F ratio can be used to test the significance of the regression.

In simple linear regression, there is only one explanatory variable. Consequently, testing for the significance of the regression using the F ratio from the ANOVA table is equivalent to the two-sided t test of the hypothesis that the slope of the regression line is 0. For multiple regression, the t tests examine the significance of *individual* terms in the regression function, and the F test examines the significance of *all* of the terms collectively.

F Test for the Significance of the Regression

In the multiple regression model, the hypotheses

$$H_0: \quad \beta_1 = \beta_2 = \cdots = \beta_p = 0$$
$$H_1: \quad \text{at least one } \beta_j \neq 0$$

are tested by the F ratio

$$F = \frac{\text{MSR}}{\text{MSE}}$$

with d.f. $= (p, n - p - 1)$. At level α, the rejection region is

$$F > F_\alpha(p, n - p - 1)$$

The **coefficient of determination*** R^2 is given by

$$R^2 = \frac{\text{SSR}}{\text{SST}} = 1 - \frac{\text{SSE}}{\text{SST}}$$

and has the same interpretation as r^2 does for simple linear regression. It represents the proportion of variation in the response y explained by the regression, or, equivalently, explained by the relationship of y with the x's.

---

*It is customary to use capital R^2 to denote the coefficient of determination in multiple regression. This notation also corresponds to the notation for the coefficient of determination in the multiple regression output for most statistical software packages.

A value of $R^2 = 1$ says that all of the observed y's fall exactly on the fitted regression function. All of the variation in the response is explained by the regression. A value of $R^2 = 0$ says that $\hat{y} = \bar{y}$, that is, SSR $= 0$, and none of the variation in y is explained by the multiple regression. Of course, in practice $0 < R^2 < 1$, and the value of R^2 must be interpreted relative to the two extremes, 0 and 1.

The square root of the coefficient of determination has an interesting interpretation for multiple regression models. The quantity $R = \sqrt{R^2}$ is called the **multiple correlation coefficient,** and it is the correlation between the responses y_i and the fitted values $\hat{y}_i$. Since the fitted values predict the responses, R is always positive so that $0 \leq R \leq 1$.

EXAMPLE 12.3 Fitting a Multiple Regression Model to the Newsprint Consumption Data

In Example 12.1, we specified a multiple regression model for the amount of newsprint consumed in a year. The data referred to in Example 12.1 are listed in Table 12.3.

TABLE 12.3 Newsprint Data

Case	x_1 Papers	x_2 LnFamily	x_3 LnRetSal	y Newsprnt
1	1	9.060	11.254	961
2	1	8.835	10.814	469
3	1	8.983	10.926	3511
4	2	10.280	12.403	9256
5	1	9.198	11.019	556
6	1	9.424	11.389	1252
7	1	8.843	11.367	902
8	1	9.530	11.154	1399
9	1	8.916	11.212	1877
10	2	10.389	12.436	13907
11	1	8.811	10.839	921
12	1	10.402	12.228	6959
13	2	9.385	11.391	2260
14	2	9.649	11.617	7255
15	1	8.912	10.998	494

Fit a multiple regression model to these data, and interpret the results.

Solution and Discussion. The Minitab output is shown here.

```
The regression equation is
① Newsprnt = - 56388 + 2385 Papers + 1859 LnFamily + 3455 LnRetSal

Predictor        Coef       Stdev      t-ratio       p         VIF
Constant       -56388       13206       -4.27      0.001
Papers           2385        1410        1.69      0.119       1.7
LnFamily         1859        2346        0.79      0.445       7.4
LnRetSal      ② 3455        2590      ③ 1.33      0.209       8.1

④ s = 1849     ⑤ R-sq = 83.5%     R-sq(adj) = 79.0%     (continued)
```

```
Analysis of Variance

SOURCE        DF              SS          MS            F          p
Regression    3         190239360     63413120   (7) 18.54     0.000
Error         11 (6)     37621488      3420135
Total         14        227860848
```

From the output, we see that:

1. The equation of the fitted regression function is

$$\text{(1)} \quad \hat{y} = -56388 + 2385x_1 + 1859x_2 + 3455x_3$$

This means that newsprint consumption is estimated to increase by 2385 if the number of papers increases by 1 while the number of families and the amount of retail sales remain fixed. Similarly, a 1-unit increase in the log of the number of families results in an increase in newsprint consumption of 1859 while the remaining explanatory variables remain fixed, and so forth.

2. The least squares estimate of β_3 is

$$\text{(2)} \quad \hat{\beta}_3 = 3455 \quad \text{with estimated standard error } s_{\hat{\beta}_3} = 2590$$

3. The t value for testing $H_0 : \beta_3 = 0$ against $H_1 : \beta_3 \neq 0$ is

$$\text{(3)} \quad t = 1.33 \quad \text{with } P\text{-value} = .209$$

With variables x_1 and x_2 in the regression function, we would not reject H_0 at any reasonable significance level. We conclude that, with x_1 and x_2 in the model, x_3 is not needed. (We must be careful about interpreting the t statistics for individual terms in the fitted function. We discuss this issue later.)

4. An estimate of σ is provided by

$$\text{(4)} \quad s = 1849$$

and the coefficient of determination is

$$\text{(5)} \quad R^2 = .835$$

About 84% of the variation in y is explained by the fitted multiple regression of y on x_1, x_2, and x_3.

5. From the ANOVA table,

$$\text{(6)} \quad \text{SSR} = 190239360 \quad \text{with d.f.} = 3 \text{ (number of } x\text{'s)}$$
$$\text{SSE} = 37621488 \quad \text{with d.f.} = 11 \text{ } (n - (\text{number of } x\text{'s}) - 1)$$
$$\text{SST} = 227860848 \quad \text{with d.f.} = 14 \text{ } (n - 1)$$

6. The F statistic for testing $H_0: \beta_1 = \beta_2 = \beta_3 = 0$ or, equivalently, for testing the significance of the regression, is

$$\text{(7)} \quad F = 18.54 \quad \text{with d.f.} = (3, 11)$$

Its P-value is .000, indicating there is strong evidence for rejecting H_0. We conclude the regression is significant.

For this example, the t statistic for each of the individual terms in the fitted regression function is not significant at the 10% level (each t statistic has a P-value greater than .10). On the other hand, the regression is clearly significant. How can this be? The individual terms are not significant, yet all the terms together are significant (the regression is significant). This apparent anomaly happens often in practice and has to do with the relations among the x's. Information about the relations among the x's is contained in the column labeled VIF. We will ignore this column temporarily and return to it in Example 12.4. One of the lessons here is that the significance of individual terms in a fitted regression equation must be interpreted with care.

In keeping with our admonition to always examine the residuals from a regression analysis, we present Figure 12.1, Minitab residual plots from our analysis of the newsprint consumption data.

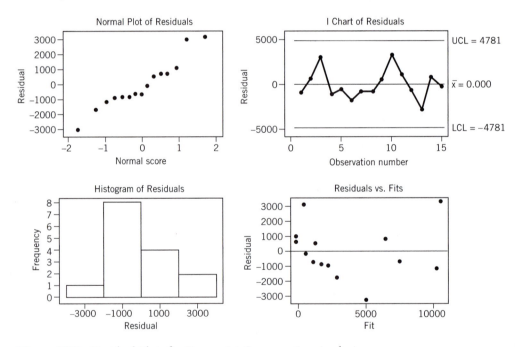

Figure 12.1 Residual Plots for Newsprint Consumption Analysis

Interpretation of these plots is straightforward, with the possible exception of the I Chart. The I stands for *individual* observation; this chart is simply a sequence plot of the residuals relative to their mean 0 with ±3 estimated standard deviation limits indicated. These limits are labeled UCL (upper control limit) and LCL (lower control limit), respectively. We see from this control chart that all the residuals are well within 3 (estimated) standard deviations of 0. This is what we would expect of normally distributed error terms.

The normal-scores plot is not particularly straight, but with only $n = 15$ observations, it is difficult to argue that the normal assumption is invalid. The remaining plots are consistent with the regression assumptions, so we conclude the regression assumptions are appropriate.

POLYNOMIAL REGRESSION

A scatterplot may indicate a relationship on a curve for which a suitable linearizing transformation of the kind discussed in Chapter 11 cannot be constructed. Another method of handling such a nonlinear relation is to include terms with higher powers of x in the model $Y = \beta_0 + \beta_1 x + \varepsilon$. For example, by including the second power of x, we obtain the **polynomial regression model**

$$Y_i = \beta_0 + \beta_1 x_i + \beta_2 x_i^2 + \varepsilon_i \qquad i = 1, 2, \ldots, n$$

This model states that aside from the error components, ε_i, the response Y is a quadratic function (or a second-degree polynomial) of the explanatory variable x. The subpopulation means of Y lie along a quadratic curve. In general, the highest power of x that occurs in the model is called the *degree* or *order* of the polynomial regression. The analysis of a polynomial regression model does not require any special techniques other than those used in multiple regression analysis. By identifying x and x^2 as the two variables x_1 and x_2, respectively, the second-degree polynomial model reduces to the form of a multiple regression model

$$Y_i = \beta_0 + \beta_1 x_{i1} + \beta_2 x_{i2} + \varepsilon_i \qquad i = 1, 2, \ldots, n$$

discussed previously.

EXERCISES

12.1 The multiple regression model $Y = \beta_0 + \beta_1 x_1 + \beta_2 x_2 + \varepsilon$ was fitted to a data set with $n = 20$ observations. The least squares estimates were

$$\hat{\beta}_0 = 4.21 \qquad \hat{\beta}_1 = 11.37 \qquad \hat{\beta}_2 = -.51$$

Predict the response for:
a. $x_1 = 8, x_2 = 30$
b. $x_1 = 8, x_2 = 50$
c. $x_1 = 3, x_2 = 50$

12.2 Consider the multiple regression model

$$Y = \beta_0 + \beta_1 x_1 + \beta_2 x_2 + \varepsilon$$

where $\beta_0 = 5$, $\beta_1 = 1$, $\beta_2 = -4$, and the normal random variable ε has standard deviation $\sigma = 2$. How much will the expected response change if
a. x_1 is increased 1 unit
b. x_2 is decreased 1 unit
c. x_1 and x_2 are both increased by 1 unit

12.3 Consider the multiple regression model

$$Y = \beta_0 + \beta_1 x_1 + \beta_2 x_2 + \varepsilon$$

where $\beta_0 = -1$, $\beta_1 = -2$, $\beta_2 = 3$, and the normal random variable ε has standard deviation $\sigma = 4$. Determine the mean of the response y for:

a. $x_1 = 15$, $x_2 = 10$

b. $x_1 = 12$, $x_2 = 10$

c. $x_1 = 12$, $x_2 = 18$

12.4 Refer to Exercise 12.3. What is the probability that the response y will exceed 20 if $x_1 = 5$ and $x_2 = 12$?

12.5 Refer to Exercise 12.1. Suppose the residual sum of squares was SSE = 46.25 and the regression sum of squares was SSR = 236.70.

a. Estimate the error standard deviation σ. State the degrees of freedom associated with your estimator.

b. Determine R^2 and interpret the result.

12.6 Refer to Exercise 12.1. Suppose the estimated standard errors of $\hat{\beta}_0$, $\hat{\beta}_1$, and $\hat{\beta}_2$ were 2.26, 1.08, and .098, respectively.

a. Construct 95% confidence intervals for β_0 and β_2.

b. Test $H_0: \beta_1 = 12$ versus $H_1: \beta_1 > 12$ with $\alpha = .05$.

Newsprin.dat

12.7 (*Minitab or similar program recommended*) Consider the newsprint data in Table 12.3. Fit the multiple regression model

$$Y = \beta_0 + \beta_1 x_1 + \beta_2 x_2 + \varepsilon$$

where Y is newsprint consumption, x_1 is the number of papers, and x_2 is the logarithm of number of families in a city.

a. Write the equation of the fitted regression function.

b. Is the regression significant? Explain.

c. Compare the estimated coefficients of "number of papers" and "log number of families" with those given for these variables in Example 12.3. Notice that the estimated coefficient of "log number of families" has changed considerably and its t value has increased dramatically. Can you think of a possible explanation?

d. What proportion of the variability of y is explained by the regression of y on x_1 and x_2?

12.8 (*Minitab or similar program recommended*) Consider the following data:

y	3.2	3.8	5.0	6.2	6.9	7.0	8.0	8.2	8.9	9.8
x	130	156	180	220	254	265	300	315	352	420
x^2										

a. Fill in the x^2 values in the table, and fit the quadratic regression model

$$Y = \beta_0 + \beta_1 x + \beta_2 x^2 + \varepsilon$$

to these data.

b. What proportion of the variability of y is explained by the quadratic regression?

c.   Is the second-order term required in this case? Explain.

d.   Examine the residuals. Are the regression assumptions appropriate?

12.9   (*Minitab or similar program recommended*) The data in the table include observations on the 20 best selling cars for 1994.

BestCar.dat

Case	95Price	HP	Weight	MPG
1	15,902	140	3118	30
2	16,294	130	2756	29
3	9,693	88	2355	34
4	14,849	125	2910	28
5	11,062	100	2325	36
6	10,919	102	2231	40
7	12,662	150	2824	30
8	12,661	155	2745	29
9	11,799	105	2315	30
10	13,930	120	2537	32
11	12,560	115	2300	37
12	14,076	150	2829	29
13	18,962	170	3449	29
14	13,907	145	3077	29
15	14,047	140	3144	30
16	14,787	120	2986	32
17	16,227	161	3310	28
18	15,711	140	3536	26
19	31,934	200	3758	26
20	14,263	160	3372	29

Here, 95Price = 1995 price in dollars, HP = horsepower, Weight = weight in pounds, and MPG = highway miles per gallon.

a.   Fit a multiple regression model linking 95Price to HP and Weight. Is the regression significant? Are the individual predictor variable terms significant? Explain.

b.   What proportion of the 95Price variability is explained by the regression on HP and Weight?

c.   Examine the residuals. Are the regression assumptions appropriate?

12.10   (*Minitab or similar program recommended*) Refer to Exercise 12.9.

BestCar.dat

a.   Fit a multiple regression linking MPG to HP and Weight. Is the regression significant? Are the individual predictor variable terms significant? Explain.

b.   Interpret the coefficient $\hat{\beta}_1$. Construct a 95% confidence interval for β_1.

c.   Examine the residuals. Are the regression assumptions appropriate?

12.11   Refer to Example 12.2. A printout from a multiple regression analysis of CEO compensation follows. Here y = LnComp (log of CEO compensation in $1000's), x_1 = LnSales (log of company's sales), x_2 = Exper (years of experience as a CEO), x_3 = Educate (educational level of CEO with 0 = no college degree, 1 = undergraduate degree, and 2 = graduate degree), and x_4 = PctOwn (percentage of company's stock owned by CEO).

```
The regression equation is
LnComp = 5.36 + 0.263 LnSales + 0.0157 Exper
             - 0.429 Educate - 0.0308 PctOwn
```

Predictor	Coef	Stdev	t-ratio	p
Constant	5.3636	0.6208	8.64	0.000
LnSales	0.26252	0.07086	3.70	0.001
Exper	0.015714	0.008576	1.83	0.074
Educate	-0.4292	0.1213	-3.54	0.001
PctOwn	-0.03077	0.01311	-2.35	0.023

```
s = 0.4831       R-sq = 46.8%       R-sq(adj) = 42.1%
```

Analysis of Variance

SOURCE	DF	SS	MS	F	p
Regression	4	9.2421	2.3105	9.90	0.000
Error	45	10.5018	0.2334		
Total	49	19.7439			

a. Identify the fitted regression function and interpret the coefficient $\hat{\beta}_3$.

b. Predict the log compensation for a CEO with company sales of $7,818 million, 6 years of experience, an undergraduate degree, and .40% of the company's stock. Convert this number to compensation (in millions of dollars).

c. Identify the proportion of variability in log compensation explained by the estimated regression function.

d. Interpret the P-value associated with the F statistic.

12.12 Refer to Exercise 12.11. Residual plots from the regression analysis described in Exercise 12.11 are shown here.

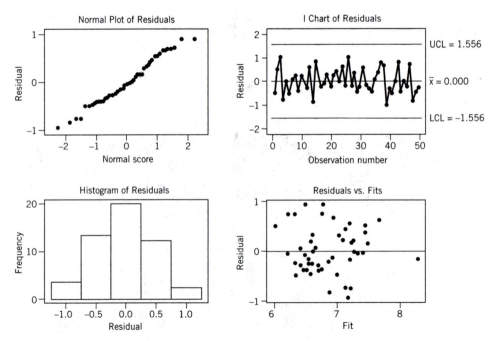

Interpret each of these plots. Is there any reason to doubt the regression model assumptions? Explain.

12.13 (*Minitab or similar program recommended*) Sometimes it is necessary in a regression analysis to account for the effects of variables that cannot be quantified or, if they can be quantified, cannot be measured for various reasons. Ignoring the effects of these variables can produce misleading results. One way to account for the effects of a nonquantifiable variable is to use an *indicator* or *dummy* variable whose numerical values indicate varying conditions.

A taxi company is interested in the relationship between mileage, measured in miles per gallon, and the age of cars in its fleet. The 12 fleet cars are the same make and size, and in good operating condition as a result of regular maintenance. The company employs both male and female drivers, and it is believed that some of the variability in mileage may be due to differences in driving techniques between the groups of drivers of opposite gender. In fact, "other things being equal," women tend to get better mileage than men. Data are generated by randomly assigning the 12 cars to the 5 female and 7 male drivers and computing miles per gallon (MPG) after 300 miles.

y (MPG)	x_1 (Age of car)	x_2 (Gender: 0 = male, 1 = female)
22.3	3	0
22.0	4	1
23.7	3	1
24.2	2	0
25.5	1	1
21.1	5	0
20.6	4	0
24.0	1	0
26.0	1	1
23.1	2	0
24.8	2	1
20.2	5	0

a. Construct a scatterplot with y as the vertical axis and x_1 as the horizontal axis. Identify the points corresponding to male and female drivers, respectively.

b. Fit the multiple regression model

$$Y = \beta_0 + \beta_1 x_1 + \beta_2 x_2 + \varepsilon$$

and interpret the coefficient $\hat{\beta}_2$.

c. Compute the fitted values for each of the (x_1, x_2) pairs, and plot the fitted values on the scatterplot. Draw straight lines through the fitted values for male drivers and female drivers, respectively. Specify the equations for these two straight lines.

d. Suppose gender is ignored. Fit the simple linear regression model $Y = \beta_0 + \beta_1 x_1 + \varepsilon$, and plot the fitted straight line on the scatterplot. Is it important to include the effects of gender in this case? Explain.

12.3   MULTICOLLINEARITY, VARIABLE SELECTION, AND REGRESSION DIAGNOSTICS

In this section, we briefly discuss some important topics in regression that are particularly relevant for multiple linear regression models.

MULTICOLLINEARITY

In many regression problems, data are routinely recorded rather than generated from preselected settings of the explanatory variables (the "designed experiment"). In these cases, the explanatory variables are frequently linearly dependent. For example, in appraisal work, the selling price of homes may be related to explanatory factors such as age, living space in square feet, number of bathrooms, number of rooms exclusive of bathrooms, lot size, and an index of construction quality. Living space, number of rooms, and number of bathrooms should certainly "move together." If one of these variables increases, the others will generally increase.

If this linear dependence in the predictor variables is less than perfect, the least squares estimates of the regression model parameters can still be obtained. However, these estimates tend to be unstable—their values can change dramatically with slight changes in the data—and inflated—their values are larger than expected. In particular, individual coefficients may have the wrong sign and the t statistics for judging the significance of individual terms may all be insignificant, yet the F test will indicate the regression is significant. Finally, the calculation of the least squares estimates is sensitive to rounding errors.

A linear relation among two or more of the explanatory variables is referred to as **multicollinearity.** The strength of the multicollinearity is measured by the **variance inflation factor** or VIF.

$$ \text{VIF}_j = \frac{1}{1 - R_j^2} \qquad j = 1, 2, \ldots, p $$

Here R_j^2 is the coefficient of determination from the regression of the jth *explanatory* variable on the remaining $p - 1$ explanatory variables. For $p = 2$ explanatory variables, r_j^2 is the square of their sample correlation coefficient r.

If the jth explanatory variable x_j is not related to the remaining x's, $R_j^2 = 0$ and $\text{VIF}_j = 1$. If there is a relationship, $\text{VIF}_j > 1$. For example, with $R_j^2 = .9$, $\text{VIF}_j = 1/[1 - (.9)^2] = 5.26$.

A VIF near 1 suggests that multicollinearity is not a problem for that explanatory variable. Its estimated coefficient and associated t value will not change much as the other explanatory variables are added to or deleted from the regression function. A VIF much greater than 1 indicates that the estimated coefficient attached to that explanatory variable is unstable. Its value and the associated t statistic may change considerably as the other explanatory variables are added to or deleted from the regression equation. A large VIF means, essentially, that there is redundant information among the predictor variables. The information being conveyed by a variable with a large VIF is already being conveyed by the remaining predictor variables.

EXAMPLE 12.4   Demonstrating Multicollinearity with the Newsprint Consumption Data

In Example 12.3, we presented a regression analysis of the amount of newsprint consumed in a year by newspaper publishers in 15 cities. A portion of the Minitab output for that analysis is reproduced here.

```
The regression equation is
Newsprnt = - 56388 + 2385 Papers + 1859 LnFamily + 3455 LnRetSal

Predictor        Coef       Stdev     t-ratio          p        VIF
Constant       -56388       13206       -4.27      0.001
Papers           2385        1410        1.69      0.119        1.7
LnFamily         1859        2346        0.79      0.445        7.4
LnRetSal         3455        2590        1.33      0.209        8.1

  s = 1849      R-sq = 83.5%      R-sq(adj) = 79.0%
```

Interpret the column labeled VIF, and suggest an alternative model for newsprint consumption that is consistent with the current model and is almost as good as measured by R^2.

Solution and Discussion.   First, let's interpret the t statistics associated with the explanatory variables. Starting with the smallest one, $t = .79$ with P-value $= .445$, we do not reject $H_0: \beta_2 = 0$ at any reasonable significance level. We conclude that the variable LnFamily (log of number of families) is not significant *provided the other predictor variables remain in the regression function.** This suggests that the term $\beta_2 x_2$ can be dropped from the regression function if we retain the remaining terms, $\beta_1 x_1$ and $\beta_3 x_3$. A similar statement can be made about the term $\beta_3 x_3$. That is, this term might be dropped from the regression model if we retain the remaining predictor variable terms. The t value associated with Papers (number of newspapers in a city) is marginally significant (we would reject $H_0: \beta_1 = 0$ if $\alpha = .12$, for example), and for the moment, we will regard this term as important.

Now turn to the VIF column. Since VIF $= 1.7$ for Papers, we conclude that Papers is very weakly related (VIF near 1) to the remaining predictor variables, LnFamily and LnRetSal. The VIF $= 7.4$ for LnFamily is large, indicating that this variable is linearly related to the remaining predictor variables. Also, the VIF $= 8.1$ for LnRetSal indicates that this variable is linearly related to the remaining predictor variables. Since Papers is weakly related to LnFamily and LnRetSal, the relationship among the predictor variables is, essentially, the relationship between LnFamily and LnRetSal. Figure 12.2 (page 638) is a scatterplot of LnFamily and LnRetSal.

The sample correlation between LnFamily and LnRetSal is $r = .93$, indicating strong linear association. These two variables are very similar in their ability to explain newsprint consumption. We need only one, not both, in the regression function. This conclusion is consistent with our previous discussion of the t statistics.

---

*The t tests compare the model involving all of the x variables with a model in which one of the x variables has been omitted.

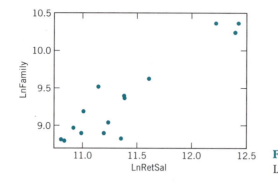

Figure 12.2 Scatterplot of LnFamily and LnRetSal

Of the two explanatory variables LnFamily and LnRetSal, LnRetSal has the larger correlation (a calculation gives $r = .88$) with the response Newsprnt (newsprint consumption). Consequently, we drop LnFamily from the regression function and consider a regression of Newsprnt on the remaining two predictors, Papers and LnRetSal. The Minitab output for this regression is shown here.

```
The regression equation is
Newsprnt = - 59766 + 2393 Papers + 5279 LnRetSal

Predictor        Coef       Stdev      t-ratio          p         VIF
Constant       -59766       12304        -4.86      0.000
Papers           2393        1388         1.72      0.110         1.7
LnRetSal         5279        1171         4.51      0.000         1.7

 s = 1820      R-sq = 82.5%      R-sq(adj) = 79.6%

Analysis of Variance

SOURCE        DF            SS           MS          F          p
Regression     2     188090480     94045240      28.38      0.000
Error         12      39770364      3314197
Total         14     227860848
```

Let's compare the $p = 2$ predictor variable regression with the $p = 3$ predictor variable regression. Notice that the coefficient of Papers is about the same for the two regressions. The coefficients of LnRetSal, however, are considerably different (3455 for $p = 3$ and 5279 for $p = 2$). Also, for the second regression, the variable LnRetSal is clearly significant ($t = 4.51$ with P-value $= .000$). With Papers in the model, LnRetSal is an additional important predictor of Newsprnt. The R^2's for the two models are nearly the same, approximately .83, as are the estimates of σ, $s = 1849$ and $s = 1820$, respectively. Finally, the common VIF for the two predictor variables in the second model is 1.7. By this measure, multicollinearity is no longer a problem.

As the reader may verify, an analysis of the residuals from the second regression indicates there is no reason to doubt the regression assumptions. For the variables considered, the regression of Newsprint on Papers and LnRetSal is entirely adequate. (For a regression of Newsprint on Papers and LnFamily, see Exercise 12.7.)

Example 12.4 illustrates the effects of multicollinearity. When severe multicollinearity is present, it is very difficult to disentangle the influences of the individual explanatory variables and to obtain reasonably precise estimates of their separate effects.

Extreme multicollinearity may not be a problem if the objective of the regression analysis is to develop a function that can be used to accurately predict the response. If the focus is prediction, it is the total contribution of the explanatory variables that is of interest, not their separate effects. A fitted function with highly correlated explanatory variables may yield a high R^2 and very stable predictions.

If estimating the separate effects of the explanatory variables is important and multicollinearity appears to be a problem, what should be done? There are several ways to deal with severe multicollinearity, as follows. None of them may be completely satisfactory or feasible.

- Create new x variables by scaling all of the explanatory variables according to the relation

$$\tilde{x}_{ij} = \frac{x_{ij} - \bar{x}_j}{\sqrt{\sum_{i=1}^{n}(x_{ij} - \bar{x}_j)^2}}, \qquad j = 1, 2, \ldots, p; \quad i = 1, 2, \ldots, n$$

  These new variables will each have a sample mean of 0 and the same standard deviation. The regression calculations with the new x variables are less sensitive to round-off error in the presence of severe multicollinearity.

- Identify and eliminate one or more of the redundant explanatory variables from the regression function. (This was the approach considered in Example 12.4.)

- Consider estimation procedures other than least squares.*

- Regress the response y on linear combinations of the x's that are uncorrelated.†

- Carefully select potential explanatory variables at the beginning of the study. Try to avoid variables that "say the same thing."

VARIABLE SELECTION

In practice, it is often difficult to formulate an appropriate regression function immediately. Which predictor variables should be included? What form should the regression function take?

When the list of possible predictor variables is very large, it is not sensible to include all the variables in the regression function. Techniques and computer programs designed to select the "best" subset of predictors are now readily available. The good ones try **all possible regressions** with the subsets: x_1 alone, x_2 alone, $\ldots$, x_1 and

---

*Alternative procedures for estimating the regression parameters are beyond the scope of this book. The interested reader should consult Draper, N. R., and Smith, H., *Applied Regression Analysis,* 2nd ed., New York: Wiley, 1981 or Bowerman, B. L., and O'Connell, R. T., *Linear Statistical Models,* 2nd ed., Boston: PWS-Kent, 1990.

†Again, the procedures for creating linear combinations of the x's that are uncorrelated are beyond the scope of this book. The book by Draper and Smith contains a discussion of these techniques.

$x_2, \ldots.$ The best choice is decided by examining some criterion like R^2. However, R^2 always increases with the inclusion of additional predictor variables. Although this problem can be circumvented by using the adjusted R^2,

$$\overline{R}^2 = 1 - (1 - R^2)\left(\frac{n-1}{n-p-1}\right)$$

(see Exercise 11.46 for $\overline{r}^2$ with $p = 1$), a better statistic for variable selection seems to be the C_p **statistic,** a measure of total prediction error:

$$C_p = \left(\frac{\begin{array}{c}\text{Residual sum of squares for subset model with} \\ p + 1 \text{ parameters, including an intercept}\end{array}}{\text{Residual mean square for full model}} \right) - (n - 2(p + 1))$$

A list or plot of the pairs $(p + 1, C_p)$, one pair for each subset of predictors, will indicate models that forecast the observed responses well. In good models, the $p + 1$ and C_p coordinates are typically about equal, or, equivalently, the points $(p + 1, C_p)$ are near the 45° line.

If the list of predictor variables is very long, time and cost considerations limit the number of models that can be examined. Another approach, called **stepwise regression,** attempts to select important predictors while considering all the possibilities. The procedure can be described by listing the basic steps (algorithm) involved in the computations:

Step 1.   All possible *simple* linear regressions are considered. The predictor variable that explains the largest significant proportion of the variation in y (has the largest correlation with the response) is the first variable to enter the regression function.

Step 2.   The next variable to enter is the one (out of those not yet included) that makes the largest significant contribution to the regression sum of squares. The significance of the contribution is determined by an F test. The value of the F statistic that must be exceeded before the contribution of a variable is deemed significant is often called the F *to enter.*

Step 3.   Once an additional variable has been included in the equation, the individual contributions to the regression sum of squares of the other variables already in the equation are checked for significance using F tests. If the F statistic is less than a value called the F *to remove,* the variable is deleted from the regression function.

Step 4.   Steps 2 and 3 are repeated until all possible additions are nonsignificant and all possible deletions are significant. At this point, the selection stops.

The values for F to enter and F to remove are supplied by the user. Some programs use the default value $F = 4$ for both of these quantities.

Because of the step-by-step procedure, there is no guarantee that stepwise regression will select, for example, the best three variables for prediction. In addition, an automatic selection method is not capable of indicating when transformations of variables are useful, nor does it necessarily avoid a multicollinearity problem.

EXAMPLE 12.5 Selecting a Regression Model for CEO Compensation

In Example 12.2, we referred to a study of CEO compensation. Exercise 12.11 contains a regression analysis linking CEO compensation (LnComp) to company sales (LnSales), experience as a CEO (Exper), CEO educational level (Educate), and amount of company stock owned (PctOwn). Data on these variables, along with the additional potential explanatory variables CEO age (Age), professional background (Backgrnd) coded for different categories, such as finance, marketing, and so forth, length of time with company (Tenure), market valuation of company stock owned (Valuate), and company profits (Profits), were collected for 50 companies. Use the all possible regressions and the stepwise regression procedures to select the "best" regression model involving log of CEO compensation (LnComp) as the response, and the nine potential predictor variables, log of company sales, experience, educational level,..., and company profits, listed previously.

Solution and Discussion.   The Minitab results for all possible regressions (Minitab calls it Best Subsets Regression) are displayed here.

Best Subsets Regression

Response is LnComp

	Vars	R-sq	Adj. R-sq	C-p	s	Age	Educate	Backgrnd	Tenure	Exper	LnSales	Valuate	PctOwn	Profits
	1	22.2	20.4	21.2	0.56634	X								
	1	18.0	16.3	24.7	0.58076						X			
✔	2	38.4	35.8	9.1	0.50878	X					X			
	2	27.5	24.4	18.5	0.55204	X							X	
	3	42.8	39.1	7.3	0.49531	X					X		X	
	3	41.0	37.1	8.9	0.50330	X						X	X	
	4	51.5	47.1	1.8	0.46149	X						X	X	X
→	4	46.8	42.1	5.9	0.48309		X			X	X		X	
	5	52.6	47.3	2.8	0.46100	X					X	X	X	X
	5	52.6	47.2	2.9	0.46139	X				X	X	X	X	
	6	53.4	46.9	4.2	0.46244	X				X	X	X	X	X
	6	52.9	46.4	4.6	0.46490	X		X			X	X	X	X
	7	53.5	45.8	6.1	0.46742	X	X			X	X	X	X	X
	7	53.4	45.7	6.1	0.46786	X			X	X	X	X	X	X
	8	53.6	44.5	8.0	0.47270	X	X		X	X	X	X	X	X
	8	53.5	44.5	8.1	0.47308	X	X	X		X	X	X	X	X
	9	53.6	43.2	10.0	0.47855	X	X	X	X	X	X	X	X	X

Not all regressions are displayed. Only the two best models for each subset of predictor variables are shown, along with the results for all nine predictors. The $p = 4$ predictor model considered in Exercise 12.11 is indicated by the arrow and can be justified by an R^2 that is not too far from the highest value for the group and by a pair $(p + 1, C_p) = (5, 5.9)$ that is close to the 45° line. (The four predictor model with Valuate replacing Exper is also attractive.)

The predictor Educate appears in all the models listed, and the predictors LnSales and PctOwn appear in almost all of the models. Of the variables considered, these three predictors appear to be the important predictors of LnComp.

The Minitab results for the stepwise regression procedure applied to these data follow.

Stepwise Regression

```
    F-to-Enter:        4.00     F-to-Remove:        4.00

    Response is  LnComp  on  9 predictors, with N =   50

          Step        1        2
    Constant      7.608    5.525

    Educate       -0.49    -0.47
    T-Ratio       -3.68    -3.94

    LnSales                0.263
    T-Ratio                 3.53

    S             0.566    0.509
    R-Sq          22.02    38.38
```

The stepwise regression algorithm stopped after two steps. This procedure selected as the best model

$$\text{LnComp} = \beta_0 + \beta_1 \text{Educate} + \beta_2 \text{LnSales} + \varepsilon$$

Notice that this is the best $p = 2$ predictor model selected by the all possible regressions procedure (indicated by a check in the printout on page 641). The Minitab output for a regression analysis of the model selected by the stepwise procedure is shown here, along with residual plots.

```
The regression equation is
LnComp = 5.52 - 0.467 Educate + 0.263 LnSales

Predictor        Coef       Stdev      t-ratio         p       VIF
Constant       5.5248      0.6208         8.90     0.000
Educate       -0.4670      0.1185        -3.94     0.000       1.0
LnSales       0.26280      0.07440         3.53     0.001       1.0

s = 0.5088      R-sq = 38.4%      R-sq(adj) = 35.8%

Analysis of Variance

SOURCE        DF           SS          MS           F         p
Regression     2       7.5776      3.7888       14.64     0.000
Error         47      12.1663      0.2589
Total         49      19.7439
```

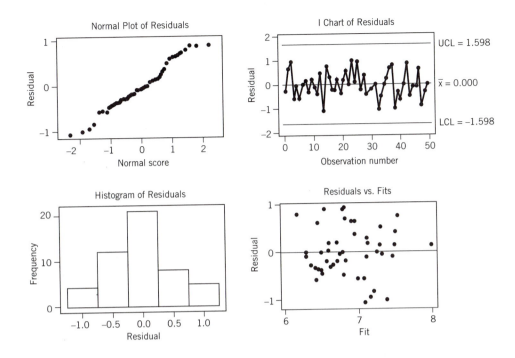

The residual plots indicate no major violations of the regression assumptions.

Although the fitted function explains only 38% of the variation in the response LnComp, the regression is significant, and so is each of the explanatory variables. The VIF = 1 indicates that Educate and LnSales are unrelated, and each variable makes its own separate contribution to the determination of LnComp.

Notice that the coefficient of Educate is negative. This somewhat surprising result means, all other things equal, that the CEO compensation decreases as his or her educational level increases.

REGRESSION DIAGNOSTICS

In keeping with the model building strategy outlined in Section 11.7 of Chapter 11, a regression analysis is not complete until one is convinced the model is an adequate representation of the data. Of course, it is imperative to examine the adequacy of the model *before* it becomes a part of the decision-making apparatus.

An examination of the residuals is a crucial component of the determination of model adequacy. We have discussed several residual plots designed to check the regression model assumptions, and we have displayed some of these plots in Examples 12.3 and 12.5 in this chapter. Also, if regression models are used with time series data, it is very important to compute the residual autocorrelations to specifically check the independence assumption. Inferences (and decisions) made with models that do not approximately conform with the regression assumptions can be grossly misleading. For example, we may conclude that the manipulation of an explanatory variable will produce a specified change in the response when, in fact, it will not, or we may conclude that a forecast is very likely (95% confident) to be within 2% of the future response when, in fact, the actual confidence is far less, and so forth.

In this section, we will provide some additional diagnostic tools that can be used to evaluate a regression model. These tools are designed to identify observations that are outlying or extreme (observations that are well separated from the remainder of the data). Outlying observations are often hidden by the fitting process and may not be easily detected from an examination of residual plots. Yet they can have a major role in determining the fitted regression function. It is important to study outlying observations to decide whether they should be retained or eliminated and, if retained, whether their influence should be reduced in the fitting process or the regression function revised.

The **leverage h_i** associated with the ith data point measures the distance between the x values for the ith observation and the means of the x values for all n observations. The leverage depends only on the predictors; it does not involve the response y. For simple linear regression with one explanatory variable, x,

$$h_i = \frac{1}{n} + \frac{(x_i - \overline{x})^2}{\sum_{i=1}^{n}(x_i - \overline{x})^2}$$

With p predictors, one can show that $0 < h_i < 1$ and that the mean leverage is $\overline{h} = (p+1)/n$. For a data point with high leverage, h_i is close to 1, and the predicted response at these x's is almost completely determined by y_i, with the rest of the data having very little influence. This follows because for each 1-unit change in y_i, there is an h_i-unit change in $\hat{y}_i$, or

$$(\text{Change in } \hat{y}_i) = h_i(\text{Change in } y_i)$$

provided the other y values remain fixed.

A rule of thumb suggests that h_i is large enough to merit checking if it is more than $2(p+1)/n$ or $3(p+1)/n$. Many software packages identify data points with $h_i \geq 3(p+1)/n$.

The detection of outlying or extreme y values based on an examination of the residuals has been considered in Chapters 3 and 11. We have used either the residuals

$$\hat{\varepsilon}_i = y_i - \hat{y}_i$$

or the standardized residuals

$$\frac{\hat{\varepsilon}_i}{s}$$

where $s = \sqrt{\text{MSE}}$ is an estimate of σ, the standard deviation of the errors. We now introduce a refinement to make the residuals more effective for identifying outlying y values.

Although s^2 estimates $\sigma^2 = \text{var}(\varepsilon_i)$, the residuals have estimated variances

$$s^2(\hat{\varepsilon}_i) = s^2(1 - h_i) \qquad i = 1, 2, \ldots, n$$

The ratio of $\hat{\varepsilon}$ to $s(\hat{\varepsilon})$ is often called the **standardized residual** and is sometimes called the **Studentized residual** by software packages.

The residuals will have substantially different estimated variances if the leverages h_i differ markedly, but the standardized residuals

$$\frac{\hat{\varepsilon}_i}{s(\hat{\varepsilon}_i)} = \frac{\hat{\varepsilon}_i}{s\sqrt{1 - h_i}} \qquad i = 1, 2, \ldots, n$$

will all have variance 1. A large standardized residual indicates that an observation has an unusual or extreme response y. (See Figure 3.22 for observations with extreme responses.)

A standardized residual is considered large (the response extreme) if

$$\left| \frac{\hat{\varepsilon}_i}{s(\hat{\varepsilon}_i)} \right| > 2$$

Observations with large standardized residuals are typically identified by statistical software packages. The y values corresponding to data points with large standardized residuals can heavily influence the fit, as we have seen in Examples 3.14 and 3.15 in Chapter 3.

EXAMPLE 12.6 Identifying Influential Observations with the CEO Compensation Data

In Example 12.5, we presented a regression relating CEO compensation, represented by the variable LnComp, to the variables CEO educational level (Educate), and company sales (LnSales). The fitted regression function was

$$\widehat{\text{LnComp}} = 5.52 - .467 \text{ Educate} + .263 \text{ LnSales}$$

Minitab identified three observations from this regression analysis that have either large standardized residuals or large leverage:

```
Unusual Observations
Obs.    Educate       LnComp        Fit    Stdev.Fit     Residual      St.Resid
 14       1.00        6.0568     7.0995       0.0949      -1.0427        -2.09R
 25       0.00        8.1342     7.9937       0.2224       0.1404         0.31 X
 33       0.00        6.3969     7.3912       0.2032      -0.9943        -2.13R

R denotes an obs. with a large st. resid.
X denotes an obs. whose X value gives it large influence.
```

Minitab marks observations with large standardized residuals with an "R" and those with large leverage with an "X." Interpret this output.

Solution and Discussion. Cases 14 and 33 have large standardized residuals. The fitted regression function is predicting (log) compensation that is too large for these two CEOs. An examination of the full data set shows that these CEOs each own relatively large percentages of their company's stock. Case 14 owns more than 10% of the company's stock, and case 33 owns more than 17% of the company's stock. These individuals are receiving much of their remuneration through long-term compensation, like stock incentives, rather than through annual salary and bonuses. Since amount of stock owned (or stock value) is not included as a variable in the regression function, it cannot be used to adjust the prediction of compensation determined by CEO education and company sales. Although education and (log) sales do not predict the compensation of these two CEOs as well as the others, there appears to be no reason to eliminate them from consideration.

Case 25 is singled out because the leverage for this data point is greater than $3(p + 1)/n = 3(3)/50 = .18$. This CEO has no college degree (Educate $= 0$) but is with a company with relatively large sales (LnSales $= 9.394$). The combination $(0, 9.394)$ is far from the point $(\bar{x}_1, \bar{x}_2)$; therefore, it is an outlier among the pairs of x's. The response associated with these x's will have a large influence on the determination of the fitted regression function. (Notice that the standardized residual for this data point is small, indicating that the predicted or fitted log compensation is close to the actual value.) This particular CEO has 30 years experience as a CEO, more experience than all but one of the CEOs in the data set. This observation is influential, but there is no reason to delete it.

Leverage tells us if an observation has unusual predictors, and a standardized residual tells us if an observation has an unusual response. These quantities can be combined into one overall measure of influence, called Cook's distance. Cook's distances can be printed out in most statistical software packages, but additional discussion is beyond the scope of this book.*

EXERCISES

StatExam.dat

12.14 (*Minitab or similar program recommended*) The scores, x_1 and x_2, for two within-term examinations, the current grade point average (GPA) x_3, and the final exam score y for 20 students in a business statistics class follow.

x_1	x_2	x_3	y	x_1	x_2	x_3	y
87	85	2.7	91	93	60	3.2	54
100	84	3.3	90	92	69	3.1	63
91	82	3.5	83	100	86	3.6	96
85	60	3.7	93	80	87	3.5	89
56	64	2.8	43	100	96	3.8	97
81	48	3.1	75	69	51	2.8	50
77	67	3.1	63	80	75	3.6	74
86	73	3.0	78	74	70	3.1	58
79	90	3.8	98	79	66	2.9	87
96	69	3.7	99	95	83	3.3	57

a. Fit a multiple linear regression model to predict the final exam score from the scores on the within-term exams and GPA. Is the regression significant? Explain.

---

*Discussion of Cook's distance and other statistics useful in checking certain features of multiple regression models can be found in Belsley, D. A., Kuh, E., and Welsch, R. E., *Regression Diagnostics*. New York: Wiley, 1980.

b. Predict the final exam score for a student with the within-term exam scores of 86 and 77, and a GPA of 3.4.

c. Compute the VIFs and examine the t statistics for checking the significance of the individual predictor variables. Is multicollinearity a problem? Explain.

 12.15 (*Minitab or similar program recommended*) Refer to Exercise 12.14.

StatExam.dat

    a. Compute the mean leverage. Are any of the observations high leverage points? Explain.

    b. Compute the standardized residuals. Identify any observation with a large standardized residual. Does the fitted model under- or overpredict the response for these observations? Why?

 **12.16** (*Minitab or similar program recommended*) Refer to Exercise 12.14. Select the "best" regression model using the stepwise regression and all possible regressions procedures. Compare the results. Are you confident using a regression model to predict the final exam score with fewer than the original 3 explanatory variables? Explain.

StatExam.dat

12.17 (*Minitab or similar program recommended*) Refer to Exercise 12.9, which has data on the 20 best selling cars for 1994.

BestCar.dat

    a. Fit a multiple linear regression model relating 1995 price in dollars to horsepower, weight, and highway miles per gallon. Calculate the VIFs. Is multicollinearity a problem? Can you estimate the separate effects of horsepower, weight, and miles per gallon on selling price? Explain.

    b. Determine and fit the "best" multiple regression model using stepwise regression. Explain any influential observations. Are you satisfied with the choice? Discuss.

12.18 (*Minitab or similar program recommended*) Refer to Example 12.5. The data relating to CEO compensation are contained in Table C.3, Appendix C. Use stepwise regression to select the "best" model with $p = 3$ predictors. Compare the stepwise result with the all possible regressions selections in Example 12.5. Fit the stepwise model and interpret the estimated coefficients. Examine the residuals. Identify and explain any influential observations. If you had to choose between this model and the $p = 2$ predictor model discussed in Example 12.5, which one would you choose? Why?

CEOComp.dat

12.4   AN INTRODUCTION TO TIME SERIES ANALYSIS

According to a recent *Wall Street Journal* story, American Airlines (AA) compared current reservations with forecasts based on projections of historical patterns. Depending on whether current reservations were lagging behind or exceeding the projections, AA adjusted the proportion of discounted seats accordingly. The adjustments were made for each flight segment in the AA system. The result was significantly more passengers and more revenue with the same number of planes. Other travel-related companies followed AA's example, including Marriott, Best Western, and National Car Rental.

As the AA story indicates, an analysis of time series can be important, with a real dollar payoff. Several examples of data collected over time have appeared in this book:

the sequence of engine inventory levels in Chapter 1; the monthly employment levels in the Wisconsin food products industry and the monthly peak power demand for the Wisconsin branch of Northern States Power in Chapter 3; the monthly returns of the S&P 500 Index in Chapter 7; and the weekly Canadian dollar to U.S. dollar exchange rate in Chapter 11.

One distinguishing feature of time series data, as opposed to data collected at a particular point in time, is that the observations are not assumed to vary independently. In fact, it is precisely the nature of the *dependence* that is of interest. In the sections that follow, we introduce models that attempt to account for this dependence. To the extent that they do, the fitted models can be used to generate forecasts of future values.

The validity of forecasting procedures developed from models that have been suggested by and fitted to historical data necessarily relies on the assumption that the future tends to behave like the past. Rarely in business is this assumption warranted for an *extended* time horizon, that is, over the *long term*. Accurate long-term forecasting is a very difficult, if not impossible, task, and successes may be followed by agonizing failures. Generating accurate short-term forecasts is, however, a very reasonable objective. Typically, long-term means several years and short-term means a year or less, but this can change depending on the context.

STATIONARY AND NONSTATIONARY TIME SERIES

If a time series appears to vary about a fixed level, the series is said to be *stationary in the mean*. On the other hand, times series that exhibit a trend or wander away from a fixed level are said to be *nonstationary in the mean*. For stationary series, the overall behavior of the observations stays roughly the same over time. Nonstationary series are those series whose statistical properties change over time. Nonstationary series can occur when the underlying physical mechanism changes—that is, when the principal movements of the series are due to a shift in factors that occur on occasion. A sudden shift in U.S. economic policy may have a severe effect on the interest rate of three-month Treasury bills; in fact, a contraction of the money supply would drive the interest rate upward.

Figure 12.3 shows three time series. The time series in Figure 12.3(a) and 12.3(b) are stationary in the mean. The time series in Figure 12.3(c) is nonstationary in the mean.

Keep in mind that stationary time series may not vary *randomly* about the mean. In fact, it is the nature of the correlation among the observations (autocorrelation) that will help us identify an appropriate time series model. As we shall see, identifying an appropriate model is often a two-step procedure. First, transform a nonstationary to a stationary series, and then select a model for the stationary series taking into account the transformation. One useful transformation for this purpose is the *difference transformation,* or the operation of creating a new series by taking the successive differences of the original series.

DIFFERENCING TO PRODUCE STATIONARITY

Many series arising in business and economics behave as if they have no fixed mean level even though parts of the series display a certain kind of homogeneity. That is, the *local* behavior for each series is similar in the sense that, for short time intervals, apart

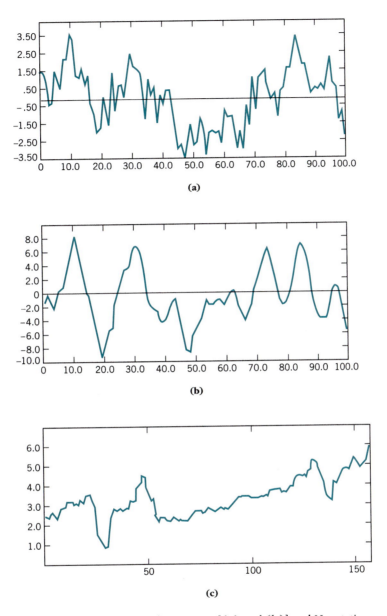

Figure 12.3   Examples of Stationary [(a) and (b)] and Nonstationary (c) Time Series

from a difference in trend, one part of the series looks very much like any other part. The situation is illustrated in Figure 12.4 (page 650), in which two typical series nonstationary in the mean are plotted. Although the level of the series in Figure 12.4(a) and the level and trend of the series in Figure 12.4(b) are constantly changing, the behavior of a given series within the blocks outlined in the figure is very similar. Models useful for representing such behavior can be obtained by supposing a suitable *difference* of the process is stationary.

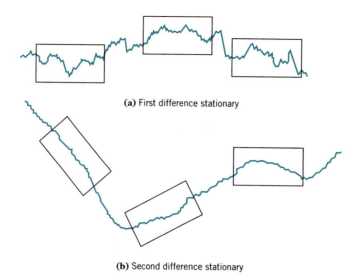

(a) First difference stationary

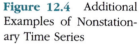

(b) Second difference stationary

Figure 12.4 Additional Examples of Nonstationary Time Series

If y_t represents the response at time t, so that $y_1, y_2, \ldots, y_t, \ldots, y_n$ denote the observed time series, the differenced series (or series of first differences) is

$$w_2 = y_2 - y_1, \; w_3 = y_3 - y_2, \ldots, w_t = y_t - y_{t-1}, \ldots, w_n = y_n - y_{n-1}$$

Notice there are $n - 1$ observations in the differenced series. Differencing the first differences produces a time series of second differences, and so forth. In practice, it is generally not necessary to go beyond second differences to achieve stationarity.

Other than looking at plots of the series, how can we tell whether a time series is stationary or nonstationary? Help is provided by the autocorrelation function of the original series and its differences. For nonstationary series, the sample autocorrelations fail to die out rapidly with increasing lag, indicating a lot of inertia or trend in the series. For stationary series, the sample autocorrelations tend to die out relatively quickly and, within error limits, they have a recognizable pattern that suggests a particular time series model. These ideas are best illustrated with an example.

EXAMPLE 12.7 Interpreting the Autocorrelation Function with the Canadian Dollar/U.S. Dollar Exchange Rate Data

Figure 11.8 (page 591) contains a plot of the Canadian dollar to U.S. dollar exchange rate, recorded weekly, for a ten-year period. This plot is reproduced in Figure 12.5(a). Figure 12.5(b) shows the series of first differences, obtained by taking the differences of consecutive exchange rates.

Calculate the sample autocorrelation function for the original series and the differenced series. Interpret the patterns in the plots and in the autocorrelations. Is the exchange rate series stationary or nonstationary?

Solution and Discussion. The sample autocorrelations for the exchange rate series and the differenced series are displayed in Figure 12.6 (pages 651–652).

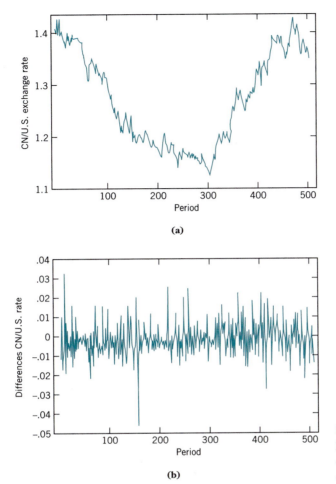

Figure 12.5 (a) Canadian Dollar/U.S. Dollar Weekly Exchange Rates and (b) Differences in Rates

k	r_k	-1.0 -0.8 -0.6 -0.4 -0.2 0.0 0.2 0.4 0.6 0.8 1.0
		+----+----+----+----+----+----+----+----+----+----+
1	0.993	XXXXXXXXXXXXXXXXXXXXXXXXX
2	0.986	XXXXXXXXXXXXXXXXXXXXXXXXX
3	0.979	XXXXXXXXXXXXXXXXXXXXXXXX
4	0.971	XXXXXXXXXXXXXXXXXXXXXXXX
5	0.963	XXXXXXXXXXXXXXXXXXXXXXXX
6	0.956	XXXXXXXXXXXXXXXXXXXXXXXX
7	0.950	XXXXXXXXXXXXXXXXXXXXXXXX
8	0.943	XXXXXXXXXXXXXXXXXXXXXXXX
9	0.934	XXXXXXXXXXXXXXXXXXXXXXX
10	0.927	XXXXXXXXXXXXXXXXXXXXXXX
11	0.919	XXXXXXXXXXXXXXXXXXXXXXX
12	0.912	XXXXXXXXXXXXXXXXXXXXXXX
13	0.905	XXXXXXXXXXXXXXXXXXXXXXX
14	0.898	XXXXXXXXXXXXXXXXXXXXXXX
15	0.891	XXXXXXXXXXXXXXXXXXXXXXX
16	0.884	XXXXXXXXXXXXXXXXXXXXXXX
17	0.878	XXXXXXXXXXXXXXXXXXXXXXX
18	0.871	XXXXXXXXXXXXXXXXXXXXXXX
19	0.865	XXXXXXXXXXXXXXXXXXXXXXX
20	0.858	XXXXXXXXXXXXXXXXXXXXXX
21	0.851	XXXXXXXXXXXXXXXXXXXXXX
22	0.844	XXXXXXXXXXXXXXXXXXXXXX
23	0.837	XXXXXXXXXXXXXXXXXXXXXX
24	0.829	XXXXXXXXXXXXXXXXXXXXXX
25	0.822	XXXXXXXXXXXXXXXXXXXXXX

Figure   12.6 (a) Autocorrelations of Exchange Rate Series

```
 k     rₖ      -1.0 -0.8 -0.6 -0.4 -0.2  0.0  0.2  0.4  0.6  0.8  1.0
                +----+----+----+----+----+----+----+----+----+----+
 1   -0.057                                XX
 2    0.019                                 X
 3   -0.025                                XX
 4    0.030                                 XX
 5   -0.084                               XXX
 6    0.039                                 XX
 7    0.036                                 XX
 8    0.060                                 XXX
 9   -0.067                               XXX
10    0.032                                 XX
11   -0.013                                 X
12   -0.038                                XX
13   -0.004                                 X
14    0.048                                 XX
15   -0.016                                 X
16    0.024                                 XX
17   -0.028                                XX
18   -0.014                                 X
19    0.009                                 X
20    0.049                                 XX
21   -0.069                               XXX
22    0.016                                 X
23   -0.021                                XX
24   -0.025                                XX
25   -0.036                                XX
```

Figure 12.6 (b) Autocorrelations for the Differenced Series

The autocorrelations for the original series in Figure 12.6(a) are uniformly large and fail to die out quickly. (The autocorrelation at lag $k = 25$, $r_k = .822$, is still substantial.) This behavior is typical of sample autocorrelations for a nonstationary series. On the other hand, the autocorrelations for the differenced series are uniformly small, and if the error bounds were computed, none of the autocorrelations would be significantly different from 0. We conclude that the differences appear to be uncorrelated at any lag. Here, the autocorrelations have certainly died out rapidly, and this behavior is typical of sample autocorrelations for a stationary series. It is important to remember that the sample autocorrelations do not all have to be near 0 to indicate stationarity. Rather, they have to die out quickly. For stationary series, there could be substantial autocorrelations at small lags, but the autocorrelations at large lags would be uniformly small.

Now turn to the plots in Figure 12.5 (page 651). The Canadian/U.S. exchange rate series drifts downward for a long period of time (recall these are weekly rates for ten years) and then wanders back up to a level almost equal to the level at the beginning of the series. This drifting behavior, or failure to vary about a fixed level, implies the series is nonstationary. The differenced series, however, clearly varies about a fixed level near 0. The differenced series is stationary.

Based on an examination of the sample autocorrelations and plots of the series, we conclude that the Canadian/U.S. exchange rate series is nonstationary in the mean. However, the series created by taking the differences of consecutive observations (the differenced series) is stationary.

SEASONAL TIME SERIES

A seasonal event is one that occurs with a more or less regular period that can be anticipated. The large movement of students into the labor market in the summer is a seasonal event. Firework sales associated with the Fourth of July in the United States or Bastille Day in France is a seasonal event. Anticipation of and planning for seasonal events is simply prudent management. Thus, forecasts of the magnitudes of the effects of seasonal events should prove valuable to management.

We have discussed two seasonal time series in this book: (1) the Wisconsin monthly employment in food and kindred products for $n = 178$ consecutive months and (2) the maximum monthly power demand for the Wisconsin branch of Northern States Power (NSP) for $n = 107$ consecutive months. Figure 12.7 contains plots of these two series.*

The Wisconsin food products series shows a rather stable level of employment with a consistently large summer peak. The NSP(Wis) power demand series has an upward trend with a consistently large peak during the winter months (associated

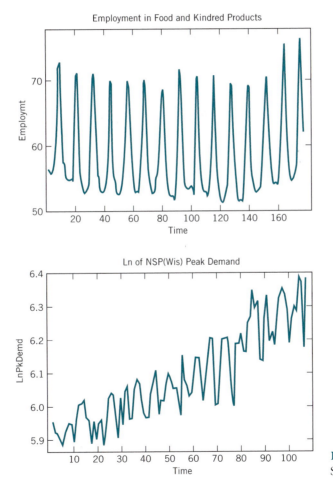

Figure 12.7 Examples of Seasonal Time Series

---

*The series plotted for NSP(Wis) peak demand is actually the natural logarithms of peak demand. Using the logarithms has the advantage of making the variation in peak demand more nearly constant throughout the series.

with heating) and a secondary peak during the summer months (associated with air conditioning).

The peak demand series is clearly nonstationary in the mean. The employment series appears to vary about a fixed level but is slightly "bowed," with the middle section of the series being lower than both ends of the series. We will return to the stationarity for the employment series later. For now we note that, for both series, observations 12 months apart—that is, observations at the seasonal lag $k = 12$—are related. Also, for both series, consecutive observations are related since neither series appears to vary *randomly* about a fixed level. This behavior has implications for identifying an appropriate model for each of these series.

TIME SERIES DECOMPOSITION

One approach to modeling and forecasting a time series is to assume that a series consists of three components: a **trend,** denoted by T, **seasonal component,** denoted by S, and an **irregular component,** denoted by I. (The irregular component is the residual or "noise.") The three components sum* to give the observed series y_t.

Additive Decomposition of a Time Series

Let $y_1, y_2, \ldots, y_t, \ldots, y_n$ denote a time series of n observations. The additive decomposition of the series is

$$y_t = T_t + S_t + I_t \qquad t = 1, 2, \ldots, n$$

where

T_t is the value of the trend at time t.

S_t is the value of the seasonal component at time t.

I_t is the value of the irregular (residual) component at time t.

The three components T, S, and I are estimated separately, beginning with the trend. The trend is then subtracted from the original series to get a "detrended" series from which the seasonal is estimated. The irregular or residual is the remainder after subtracting the trend and the seasonal components.

The trend is typically estimated by fitting a line or curve by the method of least squares. Once the trend is determined, the seasonal component is often estimated using a two-step procedure. First, the detrended series is "smoothed" by replacing the

---

*A multiplicative version of the decomposition of a time series into trend, seasonal, and irregular components exists, but the multiplicative decomposition can always be converted to an additive decomposition by taking the logarithm of the response. In many situations, it is necessary to take the logarithms of the response to stabilize the variability throughout the observation period.

current values with **moving averages** obtained by averaging consecutive groups of observations.* For example, suppose a detrended series begins with the numbers

$$8, \quad 4, \quad 5, \quad 10, \quad \text{and} \quad 9,$$

and we smooth these values using a centered moving average of length 3. The first value of the moving average is missing; the second value of the moving average is the average of 8, 4, and 5; the third value of the moving average is the average of 4, 5, and 10; the fourth value is the average of 5, 10, and 9, and so forth. (The length of the moving average used to smooth a seasonal series is the length of the seasonal period, usually 12 for monthly data.) Second, once the moving average is obtained, it is subtracted from the detrended values to get the *raw seasonals*. Within each seasonal period, the median value of the raw seasonals is determined. These medians make up the **seasonal indices.** The seasonal indices make up the seasonal component of the series and can be used to *seasonally adjust* the data.

Let $\hat{T}$ denote the estimated trend, and let $\hat{S}$ denote the estimated seasonal. Then the fitted or predicted series is given by

$$\hat{y}_t = \hat{T}_t + \hat{S}_t$$

and the residuals are

$$\hat{I}_t = \hat{y}_t - \hat{T}_t - \hat{S}_t$$

The fit of the decomposition can be judged by computing several measures of accuracy: the **mean absolute percentage error** (MAPE), the **mean absolute deviation** (MAD), and the **mean squared deviation** (MSD).

$$\text{MAPE} = \frac{\sum_{t=1}^{n} |(y_t - \hat{y}_t)/y_t|}{n} \times 100 \qquad (y_t \neq 0)$$

$$\text{MAD} = \frac{\sum_{t=1}^{n} |y_t - \hat{y}_t|}{n}$$

$$\text{MSD} = \frac{\sum_{t=1}^{n} (y_t - \hat{y}_t)^2}{n}$$

Forecasts of future values are generated by extrapolating the estimated trend and adding the estimated seasonal. Since the decomposition is not based on an underlying statistical model involving an assumed distribution for the irregular term, there is no easy way to calculate error limits or generate prediction intervals.

The decomposition of a time series is performed by many statistical software packages, including Minitab.

---

*The detrended series is smoothed to temporarily eliminate the noise.

EXAMPLE 12.8 Performing an Additive Decomposition of NSP(Wis) Peak Demand

Perform an additive decomposition of the NSP(Wis) peak demand time series displayed in Figure 12.7, and generate forecasts of the next 12 observations.

Solution and Discussion. Figure 12.8 shows Minitab plots of the original series, the detrended series, the seasonally adjusted series, and the irregular or residual series (the detrended and seasonally adjusted series). Since there are 12 seasonal indices, one for each month of the year, the seasonally adjusted series is the original series minus the seasonal indices. For example, the deseasonalized Januarys are the original Januarys minus the seasonal index for January, and so forth.

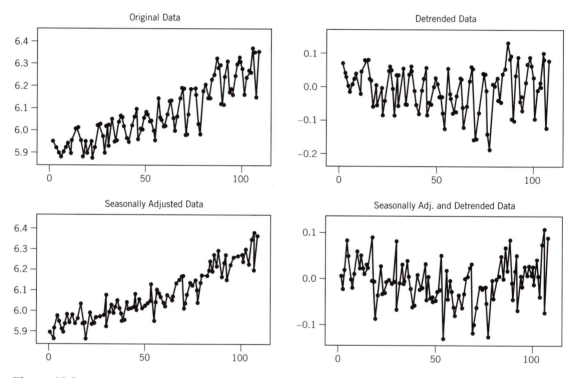

Figure 12.8 Component Analysis for Log Peak Demand

The estimated trend for this example is

$$\hat{T} = 5.8812 + .0039t$$

where $t = 1, 2, \ldots$ represents the time periods. The seasonal indices are listed in the table:

Month	Index
Jan.	.0608
Feb.	.0536
Mar.	.0016
Apr.	−.0826
May	−.0554
June	.0081
July	.0372
Aug.	.0214
Sept.	−.0354
Oct.	−.0495
Nov.	−.0116
Dec.	.0518

The seasonal indices indicate the nature of the seasonality. The cold winter months, December (12), January (1), and February (2), have positive and relatively large seasonal indices. The same is true for the warm summer months of July (7) and August (8). The peak demand is relatively high for these months. On the other hand, the seasonal indices are negative for the transition months of April (4), May (5), September (9), October (10), and November (11). The peak demand for these months is relatively low. This pattern is consistent over time and exists on top of a general overall increase in demand indicated by the trend.

The log peak demand series, the fitted series, including the trend line, and forecasts for the next 12 observations beginning with December are shown in Figure 12.9. The estimated seasonal pattern is clearly evident in the forecasts.

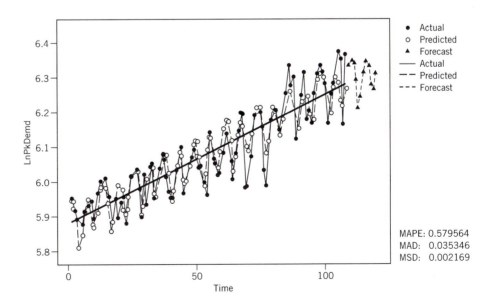

Figure 12.9   The Decomposition Fit and Forecasts for NSP(Wis) Peak Demand

To get forecasts of the actual peak demand, we must exponentiate the forecasts in Figure 12.9. These are given in the following table:

Month	Nov.	Dec.	Jan.	Feb.	Mar.	Apr.
$\ln y_t$	6.3510	6.3638	6.3606	6.3123	6.2320	6.2631
y_t	573.07	580.45	578.59	551.31	508.77	524.84

Month	May	June	July	Aug.	Sept.	Oct.
$\ln y_t$	6.3305	6.3634	6.3516	6.2986	6.2884	6.3302
y_t	561.44	580.22	573.41	543.81	538.29	561.27

Consistent with the forecasts of the log peak demand, the forecasts of the actual peak demand show a seasonal pattern superimposed on an upward trend.

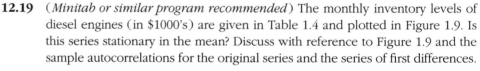

Not all series have both a trend and a consistent seasonal pattern; some series may have neither. If there is no trend, the estimated trend will be essentially horizontal. If there is no consistent seasonal pattern, the seasonal indices will all be close to zero in an additive decomposition.

EXERCISES

EngInven.dat

12.19   (*Minitab or similar program recommended*) The monthly inventory levels of diesel engines (in $1000's) are given in Table 1.4 and plotted in Figure 1.9. Is this series stationary in the mean? Discuss with reference to Figure 1.9 and the sample autocorrelations for the original series and the series of first differences.

S&P500RR.dat

12.20   (*Minitab or similar program recommended*) Monthly rates of return on the S&P 500 Index for $n = 47$ consecutive months are given in Table 7.1 of Chapter 7. Is this series stationary in the mean? Discuss with reference to a plot of the series and the sample autocorrelation function.

Toothpas.dat

12.21   (*Minitab or similar program recommended*) The weekly market share for Colgate toothpaste for $n = 276$ consecutive weeks is given in the Data Disk. Is this series stationary in the mean? Discuss with reference to a plot of the series and the sample autocorrelations of the original series and the series of first differences.

Toothpas.dat

12.22   (*Minitab or similar program recommended*) Refer to Exercise 12.21. Repeat this exercise with the weekly market shares for Crest toothpaste given in the Data Disk.

12.23   (*Class project with Minitab*) Pick your favorite stock. Collect the Friday closing price for this stock for the last three years. Plot the stock price time series. Is this series stationary in the mean? Is this series seasonal? Discuss. Now calculate the changes in the weekly stock price (the consecutive differences). Are the changes in stock price stationary? Is the differenced series seasonal? Discuss.

12.24 (*Minitab or similar program recommended*) Using the Wisconsin employment in food and kindred products data listed in Table C.8, Appendix C, perform an additive decomposition of this series. Interpret the seasonal indices. Analyze the residuals. Generate forecasts for the next 12 months.

12.5 AUTOREGRESSIVE TIME SERIES MODELS

A class of models useful for representing a wide variety of stationary time series is the class of autoregressive models. The first-order autoregressive model was introduced in Section 11.6. Recall that the order of the model refers to the time lag of the predictor variable. A **second-order autoregressive model** has the form*

$$y_t = \beta_0 + \beta_1 y_{t-1} + \beta_2 y_{t-2} + \varepsilon_t$$

Predictor variables with time lags up to and including 2 are contained in this model. In general, the **pth-order autoregressive model**

$$y_t = \beta_0 + \beta_1 y_{t-1} + \beta_2 y_{t-2} + \cdots + \beta_p y_{t-p} + \varepsilon_t$$

includes predictor variables with time lags up to and including p. The predictor variables in this case are the various lags of the response variable. We use the notation AR(p) to indicate a pth-order autoregressive model.

For time series with a seasonal pattern, the time lags of the predictor variables are often multiples of the seasonal period. For example, for monthly data and a seasonal period of 12, a first-order autoregressive model in the seasonal lag is

$$y_t = \beta_0 + \beta_1 y_{t-12} + \varepsilon_t$$

A second-order autoregressive model in the seasonal lag is

$$y_t = \beta_0 + \beta_1 y_{t-12} + \beta_2 y_{t-24} + \varepsilon_t$$

and so forth.

Finally, if it is necessary to difference the series to achieve stationarity, the response variable is a difference, for example, $w_t = y_t - y_{t-1}$, and a pth-order autoregressive model for the differences is

$$w_t = \beta_0 + \beta_1 w_{t-1} + \beta_2 w_{t-2} + \cdots + \beta_p w_{t-p} + \varepsilon_t$$

On occasion, we may have to take differences at the seasonal lag, so w_t might have the form $w_t = y_t - y_{t-12}$ or, for quarterly data, $w_t = y_t - y_{t-4}$, and so forth. These differences might then be related to one another with an autoregressive model.

---

*We adopt the convention of using the notation y_t to represent both the random response and its observed value.

An autoregressive model has the form of a multiple regression model. The errors ε_t in any autoregressive model are assumed to be independent and have a $N(0, \sigma)$ distribution. That is, we make the same assumptions that we do in multiple regression analysis.

How do we arrive at a suitable autoregressive model for a given time series? Guidance is provided by a plot of the series, and the sample autocorrelations for the original series and its differences. The sample autocorrelations r_k for series consistent with an autoregressive model have very recognizable patterns. Figure 12.10 contains the general shapes for the autocorrelations of series that can be represented by first- and second-order autoregressive models.

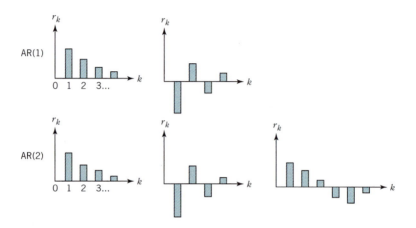

Figure 12.10 Shapes of r_k $(k > 0)$ for Series Represented by AR(1) and AR(2) Models

There are two possible patterns for AR(1) models and three possible patterns for AR(2) models. The idea is to look at a plot of the series, and the sample autocorrelations of the series and its differences. If the original series is stationary and the sample autocorrelations are consistent with one of the patterns displayed in Figure 12.10, for example, one of the AR(1) patterns, we would fit an AR(1) model to the data using least squares, check the significance of the predictor variable term, and examine the residuals. We analyze the model just as we would a multiple regression model. If we are satisfied with the fit, we can then use the model to forecast future values.

EXAMPLE 12.9 Selecting a Model for the Treasury Bill Interest Rate Series

A plot of the monthly interest rate on three-month Treasury bills for a thirteen-year period is shown in Figure 12.3(c). Identify and fit an autoregressive model to these data.

Solution and Discussion. We argued at the beginning of this section that the series displayed in Figure 12.3(c) on page 649 is nonstationary in the mean because it does not vary about a fixed level. The sample autocorrelations for the interest rate series y_t and the series of first differences $w_t = y_t - y_{t-1}$ follow.

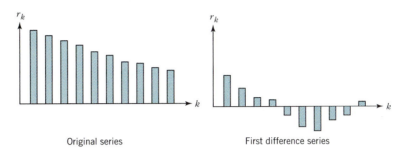

Original series   First difference series

The autocorrelations for the original series do not die out rapidly. This behavior suggests the series is nonstationary; this is consistent with the plot of the series. The autocorrelations for the differenced series die out with a sinusoidal pattern. These autocorrelations suggest that the differenced series is stationary. Moreover, the pattern of autocorrelations looks very much like one of the patterns for the autocorrelations of AR(2) processes shown in Figure 12.10. Consequently, we tentatively identify the AR(2) model

$$w_t = \beta_0 + \beta_1 w_{t-1} + \beta_2 w_{t-2} + \varepsilon_t$$

for the differenced series $w_t = y_t - y_{t-1}$. The AR(2) model was fit to the T-bill interest rate series. The fitted model, after deletion of an insignificant $\hat{\beta}_0$, is

$$\hat{w}_t = .40\, w_{t-1} + .10\, w_{t-2} \qquad t = 2, 3, \ldots, 154$$

A plot of the residual autocorrelations with approximate ± 2 standard error limits is shown here.

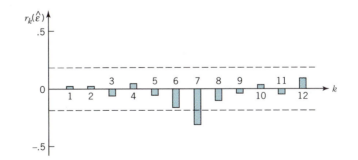

Although the residual autocorrelation at lag 7 is large, this plot and additional analyses of the residuals not shown here suggest there is no reason to doubt the model assumptions. We accept the fitted AR(2) model as an adequate representation of the T-bill interest rate series. We can now use this model to generate forecasts of future rates.

Figure 12.11 contains the sample autocorrelation function and ±2 standard error limits for the Wisconsin employment in food and kindred products time series. (These sample autocorrelations for the first 12 lags were displayed in Exercise 3.19.)

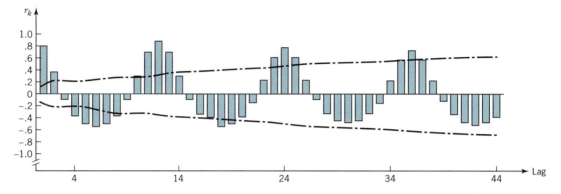

Figure 12.11 The Sample Autocorrelation Function for the Wisconsin Employment in Food Products Time Series

The sample autocorrelations do not die out quickly and have a wave-like appearance. Notice that the autocorrelation at multiples of the seasonal lag, $k = 12, 24, 36, \ldots$, are uniformly large. This behavior suggests that the series is nonstationary. The persistent autocorrelation at the seasonal lags can often be eliminated by creating differences with a lag equal to the period of the seasonality. In this case, the seasonal lag is 12, and the seasonal differences are $y_{13} - y_1, y_{14} - y_2, \ldots, y_t - y_{t-12}, \ldots, y_n - y_{n-12}$.

Remember, we are arguing that differencing can eliminate nonstationarity, and that the differences typically have a simple autocorrelation structure that can be used to identify appropriate time series models, in particular, autoregressive models. As we shall see, these models can then be used to forecast future values of the *original* series.

Figure 12.12 is a plot of the sample autocorrelation function and ±2 standard error limits for the seasonal differences of the employment series. The autocorrelations in this plot get small rather quickly, and they fall off geometrically from $r_1 = .64$ in a pattern reminiscent of one of the possibilities for an AR(1) model pictured in Figure 12.10.

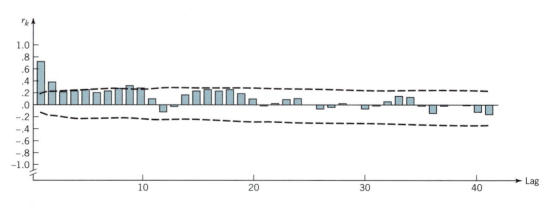

Figure 12.12 The Sample Autocorrelation for the Differences $w_t = y_t - y_{t-12}$ for the Food Products Series

The seasonally differenced series is stationary and appears to follow a first-order autoregressive model. Consequently, we would tentatively consider the model

$$w_t = \beta_0 + \beta_1 \, w_{t-1} + \varepsilon_t$$

for the seasonally differenced series $w_t = y_t - y_{t-12}$.

The autocorrelation function in Figure 12.12 has another interpretation. In Example 11.12, we presented the results of a fit of the straight-line model

$$y_t = \beta_0 + \beta_1 \, y_{t-12} + \varepsilon_t$$

to the pairs of employment observations (y_{t-12}, y_t). We concluded that β_0 was not required and that the coefficient of y_{t-12} is essentially 1. That is, $\hat{y}_t = y_{t-12}$. The residuals from this fit are displayed in Figure 3.17, and the residual autocorrelations are given in Figure 11.10(b). Because the residuals from the straight-line fit are essentially

$$y_t - \hat{y}_t = y_t - y_{t-12}$$

the seasonal differences, the autocorrelation function in Figure 11.10(b) is the auto-correlation function in Figure 12.12.

We conclude that the residuals from the straight-line fit are not independent (uncorrelated), indicating that the original model must be modified. Given the nature of the residual autocorrelation function, we must allow for correlation between successive seasonal differences, between differences two periods apart, and so forth. This is what the AR(1) model in the seasonal differences does.

EXAMPLE 12.10   Fitting a Model for the Wisconsin Employment in Food Products Series

Fit the model

$$w_t = \beta_0 + \beta_1 \, w_{t-1} + \varepsilon_t$$

with $w_t = y_t - y_{t-12}$ to the Wisconsin employment in food products time series. Interpret the results and analyze the residuals.

Solution and Discussion.   With the help of Minitab, the AR model was fit to the employment series. The results from this fit indicate that $\hat{\beta}_0$ was not significantly different from 0. The model without β_0 was then fit to the data. A brief summary of the results follows.

```
Final Estimates of Parameters
Type       Estimate       St. Dev.    t-ratio
AR    1      0.6673         0.0599      11.14


Differencing: 0 regular, 1 seasonal of order 12
No. of obs.:  Original series 178, after differencing 166
Residuals:    SS = 279.456
              MS =    1.694   DF = 165
```

We have

$$\hat{w}_t = .667\, w_{t-1}$$

or, in terms of the original observations,

$$\hat{y}_t = y_{t-12} + .667(y_{t-1} - y_{t-13}) = .667\, y_{t-1} + y_{t-12} - .667\, y_{t-13}$$

with the mean square error, MSE $= \hat{\sigma}^2 = 1.694$. The model relates the current observation to the observation in the previous time period and to the same pair of observations 12 months ago. In other words, the employment for July of the current year depends directly on the June employment and on the employment for June and July of the previous year.

Suppose we want to use the fitted model to forecast next month's employment, and next month is August. Let A denote August, J denote July, PA denote August last year (previous August), and let PJ denote July last year (previous July); then our forecast of August's Wisconsin employment in food products is

$$\hat{y}_A = .667\, y_J + y_{PA} - .667\, y_{PJ}$$

The residual autocorrelations and their ± 2 standard error limits are given here.

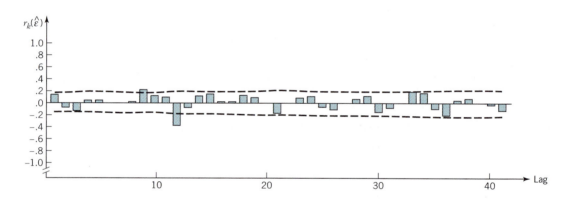

These autocorrelations are all small, with the exception of the residual autocorrelation at the seasonal lag 12, $r_{12}(\hat{\varepsilon}) = -.37$. It is possible to improve the model a little bit by adding a term to account for this autocorrelation. We will not pursue that possibility here. A histogram and a normal-scores plot of the residuals follow.

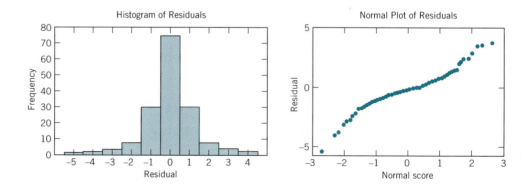

Although there are a few more extreme residuals than would be predicted by a $N(0, \hat{\sigma}) = N(0, 1.302)$ distribution, the evidence against normality is marginal. It is reasonable to assume that the errors are approximately normally distributed and that the usual procedures can be used to construct confidence intervals and test hypotheses. In short, the model may be improved slightly, but it appears to be a very adequate representation of the data.

Although differencing may be required to achieve stationarity, not every stationary time series can be represented by a low-order autoregressive model. On the other hand, autoregressive models are quite flexible and, with appropriate differencing, can represent a wide variety of time series that occur in practice. Because of their similarity with multiple linear regression models, the standard regression procedures can be used for analyzing autoregressive models.*

FORECASTING WITH AUTOREGRESSIVE MODELS

As we have said, one of the major objectives in time series analysis is to predict future observations. Very often, important business decisions are based on the "best guess" of future outcomes. For example, corporate planners are concerned with predicting future sales, earnings, costs, expenditures, and other relevant quantities.

Once an adequate time series model is in hand, it can be used to make inferences about future values. However, it is important to keep in mind that forecasting based on a model fitted to an observed time series necessarily involves the extrapolation of historical data. To the extent that the future behaves like the past and the model correctly describes the process of interest, good forecasts can be obtained. If the process changes, the current time series model may no longer be appropriate, and forecasts computed from this model may be misleading. This is particularly true for forecasts with a long lead time. We recommend a periodic monitoring of the time series model. The model and the old forecasts should be updated as new information (data) becomes available.

We introduce some new notation that makes it easier to distinguish forecasts from observations, and then we illustrate how the forecasts (and error limits) are generated for autoregressive models. We will concentrate on AR(1) and AR(2) models to demonstrate the ideas. Ordinarily, statistical software, including Minitab, would be used to generate forecasts and error limits.

Let y_n denote the last value in the time series, and suppose we are interested in forecasting the value that will be observed l time periods ($l > 0$) in the future, y_{n+l}. That is, at forecast origin $t = n$, we are interested in forecasting the future value y_{n+l}. We denote the forecast of y_{n+l} by $\hat{y}_{n+l}$. It can be shown that the "best" forecast of y_{n+l} is given by the *expected value of y_{n+l} at time n*. Keep in mind that, at time n, y_{n+l} is a random variable that has not yet been observed. Here "best" means the forecast that minimizes the (mean) square error.

*Good references for further study are: Newbold, P., and Bos, T., *Introductory Business and Economic Forecasting,* 2nd ed. Cincinnati: South-Western, 1994 and Abraham, B., and Ledolter, J., *Statistical Methods for Forecasting.* New York: Wiley, 1983.

Let E_n denote the expected value at time n, so that $E_n(y_{n+l})$ is the expected value of y_{n+l} at time n. This is really a conditional expectation since, in general, it will depend on information already available. The best forecast of y_{n+l} at time n is then

$$\hat{y}_{n+l} = E_n(y_{n+l})$$

In other words, to generate the forecast, we use the time series model to write the expression for y_{n+l} and then evaluate its expected value at time n. Let's see how this works for an AR(1) model.

The first-order autoregressive model is

$$y_t = \beta_0 + \beta_1 y_{t-1} + \varepsilon_t$$

or, for $t = n + 1$,

$$y_{n+1} = \beta_0 + \beta_1 y_n + \varepsilon_{n+1}$$

Now, suppose we are interested in forecasting the next observation y_{n+1} at the forecast origin $t = n$. The forecast is determined by computing $E_n(y_{n+1})$. Consequently,

$$\begin{aligned} \hat{y}_{n+1} = E_n(y_{n+1}) &= E_n(\beta_0 + \beta_1 y_n + \varepsilon_{n+1}) \\ &= \beta_0 + \beta_1 y_n + E_n(\varepsilon_{n+1}) = \beta_0 + \beta_1 y_n \end{aligned}$$

since β_0, β_1, and y_n are all constant* and, by assumption, $E_n(\varepsilon_{n+1}) = 0$.

Now suppose we want to forecast two steps ahead (lead time $l = 2$). We have

$$y_{n+2} = \beta_0 + \beta_1 y_{n+1} + \varepsilon_{n+2}$$

and

$$\begin{aligned} \hat{y}_{n+2} = E_n(y_{n+2}) &= E_n(\beta_0 + \beta_1 y_{n+1} + \varepsilon_{n+2}) \\ &= \beta_0 + \beta_1 E_n(y_{n+1}) + E_n(\varepsilon_{n+2}) = \beta_0 + \beta_1 \hat{y}_{n+1} \end{aligned}$$

The forecast two steps ahead can be computed using the model and the forecast one step ahead.

In general, for AR(1) models with forecast origin n,

$$\hat{y}_{n+l} = \beta_0 + \beta_1 \hat{y}_{n+l-1} \qquad l = 2, 3, \ldots$$

That is, once the forecast of the next observation is computed, additional forecasts can be generated recursively from the model. This is the kind of calculation that is easily performed by a computer.

To construct a prediction interval for a future observation, we need the estimated standard error of the forecast. In general, the standard error depends on the AR model parameters $\beta_1, \beta_2, \ldots, \beta_p$, the standard deviation of the error term, σ, and the lead

---

*At time n, y_n is a constant because it has been observed. It is the last value in the time series.

time l. The expressions for the standard error can be quite complicated, but for the AR(1) model they are rather simple.

Standard Errors for Selected AR(1) Forecasts

lead time $l = 1$ std. error $= \sigma$

lead time $l = 2$ std. error $= \sqrt{1 + \beta_1^2}\, \sigma$

lead time $l = 3$ std. error $= \sqrt{1 + \beta_1^2 + \beta_1^4}\, \sigma$

Notice that the standard errors increase with the lead time. The uncertainty associated with our forecasts increases as we forecast farther into the future.

Once the standard errors are determined, error limits given by $\pm 2(\text{standard error})$ can be calculated. At forecast origin n, an approximate 95% prediction interval for y_{n+l} is

$$\hat{y}_{n+l} \pm 2(\text{Standard error})$$

Using an AR(1) model with forecast origin n, an approximate 95% prediction interval for y_{n+1} is

$$\hat{y}_{n+1} \pm 2\sigma$$

The 95% prediction interval for y_{n+2} is

$$\hat{y}_{n+2} \pm 2\sqrt{1 + \beta_1^2}\, \sigma$$

In practice, estimates of the model parameters must be used to actually calculate the error limits and prediction intervals.

EXAMPLE 12.11   Forecasting with an AR(2) Model

A second-order autoregressive model

$$y_t = \beta_0 + \beta_1 y_{t-1} + \beta_2 y_{t-2} + \varepsilon_t$$

was fit to a time series consisting of $n = 62$ observations. The fitted model is

$$\hat{y}_t = 1.6 + 1.5 y_{t-1} - .8 y_{t-2}$$

with $\hat{\sigma} = .3$. The last two values of the time series are $y_{61} = 5.5$ and $y_{62} = 5.8$. Calculate the forecasts of y_{63}, y_{64}, and y_{65} from forecast origin 62 (the end of the series).

Solution and Discussion.   Using the estimates of the model parameters, the forecast of the next observation y_{63} is

$$\hat{y}_{63} = E_{62}(y_{63}) = E_{62}(1.6 + 1.5y_{62} - .8y_{61} + \varepsilon_{63})$$
$$= 1.6 + 1.5y_{62} - .8y_{61} + E_{62}(\varepsilon_{63}) = 1.6 + 1.5y_{62} - .8y_{61}$$
$$= 1.6 + 1.5(5.8) - .8(5.5) = 5.9$$

The forecast of y_{64} is

$$\hat{y}_{64} = E_{62}(y_{64}) = 1.6 + 1.5E_{62}(y_{63}) - .8y_{62} + E_{62}(\varepsilon_{64})$$
$$= 1.6 + 1.5\hat{y}_{63} - .8y_{62} = 1.6 + 1.5(5.9) - .8(5.8) = 5.8$$

Finally, the forecast of y_{65} is

$$\hat{y}_{65} = E_{62}(y_{65}) = 1.6 + 1.5\hat{y}_{64} - .8\hat{y}_{63} = 1.6 + 1.5(5.8) - .8(5.9) = 5.6$$

The pattern is evident. Additional forecasts can be generated recursively from the fitted model (see Exercise 12.27).

The procedure for generating forecasts from autoregressive models can be summarized as follows:

1. Using the fitted time series model, solve for y_{n+l}, where n is the forecast origin and l is the lead time.

2. Evaluate the conditional expectation $E_n(y_{n+l})$ using the relationships

$$E_n(y_{n+j}) = \begin{cases} \hat{y}_{n+j}, & j > 0 \\ y_{n+j}, & j \le 0 \end{cases}$$

and

$$E_n(\varepsilon_{n+j}) = 0, \quad j > 0$$

3. With the least squares estimates of the model parameters, evaluate the forecast of the next observation y_{n+1}. Calculate the subsequent forecasts recursively using the expression for the conditional expectation in step 2.

EXERCISES

12.25 Derive an expression for the forecast of the next observation y_{n+1} for each of the autoregressive models given here.

a. $y_t = \beta_0 + \beta_1 y_{t-1} + \beta_2 y_{t-2} + \beta_3 y_{t-3} + \varepsilon_t$

b. $w_t = \beta_0 + \beta_1 w_{t-1} + \varepsilon_t$ where $w_t = y_t - y_{t-1}$

c. $w_t = \beta_0 + \beta_1 w_{t-1} + \varepsilon_t$ where $w_t = y_t - y_{t-4}$

12.26 Refer to Exercise 12.25. Derive expressions for the forecasts at lead times $l = 2, 3$ for each of the models listed in Exercise 12.25.

12.27 We showed that AR(1) forecasts made at forecast origin n satisfy $\hat{y}_{n+l} = \beta_0 + \beta_1 \hat{y}_{n+l-1}$, $l = 2, 3, \ldots$. Develop a similar expression for AR(2) models. That is, develop an expression that can be used to recursively generate forecasts for lead times $l = 3, 4, \ldots$ if the forecasts of the next two observations, $\hat{y}_{n+1}$ and $\hat{y}_{n+2}$, are available.

12.28 Using the results for AR(1) forecasts developed in this section, show that the forecast $\hat{y}_{n+2}$ can be written entirely in terms of the model parameters and the last observation y_n. Can you generalize this result?

12.29 Refer to Example 12.11. It can be shown that an approximate 95% prediction interval for the next observation y_{n+1} for *any* autoregressive model is

$$\hat{y}_{n+1} \pm 2\hat{\sigma}$$

Using $\hat{y}_{63}$ and $\hat{\sigma}$ given in Example 12.11, construct an approximate 95% prediction interval for y_{63}. Also, using the information in Example 12.11, generate forecasts for y_{66} and y_{67}. Plot the observations y_{61} and y_{62}, and the forecasts $\hat{y}_{63}$ through $\hat{y}_{67}$. Comment on the pattern of the forecasts.

MonSaleX.dat

12.30 (*Minitab or similar program recommended*) The monthly sales for Company X ($n = 77$) are given here.

	Year						
Month	1990	1991	1992	1993	1994	1995	1996
Jan.	154	200	223	346	518	613	628
Feb.	96	118	104	261	404	392	308
Mar.	73	90	107	224	300	273	324
Apr.	49	79	85	141	210	322	248
May	36	78	75	148	196	189	272
June	59	91	99	145	186	257	
July	95	167	135	223	247	324	
Aug.	169	169	211	272	343	404	
Sept.	210	289	335	445	464	677	
Oct.	278	347	460	560	680	858	
Nov.	298	375	488	612	711	895	
Dec.	245	203	326	467	610	664	

Is this series stationary? Is it seasonal? Discuss with reference to plots and the sample autocorrelations of the original series and, if appropriate, a differenced series.

MonSaleX.dat

12.31 (*Minitab or similar program recommended*) Refer to Exercise 12.30. Identify and fit an autoregressive model to the series consisting of the monthly sales of Company X.

TBillInt.dat

12.32 (*Minitab or similar program recommended*) The table at the top of page 670 contains the monthly averages of the weekly interest rates for three-month U.S. Treasury bills for a ten-year period ($n = 120$). The period covered by this series is different from the period covered by the monthly interest rates on three-month T-bills discussed in Example 12.9.

Month	Year									
	1	2	3	4	5	6	7	8	9	10
Jan.	3.93	4.70	4.63	5.28	6.30	7.85	4.56	3.73	5.58	7.77
Feb.	4.00	4.83	4.60	5.13	6.29	7.22	3.77	3.62	5.77	7.18
Mar.	4.00	4.79	4.28	5.31	6.19	6.59	3.47	4.04	6.47	7.86
Apr.	3.99	4.73	3.93	5.47	6.15	6.49	3.92	4.25	6.52	8.29
May	3.96	4.81	3.80	5.81	6.14	7.04	4.32	4.12	6.56	8.33
June	3.87	4.66	3.80	5.68	6.75	6.89	4.88	4.29	7.19	7.93
July	3.89	4.88	4.61	5.42	7.20	6.53	5.58	4.50	8.08	7.53
Aug.	3.94	5.22	4.80	5.24	7.19	6.54	5.27	4.45	8.64	8.80
Sept.	4.04	5.78	4.94	5.26	7.30	6.49	4.94	5.09	8.49	8.22
Oct.	4.18	5.64	5.06	5.39	7.30	6.24	4.66	5.14	7.31	7.30
Nov.	4.24	5.59	5.19	5.58	7.55	5.46	4.38	5.07	7.91	7.58
Dec.	4.49	5.09	5.48	6.04	7.87	4.89	4.31	5.28	7.60	7.15

Is this series stationary? Is this series seasonal? Discuss with reference to plots and the sample autocorrelations of the original series and, if appropriate, a differenced series.

TBillInt.dat

12.33 (*Minitab or similar program recommended*) Refer to Exercise 12.32 and Example 12.9. Identify and fit an autoregressive model to the T-bill interest rate series in Exercise 12.32. Compare this model with the one for the T-bill interest rate series in Example 12.9. Using the end of the series as the forecast origin, generate forecasts and error limits for the T-bill interest rate for the next 12 months. Discuss the nature of the forecasts and their error limits.

NPowPeak.dat

12.34 (*Minitab or similar program recommended*) The NSP(Wis) peak demand time series discussed in Example 12.8 is contained in Table 3.2 in Example 3.18. Using the natural logarithms of the monthly peak demand as the response, fit the autoregressive model

$$w_t = \beta_0 + \beta_1 w_{t-1} + \varepsilon_t$$

where $w_t = y_t - y_{t-12}$ and y_t is the log of peak demand in month t. Does this model appear to adequately represent the peak demand time series? Explain. Using the end of the series as the forecast origin, generate forecasts of the log of peak demand for the next 12 months. Compare these forecasts with those generated by the additive decomposition in Example 12.8. Which forecasts do you prefer? Why?

12.6   STATISTICS IN CONTEXT

Real estate investors who also manage their rental properties must know the market. To help determine the factors that influence the amount of rent that can be charged, one investor selected a random sample of $n = 16$ apartments on the west side of a midwestern city. The monthly rent (y), apartment size in square feet (x_1), number of bedrooms (x_2), and number of bathrooms (x_3) were recorded for each apartment.* The data are given in Table 12.4.

*We have already considered elements of this problem in Exercises 11.11, 11.23, and 11.24.

TABLE 12.4 Apartment Rent Data

Rent y	SqFt x_1	No. Bed x_2	No. Bath x_3
720	1000	2	1.00
595	900	2	1.00
915	1200	2	2.00
760	810	1	1.00
1000	1210	2	2.00
790	860	1	1.00
880	1135	2	2.00
845	960	2	1.50
650	800	1	1.00
748	960	2	1.50
685	650	1	1.00
755	970	2	2.00
815	1000	2	2.00
745	1000	2	1.75
715	1000	2	1.00
885	1180	2	1.00

The investor will develop a multiple linear regression model to relate rent to apartment size, number of bedrooms, and number of bathrooms. Location is also a prime candidate for a predictor variable, but the area from which the random sample was selected is only a couple of miles square, so location is unlikely to be a major issue as long as we limit our conclusions to the west side of town. Any effect that location has on these data will be included in the error term. Also, amenities such as fireplaces or inside parking will be components of the error. (Real estate assessments, at least for homes, are often based on regression equations that include terms for these facilities.)

Scatterplots of rent versus each of the predictor variables are shown in Figure 12.13 on page 672.

The scatterplots indicate there is a tendency for rent to increase with an increase in each of size, number of bedrooms, and number of bathrooms. The sample correlations among the pairs of variables are given here.

```
          Rent     SqFt   No. Bed
SqFt      0.765
No. Bed   0.343   0.760
No. Bath  0.613   0.586   0.543
```

Consistent with the scatterplots, the association between rent and size is the strongest, followed by the association between rent and the number of bathrooms. The positive correlation between rent and the number of bedrooms is reasonably small. Not surprisingly, the number of bedrooms and the number of bathrooms are each positively correlated with size and with each other.

A fit of the multiple linear regression model

$$Y_i = \beta_0 + \beta_1 x_{i1} + \beta_2 x_{i2} + \beta_3 x_{i3} + \varepsilon_i \qquad i = 1, 2, \ldots, 16$$

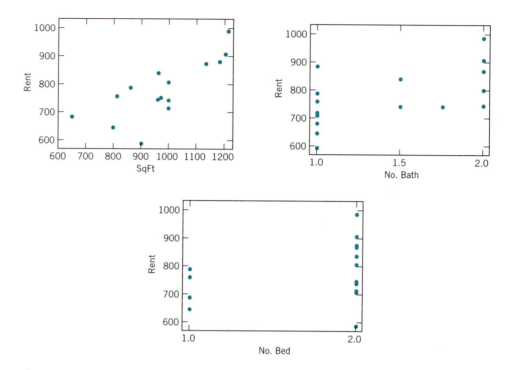

Figure 12.13   Scatterplots of Rent and Size, Rent and Bedrooms, and Rent and Bathrooms

where the ε_i are assumed to be independent $N(0, \sigma)$ random variables, produced these
results:

```
The regression equation is
Rent = 238 + 0.713 SqFt - 151 No. Bed + 78.6 No. Bath

Predictor          Coef        Stdev       t-ratio          p
Constant         238.11        89.48          2.66      0.021
SqFt             0.7127       0.1432          4.98      0.000
No. Bed         -151.33        47.79         -3.17      0.008
No. Bath          78.59        37.00          2.12      0.055

s = 52.83        R-sq = 79.6%        R-sq(adj) = 74.5%

Analysis of Variance

SOURCE         DF            SS            MS          F          p
Regression      3        130930         43643      15.64      0.000
Error          12         33486          2791
Total          15        164416

Unusual Observations
Obs.       SqFt          Rent          Fit    Stdev.Fit      Residual      St.Resid
  8         960         845.0        737.5         19.0         107.5         2.18R

R denotes an obs. with a large st. resid.
```

There is one observation with a large standardized residual. Inspection of the data shows that the fitted model underpredicts the rent for this apartment. This apartment has 2 bedrooms and $1\frac{1}{2}$ baths, but is relatively small for the rent that is being charged. The residual plots in Figure 12.14 suggest there is no reason to doubt the model assumptions.

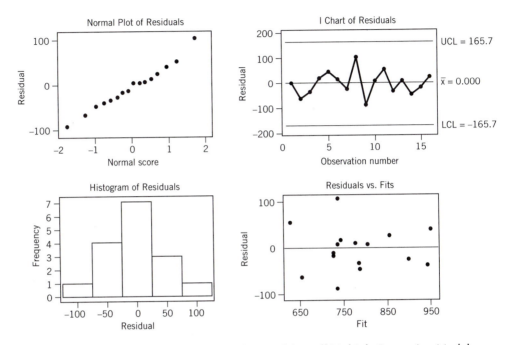

Figure 12.14 Plots of the Residuals from the Fit of the Full Multiple Regression Model

The regression is significant ($F = 15.64$ with P-value $= .000$), and $R^2 = .796$ says that about 80% of the variation in rents is explained by the (estimated) relationship of rent with size, number of bedrooms, and number of bathrooms. An apartment with 1050 square feet containing 2 bedrooms and $1\frac{1}{2}$ bathrooms would be predicted to rent for

$$\hat{y}^* = 238.11 + .713(1050) - 151.33(2) + 78.59(1.5) = 802.0$$

or about $800 per month. An interval estimate for this rent is given by the 95% prediction interval shown here. Also shown is a 95% confidence interval for the mean rent for apartments with these specifications.

```
  Fit   Stdev.Fit       95.0% C.I.              95.0% P.I.
 801.6       15.5   (   767.8,   835.4)   (    681.7,    921.6)
```

We can be 95% confident that the mean monthly rent for apartments in this area with 1050 square feet, 2 bedrooms, and $1\frac{1}{2}$ baths is between $768 and $835. The monthly rent for a single apartment with these characteristics is very likely to be in the range $682 to $922.

Returning to the regression output, we question whether all the predictor variables are necessary. The P-value for the coefficient of x_3, the number of bathrooms, is .055, so this term might be dropped. Since we have only a small number of predictor variables, we can explore this issue by using the stepwise and all possible regression procedures.

Stepwise Regression

```
Response is    Rent   on  3 predictors, with N =    16

       Step      1      2       3
   Constant   275.5   222.7   238.1

   SqFt        0.52    0.81    0.71
   T-Ratio     4.44    5.29    4.98

   No. Bed            -132    -151
   T-Ratio            -2.50   -3.17

   No. Bath                     79
   T-Ratio                    2.12

   S           69.8    59.5    52.8
   R-Sq        58.48   71.97   79.63
```

We see from the stepwise results that the best model with one predictor uses size (SqFt). The regression is significant ($t = 4.44$ with d.f. $= 14$, P-value $< .01$), and $R^2 = .58$. The best model with two predictor variables uses size (SqFt) and the number of bedrooms (No. Bed). Both predictor variables are required. For x_1 (SqFt), $t = 5.29$ with d.f. $= 13$, P-value $< .01$, and we conclude $\beta_1 \neq 0$ given that x_2 (No. Bed) is in the model. Likewise, for x_2 (No. Bed), $t = -2.50$ with d.f. $= 13$, P-value $< .05$, and we conclude $\beta_2 \neq 0$ given that x_1 (SqFt) is in the model. For this model, $R^2 = .72$. Of course, the best model with three predictor variables is the full model described previously with $R^2 = .80$.

The estimated coefficients of x_1 and x_2 do not change a great deal from the model with two predictor variables to the model with three predictor variables. This suggests that the variable x_3 (No. Bath) is contributing information not contained in x_1 and x_2. This evidence, along with the variance inflation factors (VIF) that are not shown, means that multicollinearity is not a problem.

All Possible Regressions

The Minitab output from its best subsets regression procedure follows.

Vars	R-sq	Adj. R-sq	C-p	s	SqFt	No. Bed	No. Bath
1	58.5	55.5	12.5	69.833	X		
1	37.6	33.1	24.8	85.635			X
2	72.0	67.7	6.5	59.536	X	X	
2	62.6	56.9	12.0	68.761	X		X
3	79.6	74.5	4.0	52.825	X	X	X

Again, we see that the best model using one predictor variable involves SqFt, and the best model with two predictor variables involves SqFt and No. Bed. The best model as judged by R^2, $s = \sqrt{MSE}$, and the C_p statistic is the full ($p = 3$ predictor variable) model. For the full model, $(p + 1, C_p) = (4, 4)$. This point lies on the 45° line. Moreover, C_p is a measure of the total prediction error for a model, and this statistic is smallest for the full model.

Taking all this evidence into account, we argue that, even though the coefficient of x_3 is not significantly different from 0 at the .05 level, this term improves the fit and contributes information about rent that is not contributed by the other predictor variables. The best model, among those considered, is the original model using all three predictor variables.

12.7 CHAPTER SUMMARY

In this chapter, we have learned:

- We can analyze the **multiple linear regression** model

$$Y_i = \beta_0 + \beta_1 x_{i1} + \beta_2 x_{i2} + \cdots + \beta_p x_{ip} + \varepsilon_i \qquad i = 1, 2, \ldots, n$$

where

1. Y_i is the response corresponding to the ith experimental trial in which $x_1 = x_{i1}$, $x_2 = x_{i2}, \ldots, x_p = x_{ip}$.
2. $\varepsilon_1, \varepsilon_2, \ldots, \varepsilon_n$ are the unknown error components that represent the deviations of the response from the true linear relation. We assume the errors are independent and each has a $N(0, \sigma)$ distribution.
3. The coefficients or parameters $\beta_0, \beta_1, \beta_2, \ldots, \beta_p$, which together locate the regression function, are unknown.

- A $100(1 - \alpha)\%$ **confidence interval for β_j** is

$$(\hat{\beta}_j - t_{\alpha/2} s_{\hat{\beta}_j}, \ \hat{\beta}_j + t_{\alpha/2} s_{\hat{\beta}_j})$$

where $s_{\hat{\beta}_j}$ is the estimated standard error of $\hat{\beta}_j$ and $t_{\alpha/2}$ is the upper $\alpha/2$ point of a t distribution with d.f. $= n - p - 1$.

- To test the hypothesis H_0: $\beta_j = 0$, compute the test statistic

$$t = \frac{\hat{\beta}_j}{s_{\hat{\beta}_j}}$$

For an α level test, reject H_0 if

$$|t| > t_{\alpha/2} \qquad \text{for } H_1: \beta_j \neq 0$$
$$t > t_\alpha \qquad \text{for } H_1: \beta_j > 0$$
$$t < -t_\alpha \qquad \text{for } H_1: \beta_j < 0$$

The P-value is the smallest α for which the observed t value just rejects H_0. Consequently, there is a P-value corresponding to each of these three alternative hypotheses.

- An estimator of $\sigma^2 = \text{var}(\varepsilon_i)$ is

$$s^2 = \frac{\text{SSE}}{n - p - 1} = \frac{\sum (y_i - \hat{y}_i)^2}{n - p - 1}$$

where $\hat{y}_i$ is the ith fitted value

$$\hat{y}_i = \hat{\beta}_0 + \hat{\beta}_1 x_{i1} + \hat{\beta}_2 x_{i2} + \cdots + \hat{\beta}_p x_{ip}$$

- **Confidence intervals for the mean response** $\beta_0 + \beta_1 x_1^* + \cdots + \beta_p x_p^*$ or a new response y^* at the values of the predictor variables $x_1^*, x_2^*, \ldots, x_p^*$ generally require additional input to a computer program. To have the computer generate these interval estimates, we must input the x^*'s and the confidence level $1 - \alpha$. However, the intervals have the general form

$$\hat{y}^* \pm t_{\alpha/2}(\text{Estimated standard error})$$

where

$$\hat{y}^* = \hat{\beta}_0 + \hat{\beta}_1 x_1^* + \hat{\beta}_2 x_2^* + \cdots + \hat{\beta}_p x_p^*$$

- The **analysis of variance** (ANOVA) table for multiple regression takes the form

Source	Sum of Squares	d.f.	Mean Square	F ratio
Regression	SSR	p	$\text{MSR} = \text{SSR}/p$	$F = \text{MSR}/\text{MSE}$
Error	SSE	$n - p - 1$	$\text{MSE} = \text{SSE}/(n - p - 1)$	
Total	SST	$n - 1$		

1. The coefficient of determination R^2 is

$$R^2 = \frac{\text{SSR}}{\text{SST}} = 1 - \frac{\text{SSE}}{\text{SST}}$$

2. The **F test for the significance of the regression** tests the hypothesis $H_0: \beta_1 = \beta_2 = \cdots = \beta_p = 0$ versus H_1: at least one $\beta_j \neq 0$. At level α, the rejection region is $F > F_\alpha(p, n - p - 1)$, where

$$F = \frac{\text{MSR}}{\text{MSE}}$$

with d.f. $= (p, n - p - 1)$.

- A **polynomial regression model** may be used in some cases to handle a nonlinear relation.
- A linear relation among two or more of the explanatory variables is called **multicollinearity.**
- The strength of the multicollinearity is measured by the **variance inflation factor** (VIF)

$$\text{VIF}_j = \frac{1}{1 - R_j^2} \qquad j = 1, 2, \ldots, p$$

If VIF_j is much greater than 1, then $\hat{\beta}_j$ is unstable.

- Two procedures for selecting the "best" set of explanatory variables from a group of alternatives are **stepwise regression** and **all possible** (best subset) **regressions.**
- The **leverage** h_i of the ith data point measures how far the x values for the ith observation are from the remaining x values. If the leverage is large (close to 1), the ith observation has a large role in determining the location of the fitted regression function.
- The **standardized** (or Studentized) **residuals**

$$\frac{\hat{\varepsilon}_i}{s(\hat{\varepsilon}_i)} = \frac{\hat{\varepsilon}_i}{s\sqrt{1 - h_i}} \qquad i = 1, 2, \ldots, n$$

all have variance 1. A standardized residual greater than 2, or less than -2, indicates that an observation has an unusual or extreme response y.

- A time series that varies about a fixed level is said to be **stationary in the mean.**
- **Nonstationary time series** can often be converted to stationary time series by **differencing.**
- Stationary and nonstationary time series can frequently be identified from their sample autocorrelation functions. Sample autocorrelations for stationary series tend to die out quickly. Sample autocorrelations for nonstationary series tend to persist for many time lags.
- **Seasonal time series** are time series with a pattern that repeats itself periodically.
- One approach to modeling and forecasting a time series is to assume the series is composed of a trend component (T), a seasonal component (S), and an irregular or residual component (I). The **additive decomposition** of a time series is

$$y_t = T_t + S_t + I_t \qquad t = 1, 2, \ldots, n$$

where

T_t is the value of the trend at time t

S_t is the value of the seasonal component at time t

I_t is the value of the irregular component (residual) at time t

- The fit of a time series model can be judged by several measures of accuracy: the **mean absolute percentage error** (MAPE), the **mean absolute deviation** (MAD), and the **mean squared deviation** (MSD).
- A useful class of models for representing a wide variety of stationary time series is the class of autoregressive models. The **pth-order autoregressive model** is given by

$$w_t = \beta_0 + \beta_1 w_{t-1} + \beta_2 w_{t-2} + \cdots + \beta_p w_{t-p} + \varepsilon_t$$

where w_t may be the original series y_t or a suitable difference of the original series. The errors ε_t are assumed to be independent, and each error has a $N(0, \sigma)$ distribution.

- Autoregressive models are often identified by matching the autocorrelation patterns produced by the time series with the known autocorrelation patterns of autoregressive processes.

- Because of their similarity with multiple linear regression models, the standard regression procedures can be used for analyzing autoregressive models.

- **Forecasts** from autoregressive models are computed by evaluating the **conditional expectation** $E_n(y_{n+l})$. Here n represents the forecast origin and l represents the lead time. The procedure for generating forecasts, denoted by $\hat{y}_{n+l}$, proceeds as follows:

1. Using the fitted time series model, solve for y_{n+l}, where n is the forecast origin and l is the lead time.

2. Evaluate the conditional expectation $E_n(y_{n+l})$ using the relationships

$$E_n(y_{n+j}) = \begin{cases} \hat{y}_{n+j}, & j > 0 \\ y_{n+j}, & j \le 0 \end{cases}$$

and

$$E_n(\varepsilon_{n+j}) = 0, \quad j > 0$$

3. With the least squares estimates of the model parameters, evaluate the forecast of the next observation y_{n+1}. Calculate the subsequent forecasts recursively using the expression for the conditional expectation in Step 2.

12.8 IMPORTANT CONCEPTS AND TOOLS

CONCEPTS

Irregular component, 654
Multicollinearity, 636
Multiple linear regression model, 622
Nonstationary time series, 648
Polynomial regression model, 631
pth-order autoregressive model, 659
Seasonal component, 654
Seasonal time series, 653
Second-order autoregressive model, 659
Stationary time series, 648
Trend component, 654

TOOLS

Additive decomposition of a time series, 654
All possible regressions, 639
Analysis of variance table, 627
Coefficient of determination, R^2, 627
Confidence interval for β_j, 625
C_p statistic, 640
Differencing, 649
Estimator of σ^2, 624
Forecasts for autoregressive models, 668
F test for the significance of the regression, 627

Leverage, 644
Mean absolute deviation, 655
Mean absolute percentage error, 655
Mean squared deviation, 655
Moving averages, 655
Multiple correlation coefficient, 628
Seasonal indices, 655
Standardized (Studentized) residual, 644
Stepwise regression, 640
Test statistic for H_0: $\beta_j = 0$, 625
Variance inflation factor, 636

12.9 KEY FORMULAS

Estimator of σ^2: $s^2 = \dfrac{\text{SSE}}{n - p - 1} = \dfrac{\sum(y_i - \hat{y}_i)^2}{n - p - 1}$

Estimator of σ: $s = \sqrt{s^2} = \sqrt{\dfrac{\text{SSE}}{n - p - 1}}$

A $100(1 - \alpha)\%$ confidence interval for β_j is

$$(\hat{\beta}_j - t_{\alpha/2}s_{\hat{\beta}_j}, \ \hat{\beta}_j + t_{\alpha/2}s_{\hat{\beta}_j})$$

where $s_{\hat{\beta}_j}$ is the estimated standard error of $\hat{\beta}_j$ and $t_{\alpha/2}$ is the upper $\alpha/2$ point of a t distribution with d.f. $= n - p - 1$.

To test the hypothesis H_0: $\beta_j = 0$, use the test statistic

$$t = \frac{\hat{\beta}_j}{s_{\hat{\beta}_j}} \quad \text{with d.f.} = n - p - 1$$

For an α level test, the rejection region is

$$t < -t_\alpha, \quad t > t_\alpha, \quad \text{or} \quad |t| > t_{\alpha/2}$$

according to whether the alternative hypothesis (H_1) is

$$\beta_j < 0, \quad \beta_j > 0, \quad \text{or} \quad \beta_j \neq 0$$

respectively.

The ANOVA table for multiple linear regression is

Source	Sum of Squares	d.f.	Mean Square	F ratio
Regression	SSR	p	MSR $=$ SSR$/p$	$F =$ MSR$/$MSE
Error	SSE	$n - p - 1$	MSE $=$ SSE$/(n - p - 1)$	
Total	SST	$n - 1$		

The coefficient of determination R^2 is

$$R^2 = \frac{\text{SSR}}{\text{SST}} = 1 - \frac{\text{SSE}}{\text{SST}}$$

The multiple correlation coefficient is $R = \sqrt{R^2}$.

The F test for the significance of the regression tests the hypothesis H_0: $\beta_1 = \beta_2 = \cdots = \beta_p = 0$ versus H_1: at least one $\beta_j \neq 0$. Use the F statistic

$$F = \frac{\text{MSR}}{\text{MSE}}$$

with d.f. $= (p, n - p - 1)$. At level α, the rejection region is

$$F > F_\alpha(p, n - p - 1)$$

Variance inflation factor (VIF)

$$\text{VIF}_j = \frac{1}{1 - R_j^2} \qquad j = 1, 2, \ldots, p$$

where R_j^2 is the coefficient of determination from the regression of the jth explanatory variable on the remaining $p - 1$ explanatory variables.

$$C_p = \left(\frac{\begin{array}{c}\text{Residual sum of squares for subset model with}\\ p + 1 \text{ parameters, including an intercept}\end{array}}{\text{Residual mean square for full model}} \right) - (n - 2(p + 1))$$

Standardized (Studentized) residual

$$\frac{\hat{\varepsilon}_i}{s(\hat{\varepsilon}_i)} = \frac{\hat{\varepsilon}_i}{s\sqrt{1 - h_i}} \qquad i = 1, 2, \ldots, n$$

where h_i is the leverage for the ith data point.

Additive decomposition of a time series

$$y_t = T_t + S_t + I_t \qquad t = 1, 2, \ldots, n$$

where

T_t is the value of the trend at time t

S_t is the value of the seasonal component at time t

I_t is the value of the irregular component (residual) at time t

Mean absolute deviation (MAD)

$$\text{MAD} = \frac{\sum_{t=1}^{n} |y_t - \hat{y}_t|}{n}$$

Mean absolute percentage error (MAPE)

$$\text{MAPE} = \frac{\sum_{t=1}^{n} |(y_t - \hat{y}_t)/y_t|}{n} \times 100 \qquad (y_t \neq 0)$$

Mean squared deviation (MSD)

$$\text{MSD} = \frac{\sum_{t=1}^{n} (y_t - \hat{y}_t)^2}{n}$$

Let $E_n(y_{n+l})$ denote the conditional expectation of y_{n+l} made at time $t = n$. For autoregressive models, the forecast of y_{n+l} at forecast origin n is $\hat{y}_{n+l} = E_n(y_{n+l})$, where

$$E_n(y_{n+j}) = \begin{cases} \hat{y}_{n+j}, & j > 0 \\ y_{n+j}, & j \leq 0 \end{cases}$$

and

$$E_n(\varepsilon_{n+j}) = 0, \quad j > 0$$

REVIEW EXERCISES

12.35 A portion of a time series and the corresponding fitted values produced by a time series model are shown here.

y_t	31.0	34.0	40.0	42.0	39.0	34.0	29.0	20.0
$\hat{y}_t$	29.8	35.1	38.2	40.1	40.5	31.2	27.5	22.4

y_t	17.0	14.0	15.0	17.0	23.0	28.0	33.0	35.0
$\hat{y}_t$	19.5	15.1	16.9	18.8	21.5	26.2	31.3	36.9

    a. Calculate the residuals, and plot the residuals against the fitted values. Is this plot consistent with the standard error term assumptions for a time series model? Discuss.

    b. Calculate the MAD, MAPE, and MSD. Which of these measures do you think is the best measure of accuracy? Discuss.

12.36 ApartRen.dat (*Minitab or similar program recommended*) Refer to Section 12.6, Statistics in Context. The all possible regressions procedure suggests the best model using two predictor variables is to regress Rent on SqFt and No. Bed. Using the data in Table 12.4, perform this regression. Examine the residuals, and investigate any influential observations. Does this model provide an adequate explanation of the data? Discuss.

12.37 ApartRen.dat (*Minitab or similar program recommended*) Refer to Exercise 12.36. Using the fitted model in Exercise 12.36, generate a 95% confidence interval for the mean rent corresponding to apartments with 1050 square feet of space and 2 bedrooms. Generate a 95% prediction interval for the rent of a single apartment with these characteristics. Compare these intervals with the ones generated in Section 12.6. What is the effect on these interval estimates of the additional predictor variable No. Bath?

12.38 CHealthC.dat (*Minitab or similar program recommended*) Health care decisions are made at the individual, corporate, and government levels. Different perspectives result in a variety of systems for managing health care. Comparing different health care systems can help us learn about approaches other than our own. Here we consider health care systems for 32 countries throughout the world. As a measure of quality of care, we use LifeEx, the life expectancy at birth. Potential explanatory variables include: %Urban, the percentage of the population living in urban areas; GDP, gross domestic product in billions of dollars; GDP/Cap, GDP per capita in dollars; and PSqMi, persons per square mile. The data are given in Table 12.5 on page 682.

    a. Consider first a regression of life expectancy on all the other explanatory variables. Use the natural log of GDP, call it LnGDP, instead of GDP. Compute descriptive statistics, including the sample correlations for all the variables in the data set. Fit a multiple regression model and analyze the residuals.

TABLE 12.5   Life Expectancy Data

Country	LifeEx	%Urban	GDP	GDP/Cap	PSqMi
Afghanistan	44.9	18	3	200	84
Argentina	71.4	87	185	5500	32
Australia	77.6	85	339.7	19100	6
Bangladesh	55.1	17	122	1100	2236
Belgium	77.0	97	177.5	17700	855
Brazil	62.3	77	785	5000	49
Cambodia	49.3	13	6	600	150
Canada	78.1	77	617.7	22200	7
Chile	74.5	85	96	7000	48
China	67.9	28	2610	2200	326
Denmark	75.8	85	95.6	18500	312
Egypt	60.8	44	139	2400	162
France	78.2	74	1050	18200	277
Germany	76.3	85	1331	16500	590
Greece	77.7	63	93.2	8900	209
India	58.6	26	1700	1300	766
Indonesia	60.7	31	571	2900	275
Israel	78.0	90	65.7	13350	643
Italy	77.6	68	986	16700	501
Japan	79.3	77	2550	20400	861
Malaysia	69.2	51	141	7500	155
Mexico	72.9	71	740	7800	124
Nepal	52.5	10	.021	1000	379
Nigeria	55.3	16	95.1	1000	284
Russia	68.9	73	975.4	5190	23
South Korea	70.6	74	424	9500	1188
Spain	77.7	64	498	12700	51
Switzerland	78.2	68	149.1	21300	444
Turkey	70.9	51	312.4	5100	211
United Kingdom	76.8	92	980.2	16900	619
United States	75.9	75	6380	24700	72
Vietnam	65.4	21	72	1000	585

SOURCES: 1996 *World Almanac* and *Statistical Abstract*.

b. Interpret the results of your regression. Is the regression significant? Do the estimated coefficients have the "right" signs? Is multicollinearity a problem? Can any predictor variable terms be dropped? Are there any influential observations? If there are, what should be done with these influential observations?

CHealthC.dat

12.39 (*Minitab or similar program recommended*) Refer to Exercise 12.38. Search for a better regression model using stepwise regression and the all possible regressions (best subset regression) procedures. Justify your choice. Once you have the best model, generate a 95% prediction interval for life expectancy for a hypothetical country with characteristics close to, but not identical to, those of Nigeria.

12.40 (*Minitab or similar program recommended*) In Section 11.6, we suggested that the Canadian dollar/U.S. dollar exchange rate time series (see Figure 12.5(a)) could be represented by the random walk model

$$y_t = y_{t-1} + \varepsilon_t \quad \text{or} \quad y_t - y_{t-1} = \varepsilon_t$$

CanUSExc.dat

Let $w_t = y_t - y_{t-1}$ be the series of first differences. Use the exchange rate data on the Data Disk to fit the first-order autoregressive model

$$w_t = \beta_0 + \beta_1 w_{t-1} + \varepsilon_t$$

Do your results confirm the random walk model for the Canadian dollar/U.S. dollar exchange rate series? Explain.

12.41 (*Minitab or similar program recommended*) Identify and fit an autoregressive model to the monthly inventory levels of diesel engines given in Table 1.4. Does an autoregressive model provide an adequate representation of this time series? Discuss. [*Hint:* Try models for the original series and the series of first differences.]

EngInven.dat

12.42 (*Minitab or similar program recommended*) Identify and fit an autoregressive model to the weekly market share of Colgate data on the Data Disk. Does an autoregressive model provide an adequate representation of this time series? Discuss. [*Hint:* Try models for the original series and the series of first differences.]

Toothpas.dat

After reading this chapter, you should be able to:

- Distinguish among the sources of variation.
- Make variation visible with a control chart.
- Interpret tests for special causes of variation.
- Understand how to react to variation.
- Discuss strategies for reducing variation.
- Use Deming's PDCA wheel.
- Implement a framework for process improvement.

CHAPTER THIRTEEN

Management and Statistics

13.1 INTRODUCTION

The primary focus of this book has been about ways to generate, summarize, model, and make informed generalizations from data. The goal has been to develop information about a situation, problem, or condition that will be useful to business decision makers. From a management perspective, the ultimate goal of the firm is to be able to offer desirable products and services as economically as possible. How do the roles of the statistician and the manager fit together to accomplish this goal? Should all managers be statisticians? No. Should all managers know something about statistics? Yes.

Change and variation are a necessary part of any business environment—indeed, a necessary part of everyday life. Nothing remains the same. Variation creates uncertainty because we do not know enough to account precisely for all of the variation. Recall from Chapter 1, for example, the discussion about the power company that must plan for the amounts of natural gas to be shipped on a daily basis for winter heating. This example illustrates that key business decisions must invariably be made in an atmosphere of uncertainty.* In this chapter, we attempt to link management and statistics. We will argue, once again, that the careful generation and analysis of data reduces uncertainty and leads to rapid learning and opportunities for improvement that are generally not apparent from intuition, hearsay, or reports.

As illustrated in Figure 1.4, Dr. Deming viewed the firm as a system of inter-connected processes within which people work. This system takes inputs and turns them into products and services. To succeed, the interconnected elements must work together with a common aim. People must break down the barriers to communication and view improvements to processes with a system perspective. A particular solution to an isolated problem may not be in the best interests of the entire firm (system). We present a framework for making improvements that incorporates the use of statistics and promotes a system perspective. This framework is summarized by the flow diagram in Figure 13.5 on page 706.

To improve the quality of products and services, we can use data to guide our search for the causes of variation and to evaluate change. To be effective, this activity must be part of a reasoned approach (the scientific method) to problem solving that has the support of top management, and involves teams that incorporate both statistical and subject matter expertise. Some CEOs recognize this necessity. Consider the following example from the semiconductor industry.

The electronics products and services industry is the largest employer in the United States, with over 2.2 million employees in 1995 and a $257 billion share of the annual gross national product. This industry depends heavily on semiconductor manufacturing. SEMATECH is a consortium founded in 1987 by the U.S. government and the major U.S. semiconductor manufacturing companies. From the start, the use of applied statistics was integrated within all the process and tool improvement projects at SEMATECH, creating a partnership among statisticians, engineers, and technicians. Statisticians have learned about semiconductor manufacturing, and engineers have learned about statistics so they can communicate and work effectively together.

At the end of a paper describing the use of statistical methods at SEMATECH, William Spencer, Chief Executive Officer, and Paul Tobias, Manager, Statistical Methods Group, declare: "Intense competition in the worldwide marketplace is a never-ending fact of life in the semiconductor industry. While we have a good idea where the technology is going over the next 15 years, the key to success will be maintaining a cost-effective manufacturing capability, and using this to financially fuel the development of the tools and processes needed for the next generations.... Statistics will continue to play a major role in optimizing day-to-day manufacturing operations and assisting managers in making intelligent decisions based on adequate and relevant data."[†]

---

*A quote attributed to Arthur Radford (1957) supports this notion: "A decision is the action an executive must take when he has information so incomplete that the answer does not suggest itself."
†SOURCE: Spencer, W. J., and Tobias, P. A., "Statistics in the semiconductor industry: A competitive necessity," *The American Statistician,* Vol. 49, No. 3, Aug. 1995.

As is the case at SEMATECH, if the results of a statistical analysis are to be helpful to the manager, they must be trusted and used. They must be part of the day-to-day process of learning.

13.2   UNDERSTANDING VARIATION

In Chapter 1, we reported that a Director of Statistical Methods for Nashua Corporation claimed:

Failure to understand variation is a central problem of management.

We agree. Consider the following scenarios:

- A department head budgeted $50,000 for travel, but the actual expenditures were $57,000. She was not sure whether to tell her staff that they would have only $43,000 for travel this coming year (so that if they came in $7,000 over again, they would hit the real target of $50,000), or to be realistic and set the travel budget at $57,000 since that is what it seemed to take.

- A team had four months to finish a project, but they finished in three months. Based on this experience, their manager scheduled the next similar project for three months.

- As part of the evaluation of one of his managers, a division head periodically surveyed the manager's staff. This year's mean response on one key leadership quality question is 3.7 (on a scale of 1–5, with 5 representing "excellent"). The mean response last year was 4.1. What has happened? Should he penalize the manager? Should he look for a replacement?

- Diane was upset. As sales manager, she is concerned about the performance of one of her salesmen. Patrick's sales are down from last month, although the number of his contacts is roughly the same. This is particularly disappointing because last month's sales were up from his sales two months ago. Should she give him a little pep talk? Does he need more training? Should he be reassigned to a different territory?

Like these people, we react, or contemplate reacting, to the information that we receive. The question is whether our decisions make things better, have no effect, or make things worse. To answer that question, we must understand a few basic concepts about variation in the data that describe the problem we are studying.

SOURCES OF VARIATION

Diane's concern about Patrick's sales figures is prompted by variation. Patrick's sales for the last several months are shown in Figure 13.1 (page 688).

The sales vary about a horizontal line, with all sales contained within a band with a lower limit of about 20 and an upper limit of about 100. Patrick's sales for the last 3 months are circled in the figure. These are the numbers that bothered Diane.

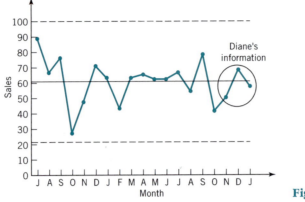

Figure 13.1   Patrick's Sales

Think about the possible things that might affect Patrick's sales: the number of unannounced or "cold" calls, the amount of inventory remaining from last month, the number of referrals, the weather, availability of new or updated products, delays in processing orders, and so forth. These are called **common causes of variation.** Common causes have these characteristics:

- They are present all the time in a process, although their impact varies.
- *Individually,* they have a small effect on the variation.
- *Collectively,* they can produce quite a bit of variation.

All processes have common causes of variation. Some also have other causes of variation. Consider Figure 13.2, which shows 2 additional months of Patrick's sales data. The time when Patrick entered the hospital to have a scheduled operation that kept him off his feet for 2 weeks is also indicated.

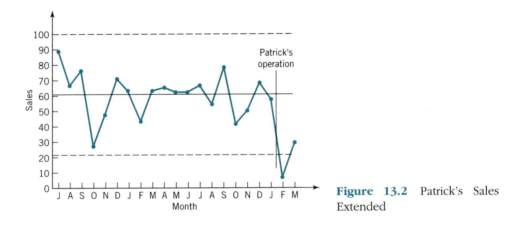

Figure 13.2   Patrick's Sales Extended

The factor—Patrick's operation—that led to the abnormally low sales for February is called a **special cause of variation.** Special causes have the following characteristics:

- They are not always present in the process; they appear sporadically.
- They come from *outside* the usual process (for example, the operation was outside Patrick's usual process of selling products).

- They can contribute either a small or large amount to the total variation, but usually have a bigger impact on variation than any single common cause.

Factors that are always present in the work, and whose impact varies day to day or month to month are common causes. Factors that interrupt the usual flow of events are special causes.

Processes that have only common cause variation are said to be **stable** or **predictable.** Stable processes are said to be **in statistical control.** Processes with both common causes and special causes are said to be **unstable** or **unpredictable.** These processes are not in statistical control.

According to Brian Joiner,* we can imagine a plot of the variation from a stable process as a straight highway across the desert. We are not sure where the next point will fall, but we are pretty sure it will fall somewhere on the highway.

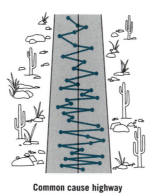

Common cause highway

On the other hand, a plot of the variation from an unstable process will look something like a highway across the desert interrupted by a major fault—a highway that shifts suddenly to one side by several feet or more.

Special cause highway

Variation due entirely to common causes is what we usually think of as random variation, that is, variation that can be modeled as independent drawings from a

---

*Much of the discussion in this section is based on the book by B. L. Joiner entitled *Fourth Generation Management.* New York: McGraw–Hill, Inc., 1994.

probability distribution with a particular mean and standard deviation. Starting with a stable process, statistical methods can point out the existence of special causes of variation: the point outside the prediction interval, the significant result of a test of hypotheses, the long sequence of points on one side of the mean, and so forth. In general, we learn something from understanding the causes of variation, and this knowledge allows us to increase quality, reduce costs, improve productivity—the Deming chain reaction shown in Figure 1.5.

Common cause variation is usually harder to deal with than special cause variation. As we shall discuss, common cause variation cannot be reduced or eliminated without changing the characteristics of the work environment.

Many processes have another source of variation, called **structural variation.** Structural variation is a consistent pattern that is present, because of natural laws or an established cause-and-effect relation in all of the data. Trend and seasonality are examples of structural variation. In regression models, structural variation is modeled by the regression function, and the remaining variation due to common causes is modeled by the error component (see Section 11.2 or Section 12.2). Data not consistent with these sources of variation imply the existence of one or more special causes.

Before we consider how managers should react to variation, we must make them aware of the nature of the variation. That is, we must make the variation visible or plot the highway across the desert.

MAKING VARIATION VISIBLE—CONTROL CHARTS

Figure 2.20 (page 90) contains a plot of the amounts of radiation escaping through the closed doors of 42 microwave ovens. This control chart of the (transformed) radiation measurements is reproduced in Figure 13.3.

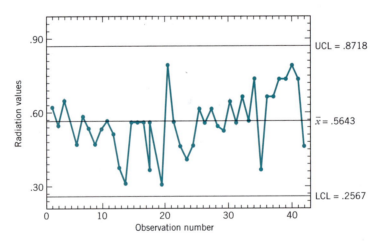

Figure 13.3   Control Chart for Radiation Measurements

Control charts are useful devices for displaying variation, and we have used them on occasion in this book. Although there are different kinds of control charts, depending on the variable or characteristic being monitored, any **control chart** has

- data plotted in time order,
- a centerline, usually the sample mean, and

- horizontal lines, called control limits, that indicate the width of the common cause variation.

The upper and lower control limits are typically located at three standard deviations on each side of the mean, and various methods may be used to estimate the standard deviation.

Creating a control chart is not difficult, but the calculations can be left to a computer. Most statistical software packages, including Minitab, will create a control chart.

Control charts make the variation in the process data visible. They indicate at a glance what is to be expected if the process is stable, and they help to distinguish common cause variation from variation due to special causes. Recall that common causes are a lot of small things that add up one way one day and another way the next day. They affect all of the data and create variation that wanders about the centerline of the highway across the desert. As we have suggested, special causes create patterns that deviate from the ordinary. They typically affect only a few of the observations, and create a break in the road, or points on the shoulder, or several consecutive observations only in the left-hand lane, and so forth.

How do we distinguish special causes from common causes? There are several tests available. The tests are designed to detect patterns of various types. The occurrence of a pattern suggests a special cause of variation that should be investigated. Four **tests for special causes** are summarized in Figure 13.4. The upper and lower control limits (UCL and LCL) are positioned at $\pm 3\sigma$ from the mean.

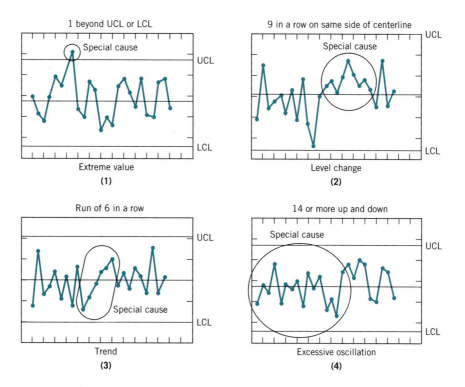

Figure 13.4   Four Tests for Special Causes

These tests for special causes are not infallible. We might miss an occasional special cause, or react to one of the signals in Figure 13.4 that ends up being only common cause variation. However, although not perfect, the special cause tests enhance our ability to react appropriately, particularly when compared to intuition or traditional managerial reports of short-term performance.

EXAMPLE 13.1   Testing for Special Causes with the Radiation Data

Test for special causes of variation using the radiation measurements shown on the control chart in Figure 13.3.

Solution and Discussion.   Using Minitab, we find that the radiation measurements fail Test 2. The level of the radiation measurements is apparently different (lower) in this shaded area than it is for the remainder of the measurements. The control chart and the Minitab summary are shown here.

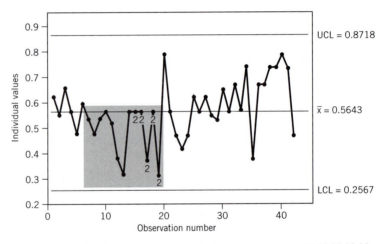

TEST 2. Nine points in a row on one side of CL. Test Failed at points: 15 16 17 18 19

Our goal is to identify the special causes that appear to be responsible for the apparent change in the radiation through the closed doors of the microwave ovens. As we discussed in Chapter 2, ovens near the beginning of the series (roughly, observations 10–20 that failed Test 2) appear to emit lower than average radiation, and ovens near the end of the series (roughly, observations 33–41) appear to emit higher than average radiation. Has there been a change in the supplier of the door components? Has there been a change in the assembly procedure? Are we mixing ovens from two different production runs? Questions such as these lead to the special causes of the inconsistent variation. Once the causes are identified, appropriate action can be taken to resolve the difficulty.

Special causes offer the opportunity for rapid learning and timely fixes. However, it is better to work on the source of the special cause to prevent recurrence rather than to change the process to accommodate the special cause. Changing the process to accommodate a special cause typically adds complexity and increases cost.

Though some variation is inevitable, we can improve quality and lower costs by eliminating as much variation as possible. However, if the variation is not visible and the causes of the variation are not identified, we have no hope of reducing it. In fact, typical reactions to variation can actually make things worse.

THE WRONG REACTION TO VARIATION—TAMPERING

Let's return to Diane's problem with Patrick's sales performance. Recall the circled sales figures in Figure 13.1. Diane was concerned because, after an increase from November to December, Patrick's sales for January were down (relative to his December sales). With only two data points, it is easy to compute a trend. Diane's reaction was to give Patrick a pep talk and schedule him for a three-day training program offered by a consulting firm at an additional cost to the company. Diane felt good about the decision. Patrick thought he did not learn anything new, and he was unable to make any sales calls for three days.

Did Diane do the right thing? Apart from the decrease in sales caused by Patrick's operation (see Figure 13.2), should she be surprised if Patrick's sales for the next few months were not appreciably different from his sales for January? What should she do at that point, fire Patrick and hire (and train) a new person?

Diane is overreacting to common cause variation or **tampering.** She is trying to adjust a stable system to make things better. Instead, she is making the situation worse. She has incurred the added cost of training that was not helpful and has created a disgruntled employee. Tampering can be done by anyone—a manager, an employee, or even a machine.

If we look at Patrick's monthly sales for the 19 months shown in Figure 13.1, we see that the circled numbers are generally consistent with the other numbers and well within the common cause highway. Diane should not have been alarmed by the variation in the sales figures for November, December, and January. Patrick's sales represent a stable process. We learn nothing of importance by comparing two results from a stable process, because we are essentially looking at random variation produced by a host of ever-present common causes.

The management lesson to be learned is to plot the data and stop tampering.

Failure to overreact to variation is progress, but it will not lead to rapid, sustained improvement. To improve processes, we must not only describe or explain variability (a role for statistics), we must seek to reduce it (a role for management).

REDUCING VARIATION

Most problems arise from common causes, yet it pays to work on special causes first. Special causes—the occasional jolts—give us a chance to learn the easy way. We can often readily identify the source of special cause variation. We simply have to determine what was different when the special cause appeared: the accident on the freeway, the computer that crashed, the change in tax policy, the defective raw material, and so forth. Although it may have a positive impact, a special cause typically produces a fire that has to be put out.

There is no such thing as THE common cause. As we have said, it is just a lot of small things that add up differently each time. Dealing with common cause variation is much more difficult. The answers are often more subtle. A different strategy is required for dealing with common cause variation than with special cause variation. Changing the common cause variation requires a reconfiguration of the work environment or system.

In addition, if we fail to deal with special cause variation first, our vision may be clouded, and we may not be able to determine what the common cause variation is saying. It will be difficult to judge the effect of changes.

Joiner developed a special cause **strategy for improving an unstable process,** as follows:

- *Get timely data.* Special causes should be signalled quickly so that action can be taken before the trail gets cold. We might use an approximate figure— *projected* orders, for instance—that is available immediately rather than waiting days or weeks for a more accurate figure.

- *Act immediately to contain any damage.* Put out the fire. For example, take care of the angry customer, recall and fix (replace) the defective product, assign additional people to meet the deadline, and so forth.

- *Search for the cause.* See what was different. What occurred, when, where, and with whom? What did not occur that might have been expected to occur? Which groups were not affected by the problem? Look for deep causes. Keep asking "why? why? why?" until you get the deepest cause (output, process, or system) that you can detect.

- *Develop a longer-term remedy.* Once the source of the special cause variation has been identified, develop a long-term fix to prevent recurrence. If the source of the special cause variation is outside of the system—a competitor's sudden price reduction, for example—make a plan to minimize the effect. If the results are good, develop a solution to preserve and maintain the benefit.

Remedies for special causes may involve high-level, wide-impact policies and practices that reach well beyond the individual employee. A computer malfunction during payroll processing looks like a special cause that may be handled by purchasing a new computer, but a higher-level manager may notice that this problem is consistent with similar problems with computers purchased from the same "least-cost" vendor. Perhaps it is time to change the purchasing policy.

Management must be involved in tracking down and eliminating the sources of special causes, or in helping to capture a favorable special cause and making sure it continues to happen. It is also management's responsibility to verify (with the help of data) the effectiveness of any changes and to ensure that any improvements are maintained.

A stable process with only common cause variation is predictable. The results will fall somewhere on the common cause highway. Unfortunately, just because a process is stable does not mean it meets the customer's needs or the firm's needs. Knowing a process is stable does not tell us how wide the variation is or whether the mean is at an appropriate level. Discovering a process is stable does not mean we should be satisfied with its variation or its level. *Leaving the process alone is not improvement.*

Improving a stable process—reducing the variation, changing the level—is different from improving an unstable process. The same set of variables is operating all the time, so every data point has information and all the data are relevant and useful. There is nothing special about the highest point, or the lowest point, or the latest point, or the points we do not like. Unlike special causes, there is no obvious signal that says, "Here's a common cause, come look." Instead, we need strategies that help us understand the relationships among the variables that are present all the time in the system. It is at this point where planned experiments and statistical models are particularly useful. Management must be involved because these strategies may require collecting additional data and may even require disrupting a process temporarily.

The **strategies for improving stable processes** fall into these three categories:

- *Stratify*. Sort data into groups or categories based on different factors; look for patterns.
- *Experiment*. Make planned changes in several factors and look for the effects.
- *Disaggregate*. Divide the process into component pieces and manage the pieces. This strategy requires a management system to keep the pieces integrated, so that we do not fix each piece without looking at the process as a whole.

These strategies may be used individually or in combination. We might disaggregate, and then run experiments within some of the component pieces. The idea is to generate thoughts about the causes of variation and potential solutions, separating those that yield a payoff from those that lead nowhere. Once we have pinpointed the common cause variation at its source, we can develop measures to eliminate it or at least to minimize its effects. Generally, these measures require making fundamental changes in the system.

EXAMPLE 13.2 Stratifying to Eliminate Variation

A firm manufactures cardboard mailing tubes. The firm is concerned about the strength of the tubes. It seems that some of the tubes have deteriorated in the mail, generating a number of customer complaints. This has been going on for some time and appears to be affecting the sales of the tubes to intermediaries. The cardboard for the tubes is made by gluing layers of paper. Identify potential causes of variation in strength, and suggest a strategy for dealing with this variation.

Solution and Discussion. Let's agree, without information to the contrary, that the strength of a tube is determined by the strength of the cardboard. Let's also agree that the strength of the paper (cardboard) is determined by two measurements: strength in the machine direction and strength in the cross-direction (see Example 2.6). Ideally, we should have control charts showing over time the strengths of the cardboard for individual tubes, or the average strengths of the cardboard for small individual samples of tubes. It would then be easier to determine whether the variation in strengths is due only to common causes (a stable system) or to both common and special causes (an unstable system). Without control charts, we have to guess.

Since the problem with strengths has apparently been occurring for some time, we will assume that the variation in strengths is common cause variation and that the system is stable. Potential causes of variation might include the glue, the paper, the temperature, the humidity, the drying time, the assembly line, and the production shift. One way to determine the effect of these factors on strength would be to run planned experiments with the factors set at different levels and to compare the strengths of cardboard produced at the various combinations of factor levels. However, this strategy is likely to be time-consuming and will necessarily require an interruption of the current production process (that is, costly). A strategy that requires less investment of time and resources is stratification.

After a review of company records, it is determined that most of the complaints are associated with cardboard manufactured on Production line 2 on the third shift. We have now stratified; that is, we have grouped the data according to whether the cardboard was produced during the third shift on Production line 2.

What is it about the third shift on Production line 2 that could lead to problems with cardboard strength? A review of the procedure used to assemble the cardboard seemed to be in order. The procedure was the same one used during other shifts and on other production lines. The temperature seemed to be OK, the humidity readings were consistent with the humidity readings for the other shifts, and the glue came from the same source as the glue used on the other lines. However, a discussion with the third-shift supervisor revealed that he was "helping the company" by slowly getting rid of a large inventory of "old" paper—paper from a supplier the company no longer used. The supervisor was mixing the old paper with the "new" paper from the current supplier. Once this practice was eliminated, subsequent tests showed that the strengths of cardboard produced during the third shift on Production line 2 were not appreciably different from the strengths of cardboard produced on other lines at other times. The variability in the strengths of the mailing tubes was greatly reduced, and the customer complaints declined.

Stratification helps us to identify and eliminate common cause variation by revealing patterns in the data that let us focus on the source of the trouble. Focusing allows us to determine the leverage points where a little effort brings major improvement.

To do a stratification analysis, we must have information on conditions related to the data, such as the production line, the day of the week, equipment, supplier, employee, weather, and so on. If this information is not available, or not accessible, then we may need to collect new data.

We discussed planned experiments in Section 4.5, and in Chapter 9, we considered inferences about means for completely randomized designs and paired samples. We do not intend to say much more about experimentation here, except that it is a very powerful tool for determining cause-and-effect relations. If time and resources permit, even small-scale experimentation (a pilot plant or laboratory operation) can produce impressive results when the goal is to explain the variation in a response, and ultimately move the centerline in the common cause highway or reduce the width of the highway.

As the next example illustrates, eliminating unwanted variation by disaggregation works when each piece of the process has an aim tied to serving the next step and when these aims are consistent with the overall objective of the process.

EXAMPLE 13.3   Disaggregating to Eliminate Variation

In Section 8.8, entitled Statistics in Context, we considered the problem of reducing the total time taken to process credit card applications at local credit unions. Since many local credit unions do not have the resources to handle the applications "in house," most of the processing is done by the association of credit unions national organization. With the information in Section 8.8, identify the strategy used to reduce the variation in the total time required to process credit card applications, and pinpoint the action(s) taken to improve the process.

Solution and Discussion. In the search for the causes of variation in the total time required to process applications, the quality team broke the application process into separate steps: application data entry, application review, local credit union recommendation, account data entry, account posting, plastic card generation, and postal handling. That is, the process was disaggregated into its component pieces. The strategy to *disaggregate* is a natural one, in this case, to study process improvement. The steps are sequential—the outcome from one step providing input for the next step—and some steps are handled at the national organization, some at the local credit union.

A review of the data collected on the amount of time required to complete each step suggested that the time to complete the local credit union recommendation (a step required by law) was inordinately long—approximately 5 working days. Consequently, the quality team concentrated on the recommendation step. After reviewing a cause-and-effect or fishbone diagram showing the potential causes of variation in the recommendation cycle times, a change in the way the local credit union communicated with the national organization was recommended. This recommendation led to the policy requiring communication by fax. Data collected to check the effectiveness of the new policy showed that the communication change cut the average recommendation cycle time approximately in half and saved tens of thousands of dollars in the total cost of processing credit card applications.

EXERCISES

13.1 Sit in a restaurant and consider the process for ordering and delivering your meal. Consider the time it takes to get your order. At what points does the process seem to have problems? List some of the causes of the problems that you see. Suggest a way to demonstrate that the problems really exist, and give a strategy for dealing with the problem(s).

13.2 Consider the two-way table of the NSP (Wisc) peak demand given in Chapter 3, Table 3.2, reproduced here.

Month	1970	1971	1972	1973	1974	1975	1976	1977	1978	Average
January	385	406	420	432	446	468	496	572	574	466.6
February	375	411	418	412	440	467	498	543	564	458.7
March	372	388	397	396	426	433	477	554	544	443.0
April	365	387	368	390	428	411	423	464	486	413.6
May	360	361	415	390	409	440	405	462	527	418.8
June	370	386	381	418	393	473	490	527	546	442.7
July	376	367	420	434	471	496	489	562	539	461.6
August	383	382	429	451	438	495	504	492	597	463.4
September	382	387	389	395	431	403	476	504	586	439.2
October	365	360	390	412	417	406	476	487	483	421.8
November	391	377	424	410	421	440	518	530	593	456.0
December	406	412	438	433	442	495	528	560	*	464.3
Average	377.5	385.3	407.4	414.4	430.2	452.3	481.7	521.4	549.0	

The variation in peak demand is displayed by month and year. What strategy for searching for common causes is represented by this table? Suggest some causes of the variation in peak demand, and classify them by type.

13.3   Money managers are always looking for an edge. Can a money manager create a portfolio of stocks that will produce higher than normal returns with low risk? The *efficient markets hypothesis* says No! If you want higher returns, you must be willing to accept higher risk. That is, differences in risk should be the sole determinant of differences in expected return. However, some would argue that the stock market is not efficient, and that the variation in a cross section of stock returns can be partially explained by variables (factors) that can be classified into five broad categories: risk, liquidity, price level, growth potential, and price history. Suppose this is true. Are these variables responsible for common cause variation or special cause variation? Which strategy might you use to manage the causes of variation? That is, which strategy might you use to create a portfolio of Super Stocks—a portfolio with abnormally high returns with little risk (variability)? Discuss.

13.4   (*Class project*) Consider the process of receiving a final grade in this course. What factors contribute to variation in the final course grade? Show these factors on a cause-and-effect diagram. Suggest a strategy for improving the process, that is, for eliminating or reducing some of the undesirable causes of variation. For those factors that relate to the delivery of the course material, work with your instructor to make any agreed-upon changes. How might you collect data to demonstrate that improvement has occurred? [*Hint:* Consider factors like exams, homework or projects, lecture attendance, professor's attitude, and performance of other students.]

EngInven.dat

13.5   (*Minitab or similar program recommended*) Construct a control chart for the monthly engine inventory levels given in Chapter 1, Table 1.4 and reproduced here (read across).

772	701	681	620	618	543	551
848	1114	1079	1143	1040	1018	923
862	881	903	948	952	915	1096
965	1067	1049	948	863	1072	1440
1638	1669	1640	1699	1714	1571	1583
1481	1418	1255	1166	1037	914	993
1008	1094	1454	1334	1184	1180	1033
994	847	719	778	866	804	

We said in Example 1.8 that $\bar{x}$ and s did not provide a good summary of these data because of the apparent change in level of the inventory series. Does the control chart confirm this statement? Specifically, conduct tests for special causes. If a special cause is indicated, comment on its effect (levels higher than usual, a run of decreasing amounts, and so forth).

Toothpas.dat

13.6   (*Minitab or similar program recommended*) Construct a control chart for the Colgate market share for weeks 115–155 given on the Data Disk. Conduct tests for special causes. If a special cause is indicated, comment on its effect (levels higher than usual, a run of decreasing amounts, and so forth). (The American Dental Association endorsement of Crest toothpaste occurred at about week 135.)

 13.7   (*Minitab or similar program recommended*) Pick a process with some measurable characteristic of interest to you. Examples are the amount of time spent studying on individual weekdays Monday through Thursday, the time required to jog around a given course, the daily closing price of a particular stock, the amount (in ounces) of soft drinks consumed daily, the number of minutes early ($+3$, for example) or late (-2, for example) to your first class of the day, and so forth. Try to collect 20 or more observations, and construct a control chart. Conduct tests for special causes. If a special cause is indicated, identify it.

13.3   A FRAMEWORK FOR IMPROVING PROCESSES

We have discussed methods for learning from data and using this knowledge to make decisions that lead to improvements, that is, that make things better. Learning and improvement are not one-shot concepts. Rather, they are part of a never-ending cycle of discovery, careful planning, experimenting, summarizing, checking, determining new standards and policies, and looking for new ways to improve (discovery again). These ideas were actually introduced and developed in the 1920s by Walter A. Shewhart,* an engineer working for Bell Telephone Labs in New York, in the context of improving manufactured products. The **Shewhart PDCA (Plan, Do, Check, Act) cycle** for rapid learning and improvement was embraced and expanded by Dr. Deming and has now become known as "Deming's wheel." **Deming's wheel** is an outline of the application of the scientific method to process improvement. It is a simple, flexible model that can be used as a guide for small-scale operations, as well as for managing major organizational changes. Let's explore the components of Deming's wheel.

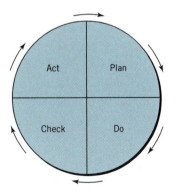

Plan. Assess the situation. What are the problems? Determine the objectives. What are the most important accomplishments? Develop a procedure for identifying and

*See the book by W. A. Shewhart entitled *Economic Control of Quality of Manufactured Product,* New York: Van Nostrand, 1931.

making desirable changes. What data are available? Are new data required? How will we use the observations? Develop a way to determine whether the plan works. How will we evaluate the result of our effort?

Do. Carry out the plan. That is, organize teams and support systems, collect data required by the plan, and, if necessary, carry out small-scale changes or tests.

Check. Study the outcome(s). Evaluate the data. What did we learn from the results? Audit progress toward objectives.

Act. Take action. That is, select the best solution, make the required changes, and predict the effects.

Predicting the effects at the Act phase leads to a new Plan and another repetition of the cycle. The Deming wheel revolves, depicting the concept of "never-ending improvement."

All the steps in the Deming wheel are important for rapid improvement, but the Check step is the driver. Without it, improvement is nearly impossible. Many organizations implement only the Plan and Do part of PDCA. This incomplete execution of PDCA is what many regard as decision making. Being conscientious about Check means treating Do decisions as experiments from which we can learn. Once this is done, all the components of PDCA fall into place.* A painstaking Check creates the energy to do a better job of the three phases Act, Plan, and Do.

No organization has the resources to launch major improvement projects for every process. Successful management finds the *fundamental* processes, whose improvement has a sizable impact on the goals of the organization, and makes the control of these processes the top priority. Many business scholars recommend that quality improvement be the guide in seeking the fundamental processes of a firm. A worldwide study of factors that make business firms competitive, conducted under the auspices of the Strategic Planning Institute, a nonprofit corporation governed by its member companies, reached the following significant conclusions:

> *In the long run, the most important single factor affecting a Business Unit's performance is the Quality of its products and services relative to those of competitors.*

and

> *[M]arket share is key to a company's growth and profitability ... one factor above all others, quality, drives market share. And when superior quality and large market share are both present, profitability is virtually guaranteed.*

Acknowledging that it is difficult to identify the fundamental processes of the firm—the processes that provide quality and economic advantages—in an increasingly complex and globally competitive market, we are now in a position to tie together the elements of process improvement. You will see specifically where statistical methods play an important role.

---

*Our statistical model building strategy outlined in Chapter 11, Section 11.7, is essentially PDCA with different words. For example, Check (in PDCA) is equivalent to Step 3: Review model by examining residuals (in the model building strategy).

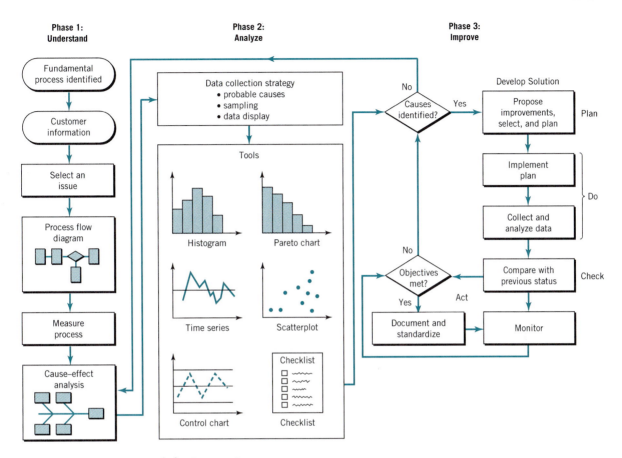

Figure 13.5   A Framework for Process Improvement

Figure 13.5 contains a flow diagram for a process improvement model. The **framework for process improvement** is divided into three phases: *Understand, Analyze,* and *Improve.* The *Understand* phase starts with the identification of the fundamental process to be studied, using quality improvement as a guide. Customer information, perhaps obtained from a sample survey, is used to select the particular problem(s) to be addressed. A process flow diagram shows how the components of the process are sequenced and how they relate to one another. Process performance measures are established so that the improvement objectives can be evaluated. Finally, a cause-and-effect diagram, or fishbone chart, is constructed to represent the relationship between the problem or condition (effect) to be addressed and all the possible factors (causes) influencing it.

The *Analyze* phase is concerned with verifying that potential causes are, indeed, causes, and with separating important causes—those whose study will lead to the greatest improvement—from those that are unimportant. During this phase, the focus is on explaining the process variation. Consequently, data are collected (experiments may be run, additional surveys may be conducted), displayed, and analyzed. Often, nothing more elaborate than simple displays like histograms, Pareto charts, scatterplots, time series graphs, and control charts are required to identify those causes that have the potential for the greatest gain. Some of the statistical methods discussed in this book are valuable tools in the Analyze phase.

The *Improve* phase is concerned with developing, implementing, and monitoring a solution for process improvement. As we have discussed, the solution will generally involve eliminating special or important common causes of variation and will often lead to a reconfiguration of the entire process—a different way of doing things. Collecting and analyzing data (statistical methods) are a vital part of determining whether the solution is a good one. We must compare the proposed solution with the status quo to verify that improvement has taken place and that the performance objectives have been met. (Notice we have identified the Plan, Do, Check, and Act components of the Deming wheel with regard to the solution development and implementation.) Once we have agreed that the solution will lead to an improved process, new procedures are documented and certain methods may be standardized to ensure consistency and maximize efficiency.

Quality improvement is a never-ending process. The framework for improvement that we have presented, may, itself, be viewed as an application of Deming's wheel, that is, a cycle to be repeated regularly.

EXERCISES

13.8 (*Class project*) The percentages of on-time arrivals and departures for major U.S. airlines are published periodically. Consider the boxes labeled Measure Process and Cause–Effect Analysis in the Understand phase of the framework for improving processes (Fig. 13.5, page 701). Indicate the issues involved in measuring the process (and establishing performance standards) of on-time arrivals for an airline. [*Hint:* What does on-time mean?] Construct a cause-and-effect diagram for on-time arrivals.

13.9 *Conformance analysis* is the collection of data to determine whether standards for a process are met. It is generally part of the Measure Process and Monitor boxes in the framework for process improvement. Consider the radiation through the closed doors of microwave ovens. What are the issues involved in determining whether the microwave ovens conform to government standards for emitted radiation? How would you convince a government auditor that your microwave ovens meet the standards?

13.10 Select a process of interest to you, for example, getting to your first class on time, baking a cake, budgeting your monthly expenses, scoring well in golf, and so forth, and discuss how you would implement the framework for process improvement. Draw a process flow diagram, indicate the potential causes of variation with a cause-and-effect diagram, suggest data that might be collected and tell how it should be used. Develop a solution that is likely to improve your process.

13.4 STATISTICS IN CONTEXT

Shortly after the end of World War II, American automobile manufacturers switched production to domestic automobiles. Because no automobiles had been made for several years, there was a large pent-up domestic demand for cars. Using the techniques of mass production, manufacturers tried to keep up with the demand, but the emphasis was on quantity not quality. American manufacturers dominated the domestic market throughout the 1970s.

Overall quality can be measured in several ways. One measure of quality used by the industry is the number of owner-reported things-gone-wrong in the last six months for new cars purchased in the United States. This number, per 100 new cars, remained relatively stable for the major automobile manufacturers for a number of years. The values for Ford Motor Company* are graphed in Figure 13.6.

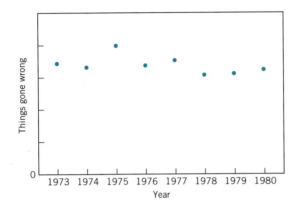

Figure   13.6   Things-Gone-Wrong per 100 Ford Cars

If the data in Figure 13.6 are plotted on a control chart, the result looks like a common cause highway with all the data points well within the upper and lower control limits. The things-gone-wrong process is relatively stable through many model changes. But, stable may not be good enough!

What was the competition doing? General Motors Corporation had a similar record, and the figures for Chrysler Corporation were a little higher. What about manufacturers in Japan? The Japanese began by producing poor quality automobiles that did not sell well in the United States or Europe. However, companies in Japan adopted the Deming philosophy of continuous quality improvement. This emphasis enabled the Japanese to produce better and better quality automobiles. Their progress, in terms of the number of owner-reported things-gone-wrong, is shown in Figure 13.7, where the data for Ford are reproduced for comparison.

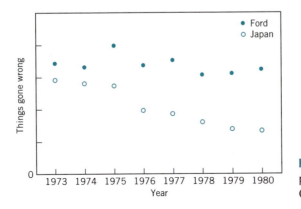

Figure   13.7   Things-Gone-Wrong per 100 Japanese Cars and 100 Ford Cars

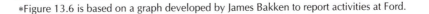

*Figure 13.6 is based on a graph developed by James Bakken to report activities at Ford.

It is clear from Figure 13.7 that Ford needed to do something, and this was not lost on Ford management. They hired Dr. Deming as a consultant and started a major quality and productivity improvement program. This decision was further motivated by the fact that U.S. consumers had already recognized the recent quality differential, and Ford, as well as General Motors and Chrysler, had lost substantial market share to the Japanese automobile companies.

Over the period 1981 to 1988, Ford made substantial improvements in their cars and, consequently, the numbers of things-gone-wrong declined. Figure 13.8 shows the Ford data from the relatively stable 1973–1980 period along with the data from the 1981–1988 quality improvement period.

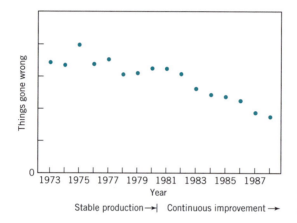

Figure 13.8   Improvement in Things-Gone-Wrong per 100 Ford Cars

Ford is still chasing a moving target. The things-gone-wrong value for Japanese cars was somewhat below that for Ford cars at the end of 1988. Quality improvement is a continuous project at Ford, and at the other U.S. automobile manufacturers. The quality improvement in automobiles is a major success story from which all car owners have benefited.

13.5   CHAPTER SUMMARY

In this chapter, we have learned:

- There are several causes of variation. These causes can be categorized as **common causes of variation, special causes of variation,** and **structural variation.**
- Common causes of variation:

  1. Are present all the time in a process, although their impact varies
  2. Individually, have a small effect on the variation
  3. Collectively, can produce quite a bit of variation

- Special causes of variation:

  1. Are not always present in the process; they appear sporadically
  2. Come from outside the usual process

3. Can contribute a small or large amount to the total variation, but usually have a bigger impact on variation than any single common cause

• Structural variation is a consistent pattern that is present, because of natural laws or an established cause-and-effect relation, in all of the process data.

• Processes that have only common cause variation are said to be **stable** or **predictable.** Stable processes are said to be in **statistical control.**

• Processes with both common cause and special cause variation are said to be **unstable** or **unpredictable.**

• **Control charts** provide a way to make variation visible.

• Any control chart has:

1. Data plotted in time order

2. A centerline, usually the sample mean

3. Horizontal lines, called control limits, that indicate the width of the common cause variation

• There are several tests available for distinguishing special cause variation from common cause variation.

• **Tampering**—that is, producing quick solutions to common cause variation—can actually make things worse.

• Eliminating or reducing variation due to special causes should be done before investigating common causes of variation.

• A strategy for eliminating special causes consists of the steps:

1. Get timely data.

2. Act immediately to contain any damage.

3. Search for the cause.

4. Develop a longer-term remedy.

• Strategies for improving stable (common cause) processes fall into three categories:

1. **Stratify.** Sort data into groups or categories based on different factors; look for patterns.

2. **Experiment.** Make planned changes in several factors and look for the effects.

3. **Disaggregate.** Divide the process into component pieces and manage the pieces. This strategy requires a management system to keep the pieces integrated so that we do not fix each piece without looking at the process as a whole.

• **Deming's wheel** is an outline of the application of the scientific method to process improvement. It is a cycle of rapid learning and improvement consisting of the components Plan, Do, Check, and Act.

• Improving quality should be the guide for seeking those fundamental processes whose improvement will have the greatest impact on the goals of the organization.

• A useful framework for process improvement consists of the phases Understand, Analyze, and Improve. This framework essentially involves implementation of the Deming wheel on several levels; it explicitly recognizes the role of statistical methods.

• Quality improvement is a never-ending process.

13.6   IMPORTANT CONCEPTS AND TOOLS

CONCEPTS

Common cause of variation, 688
In statistical control, 689
Shewhart's Plan, Do, Check,
    Act cycle, 699
Special cause of variation, 688
Stable (predictable) process, 689
Structural variation, 690
Tampering, 693
Unstable (unpredictable) process,
    689

TOOLS

Control chart, 690
Deming's PDCA wheel, 699
Framework for process improvement,
    701
Strategies for improving stable pro-
    cesses, 695
Strategy for improving an unstable
    process, 694
Tests for special causes, 691

REVIEW EXERCISES

13.11   As we have discussed, a Pareto chart is a special form of a vertical bar chart that displays the relative importance of problems or conditions. Some have suggested that a Pareto analysis take the costs of the activities into account. A very frequent problem may imply less overall cost than a relatively rare, but potentially disastrous problem. Give an example of a situation where you might be willing to put up with a frequent but "low-cost" problem in return for avoiding an infrequent "high-cost" problem. Suggest a modification of the usual Pareto chart (with frequency on the vertical axis) to account for costs.

13.12   Pick a process that interests you and that you can observe. Draw a flow diagram (a series of boxes connected by arrows) of how the process works. How would you collect data from the process to determine the steps or causes that must, in your judgment, be modified to improve the process? What data are necessary to verify that improvement has taken place?

13.13   Find a report of quality improvement in the popular press (for example, *Harvard Business Review, Forbes, Business Week, Time,* or *Newsweek*). The report should explicitly mention a management philosophy and detail the major steps taken to improve quality. A report that simply says "improving quality is a good thing" is not appropriate. Prepare a short summary of the report, identifying, if possible, places where the PDCA components of Deming's wheel were applied. Does it appear that organization followed the framework for process improvement shown in Figure 13.5?

13.14   Based on your experience, do you think the statement "Failure to understand variation is a central problem of management" is true? Interpreting "management" very broadly, give an example of an action that indicates management failed to understand variation.

13.15   Explain why quality improvement is a never-ending cycle of PDCA.

13.16   (*Class or team project*) With the help of a local business, identify a competitively significant fundamental process. Study the process and suggest ways to improve it. Prepare a report for the business with your recommendations.

APPENDIX A

Summation Notation

A.1   SUMMATION AND ITS PROPERTIES

The addition of numbers is basic to our study of statistics. To avoid a detailed and repeated writing of this operation, the symbol $\sum$ (the Greek capital letter sigma) is used as mathematical shorthand for the operation of addition.

Summation Notation Σ

The notation $\sum_{i=1}^{n} x_i$ represents the sum of n numbers $x_1, x_2, \ldots, x_n$ and is read as the sum of all x_i with i ranging from 1 to n.

$$\sum_{i=1}^{n} x_i = x_1 + x_2 + \cdots + x_n$$

The term following the sign Σ indicates the quantities that are being summed, and the notations on the bottom and the top of the Σ specify the range of the terms being added. For instance,

$$\sum_{i=1}^{3} x_i = x_1 + x_2 + x_3$$

$$\sum_{i=1}^{4} (x_i - 3) = (x_1 - 3) + (x_2 - 3) + (x_3 - 3) + (x_4 - 3)$$

Example

Suppose that the four measurements in a data set are given as $x_1 = 2$, $x_2 = 5$, $x_3 = 3$, $x_4 = 4$. Compute the numerical values of:

a. $\displaystyle\sum_{i=1}^{4} x_i$ b. $\displaystyle\sum_{i=1}^{4} 6$

c. $\displaystyle\sum_{i=1}^{4} 2x_i$ d. $\displaystyle\sum_{i=1}^{4} (x_i - 3)$

e. $\displaystyle\sum_{i=1}^{4} x_i^2$ f. $\displaystyle\sum_{i=1}^{4} (x_i - 3)^2$

Solution and Discussion.

a. $\displaystyle\sum_{i=1}^{4} x_i = x_1 + x_2 + x_3 + x_4 = 2 + 5 + 3 + 4 = 14$

b. $\displaystyle\sum_{i=1}^{4} 6 = 6 + 6 + 6 + 6 = 4(6) = 24$

c. $\displaystyle\sum_{i=1}^{4} 2x_i = 2x_1 + 2x_2 + 2x_3 + 2x_4 = 2\left(\sum_{i=1}^{4} x_i\right) = 2 \times 14 = 28$

d. $\displaystyle\sum_{i=1}^{4} (x_i - 3) = (x_1 - 3) + (x_2 - 3) + (x_3 - 3) + (x_4 - 3)$

$$= \sum_{i=1}^{4} x_i - 4(3) = 14 - 12 = 2$$

e. $\displaystyle\sum_{i=1}^{4} x_i^2 = x_1^2 + x_2^2 + x_3^2 + x_4^2 = 2^2 + 5^2 + 3^2 + 4^2 = 54$

f. $\displaystyle\sum_{i=1}^{4} (x_i - 3)^2 = (x_1 - 3)^2 + (x_2 - 3)^2 + (x_3 - 3)^2 + (x_4 - 3)^2$

$$= (2 - 3)^2 + (5 - 3)^2 + (3 - 3)^2 + (4 - 3)^2$$
$$= 1 + 4 + 0 + 1 = 6$$

Alternatively, noting that $(x_i - 3)^2 = x_i^2 - 6x_i + 9$, we can write

$$\sum_{i=1}^{4} (x_i - 3)^2 = \sum_{i=1}^{4} (x_i^2 - 6x_i + 9)$$

$$= (x_1^2 - 6x_1 + 9) + (x_2^2 - 6x_2 + 9) + (x_3^2 - 6x_3 + 9) + (x_4^2 - 6x_4 + 9)$$

$$= \sum_{i=1}^{4} x_i^2 - 6\left(\sum_{i=1}^{4} x_i\right) + 4(9)$$

$$= 54 - 6(14) + 36 = 6$$

A few basic properties of the summation operation are apparent from the numerical demonstrations in the example.

Some Basic Properties of Summation

If a and b are fixed numbers,

$$\sum_{i=1}^{n} bx_i = b\sum_{i=1}^{n} x_i$$

$$\sum_{i=1}^{n} (bx_i + a) = b\sum_{i=1}^{n} x_i + na$$

$$\sum_{i=1}^{n} (x_i - a)^2 = \sum_{i=1}^{n} x_i^2 - 2a\sum_{i=1}^{n} x_i + na^2$$

EXERCISES

1. Demonstrate your familiarity with the summation notation by evaluating the following expressions when $x_1 = 4$, $x_2 = -2$, $x_3 = 1$.

   a. $\displaystyle\sum_{i=1}^{3} x_i$

   b. $\displaystyle\sum_{i=1}^{3} 7$

   c. $\displaystyle\sum_{i=1}^{3} 5x_i$

   d. $\displaystyle\sum_{i=1}^{3} (x_i - 2)$

   e. $\displaystyle\sum_{i=1}^{3} (x_i - 3)$

   f. $\displaystyle\sum_{i=1}^{3} (x_i - 2)^2$

   g. $\displaystyle\sum_{i=1}^{3} x_i^2$

   h. $\displaystyle\sum_{i=1}^{3} (x_i - 3)^2$

   i. $\displaystyle\sum_{i=1}^{3} (x_i^2 - 6x_i + 9)$

2. Five measurements in a data set are $x_1 = 4$, $x_2 = 3$, $x_3 = 6$, $x_4 = 5$, $x_5 = 7$. Determine:

a. $\sum\limits_{i=1}^{5} x_i$

b. $\sum\limits_{i=2}^{3} x_i$

c. $\sum\limits_{i=1}^{5} 2$

d. $\sum\limits_{i=1}^{5} (x_i - 6)$

e. $\sum\limits_{i=1}^{5} (x_i - 6)^2$

f. $\sum\limits_{i=1}^{4} (x_i - 5)^2$

A.2   SOME BASIC USES OF $\sum$ IN STATISTICS

Let's use the summation notation and its properties to verify some computational facts about the sample mean and variance.

$\sum(x_i - \bar{x}) = 0$

The total of the deviations about the sample mean is always zero. Since $\bar{x} = (x_1 + x_2 + \cdots + x_n)/n$, we can write

$$\sum_{i=1}^{n} x_i = x_1 + x_2 + \cdots + x_n = n\bar{x}$$

Consequently, whatever the observations,

$$\sum_{i=1}^{n} (x_i - \bar{x}) = (x_1 - \bar{x}) + (x_2 - \bar{x}) + \cdots + (x_n - \bar{x})$$

$$= x_1 + x_2 + \cdots + x_n - n\bar{x}$$

$$= n\bar{x} - n\bar{x} = 0$$

We could also verify this directly with the second property for summation in A.1, when $b = 1$ and $a = -\bar{x}$.

ALTERNATIVE FORMULA FOR s^2

By the rule for squaring a difference,

$$(x_i - \bar{x})^2 = x_i^2 - 2\bar{x}x_i + \bar{x}^2$$

Therefore,

$$\sum(x_i - \bar{x})^2 = \sum x_i^2 - \sum 2\bar{x}x_i + \sum \bar{x}^2$$

$$= \sum x_i^2 - 2\bar{x}\sum x_i + n\bar{x}^2$$

Using $(\sum x_i)/n$ in place of $\bar{x}$, we get

$$\sum (x_i - \bar{x})^2 = \sum x_i^2 - \frac{2(\sum x_i)^2}{n} + \frac{n(\sum x_i)^2}{n^2}$$

$$= \sum x_i^2 - \frac{2(\sum x_i)^2}{n} + \frac{(\sum x_i)^2}{n}$$

$$= \sum x_i^2 - \frac{(\sum x_i)^2}{n}$$

We could also verify this directly from the third property for summation, in A.1, with $a = \bar{x}$.

This result establishes that

$$s^2 = \frac{\sum_{i=1}^{n}(x_i - \bar{x})^2}{n - 1} = \frac{\sum x_i^2 - (\sum x_i)^2/n}{n - 1}$$

so the two forms of s^2 are equivalent.

SAMPLE CORRELATION COEFFICIENT

The sample correlation coefficient and the slope of the fitted regression line contain a term

$$S_{xy} = \sum_{i=1}^{n}(x_i - \bar{x})(y_i - \bar{y})$$

which is a sum of the products of the deviations. To obtain the alternative form, first note that

$$(x_i - \bar{x})(y_i - \bar{y}) = x_i y_i - x_i \bar{y} - \bar{x} y_i + \bar{x}\bar{y}$$

We treat $x_i y_i$ as a single number, with index i, and conclude that

$$\sum (x_i - \bar{x})(y_i - \bar{y}) = \sum x_i y_i - \sum x_i \bar{y} - \sum \bar{x} y_i + \sum \bar{x}\bar{y}$$

$$= \sum x_i y_i - \bar{y} \sum x_i - \bar{x} \sum y_i + n\bar{x}\bar{y}$$

Since $\bar{x} = (\sum x_i)/n$ and $\bar{y} = (\sum y_i)/n$,

$$\sum (x_i - \bar{x})(y_i - \bar{y}) = \sum x_i y_i - \frac{(\sum y_i)}{n} \sum x_i - \frac{(\sum x_i)}{n} \sum y_i + \frac{n(\sum x_i)(\sum y_i)}{n \quad n}$$

$$= \sum x_i y_i - \frac{(\sum x_i)(\sum y_i)}{n}$$

Consequently, either $\sum (x_i - \bar{x})(y_i - \bar{y})$ or $\sum x_i y_i - (\sum x_i)(\sum y_i)/n$ can be used for the calculation of S_{xy}. Similar expressions hold for S_{xx} and S_{yy} in the calculation of r.

APPENDIX B

Tables

TABLE 1   Random Digits

Row										
1	0695	7741	8254	4297	0000	5277	6563	9265	1023	5925
2	0437	5434	8503	3928	6979	9393	8936	9088	5744	4790
3	6242	2998	0205	5469	3365	7950	7256	3716	8385	0253
4	7090	4074	1257	7175	3310	0712	4748	4226	0604	3804
5	0683	6999	4828	7888	0087	9288	7855	2678	3315	6718
6	7013	4300	3768	2572	6473	2411	6285	0069	5422	6175
7	8808	2786	5369	9571	3412	2465	6419	3990	0294	0896
8	9876	3602	5812	0124	1997	6445	3176	2682	1259	1728
9	1873	1065	8976	1295	9434	3178	0602	0732	6616	7972
10	2581	3075	4622	2974	7069	5605	0420	2949	4387	7679
11	3785	6401	0540	5077	7132	4135	4646	3834	6753	1593
12	8626	4017	1544	4202	8986	1432	2810	2418	8052	2710
13	6253	0726	9483	6753	4732	2284	0421	3010	7885	8436
14	0113	4546	2212	9829	2351	1370	2707	3329	6574	7002
15	4646	6474	9983	8738	1603	8671	0489	9588	3309	5860
16	7873	7343	4432	2866	7973	3765	2888	5154	2250	4339
17	3756	9204	2590	6577	2409	8234	8656	2336	7948	7478
18	2673	7115	5526	0747	3952	6804	3671	7486	3024	9858
19	0187	7045	2711	0349	7734	4396	0988	4887	7682	8990
20	7976	3862	8323	5997	6904	4977	1056	6638	6398	4552
21	5605	1819	8926	9557	2905	0802	7749	0845	1710	4125
22	2225	5556	2545	7480	8804	4161	0084	0787	2561	5113
23	2549	4166	1609	7570	4223	0032	4236	0169	4673	8034
24	6113	1312	5777	7058	2413	3932	5144	5998	7183	5210
25	2028	2537	9819	9215	9327	6640	5986	7935	2750	2981
26	7818	3655	5771	4026	5757	3171	6435	2990	1860	1796
27	9629	3383	1931	2631	5903	9372	1307	4061	5443	8663
28	6657	5967	3277	7141	3628	2588	9320	1972	7683	7544
29	4344	7388	2978	3945	0471	4882	1619	0093	2282	7024
30	3145	8720	2131	1614	1575	5239	0766	0404	4873	7986
31	1848	4094	9168	0903	6451	2823	7566	6644	1157	8889
32	0915	5578	0822	5887	5354	3632	4617	6016	8989	9482
33	1430	4755	7551	9019	8233	9625	6361	2589	2496	7268
34	3473	7966	7249	0555	6307	9524	4888	4939	1641	1573
35	3312	0773	6296	1348	5483	5824	3353	4587	1019	9677
36	6255	4204	5890	9273	0634	9992	3834	2283	1202	4849
37	0562	2546	8559	0480	9379	9282	8257	3054	4272	9311
38	1957	6783	4105	8976	8035	0883	8971	0017	6476	2895
39	7333	1083	0398	8841	0017	4135	4043	8157	4672	2424
40	4601	8908	1781	4287	2681	6223	0814	4477	3798	4437

(*continued*)

TABLE 1   RANDOM DIGITS   **715**

TABLE 1   (*Continued*)

Row										
41	2628	2233	0708	0900	1698	2818	3931	6930	9273	6749
42	5318	8865	6057	8422	6992	9697	0508	3370	5522	9250
43	6335	0852	8657	8374	0311	6012	9477	0112	8976	3312
44	0301	8333	0327	0467	6186	1770	4099	9588	5382	8958
45	1719	9775	1566	7020	4535	2850	0207	4792	6405	1472
46	8907	8226	4249	6340	9062	3572	7655	6707	3685	1282
47	6129	5927	3731	1125	0081	1241	2772	6458	9157	4543
48	7376	3150	8985	8318	8003	6106	4952	8492	2804	3867
49	9093	3407	4127	9258	3687	5631	5102	1546	2659	0831
50	1133	3086	9380	5431	8647	0910	6948	2257	0946	1245
51	4567	0910	8495	2410	1088	7067	8505	9083	4339	2440
52	6141	8380	2302	4608	7209	5738	9765	3435	9657	6061
53	1514	8309	8743	3096	0682	7902	8204	7508	8330	1681
54	7277	1634	7866	9883	0916	6363	5391	6184	8040	3135
55	4568	4758	0166	1509	2105	0976	0269	0278	7443	2431
56	9200	7599	7754	4534	4532	3102	6831	2387	4147	2455
57	3971	8149	4431	2345	6436	0627	0410	1348	6599	1296
58	2672	9661	2359	8477	3425	8150	6918	8883	1518	4708
59	1524	3268	3798	3360	2255	0371	7610	9114	9466	0901
60	6817	9007	5959	0767	1166	7317	7502	0274	6340	0427
61	6762	3502	9559	4279	9271	9595	3053	4918	7503	5169
62	5264	0075	6655	4563	7112	7264	3240	2150	8180	1361
63	5070	8428	5149	2137	8728	9110	2334	9709	8134	3925
64	1664	3379	5273	9367	6950	6828	1711	7082	4783	0147
65	6962	7141	1904	6648	7328	2901	6396	9949	6274	1672
66	7541	4289	4970	2922	6670	8540	9053	3219	8881	1897
67	5244	4651	2934	6700	8869	0926	4191	1364	0926	2874
68	2939	3890	0745	2577	7931	3913	7877	2837	2500	8774
69	4266	6207	8083	6564	5336	5303	7503	6627	6055	3606
70	7848	5477	5588	3490	0294	3609	1632	5684	1719	6162
71	3009	1879	0440	7916	6643	9723	5933	0574	2480	6893
72	9865	7813	7468	8493	3293	1071	7183	9462	2363	6529
73	1196	1251	2368	1262	5769	9450	7485	4039	4985	6612
74	1067	3716	8897	1970	8799	5718	4792	7292	4589	4554
75	5160	5563	6527	7861	3477	6735	7748	4913	6370	2258
76	4560	0094	8284	7604	1667	9286	2228	9507	1838	4646
77	7697	2151	4860	0739	4370	3992	8121	2502	7670	4470
78	8675	2997	9783	7306	4116	6432	7233	4611	7121	9412
79	3597	3520	5995	0892	3470	4581	1068	8801	1254	8607
80	4281	8802	5880	6212	6818	8162	0052	1755	7107	5197

TABLE 2 Cumulative Binomial Probabilities

$$P[X \le c] = \sum_{x=0}^{c} \binom{n}{x} p^x (1-p)^{n-x}$$

	c	.05	.10	.20	.30	.40	.50	.60	.70	.80	.90	.95
$n=1$	0	.950	.900	.800	.700	.600	.500	.400	.300	.200	.100	.050
	1	1.000	1.000	1.000	1.000	1.000	1.000	1.000	1.000	1.000	1.000	1.000
$n=2$	0	.902	.810	.640	.490	.360	.250	.160	.090	.040	.010	.002
	1	.997	.990	.960	.910	.840	.750	.640	.510	.360	.190	.097
	2	1.000	1.000	1.000	1.000	1.000	1.000	1.000	1.000	1.000	1.000	1.000
$n=3$	0	.857	.729	.512	.343	.216	.125	.064	.027	.008	.001	.000
	1	.993	.972	.896	.784	.648	.500	.352	.216	.104	.028	.007
	2	1.000	.999	.992	.973	.936	.875	.784	.657	.488	.271	.143
	3	1.000	1.000	1.000	1.000	1.000	1.000	1.000	1.000	1.000	1.000	1.000
$n=4$	0	.815	.656	.410	.240	.130	.063	.026	.008	.002	.000	.000
	1	.986	.948	.819	.652	.475	.313	.179	.084	.027	.004	.000
	2	1.000	.996	.973	.916	.821	.688	.525	.348	.181	.052	.014
	3	1.000	1.000	.998	.992	.974	.938	.870	.760	.590	.344	.185
	4	1.000	1.000	1.000	1.000	1.000	1.000	1.000	1.000	1.000	1.000	1.000
$n=5$	0	.774	.590	.328	.168	.078	.031	.010	.002	.000	.000	.000
	1	.977	.919	.737	.528	.337	.188	.087	.031	.007	.000	.000
	2	.999	.991	.942	.837	.683	.500	.317	.163	.058	.009	.001
	3	1.000	1.000	.993	.969	.913	.813	.663	.472	.263	.081	.023
	4	1.000	1.000	1.000	.998	.990	.969	.922	.832	.672	.410	.226
	5	1.000	1.000	1.000	1.000	1.000	1.000	1.000	1.000	1.000	1.000	1.000
$n=6$	0	.735	.531	.262	.118	.047	.016	.004	.001	.000	.000	.000
	1	.967	.886	.655	.420	.233	.109	.041	.011	.002	.000	.000
	2	.998	.984	.901	.744	.544	.344	.179	.070	.017	.001	.000
	3	1.000	.999	.983	.930	.821	.656	.456	.256	.099	.016	.002
	4	1.000	1.000	.998	.989	.959	.891	.767	.580	.345	.114	.033
	5	1.000	1.000	1.000	.999	.996	.984	.953	.882	.738	.469	.265
	6	1.000	1.000	1.000	1.000	1.000	1.000	1.000	1.000	1.000	1.000	1.000
$n=7$	0	.698	.478	.210	.082	.028	.008	.002	.000	.000	.000	.000
	1	.956	.850	.577	.329	.159	.063	.019	.004	.000	.000	.000
	2	.996	.974	.852	.647	.420	.227	.096	.029	.005	.000	.000
	3	1.000	.997	.967	.874	.710	.500	.290	.126	.033	.003	.000
	4	1.000	1.000	.995	.971	.904	.773	.580	.353	.148	.026	.004
	5	1.000	1.000	1.000	.996	.981	.938	.841	.671	.423	.150	.044
	6	1.000	1.000	1.000	1.000	.998	.992	.972	.918	.790	.522	.302
	7	1.000	1.000	1.000	1.000	1.000	1.000	1.000	1.000	1.000	1.000	1.000

(continued)

TABLE 2   CUMULATIVE BINOMIAL PROBABILITIES   **717**

TABLE 2   (*Continued*)

						p						
		.05	.10	.20	.30	.40	.50	.60	.70	.80	.90	.95
	c											
$n = 8$	0	.663	.430	.168	.058	.017	.004	.001	.000	.000	.000	.000
	1	.943	.813	.503	.255	.106	.035	.009	.001	.000	.000	.000
	2	.994	.962	.797	.552	.315	.145	.050	.011	.001	.000	.000
	3	1.000	.995	.944	.806	.594	.363	.174	.058	.010	.000	.000
	4	1.000	1.000	.990	.942	.826	.637	.406	.194	.056	.005	.000
	5	1.000	1.000	.999	.989	.950	.855	.685	.448	.203	.038	.006
	6	1.000	1.000	1.000	.999	.991	.965	.894	.745	.497	.187	.057
	7	1.000	1.000	1.000	1.000	.999	.996	.983	.942	.832	.570	.337
	8	1.000	1.000	1.000	1.000	1.000	1.000	1.000	1.000	1.000	1.000	1.000
$n = 9$	0	.630	.387	.134	.040	.010	.002	.000	.000	.000	.000	.000
	1	.929	.775	.436	.196	.071	.020	.004	.000	.000	.000	.000
	2	.992	.947	.738	.463	.232	.090	.025	.004	.000	.000	.000
	3	.999	.992	.914	.730	.483	.254	.099	.025	.003	.000	.000
	4	1.000	.999	.980	.901	.733	.500	.267	.099	.020	.001	.000
	5	1.000	1.000	.997	.975	.901	.746	.517	.270	.086	.008	.001
	6	1.000	1.000	1.000	.996	.975	.910	.768	.537	.262	.053	.008
	7	1.000	1.000	1.000	1.000	.996	.980	.929	.804	.564	.225	.071
	8	1.000	1.000	1.000	1.000	1.000	.998	.990	.960	.866	.613	.370
	9	1.000	1.000	1.000	1.000	1.000	1.000	1.000	1.000	1.000	1.000	1.000
$n = 10$	0	.599	.349	.107	.028	.006	.001	.000	.000	.000	.000	.000
	1	.914	.736	.376	.149	.046	.011	.002	.000	.000	.000	.000
	2	.988	.930	.678	.383	.167	.055	.012	.002	.000	.000	.000
	3	.999	.987	.879	.650	.382	.172	.055	.011	.001	.000	.000
	4	1.000	.998	.967	.850	.633	.377	.166	.047	.006	.000	.000
	5	1.000	1.000	.994	.953	.834	.623	.367	.150	.033	.002	.000
	6	1.000	1.000	.999	.989	.945	.828	.618	.350	.121	.013	.001
	7	1.000	1.000	1.000	.998	.988	.945	.833	.617	.322	.070	.012
	8	1.000	1.000	1.000	1.000	.998	.989	.954	.851	.624	.264	.086
	9	1.000	1.000	1.000	1.000	1.000	.999	.994	.972	.893	.651	.401
	10	1.000	1.000	1.000	1.000	1.000	1.000	1.000	1.000	1.000	1.000	1.000
$n = 11$	0	.569	.314	.086	.020	.004	.000	.000	.000	.000	.000	.000
	1	.898	.697	.322	.113	.030	.006	.001	.000	.000	.000	.000
	2	.985	.910	.617	.313	.119	.033	.006	.001	.000	.000	.000
	3	.998	.981	.839	.570	.296	.113	.029	.004	.000	.000	.000
	4	1.000	.997	.950	.790	.533	.274	.099	.022	.002	.000	.000
	5	1.000	1.000	.988	.922	.753	.500	.247	.078	.012	.000	.000
	6	1.000	1.000	.998	.978	.901	.726	.467	.210	.050	.003	.000
	7	1.000	1.000	1.000	.996	.971	.887	.704	.430	.161	.019	.002
	8	1.000	1.000	1.000	.999	.994	.967	.881	.687	.383	.090	.015
	9	1.000	1.000	1.000	1.000	.999	.994	.970	.887	.678	.303	.102
	10	1.000	1.000	1.000	1.000	1.000	1.000	.996	.980	.914	.686	.431
	11	1.000	1.000	1.000	1.000	1.000	1.000	1.000	1.000	1.000	1.000	1.000

(*continued*)

TABLE 2 (*Continued*)

	c	.05	.10	.20	.30	.40	.50	.60	.70	.80	.90	.95
$n = 12$	0	.540	.282	.069	.014	.002	.000	.000	.000	.000	.000	.000
	1	.882	.659	.275	.085	.020	.003	.000	.000	.000	.000	.000
	2	.980	.889	.558	.253	.083	.019	.003	.000	.000	.000	.000
	3	.998	.974	.795	.493	.225	.073	.015	.002	.000	.000	.000
	4	1.000	.996	.927	.724	.438	.194	.057	.009	.001	.000	.000
	5	1.000	.999	.981	.882	.665	.387	.158	.039	.004	.000	.000
	6	1.000	1.000	.996	.961	.842	.613	.335	.118	.019	.001	.000
	7	1.000	1.000	.999	.991	.943	.806	.562	.276	.073	.004	.000
	8	1.000	1.000	1.000	.998	.985	.927	.775	.507	.205	.026	.002
	9	1.000	1.000	1.000	1.000	.997	.981	.917	.747	.442	.111	.020
	10	1.000	1.000	1.000	1.000	1.000	.997	.980	.915	.725	.341	.118
	11	1.000	1.000	1.000	1.000	1.000	1.000	.998	.986	.931	.718	.460
	12	1.000	1.000	1.000	1.000	1.000	1.000	1.000	1.000	1.000	1.000	1.000
$n = 13$	0	.513	.254	.055	.010	.001	.000	.000	.000	.000	.000	.000
	1	.865	.621	.234	.064	.013	.002	.000	.000	.000	.000	.000
	2	.975	.866	.502	.202	.058	.011	.001	.000	.000	.000	.000
	3	.997	.966	.747	.421	.169	.046	.008	.001	.000	.000	.000
	4	1.000	.994	.901	.654	.353	.133	.032	.004	.000	.000	.000
	5	1.000	.999	.970	.835	.574	.291	.098	.018	.001	.000	.000
	6	1.000	1.000	.993	.938	.771	.500	.229	.062	.007	.000	.000
	7	1.000	1.000	.999	.982	.902	.709	.426	.165	.030	.001	.000
	8	1.000	1.000	1.000	.996	.968	.867	.647	.346	.099	.006	.000
	9	1.000	1.000	1.000	.999	.992	.954	.831	.579	.253	.034	.003
	10	1.000	1.000	1.000	1.000	.999	.989	.942	.798	.498	.134	.025
	11	1.000	1.000	1.000	1.000	1.000	.998	.987	.936	.766	.379	.135
	12	1.000	1.000	1.000	1.000	1.000	1.000	.999	.990	.945	.746	.487
	13	1.000	1.000	1.000	1.000	1.000	1.000	1.000	1.000	1.000	1.000	1.000
$n = 14$	0	.488	.229	.044	.007	.001	.000	.000	.000	.000	.000	.000
	1	.847	.585	.198	.047	.008	.001	.000	.000	.000	.000	.000
	2	.970	.842	.448	.161	.040	.006	.001	.000	.000	.000	.000
	3	.996	.956	.698	.355	.124	.029	.004	.000	.000	.000	.000
	4	1.000	.991	.870	.584	.279	.090	.018	.002	.000	.000	.000
	5	1.000	.999	.956	.781	.486	.212	.058	.008	.000	.000	.000
	6	1.000	1.000	.988	.907	.692	.395	.150	.031	.002	.000	.000
	7	1.000	1.000	.998	.969	.850	.605	.308	.093	.012	.000	.000
	8	1.000	1.000	1.000	.992	.942	.788	.514	.219	.044	.001	.000
	9	1.000	1.000	1.000	.998	.982	.910	.721	.416	.130	.009	.000
	10	1.000	1.000	1.000	1.000	.996	.971	.876	.645	.302	.044	.004
	11	1.000	1.000	1.000	1.000	.999	.994	.960	.839	.552	.158	.030
	12	1.000	1.000	1.000	1.000	1.000	.999	.992	.953	.802	.415	.153
	13	1.000	1.000	1.000	1.000	1.000	1.000	.999	.993	.956	.771	.512
	14	1.000	1.000	1.000	1.000	1.000	1.000	1.000	1.000	1.000	1.000	1.000

(*continued*)

TABLE 2   CUMULATIVE BINOMIAL PROBABILITIES   **719**

TABLE 2   (*Continued*)

		p									
		.05	.10	.20	.30	.40	.50	.60	.70	.80	.90	.95
	c											
$n = 15$	0	.463	.206	.035	.005	.000	.000	.000	.000	.000	.000	.000
	1	.829	.549	.167	.035	.005	.000	.000	.000	.000	.000	.000
	2	.964	.816	.398	.127	.027	.004	.000	.000	.000	.000	.000
	3	.995	.944	.648	.297	.091	.018	.002	.000	.000	.000	.000
	4	.999	.987	.836	.515	.217	.059	.009	.001	.000	.000	.000
	5	1.000	.998	.939	.722	.403	.151	.034	.004	.000	.000	.000
	6	1.000	1.000	.982	.869	.610	.304	.095	.015	.001	.000	.000
	7	1.000	1.000	.996	.950	.787	.500	.213	.050	.004	.000	.000
	8	1.000	1.000	.999	.985	.905	.696	.390	.131	.018	.000	.000
	9	1.000	1.000	1.000	.996	.966	.849	.597	.278	.061	.002	.000
	10	1.000	1.000	1.000	.999	.991	.941	.783	.485	.164	.013	.001
	11	1.000	1.000	1.000	1.000	.998	.982	.909	.703	.352	.056	.005
	12	1.000	1.000	1.000	1.000	1.000	.996	.973	.873	.602	.184	.036
	13	1.000	1.000	1.000	1.000	1.000	1.000	.995	.965	.833	.451	.171
	14	1.000	1.000	1.000	1.000	1.000	1.000	1.000	.995	.965	.794	.537
	15	1.000	1.000	1.000	1.000	1.000	1.000	1.000	1.000	1.000	1.000	1.000
$n = 16$	0	.440	.185	.028	.003	.000	.000	.000	.000	.000	.000	.000
	1	.811	.515	.141	.026	.003	.000	.000	.000	.000	.000	.000
	2	.957	.789	.352	.099	.018	.002	.000	.000	.000	.000	.000
	3	.993	.932	.598	.246	.065	.011	.001	.000	.000	.000	.000
	4	.999	.983	.798	.450	.167	.038	.005	.000	.000	.000	.000
	5	1.000	.997	.918	.660	.329	.105	.019	.002	.000	.000	.000
	6	1.000	.999	.973	.825	.527	.227	.058	.007	.000	.000	.000
	7	1.000	1.000	.993	.926	.716	.402	.142	.026	.001	.000	.000
	8	1.000	1.000	.999	.974	.858	.598	.284	.074	.007	.000	.000
	9	1.000	1.000	1.000	.993	.942	.773	.473	.175	.027	.001	.000
	10	1.000	1.000	1.000	.998	.981	.895	.671	.340	.082	.003	.000
	11	1.000	1.000	1.000	1.000	.995	.962	.833	.550	.202	.017	.001
	12	1.000	1.000	1.000	1.000	.999	.989	.935	.754	.402	.068	.007
	13	1.000	1.000	1.000	1.000	1.000	.998	.982	.901	.648	.211	.043
	14	1.000	1.000	1.000	1.000	1.000	1.000	.997	.974	.859	.485	.189
	15	1.000	1.000	1.000	1.000	1.000	1.000	1.000	.997	.972	.815	.560
	16	1.000	1.000	1.000	1.000	1.000	1.000	1.000	1.000	1.000	1.000	1.000

(*continued*)

TABLE 2   (*Continued*)

	c	.05	.10	.20	.30	.40	.50	.60	.70	.80	.90	.95
								p				
$n = 17$	0	.418	.167	.023	.002	.000	.000	.000	.000	.000	.000	.000
	1	.792	.482	.118	.019	.002	.000	.000	.000	.000	.000	.000
	2	.950	.762	.310	.077	.012	.001	.000	.000	.000	.000	.000
	3	.991	.917	.549	.202	.046	.006	.000	.000	.000	.000	.000
	4	.999	.978	.758	.389	.126	.025	.003	.000	.000	.000	.000
	5	1.000	.995	.894	.597	.264	.072	.011	.001	.000	.000	.000
	6	1.000	.999	.962	.775	.448	.166	.035	.003	.000	.000	.000
	7	1.000	1.000	.989	.895	.641	.315	.092	.013	.000	.000	.000
	8	1.000	1.000	.997	.960	.801	.500	.199	.040	.003	.000	.000
	9	1.000	1.000	1.000	.987	.908	.685	.359	.105	.011	.000	.000
	10	1.000	1.000	1.000	.997	.965	.834	.552	.225	.038	.001	.000
	11	1.000	1.000	1.000	.999	.989	.928	.736	.403	.106	.005	.000
	12	1.000	1.000	1.000	1.000	.997	.975	.874	.611	.242	.022	.001
	13	1.000	1.000	1.000	1.000	1.000	.994	.954	.798	.451	.083	.009
	14	1.000	1.000	1.000	1.000	1.000	.999	.988	.923	.690	.238	.050
	15	1.000	1.000	1.000	1.000	1.000	1.000	.998	.981	.882	.518	.208
	16	1.000	1.000	1.000	1.000	1.000	1.000	1.000	.998	.977	.833	.582
	17	1.000	1.000	1.000	1.000	1.000	1.000	1.000	1.000	1.000	1.000	1.000
$n = 18$	0	.397	.150	.018	.002	.000	.000	.000	.000	.000	.000	.000
	1	.774	.450	.099	.014	.001	.000	.000	.000	.000	.000	.000
	2	.942	.734	.271	.060	.008	.001	.000	.000	.000	.000	.000
	3	.989	.902	.501	.165	.033	.004	.000	.000	.000	.000	.000
	4	.998	.972	.716	.333	.094	.015	.001	.000	.000	.000	.000
	5	1.000	.994	.867	.534	.209	.048	.006	.000	.000	.000	.000
	6	1.000	.999	.949	.722	.374	.119	.020	.001	.000	.000	.000
	7	1.000	1.000	.984	.859	.563	.240	.058	.006	.000	.000	.000
	8	1.000	1.000	.996	.940	.737	.407	.135	.021	.001	.000	.000
	9	1.000	1.000	.999	.979	.865	.593	.263	.060	.004	.000	.000
	10	1.000	1.000	1.000	.994	.942	.760	.437	.141	.016	.000	.000
	11	1.000	1.000	1.000	.999	.980	.881	.626	.278	.051	.001	.000
	12	1.000	1.000	1.000	1.000	.994	.952	.791	.466	.133	.006	.000
	13	1.000	1.000	1.000	1.000	.999	.985	.906	.667	.284	.028	.002
	14	1.000	1.000	1.000	1.000	1.000	.996	.967	.835	.499	.098	.011
	15	1.000	1.000	1.000	1.000	1.000	.999	.992	.940	.729	.266	.058
	16	1.000	1.000	1.000	1.000	1.000	1.000	.999	.986	.901	.550	.226
	17	1.000	1.000	1.000	1.000	1.000	1.000	1.000	.998	.982	.850	.603
	18	1.000	1.000	1.000	1.000	1.000	1.000	1.000	1.000	1.000	1.000	1.000

(*continued*)

TABLE 2 CUMULATIVE BINOMIAL PROBABILITIES **721**

TABLE 2 (*Continued*)

		.05	.10	.20	.30	.40	.50	.60	.70	.80	.90	.95
							p					
	c											
$n = 19$	0	.377	.135	.014	.001	.000	.000	.000	.000	.000	.000	.000
	1	.755	.420	.083	.010	.001	.000	.000	.000	.000	.000	.000
	2	.933	.705	.237	.046	.005	.000	.000	.000	.000	.000	.000
	3	.987	.885	.455	.133	.023	.002	.000	.000	.000	.000	.000
	4	.998	.965	.673	.282	.070	.010	.001	.000	.000	.000	.000
	5	1.000	.991	.837	.474	.163	.032	.003	.000	.000	.000	.000
	6	1.000	.998	.932	.666	.308	.084	.012	.001	.000	.000	.000
	7	1.000	1.000	.977	.818	.488	.180	.035	.003	.000	.000	.000
	8	1.000	1.000	.993	.916	.667	.324	.088	.011	.000	.000	.000
	9	1.000	1.000	.998	.967	.814	.500	.186	.033	.002	.000	.000
	10	1.000	1.000	1.000	.989	.912	.676	.333	.084	.007	.000	.000
	11	1.000	1.000	1.000	.997	.965	.820	.512	.182	.023	.000	.000
	12	1.000	1.000	1.000	.999	.988	.916	.692	.334	.068	.002	.000
	13	1.000	1.000	1.000	1.000	.997	.968	.837	.526	.163	.009	.000
	14	1.000	1.000	1.000	1.000	.999	.990	.930	.718	.327	.035	.002
	15	1.000	1.000	1.000	1.000	1.000	.998	.977	.867	.545	.115	.013
	16	1.000	1.000	1.000	1.000	1.000	1.000	.995	.954	.763	.295	.067
	17	1.000	1.000	1.000	1.000	1.000	1.000	.999	.990	.917	.580	.245
	18	1.000	1.000	1.000	1.000	1.000	1.000	1.000	.999	.986	.865	.623
	19	1.000	1.000	1.000	1.000	1.000	1.000	1.000	1.000	1.000	1.000	1.000
$n = 20$	0	.358	.122	.012	.001	.000	.000	.000	.000	.000	.000	.000
	1	.736	.392	.069	.008	.001	.000	.000	.000	.000	.000	.000
	2	.925	.677	.206	.035	.004	.000	.000	.000	.000	.000	.000
	3	.984	.867	.411	.107	.016	.001	.000	.000	.000	.000	.000
	4	.997	.957	.630	.238	.051	.006	.000	.000	.000	.000	.000
	5	1.000	.989	.804	.416	.126	.021	.002	.000	.000	.000	.000
	6	1.000	.998	.913	.608	.250	.058	.006	.000	.000	.000	.000
	7	1.000	1.000	.968	.772	.416	.132	.021	.001	.000	.000	.000
	8	1.000	1.000	.990	.887	.596	.252	.057	.005	.000	.000	.000
	9	1.000	1.000	.997	.952	.755	.412	.128	.017	.001	.000	.000
	10	1.000	1.000	.999	.983	.872	.588	.245	.048	.003	.000	.000
	11	1.000	1.000	1.000	.995	.943	.748	.404	.113	.010	.000	.000
	12	1.000	1.000	1.000	.999	.979	.868	.584	.228	.032	.000	.000
	13	1.000	1.000	1.000	1.000	.994	.942	.750	.392	.087	.002	.000
	14	1.000	1.000	1.000	1.000	.998	.979	.874	.584	.196	.011	.000
	15	1.000	1.000	1.000	1.000	1.000	.994	.949	.762	.370	.043	.003
	16	1.000	1.000	1.000	1.000	1.000	.999	.984	.893	.589	.133	.016
	17	1.000	1.000	1.000	1.000	1.000	1.000	.996	.965	.794	.323	.075
	18	1.000	1.000	1.000	1.000	1.000	1.000	.999	.992	.931	.608	.264
	19	1.000	1.000	1.000	1.000	1.000	1.000	1.000	.999	.988	.878	.642
	20	1.000	1.000	1.000	1.000	1.000	1.000	1.000	1.000	1.000	1.000	1.000

(*continued*)

TABLE 2   (*Continued*)

							p					
		.05	.10	.20	.30	.40	.50	.60	.70	.80	.90	.95
	c											
$n = 25$	0	.277	.072	.004	.000	.000	.000	.000	.000	.000	.000	.000
	1	.642	.271	.027	.002	.000	.000	.000	.000	.000	.000	.000
	2	.873	.537	.098	.009	.000	.000	.000	.000	.000	.000	.000
	3	.966	.764	.234	.033	.002	.000	.000	.000	.000	.000	.000
	4	.993	.902	.421	.090	.009	.000	.000	.000	.000	.000	.000
	5	.999	.967	.617	.193	.029	.002	.000	.000	.000	.000	.000
	6	1.000	.991	.780	.341	.074	.007	.000	.000	.000	.000	.000
	7	1.000	.998	.891	.512	.154	.022	.001	.000	.000	.000	.000
	8	1.000	1.000	.953	.677	.274	.054	.004	.000	.000	.000	.000
	9	1.000	1.000	.983	.811	.425	.115	.013	.000	.000	.000	.000
	10	1.000	1.000	.994	.902	.586	.212	.034	.002	.000	.000	.000
	11	1.000	1.000	.998	.956	.732	.345	.078	.006	.000	.000	.000
	12	1.000	1.000	1.000	.983	.846	.500	.154	.017	.000	.000	.000
	13	1.000	1.000	1.000	.994	.922	.655	.268	.044	.002	.000	.000
	14	1.000	1.000	1.000	.998	.966	.788	.414	.098	.006	.000	.000
	15	1.000	1.000	1.000	1.000	.987	.885	.575	.189	.017	.000	.000
	16	1.000	1.000	1.000	1.000	.996	.946	.726	.323	.047	.000	.000
	17	1.000	1.000	1.000	1.000	.999	.978	.846	.488	.109	.002	.000
	18	1.000	1.000	1.000	1.000	1.000	.993	.926	.659	.220	.009	.000
	19	1.000	1.000	1.000	1.000	1.000	.998	.971	.807	.383	.033	.001
	20	1.000	1.000	1.000	1.000	1.000	1.000	.991	.910	.579	.098	.007
	21	1.000	1.000	1.000	1.000	1.000	1.000	.998	.967	.766	.236	.034
	22	1.000	1.000	1.000	1.000	1.000	1.000	1.000	.991	.902	.463	.127
	23	1.000	1.000	1.000	1.000	1.000	1.000	1.000	.998	.973	.729	.358
	24	1.000	1.000	1.000	1.000	1.000	1.000	1.000	1.000	.996	.928	.723
	25	1.000	1.000	1.000	1.000	1.000	1.000	1.000	1.000	1.000	1.000	1.000

TABLE 3   STANDARD NORMAL PROBABILITIES   **723**

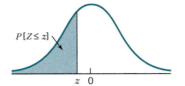

$P[Z \leq z]$

TABLE 3   Standard Normal Probabilities

z	.00	.01	.02	.03	.04	.05	.06	.07	.08	.09
−3.5	.0002	.0002	.0002	.0002	.0002	.0002	.0002	.0002	.0002	.0002
−3.4	.0003	.0003	.0003	.0003	.0003	.0003	.0003	.0003	.0003	.0002
−3.3	.0005	.0005	.0005	.0004	.0004	.0004	.0004	.0004	.0004	.0003
−3.2	.0007	.0007	.0006	.0006	.0006	.0006	.0006	.0005	.0005	.0005
−3.1	.0010	.0009	.0009	.0009	.0008	.0008	.0008	.0008	.0007	.0007
−3.0	.0013	.0013	.0013	.0012	.0012	.0011	.0011	.0011	.0010	.0010
−2.9	.0019	.0018	.0018	.0017	.0016	.0016	.0015	.0015	.0014	.0014
−2.8	.0026	.0025	.0024	.0023	.0023	.0022	.0021	.0021	.0020	.0019
−2.7	.0035	.0034	.0033	.0032	.0031	.0030	.0029	.0028	.0027	.0026
−2.6	.0047	.0045	.0044	.0043	.0041	.0040	.0039	.0038	.0037	.0036
−2.5	.0062	.0060	.0059	.0057	.0055	.0054	.0052	.0051	.0049	.0048
−2.4	.0082	.0080	.0078	.0075	.0073	.0071	.0069	.0068	.0066	.0064
−2.3	.0107	.0104	.0102	.0099	.0096	.0094	.0091	.0089	.0087	.0084
−2.2	.0139	.0136	.0132	.0129	.0125	.0122	.0119	.0116	.0113	.0110
−2.1	.0179	.0174	.0170	.0166	.0162	.0158	.0154	.0150	.0146	.0143
−2.0	.0228	.0222	.0217	.0212	.0207	.0202	.0197	.0192	.0188	.0183
−1.9	.0287	.0281	.0274	.0268	.0262	.0256	.0250	.0244	.0239	.0233
−1.8	.0359	.0351	.0344	.0336	.0329	.0322	.0314	.0307	.0301	.0294
−1.7	.0446	.0436	.0427	.0418	.0409	.0401	.0392	.0384	.0375	.0367
−1.6	.0548	.0537	.0526	.0516	.0505	.0495	.0485	.0475	.0465	.0455
−1.5	.0668	.0655	.0643	.0630	.0618	.0606	.0594	.0582	.0571	.0559
−1.4	.0808	.0793	.0778	.0764	.0749	.0735	.0721	.0708	.0694	.0681
−1.3	.0968	.0951	.0934	.0918	.0901	.0885	.0869	.0853	.0838	.0823
−1.2	.1151	.1131	.1112	.1093	.1075	.1056	.1038	.1020	.1003	.0985
−1.1	.1357	.1335	.1314	.1292	.1271	.1251	.1230	.1210	.1190	.1170
−1.0	.1587	.1562	.1539	.1515	.1492	.1469	.1446	.1423	.1401	.1379
− .9	.1841	.1814	.1788	.1762	.1736	.1711	.1685	.1660	.1635	.1611
− .8	.2119	.2090	.2061	.2033	.2005	.1977	.1949	.1922	.1894	.1867
− .7	.2420	.2389	.2358	.2327	.2297	.2266	.2236	.2206	.2177	.2148
− .6	.2743	.2709	.2676	.2643	.2611	.2578	.2546	.2514	.2483	.2451
− .5	.3085	.3050	.3015	.2981	.2946	.2912	.2877	.2843	.2810	.2776
− .4	.3446	.3409	.3372	.3336	.3300	.3264	.3228	.3192	.3156	.3121
− .3	.3821	.3783	.3745	.3707	.3669	.3632	.3594	.3557	.3520	.3483
− .2	.4207	.4168	.4129	.4090	.4052	.4013	.3974	.3936	.3897	.3859
− .1	.4602	.4562	.4522	.4483	.4443	.4404	.4364	.4325	.4286	.4247
− .0	.5000	.4960	.4920	.4880	.4840	.4801	.4761	.4721	.4681	.4641

(continued)

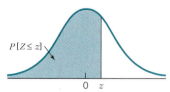

$P[Z \le z]$

0   z

TABLE 3   *(Continued)*

z	.00	.01	.02	.03	.04	.05	.06	.07	.08	.09
.0	.5000	.5040	.5080	.5120	.5160	.5199	.5239	.5279	.5319	.5359
.1	.5398	.5438	.5478	.5517	.5557	.5596	.5636	.5675	.5714	.5753
.2	.5793	.5832	.5871	.5910	.5948	.5987	.6026	.6064	.6103	.6141
.3	.6179	.6217	.6255	.6293	.6331	.6368	.6406	.6443	.6480	.6517
.4	.6554	.6591	.6628	.6664	.6700	.6736	.6772	.6808	.6844	.6879
.5	.6915	.6950	.6985	.7019	.7054	.7088	.7123	.7157	.7190	.7224
.6	.7257	.7291	.7324	.7357	.7389	.7422	.7454	.7486	.7517	.7549
.7	.7580	.7611	.7642	.7673	.7703	.7734	.7764	.7794	.7823	.7852
.8	.7881	.7910	.7939	.7967	.7995	.8023	.8051	.8078	.8106	.8133
.9	.8159	.8186	.8212	.8238	.8264	.8289	.8315	.8340	.8365	.8389
1.0	.8413	.8438	.8461	.8485	.8508	.8531	.8554	.8577	.8599	.8621
1.1	.8643	.8665	.8686	.8708	.8729	.8749	.8770	.8790	.8810	.8830
1.2	.8849	.8869	.8888	.8907	.8925	.8944	.8962	.8980	.8997	.9015
1.3	.9032	.9049	.9066	.9082	.9099	.9115	.9131	.9147	.9162	.9177
1.4	.9192	.9207	.9222	.9236	.9251	.9265	.9279	.9292	.9306	.9319
1.5	.9332	.9345	.9357	.9370	.9382	.9394	.9406	.9418	.9429	.9441
1.6	.9452	.9463	.9474	.9484	.9495	.9505	.9515	.9525	.9535	.9545
1.7	.9554	.9564	.9573	.9582	.9591	.9599	.9608	.9616	.9625	.9633
1.8	.9641	.9649	.9656	.9664	.9671	.9678	.9686	.9693	.9699	.9706
1.9	.9713	.9719	.9726	.9732	.9738	.9744	.9750	.9756	.9761	.9767
2.0	.9772	.9778	.9783	.9788	.9793	.9798	.9803	.9808	.9812	.9817
2.1	.9821	.9826	.9830	.9834	.9838	.9842	.9846	.9850	.9854	.9857
2.2	.9861	.9864	.9868	.9871	.9875	.9878	.9881	.9884	.9887	.9890
2.3	.9893	.9896	.9898	.9901	.9904	.9906	.9909	.9911	.9913	.9916
2.4	.9918	.9920	.9922	.9925	.9927	.9929	.9931	.9932	.9934	.9936
2.5	.9938	.9940	.9941	.9943	.9945	.9946	.9948	.9949	.9951	.9952
2.6	.9953	.9955	.9956	.9957	.9959	.9960	.9961	.9962	.9963	.9964
2.7	.9965	.9966	.9967	.9968	.9969	.9970	.9971	.9972	.9973	.9974
2.8	.9974	.9975	.9976	.9977	.9977	.9978	.9979	.9979	.9980	.9981
2.9	.9981	.9982	.9982	.9983	.9984	.9984	.9985	.9985	.9986	.9986
3.0	.9987	.9987	.9987	.9988	.9988	.9989	.9989	.9989	.9990	.9990
3.1	.9990	.9991	.9991	.9991	.9992	.9992	.9992	.9992	.9993	.9993
3.2	.9993	.9993	.9994	.9994	.9994	.9994	.9994	.9995	.9995	.9995
3.3	.9995	.9995	.9995	.9996	.9996	.9996	.9996	.9996	.9996	.9997
3.4	.9997	.9997	.9997	.9997	.9997	.9997	.9997	.9997	.9997	.9998
3.5	.9998	.9998	.9998	.9998	.9998	.9998	.9998	.9998	.9998	.9998

TABLE 4 PERCENTAGE POINTS OF t DISTRIBUTIONS **725**

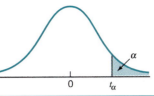

TABLE 4 Percentage Points of t Distributions

α d.f.	.25	.10	.05	.025	.01	.00833	.00625	.005	.0025
1	1.000	3.078	6.314	12.706	31.821	38.188	50.923	63.657	127.321
2	.816	1.886	2.920	4.303	6.965	7.649	8.860	9.925	14.089
3	.765	1.638	2.353	3.182	4.541	4.857	5.392	5.841	7.453
4	.741	1.533	2.132	2.776	3.747	3.961	4.315	4.604	5.598
5	.727	1.476	2.015	2.571	3.365	3.534	3.810	4.032	4.773
6	.718	1.440	1.943	2.447	3.143	3.287	3.521	3.707	4.317
7	.711	1.415	1.895	2.365	2.998	3.128	3.335	3.499	4.029
8	.706	1.397	1.860	2.306	2.896	3.016	3.206	3.355	3.833
9	.703	1.383	1.833	2.262	2.821	2.933	3.111	3.250	3.690
10	.700	1.372	1.812	2.228	2.764	2.870	3.038	3.169	3.581
11	.697	1.363	1.796	2.201	2.718	2.820	2.981	3.106	3.497
12	.695	1.356	1.782	2.179	2.681	2.779	2.934	3.055	3.428
13	.694	1.350	1.771	2.160	2.650	2.746	2.896	3.012	3.372
14	.692	1.345	1.761	2.145	2.624	2.718	2.864	2.977	3.326
15	.691	1.341	1.753	2.131	2.602	2.694	2.837	2.947	3.286
16	.690	1.337	1.746	2.120	2.583	2.673	2.813	2.921	3.252
17	.689	1.333	1.740	2.110	2.567	2.655	2.793	2.898	3.222
18	.688	1.330	1.734	2.101	2.552	2.639	2.775	2.878	3.197
19	.688	1.328	1.729	2.093	2.539	2.625	2.759	2.861	3.174
20	.687	1.325	1.725	2.086	2.528	2.613	2.744	2.845	3.153
21	.686	1.323	1.721	2.080	2.518	2.601	2.732	2.831	3.135
22	.686	1.321	1.717	2.074	2.508	2.591	2.720	2.819	3.119
23	.685	1.319	1.714	2.069	2.500	2.582	2.710	2.807	3.104
24	.685	1.318	1.711	2.064	2.492	2.574	2.700	2.797	3.091
25	.684	1.316	1.708	2.060	2.485	2.566	2.692	2.787	3.078
26	.684	1.315	1.706	2.056	2.479	2.559	2.684	2.779	3.067
27	.684	1.314	1.703	2.052	2.473	2.552	2.676	2.771	3.057
28	.683	1.313	1.701	2.048	2.467	2.546	2.669	2.763	3.047
29	.683	1.311	1.699	2.045	2.462	2.541	2.663	2.756	3.038
30	.683	1.310	1.697	2.042	2.457	2.536	2.657	2.750	3.030
40	.681	1.303	1.684	2.021	2.423	2.499	2.616	2.704	2.971
60	.679	1.296	1.671	2.000	2.390	2.463	2.575	2.660	2.915
120	.677	1.289	1.658	1.980	2.358	2.428	2.536	2.617	2.860
∞	.674	1.282	1.645	1.960	2.326	2.394	2.498	2.576	2.813

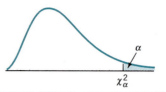

TABLE 5 Percentage Points of χ^2 Distributions

d.f. \ α	.99	.975	.95	.90	.50	.10	.05	.025	.01
1	.0002	.001	.004	.02	.45	2.71	3.84	5.02	6.63
2	.02	.05	.10	.21	1.39	4.61	5.99	7.38	9.21
3	.11	.22	.35	.58	2.37	6.25	7.81	9.35	11.34
4	.30	.48	.71	1.06	3.36	7.78	9.49	11.14	13.28
5	.55	.83	1.15	1.61	4.35	9.24	11.07	12.83	15.09
6	.87	1.24	1.64	2.20	5.35	10.64	12.59	14.45	16.81
7	1.24	1.69	2.17	2.83	6.35	12.02	14.07	16.01	18.48
8	1.65	2.18	2.73	3.49	7.34	13.36	15.51	17.53	20.09
9	2.09	2.70	3.33	4.17	8.34	14.68	16.92	19.02	21.67
10	2.56	3.24	3.94	4.87	9.34	15.99	18.31	20.48	23.21
11	3.05	3.81	4.57	5.58	10.34	17.28	19.68	21.92	24.72
12	3.57	4.40	5.23	6.30	11.34	18.55	21.03	23.34	26.22
13	4.11	5.01	5.89	7.04	12.34	19.81	22.36	24.74	27.69
14	4.66	5.62	6.57	7.79	13.34	21.06	23.68	26.12	29.14
15	5.23	6.26	7.26	8.55	14.34	22.31	25.00	27.49	30.58
16	5.81	6.90	7.96	9.31	15.34	23.54	26.30	28.85	32.00
17	6.41	7.56	8.67	10.09	16.34	24.77	27.59	30.19	33.41
18	7.01	8.23	9.39	10.86	17.34	25.99	28.87	31.53	34.81
19	7.63	8.90	10.12	11.65	18.34	27.20	30.14	32.85	36.19
20	8.26	9.59	10.85	12.44	19.34	28.41	31.41	34.17	37.57
21	8.90	10.28	11.59	13.24	20.34	29.62	32.67	35.48	38.93
22	9.54	10.98	12.34	14.04	21.34	30.81	33.92	36.78	40.29
23	10.20	11.69	13.09	14.85	22.34	32.01	35.17	38.08	41.64
24	10.86	12.40	13.85	15.66	23.34	33.20	36.42	39.36	42.98
25	11.52	13.11	14.61	16.47	24.34	34.38	37.65	40.65	44.31
26	12.20	13.84	15.38	17.29	25.34	35.56	38.89	41.92	45.64
27	12.88	14.57	16.15	18.11	26.34	36.74	40.11	43.19	46.96
28	13.56	15.30	16.93	18.94	27.34	37.92	41.34	44.46	48.28
29	14.26	16.04	17.71	19.77	28.34	39.09	42.56	45.72	49.59
30	14.95	16.78	18.49	20.60	29.34	40.26	43.77	46.98	50.89
40	22.16	24.42	26.51	29.05	39.34	51.81	55.76	59.34	63.69
50	29.71	32.35	34.76	37.69	49.33	63.17	67.50	71.42	76.15
60	37.48	40.47	43.19	46.46	59.33	74.40	79.08	83.30	88.38
70	45.44	48.75	51.74	55.33	69.33	85.53	90.53	95.02	100.43
80	53.54	57.15	60.39	64.28	79.33	96.58	101.88	106.63	112.33
90	61.75	65.64	69.13	73.29	89.33	107.57	113.15	118.14	124.12
100	70.06	74.22	77.93	82.36	99.33	118.50	124.34	129.56	135.81

TABLE 6 Percentage Points of $F(\nu_1, \nu_2)$ Distributions $\boxed{\alpha = .10}$

$F_\alpha(\nu_1, \nu_2)$

$\nu_2 \backslash \nu_1$	1	2	3	4	5	6	7	8	9	10	12	15	20	25	30	40	60
1	39.86	49.50	53.59	55.83	57.24	58.20	58.91	59.44	59.86	60.19	60.71	61.22	61.74	62.05	62.26	62.53	62.79
2	8.53	9.00	9.16	9.24	9.29	9.33	9.35	9.37	9.38	9.39	9.41	9.42	9.44	9.45	9.46	9.47	9.47
3	5.54	5.46	5.39	5.34	5.31	5.28	5.27	5.25	5.24	5.23	5.22	5.20	5.18	5.17	5.17	5.16	5.15
4	4.54	4.32	4.19	4.11	4.05	4.01	3.98	3.95	3.94	3.92	3.90	3.87	3.84	3.83	3.82	3.80	3.79
5	4.06	3.78	3.62	3.52	3.45	3.40	3.37	3.34	3.32	3.30	3.27	3.24	3.21	3.19	3.17	3.16	3.14
6	3.78	3.46	3.29	3.18	3.11	3.05	3.01	2.98	2.96	2.94	2.90	2.87	2.84	2.81	2.80	2.78	2.76
7	3.59	3.26	3.07	2.96	2.88	2.83	2.78	2.75	2.72	2.70	2.67	2.63	2.59	2.57	2.56	2.54	2.51
8	3.46	3.11	2.92	2.81	2.73	2.67	2.62	2.59	2.56	2.54	2.50	2.46	2.42	2.40	2.38	2.36	2.34
9	3.36	3.01	2.81	2.69	2.61	2.55	2.51	2.47	2.44	2.42	2.38	2.34	2.30	2.27	2.25	2.23	2.21
10	3.29	2.92	2.73	2.61	2.52	2.46	2.41	2.38	2.35	2.32	2.28	2.24	2.20	2.17	2.16	2.13	2.11
11	3.23	2.86	2.66	2.54	2.45	2.39	2.34	2.30	2.27	2.25	2.21	2.17	2.12	2.10	2.08	2.05	2.03
12	3.18	2.81	2.61	2.48	2.39	2.33	2.28	2.24	2.21	2.19	2.15	2.10	2.06	2.03	2.01	1.99	1.96
13	3.14	2.76	2.56	2.43	2.35	2.28	2.23	2.20	2.16	2.14	2.10	2.05	2.01	1.98	1.96	1.93	1.90
14	3.10	2.73	2.52	2.39	2.31	2.24	2.19	2.15	2.12	2.10	2.05	2.01	1.96	1.93	1.91	1.89	1.86
15	3.07	2.70	2.49	2.36	2.27	2.21	2.16	2.12	2.09	2.06	2.02	1.97	1.92	1.89	1.87	1.85	1.82
16	3.05	2.67	2.46	2.33	2.24	2.18	2.13	2.09	2.06	2.03	1.99	1.94	1.89	1.86	1.84	1.81	1.78
17	3.03	2.64	2.44	2.31	2.22	2.15	2.10	2.06	2.03	2.00	1.96	1.91	1.86	1.83	1.81	1.78	1.75
18	3.01	2.62	2.42	2.29	2.20	2.13	2.08	2.04	2.00	1.98	1.93	1.89	1.84	1.80	1.78	1.75	1.72
19	2.99	2.61	2.40	2.27	2.18	2.11	2.06	2.02	1.98	1.96	1.91	1.86	1.81	1.78	1.76	1.73	1.70
20	2.97	2.59	2.38	2.25	2.16	2.09	2.04	2.00	1.96	1.94	1.89	1.84	1.79	1.76	1.74	1.71	1.68
21	2.96	2.57	2.36	2.23	2.14	2.08	2.02	1.98	1.95	1.92	1.87	1.83	1.78	1.74	1.72	1.69	1.66
22	2.95	2.56	2.35	2.22	2.13	2.06	2.01	1.97	1.93	1.90	1.86	1.81	1.76	1.73	1.70	1.67	1.64
23	2.94	2.55	2.34	2.21	2.11	2.05	1.99	1.95	1.92	1.89	1.84	1.80	1.74	1.71	1.69	1.66	1.62
24	2.93	2.54	2.33	2.19	2.10	2.04	1.98	1.94	1.91	1.88	1.83	1.78	1.73	1.70	1.67	1.64	1.61
25	2.92	2.53	2.32	2.18	2.09	2.02	1.97	1.93	1.89	1.87	1.82	1.77	1.72	1.68	1.66	1.63	1.59
26	2.91	2.52	2.31	2.17	2.08	2.01	1.96	1.92	1.88	1.86	1.81	1.76	1.71	1.67	1.65	1.61	1.58
27	2.90	2.51	2.30	2.17	2.07	2.00	1.95	1.91	1.87	1.85	1.80	1.75	1.70	1.66	1.64	1.60	1.57
28	2.89	2.50	2.29	2.16	2.06	2.00	1.94	1.90	1.87	1.84	1.79	1.74	1.69	1.65	1.63	1.59	1.56
29	2.89	2.50	2.28	2.15	2.06	1.99	1.93	1.89	1.86	1.83	1.78	1.73	1.68	1.64	1.62	1.58	1.55
30	2.88	2.49	2.28	2.14	2.05	1.98	1.93	1.88	1.85	1.82	1.77	1.72	1.67	1.63	1.61	1.57	1.54
40	2.84	2.44	2.23	2.09	2.00	1.93	1.87	1.83	1.79	1.76	1.71	1.66	1.61	1.57	1.54	1.51	1.47
60	2.79	2.39	2.18	2.04	1.95	1.87	1.82	1.77	1.74	1.71	1.66	1.60	1.54	1.50	1.48	1.44	1.40
120	2.75	2.35	2.13	1.99	1.90	1.82	1.77	1.72	1.68	1.65	1.60	1.55	1.48	1.45	1.41	1.37	1.32
∞	2.71	2.30	2.08	1.94	1.85	1.77	1.72	1.67	1.63	1.60	1.55	1.49	1.42	1.38	1.34	1.30	1.24

(continued)

TABLE 6 (*Continued*) Percentage Points of $F(v_1, v_2)$ Distributions $\alpha = .05$

v_2 \ v_1	1	2	3	4	5	6	7	8	9	10	12	15	20	25	30	40	60
1	161.5	199.5	215.7	224.6	230.2	234.0	236.8	238.9	240.5	241.9	243.9	246.0	248.0	249.3	250.1	251.1	252.2
2	18.51	19.00	19.16	19.25	19.30	19.33	19.35	19.37	19.38	19.40	19.41	19.43	19.45	19.46	19.46	19.47	19.48
3	10.13	9.55	9.28	9.12	9.01	8.94	8.89	8.85	8.81	8.79	8.74	8.70	8.66	8.63	8.62	8.59	8.57
4	7.71	6.94	6.59	6.39	6.26	6.16	6.09	6.04	6.00	5.96	5.91	5.86	5.80	5.77	5.75	5.72	5.69
5	6.61	5.79	5.41	5.19	5.05	4.95	4.88	4.82	4.77	4.74	4.68	4.62	4.56	4.52	4.50	4.46	4.43
6	5.99	5.14	4.76	4.53	4.39	4.28	4.21	4.15	4.10	4.06	4.00	3.94	3.87	3.83	3.81	3.77	3.74
7	5.59	4.74	4.35	4.12	3.97	3.87	3.79	3.73	3.68	3.64	3.57	3.51	3.44	3.40	3.38	3.34	3.30
8	5.32	4.46	4.07	3.84	3.69	3.58	3.50	3.44	3.39	3.35	3.28	3.22	3.15	3.11	3.08	3.04	3.01
9	5.12	4.26	3.86	3.63	3.48	3.37	3.29	3.23	3.18	3.14	3.07	3.01	2.94	2.89	2.86	2.83	2.79
10	4.96	4.10	3.71	3.48	3.33	3.22	3.14	3.07	3.02	2.98	2.91	2.85	2.77	2.73	2.70	2.66	2.62
11	4.84	3.98	3.59	3.36	3.20	3.09	3.01	2.95	2.90	2.85	2.79	2.72	2.65	2.60	2.57	2.53	2.49
12	4.75	3.89	3.49	3.26	3.11	3.00	2.91	2.85	2.80	2.75	2.69	2.62	2.54	2.50	2.47	2.43	2.38
13	4.67	3.81	3.41	3.18	3.03	2.92	2.83	2.77	2.71	2.67	2.60	2.53	2.46	2.41	2.38	2.34	2.30
14	4.60	3.74	3.34	3.11	2.96	2.85	2.76	2.70	2.65	2.60	2.53	2.46	2.39	2.34	2.31	2.27	2.22
15	4.54	3.68	3.29	3.06	2.90	2.79	2.71	2.64	2.59	2.54	2.48	2.40	2.33	2.28	2.25	2.20	2.16
16	4.49	3.63	3.24	3.01	2.85	2.74	2.66	2.59	2.54	2.49	2.42	2.35	2.28	2.23	2.19	2.15	2.11
17	4.45	3.59	3.20	2.96	2.81	2.70	2.61	2.55	2.49	2.45	2.38	2.31	2.23	2.18	2.15	2.10	2.06
18	4.41	3.55	3.16	2.93	2.77	2.66	2.58	2.51	2.46	2.41	2.34	2.27	2.19	2.14	2.11	2.06	2.02
19	4.38	3.52	3.13	2.90	2.74	2.63	2.54	2.48	2.42	2.38	2.31	2.23	2.16	2.11	2.07	2.03	1.98
20	4.35	3.49	3.10	2.87	2.71	2.60	2.51	2.45	2.39	2.35	2.28	2.20	2.12	2.07	2.04	1.99	1.95
21	4.32	3.47	3.07	2.84	2.68	2.57	2.49	2.42	2.37	2.32	2.25	2.18	2.10	2.05	2.01	1.96	1.92
22	4.30	3.44	3.05	2.82	2.66	2.55	2.46	2.40	2.34	2.30	2.23	2.15	2.07	2.02	1.98	1.94	1.89
23	4.28	3.42	3.03	2.80	2.64	2.53	2.44	2.37	2.32	2.27	2.20	2.13	2.05	2.00	1.96	1.91	1.86
24	4.26	3.40	3.01	2.78	2.62	2.51	2.42	2.36	2.30	2.25	2.18	2.11	2.03	1.97	1.94	1.89	1.84
25	4.24	3.39	2.99	2.76	2.60	2.49	2.40	2.34	2.28	2.24	2.16	2.09	2.01	1.96	1.92	1.87	1.82
26	4.23	3.37	2.98	2.74	2.59	2.47	2.39	2.32	2.27	2.22	2.15	2.07	1.99	1.94	1.90	1.85	1.80
27	4.21	3.35	2.96	2.73	2.57	2.46	2.37	2.31	2.25	2.20	2.13	2.06	1.97	1.92	1.88	1.84	1.79
28	4.20	3.34	2.95	2.71	2.56	2.45	2.36	2.29	2.24	2.19	2.12	2.04	1.96	1.91	1.87	1.82	1.77
29	4.18	3.33	2.93	2.70	2.55	2.43	2.35	2.28	2.22	2.18	2.10	2.03	1.94	1.89	1.85	1.81	1.75
30	4.17	3.32	2.92	2.69	2.53	2.42	2.33	2.27	2.21	2.16	2.09	2.01	1.93	1.88	1.84	1.79	1.74
40	4.08	3.23	2.84	2.61	2.45	2.34	2.25	2.18	2.12	2.08	2.00	1.92	1.84	1.78	1.74	1.69	1.64
60	4.00	3.15	2.76	2.53	2.37	2.25	2.17	2.10	2.04	1.99	1.92	1.84	1.75	1.69	1.65	1.59	1.53
120	3.92	3.07	2.68	2.45	2.29	2.18	2.09	2.02	1.96	1.91	1.83	1.75	1.66	1.60	1.55	1.50	1.43
∞	3.84	3.00	2.61	2.37	2.21	2.10	2.01	1.94	1.88	1.83	1.75	1.67	1.57	1.51	1.46	1.39	1.32

Data Bank

BANKING DATA (BankSamp.dat)

Some of the responses to a sample survey of bank services are given in Table C.1. The data are categorical, and the category definitions for each variable follow. There are more cases on the data disk. (Courtesy of Gilbert Churchill, Jr.)

$$
\text{Age} = \begin{cases}
1 & 18\text{--}21 \text{ yr.} \\
2 & 22\text{--}30 \text{ yr} \\
3 & 31\text{--}40 \text{ yr} \\
4 & 41\text{--}50 \text{ yr.} \\
5 & 51\text{--}64 \text{ yr.} \\
6 & 65 \text{ yr. or more}
\end{cases}
$$

$$
\text{Service rating} = \begin{cases}
1 & \text{Excellent} \\
2 & \text{Good} \\
3 & \text{Acceptable} \\
4 & \text{Poor}
\end{cases}
$$

$$
\text{Savings account} = \begin{cases}
0 & \text{American Trust} \\
1 & \text{Elsewhere}
\end{cases}
$$

$$
\text{Checking account} = \begin{cases}
0 & \text{American Trust} \\
1 & \text{Elsewhere}
\end{cases}
$$

$$
\text{Years living in area (YrsLivAr)} = \begin{cases}
1 & 1 \text{ yr. or less} \\
2 & 1\text{--}3 \text{ yr.} \\
3 & 4\text{--}5 \text{ yr.} \\
4 & 6\text{--}10 \text{ yr.} \\
5 & 10 \text{ yr. or more}
\end{cases}
$$

TABLE C.1   BANKING SAMPLE SURVEY RESULTS   **731**

TABLE C.1   Banking Sample Survey Results

Age	Service Rating	Savings	Checking	YrsLivAr	Age	Service Rating	Savings	Checking	YrsLivAr	Age	Service Rating	Savings	Checking	YrsLivAr
3	1	0	1	5	1	2	1	0	2	6	1	0	1	1
3	2	0	0	5	6	1	1	0	5	4	2	1	1	5
3	2	1	1	5	2	1	1	0	5	5	3	0	1	5
3	4	1	1	2	2	2	0	0	5	6	1	1	0	5
3	2	1	1	4	1	1	1	0	1	1	1	0	0	2
3	2	1	1	5	3	1	1	0	5	4	1	0	0	5
5	2	1	1	5	2	2	1	0	2	6	2	1	0	5
2	1	0	0	4	1	3	0	0	3	3	2	1	1	3
2	3	1	1	4	6	1	1	1	5	3	2	1	0	5
3	2	1	0	5	5	1	0	0	5	6	1	1	1	5
6	1	1	0	5	2	2	1	0	3	2	1	0	0	5
2	3	1	1	3	6	1	1	1	5	2	2	1	0	5
5	1	0	0	5	6	1	0	1	5	4	2	1	1	5
6	1	0	0	5	3	3	1	0	4	3	1	1	0	3
5	2	1	1	5	2	3	1	0	5	6	1	0	0	5
3	1	1	1	2	5	3	0	0	5	3	1	0	0	4
2	1	0	0	5	2	1	0	0	2	5	1	0	0	5
3	2	1	0	2	3	2	1	0	5	2	1	0	1	3
5	1	0	0	5	5	1	0	0	5	5	2	1	1	5
1	2	1	0	1	3	2	1	0	5	1	2	1	0	2
3	2	1	0	3	4	3	1	0	5	6	2	0	0	5
6	1	1	0	5	4	1	1	0	5	2	3	0	0	4
4	1	0	0	5	2	1	0	0	2	5	1	1	0	5
4	1	0	1	5	2	2	0	1	2	5	2	0	1	5
4	3	0	1	3	2	3	0	1	4	4	2	1	0	5
2	2	1	0	5	5	1	0	0	5	6	3	0	1	5
3	2	1	0	5	2	2	1	0	2	5	2	0	1	5
5	1	0	1	5	6	1	1	0	5	3	2	1	1	5
2	1	0	0	4	4	1	0	0	5	4	2	0	0	5
5	1	1	1	5	4	2	1	0	5	3	1	1	0	5
3	2	1	0	5	3	1	1	0	3	3	1	1	0	4
3	1	1	1	5	3	2	1	1	5	2	1	1	0	2
3	2	1	0	3	2	1	1	1	4	6	1	0	0	5
3	2	1	0	5	1	2	0	0	2	6	1	0	1	5
5	2	0	0	5	4	1	0	0	2	2	2	1	0	5
5	1	1	1	5	2	3	0	0	2	4	1	0	0	5
2	1	1	0	5	2	1	0	1	5	3	1	1	0	5
2	1	0	0	5	2	1	0	0	5	2	2	0	0	4
6	1	1	0	5	3	2	0	0	5	6	1	1	0	5
1	3	0	0	1	6	1	1	0	5	3	1	1	0	5
2	1	0	0	4	2	2	1	0	5	1	3	1	1	5
2	3	0	0	1	3	3	1	0	5	4	1	1	1	5
3	3	1	0	5	6	1	0	0	5	6	1	1	1	5
2	1	0	1	4	5	1	1	0	5	5	1	1	1	5
5	1	0	1	5	6	2	1	1	5	2	2	1	0	2
3	2	1	0	5	5	3	0	1	5	2	1	1	0	4
6	1	1	0	5	4	3	1	1	5	6	1	0	0	5
5	2	1	1	5	2	1	0	0	4	3	2	1	1	4
2	2	0	0	2	6	1	0	0	5	3	1	1	0	5
5	1	0	0	5	5	2	1	1	5	3	2	1	0	5

COMPUTER ATTITUDE AND ANXIETY (CompAtti.dat)

Beginning accounting students need to learn to audit in a computerized environment. A sample of beginning students took a test that is summarized by two scores shown in Table C.2: the Computer Attitude Scale (CAS), based on 20 questions, and the Computer Anxiety Rating Scale (CARS), based on 19 questions. Males are coded as 1 and females as 0. (Courtesy of Douglas Stein)

TABLE C.2   Computer Attitude and Anxiety Scores

Gender	CAS	CARS	Gender	CAS	CARS
0	2.85	2.90	1	3.30	3.47
1	2.60	2.32	1	2.90	3.05
0	2.20	1.00	1	2.60	2.68
1	2.65	2.58	0	2.25	1.90
1	2.60	2.58	0	1.90	1.84
1	3.20	3.05	1	2.20	1.74
1	3.65	3.74	0	2.30	2.58
0	2.55	1.90	0	1.80	1.58
1	3.15	3.32	1	3.05	2.47
1	2.80	2.74	1	3.15	3.32
0	2.40	2.37	0	2.80	2.90
1	3.20	3.11	0	2.35	2.42
0	3.05	3.32	1	3.70	3.47
1	2.60	2.79	1	2.60	4.00
1	3.35	2.95	0	3.50	3.42
0	3.75	3.79	0	2.95	2.53
0	3.00	3.26	1	2.80	2.68
1	2.80	3.21			

CEO COMPENSATION (CEOComp.dat)

The compensation for chief executive officers (CEOs) varies widely, and contains several components. CEO compensation seems to depend on certain characteristics of the executive and measures of firm performance. The outcomes for several CEOs are given in Table C.3. (Source: *Forbes*, May 22, 1995)

$$\text{Education} = \begin{cases} 0 & \text{No college degree} \\ 1 & \text{Undergraduate degree} \\ 2 & \text{Graduate degree} \end{cases}$$

Professional Backgrnd = Categorical variable indicating professional background such as finance, insurance, marketing, and so forth

OtherCom = Other Compensation   TotalCompens = Total Compensation

Tenure = Time with firm in years   Exper = Experience as CEO in years

Market Valuation = Market value of firm stock owned by CEO

PctOwn = Percentage of firm stock owned by CEO

TABLE C.3 Executive (CEO) Compensation

Salary ($1,000's)	Bonus ($1,000's)	OtherCom ($1,000's)	Total Compens ($1,000's)	Age	Education	Professional Backgrnd	Tenure	Exper	Market Valuation ($1,000,000's)	PctOwn	Firm Profits ($1,000,000's)	Firm Sales ($1,000,000's)
173	275	5	453	64	2	3	40	26	54.5	3.14	91	872
1441	429	78	1948	55	1	1	23	23	7.6	.55	145	1227
1646	0	89	1735	47	2	7	5	5	21.7	.52	−47	1712
294	325	24	643	65	1	3	29	23	8.9	.89	44	1681
1254	105	102	1461	63	1	6	23	8	3.6	.05	201	5673
325	25	7	357	54	2	5	20	1	.5	.06	71	1117
658	0	11	669	61	2	5	2	2	.7	.05	−187	1475
1723	289	82	2094	63	1	3	41	8	5.9	.04	1166	10818
504	69	24	597	57	2	5	27	13	1.4	.03	377	2686
822	38	29	889	56	2	1	5	5	.7	.03	224	2201
374	129	11	514	57	2	4	3	3	4.1	.17	79	661
447	11	8	466	48	2	1	17	1	.2	.01	189	1539
2781	0	52	2833	50	1	3	4	4	11.7	.39	−332	11663
128	282	17	427	54	1	8	31	15	71.4	10.09	55	2366
1782	0	74	1856	60	2	7	33	3	.4	.03	−507	4864
1137	423	92	1652	60	2	1	34	14	11.5	.06	856	14949
761	20	1	782	49	2	9	18	9	1.3	.07	14	5061
505	0	108	613	56	2	9	8	1	.1	.02	−29	1929
976	448	64	1488	58	1	3	9	8	9.4	.56	126	2643
434	12	1	447	50	2	9	5	1	.3	.03	54	1084
1010	687	55	1752	63	1	7	14	14	534.2	3.99	249	5137
956	1452	89	2497	64	0	1	28	28	221.1	3.98	91	844
700	37	31	768	60	2	9	30	8	.7	.02	322	2097
1813	489	40	2342	71	1	4	46	34	9.6	.83	99	835
3396	0	13	3409	64	0	9	30	30	29.4	.31	−99	12021

(*continued*)

733

TABLE C.3 Continued

Salary ($1,000's)	Bonus ($1,000's)	OtherCom ($1,000's)	Total Compens ($1,000's)	Age	Education	Professional Backgrnd	Tenure	Exper	Market Valuation ($1,000,000's)	PctOwn	Firm Profits ($1,000,000's)	Firm Sales ($1,000,000's)
2108	38	98	2244	64	2	5	41	5	4.0	.04	30	4451
597	0	4	601	59	2	4	35	5	.1	.12	-85	1911
616	862	76	1554	61	1	8	41	17	30.6	2.23	82	1435
237	221	4	462	61	2	5	25	11	16.8	1.03	27	1314
571	0	16	587	55	2	4	5	5	1.6	.17	-76	2301
269	391	28	688	54	2	9	28	28	1689.0	34.04	317	3277
721	101	71	893	60	2	5	36	15	2.0	.04	417	4444
328	238	34	600	60	0	7	42	1	85.6	17.66	43	1214
538	25	7	570	60	1	4	3	3	.2	.21	49	804
741	104	9	854	62	1	7	30	3	2.6	.17	81	669
607	380	47	1034	51	1	6	23	3	7.0	.83	82	578
1044	107	36	1187	55	2	8	2	1	3.1	1.21	10	1214
2409	1487	143	4039	59	1	7	32	17	35.2	.29	715	12651
287	198	32	517	51	1	8	37	21	181.0	6.70	136	3180
567	15	34	616	62	2	1	16	9	.3	.01	237	2754
682	0	2	684	52	2	1	36	2	.8	.01	-1086	12794
1226	174	56	1456	45	1	4	30	10	6.0	.17	98	4439
952	80	56	1088	50	2	7	11	11	2.6	.17	48	415
432	0	12	444	57	2	7	25	3	.1	.01	-50	1569
1085	440	97	1622	64	1	8	29	5	9.7	.19	347	9886
1009	117	0	1126	62	1	3	28	14	3.4	.21	63	2545
1711	182	134	2027	52	2	2	25	5	3.4	.04	806	8379
408	183	9	600	62	2	7	12	2	4.2	.26	10	21351
543	13	2	558	62	2	5	34	12	.2	.01	265	2359
278	209	74	561	61	2	6	24	24	15.4	.95	52	695

TABLE C.4   HEALTH INSURANCE CLAIM TURNAROUND TIMES   **735**

HEALTH INSURANCE TURNAROUND TIMES (HealthTu.dat)

It often takes several days to process health insurance claims. The turnaround times (in days) to process a large number of claims at one company are given in Table C.4.

TABLE C.4   Health Insurance Claim Turnaround Times

1	1	1	2	2	2	3	3	3	3	3
3	4	4	4	4	4	5	5	5	5	6
6	6	6	6	7	7	7	7	7	7	7
7	7	7	8	8	8	8	8	8	8	8
8	8	9	9	10	10	10	10	10	10	10
10	10	11	11	11	11	11	11	11	11	11
11	11	11	11	11	11	11	11	11	11	11
11	11	11	12	12	12	12	12	13	13	13
14	14	14	14	14	14	14	14	14	14	14
15	15	15	15	15	15	15	15	15	15	15
16	16	16	16	16	16	16	16	17	17	17
17	17	17	17	18	18	18	18	18	18	18
18	19	19	19	19	20	20	20	20	20	21
21	21	21	21	21	21	21	22	22	22	22
22	22	22	23	23	23	24	24	24	24	25
25	25	26	26	27	27	27	27	27	28	28
28	28	28	29	29	30	31	32	32	32	35
37	38	38	38	43	46	46	48	48	49	52
52	53	53	55	63	69	73	74	77	95	177
219	270	292								

LIFE INSURANCE DATA (LifeIns.dat)

Whole life insurance policies differ by company. One way to compare policies is to examine the guaranteed accumulated cash values after certain periods of time and to look at the current rates of interest the companies are paying on accumulated funds. Table C.5 (page 736) contains the current interest rate (CurrInRt) and the guaranteed accumulated cash value after 10 years (GurAcc10) for the whole life policies of a large number of insurance companies.

TABLE C.5   Life Insurance Policy Characteristics

CurrInRt	GurAcc10	CurrInRt	GurAcc10	CurrInRt	GurAcc10	CurrInRt	GurAcc10
7.50	12428	7.75	11402	8.00	12197	8.75	8922
8.00	7703	6.88	12974	7.25	9294	7.25	11756
9.00	10308	6.75	10403	7.60	11266	7.50	11386
7.50	11090	7.00	17059	7.50	12828	7.00	13396
7.50	10786	8.35	11569	7.00	10864	7.00	12755
7.50	11889	7.50	11771	7.00	12116	8.00	10546
7.50	10654	7.50	11949	8.00	10930	8.00	8873
7.50	9559	7.75	12622	8.50	13695	8.00	10803
8.00	14881	7.50	10270	8.20	10139	8.00	11008
7.25	11064	7.00	7325	7.25	13005	8.50	10930
7.50	13043	7.00	11053	8.00	11846	7.50	12016
7.50	11350	6.75	11210	8.25	12698	7.50	11209
7.50	10600	7.60	10957	8.25	12742	7.50	9991
7.50	9991	7.50	9695	8.00	11307	6.75	13327
7.40	9231	7.00	12889	7.90	9983	8.00	8580
7.40	11941	7.00	11444	8.50	7300	7.50	10024
7.50	12248	7.80	12263	7.50	12020	8.00	10689
8.00	11292	8.05	12947	7.50	13691	7.25	10912
7.70	12849	7.75	12709	8.00	11618	7.50	11847
7.00	11884	7.85	10372	7.00	8572	7.75	9804
8.15	10405	8.10	10372	8.00	11049	8.20	9851
7.50	11418	7.25	12509	7.50	11215	7.25	11082
7.00	7438	7.25	12205	8.25	12882	7.25	11610
7.50	11727	8.05	12710	7.20	10534	7.25	11871
7.90	10552	8.00	10561	8.25	10170	7.80	12963
8.00	11029	8.25	12633	7.50	9382	8.75	11164
7.75	12434	7.00	8572	7.00	12248	7.65	10887
7.25	12260	7.00	8949	7.50	12137	7.75	10588
7.25	10793	8.25	10686	7.60	11275	7.00	12094
7.75	12127	8.25	12481	7.60	12730	7.00	12338
6.85	11433	8.50	9816	6.75	9131	7.00	10918
7.55	11020	6.70	12162	6.25	12040	8.00	11066
7.80	12006	7.75	11782	7.00	11758	8.00	13005
8.00	12013	8.40	12054	7.00	11816	8.00	11079
8.25	10686	5.75	9688	7.50	12898	7.50	11053
8.25	12481	8.10	9329	8.90	7172	7.25	10396
7.50	10622	8.40	10747	7.25	11856	7.75	10556
7.25	10951	7.25	11203	7.00	9095	7.30	11769
7.50	13596	8.85	8886	8.05	12934	7.60	8713
8.00	14512	8.00	13222	6.15	10871	7.60	12011
7.75	12082	8.00	14285	7.25	10395	8.00	11641
8.00	10200	8.25	11877	7.25	11456	6.75	11481
8.00	11605	8.40	9711	7.75	10993	7.90	12604
7.20	9656	8.25	12580	7.55	10190	8.10	12604
7.55	11272	8.05	13695	6.75	11374	7.75	11381
8.00	11917	8.05	9567				

TABLE C.6   PAPER STRENGTHS   **737**

PAPER STRENGTHS (PaprStrg.dat)

Paper is measured in continuous sheets several feet wide. Because of the orientation of the fibers, it has a different strength when measured in the direction produced by the machine (strength in machine direction or StrengMa here) than when measured at right angles to the machine direction (strength in the cross direction or StrengCr here). The strengths are measured in pounds and are listed in Table C.6. Here TypePap = 1 if new paper and TypePap = 2 if old paper. (Data courtesy of SONOCO Products, Inc.)

TABLE C.6   Paper Strengths

StrengMa	StrengCr	TypePap	StrengMa	StrengCr	TypePap	StrengMa	StrengCr	TypePap
121.41	70.42	1	117.51	71.62	1	121.91	73.68	1
127.70	72.47	1	118.00	70.70	1	122.31	74.93	1
129.20	78.20	1	131.00	74.35	1	109.81	53.10	2
131.80	74.89	1	125.70	68.29	1	109.10	50.85	2
135.10	71.21	1	126.10	72.10	1	115.10	51.68	2
131.50	78.39	1	125.80	70.64	1	118.31	50.60	2
126.70	69.02	1	125.50	76.33	1	112.60	53.51	2
115.10	73.10	1	127.80	76.75	1	116.20	56.53	2
130.80	79.28	1	130.50	80.33	1	107.40	54.42	2
124.60	76.48	1	127.90	75.68	1	110.60	53.52	2
118.31	70.25	1	123.90	78.54	1	103.51	48.93	2
114.20	72.88	1	124.10	71.91	1	110.71	53.67	2
120.30	68.23	1	120.80	68.22	1	113.80	52.42	2
115.70	68.12	1	120.70	70.41	1			

SPORT FRANCHISES DATA (SportFrn.dat)

Do owners of sport franchises make a lot of money? You be the judge. The accounting numbers for Major League Baseball (MLB), the National Basketball Association (NBA), the National Football League (NFL), and the National Hockey League (NHL) for 1991 are given in Table C.7 (page 738). All figures are in $1,000,000's. (Source: M. Ozanian and S. Taub, "Big Leagues, Bad Business," *Financial World,* July 7, 1992, pp. 34–51)

$$\text{FranType} = \text{Franchise Type} = \begin{cases} 1 & \text{MLB} \\ 2 & \text{NBA} \\ 3 & \text{NFL} \\ 4 & \text{NHL} \end{cases}$$

GateRec = Gate Receipts   MediaRev = Media Revenues

StadRev = Stadium Revenues   TotalRev = Total Revenues

PlayerCt = Player Costs   OpExpens = Operating Expenses

OpIncome = Operating Income   ValuFran = Value of Franchise

Franchis = Abbreviated name of team

TABLE C.7   Sport Franchises

GateRec	MediaRev	StadRev	TotalRev	PlayerCt	OpExpens	OpIncome	ValueFran	Franchis	FranType
19.4	61.0	7.4	90.0	29.8	59.6	30.4	200	NyYank	1
26.6	32.5	18.0	79.3	36.0	72.0	7.3	180	LADodge	1
22.9	50.0	16.0	91.1	35.2	70.4	20.7	170	NYMets	1
44.5	30.0	12.0	88.7	29.7	62.4	26.3	160	TorBlJay	1
24.5	40.5	14.3	81.5	35.4	70.8	10.7	160	BosRdSox	1
19.0	24.4	5.0	50.6	15.8	39.5	11.1	140	BaltOrio	1
27.5	25.7	19.3	78.0	18.0	60.0	18.0	140	ChWhSox	1
19.9	25.0	12.0	59.1	23.2	46.4	12.7	132	StLCard	1
22.8	27.5	12.0	64.5	29.0	58.0	6.5	132	ChCubs	1
19.0	25.5	14.0	61.5	20.7	47.6	13.9	123	TxRanger	1
16.9	20.5	14.0	53.6	30.4	60.8	−7.2	117	KCRoyals	1
15.2	23.2	7.6	48.2	21.7	43.4	4.8	115	PhilPhil	1
25.7	27.0	10.0	64.9	39.2	66.6	−1.7	115	OakAthlt	1
19.0	27.9	5.0	54.1	34.3	61.7	−7.6	103	CalAngls	1
15.5	26.2	5.0	48.9	33.3	53.3	−4.4	99	SFGiants	1
17.1	24.4	5.3	49.0	27.1	48.8	.2	98	CinnReds	1
15.6	23.1	7.5	48.4	24.4	48.8	−.4	96	SDPadres	1
10.6	25.2	8.0	46.0	12.1	31.5	14.5	95	HousAstr	1
16.2	21.9	5.5	45.8	24.9	49.8	−4.0	87	PittPirt	1
15.6	28.8	5.0	51.6	31.1	54.4	−2.8	85	DetTiger	1
15.4	18.9	3.8	40.3	20.4	40.8	−.5	83	AtBraves	1
18.2	20.5	3.2	44.1	24.1	48.2	−4.1	83	MinnTwin	1
15.5	22.0	5.0	44.7	17.4	41.8	2.9	79	SeatMar	1
14.2	19.4	3.0	38.8	26.4	50.2	−11.4	77	MilBrews	1
9.5	23.7	6.6	42.0	19.5	46.8	−4.8	77	ClevIndn	1
10.7	23.5	3.0	39.4	21.8	43.6	−4.2	75	MonExpos	1
28.4	25.1	5.0	62.6	13.0	32.5	30.1	150	LALakers	2
23.2	15.5	5.0	45.0	14.1	29.6	15.4	120	DetPistn	2
16.4	18.0	2.0	41.8	14.5	27.6	14.2	110	BosCelt	2
19.9	14.6	4.0	41.2	10.8	24.3	16.9	100	ChiBulls	2
13.3	13.1	6.0	33.8	14.8	28.1	5.7	83	NYKnicks	2
12.2	13.9	8.0	35.3	15.6	29.6	5.7	81	ClevCavs	2
12.1	16.2	.5	29.9	12.4	24.8	5.1	80	PheonSun	2
12.4	18.4	4.0	36.2	12.4	25.8	10.4	78	PtTrailB	2
21.7	9.6	1.9	34.4	11.4	25.1	9.3	74	CharHorn	2
13.7	9.4	2.0	26.3	11.9	26.2	.1	63	SacKings	2
11.9	14.3	2.2	30.1	13.4	26.8	3.3	63	Phil76s	2
12.8	14.1	2.2	30.8	12.7	25.4	5.4	63	GSWarrio	2
15.4	12.8	3.3	33.0	12.7	25.4	7.6	63	SASpurs	2
10.7	12.9	2.5	27.3	8.5	18.7	8.6	62	OrlMagic	2
12.5	18.5	.5	32.7	8.7	20.0	12.7	62	MinnTWol	2
11.5	13.8	1.6	28.4	12.9	25.8	2.6	61	HousRock	2
13.1	14.0	1.0	29.3	12.7	25.4	3.9	60	DallMavs	2
10.0	12.2	2.9	26.3	9.6	21.1	5.2	60	MiamiHea	2
9.5	12.5	1.5	24.7	12.9	25.8	−1.1	57	AtlHawks	2
11.6	9.7	1.5	24.2	12.7	25.4	−1.2	56	MilwBuck	2
9.9	13.7	2.0	26.8	12.8	25.6	1.2	54	NJNets	2
10.5	15.6	1.0	28.3	11.5	25.3	3.0	54	LAClippr	2
11.7	11.9	2.0	27.5	12.1	24.2	3.3	52	UtahJazz	2

(*continued*)

TABLE C.7 Continued

GateRec	MediaRev	StadRev	TotalRev	PlayerCt	OpExpens	OpIncome	ValueFran	Franchis	FranType
7.6	11.5	1.2	21.5	12.4	24.8	−3.3	46	DenNuggt	2
8.3	10.6	1.5	21.6	10.4	22.9	−1.3	46	WashBull	2
9.5	9.7	1.8	22.4	11.8	26.0	−3.6	45	SeatSupS	2
8.0	11.0	1.0	21.7	12.2	24.4	−2.7	43	IndPacer	2
12.3	32.0	18.0	66.0	25.7	51.4	14.6	150	MiamiDol	3
13.5	34.0	5.5	56.7	28.1	47.8	8.9	150	NYGiants	3
13.9	34.2	4.0	55.8	26.6	47.9	7.9	146	DallasCo	3
13.9	31.9	7.9	57.4	21.3	44.7	12.7	146	PhilEagl	3
13.5	33.6	5.8	56.6	22.4	44.8	11.8	139	ChBears	3
15.5	33.0	3.3	55.5	32.6	52.2	3.3	134	SF49ers	3
12.4	31.8	4.7	52.6	22.9	45.8	6.8	130	SeatSeaH	3
14.5	33.8	4.8	56.8	23.3	46.6	10.2	128	HousOilr	3
12.2	32.7	3.3	51.9	26.8	45.6	6.3	128	LARaider	3
10.4	32.7	4.8	51.6	24.6	44.8	6.8	126	LARams	3
22.7	31.6	3.0	61.0	29.5	50.2	10.9	125	BuffBill	3
11.9	31.6	12.6	59.8	25.8	51.6	8.2	125	ClBrowns	3
12.4	31.3	3.1	50.5	22.7	45.4	5.1	123	NOSaints	3
12.2	31.2	3.5	50.6	23.8	42.8	7.8	123	KanCtChf	3
12.4	32.1	2.0	50.2	19.0	39.9	10.3	121	PittStel	3
9.5	31.0	4.0	48.2	26.7	42.7	5.5	121	InColts	3
10.6	32.2	3.3	50.5	28.1	45.0	5.5	120	MinnViks	3
10.7	30.9	4.5	49.8	25.6	43.5	6.3	120	PhCards	3
10.2	32.0	3.0	48.9	24.8	44.6	4.3	120	AtlFalcn	3
13.3	33.2	2.0	52.2	27.9	44.6	7.6	117	WashRed	3
11.7	32.4	2.1	49.0	22.5	45.0	4.0	117	NYJets	3
9.3	30.9	1.1	45.0	23.9	43.0	2.0	115	GBPacker	3
16.0	31.2	3.0	53.9	30.6	52.0	1.9	115	CinBengl	3
9.3	31.8	3.5	48.3	21.6	43.2	5.1	115	SBChargr	3
13.3	32.6	.0	49.6	20.7	43.5	6.1	114	DenBronc	3
8.8	31.2	3.0	46.7	19.9	41.8	4.9	113	TBBucc	3
9.8	31.8	3.0	48.3	24.3	43.7	4.6	110	DetLions	3
9.9	31.0	1.0	45.6	21.2	46.6	−1.0	103	NEPatrit	3
29.3	4.3	8.0	42.6	10.0	27.0	15.6	70	DetRdWin	4
22.0	10.0	.0	32.0	8.0	20.9	11.5	67	BosBruin	4
20.0	6.0	.3	27.0	11.0	21.0	6.0	62	NYRanger	4
17.6	7.2	3.3	29.0	8.0	22.1	6.9	62	MontCana	4
19.4	3.5	2.0	25.3	7.2	18.2	7.1	61	ChiBlHaw	4
20.2	6.2	6.0	35.7	10.5	25.2	10.5	60	LAKings	4
15.9	5.0	3.1	24.1	6.5	19.4	4.7	55	CalFlame	4
16.0	2.6	1.3	21.6	6.0	18.4	3.2	55	EdmonOil	4
13.1	8.1	2.5	23.8	5.5	17.4	6.4	54	TorMapLv	4
11.5	7.0	4.1	24.2	6.0	17.4	6.8	53	NYIsland	4
13.8	7.9	.3	23.1	7.6	21.9	1.2	51	PhilFlyr	4
13.8	2.0	7.3	23.6	11.2	20.5	3.1	49	HartWhal	4
8.7	6.3	1.3	18.0	7.1	17.7	.3	45	QuebNord	4
12.3	5.1	4.5	22.1	4.7	22.8	−.8	45	VanCanuk	4
15.3	4.3	1.3	22.5	6.0	19.8	2.7	41	NJDevils	4
14.8	4.2	2.8	22.2	9.8	17.8	4.4	41	PittPeng	4
13.2	4.4	0.0	19.9	7.3	21.1	−1.2	40	WashCaps	4

(continued)

TABLE C.7 Continued

GateRec	MediaRev	StadRev	TotalRev	PlayerCt	OpExpens	OpIncome	ValueFran	Franchis	FranType
12.5	4.8	2.8	20.5	8.5	19.7	.8	39	BuffSabr	4
18.6	3.5	.0	22.7	10.0	21.9	.8	39	StLBlues	4
10.5	4.5	2.9	21.2	7.9	22.5	−1.3	34	MinnNStr	4
10.5	4.5	.5	16.6	10.0	18.1	−1.5	30	WinnJets	4

WISCONSIN EMPLOYMENT IN FOOD PRODUCTS (WiscEmpl.dat)

Employment in the food industry in Wisconsin varies greatly by season. Employment is high in the summer because of the summer harvest of fruits and vegetables. The number of people employed in food and kindred products in Wisconsin (units of 1000 employees) is shown in Table C.8 for a particular period of time.

TABLE C.8 Wisconsin Employment in Food and Kindred Products

Month	1961	1962	1963	1964	1965	1966	1967	1968	1969	1970	1971	1972	1973	1974	1975
January	56.3	55.3	53.3	53.4	52.9	53.4	52.8	52.6	53.6	53.5	52.1	52.3	53.3	54.8	55.8
February	55.7	54.9	52.8	53.0	52.6	52.7	52.8	52.1	53.4	53.0	51.5	51.5	53.1	54.2	54.7
March	55.8	54.9	53.0	53.0	52.8	53.0	53.2	52.4	53.5	53.2	51.5	51.7	53.5	54.6	55.0
April	56.3	54.9	53.4	53.2	53.0	52.9	55.3	51.6	53.3	52.5	52.4	51.5	53.5	54.3	55.6
May	57.2	54.6	54.3	54.2	53.6	55.4	55.8	52.7	53.9	53.4	53.3	52.2	53.9	54.8	56.4
June	59.1	57.7	58.2	58.0	56.1	58.7	58.2	57.3	52.7	56.5	55.5	57.1	57.1	58.1	60.6
July	71.5	68.2	67.4	67.5	66.1	67.9	65.3	65.1	61.0	65.3	64.2	63.6	64.7	68.1	70.8
August	72.2	70.6	71.0	70.1	69.8	70.0	67.9	71.5	69.9	70.7	69.6	68.8	69.4	73.3	76.4
September	72.7	71.0	69.8	68.2	69.3	68.7	68.3	69.9	70.4	66.9	69.3	68.9	70.3	75.5	74.8
October	61.5	60.0	59.4	56.6	61.2	59.3	61.7	61.9	59.4	58.2	58.5	60.1	62.6	66.4	62.2
November	57.4	56.0	55.6	54.9	57.5	56.4	56.4	57.3	56.3	55.3	55.3	55.6	57.9	60.5	
December	56.9	54.4	54.6	54.0	54.9	54.5	53.9	55.1	54.3	53.4	53.6	53.9	55.8	57.7	

TABLE C.9   Data Sets in Data Disk

(In order of appearance in text)	File Name
1. Diversified Service Companies	DivSerCo.dat
2. Largest Banks	LargBank.dat
3. Engine Inventory Levels	EngInven.dat
4. National 800-m Records for Women	Nat800m.dat
5. Paper Strengths	PaprStrg.dat
6. Sport Franchises	SportFrn.dat
7. Fuel Costs	FuelCost.dat
8. Bankruptcy Ratios	Bankrupt.dat
9. Death Claim Amounts	DeathClm.dat
10. Utility Kilowatt Capacities	UtilKilo.dat
11. Age of Presidents at Inauguration	AgePres.dat
12. Cities and Percent Employees with Graduate Degree	CitGrad.dat
13. Microwave Oven Radiation	MicroRad.dat
14. Cities and Percent Employees with BA and Higher Degree	CitiesBA.dat
15. Life Insurance Policy Characteristics	LifeIns.dat
16. Construction Costs	ConsCost.dat
17. Wisconsin Employment in Food and Kindred Products	WiscEmpl.dat
18. Profits and Employees in Publishing Firms	ProfitPu.dat
19. GPA and GMAT Scores for Business Students	GPAGMAT.dat
20. S&P 500 Rates of Return	S&P500RR.dat
21. Telephone Wire Splices	TeleWire.dat
22. Anscombe Regression Sets	Anscombe.dat
23. Market and Assessed Values for Homes	MarketAs.dat
24. State SAT Rank and Education Expenditures	StSATExp.dat
25. Northern States Power (Wisconsin) Peak Demand	NPowPeak.dat
26. Capital Expenditures for Farm Equipment	CapExpFa.dat
27. Health Insurance Claim Turnaround Times	HealthTu.dat
28. Computer Attitude and Anxiety Scores	CompAtti.dat
29. Calls per Shift to Mail Order Company	CallsMai.dat
30. Construction Company Bids and Earnings	ConstBid.dat
31. Credit Union Approval Recommendation Cycle Times	CreditUn.dat
32. Labor Costs	LaborCos.dat
33. Brand Loyalty Measurements	BrandLoy.dat
34. Times to Return Phone Calls for Health Facility	TimesRet.dat
35. Thickness Measurements	Thicknes.dat
36. Burn Times	BurnTime.dat
37. Banking Sample Survey Results	BankSamp.dat
38. Apartment Rents and Characteristics	ApartRen.dat
39. Market Shares for Toothpaste	Toothpas.dat
40. Canadian Dollar/U.S. Dollar Exchange Rates	CanUSExc.dat
41. U.S. and Japan Economic Indices	USJapInd.dat
42. U.S. and Mexico Economic Indices	USMexInd.dat
43. State SAT and Percent Students Taking SAT	StSAT%.dat
44. Newsprint Consumptions	Newsprin.dat
45. Best Selling Car Characteristics	BestCar.dat
46. Executive (CEO) Compensations	CEOComp.dat
47. Statistics Exam Scores	StatExam.dat
48. Monthly Sales for Company X	MonSaleX.dat
49. T-bill Interest Rates	TBillInt.dat
50. Country Health Care Measurements	CHealthC.dat

ANSWERS TO SELECTED EXERCISES

CHAPTER 1

1.1

Country	Proportion
United States	.270
Japan	.256
Germany	.090
Britain	.084
France	.066
Canada	.036
Spain	.032
Italy	.030
Switzerland	.030
Other	.106
Total	1.000

1.3 The proportion of banks from Japan is .64.

1.5 There are gaps in the asset pattern. The group of largest banks, greater than $450 billion, includes 6 banks. Japan dominates this group.

1.7 .294

1.15 Sample mean = 1
Sample variance = 7.5
Sample standard deviation $\cong$ 2.74

1.17 Sample mean = 3.525
Sample variance = .3358
Sample standard deviation $\cong$ .580

1.19 Mean for five plants = 808.8

1.27 Anecdotal data are given in (a) and (c), whereas (b) is based on a sample.

1.37 b. Sample mean = 4.192
Sample standard deviation = 1.819
c. Sample mean = 3.7
Standard deviation = .671

1.39 b. Mean = 5.857; Standard deviation = 2.931

1.41 a. Standard deviation = 8.794
b. In general, multiplying each number in a data set by a positive constant c will increase the standard deviation by a multiple of c.
c. Adding a constant, c, to each number in a data set does not change the standard deviation.

CHAPTER 2

2.1 a. Enumerative
b. Enumerative

c. Analytical
d. Analytical

2.3 a. Quantitative and discrete
b. Quantitative and discrete
c. Quantitative and continuous
d. Quantitative and discrete

2.7 a. Seven out of ten recent accounting graduates were satisfied with their jobs. This can be interpreted as seventy percent of new accounting graduates are satisfied with their jobs.
b. Sample mean = .70

2.19

	Sample mean	Variance	Standard deviation
a.	9	9.5	3.082
b.	25	10	3.162
c.	.8	2.415	1.554

2.21 First quartile: 190
Median: 240
Third quartile: 300

2.23 a. Sample median = 3.2
First quartile = 1.0
Third quartile = 7.6
b. Range = 26.9
Interquartile range = 6.6
c. 90th percentile = 14.9

2.25 a. Mean of Workers = 2.513
b. The 5% trimmed mean = 2.5262
c. Median of Workers = 2.505. The data are skewed to the right.

2.27 a. Mean of Claims = 16,653
5% trimmed mean = 12,094
b. First quartile = 4,375
Third quartile = 13,125
Interquartile range = 8,750

2.31 b. Median of Age = 55
First quartile = 51
Third quartile = 58

2.35 a. .7794
b. .9535
c. .4168
d. .0823

2.37 a. .4168
b. .0212

c. .7486
d. .8676

2.39 a. .4968
b. .2318
c. .2794
d. .2159

2.41 a. $z = -.8418$
b. $z = 1.1503$
c. $z = .97$
d. $z = -1.3457$

2.43 a. The area is .6368.
b. The 35th percentile is $-.3853$.
c. The area is .7257.
d. The 60th percentile is .2533.

2.45 a. Mean = 160;
Standard deviation = 60
b. Mean = -40;
Standard deviation = 4
c. Mean = 12.5;
Standard deviation = 10
d. Mean = -200;
Standard deviation = 80

2.47 a. Area = .8413
b. Area = .9522
c. Area = .2514
d. Area = .5
e. Area = .9087
f. Area = .4706

2.49 a. 204.0794
b. 199.0929
c. 190.9195
d. 202.9593

2.51 a. Probability$(> 25) = .0918$
b. Probability$(< 20) = .3707$
c. Probability(score between 19 and 27) = .7258

2.53 a. Analytical
b. Enumerative

2.55 a.

Frequency	Relative frequency	Density
8	.133	.013
17	.283	.028
14	.233	.023
10	.167	.017
11	.183	.009

2.57 a. Sample mean = 3; Median = 3
b. s^2 using the definitional formula = 6.67
c. s^2 using the computing formula = 6.67

2.61 a. These measurements are not normal.

b. These measurements are not strictly speaking normal. However, the transformed measurements are more nearly normal than the original data.

2.65 The first ten cities appear to have a larger percentage of workers with college degrees.

2.67 a. The minimum percentage is 13.3.
The maximum percentage is 37.0.
The first quartile is 18.8.
The third quartile is 25.0.
b. The interquartile range is 6.2.

2.69 a. These data are not normal and are skewed to the right.
b. There are outliers for basketball and football.
c. The mean is larger than the median for all sports. The data are skewed to the right.

CHAPTER 3

3.1 a. Positive correlation
b. Positive correlation
c. Positive correlation
d. May give a positive or negative correlation

3.3 b. The correlation coefficient is negative.
c. $r = -.931$

3.5 Correlation of x and y is .837.

3.7 b. Mean of x: 5.167
Mean of y: 5.800
Standard deviation of x: 3.271
Standard deviation of y: 3.792
Correlation of x and y: $r = -.791$

3.9 $r = -.957$

3.11 The sign of the correlation coefficient is negative. The key to prosperity is not to reduce the number of central bankers per capita to increase the GDP growth rate.

3.13 a. Correlation = $-.387$
b. Correlation = $-.561$
c. Correlation = .219. The correlation coefficient has changed from negative to positive. The addition of two outlying points can have a drastic effect on the correlation coefficient.

3.15

	r value	Diagram
a.	$r = -.7$	(c)
b.	$r = .9$	(d)
c.	$r = .5$	(a)
d.	$r = 0$	(b)

3.17 a. Correlation of x (GPA) and y (GMAT) is $-.158$.

b. There should be a strong positive correlation between GPA and GMAT for students accepted to the graduate program, but the negative correlation in the admitted students leaves doubt about the students who were not admitted.

c. Variables that could be plotted against GPA and/or GMAT scores include work experience in the business world, interpersonal skills profile score, and writing ability (essay) score.

3.19 a. The r_1 and r_{12} values for Example 3.6 are .77 and .88.

b. The lag 1 correlation coefficient is .773.

3.21 a. Slope = 7; y-intercept = 3
b. Slope = 2; y-intercept = -4
c. Slope = -1; y-intercept = 7

3.23 b. The slope is positive.
c. $y = -2.3 + 2.1x$
d. When $x = 4$, $y = 6.1$.

3.25 a. Residuals: .2, .1, -1.0, .9, $-.2$
b. Standard deviation of the residuals: .689

3.27 a. Slope = -3; y-intercept = 162
b. Slope = -3

3.29 a. $y = .683 + .992x$
b. Estimated costs are better predictors of actual costs for smaller projects.

3.31 a. **The regression equation is Actual = 0.948 Estimate**
b. The least squares line from Ex. 3.29a is the best fit.
c. Sum of residuals: 7.7518

3.33 a. The risk-free rate = 4.5%
b. If the systematic risk = .70, the required rate of return is $y = .1038$.

3.35 a. Least squares equation:
OpExBsbl = 18.9 + 1.30 PlCtBsbl
b. For a baseball team with a player cost of 15 million dollars, operating expense = 38.407.
c. Residual standard deviation: $s = 5.273$. The residuals are generally within a horizontal band centered at zero. This is important since any deviation from a horizontal band would indicate a need for adjusting the original model to accommodate the displayed pattern.
d. The empirical rule states that about 68% and 95% of the data will be within one and two standard deviations of zero, respectively. The

actual numbers are 77% and 96%. There are more observations within one standard deviation of zero than predicted by the empirical rule.

3.37 a. and b. Least squares line: $y = 3 + .5x$. The first data set seems to be best represented by the least squares line for the range of x values considered.

c. The first data set still appears to be best represented by the least squares line just as it was in part b. The residual plots for the last three data sets indicate an inadequate model (second data set) or potential outliers or unrepresentative observations.

d. The influential observation in data set 4 is the point (19, 12.50) since it is the only point without 8 as the first coordinate. It determines the slope of the fitted line.

3.39 a. **The regression equation is Yt = 1.27 - 0.217 Yt-1**
b. The lag 1 autocorrelation coefficient is .028. There is no obvious pattern in the residuals that appears over time. The residuals appear to vary randomly.
c. and d.

Month	Actual rate of return	Forecast rates of return	
		Least squares equation	Random walk model
Jan. 91	4.07	.73835	2.45
Mar. 91	2.20	$-.14267$	6.51
Jun. 91	-4.91	.44757	3.79
Sep. 91	-1.93	.84685	1.95

Month	Error in forecast rate of return	
	Least squares equation	Random walk model
Jan. 91	3.33165	1.6200
Mar. 91	2.34267	-4.3100
Jun. 91	-5.35757	-8.7000
Sep. 91	-2.77685	-3.8800

The least squares equation gives the slightly better forecast.

3.41 c. The largest percentage of criminal types discharged is burglary, followed by drugs. The largest percentage received is other, followed by burglary.

3.43 a. and b.

Problem	Volume		
	Low	**High**	**Total**
No	180	120	300
	(45%)	(30%)	(75%)
Yes	60	40	100
	(15%)	(10%)	(25%)
Total	240	160	400
	(60%)	(40%)	(100%)

c. Customers who experience problems do proportionately as much low (high) volume business as those who are not experiencing problems. That is, there appears to be no relationship between problems and volume.

3.45 Hospital I had $88/2200 = 4\%$ of surgery patients who died. Hospital II had $21/700 = 3\%$ of surgery patients who died. From this information, Hospital II is preferred as a location for surgery.

3.47 a. There does not appear to be any association between promotional expenditure and sales. Marginal totals cannot change since there still must be half of the expenditures and sales below the median and half above the median by the definition of median.

b.

Price	Sales		
	Below median	**Above median**	**Total**
Below median	30	70	100
Above median	60	40	100
Total	90	110	200

The largest group of sales/price combination is for the sales above the median and price below the median, i.e., low price and high promotions create high sales.

c.

Price	Sales		
	Below median	**Above median**	**Total**
Below median	45	55	100
Above median	65	35	100
Total	110	90	200

The largest group is for high price and low sales, followed by low price and high sales. Therefore, without as much promotion, low sales are associated with high price and high sales are associated with low price.

d. Promotion increases sales from 55 to 70 when the price is low. The manager should increase promotion and lower price to increase sales.

3.49 There are higher inventory levels in July through November and lower levels in December through April.

3.51 a. Correlation coefficient: $r = .993$
b. The correlation coefficient remains $r = .993$.
c. The correlation changes to $-.993$.

3.53 The correlation coefficient is $r = -.797$.

3.55 b. The sign of the correlation coefficient and the slope of the least squares lines are both positive.
c. Least squares line: $y = 3 + 2x$
d. When $x = 1.5$, $y = 6$.

3.57 a. The residuals are 2, -1, -3, 1, and 1.
b. Standard deviation of the residuals: $s = 2$

3.59

	Sales		
	<50 billion	**50 billion or more**	**Total**
Japan	7	9	16
	(28%)	(36%)	(64%)
U.S.	3	1	4
	(12%)	(4%)	(16%)
Other	5	0	5
	(20%)	(0%)	(20%)
Total	15	10	25
	(60%)	(40%)	(100%)

The largest percentage of sales remains that of Japan (50 billion or more). The smallest now is Other (50 billion or more).

3.61 b. The correlation coefficient is $-.345$.

3.63 The lurking variable is the type of individuals who are likely to drive Corvettes, Camaros, Chargers, and Mustangs, or the attitude of those who drive this list of cars. Young drivers are more likely to drive these cars and more likely to have fatal accidents.

3.65 a. The regression equation is the same as that in Example 3.9.
b. $b = .701$

3.67 a.

Lag	Correlation	Lag	Correlation
1	.83	8	.59
2	.73	9	.52
3	.66	10	.53
4	.65	11	.59
5	.70	12	.61
6	.73		
7	.66		

There is a strong annual seasonal pattern since the autocorrelation coefficients for lags 1–12 are large. The autocorrelation is largest for lag 1, which means that the association between the peak demands in adjacent months is stronger than for the peak demands separated by more than one month.

b. Least squares equation: $y = 3.682 + 1.042x$

c. There appears to be some correlation among the residuals. The model could be improved by including the peak demand from one or two months ago in predicting the next month's demand.

d. Next May's peak demand is predicted to be $y = 524.607$.

3.69 The fitted line does appear to adequately represent the data since the residuals are random and within a horizontal band about zero.

CHAPTER 4

4.1 I agree with the statement. Data collected directly by one person are primary data to that person. When the data are used by another person, they become secondary data to the second person.

4.5 Factors that influence the choice of a method for collecting data include objectives of the study, cost, structure of the population, type of information sought, administrative facilities, and personnel available to carry out the plan.

4.7 Additional questions on the GMAT exam could be asked to determine the income level of the student's family, work experience, and other experiences that could affect performance on the exam.

4.9 a. Nonprobability sample
 b. Nonprobability sample
 c. Probability sample

4.11 a. Nonprobability sample
 b. Nonprobability sample
 c. Systematic random sample

4.21 c. Means: Small, 27.702; Medium, 36.693; Large, 58.904. The population mean is 37.092.

4.23 a. The statement can compare the mean age of the users to the mean age of nonusers.
 b. The image is a qualitative description, not related to a numerical measurement, so the company cannot legitimately make a statement involving the phrase "twice as positive."

4.37 a. The explanatory variable is whether the area was wired for cable. The response variable is the number of Duran Duran albums purchased.
 b. The explanatory variable is the number of calls per customer. The response variable is sales.
 c. The explanatory variable is the payment terms. The response variable is the "days until payment" for each distributor.

4.43

Age group	Excellent or good	Other	% Exc. or good
Under 18	0	1	0.00%
18–21	23	8	74.19%
22–30	129	31	80.63%
31–40	114	28	80.28%
41–50	56	8	87.50%
51 plus	224	15	93.72%
No reply	39	4	90.70%

Therefore these older customers tend to have a more favorable image of the bank's services relative to those customers in other age groups.

CHAPTER 5

5.1 a. ii
 b. iv
 c. vi
 d. vi
 e. v
 f. iii
 g. i

5.3 a. ii
 b. iii
 c. i

5.5 a. $\{0, 1\}$
 b. $\{\text{number} < 345\}$
 c. $\{90 < \text{number} < 425.4\}$

5.7 a. 2 sales—stop (e_1)
 1 sale—contact one more customer (e_2)
 0 sales—contact two more customers (e_3)
 Sample space $= \{e_1, e_2, e_3\}$
 b. $A = \{e_1\}; B = \{e_3\}$

5.9 $P(e_1) = P(e_2) = P(e_3) = .333$

5.11 a. $P(e_1) = .125$; $P(e_2) = .250$; $P(e_3) = .500$; $P(e_4) = .125$
b. $P(A) = .625$

5.13 a. $P(\text{Nancy will be promoted}) = .667$
b. $P(\text{delay funding}) = .714$

5.15 b. The elementary outcomes are HHH, HHT, HTH, HTT, THH, THT, TTH, and TTT. Each elementary outcome occurs with the probability $\frac{1}{8}$.
c. $P(\text{one head}) = \frac{3}{8}$

5.17 a. $S = \{1, 1, 1, 2, 2, 3, 3, 3, \}$; $P(1) = \frac{3}{8}$; $P(2) = \frac{1}{4}$; $P(3) = \frac{3}{8}$
b. $P(\text{odd number ticket}) = \frac{3}{4}$

5.19 a. $P(\text{only you pay}) = \frac{1}{4}$
b. $P(\text{all three pay}) = \frac{1}{4}$

5.21 a. $P(\text{IBM}) = .073$
b. $P(\text{Japanese company}) = .519$

5.23 a. $P(\text{managerial/professional}) = .294$
b. $P(\text{service}) = .119$

5.25 a. The Dow Jones average increases over a long term, so a long-run relative frequency interpretation of probability does not apply in this situation.
b. Collecting the data over a slack period is not a good predictor for the entire year's tax returns.
c. This sample is not representative of the entire population since the mechanics have checked and repaired the emission systems on this group of cars on a regular basis.

5.27 b. (i) $A \cap B = \{e_2, e_5\}$
(ii) $\overline{B} = \{e_3, e_4, e_6, e_7\}$
(iii) $A \cap \overline{B} = \{e_4, e_7\}$
(iv) $A \cup B = \{e_1, e_2, e_4, e_5, e_7\}$

5.29 a. C does not occur: $\overline{C} = \{e_1, e_2, e_3, e_4, e_5, e_7\}$; $P(\overline{C}) = .7$
b. Both A and B occur: $A \cap B = \{e_2, e_6, e_7\}$; $P(A \cap B) = .38$
c. A occurs and B does not occur: $A \cap \overline{B} = \{e_1, e_5\}$; $P(A \cap \overline{B}) = .31$
d. Neither A nor C occurs: $\overline{A} \cap \overline{C} = \{e_3, e_4\}$; $P(\overline{A} \cap \overline{C}) = .16$

5.31 b. $A \cup C = \{e_1, e_2, e_3, e_4\}$; $A \cap B = \{e_3\}$

5.33 a. $P(\text{at least one fund}) = .8$
b. $P(\text{neither of the two funds}) = .2$

5.35 a. $P(A) = .25$; $P(B) = .32$; $P(A \cap B) = .17$
b. $P(A \cup B) = .4$
c. $P(A \cup B) = .4$
d. $P(\overline{B}) = .68$

5.37 a. $P(H \cap R) = P(H) + P(R) - P(H \cup R) = 1.2$. This is impossible since a probability cannot be greater than 1.
b. These probabilities sum to 1.03, which is impossible since the intersection of the events is empty.

5.39 a.

	B	$\overline{B}$	Total
A	.20	.32	.52
$\overline{A}$	.16	.32	.48
	.36	.64	1.00

b. $P(A \cap \overline{B}) = .32$; $P(\overline{A} \cap B) = .16$; $P(\overline{A} \cap \overline{B}) = .32$

5.41 a.

	B	$\overline{B}$	Total
A	.25	.12	.37
$\overline{A}$	.15	.48	.63
Total	.40	.60	1.0

b. $P(A \cap \overline{B}) = .12$
c. $P(A \cup B) = .52$
d. $P(A \cap \overline{B}) + P(\overline{A} \cap B) = .27$

5.43 A and B cannot be incompatible since they have some elementary events in common.

5.45 Let A = violation of sanitary standards; B = violation of security standards.

	B	$\overline{B}$	Total
A	5	1	6
$\overline{A}$	3	10	13
Total	8	11	19

(Divide all numbers by 19 to get probabilities.) $P(\overline{A} \cap \overline{B}) = .526$

5.47 a. i. $P(A) = .239$
ii. $P(C) = .169$
iii. $P(B \cap C) = .086$
iv. $P(A \cap B \cap C) = .032$
b. i. $\overline{A} \cap \overline{B}$ means the set of events that are not in A and are also not in B; $P(\overline{A} \cap \overline{B}) = .644$
ii. $\overline{A} \cup \overline{C}$ means the set of events that are not in A or not in C; $P(\overline{A} \cup \overline{C}) = .831$
iii. $\overline{A} \cap \overline{B} \cap \overline{C}$ means the set of events that are at the same time not in A, not in B, and not in C; $P(\overline{A} \cap \overline{B} \cap \overline{C}) = .408$

5.49 a. $P(B \mid A) = .582$
b. $P(\overline{B} \mid A) = .529$
c. $P(B \mid \overline{A}) = .719$

5.51 $P(B \mid A) = .010$;
These events are not independent events since $P(B \mid A)$ is not equal to $P(B)$.

5.53
a. $P(\overline{A}) = .5$
b. $P(A \cap B) = .2$
c. $P(A \cup B) = .55$

5.55

	B	**$\overline{B}$**	**Total**
A	.2	.3	.5
$\overline{A}$	.3	.2	.5
Total	.5	.5	1

a. A and B are not independent since $P(A \mid B) = .4$, which is not equal to $P(A) = .5$.
b. A and B are not incompatible since they have elementary events in common.

5.57
a. $P(\text{precision} \mid \text{female}) = .022$; The condition is that the worker is a female.
b.   i. $P(A \mid B) = .022$
     ii. $P(\overline{A} \mid B) = .978$
     iii. $P(C \mid A) = 0$
c. A and B are not independent since $P(A \mid B)$ is not equal to $P(A)$, which is equal to .452.

5.59 D represents delinquent; G represents good, the subscript represents first or second.
a. $P(D_1) = .267$
b. $P(D_1 \cap G_2) = .210$
c. $P(D_1 \cap D_2) = .057$
d. $P(D_2) = .267$
e. $P(D_1 \cap G_2) + P(G_1 \cap D_2) = .420$

5.61
a. $P(\text{batch passed if 5\% of the bills are irregular}) = .815$
b. $P(\text{batch passed if 20\% of the bills are irregular}) = .410$

5.63
a. $S = \{GG, GB, GD, BG, BB, BD, DG, DB, DD\}$; $P(GG) = .5625$; $P(GB) = P(BG) = .1125$; $P(GD) = P(DG) = .075$; $P(BB) = .0225$; $P(BD) = P(DB) = .015$; $P(DD) = .010$
b. $P(GB) + P(BG) + P(BB) + P(BD) + P(DB) = .2775$
c. $P(\text{neither is good}) = .0625$

5.65 $P(\text{late}) = .040$

5.67 $P(\text{parcel} \mid \text{late}) = .300$

5.69
a. $S = \{(a, b), (a, c), (a, d), (a, e), (b, c), (b, d), (b, e), (c, d), (c, e), (d, e)\}$
b. $S = \{(a, b, c), (a, b, d), (a, b, e), (a, c, d), (a, c, e), (a, d, e), (b, c, d), (b, c, e), (b, d, e), (c, d, e)\}$

5.71 $\binom{12}{4} = 495$

5.73 $P(\text{0 females}) = .041$
It is very unlikely to have no females.

5.75
a. $P(G_1 G_2 G_3) = .446 = P(A)$
b. $P(\text{2 defectives}) = .103 = P(B)$

5.77
a. This is not a random sample since only a portion of students who enjoy throwing flying disks on the mall will be chosen.
b. This is not a random sample since only a portion of students who study at the library on Friday night can be chosen.
c. This is again not a random sample since all students are not in your statistics course.

5.79 $\binom{30}{5} = 142,506$

5.83
a. $S = \{(1 \text{ win}, 0 \text{ losses}, 0 \text{ ties}), (0 \text{ wins}, 1 \text{ loss}, 0 \text{ ties}), (0 \text{ wins}, 0 \text{ losses}, 1 \text{ tie})\}$
b. $S = \{1, 2, 3, 4, 5, 6, 7, 8, 9, 10, 11, 12, 13, 14, 15, 16, 17, 18, 19, 20\}$
c. $S = \{\text{the set of all numbers between 1 and 1000 persons, inclusive}\}$
d. $S = \{\text{the interval of measurements possible for cubic feet of gas in an area}\}$

5.85
a. Don't lose $= \{(1 \text{ win}, 0 \text{ losses}, 0 \text{ ties}), (0 \text{ wins}, 0 \text{ losses}, 1 \text{ tie})\}$
b. At least half are excellent $= \{10, 11, 12, 13, 14, 15, 16, 17, 18, 19, 20\}$

5.87
a. Two elementary outcomes yield three sets. Six elementary outcomes yield four sets.
b. $P(\text{four sets}) = .75$

5.89
a. $S = \{(156), (165), (516), (561), (615), (651)\}$
b. $P(\text{larger than 400}) = .667$
c. $P(\text{even}) = .333$

5.91
a. $P(\text{Japan}) = .250$
b. $P(\text{not Japan}) = .750$
c. $P(\text{Japan or Hong Kong}) = .321$
d. $P(\text{Hong Kong} \mid \text{not Japan}) = .094$

5.93
a. $P(\text{computer}) = .699$
b. $P(\text{not computer}) = .301$
c. $P(\text{General Motors} \mid \text{not computer}) = .229$

5.95
a. $P(A \cup B) = .668$
b. $P(\overline{A} \cup \overline{B}) = .674$
c. $P(A \mid B) = .674$
d. $P(A)$ is not equal to $P(A \mid B)$, so these events are not independent.

5.97 $P(\text{claim} \mid \text{high performance}) = .208$; $P(\text{claim}) = .169$. Since $P(\text{claim})$ is not equal to $P(\text{claim} \mid \text{high performance})$, these are not independent events.

5.99
a. $P(C \mid M) = .323$; $P(C \mid F) = .460$
b. $P(F \cap C) = .208$

c.

	Use computer	Don't use computer	Total
Male	.177	.371	.548
Female	.208	.244	.452
Total	.385	.615	1.000

5.101 $\binom{16}{2} = 120$

5.103 $P(2 \text{ good, then 2 illegal}) = .066$

5.105
a. $P(2 \text{ out of 3 have same birthday}) = .005$
b. $P(\text{no common birthday for 3}) = .992$;
For $N - 1$: $P(\text{no common birthday for } N-1) = (365 \cdot 364 \cdot \cdots \cdot (365 - N + 2)) \div (365)^{N-1}$
For N: $P(\text{no common birthday for } N) = (365 \cdot 364 \cdot \cdots \cdot (364 - N + 1))/(365)^N$
c. $P(\text{no common birthday for 5}) = .973$
$P(\text{no common birthday for 9}) = .905$
$P(\text{no common birthday for 18}) = .653$
$P(\text{no common birthday for 22}) = .524$
$P(\text{no common birthday for 23}) = .493$

CHAPTER 6

6.1
a. Discrete
b. Continuous
c. Discrete
d. Continuous
e. Discrete
f. Discrete

6.3
a.

Elementary outcomes	x = Difference
2, 4	2
2, 6	4
2, 7	5
2, 8	6
4, 6	2
4, 7	3
4, 8	4
6, 7	1
6, 8	2
7, 8	1

b.

x	$P(x)$
1	.2
2	.3
3	.1
4	.2
5	.1
6	.1

6.5
a. All ratings that A can receive: (1,1,1,1), (1,1,1,2), (1,1,2,1), (1,1,2,2), (1,2,1,1), (1,2,1,2), (1,2,2,1), (1,2,2,2), (2,1,1,1), (2,1,1,2), (2,1,2,1), (2,1,2,2), (2,2,1,1), (2,2,1,2), (2,2,2,1), (2,2,2,2)
b. All distinct values of X: 4, 5, 6, 7, 8

6.7
a. $S = \{\text{CCC, CCB, CBB, CBC, BCC, BCB, BBC, BBB}\}$
b. Number of switches: CCC (0), CCB (1), CBB (1), CBC (2), BCC (1), BCB (2), BBC (1), BBB (0)

6.9

x	$f(x)$
0	.61
2	.23
4	.16

6.11
a. $P(X \leq 3) = .50$
b. $P(X \geq 5) = .25$
c. $P(2 \leq X \leq 5) = .75$

6.13
a.

x	$f(x)$
3	.1
4	.2
5	.3
6	.4

This is a legitimate probability distribution since the probabilities sum to 1.

b.

x	$f(x)$
1	−.5
2	0
3	.5
4	1.0

This is not a legitimate probability distribution since there cannot be a negative number as a probability.

c.

x	$f(x)$
−2	0
−1	.1
0	.2
1	.3
2	.4

This is a legitimate probability distribution.

d.

x	$f(x)$
2	.75
3	.375
4	.1875
5	.09375

This is not a legitimate probability distribution since the probabilities do not sum to 1.

6.15

x = # of switches	f(x)
0	.25
1	.50
2	.25

6.17

x	f(x)
0	.2
1	.4
4	.4

6.19 a. X = 0, 1, 2, or 3 questions can be answered correctly.

b.

x	f(x)
0	.222
1	.444
2	.278
3	.056

c. $P(X \geq 1) = .778$

6.21

x	f(x)
1	.25
2	.28
3	.30
4	.17

6.23 a.

x	f(x)
0	.35
1	.42
2	.18
3	.05

b. $P(X \geq 2) = .23$

6.25 a. $P(X \leq 3) = .92$
b. $P(X \geq 2) = .63$
c. $P(1 \leq X \leq 3) = .80$

6.27 a. $P(X \geq 3) = .45$
b. $P(X < 5) = .95$
c. The capacity must increase to 4 customers.

6.29 b. $E(X) = 1; \sigma^2 = 1; \sigma = 1$

6.31 $E(X) = \$12,125.00$

6.33 $E(X) = 1.2; \sigma = .917$

6.35 a. $P(\text{win A and win B}) = .325$
$P(\text{win A and lose B}) = .175$
$P(\text{lose A and win B}) = .325$
$P(\text{lose A and lose B}) = .175$

b.

Event	x	f(x)
win A, win B	195,000	.325
win A, lose B	75,000	.175
lose A, win B	120,000	.325
lose A, lose B	0	.175
Total		1.000

c.

Event	x	f(x)	xf(x)
win A, win B	193,000	.325	62725
win A, lose B	73,000	.175	12775
lose A, win B	118,000	.325	38350
lose A, lose B	−2000	.175	−350
Total		1.000	113,500

Expected net profit = \$113,500

6.37 a. Expected value = 1.420
b. Standard deviation of X: 1.351

6.39 a.

x	f(x)	xf(x)	x²f(x)
0	.04762	.0000	.0000
1	.35714	.3571	.3571
2	.47619	.9524	1.9048
3	.11905	.3572	1.0714
Total	1.00000	1.667	3.3333

b. Mean = 1.667;
Standard deviation = .745

6.41 Mean = 2.400
Variance = 1.540
Standard deviation = 1.241

6.43 a. Mean of x: 1.200;
Standard deviation of x: .557
b. Mean = 1.040;
Standard deviation = .529

6.45 a.

y	f(y)	yf(y)
\$ 0	.4096	\$ 0
\$2000	.4096	\$ 819.20
\$4000	.1536	\$ 614.40
\$6000	.0256	\$ 153.60
\$8000	.0016	\$ 12.80
Total	1.00	\$1600.00

b. Expected value of Y: 1600

6.47 a. These are not Bernoulli trials.
b. These are not Bernoulli trials.
c. These are Bernoulli trials.
d. These are not Bernoulli trials.

6.49 a. These are Bernoulli trials; $p = .4$.
        b. These are not Bernoulli trials since the probability changes with each trial.
        c. These are not Bernoulli trials since the probability changes with each trial.

6.51 a. These are not Bernoulli trials since there is a lack of independence between trials for various customers.
        b. These are Bernoulli trials since the trials are independent.

6.53 a. $P(X = 0) = .316$
        b. P(second four are successes | first four are failures) = P(four successes) = $.0039$
        c. $P(FFFS) = .105$

6.55 a. $S = \{CC, CNC, CNN, NCN, NCC, NNCC, NNCN,$ $NNNC, NNNN\}$
        b. $P(CC) = .111$
            $P(CNC) = .074$
            $P(CNN) = .148$
            $P(NCN) = .148$
            $P(NCC) = .074$
            $P(NNCC) = .049$
            $P(NNCN) = .099$
            $P(NNNC) = .099$
            $P(NNNN) = .198$
        c.

x	$f(x)$
0	.1976
1	.4938
2	.3087

6.57 a. This is a binomial distribution with $n = 9$; $p = \frac{1}{6}$.
        b. This is not a binomial distribution.
        c. This is a binomial distribution with $n = 3$; $p = .6$.
        d. This is not a binomial distribution.

6.59 a. $P(X = 2) = .296$
        b. $P(X = 3) = .132$
        c. $P(X = 2) = .033$

6.61 a. $P(X \le 2) = .765$
        b. $P(X \ge 2) = .572$
        c. $P(X = 2 \text{ or } 4) = .385$

6.63 a. $P(X = 3) = .097$
        b. $P(X = 1) = .402$

6.65 a. $P(X = 3) = .027$
        b. $P(X = 3) = .186$

6.67 a. $P(X = 0) = .012$
        b. $P(X \ge 7) = .087$
        c. Mean = 4; Standard deviation = 1.789

6.69 a. Mean = 2.5; Standard deviation = 1.369

        b. Mean = 12.308; Standard deviation = 2.919
        c. Mean = 32.5; Standard deviation = 2.469

6.71 a.

x	$f(x)$
0	.064
1	.288
2	.432
3	.216

        b. Mean = 1.8; Standard deviation = .849
        c. Mean = 1.8; Standard deviation = .849

6.73 a. $P(X = 0) = .05$
        b. $P(X = 1) = .15$

6.75 a. Mean = 28; Standard deviation = 4.266
        b. $p = .333$; $n = 162$

6.77 Under 25: $P(X \ge 2) = .024$;
        Over 25: $P(X \ge 2) = .014$.
        Older drivers are likely to have fewer claims per policy.

6.79 a. Possible values of X: $-3, -1, 1, 3$
        b.

X	Elementary outcomes
-3	TTT
-1	HTT, THT, TTH
1	HHT, HTH, THH
3	HHH

6.81

W = # defective	$f(x)$
0	.605
1	.350
2	.045

6.83 a. Mean = 1
        b. Variance = .6; Standard deviation = .775

6.85 a. Within this interval are: 3, 4 and 5.
            $P(\mu - \sigma \le X \le \mu + \sigma) = .8$
        b. Within this interval are 2, 3, 4, 5, 6.
            $P(\mu - 2\sigma \le X \le \mu + 2\sigma) = 1$

6.87 a. Expected gain = \$4500
        b. Expected net gain = \$2000

6.89 a.

x	$f(x)$
4000	.0002
1000	.0006
100	.0190
5	.0850
0	.8952

        b. Mean = 3.725
        c. P(lose money) = .980

6.91 a. $f(4) = .316$
        b. $P(X \ge 2) = .5625$

c. $E(X) = 2.051$

d. $sd(X) = 1.599$

6.93   a. $P(X = 0) = .9$

b. $P(X \geq 2) = .05$

c. $P(1 \leq X \leq 2) = .08$

6.95   This is not a Bernoulli trial since the trials are not independent, i.e., the probability of success changes since there is no replacement.

6.99 $P(\text{first basket on third possession}) = .144$

6.101 $P(12 \text{ or fewer agree}) = .032$. The claim is not very plausible since it is not very likely that 12 or fewer students agree.

6.103   a.

x	$f(x)$
0	.078
1	.259
2	.346
3	.230
4	.077
5	.010

c.   Expected value = 2;
Variance = 1.200;
Standard deviation = 1.095

d. $E(X) = 2$; $var(X) = 1.2$

6.105   a.

p	P(three or fewer successes)
.1	.974
.2	.795
.3	.493
.4	.225
.5	.073

b.

p	P(three or fewer successes)
.1	.902
.2	.501
.3	.165
.4	.033
.5	.004

6.107   Expected value = 3.2;
Standard deviation = 1.6

CHAPTER 7

7.1   a.   This is a probability density function.

b.   This is not a probability density function.

c.   This is a probability density function.

d.   This is not a probability density function.

7.3   The interval $(1.5 < X < 2)$ is assigned a higher probability than $(0 < X < .5)$ since the area under the curve is larger over $(1.5 < X < 2)$.

7.5   First quartile = 1;
Median = Second quartile = 1.414;
Third quartile = 1.732

7.7   a.   The median is later than 1:20 P.M.

b.   The median cannot be determined.

7.9   a. $Z = (X - 15)/4$

b. $Z = (X + 9)/7$

c. $Z = (X - 151)/5$

7.11   a. $Z = (X - 70)/2.8$

b. $Z = (X - 65)/2.4$

c. $Z = -1.429$

d. $Z = .417$

7.13 $P(62.5 < Z < 67.7) = .940$

7.15   a. $P(X > .75) = .1056$

b. $P(\text{two rates of return are both larger than } .6\%) = .095$

c.   .1056

7.17   a. $P(\text{overstated weight}) = .5$

b. $P(|X| > 2.8) = .0672$

c. $x = 1.31$

7.19   a. $P(X < 25) = .040$

b. $P(X < 35) = .773$

7.21   a. $P(X = 15) = .091$;
$P(13 \leq X \leq 19) = .790$;
$P(13 < X < 19) = .615$

b. $P(X = 15) = .097$;
$P(13 \leq X \leq 19) = .717$;
$P(13 < X < 19) = .524$

7.23   a. $P(X = 140) = .017$

b. $P(X \leq 160) = .948$

c. $P(137 \leq X \leq 162) = .958$

7.25   a.   Yes

b.   No

c.   No

d.   No

e.   Yes

7.27 $P(X \geq 110) = .079$

7.29 $P(X > 20) = .166$

7.31 $x_0 = 3158$

7.33 $P(X \geq 41) = .113$

7.37   The plot is not very straight, but the sample size is small, so it is difficult to argue against normality.

7.39   The graph is nearly straight, therefore the data are nearly normal.

7.43   The normal scores plot is fairly straight; therefore the data are normal.

7.45   The nonnormality of the full data set is related to the four largest numbers. Without these numbers, the normal scores plot is closer to a straight line, indicating that these data are closer to normal.

7.47 $P(X > 14^2) = .536$

7.49 a. The 11 persons who served on the Supreme Court are the population.
b. The fact that 185 out of 1000 were out of work is a statistic.
c. The 46 out of 100 who read mail advertisements is a statistic.

7.51 a.

Sample	Sample mean	Sample variance
2, 2	2	0
2, 4	3	2
2, 6	4	8
4, 2	3	2
4, 4	4	0
4, 6	5	2
6, 2	4	8
6, 4	5	2
6, 6	6	0

b.

Value of $\overline{X}$	Probability
2	$\frac{1}{9}$
3	$\frac{2}{9}$
4	$\frac{1}{3}$
5	$\frac{2}{9}$
6	$\frac{1}{9}$

c.

Value of s^2	Probability
0	$\frac{1}{3}$
2	$\frac{4}{9}$
8	$\frac{2}{9}$

7.53 To get a random sample, the times should be chosen randomly instead of at regular time periods.

7.55 a. $E(\overline{X}) = 99$; $\text{sd}(\overline{X}) = 3.5$
b. $E(\overline{X}) = 99$; $\text{sd}(\overline{X}) = 1.4$

7.57 a. $\text{sd}(\overline{X}) = 2$
b. $\text{sd}(\overline{X}) = 1$
c. $\text{sd}(\overline{X}) = .5$

7.59 $E(\overline{X}) = 3 = \mu$; $\text{sd}(\overline{X}) = 1.155$

7.61 a. $E(\overline{X}) = 27$
b. $\text{sd}(\overline{X}) = 1.5$
c. The distribution of $\overline{X}$ is approximately normal.

7.63 $\text{sd}(\overline{X}) = 9.839$; $P(\overline{X} > 140) = .271$

7.65 a. $\mu = 16.084$
b. In the long run, 2% of the bags will have less than 16 ounces of chips in them.

7.67 a. Since the sample size is large, the Central Limit Theorem states that the population distribution of the sample mean is approximately normal.
b. $P(\overline{X} > 31,500) = .159$

7.69 $P(\overline{X} < 5) = .0418$

7.71 $P(34.1 < \overline{X} < 35.2) = .058$

7.73 c. The sampling distribution of the sample mean has a variance smaller than that of the sample median.

7.75 a. Median $= .5$
b. First quartile $= .25$; Third quartile $= .75$

7.77 a. $P(Z < 1.31) = .905$
b. $P(Z > 1.205) = .114$
c. $P(.67 < Z < 1.98) = .228$
d. $P(-1.32 < Z < 1.055) = .761$

7.79 a. $P(X < 107) = .809$
b. $P(X < 97) = .354$
c. $P(X > 110) = .106$
d. $P(X > 90) = .894$
e. $P(95 < X < 106) = .507$
f. $P(103 < X < 114) = .312$
g. $P(88 < X < 100) = .433$
h. $P(60 < X < 108) = .841$

7.81 $P(X \leq 98) = .401$

7.83 $P(X \geq 730) = .023$

7.85 a. i. $P(X \leq 5) = .029$
ii. $P(11 \leq X \leq 17) = .917$
iii. $P(X \geq 11) = .105$
b. i. $P(X \leq 5) = .021$
ii. $P(11 \leq X \leq 17) = .856$
iii. $P(X \geq 11) = .067$

7.87 a. $P(\overline{X} \leq 104) = .040$

7.89 a. $P(X > 370) = 1.00$
b. $P(X < 350) = 0$

7.91 a.

Samples	Sample range	Samples	Sample range
2, 2	0	6, 2	4
2, 4	2	6, 4	2
2, 6	4	6, 6	0
2, 8	6	6, 8	2
4, 2	2	8, 2	6
4, 4	0	8, 4	4
4, 6	2	8, 6	2
4, 8	4	8, 8	0

b.

Possible range	Probability of sampling distribution of R
0	$\frac{1}{4}$
2	$\frac{3}{8}$
4	$\frac{1}{4}$
6	$\frac{1}{8}$

7.93   a.   16
      b.   64
      c.   44.444

7.95   a. $P(.28 < X < .34) = .290$
      b. $P(.28 < \overline{X} < .34) = .533$

7.97   a. $E(\overline{X}) = 94$; $\text{Var}(\overline{X}) = 1.111$
      b.   The distribution of $\overline{X}$ is approximately normal by the Central Limit Theorem.

7.99   a. $P(54 < \overline{X} < 56) = .632$
      b. $P(-57.170 < \overline{X} < 57.170) = .95$

7.101 $P(1.8 < \overline{X} < 2.25) = .989$

7.105   The normal scores plot is nearly a straight line, so the data are nearly normal.

7.107   Dropping the four largest observations changes the distribution of turnaround times a little.

CHAPTER 8

8.1

	Standard error of $\overline{X}$	$100(1 - \alpha)\%$ error margin
a.	1.512	2.963
b.	.532	.931
c.	4.455	11.471

8.3

	Point estimate of μ	Estimated standard error
a.	22.147	2.209
b.	15.231	1.414
c.	15.397	1.704

8.5   Population mean weekly earnings = 624; Error margin = 12.196

8.7   a. $n = 118$
      b. $n = 4673$
      c. $n = 793$

8.9 $n = 520$

8.11   a.   Estimate of the mean number of copies per day = 382.7; Error margin = 13.471
      b.   Estimate of the mean number of copies per 5 days = 1913.5; Error margin = 6.024
      c.   The error margin is smaller in part b. This result is due to that fact that the larger sample size in part b creates smaller variance.

8.13   s.e.$(\overline{X}) = \sigma/\sqrt{n}$ indicates that
$P(-1 < (\overline{X} - \mu)/(\sigma/\sqrt{n}) < 1)$;
$P(-1 < Z < 1) = .6826$

8.15 $(36.97, 39.83)$

8.17   360 of the intervals will cover the true mean.

8.19   347 of the intervals will cover the true mean.

8.21   a.   Yes, the statement is correct.
      b.   We do not know whether this interval covers the true mean. 90% of the intervals constructed in this manner based on the means of random samples will cover the true mean.

8.23 $(2.46, 2.94)$

8.25   a. $(1158.80, 1309.20)$
      b. $(1170.89, 1297.11)$

8.27   a.   Point estimate for the population mean = 63; Error margin = 39.59
      b. $(29.77, 96.23)$

8.29   Confidence level = .881

8.31   a.   Cannot tell
      b.   Yes
      c.   Cannot tell
      d.   No
      e.   Yes

8.33   a. $H_0 : \mu = 9.5$ versus $H_1 : \mu < 9.5$
      b. $H_0 : \mu = 7.40$ versus $H_1 : \mu > 7.40$
      c. $H_0 : \mu = 3.4$ versus $H_1 : \mu \neq 3.4$
      d. $H_0 : \mu = 35$ versus $H_1 : \mu > 35$

8.37   a.   The rejected region is one-sided to the left.
      b.   The rejected region is one-sided to the right.
      c.   The rejected region is two-sided.
      d.   The rejected region is one-sided to the right.

8.39 P-value = .031

8.41   Test statistic: $z = -1.69$; reject the null hypothesis

8.43   Test statistic: $z = 4.13$;
P-value = 0;
the evidence against the null hypothesis is very strong.

8.45 a. Yes
b. Cannot tell
c. No

8.47 a. Reject the null hypothesis since -4 is not in the confidence interval.
b. Do not reject the null hypothesis since 1 is in the confidence interval.

8.49 Yes, 16 would fall in the confidence interval since the null hypothesis was not rejected.

8.51 a. 1.740
b. 1.325
c. ± 2.052
d. -1.729

8.53 a. $P(t < -1.740) = .05$
b. $P(|t| > 3.143) = .02$
c. $P(-1.330 < t < 1.330) = .8$
d. $(-1.372 < t < 2.764) = .89$

8.55

d.f.	5	10	15	20	29
$t_{.05}$ **values**	2.015	1.812	1.753	1.725	1.699

The percentile decreases as the degrees of freedom increase.

8.57 a. c is between 2.015 and 2.571 because $t_{.05} = 2.015$ and $t_{.025} = 2.571$.
b. c is between 2.262 and 2.821 because $t_{.025} = 2.262$ and $t_{.01} = 2.821$.
c. c is greater than 3.055 because $t_{.005} = 3.055$.
d. $P(t > c) = .015$; c is between 2.571 and 3.365 because $t_{.025} = 2.571$ and $t_{.01} = 3.365$.
e. $P(t > c) = .02$; c is between 2.080 and 3.365 because $t_{.025} = 2.080$ and $t_{.01} = 2.518$.

8.59 90% C.I.: $(6.39, 15.61)$

8.61 90% C.I.: $(33.52, 37.88)$

8.63 90% C.I.: $(16.51, 26.29)$

8.65 95.0% C.I.: $(56.54, 99.13)$. Normality is a reasonable assumption. The normal scores plot is relatively straight.

8.67 95% C.I.: $(5.27, 11.13)$. We assumed that the original population was normal.

8.69 Test statistic $t = -2.07$;
reject the null hypothesis.
P-value is between .025 and .05. The evidence against the null hypothesis is quite strong.

8.71 Test statistic: $t = 1.948$;
do not reject the null hypothesis.
P-value is between .05 and .1.

8.73 Test statistic: $t = 1.59$;
P-value is between .05 and .1.
Do not reject the null hypothesis.

8.75 Confidence interval: $\left(\bar{x} - t_{\alpha/2} \dfrac{s}{\sqrt{n}}, \ \bar{x} + t_{\alpha/2} \dfrac{s}{\sqrt{n}} \right)$

8.77 Test statistic: $t = 1.84$;
P-value is between .05 and .1.

8.79 a. 90.0% C.I.: $(86.27, 92.93)$
b. 95.0% C.I.: $(9.202, 11.009)$; Yes

8.81 a. Point estimate of $\mu = 16.467$;
Estimated standard error $= .212$
b. Point estimate of $\mu = 1.846$;
Estimated standard error $= .369$

8.83 a. 771
b. 347
c. 46

8.85 a. Cannot tell
b. Yes
c. No

8.87 a. Test statistic $Z = (\bar{X} - 102)/(S/\sqrt{n})$;
Rejection region: $|z| > 1.645$
b. Test statistic $Z = (\bar{X} - 6.4)/(S/\sqrt{n})$;
Rejection region: $z > 1.34$

8.89 90% C.I.: $(13.63, 18.19)$

8.91 $z = 2.30$; P-value .021;
The evidence against the null hypothesis is strong.

8.93 a. Accept the null hypothesis of $\mu = 9$ since 9.0 is in the confidence interval.
b. Reject the null hypothesis of $\mu = 9.4$ since 9.4 is not in the confidence interval.

8.95 95% C.I.: $(7.72, 9.72)$

8.97 Assumption: The data are from a normal population. 95% C.I.: $(25.70, 38.50)$

8.99 Assumption: The data are from a normal population.
95% C.I.: $(207.91, 245.29)$

8.101 $H_0 : \mu = 1.5$ versus $H_1 : \mu < 1.5$

CHAPTER 9

9.1 a. Point estimate of difference of population means: 8;
Standard error: 2.425
b. 95% C.I. for the difference in population means: $(3.25, 12.75)$

9.3   a. $z = -3.370$;
reject the null hypothesis.
b.   95% C.I.: $(-.74, -.20)$

9.5   95% C.I.: $(-.93, .03)$. The P-value is .064, therefore do not reject the null hypothesis of equality of mean computer anxiety scores for male and female accounting students at $\alpha = .05$. However, the evidence against H_0 is moderately strong.

9.7   95% C.I.: $(-.65, .05)$; $t = -1.80$.
The P-value is .085. Do not reject the null hypothesis of equality of means at $\alpha = .05$. However, the evidence against H_0 is moderately strong.

9.9   98% C.I.: $(-38.91, .91)$

9.11   95% C.I.: $(-224.81, 284.81)$

9.13   a.   Point estimate of $\mu_1 - \mu_2$: 8.070;
Standard error: .607
b.   90% C.I.: $(7.07, 9.07)$

9.15   a.   95% C.I.: $(10.28, 13.64)$
b.   Test statistic: 15.367;
P-value $= 0$;
reject the null hypothesis.

9.17   a.   Test statistic: $t = -1.805$;
reject the null hypothesis.
b.   The assumptions that must be made are equal population variances and normal populations.
c.   95% C.I.: $(-9.09, .69)$

9.19   a.   Test statistic: -1.581;
P-value is between .1 and .2.
Do not reject the null hypothesis.
b.   Test statistic: 1.579;
P-value is between .1 and .2.
Do not reject the null hypothesis.

9.21   a. $t = -.226$
b.   d.f. $= 3$

9.23   a.   Test statistic: 1.856;
P-value is between .025 amd .05.
The evidence against the null hypothesis is quite strong.
b.   95% C.I.: $(-.98, 11.48)$

9.25   The P-value of .10 is larger than $\alpha = .05$, so do not reject the null hypothesis.

9.27 $t = 1.49$; P-value $= .18$
With a P-value of .18, do not reject the null hypothesis.

9.29   The P-value, .043, indicates moderately strong evidence against the null hypothesis.

9.31   a.   95% C.I.: $(18.3, 67.5)$
b. $t = 3.95$; P-value $= .0034$
Reject the null hypothesis of equal means.
c.   There is no randomization as to which treatment is received first in this experiment.
d.   The results in parts a and b could be misleading if the fact that one year was hotter than another caused greater electricity usage.

9.33   a. $\begin{bmatrix} 6 & 10 \\ 9 & 5 \\ 9 & 7 \\ 4 & 6 \end{bmatrix} =$

$\begin{bmatrix} 7 & 7 \\ 7 & 7 \\ 7 & 7 \\ 7 & 7 \end{bmatrix} + \begin{bmatrix} 1 & 1 \\ 0 & 0 \\ 1 & 1 \\ -2 & -2 \end{bmatrix} + \begin{bmatrix} -2 & 2 \\ 2 & -2 \\ 1 & -1 \\ -1 & 1 \end{bmatrix}$

b. and c.   Treament sum of squares $= 12$, d.f. $= 3$;
Error sum of squares $= 20$, d.f. $= 4$;
Total sum of squares $= 32$, d.f. $= 7$

d.

Source	Sum of squares	d.f.
Treatment	12	3
Error	20	4
Total	32	7

9.35   a. $\begin{bmatrix} 5 & 3 & 2 & 2 \\ 5 & 0 & 1 \\ 2 & 1 & 0 & 1 \end{bmatrix} = \begin{bmatrix} 2 & 2 & 2 & 2 \\ 2 & 2 & 2 \\ 2 & 2 & 2 & 2 \end{bmatrix}$

$+ \begin{bmatrix} 1 & 1 & 1 & 1 \\ 0 & 0 & 0 \\ -1 & -1 & -1 & -1 \end{bmatrix}$

$+ \begin{bmatrix} 2 & 0 & -1 & -1 \\ 3 & -2 & -1 \\ 1 & 0 & -1 & 0 \end{bmatrix}$

b.   Treatment sum of squares $= 8$;
Error sum of squares $= 22$;
Total sum of squares $= 30$
c.   d.f.(treatment) $= 2$;
d.f.(error) $= 8$;
d.f.(total) $= 10$

d.

Source	Sum of squares	d.f.
Treatment	8	2
Error	22	8
Total	30	10

9.37
$$\begin{bmatrix} 2 & 1 & 3 \\ 1 & 5 \\ 9 & 5 & 6 & 4 \\ 3 & 4 & 5 \end{bmatrix} = \begin{bmatrix} 4 & 4 & 4 \\ 4 & 4 \\ 4 & 4 & 4 & 4 \\ 4 & 4 & 4 \end{bmatrix}$$

$$+ \begin{bmatrix} -2 & -2 & -2 \\ -1 & -1 \\ 2 & 2 & 2 & 2 \\ 0 & 0 & 0 \end{bmatrix}$$

$$+ \begin{bmatrix} 0 & -1 & 1 \\ -2 & 2 \\ 3 & -1 & 0 & -2 \\ -1 & 0 & 1 \end{bmatrix}$$

Treatment sum of squares = 30;
Error sum of squares = 26;
Total sum of squares = 56;
d.f.(treatment) = 3;
d.f.(error) = 8;
d.f.(total) = 11

Source	Sum of squares	d.f.
Treatment	30	3
Error	26	8
Total	56	11

9.39 a. 3.33
b. 4.74

9.41

Source	Sum of squares	d.f.	Mean square	F-ratio
Treatment	104	5	20.8	3.817
Error	109	20	5.45	
Total	213	25		

Tabulated F-value = 2.16; reject the null hypothesis.

9.43

Source	Sum of squares	d.f.	Mean square	F-ratio
Treatment	12	3	4	.8
Error	20	4	5	
Total	32	7		

Tabulated F-value = 6.59; do not reject the null hypothesis.

9.45

Source	Sum of squares	d.f.	Mean square	F-ratio
Treatment	8	2	4	1.455
Error	22	8	2.75	
Total	30	10		

Tabulated F-value = 4.46. Do not reject the null hypothesis.

9.47 a. $\alpha/(2m) = .0083$
b. $\alpha/(2m) = .005$

9.49 Label the Means: M1, M2, M3, M4, M5, and M6.
a. Six confidence intervals:
M1 − M2: $(10.41, 13.59)$
M1 − M3: $(4.54, 7.46)$
M1 − M4: $(19.87, 24.13)$
M2 − M3: $(−7.67, −4.33)$
M2 − M4: $(7.73, 12.27)$
M3 − M4: $(13.82, 18.18)$
b. Multiple-t 95% confidence intervals:
M1 − M2: $(9.67, 14.33)$
M1 − M3: $(3.86, 8.14)$
M1 − M4: $(18.89, 25.11)$
M2 − M3: $(−8.44, −3.56)$
M2 − M4: $(6.67, 13.33)$
M3 − M4: $(12.80, 19.20)$

9.51 a.

Source	Sum of squares	d.f.	Mean square	F-ratio
Treatment	867.01055	2	433.5052761	19.72086
Error	7100.2089	323	21.9820709	
Total	7967.21945	325		

b. Am. − Ch.: $(−6.79, −3.01)$
Am. − HK: $(−3.95, −.65)$
Ch. − HK: $(1.11, 4.09)$
These confidence intervals indicate that there is a difference in the means.

9.55 a. 98% C.I.: $(24.58, 33.43)$
b. Test statistic: $−3.16$;
reject the null hypothesis.
c. Test statistic: $−3.16$;
reject the null hypothesis.

9.57 95% C.I.: $(−13.14, −10.12)$

9.59 a. $s^2_{pooled} = 3.6000$
b. Test statistic: 1.64

9.61 95% C.I. for design 1: $(67.44, 89.16)$;
95% C.I. for design 2: $(71.44, 99.76)$

9.63 Population 1 does not have a higher mean than Population 2 since zero is in the confidence interval.

9.65 a. $t = 1.85$; P-value = .10.
The P-value, .10, is not smaller than $\alpha = .02$, so do not reject the null hypothesis of equal means.
b. 90.0% C.I.: $(−.005, 2.403)$;
do not reject the hypothesis of equal means.

9.67 a. $t = -2.95$, $P = .011$, d.f. $= 13$.
The evidence against the null hypothesis is strong.

b. 95% C.I. for $\mu_s - \mu_n$: $(-10.8, -1.7)$

9.69

Source	Sum of squares	d.f.	Mean square	F-ratio
Treatment	90	2	45	8.44
Error	64	12	5.33	
Total	154	14		

9.71 a. These data confirm that managers differ from country to country with respect to the mean response on the human-heartedness scale.

Source	Sum of squares	d.f.	Mean square	F-ratio
Treatment	37.6137	2	18.8069	38.8601
Error	156.3202	323	.4840	
Total	193.9339	325		

b. Am. $-$ Ch: $(.720, 1.280)$
Am. $-$ HK: $(.155, .645)$
Ch. $-$ HK: $(-.822, -.378)$

9.73 a. Analysis of Variance

Source	d.f.	SS	MS	F	p
Factor	2	743.02	371.51	56.00	0.000
Error	87	577.20	6.63		
Total	89	1320.22			

Since $F = 56 > 3.15$, reject the null hypothesis.

b. The statistical model assumes the data come from normal populations with possibly different means, but with equal variances. The normal scores plots are fairly straight, implying that the data are nearly normal.

c. Individual 95% CIs for the Population Means

The target thickness is not being achieved for the wafers subjected to this grinding process since none of these confidence intervals contain 244.

CHAPTER 10

10.1 a. $\hat{p} = .583$;
95% error margin: .125

b. $\hat{p} = .121$;
95% error margin: .031

c. $\hat{p} = .589$;
95% error margin: .024

10.3 95% confidence intervals:

a. $(.46, .71)$

b. $(.09, .15)$

c. $(.56, .61)$

10.5 95% C.I.: $(.51, .64)$

10.7 95% C.I.: $(.55, .72)$

10.9 a. $n = 9996$

b. $n = 19600$

10.11 a. $n = 385$

b. $n = 139$

c. $n = 114$

10.13 a. $\alpha = .079$

b. $c = .474$

10.15 a. Null hypothesis: $p = .35$;
Alternative hypothesis: $p > .35$

b. Test statistic: 2.11;
reject the null hypothesis.

10.17 P-value: .218. This is a large P-value, indicating weak evidence against the null hypothesis.

10.19 a. $\hat{p} = .467$; s.e. $= .034$

b. 95% C.I.: $(.40, .53)$

c. Test statistic: -12.62;
reject the null hypothesis.

10.21 a. 90% C.I.: $(.23, .47)$

b. Test statistic: 4.56;
reject the null hypothesis.
P-value: 0.
The evidence against the null hypothesis is very strong.

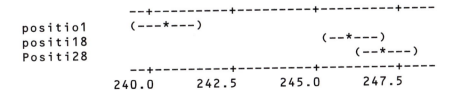

```
                --+---------+---------+---------+----
positio1       (---*---)
positi18                                 (--*---)
Positi28                                   (--*---)
                --+---------+---------+---------+----
                240.0     242.5     245.0     247.5
```

10.23 95% C.I.: (.06, .35)

10.25 95% C.I.: (.09, .30)

10.27 a. $\chi^2 = 12.789$;
   reject the null hypothesis.
   b. Test statistic: 3.576;
   reject the null hypothesis; $Z^2 = 12.789$

10.29 a. $\chi^2 = 37.641$;
   reject the null hypothesis.
   b. 95% C.I.: $(-.25, -.15)$

10.31 a. $\chi^2 = 19.263$;
   reject the hypothesis of equal means.
   The extremely small P-value of .004 indicates strong evidence against the null hypothesis.
   b. Germany, Japan, and Europe have a larger portion of settlement agreements, but Taiwan has a larger number of exclusion orders.

10.33 a. $\chi^2 = 9.179$;
   reject the null hypothesis.
   b. 95% C.I. for I minus II: $(-.31, .07)$
   95% C.I. for I minus III: $(-.49, -.11)$
   95% C.I. for II minus III: $(-.37, .01)$

10.35 $\chi^2 = 8.620$;
   reject the null hypothesis.
   The P-value, .003, is extremely small, indicating very strong evidence against the null hypothesis.

10.37 a. P-value = .032;
   reject the null hypothesis since the calculated value is larger than the tabled value.
   b. $\chi^2 = 0.000$;
   do not reject the null hypothesis.

10.39 $\chi^2 = 2.058$;
   do not reject the null hypothesis.
   The large P-value, .725, indicates extremely weak evidence against the null hypothesis.

10.41 P-value = .927

10.43 b. $\chi^2 = .828$;
   do not reject the null hypothesis.

10.45 a. 99% error margin = .175
   b. 99% error margin = .071
   c. 99% error margin = .023

10.47 a. $n = 897$
   b. $n = 1068$

10.49 90% C.I.: (.5021, .5751)

10.51 95% C.I.: (.4674, .5544)

10.53 a. 95% C.I.: (.0004, .0262)
   b. Point estimate 545.3

10.55 $\chi^2 = 16.773$;
reject the null hypothesis. The proportions are dependent.

10.57 $\chi^2 = 17.122$;
reject the null hypothesis. These characteristics are dependent.

10.59 The calculations leading to the chi-square test for homogeneity and the chi-square test for independence are the same but the sampling schemes and the null hypotheses are different.

CHAPTER 11

11.1 y-intercept = 3; Slope = 2

11.3 $\beta_0 = 7$; $\beta_1 = -6$; $\sigma = 4$

11.5 a. Mean = 6; Standard deviation = 3
   b. Mean = -6; Standard deviation = 3

11.9 a. When $x = 4$, $y = 19$. When $x = 5$, $y = 23$.
   b. The response at $x = 5$ will not always be larger than the response at $x = 4$.

11.11 a. $Y = \beta_0 + \beta_1 x + \varepsilon$, where β_0 represents the fixed costs such as location, β_1 represents the variable costs related to the number of square feet, ε represents the unexpected variations such as condition and type of construction, and Y represents the total cost.
   b. β_1 represents the number of additional dollars of rent for each additional square foot of apartment.
   c. One component variable that might be included in the error term ε is the condition of the apartment.

11.13 b. $\bar{x} = 3$;
   $\bar{y} = 3.5$,
   $S_{xx} = 10$;
   $S_{yy} = 39.5$;
   $S_{xy} = -18$
   c. $\hat{\beta}_0 = 8.9$; $\hat{\beta}_1 = -1.8$
   d. The regression equation is $\hat{y} = 8.90 - 1.80x$.

11.15 a.

x	y	Residuals
1	8	.9
2	4	-1.3
3	5	1.5
3	2	-1.5
4	2	.3
5	0	.1

Sum of squares of residuals = 7.1
   b. SSE = 7.100
   c. $s^2 = 1.775$

11.17 a. $\bar{x} = 3.4$;
$\bar{y} = 6$;
$S_{xx} = 29.2$;
$S_{yy} = 26$;
$S_{xy} = 25$
b. $\hat{\beta}_1 = .856$; $\hat{\beta}_0 = 3.089$
c. $\hat{y} = 3.089 + .856x$

11.19 a. $\hat{\beta}_1 = .133$; $\hat{\beta}_0 = 4.794$
b. SSE $= 4.393$
c. $s^2 = .338$

11.21 $\bar{y} = \hat{\beta}_0 + \hat{\beta}_1\bar{x} = (\bar{y} - \hat{\beta}_1\bar{x}) + \hat{\beta}_1\bar{x}$

11.23 **The regression equation is**
Rent = 276 + 0.518 Sqft
b. .518 is the estimated mean rent for an additional sqaure foot of space.
c. SSE $= 68273$; $s^2 = 4876.643$

11.25 a. $\hat{\beta}_1 = -.615$; $\hat{\beta}_0 = 4.85$; $s^2 = .051$
b. Value of test statistic: -13.845;
reject the null hypothesis.
c. 90% C.I.: $(4.46, 5.24)$
d. When $x^* = 2.5$, $\hat{y} = 3.313$.
90% C.I.: $(3.07, 3.55)$

11.27 a. $\hat{\beta}_0 = .4$; $\hat{\beta}_1 = .7$; $s^2 = .053$
b. Test statistic: -4.109;
reject the null hypothesis that the slope is 1.
c. 90% C.I.: $(.53, .87)$
d. When $x = 3.5$, $\hat{y} = 2.85$;
95% C.I.: $(2.50, 3.20)$

11.29 a. When $x = \$90.0$, $\hat{y} = 93.710$;
95% C.I.: $(91.313, 96.108)$
b. 95% prediction interval: $(87.295, 100.125)$

11.31 a. Slope $= -.271$; Y-intercept $= 18.0$;
Equation of the fitted line:
$\hat{y} = 18.0 - .271x$
b. $s = 10.61$
c. Test statistic: -1.571;
do not reject the null hypothesis.

11.33 a. Equation of the fitted least squares line:
$\hat{y} = 1.65 + .002x$
b. 90% C.I.: $(-5261.058, 5261.062)$
c. When $x = 948$, $\hat{y} = 3.565$;
95% C.I.: $(.93, 6.20)$

11.35 a. Predicted actual cost $= 9.318$
b. 90% C.I. for y when $x = 10$: $(7.576, 9.994)$

11.37

Source	Sum of squares	d.f.	Mean square	F-ratio
Regression	.378	1	.378	2.779
Error	1.632	12	.136	
Total	2.010	13		

11.39

Source	Sum of squares	d.f.	Mean square	F-ratio
Regression	278.261	1	278.261	48.259
Error	178.739	31	5.766	
Total	457	32		

11.41 a. $r^2 = .985$
b. $r = -.992$
c. Test statistic: 13.611;
reject the null hypothesis.

11.43 a. $r^2 = .791$
b. $F = 49.34$; the regression is significant at α close to 0.
c. $t = -7.02$, $t^2 = 49.3 = F$

11.45 a. $r^2 = .528$; this means that 52.8% of the variability in y is explained by the fitted straight line.
b. $r = .727$
c. The P-value related to the F-ratio is essentially 0, indicating that the regression is significant at the 1% level.
d. $t = 6.260$; reject the null hypothesis.

11.49 **The regression equation is**
Ln $\hat{y}$ = 2.54 + .288 Year
a. Test statistic: 4.25;
reject the null hypothesis.
b. 90% C.I. for γ: $(1.29, 1.37)$

11.51 a. Regression analysis:
$y_t = 1.27 - .217y_{t-1}$
b. We cannot reject $H_0 : \beta_1 = 0$ at the 10% level. Also, $r^2 = .053$. (Very little of the variation in Y_t is explained by Y_{t-1}.) Both of these suggest that the model $y_t = \beta_0 + \varepsilon_t$ is adequate for these data. That is, successive S&P 500 monthly returns are essentially independent.
c. The assumption of independent errors is warranted since the autocorrelation coefficients are between ± 2 standard errors $(\pm 2/\sqrt{46}) = .295$ of zero.

11.53 b. $\hat{y}' = .129 + .184x$
c. 93.8% of the variability in the response y is explained by the fitted straight line. This transformation is a better fit than the original equation.
d. The transformed data appear to be consistent with a straight-line model since the residuals are scattered in a horizontal band about zero.

11.55 b. $\hat{y}' = -.167 + .237x$

c. $r^2 = .925$ so 92.5% of the variability is explained by the fitted line equation. This is an adequate fit.

d. The transformed data appear to be consistent with a straight-line model since the residuals are scattered in a horizontal band about zero.

11.59 Value of test statistic: $-.755$; do not reject the null hypothesis.

11.61 a. The regression equation is ExRateY = 0.975 x

b. 95% C.I. for β: $(.96, .99)$; $\beta = 1$ is not in the confidence interval.

c. The linear relationship between Mexico and the United States is stronger than the relation between Japan and the United States.

11.63 b. The regression equation is TotSAT = 1053 − 2.51 PercGrad

$r^2 = .782$ so 78.2% of the variability in the response y is explained by the fitted straight line. A fairly strong linear relation.

c. Value of the test statistic for significant regression: $F = 175.38$; reject the null hypothesis $H_0 : \beta_1 = 0$.

d. Since the graph is nearly a straight line, the normal assumption for the errors (responses) seems reasonable.

11.65 a. The regression equation is OpExBsbl = 18.9 + 1.30 PlCtBsbl

$r^2 = .751$ so 75.1% of the variability of the response y is explained by the fitted straight line. This is a fairly strong linear relation.

b. Value of the test statistic for $H_0 : \rho = 0$: $t = 8.512$; reject the null hypothesis.

c. We cannot conclude that operating costs are roughly twice player costs.

d. 95.0% P.I.: $(47.18, 69.98)$

e. **Unusual Observations**

Obs.	PlCtBsbl	OpExBsbl	Fit
7	18.0	60.00	42.31

Stdev.Fit	Residual	St.Resid
1.64	17.69	3.45R

R denotes an obs. with a large st. resid.

11.67 a. 95% C.I. for $\gamma = (.543, .609)$; .5 is not a plausible value for γ since it is not in the confidence interval.

b. lnCoBars = 6.915; Prediction interval: $(6.7589, 6.9913)$; Number of coffee bars: $(861.69, 1087.13)$

c. Coffee Bars = 6217; I do not have much faith in this prediction since it is an extrapolation.

CHAPTER 12

12.1 a. $\hat{y} = 79.9$
b. $\hat{y} = 69.7$
c. $\hat{y} = 12.8$

12.3 a. $E(Y) = -1$
b. $E(Y) = 8$
c. $E(Y) = 29$

12.5 a. $s = 1.649$
b. $R^2 = .837$; 83.7% of the variability in the response y is explained by the fitted multiple regression equation.

12.7 a. The regression equation is Newsprnt = −43492 + 3853 Papers + 4508 LnFamily

b. $F = 17.31$ and its associated P-value of 0 indicate that there is strong evidence for rejecting the null hypothesis $H_0 : \beta_1 = \beta_2 = 0$. The regression is significant.

c. The independent variables are related.

d. 74.3% of the variability in the response y is explained by the fitted multiple regression equation.

12.9 a. The regression equation is 95Price = −5426 + 90.1 HP + 2.76 Weight

$F = 13.66$ and its associated P-value of 0 indicate that the regression is significant.

b. 61.6% of the variability in the response of y is explained by the fitted multiple regression equation.

c. The residual plots identify one observation as an outlier. Observation 19 has a large 95Price relative to the other cars in the sample. Without this observation, the regression assumptions are reasonable.

12.11 a. Fitted regression function: LnComp = 5.36 + .263 LnSales + .0157 Exper − .429 Educate − .0308 PctOwn; $\hat{\beta}_3 = -.429$ indicates that the mean log compensation decreases by .429 unit for each unit increase in the level of education.

b. LnComp $= 5.36 + .263\ln(7818) +$ $.0157(6) - .429(1) - .0308(.004) = 7.382;$ Compensation in millions of dollars: $1.608 or $1,608,000.

c. 46.8% of the variability in log compensation is explained by the fitted regression function.

d. The *P*-value associated with the *F* statistic is 0, indicating that the regression is significant.

12.13 b. `The regression equation is Y(MPG) = 25.5 - 1.04 X1(Age) + 1.21 X2(Gend)`

Gender appears to make a difference in MPG. Female drivers increase mean MPG by $\hat{\beta}_2 = 1.21$ miles per gallon for all ages of taxis considered.

d. `The regression equation is Y(MPG) = 26.4 - 1.18 X1 (Age)`

Gender is important. If gender is ignored, the fitted straight line tends to overestimate MPG for male drivers and underestimate MPG for female drivers.

12.15 a. The mean leverage is .20. None of the observations are high leverage points.

b. `Unusual Observations`
`Obs.  X1    Y   Fit`
`20    95 57.00 84.43`

`Stdev.Fit Residual  St.Resid`
`  4.73  -27.43   -2.10R`

R denotes an obs. with a large st. resid.
The fitted model overpredicted the response for this observation since the residual, $y - \hat{y}$, is negative. Given the first two exam scores and the current GPA, this student's final exam score should have been higher according to the fitted regression function.

12.17 a. `The regression equation is 95Price = -12943 + 93.8 HP + 3.55 Weight + 155 MPG`

Multicollinearity is a problem since the VIF values of 3.8, 2.8, and 2.7 are large.

b. **Stepwise Regression**
```
Step          1
Constant   -2771
HP           129
T-Ratio     5.15
S           2991
R-Sq       59.59
```

Regression analysis:
`The regression equation is 95Price = -2771 + 129 HP; R-sq = 59.6%`
This choice seems reasonable.

12.19 The series is stationary in the mean. The autocorrelations for the series of the first differences are all fairly small relative to twice their standard errors.

12.21 The series is nonstationary in the mean since the level of the series seems to change and the autocorrelations do not die out rapidly.

12.25 a. $\hat{y}_{n+1} = \beta_0 + \beta_1 y_n + \beta_2 y_{n-1} + \beta_3 y_{n-2}$
b. $\hat{y}_{n+1} = \beta_0 + y_n + \beta_1(y_n - y_{n-1})$
c. $\hat{y}_{n+1} = \beta_0 + y_{n-3} + \beta_1(y_n - y_{n-4})$

12.27 $\hat{y}_{n+l} = \beta_0 + \beta_1\hat{y}_{n+l-1} + \beta_2\hat{y}_{n+l-2}$, for $l = 3, 4, \ldots$

12.29 95% C.I. for y_{63}: (5.3, 6.5)

Element #	Forecast
$\hat{y}_{61}$	5.5
$\hat{y}_{62}$	5.8
$\hat{y}_{63}$	5.9
$\hat{y}_{64}$	5.81
$\hat{y}_{65}$	5.595
$\hat{y}_{66}$	5.3445
$\hat{y}_{67}$	5.14075

The forecasts tend to the series mean as the lead time increases.

12.31 Some significant residual autocorrelation is remaining. This implies the model can be improved; however, the AR(1) model fit to the seasonally differenced data does a fairly good job of explaining the variation in the monthly sales of Company X.

12.33 **ARIMA Model (Fit AR(1) to differences in TBillInt.)**
The fitted model is $\hat{w}_t = .021 + .196w_{t-1}$ where $w_t = y_t - y_{t-1}$. Since $\beta_0 = .021$ is not significantly different from 0, drop this term and then we have, in terms of the original observations, $\hat{y}_t - y_{t-1} = .196(y_{t-1} - y_{t-2})$ or $\hat{y}_t = 1.196y_{t-1} - .196y_{t-2}$.
ARIMA Model (Fit AR(2) model to original series TBillInt.)
The fitted model is $\hat{y}_t = .225 + 1.199y_{t-1} - .239y_{t-2}$ or $\hat{y}_t - 5.615 = 1.199(y_{t-1} - 5.615) - .239(y_{t-2} - 5.615)$ where $5.615 = \bar{y}$ is the sample mean. This stationary model is nearly the same as the nonstationary model involving the series of differences. Notice there is no mean

in the model involving the differences since a nonstationary series has no mean. In this case, it is difficult to select one model over the other on the basis of the fit. The selection may have to be made on the basis of the nature of the forecasts.

12.35 a. The residuals are positive for the middle values of $\hat{y}_t$ and negative for small and large values of $\hat{y}_t$. This information suggests the fitted model may be improved. The residuals are not randomly distributed in a band about zero as the error term assumptions would suggest.

b. MAPE = 7.171; MAD = 1.775; MSD = 3.369;

It is difficult to select a best measure of accuracy without the context of the investigation.

12.37 RentY = 807.2;

95.0% C.I.: (770.0, 844.4);

95.0% P.I.: (673.3, 941.2)

These intervals are smaller than the ones in Section 12.6. The predictor variable No.Bath contains additional information and the effect is to narrow the intervals.

12.39 a. **Stepwise regression**

Step	1	2	3
Constant	51.16	52.45	49.93
%Urban	0.312	0.218	0.197
T-Ratio	9.93	4.76	4.48
GDP/Cap		0.00043	0.00037
T-Ratio		2.64	2.44
LnGDP			0.79
T-Ratio			2.18
S	4.80	4.37	4.11
R-Sq	77.28	81.80	84.53

The regression equation is
LifeEx = 49.9 + 0.197 %Urban + 0.000375 GDP/Cap + 0.794 LnGDP

These data are nearly normal since the normal scores plot is a fairly straight line.

b. $F = 49.16$, and its associated P-value $= 0$, show that the regression is significant.

12.41 **ARIMA model (original series):**

The fitted model is $\hat{y} = 111.70 + 1.249y_{t-1} - .358y_{t-2}$.

ARIMA model (First differences)

The fitted model, ignoring the nonsignificant constant, is $\hat{w}_t = .295w_{t-1}$ or $\hat{y}_t - y_{t-1} = .295(y_{t-1} - y_{t-2})$ or $\hat{y}_t = 1.295y_{t-1} - .295y_{t-2}$. The two fitted models are very similar. It is difficult to distinguish the models based on the fits. Since one is a stationary model and the other is a nonstationary model, you may have to select one based on the nature of the forecasts.

CHAPTER 13

13.6

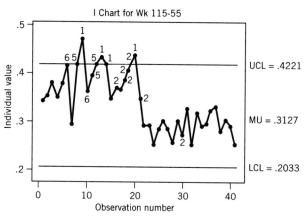

TEST 1. One point beyond LCL or UCL.

TEST 2. Nine points in a row on same side of center line.

Tests indicate the presence of special causes. The major pattern here is a clear shift in level of the series at about sample number 20 (about week 135 in the original data set).

INDEX

Random Digits

Row										
1	0695	7741	8254	4297	0000	5277	6563	9265	1023	5925
2	0437	5434	8503	3928	6979	9393	8936	9088	5744	4790
3	6242	2998	0205	5469	3365	7950	7256	3716	8385	0253
4	7090	4074	1257	7175	3310	0712	4748	4226	0604	3804
5	0683	6999	4828	7888	0087	9288	7855	2678	3315	6718
6	7013	4300	3768	2572	6473	2411	6285	0069	5422	6175
7	8808	2786	5369	9571	3412	2465	6419	3990	0294	0896
8	9876	3602	5812	0124	1997	6445	3176	2682	1259	1728
9	1873	1065	8976	1295	9434	3178	0602	0732	6616	7972
10	2581	3075	4622	2974	7069	5605	0420	2949	4387	7679
11	3785	6401	0540	5077	7132	4135	4646	3834	6753	1593
12	8626	4017	1544	4202	8986	1432	2810	2418	8052	2710
13	6253	0726	9483	6753	4732	2284	0421	3010	7885	8436
14	0113	4546	2212	9829	2351	1370	2707	3329	6574	7002
15	4646	6474	9983	8738	1603	8671	0489	9588	3309	5860
16	7873	7343	4432	2866	7973	3765	2888	5154	2250	4339
17	3756	9204	2590	6577	2409	8234	8656	2336	7948	7478
18	2673	7115	5526	0747	3952	6804	3671	7486	3024	9858
19	0187	7045	2711	0349	7734	4396	0988	4887	7682	8990
20	7976	3862	8323	5997	6904	4977	1056	6638	6398	4552
21	5605	1819	8926	9557	2905	0802	7749	0845	1710	4125
22	2225	5556	2545	7480	8804	4161	0084	0787	2561	5113
23	2549	4166	1609	7570	4223	0032	4236	0169	4673	8034
24	6113	1312	5777	7058	2413	3932	5144	5998	7183	5210
25	2028	2537	9819	9215	9327	6640	5986	7935	2750	2981
26	7818	3655	5771	4026	5757	3171	6435	2990	1860	1796
27	9629	3383	1931	2631	5903	9372	1307	4061	5443	8663
28	6657	5967	3277	7141	3628	2588	9320	1972	7683	7544
29	4344	7388	2978	3945	0471	4882	1619	0093	2282	7024
30	3145	8720	2131	1614	1575	5239	0766	0404	4873	7986
31	1848	4094	9168	0903	6451	2823	7566	6644	1157	8889
32	0915	5578	0822	5887	5354	3632	4617	6016	8989	9482
33	1430	4755	7551	9019	8233	9625	6361	2589	2496	7268
34	3473	7966	7249	0555	6307	9524	4888	4939	1641	1573
35	3312	0773	6296	1348	5483	5824	3353	4587	1019	9677
36	6255	4204	5890	9273	0634	9992	3834	2283	1202	4849
37	0562	2546	8559	0480	9379	9282	8257	3054	4272	9311
38	1957	6783	4105	8976	8035	0883	8971	0017	6476	2895
39	7333	1083	0398	8841	0017	4135	4043	8157	4672	2424
40	4601	8908	1781	4287	2681	6223	0814	4477	3798	4437